Uncle John's CANORAMIC BATHROOM READER

D0981329

By the Bathroom Readers' Institute

Bathroom Readers' Press
Ashland, Oregon

OUR "REGULAR" READERS RAVE!

"I love your books!!!! Absolutely fantastic!!!! What a joy they are. I bet I am responsible for at least 150 more *Bathroom Readers* because I take every opportunity to tell anyone I can what fun they are. I am a much smarter cookie for having read them."

—**Kathy L.**

"My husband has several of your *Readers* and we both enjoy them. Our compliments on the many interesting books and we look forward to future editions."

—**Deb B.**

"I've LOVED your books for the longest time. I just wanted to write to you guys and gals over at the BRI and tell you how much of an impact you've had on my life. Thank you so much!"

—**David K.**

"A staple of my library...er...reading room!"

—**Lee W.**

"I'm a doctor at an elderly-heavy practice, and the problem of bedsores has been epidemic. However, I saw the reference to the Smart-E-Pants in the *Perpetually Pleasing BR*, and now we're going to try them here. Congratulations, your book not only saves me from boredom, but it may save some lives! Keep 'em flushin'!"

—**Casey D., MD**

"I have read all of your books, some more than once. They are amazing! Please keep up the good work!"

—**Cathy N.**

"I got the *Perpetually Pleasing Bathroom Reader* for Christmas. I said, 'See you next year!' and then walked into the bathroom."

—**Brian F.**

UNCLE JOHN'S CANORAMIC
BATHROOM READER®

For Ann Dollison

For information, write:
The Bathroom Readers' Institute,
P.O. Box 1117,
Ashland, OR 97520
www.bathroomreader.com

Cover design and illustration by Ned Levine
BRI "technician" on the back cover: Larry Kelp

ISBN-13: 978-1-62686-074-9 / ISBN-10: 1-62686-174-9

Library of Congress Cataloging-in-Publication Data

Uncle John's Canoramic bathroom reader.
    pages cm
  ISBN 978-1-62686-174-9 (pbk.)
1. American wit and humor. 2. Curiosities and wonders.
I. Bathroom Readers' Institute (Ashland, Or.) II. Title: Canoramic bathroom reader.
  PN6165.U5325 2014
  081--dc23
                                    2014001198
Printed in the United States of America
First Printing
1 2 3 4 5 6 7 8   18 17 16 15 14

THANK YOU!

*The Bathroom Readers' Institute sincerely thanks the people
whose advice and assistance made this book possible.*

Gordon Javna

John Dollison

Jay Newman

Brian Boone

Trina "Bookie" Janssen

Kim Griswell

Thom Little

Brandon Hartley

Jack Mingo

Megan Todd

Pablo Goldstein

Eleanor Pierce

Jahnna Beecham

Tracy Vonder Brink

Andy Boyles

Adam Bolivar

Jolly Jeff Cheek

Aaron Guzman

Jill Bellrose

Dan Mansfield

Joan Kyzer

JoAnn and Melinda

Ned Levine

Ginger, Jennifer,
and Mana

Lilian Nordland

Blake Mitchum

Maggie Javna

Peter Norton

Mighty John Marshall

Rusty von Dyl

Brandon Walker

Gwen Walters

Sam & Gid

"Deacon" Brodie Hefner

Ryan Bouslaugh

Media Masters

Publishers Group West

Porter's Ghost

Raincoast Books

Thomas Crapper

*   *   *

"There is no friend as loyal as a book." —**Ernest Hemingway**

v

CONTENTS

Because the BRI understands your reading needs, we've
divided the contents by length as well as subject.

Short—a quick read

Medium—2 to 3 pages

Long—for those extended visits, when something
a little more involved is required

* Extended—for those leg-numbing experiences

*   *   *

"I had my mom fax me something recently. And then she called me
and said, 'Hey, Mike, could you fax that back? That's my only copy.'"
—**Mike Birbiglia**

COME IN AND HAVE A SEAT

Holy *Bathroom Reader*, Batman! We really opened up a can of worms this time! That phrase, by the way, comes from fishing: Before live bait came in sealable plastic containers, it was often sold in used metal coffee cans, and once opened, it was tough to keep the worms from crawling out. That's officially the first time I've shared a random fact in the first paragraph of my intro, but as longtime *Bathroom Reader* fans know, I just can't help myself. In fact, all of us here at the BRI share a passion for collecting and dispensing obscure information. And for making each other laugh.

That's how we came up with the name *Canoramic*. After 26 annual *Bathroom Readers*, choosing a new title has become quite a task. So, as I do every year, I called a staff meeting where we all shouted out title after title until one of them 1) described the book; 2) included a silly pun; and 3) made us laugh. When someone blurted out "Canoramic," we knew we had a winner. Not only is the title a bathroom pun, but it encapsulates our goal in putting this book together: *Canoramic* will give you a panoramic view of the world around you from the comfort of your can!

The ongoing mission of the Bathroom Readers' Institute: to stuff so many topics into a *Bathroom Reader* that there's something for everyone. For instance, whether you love or hate reality shows, you might be interested to know just how rigged they are. (Spoiler alert: a lot.) TV not your cup of tea? Then you might enjoy the mystery of the priceless violin that survived the *Titanic*…or did it? Prefer something lighter? You'll find funny street names, bizarre book titles, and funny names of real law firms (like "Dumas & McPhail"). The great thing about information is that none of it useless. When you learn something new, your world becomes a bigger place.

Not to toot our own horn, but…TOOT! Our *Fully-Loaded 25th Anniversary Bathroom Reader* won a Benjamin Franklin (gold medal) Award from the Independent Book Publishers Association. More tooting (excuse me): Our *Smell-O-Scopic Bathroom Reader For Kids Only!* also took gold. So now when I say we're an award-winning series I'm actually telling the truth.

In other news, we're really rolling along on the ol' Interwebs. Our Facebook page is growing bigger (and weirder) every day, as is Uncle John's Blog (which can be conveniently accessed via our Facebook page). We enjoy tweeting, too, for those who enjoy being tweeted to (@Bathroom_Reader). And in the digital publishing realm, we have a little series of e-books called "Facts To Go" that feature long-lost articles and e-pages of new material.

But awards and e-books aside, everything we do comes back to the big book you're holding in your hands. It's hard to believe that back in 1988 when we put together the first *Bathroom Reader*, it was only about 200 pages long. As we're approaching 30 years in the book biz, we've amassed more than *40,000 pages* of bathroom reading! If all the pages from all the books we've ever printed were laid end to end…it would be a huge waste of great books. Better to just read them instead.

So as we put the finishing touches on *Canoramic*, I'd like to once again thank my crack(pot) team of writers and researchers. You really do get better every year! All of the hard days and late nights (and long title meetings) become worth it when one of our faithful fans takes the time to tell us how much we mean to them—like reader Seth G., who recently wrote on our Facebook page, "Life without a *Bathroom Reader* would be like a broken pencil…point-less." Well said, Seth! To all of our fans: As you enjoy the view from your reading room, know that we've put our hearts and souls into every single page of *Canoramic* to make it as fun and absorbing as we possibly…can.

As always,

> *Go with the Flow!*

> **—Uncle John, the BRI staff, and Felix the Dog**

YOU'RE MY INSPIRATION

It's always interesting to find out where the architects of pop culture get their ideas. Some of these may surprise you.

BIFF TANNEN. The jerk played by Tom Wilson in the 1985 film *Back to the Future* was named after studio executive Ned Tannen, who once acted like a jerk to director Robert Zemeckis and writer Bob Gale during a pitch meeting in the 1970s.

"ALL RIGHT, ALL RIGHT, ALL RIGHT!" Matthew McConaughey improvised his signature catchphrase in 1993's *Dazed and Confused*. Shortly before the first movie scene he ever filmed, he was listening to a live Doors album. In between songs, singer Jim Morrison said, "All right, all right, all right!" and McConaughey parroted it.

PATSEY THE SLAVE. For her Oscar-winning portrayal of the childlike Patsey in 2013's *12 Years a Slave*, Lupita Nyong'o took inspiration from the late King of Pop: "There's something very Michael Jackson–like about Patsey. She had her childhood stripped away from her suddenly as soon as she became of sexual age."

QUASIMODO. In the 1830s, French novelist Victor Hugo spent a lot of time at Paris's Notre Dame Cathedral while it was undergoing renovations. Historians believe that one of the workers—a shy *bossu*, which means "hunchback" in French—was the inspiration for one of literature's most famous characters.

LOKI. Actor Tom Hiddleston drew from three Hollywood greats for his portrayal of the maligned god in the *Thor* and *Avengers* movies: "Peter O'Toole (enigmatic reckless), Jack Nicholson (edgy and near-insane), and Clint Eastwood (simmering anger)."

DUNGEONS & DRAGONS DRAGONS. In 1977 Gary Gygax was having trouble creating all the strange creatures for his seminal role-playing game…until he found a 99-cent bag of toy monsters made in China. His friend Tim Kask recalls that the 37-year-old Gygax "ran home, eager as a kid to open his baseball cards, and then proceeded to invent the Carrion Crawler, Umber Hulk, Rust Monster, and Purple Worm—all based on those silly plastic figures."

CORNER OF THIS & THAT

Believe it or not, all of these street names are real.

Old Guy Road
(Damon, Texas)

Pe'e Pe'e Place
(Hilo, Hawaii)

Wong Way
(Riverside, California;
in 1999 it was changed
to Wong Street)

Weiner Cutoff Road
(Harrisburg, Arkansas)

Rue du Hâ Hâ
(Chéroy, France)

Spanker Lane
(Derbyshire, England)

Awesome Street
(Cary, North Carolina)

Kickapoo Drive
(Fort Worth, Texas)

Farfrompoopen Road
(only road to Constipation
Ridge in Story, Arkansas)

Inyo Street
(Bakersfield, California;
intersects with Butte Street)

Butt Hollow Road
(Salem, Virginia)

Booger Branch Road
(Six Mile, South Carolina; also
in Crandall, Georgia)

Tater Peeler Road
(Lebanon, Tennessee)

His Way
(Lake Jackson, Texas;
behind a church)

Dumb Woman's Lane
(East Sussex, England)

Morningwood Way
(Bend, Oregon)

Unexpected Road
(Buena, New Jersey)

Kitchen-Dick Road
(Sequim, Washington)

Butts Wynd Street
(St. Andrews, Scotland)

Crotch Crescent
(Oxfordshire, England)

**This Street, That Street,
and The Other Street**
(three actual streets in
Porters Lake, Nova Scotia)

Fangboner Road
(Fremont, Ohio)

Divorce Court
(Heather Highlands,
Pennsylvania)

Psycho Path
(Traverse City, Michigan)

Small world: Walt Disney was a direct descendant of King Edward I.

PERSONAL SPACE

There's not much room on space vehicles, but NASA allows astronauts up to 1.5 pounds of personal items. Here's what went up on these flights.

• To note the historical significance of the first flight to the Moon, the *Apollo 11* crew brought a piece of wood from the Wright brothers' 1903 airplane.

• In 2008 the space shuttle *Atlantis* carried three NASCAR starter flags, commemorating the 50th anniversary of the Daytona 500. One of the flags was given to that year's Daytona winner, Ryan Newman.

• The 1971 *Apollo 15* voyage took University of Michigan alumni-chapter documents to the Moon—so now the school can claim it has a branch on the Moon.

• Cornell University founder Ezra Cornell wore a pair of tan silk socks on his wedding day in 1831. In 1990 Cornell graduate G. David Low boarded the space shuttle… carrying Cornell's socks.

• The space shuttle *Atlantis* (March 2007) brought a lead cargo tag from Jamestown colony in honor of the history of American exploration.

• In 2011 flight engineer Satoshi Furukawa represented Japan on the International Space Station. His item: a box of Legos. He used them to make a replica of the ISS.

• In 2008 Garrett Reisman, a New York Yankees fan, brought a vial of dirt from Yankee Stadium onto *Discovery*.

• Pete Conrad took matching beanie hats for his crew on *Apollo 12* in 1969. Well, not entirely matching, because Conrad's had a propeller.

• Gregory Johnson (*Endeavour*, 2008) took the title page of *Expedition 6*, actor Bill Pullman's play about life on the International Space Station.

• Pilot John Young was reprimanded for sneaking a corned beef sandwich onto the 1965 *Gemini 3* flight. Crumbs are hazardous on a space capsule. (Space food is crumb-free.)

• The 2007 space shuttle *Discovery* carried the prop lightsaber used by Mark Hamill (Luke Skywalker) in *Star Wars*—a fake space relic in real space.

Icing a burn slows the healing process. Running cold water over it works better.

BORROWED WORDS

English is a mash-up of words from other languages and cultures around the world, added through colonization, immigration, and importation. Some gave us hundreds of words; others, only a few.

- **WICKER**—bendable branches or twigs, usually willow, used to make furniture—comes from two Swedish words: *viker* (willow) and *vika*, (to bend).

- **TREK** is from Afrikaans, the form of Dutch spoken by white settlers in South Africa. It means "travel."

- **DOLLAR** comes from *tolar*, the Czech name for a coin made in Bohemia (now part of the Czech Republic) in the sixteenth century.

- **CHEETAH** is derived from the ancient Indian language of Sanskrit word *chitra-s*. It means "uniquely marked."

- **COOTIES** comes to English from *kutu*, a word in the Malay language (spoken in Malaysia and Indonesia) meaning "lice." Another Malay word imported into English: **BAMBOO**, from their word *bambu*.

- **CORGI**, the name of the short-legged dog breed, is a fitting portmanteau of two Welsh words: *cor* (dwarf) and *gi* (dog).

- **COACH**, as in the horse-drawn carriage, comes from *kocsi*, the Hungarian word for the vehicle. It's named after Kocs, the city where it was invented.

- **KIWI**—the bird, not the fruit—comes directly from Maori, a language of the native people of New Zealand.

- **HORDE** is from the Polish *horda*, indicating a large nomadic tribe.

- **SAUNA**, a small room used for hot-air or steam baths, is from the Finnish word *sauna*. (And it means the same thing.)

- **TYCOON** is an anglicized spelling of the Japanese word *taikun*, or "high commander."

- **VERANDA**, a fancy word for "deck" or "patio," derives from the Portuguese word *varanda*…which describes a deck or patio.

- **DRAG**, meaning to wear clothes more associated with the opposite sex, is a shortened form of the Romani word *indraka*, which means "dress."

Ronald Reagan was born 6 years before John F. Kennedy.

OOPS!

Everyone's amused by tales of somebody else's outrageous blunders—probably because it's comforting to know that someone out there is screwing up worse than you. So go ahead and feel superior for a few minutes.

ONE BAD APPLE

In September 2013, a motorist entered "Fairbanks Airport" into the Apple Maps app on his smartphone and started off, following the directions that he assumed would take him to Fairbanks International Airport in Alaska. They did. He soon found himself within sight of the terminal, so he drove to the terminal… except that he was driving straight across Taxiway Bravo—one of the airport's runways—to the *airplane side* of the terminal. It turns out the GPS location that the app was using to locate the airport was an arbitrary spot right in the middle of the entire airport complex. The app simply found the straightest path there, which means that if a person comes from the right (or *wrong*) direction— he could end up on the access road to the runway, rather than the passenger entrance to the airport. Fairbanks Airport officials called Apple and told them about the very dangerous problem—Apple said they'd take care of it.

Update: Apple didn't take care of it. Three weeks later someone did the exact same thing—driving straight across the airport runway— and officials had to call Apple again. *That* time Apple fixed the problem. And just to be safe, airport officials decided to close the access road to the runway. (They also put out a notice to all pilots to be on the lookout for cars on the runway.)

DUMBOLITION

On Friday, July 12, 2013, David and Valerie Underwood of Fort Worth, Texas, went to cut the grass at the house David's grandmother had left him when she died. It wasn't far from their own home, and they were planning to renovate the three-bedroom ranch house and rent it out for some extra income. But when they arrived at the address, the house was gone: All that was left was a concrete slab. "As we left, I saw two city marshals on patrol," David Underwood told reporters later, "and I said, 'Hey, what happened?

The one day of the year weddings are permitted at the Empire State Building: Valentine's Day.

Somebody tore down our house,' and he goes, 'That was your house? Oops.'" The Underwoods had to contact their city council representative to find out what happened. It turned out that the house next door to theirs had been condemned, and a demolition crew had been sent out to destroy it, but had been given the wrong address. And it wasn't as if the Underwoods' house was a dump. The home was in decent condition and was worth about $80,000, while the house next door—the one that was *supposed* to be destroyed— was an old, dilapidated structure with a bunch of broken windows. The City of Fort Worth acknowledged the error and promised to reimburse the Underwoods for the loss.

HONK IF THIS CAR IS STOLEN

Alex Walden and her boyfriend stepped out of their Boulder, Colorado, apartment one morning in September 2013 and discovered that Alex's car, a Volkswagen Jetta, had been stolen. Alex called the police to report the theft, and then the couple walked down the road. Just minutes later, as they were about to cross the street, a driver slowed to a stop to allow them to pass. It was the thief…in Alex's car. "I asked him what he was doing," Alex told reporters later, "and he said, 'I'm trying to let y'all cross.'" She told him to get out of her car, but the thief refused—indignantly acting as if it was his car. That's when Alex's boyfriend, Ryan Tippetts, dove headfirst into the passenger window of the car—landing in the lap of the woman in the passenger seat—and grabbed the steering wheel. The thief started driving away with Tippetts's feet hanging out the window, while beating Tippetts in the head and yelling that he was going to call the cops. The woman in the passenger seat, in the meantime, was screaming her head off. The thief, 20-year-old Davien Payne, finally stopped the car and tried to run away—but police were there by that time and Payne was captured and charged with several felonies. The woman in the car wasn't arrested, apparently unaware that the car was stolen. Tippetts, for his heroics, required surgery—and six titanium plates in his throat—to repair the broken larynx he suffered at Payne's hands. Payne told arresting officers that *he* was the real victim—he was only a passenger in the car, he said, having been offered a ride by a friend, who then ran away when Walden and Tippetts appeared. (The cops didn't believe him.)

I'LL BELIEVE IT WHEN...

Phrases like "when pigs fly" and "when hell freezes over" are called adynata
(from the Greek word for "impossible"). And they're common all over the world.

In Turkey:
"When the garden is full of ducks, holding pastry in their hands"

In Serbia:
"When the willow bears grapes"

In China:
"When the sun rises in the west"

In Algeria:
"When salt blossoms"

In Germany:
"When dogs bark with their tails"

In Latvia:
"When the owl's tail blossoms"

In Denmark:
"When there are two Wednesdays in a week"

In Bulgaria:
"When the pig climbs the pear tree in yellow slippers"

In Russia:
"When the crawfish whistles on the mountain"

In Portugal:
"In the afternoon of Saint Never's Day"

In France:
"When chickens have teeth"

In the Netherlands:
"On St. Juttemis Day, when the calves dance on the ice" (The holiday is in August.)

In India:
"When the crow flies upside down"

In Hungary:
"When gypsy children are streaming from the sky"

In Spain:
"When frogs grow hair"

In Colombia:
"When St. John lowers a finger" (Statues of St. John always show him with fingers raised in a benediction.)

In Italy:
"When geese piss"

In Ukraine:
"When the louse sneezes"

In the Seychelles:
"In the year two-thousand-and-never"

In Thailand:
"When the 7-Eleven closes"

The famed Hatfield–McCoy feud started over a pig.

PLANT TRICKSTERS

Plant seeds have ingenious ways of traveling from their parents to faraway places. The dandelion seed has a fluffy parachute to sail on the wind. Maple tree seeds fly away on a helicopter blade. Apples and berries employ animals to disperse seeds in their scat (complete with fertilizer). Here are some more.

• Want help with planting? Look to the ants. That's what many wildflowers do. Seeking the nutritious *elaiosomes* that are attached to the plants' seeds, ants cart the seeds into their nest, feed the elaiosomes to their larvae, and then toss the seeds on their underground trash pile. It's an ideal spot for sprouting—an underground mound of ant poop in a fiercely protected nest.

• For the many types of plants that have the aboveground structure of the tumbleweed, rolling along is a way to keep the population alive. After the plant's flowers wither and the seeds grow, the plant dries up and breaks off at the stem. Then it rolls where the wind blows, dropping seeds as it goes.

• The coconut has two things going for it: it has a tough skin and it floats. A coconut can float on ocean currents that take it far from home. As it does, its outer hull will protect it from corrosive salt water for months. It goes dormant until it reaches fresh water.

• One kind of prairie-grass seed (*redstem filaree*) has a long corkscrew-shaped bristle that propels the seed as far as 16 inches from the plant. With each change in humidity, the corkscrew straightens out and curls up, drilling its way into the ground to plant its seed.

• *Dorstenia gigas* is a large succulent that grows naturally in only one place: Socotra, an island off the Arabian peninsula. The plant's pot-bellied trunk clings to cracks in limestone cliff faces. Seeds shoot out of its saucer-shaped flowers by way of hydraulic pressure and can land in crevices more than three feet away from the parent plant.

• The ball-shaped spores of the prehistoric horsetail plant are only as big around as a human hair, but they have four ribbon-like "legs" that curl up and spring out with changes in humidity, letting them walk and hop around randomly in search of new places to put down roots. Sometimes, they jump high enough to be caught by the wind and carried away. (No wonder they outlived *T. rex*.)

First author to earn $1 million for writing: Jack London.

I'LL HAVE A DUST SUCKER

You know that Danish pastry is associated with Denmark, but we'll bet ten kopeks that you've never heard of these regional pastry favorites.

Pastry: *Coussin de Lyon* ("Cushion of Lyon")
Native to: Lyon, France
Details: When a plague swept through southern France in 1643, the citizens of Lyon organized a religious procession to a cathedral dedicated to the Virgin Mary, and asked for her help in protecting the city. They carried with them a seven-pound candle and a gold coin on a green silk cushion. The plague ended more than 350 years ago, but every year on December 8, the citizens of Lyon commemorate their deliverance by placing lit candles outside their homes and by eating these green pillow-shaped treats, which are made of *marzipan* (almond paste) and filled with *ganache* (chocolate and cream) flavored with curaçao liqueur.

Pastry: *Kürtoskalács* ("Chimney Cake")
Native to: Transylvania, Romania
Details: Chimney cakes are baked using a special tool that consists of a wood or metal cylinder at the end of a metal rod. A sweet yeast dough is rolled into a snakelike strip several feet long, then wound around the cylinder, rolled in granulated sugar, and roasted over an open fire. As soon as the sugar starts to brown, the dough is basted with butter and cooked to a golden brown. Then it's slid off of the cylinder and served upright, giving the finished cake a hollow cylindrical shape similar to a chimney—which is how it got its name.

Pastry: *Wachauer Marillenknödel* ("Wachau Apricot Dumplings")
Native to: The Wachau Valley in lower Austria
Details: These dumplings are made by removing the pit from an apricot and replacing it with a lump of sugar, then wrapping the apricot in dough containing *quark*, a sour cheese similar in texture to ricotta. After simmering in water for about 15 minutes, the dumplings are rolled in sugary cinnamon-flavored browned bread crumbs and dusted with confectioners' sugar, then served hot—not always as a dessert, but sometimes as the main course.

24% of California is desert.

Pastry: *Paris-Brest*

Native to: Paris and the port city of Brest, in northwest France

Details: What better way to commemorate the 1891 Paris-to-Brest bicycle race than with a dessert that looks like a bicycle wheel? Made with *choux* batter (also used for éclairs), the Paris-Brest looks like a bagel, except that it's sliced in half and served with a praline cream filling. Paris-Brests were so rich that the bicyclists took to eating them as energy food while racing, and the treats soon spread (presumably by bicycle) to bakeries in every corner of France.

Pastry: *Leipziger Lerche* ("Leipzig Lark")

Native to: Leipzig, in Saxony (east-central Germany)

Details: This pie really did contain larks until 1876, when King Albert of Saxony outlawed the hunting of the songbirds for food. Today the pies contain no larks or any other kind of meat—just ground nuts mixed with eggs, sugar, butter, and brandy, plus a single cherry or dollop of jam, which symbolizes a lark's heart.

Pastry: *Schneeball* ("Snowball")

Native to: Rothenburg ob der Tauber, a town in Bavaria

Details: What do you do with your leftover scraps of pie crust? In Rothenburg ob der Tauber, they crumple them loosely into a ball, then fry them in oil using a special holder called a *schneeballeneisen* ("snowball iron") that keeps the ball from unraveling as it cooks. After the dough has been fried to a golden brown, it's dusted with confectioners' sugar and served hot.

Pastry: *Dammsugare* ("Dust Suckers"/"Vacuum Cleaners")

Native to: Sweden

Details: According to legend, this small pastry was invented by a confectioner who wanted to find a use for the crumbs that fell on his floor during the day. Bakers no longer use stale crumbs sucked up with a vacuum cleaner (or "dust sucker," as they're called in Sweden) to make the *dammsugare*—they use fresh cake and cookie crumbs. But they're still drenched in *arrak* liqueur, mixed with cocoa powder and whipped butter, then molded into long, slender fingers, which are wrapped in sheets of green marzipan. For a final touch, both ends of the finger are dipped in melted dark chocolate. (Want to try one, but can't get to Sweden? They're sold at Ikea.)

FOUR FORGOTTEN FIRSTS

We've covered a lot of "first" stories over the years—the first car, the first camera, the first Playstation, the first toilet, and dozens more. But some stories seem to have fallen through the cracks—possibly because who (besides us) would even think of asking who made the first singing-fish wall ornament?

THE FIRST FIRE HYDRANT

The forerunners of the modern fire hydrant were simple cisterns (water-storage tanks), placed in strategic locations around a town or city, which could be utilized by a bucket brigade in case of fire. Cisterns were used by many different cultures around the world for thousands of years. In the 1600s, big cities like London had underground water mains made from hollowed-out wooden logs. When a fire broke out, firefighters dug down to one of those mains and used a hand drill to bore a hole in it, allowing the water to be used to fight the fire. Afterward, the firefighters would repair the hole with a wooden plug—and that's the origin of the term "fire plug." This evolved to the placement of permanent plugs that rose aboveground and had fixtures in them to which firefighters could attach what were basically faucets. Those led to the invention of the permanent fire hydrant, which is commonly attributed to a man named Frederick Graff Sr., the chief engineer of the Philadelphia Water Works in the late 1700s. Graff was apparently issued a patent for a permanently connected standing faucet around 1801 but that can't be confirmed because some years later the patent records were destroyed in a fire. (You may refer to this as *firony*.) The modern, stout, cast-iron fire hydrant most people are familiar with dates to around the 1830s. It became common around the United States in the 1850s, and around the world by the late 1900s.

THE FIRST BALLISTIC MISSILE

"Ballistic missile" is a name given to a type of military missile that flies in a *ballistic trajectory*. Such a missile is shot up high into the air—the only part of its flight that is powered—after which it is meant to fall, under the force of gravity, onto its target. The missile's flight path is governed by the physical laws of flight, known as *ballistics*. This is opposed to a *guided* missile, whose flight is powered

---

for all or most of its time in the air, which means it doesn't have to be shot high into the air. A guided missile can fly on a very low trajectory, and its flight path can be altered during flight. The first ballistic missile ever produced was the German Vergeltungswaffe 2—the "Vengeance Weapon 2"—better known as the V-2 rocket, developed by Nazi scientists in 1942 and first put into use in 1944. Weighing more than 12,000 pounds, the V-2 was about 46 feet long, could cover about 200 miles at speeds of more than 3,500 miles per hour, and carried a 2,200-pound warhead. More than 3,000 of them were launched during World War II. They were aimed at targets in northern Europe, including London, and killed an estimated 9,000 people overall. (Fortunately, the war was almost over by the time they came into use.)

Its horrors aside, the V-2 was a remarkable scientific achievement: It could reach an altitude of more than 60 miles—making it the first rocket ever to make it to space. After the war, the V-2 became the foundation for the space programs of the United States and the Soviet Union. There are many different kinds of ballistic missiles in use around the world today, one of the most powerful being the Trident II, an American submarine-launched ICBM (intercontinental ballistic missile), which can travel distances of more than 7,000 miles at speeds greater than 13,000 miles per hour…and which carry nuclear warheads.

THE FIRST MINIVAN

The simple definition of a "minivan": a small van with an interior designed like a car. If you think the first one was the Dodge Caravan or the Plymouth Voyager, think again. According to automotive historians, the Stout Scarab, designed in 1934 by William Stout, should be called the very first minivan. The Scarab was a beetle-shaped (hence the name) vehicle, meant to be a "mobile office," that had seats for several passengers. But the Scarab did not have what we think of as the classic minivan body shape, and only nine were ever produced. A better candidate for the very first minivan: Germany's DKW Schnellaster (Rapid Transporter), made from 1949 until 1962. The Schnellaster was not just a small passenger van, it also had several other features closely associated with modern minivans, including a transverse (sideways-situated) front engine, front-wheel drive, three rows of bench seats—and even a forward-slanted face, just like the Dodge Caravan.

THE FIRST SINGING-FISH WALL PLAQUE

This bizarre product became a sensation starting in 2000. Where did it come from? Joe Pellettieri, vice president of Gemmy Industries, a novelty gift company based in Irving, Texas. In 1998 Pellettieri and his wife, Barbara, were trying to come up with ideas for gifts when Barbara saw the logo of Bass Pro Shops store, which features a bass with an open mouth, and said, "How about a singing fish?" Pellettieri actually spent the next two years developing the idea, and in April 2000, the Big Mouth Billy Bass was released. Amazingly, more than a million sold in just that first year alone, and millions more have sold since. Gemmy—and its competitors—have released numerous related singing-critter models in the years since—including Travis the Singing Trout (it sings "Doo Wah Diddy"), Cool Catfish (it raps), Sammy the Salmon, Jaws (a shark), Larry the Lobster (it sings "Rock the Boat"), Frankie the Filet-o-Fish (a promotional item available only at MacDonald's), Buck the Deer (it sings "Rawhide"), and Billy Bones—a singing fish skeleton.

* * *

ALL THE NEWS THAT'S FRIT TO PINT

Embarrassing goofs from the Fourth Estate.

• The *Toronto Sun* issued a correction noting that teachers did not get paid during a strike. That's not a grievous (or funny) error. So why mention it? It was listed under the heading "Correrction."

• From an article in the *Huffington Post*: "Older adults: If you feel cold, put on a sweater, crap yourself in a blanket, or turn on the heat, recommend the physicians."

• After the satirical U.S. news site, *The Onion*, reported in 2012 that North Korean leader Kim Jong Un had been named "Sexiest Man Alive," the Chinese news agency, *The People's Daily*, ran a flattering photo spread of Un, and quoted directly from *The Onion*: "With his devastatingly handsome, round face, his boyish charm, and his strong, sturdy frame, this Pyongyang-bred heart-throb is every woman's dream come true." *The People's Daily* pulled the story when informed it was a joke.

• "He and his wife Gllian have three children, Gavin, 3, and 11-year-old twins Helen and ugh." (*Oprington News Shopper*)

Most poisonous plant native to North America: water hemlock—you can die from touching it.

TAKE MY KID, PLEASE

Parents say the darndest things.

"I want my children to have all the things I couldn't afford. Then I want to move in with them."
—**Phyllis Diller**

"As someone very sagely said during the patricide trials of the Menendez brothers: any time your kids kill you, you are at least partly to blame."
—**Elizabeth Wurtzel**

"The nature of parents is to embarrass merely by existing."
—**Neil Gaiman**

"A father has to be a provider, a teacher, a role model, but most importantly, a distant authority figure who can never be pleased. Otherwise, how will children ever understand the concept of God?"
—**Stephen Colbert**

"The value of marriage is not that adults produce children, but that children produce adults."
—**Peter De Vries**

"Raising a teenager is like nailing Jell-O to the wall."
—**Bill Cosby**

"You can't make your kids do anything. All you can do is make them wish they had. And then, they will make you wish you hadn't made them wish they had."
—**Marshall B. Rosenberg**

"Having a two-year-old is like having a blender that you don't have the top for."
—**Jerry Seinfeld**

"Parenting is the one job where, the better you are, the more surely you won't be needed in the long run."
—**Barbara Kingsolver**

"All of us have moments in our lives that test our courage. Taking children into a house with a white carpet is one of them."
—**Erma Bombeck**

"Having children is like living in a frat house. Nobody sleeps, everything's broken, and there's a lot of throwing up."
—**Ray Romano**

"What is a home without children? Quiet."
—**Henny Youngman**

Odds that a grandfather, father, and son all have the same birthday: 1 in 160,000.

SCAMMED!

*Need proof that if something seems too good to be true, it probably is?
Here are four classic scams that promise financial rewards or
some other benefit…only to part you from your money.*

BLACK BILLS

Setup: When worn-out American currency is taken out of circulation, it's shredded and either sent to a landfill or recycled. But this scam counts on the "mark," or victim of the scam, not knowing this. The con artist explains to the mark that the U.S. government destroys paper money by soaking it in permanent black ink. Guess what! The con artist has figured out a way to remove the ink and has a friend at the mint who steals the bills. He demonstrates by removing ink from a strip of black paper that turns out to be a genuine $100 bill. And is this the mark's lucky day! The con artist explains that because he has more bills than he can clean himself, he's willing to part with some of them, plus the ink remover…for a reasonable price.

Scammed! The ink-soaked $100 bill was genuine, all right, but as the mark will soon discover, the strips he bought are made of worthless paper. But he isn't likely to go to the cops, because then he would have to admit to attempting to break the law.

THE FIDDLER

Setup: Two con artists pretending not to know each other enter a restaurant separately and dine at different tables. One man has a violin and appears to be a musician. When it's time to pay up, the musician tells the waiter, the restaurant owner, or some other mark that he's left his wallet at home. He offers to leave his violin as collateral while he goes and gets his wallet.

After he leaves, the second con artist asks to see the violin and exclaims that it's a lot more valuable than the musician realizes. The con artist estimates its value at $10,000 or some other huge sum and tells the mark he wants to buy it, but he can't wait for the musician to come back, so he gives his business card to the mark and asks him to tell the man to call him.

Scammed! In order to work, this one, like the black-money scam, relies upon the greed and dishonesty of the mark. The two con artists are counting on the mark to buy the violin himself. He may offer the musician $100, or $200 or even $1,000, in the belief that he can sell it to the second con man for thousands more and pocket the difference. When the musician returns to the restaurant, he pretends to resist selling his beloved violin, but finally agrees to part with it…and walks out of the restaurant with a good chunk of the mark's money. Only later does the mark realize the "buyer" will never return and the violin is a piece of junk.

THE BANK EXAMINER

Setup: A con artist posing as a bank examiner or a law enforcement officer flashes some credentials to a bank teller. He informs them that one of the other tellers is suspected of stealing money from the till and replacing it with counterfeit bills. They need the honest teller's help in catching the crook.

Scammed! How are they going to catch the dishonest teller? By marking the money in the honest teller's drawer. To prevent the dishonest teller from suspecting anything, the bank examiner takes the money out of the bank to mark it in their car…and is never seen again.

SNAKES ON THE LOOSE

Setup: This scam hit parts of the San Francisco Bay Area in 2013. Two scammers, one dressed as an animal-control officer and another dressed as a supervisor, knock at the doors of unsuspecting homeowners and ask for permission to search their property for an escaped pet rattlesnake that bit a little girl nearby. The duo ask that everyone in the house help the animal-control officer search the backyard while the supervisor searches the front yard.

Scammed! After the homeowner leads the animal-control officer and anyone else in the house out to the backyard, the supervisor enters the empty home through the open front door and steals whatever cash, jewelry, and valuables they can find.

*   *   *

"Freedom means the right to be stupid." —**Penn Jillette**

Under federal law, clothing tags must last the lifetime of the garment.

CELEBRITY MUSEUMS

You've been to Graceland and you've visited the Roy Rogers Museum, but you're still hungry for a celebrity fix? Here are some other destinations for your next road trip.

THE ERNEST HEMINGWAY HOUSE

Location: Key West, Florida

Features: Hemingway, his wife Pauline, and their two sons lived in this two-story Spanish Colonial-style home from 1931 to 1939. It was given to the Hemingways as a wedding gift from Pauline's Uncle Gus. (He paid $8,000 for it.) The Nobel Prize-winning author owned and regularly visited the house until his death in 1961. You can see much of the home's original furniture, including the studio, desk, and typewriter "Papa" used to produce some of his most famous works, including *Death in the Afternoon* (1932) and *To Have and Have Not* (1937). Also on display are several Hemingway family photographs, stuffed and mounted heads and skins of animals killed by Hemingway on African safaris, as well as artworks, antiques, and curios the couple bought on their many trips around the world. Admission: $13.

Be Sure to See: The odd-looking fountain in the home's backyard. It's made from a urinal taken from Hemingway's favorite Key West haunt, Sloppy Joe's Bar.

Bonus: There's also a huge in-ground pool (65 feet long), which Pauline had installed in 1937 while Hemingway was in Spain covering the Spanish Civil War. It was the first residential pool in Key West and cost about $20,000 to install (about $320,000 in today's money). Upon returning home, Hemingway was reportedly so enraged at the expense that he threw a penny at Pauline's feet, telling her she may as well take it, as it was now the last one he had. Be sure to look for that penny. Pauline had it embedded in the concrete rim of the pool.

THE ARNOLD SCHWARZENEGGER MUSEUM

Location: Thal, Austria

Features: This is the house Schwarzenegger grew up in. He lived here from his birth in 1947 until he left for America in 1968.

Spell-check: A person from Nigeria is a Nigerian; a person from Niger is a Nigerien.

The home was turned into a museum, with the star's blessing, in 2011. In it you can see the small metal-frame bed Schwarzenegger slept on as a boy, the dumbbell sets he worked out with as a teen, trophies from his bodybuilding days, and memorabilia from his Hollywood career—including a sword he used in his first hit film, *Conan the Barbarian* (1982) and one of the Harley-Davidson Fat Boy motorcycles he rode in *Terminator 2* (1991). There are also several life-size replicas of Schwarzenegger as a bodybuilder and his movie characters, including the cyborg in *Terminator*. And there's an entire room dedicated to Schwarzenegger's term as governor of California, complete with a replica of the desk he used in the governor's mansion. Admission: € 6.50 (about $9).

Be Sure to See: The "pit toilet." When Schwarzenegger lived there, the home had no running water (or electricity)—and the toilet in the family bathroom consisted of a hole in the ground with a simple wooden bench above it.

THE THREE STOOGES MUSEUM

Location: Ambler, Pennsylvania

Features: The "Stoogeum," as it is known, was founded in 2004 by Gary Lassin, who is married to the grandniece of Larry Fine—the "Larry" of Curly, Larry, and Moe. (Fine grew up in nearby Philadelphia.) This is not someone's home converted into a makeshift museum. It is a full-on, professionally set-up, 10,000-square-foot, three-story museum, with an enormous collection—about 100,000 pieces of Stooges memorabilia dating all the way back to 1918. The collection includes Stooges movie posters, costumes and props from Stooges films, a research library with thousands of photographs and news clippings, interactive displays, vintage Stooges toys, and a film vault where hundreds of 16-millimeter Stooges films are preserved. The Stoogeum is open on Thursdays. Admission: $10.

Be Sure to See: The 85-seat movie theater for special film screenings and lectures. They give lectures about the Three Stooges? Soitenly.

Bonus: The Stoogeum is also the headquarters of the international Three Stooges Fan Club, which was founded in 1974 with the official endorsement of Larry Fine and Moe Howard, and is the location of the club's annual meetings. Highlight of the meetings: Stooges impersonators, you lame brain! (Nyuk nyuk nyuk…)

Actor Will Smith can solve a Rubik's Cube in one minute.

IT'S A BAD IDEA CHARLIE BROWN!

Since the 1965 debut of A Charlie Brown Christmas, *Charles Schulz's* Peanuts *characters have appeared in more than 40 animated specials. The classics leave us feeling warm and fuzzy; others leave us wondering, "What were you thinking, Charlie Brown?"*

CHARLIE BROWN'S ALL STARS! (1966)

Plot: A recurring storyline in the *Peanuts* comic strip is Charlie Brown's woefully bad management of his woefully bad baseball team. In this special, Charlie Brown quits baseball for good after his team loses by more than 100 runs. He's coaxed out of retirement by Mr. Hennessey (voiced by a trombone, of course), a hardware-store owner, who offers to sponsor Charlie Brown's team and give them new uniforms. But there's a catch—the league is "boys only," so he'd have to cut Lucy, Violet, Frieda, Patty, and even Snoopy. Unwilling to sell out his friends, Charlie Brown turns down Mr. Hennessey. To cheer him up, his teammates make him a new uniform...out of Linus's security blanket. (Linus is traumatized.)

HE'S YOUR DOG, CHARLIE BROWN! (1968)

Plot: After becoming increasingly annoyed by Snoopy's getting into mischief, the Peanuts gang insists that Charlie Brown take action. Caving to their demand, Charlie Brown arranges to send Snoopy to the Daisy Hill Puppy Farm for obedience training. Instead, Snoopy runs off and hides out at Peppermint Patty's house. After he wears out his welcome by using her pool and drinking all her root beer, Peppermint Patty forces Snoopy to earn his keep as her maid. A few days later, when Snoopy breaks some dishes, Peppermint Patty sends him to the garage. He realizes he's better off with Charlie Brown and runs away, back home to his doghouse. Everybody's happy to see him again and assumes he's learned his lesson, but he soon returns to his bad behavior. No lessons are imparted.

PLAY IT AGAIN, CHARLIE BROWN (1971)

Plot: Frustrated by the fact that her crush, Schroeder, never notices

---

Fewer than 20 existing paintings have been attributed to Leonardo da Vinci.

her, Lucy commiserates with Sally and Peppermint Patty, and Patty comes up with a plan: Schroeder, she says, will fall for Lucy if she can get him to play piano at a PTA concert. Schroeder agrees and it looks like love is in the air…until Patty tells Lucy that the PTA wants rock 'n' roll, not classical music, and that Schroeder can't play any Beethoven (his favorite). Lucy hires Charlie Brown, Snoopy, and Pig Pen to be Schroeder's backing band, but Schroeder, unwilling to compromise his musical integrity, refuses to perform at the last minute. Patty is upset that the PTA is without a program; Lucy saves the day by whipping out a spray can of "PTA program entertainment." (Really.) The next day, Lucy insults Schroeder by telling him that Beethoven "never would have made it in Nashville" because he didn't have "the Nashville sound." Schroeder storms off.

THERE'S NO TIME FOR LOVE, CHARLIE BROWN (1973)

Plot: Overwhelmed by schoolwork, Charlie Brown decides he'll improve his grades with an elaborate class project about a local art museum. Complicating matters, both Peppermint Patty and Marcie have feelings for him and decide to help him out. Together, they take photos of the art museum's displays…unaware that they are actually in a supermarket and are taking pictures of the store's shelves. He realizes the goof too late and has to move ahead with his project, which his teacher (voice of a trombone) loves, assuming it to be some sort of Warhol-esque commentary on modern art. Result: Charlie Brown gets an A. He doesn't get the girls, though—he rebuffs both Patty and Marcie, declaring his undying love for "the Little Red Haired Girl."

IT'S ARBOR DAY, CHARLIE BROWN (1976)

Plot: By 1976 the Peanuts gang had celebrated Christmas, Halloween, Easter, Valentine's Day, and Election Day, and was starting to run out of holidays with which they could impart "the true meaning." In honor of Arbor Day, Charlie Brown and his friends decide to plant trees…in the middle of their baseball field. Only problem: they have a game against Peppermint Patty's baseball team scheduled. Charlie Brown comes up with a plan: outfit the trees with baseball gloves and caps. Amazingly, Patty's team is unable to score against an outfield full of trees. Meanwhile, Lucy, having been promised a kiss from Schroeder if she hits a home run, knocks one

Although oil is known as "black gold," it can also be green, brown, or red.

out of the park. Just as Charlie Brown's team is about to win their first game ever, it starts to pour and the game is canceled.

WHAT HAVE WE LEARNED, CHARLIE BROWN? (1983)

Plot: In this one, Charlie Brown learns the true meaning of Memorial Day and commemorates the 39th anniversary of the invasion of Normandy. This one takes place after the events of the theatrical film *Bon Voyage, Charlie Brown (and Don't Come Back)!*, in which Charlie Brown, Linus, Peppermint Patty, Marcie, Snoopy, and Woodstock go to France. When their car breaks down; the gang winds up stuck in a small French town. Snoopy goes into his "World War I Flying Ace" persona, convincing a French lady that he's a real pilot, and she rents the group a replacement vehicle. They continue their journey and go to a beach—Omaha Beach—where Linus teaches the gang about the horrors of combat. Then Linus recites "In Flanders Fields," a famous World War I poem about the inevitable result of war. At the end of the special, Linus and Charlie Brown stand in a field of red poppies on an old battlefield. Linus asks, "What have we learned, Charlie Brown?" Charlie Brown's sister, Sally, to whom he's been telling the story and showing photos of the trip as he puts them in an album, responds with, "You're pasting your pictures in upside down."

WHY, CHARLIE BROWN, WHY? (1990)

Plot: If you think the horrors of war are too heavy for a children's special, you might want to skip this one. In this special, Charlie Brown and his friends learn about childhood cancer. Linus befriends Janice, a new girl in school. One day, she's not feeling well and leaves school. Later that week, Linus's teacher informs their class that Janice is in the hospital. Charlie Brown and Linus visit Janice in her hospital room, where she tells them she has leukemia and explains her chemotherapy treatment program. In a particularly poignant scene, Linus asks Charlie Brown the existential question "Why?" Of course, he has no answer, leaving Linus to ponder his mortality. In another scene, after Janice returns to school, she is taunted by a playground bully when he discovers she's lost her hair because of chemo. Fortunately, the producers pulled their punches in the finale—Janice recovers, grows her hair back, and happily joins Linus at the swing set.

Utah was almost named Deseret, which Mormons believe is an ancient word for "honeybee."

THE DEVIL'S BATHTUB

Thousands of geographic features in the U.S. are named after the devil. Some were areas sacred to "godless" natives, renamed by Christian settlers. Others got their names because they resembled something. Here are some odd ones.

- **Devil's Washdish** (a narrow lake in northeastern New York)

- **Devil's Churn** (a choppy ocean inlet on Oregon's coast)

- **Devil's Tea Table** (flat-topped rock formation in New Jersey)

- **Devil's Tater Patch** (a mountain in North Carolina)

- **Devil's Postpile** (a basalt formation in eastern California)

- **Devil's Rock Pile** (a craggy rock pile in eastern Missouri)

- **Devil's Trash Pile** (a spot on Georgia's Oconee River where logs and limbs accumulate)

- **Devil's Bathtub** (a lake near Rochester, New York)

- **Devil's Ribs** (a rock formation in northern California)

- **Devil's Golf Ball** (a naturally-occuring round rock atop a rock tower in eastern Utah)

- **Devil's Prongs** (a rock formation on Kodiak Island off the coast of Alaska)

- **Devil's Belt** (another name for Long Island Sound)

- **Devil's Dripping Pan** (a flat area in northeast Connecticut)

- **Devil's Rocking Chair** (a pillar in Colorado)

- **Devil's Racetrack** (a dyke in southern New Mexico)

- **Devil's Cash Box** (a box-shaped ridge in south Arizona)

- **Devil's Bake Oven** (a cave in western Illinois)

- **Devil's Dutch Oven** (a round mountain in central Utah)

- **Devil's Tooth** (a tooth-shaped peak, part of Idaho's "Seven Devils" chain that also includes the Ogre, the Goblin, and the Devil's Throne)

- **Devil's Nose** (a bluff that juts out in southern Wisconsin)

- **Devil's Toenail** (a tall, narrow rock formation in Texas)

- **Devil's Throat** (a gigantic hole in the ground in Hawaii that leads to…)

Only a few species of piranha are flesh eaters. Most eat only plants or insects.

DR. TECHNOLOGY

Here's how science fiction may become science fact,
coming soon to a doctor's office near you.

LASERS VS. MALARIA
Malaria kills more than a million people each year. About 90 percent of victims are in Africa, and 85 percent are children. Eradicating malaria is one of the chief aims of the Bill and Melinda Gates Foundation, and in 2011, it awarded a $1-million grant to Columbia University astrophysics professor Szabolcs Marka, who in a video pitch said he wanted to apply "my optics and laser experience towards some humanitarian goal that can help people." Marka's previous research had shown that laser light repels insects. With the grant, Marka and his team created a laser light *wall.* Emitting a light outside of the visible human spectrum, the light wall repels mosquitos, which carry malaria. Marka doesn't really know why the light wall works—mosquitos (and other insects) approach the laser light, as they do with other lights, but once they reach it, they immediately turn back. A simple, cheap, healthy, and even humane way to fight malaria, one of Marka's lasers—made in a cone-shape and the size of a lightbulb—could protect a family's entire sleeping area from malaria-carrying bugs.

CONTACT LENSES VS. DIABETES

There are more than 20 million people in the United States afflicted with diabetes. Controlling the disease involves maintaining normal blood glucose levels, which are monitored by drawing a drop of blood and testing it in an electronic meter multiple times a day. The more testing, the tighter the control; the tighter the control, the better the patient's health. Google(X) Labs is developing a system that would allow for more regular glucose testing: once a second, every second. Researchers have created a contact lens fitted with tiny microchips and glucose sensors. A tiny hole in the lens allows the wearer's tears to seep in, and the sensors measure the body's glucose levels once per second. A tiny antenna then sends data to an external device for record keeping. If the glucose levels get too high or too low, a tiny LED light in the contact lens flashes to alert the wearer.

Heart attack victims in good relationships are half as likely to suffer a second heart attack.

TURBINES VS. HEART DISEASE

Every year, about 3,000 Americans are placed on the waiting list for a heart transplant. How many donor hearts are available each year? On average, about 2,000. Artificial hearts, such as the Jarvik-7, do exist, but they may cost a few hundred thousand dollars, require an external air compressor to work, and need regular surgeries for routine maintenance because the many moving parts tend to wear out. Researchers at Houston's Texas Heart Institute have developed an alternative: an artificial heart…that doesn't beat. While the Jarvik-7 imitates the structure of a heart, THI's beatless heart has no valves, no chambers, and very few moving parts. It consists of two turbines set inside a magnetic field that makes them spin rapidly, constantly pushing blood through the body at a steady rate. (Oddly, because it doesn't mimic the natural "pump-stop" motion of a real heart, the user doesn't have a pulse.) THI has successfully tested the turbine heart on more than 70 calves. The first human with the turbine heart lived an additional five months, enough to propel the beatless heart into wider human trials.

ELECTRICITY VS. OSTEOARTHRITIS

Osteoarthritis—a degenerative joint disease in which the cartilage in the body's joints breaks down—most commonly presents in the sufferer's knees. As the cartilage wears away, the arthritis symptoms become increasingly worse, making even walking extremely painful. Apart from drugs that treat the symptoms (which can cause stomach and heart problems), the only real solution has been a surgical reworking of the knee or placement of an artificial joint. A company called VQ Orthocare has developed a noninvasive alternative—an electronic sleeve. Worn around the knee, it sends an electronic current to the joint. The patient can't feel it, but that electricity actually stimulates the dwindling cartilage to stop dwindling and even grow. Once the cartilage has sufficiently replenished itself—after about six months of daily wear of the sleeve, according to the manufacturers—patients report less pain and increased joint function.

*　　*　　*

Loony Law: Men in Carmel, California, may not go out wearing an unmatching jacket and pants.

COOL BUSINESS CARDS

Some businesses have their business information printed on rectangular pieces of heavy paper. Some businesses get a little more creative...

Schwimmer Pool Service (Oakville, Ontario). This company's cards look like normal business cards, with a nice "Schwimmer Pool Service" logo and appropriate contact information. But there's more. Dip the card in your pool's water, compare the color it turns to the color code on the back of the card—and it tells you what the water's pH level is and if you need service.

Baywood Clinic Laser Tattoo Removal (Toronto, Ontario). Place Baywood Clinic's business card over a tattoo you're thinking of having removed, add a little water, press firmly, and wait about 30 seconds. Then peel the card away from the skin-colored sticker on the back of the card. That allows you to see what you'd look like if the tattoo wasn't there. The cards come in five different skin tones, for different skin-toned people. (If you have a really big tattoo, you're probably going to need a bunch of business cards.)

Sergio Freitas, Dog Coach (Joinville, Brazil). All dog trainer Sergio Freitas's business cards say is "Sergio Freitas, Dog Coach," along with his phone number. What's special about that? Nothing...except that his business cards are actual dog treats—bone-shaped—with the words printed on them.

Laser Printing Inc. (Dallas, Texas). This clever card mimics what you would see if you looked for a printer in Dallas—on Google. At the top it says "Google," and next to that is a search box with the words "Dallas printer" entered. Under that it says, "Did you mean: *LaserPrintingInc.com?*" and below that are the company's address and phone number.

Mitnick Security Consulting, LLC (Henderson, Nevada). Kevin Mitnick is a security expert. His business card is made of metal, and die-cut into it is a set of punch-out lockpicks. (You can actually snap them out of the card.) They've been tested...and they work. Mitnick is an *Internet* security expert, so the lock picks actually

---

The first "Avon lady" was actually a man: company founder David McConnell, in 1886.

have nothing to do with his business—it's just a gimmick. (Note: Before he got into Internet security consulting, Mitnick was the most wanted computer hacker in the United States, and after he was captured in 1995, he served five years in federal prison. He probably could have used his business card back then.)

Ramiro Veredas, Computer Expert (Spain). This business card is shaped like a normal business card—but it's an actual circuit board, with a bunch of soldered electronic parts all over it. The only printing on the card instructs readers to go to Veredas's website, where they are told to break off the tabs on two of the card's corners, and then to plug the remaining nub into the USB port in their computers. When plugged in, the card becomes a flash drive containing Veredas's cover letter, résumé, and portfolio, which then open automatically on the computer. (Cost: $7.50 per card.)

Dr. Hajnal Kiprov, Plastic Surgeon (Vienna, Austria). Dr. Kiprov's business information is on one side of this business card, and on the other is just a pink silhouette of a woman, from the waist up. There are two holes cut into the card, about where the woman's breasts would be, with stretchy rubber filling in the die-cut holes. Push your fingertips into the rubber inserts from the back of the card…and you can "enhance" the woman's breasts.

Your name here? If you want your own interesting business card, you might consider MeatCards.com. They make business cards… out of meat. Flat slabs of beef jerky, four inches wide by eight inches long, on which, for a fee, they will print your business info using a laser printer. (Four cards to a slab.)

Gengavan Second Hand (Karlstad, Sweden). It looks like a second-hand card for a second-hand shop: On one side, the contact info for an employee of "MG Electronics" is crossed out, and on the reverse side Gengavan Second Hand's contact info appears to be handwritten in pen.

Bon Vivant (Curitia, Brazil). This cheese shop has a really grate business card. It's made of metal, has the store's business info printed on it, and has a series of small, convex blades pushed out. In other words, it's an actual cheese grater. (Bet you didn't see that coming.)

Better safe than sorry: The average American home has 8 spare rolls of toilet paper.

PILLBILLIES & DEWEYS

It stands to reason that a profession that deals with, shall we say, "interesting" people and situations would have a language all its own. Book 'em, Dan–o!

Cash Register: A spot where traffic laws are routinely broken; an easy place to write tickets

Zone Poaching: Detouring into another officer's assigned area because yours is too quiet

Stop and Rob: A convenience store

Boozer Cruiser: A bicycle or other non-car vehicle used by someone who's lost their driver's license due to a D.U.I.

Loser Cruiser: An ex-police car, still painted in police colors but lacking lights and other police gear, driven by a civilian wannabe cop

Novertime: Unpaid overtime

Dogworthy: A situation that justifies the time and trouble of calling in a search dog

U-Boat: Unmarked police car

Pillbilly: A redneck (hillbilly) who abuses prescription drugs

Car Fisher: A criminal who steals things from parked, unlocked cars

Mirror Meeting: When two patrol cars park driver's side to driver's side so that the officers can exchange information

Blue Steel: An officer's service handgun

Mud Shark: A "nice girl" who has a criminal for a boyfriend

Shingle or Banana: A citation or traffic ticket

Movie Ticket: One gram of cocaine (a kilogram is a "pigeon")

Double Deuce: A .22-caliber handgun

Dewey: Driving While Under the Influence

DWO: A motorist who is thought to be a Dewey (swerving, etc.) but turns out to be Driving While Old

NBSS: A crime with lots of witnesses but no one willing to testify ("Nobody Saw Sh*t")

Birthing: Pulling a suspect out of an open car window after he/she refuses to open the door and step out of the car

Longest, heaviest dinosaur ever: *Amphicoelias fragillimus* (length: 190 feet; weight: 122 tons).

GOING MY WAY

Anyone can make a name for themselves with the things they do in life. It takes real creativity (and an accommodating undertaker) to make your biggest splash after you've departed this world.

Deceased: Lonnie Holloway of Saluda, South Carolina
Details: In 1973 Holloway bought a brand-new emerald-green Pontiac Catalina coupe. He'd purchased other cars over the years, but he really loved that Catalina and drove it for the rest of his life. And before he died in 2009 at the age of 90, he told his family he wanted to be buried in it.
Going His Way: The Rock Hill Baptist Church, which owned the cemetery where Holloway wanted to be buried, had no objection. So Holloway was propped up in the front seat of his Catalina with his favorite hat on his head, $100 in his pocket, and his hands gripping the wheel, and then a construction crane lowered the car into the ground. The trunk of the Catalina was filled with Holloway's extensive collection of guns (not because Holloway had asked to be buried with them but because "somebody might take them and shoot somebody," his cousin Johnny McCloud explained). The grave was covered with a slab of concrete to keep people from stealing the guns, the car, or the $100.
Note: Holloway and his Catalina were laid to rest right beside the grave of his wife, Alice, who died in 2007. Alice did not join her husband in the Catalina; she's still in her coffin alongside the car. (No word on whether that was her decision or Holloway's.)

Deceased: Irene Bowler of Ramsgate, Kent, in southeastern England
Details: Not long before she died in 1998 at the age of 76, Bowler read an article about people scattering the ashes of loved ones by putting them into fireworks and shooting them into the sky. She told her family that she, too, wanted to go out with a BANG!
Going Her Way: Bowler's daughter, Judith Summers, needed some time to adjust to the idea of having her mother made into a giant firework. But then she found a company called Theatrical Pyrotechnics that was willing to inter her mother in a rocket

and shoot it 500 feet into the sky on the evening of her memorial service. "It was all very impressive," Summers told London's *Evening Standard* newspaper. "It went with a real bang followed by a spectacular starburst. I know it is unusual, but I suppose it is just another way of scattering ashes."

Deceased: James Henry Smith of Pittsburgh, Pennsylvania
Details: Before he died from prostate cancer in 2005 at the age of 55, Smith told his family that he didn't want an ordinary viewing with people filing past his open coffin. Instead, he wanted to go out the way he'd spent so many pleasant Sunday afternoons: dressed in his robe and Pittsburgh Steelers pajamas and watching his beloved Black and Gold on TV.
Going His Way: A room at the funeral home was redecorated to look like Smith's living room. Then he was dressed in his game-day robe and jammies and laid out, sitting in his recliner, legs crossed with a remote control in his hand and a beer and cigarettes within easy reach, in front of a television playing Steelers highlights. His favorite Steelers blanket was draped over the side of the chair. "I saw it and I couldn't even cry," Smith's friend Mary Jones told the *Pittsburgh Post-Gazette*. "People will see him the way he was."

Deceased: Jack Woodward, the former proprietor of the Boat Inn in Northamptonshire, England
Details: The Boat Inn has been in Woodward's family since 1877. He was born in the pub and tended bar there from the age of 14 until he retired. After that he was a regular at the pub until shortly before his death in 2008 at the age of 83.
Going My Way: In his will, Woodward asked that his ashes be buried beneath the pub's floorboards. His son Andrew, who took over the running of the inn, was happy to oblige. The spot in the floor is marked with a brass plaque that reads "Stand here and have a drink on me. Jack 1924–2008." Patrons of the bar have been having drinks on Jack ever since.

*　　*　　*

"The truth does not change according to our ability to stomach it."
—**Flannery O'Connor**

Studies show that men can have up to a 25% surge in testosterone when their sports team wins.

FOR MEN ONLY

Why are G.I. Joes called "action figures"? Because Hasbro knew that if they called it a "doll," parents would never buy it for their sons. Here are some other products that have been given the MAN treatment.

- **YOGURT.** Yogurt is commonly marketed toward women (have you ever seen a man in a yogurt commercial?), but the makers of Powerful Yogurt want to change that. Their Greek yogurt is packed with protein, which they claim will help tone men's abs. The packages are black with pictures of bulls on them.

- **DIET SODA.** Soda industry market research has shown that the word "diet" reads as feminine, so companies have had to come up with creative ways to pitch low-calorie drinks to guys. Coca-Cola launched Coke Zero (in a black can), Pepsi launched Pepsi Max (in a black can), and Dr Pepper markets Dr Pepper Ten with the slogans, "Just 10 manly calories" and "It's not for women."

- **DIETS.** "Dieting" is also seen as feminine. Weight Watchers for Men is almost exactly the same as the program for women, except that it doesn't use the word "diet" in its marketing materials and it has an online "cheat sheet" showing men how to eat healthy while still consuming beer and grilled meat.

- **SPANX.** These modern-day girdles fit tightly around a midsection and give a slimming effect. And almost all of its customers are women. When Spanx introduced products for men, they created an upper-body undergarment and called it a "compression shirt."

- **YOGA.** There's a new fitness trend in Boston: Broga. It's yoga for men ("bros"). It's the same yoga that's been practiced for thousands of years, but with the addition of squat thrusts and push-ups.

- **SHOWER ACCESSORIES.** How do you get men to buy bath products? Call them "tools" and make them look like auto parts. The Axe Detailer Shower Tool is a black plastic ring that looks like a monster truck tire small enough to fit in your hand. On one side is a red sponge to clean "sensitive" areas, and on the other side is a piece of black nylon mesh to scrub "your extra dirty parts."

Honest! Only U.S. president who was also a licensed bartender: Abraham Lincoln.

RAIN OF FALAFEL

American movies are released all over the world, but their titles often use phrases that are unfamiliar in other languages. Result: bizarre title changes. Here are some of the funniest ones we found, translated back into English.

Hollywood: *Austin Powers: The Spy Who Shagged Me*
Malaysia: *Austin Powers: The Spy Who Behaved Very Nicely Around Me*

Hollywood: *The Dark Knight*
Venezuela: *The Knight of the Night*

Hollywood: *Airplane!*
Germany: *The Unbelievable Journey in a Crazy Airplane*

Hollywood: *Legally Blonde*
Japan: *Cutie Blonde*

Hollywood: *Captain America: The First Avenger*
Russia: *The First Avenger*

Hollywood: *Finding Nemo*
India: *Nemo's Missing, Did You See?*

Hollywood: *Despicable Me*
Poland: *How to Steal the Moon*

Hollywood: *101 Dalmatians*
Iceland: *Puppies*

Hollywood: *Annie Hall*
Portugal: *Neurotic Fiancé, Nervous Fiancé*

Hollywood: *Pretty Woman*
China: *I Will Marry a Prostitute to Save Money*

Hollywood: *Willy Wonka and the Chocolate Factory*
Denmark: *The Boy Who Drowned in Chocolate Sauce*

Hollywood: *Cloudy with a Chance of Meatballs*
Israel: *Rain of Falafel*

Hollywood: *Tremors*
Germany: *In the Country of Rocket-Worms*

Hollywood: *The Horse Whisperer*
Japan: *Held by Wind in Montana*

Hollywood: *Never Been Kissed*
Philippines: *Because She's Ugly*

Hollywood: *The Sixth Sense*
China: *He's a Ghost!*

Weight of a great white shark's brain: 34 grams, about as much as two DVDs.

LOOK WHAT I FOUND!

*We all like the idea of searching for buried treasure,
but we like the idea of finding it by accident
even more (except when it's not treasure).*

Found: A Norman Rockwell painting

Where: Behind a false wall

Story: Don Trachte was the illustrator of the *Henry* Sunday comic strip from 1942 to 2005. He was also an avid collector of other artists' and illustrators' work. His prize possession: Norman Rockwell's *Breaking Home Ties*, a painting that depicted a farmer and his college-bound son waiting for the train. Trachte had purchased it from Rockwell in 1960 for $900. When Trachte and his wife, Elizabeth, were divorcing in 1970, he was so certain that she would try to take his art collection that he secretly painted copies of his eight favorite paintings and replaced the originals on the walls of their Sandgate, Vermont, home with the fakes. When they divvied up the art, the unsuspecting Mrs. Trachte took seven forgeries to her new home while he kept the Rockwell. Trachte never told a soul what he had done, and the fake Rockwell hung on his wall until he died in 2005. A year after their father's death, Trachte's sons, Dave and Don Jr., discovered a fake wall behind the bookcase in his art studio. Behind that wall were the eight original paintings—works by well-known illustrators Mead Schaeffer, George Hughes, Gene Pelham, Lea Ehrich...and Norman Rockwell. The art had been hidden for more than 35 years. It was worth the wait. On November 29, 2006, Sotheby's Auction House sold the Rockwell painting for $15.4 million. (No word on what happened to the forgeries.)

Found: A decomposed body

Where: Behind a basement wall

Story: On December 21, 1985, JoAnn Nichols of Poughkeepsie, New York, left for a hairdresser appointment...and never returned. After a friend reported her missing, her husband, James Nichols, told police that she'd left a farewell note on the computer and that he'd spoken to her on Christmas Eve, but she wouldn't tell him where she was. After investigating, police determined there was no sign of foul play. Twenty-eight years later, Nichols, 82, died peacefully at home of natural causes. His wife wasn't so lucky. A contractor hired to clean out the house discovered her body behind a false wall in the basement. Turned out the 55-year-old first-grade teacher had been murdered by a blow to the head with a blunt instrument and her body put in a plastic container, where it sat, decaying, for nearly 30 years within the walls of her own home.

Found: Several jars of gold dust

Where: Under a heating grate

Story: In September 2012, two HVAC workers from Clark & Rush of Sacramento, California, were installing a new heating and air-conditioning system in an old home, when they found 12 baby food jars filled to the brim with gold dust. One of the men, Steve Otley, later told a local TV reporter that they were used to finding odd things in heating grates but had never seen anything like this. Otley also admitted that he and his partner did have a weak moment when they thought of taking the gold for themselves (who wouldn't?), but ultimately handed the jars over to the owners. The HVAC installation cost $6,500, but the owners didn't mind—they cashed in the gold for a whopping $300,000.

Found: A Korean War missile

Where: Inside a bathroom wall

Story: It was probably the last thing William Wittman of St. Francis, Wisconsin, expected to find. While remodeling his bathroom in 2011, he was tearing the insulation out of a wall when he found a small green projectile. It measured 20 inches across, and had four tail fins and a 5-inch explosive head. (And it was live.) Wittman showed it to his wife, who calmly carried the 50-year-old missile out to the grass beside their detached garage and called the police. They evacuated the neighborhood and alerted the bomb squad, who took it to the department of public works and detonated it, shaking the windows all over town. According to neighbors, the previous owner's sons fought in Korea, and "the boys" liked to bring back war souvenirs as gifts for neighbors and friends. How they were able to bring home a live missile and why they walled it up in the bathroom remains a mystery.

Do poets know it? According to researchers, poets die younger than writers of other genres.

Found: Some cash

Where: In a hatbox in the attic

Story: A young couple in New Jersey bought an older home and hired an electrical contractor to do some upgrades. While trying to pull a wire out of the wall, the electrician realized something was making it stick. He went into the attic and found the obstruction: a hatbox. Curious, he opened the box and found a stack of love letters written in the 1960s, along with $10,000 in cash. The letters revealed that a man who once lived in the house had been having an affair with the woman next door. The lovers had planned to leave their spouses and run away together, but the man died unexpectedly, and their secret letters and getaway stash remained hidden for decades. The new homeowners used the money to cover expensive medical bills for their two children. (The electrician who found the loot got a $1,000 reward.)

Found: A mummified cat

Where: In the bathroom of an English cottage

Story: Richard Parson, who lived in the village of Ugborough in Devon, England, was having his upstairs bathroom redone when the builders made a horrifying discovery: A perfectly preserved 400-year-old mummified cat was entombed in the wall. "It was quite scary looking and a lot bigger than a normal domestic cat," reported Parson. (He should know scary—he's an undertaker.) The cat was hairless but still had all of its teeth and claws and was posed in the archetypal Halloween cat stance, with back arched, mouth open, and one paw extended. According to local villagers, it was common in the 1600s throughout Europe to place a dead cat in the wall or ceiling as a charm to ward off witches. "It clearly works," said Parson. "Since we have lived in the village, we have not seen sight or sound of any witches."

*　　*　　*

"I've been reading the '50 Most Beautiful People' issue for years, and there's always one person on the list who makes you think, 'Oh, give me a @#$* break.' This year, I'm proud to be that person."

—**Tina Fey**

The Finnish language has no future tense.

THE PHANTOM GAMBLER

*In the early 1980s, newspapers around the world told the evolving story
of a man dubbed "the Phantom Gambler"—an anonymous Texan
who went to a Vegas casino and...well, here's the story.*

STRANGER IN TOWN

On September 24, 1980, a man walked into the Binion's Horseshoe Casino in downtown Las Vegas carrying two suitcases. He asked a cashier to send for the casino's owner, Ted Binion. The man told Binion he had anonymously contacted the casino several weeks earlier to ask if he could make a *substantial* wager at the casino, and was told he could. (Binion had just recently instituted a policy of allowing a one-time bet of any size; most other casinos had limits—usually no more than $10,000.) The man showed Binion what was in the suitcases: one was empty; the other contained $777,000 in cash.

Binion ordered a cashier to change the money into chips, then escorted the man to a craps table in the middle of the casino hall. Another gambler, a woman, was shooting (throwing) the dice at the time. The man placed all his chips—all $777,000 worth—on the Don't Pass line on the table. Betting "Don't Pass" means you think the person shooting will lose. If you win a Don't Pass bet, you double your money. If you lose, you lose it all. In three gripping rolls of the dice...the woman lost. (She rolled a 6, a 9, and then lost with a 7.) Binion escorted the man back to the cashier, helped him pack $1,554,000 in cash into his two suitcases, helped him carry the heavy suitcases to his car, and then the man drove off without a word. "He took off like a bandit," Binion told reporters.

THE RETURN

The next day newspapers and TV programs all over the country—then all over the world—told the story of "the Phantom Gambler," whom Binion described to reporters as a slim, fair-haired Texan who had ambled into his Las Vegas casino and casually made the largest single bet on a game of craps in Las Vegas history—and won. But the story wasn't over.

Almost four years passed.

Fame-talities: The average North American lives 13 years longer than the average celebrity.

On March 24, 1984, the anonymous Texan walked back into the Horseshoe Casino. Once again he asked for Binion, and once again he told the casino owner that he wanted to make a very large wager—but only if Binion first took him (and his mother) to see Willie Nelson, who was playing at the nearby Golden Nugget. Binion agreed, and afterward the mystery man exchanged $538,000 cash for chips, and bet it all on one all-or-nothing game of craps, with someone else shooting and all of his chips on the Don't Pass line. And, same as last time…he won. The Phantom Gambler's total winnings, in just two craps games: $1.3 million.

This time the mystery man stuck around for a few days, and Binion got to know him a little. Meanwhile, the man made three more bets at the craps table, winning an additional $120,000. (And, oddly, he didn't tell his mother about the bets.)

KNOW WHEN TO HOLD 'EM

William Lee Bergstrom was born to an upper-middle-class family in Austin, Texas. He graduated from Austin High School in 1969, got married in 1972, divorced in 1974, started investing in real estate, and, according to friends, by the end of the 1970s had $1 million in the bank. But, according to Binion, he lost it all on bad investments in gold and silver shortly before his first bet at the Horseshoe. So where'd he get the $777,000 to bet on that first craps game? He had borrowed it from a bank. And if he'd lost, Binion said, Bergstrom told him he had planned to kill himself.

In the years between his two spectacular gambling wins, in 1980 and 1984, Bergstrom—after repaying the bank loan—took his fortune and traveled the world. He went to Europe, the Middle East, and the Far East, and even bought a house in Hawaii and lived there for a while. After the second win, he and a friend named John traveled around the U.S. for a few months. Then, that November, Bergstrom called Ted Binion again. He wanted to make another bet, he said—his biggest one yet.

KNOW WHEN TO FOLD 'EM

On November 16, 1984, Bergstrom showed up at the Horseshoe Casino with two suitcases. Again, one was empty. The other contained $550,000 in cash, $140,000 in South African krugerrands, and $310,000 in cashier's checks—exactly $1 million. Just as with

---

If you soaked a bone in hydrochloric acid overnight, you could tie it in a knot the next morning.

his previous two visits, Bergstrom bet the entire amount on a single, all-or-nothing game of craps, putting it all on the Don't Pass line. Except this time, *he* was throwing the dice, meaning he was betting that he would lose. As security guards attempted to hold back the huge crowd that had gathered around the table, Bergstrom threw a 7 on his very first roll, meaning he had won the game…and lost the gamble. Bergstrom had just made the single largest bet in Las Vegas craps history—and had lost $1 million in a single roll of the dice. He thanked Binion, picked up the enchiladas he had ordered before the game, and walked out the door. Newspapers worldwide told the story of the Phantom Gambler again, only this time the story had a very different ending.

KNOW WHEN TO WALK AWAY

A week later, on Thanksgiving night, November 22, 1984, police in Austin, Texas, received an anonymous tip from someone reporting a possible suicide at an Austin hotel. The *Dallas Times* reported that police officers found Bergstrom in a chair, unconscious. Two 12-gauge shotguns had been taped to a table in front of him, both of them aimed at his chest and rigged to go off when and if Bergstrom slumped forward. Luckily, he had not. After a brief period of hospitalization and psychiatric treatment, Bergstrom was released. Two months later, on February 2, 1985, he was back at the Horseshoe, this time with a cashier's check for $1.3 million, trying to make another bet. The check was a fake; Binion turned him down.

KNOW WHEN TO RUN

On Sunday, February 3, 1985, Bill Bergstrom, age 33, committed suicide in a Las Vegas hotel room, taking an overdose of pills. A maid found his body the next morning. Bergstrom had written a letter to his family and friends, telling them for the first time that the man he'd been traveling with, John, was actually his lover, and that the reason he'd made that final bet was because John had left him. Until that moment, Bergstrom's friends and family had no idea that he was the mysterious Texan who had been making headlines for the last four years. Bergstrom's letter also requested that he be cremated, and that his ashes be placed in an urn with the inscription: "The Phantom Gambler of the Horseshoe, Who Bet $1 Million on Nov. 16, 1984."

Energy-efficient: Your brain uses only about 1/10 of a calorie per minute.

URBAN JUNGLES

What happens when wild animals get lost in the "concrete jungle"?

• **Lions in L.A.** Griffith Park is Los Angeles's beautifully rugged 4,000-acre answer to New York's Central Park. While the terrain offers open spaces for joggers and hikers, it's also home to most of L.A.'s wildlife. Deer and coyotes are common sights; so are bobcats. But in 2012, National Park Service researchers spotted something new: a 125-pound mountain lion, living just minutes away from Hollywood Boulevard. Mountain lions are native to Southern California, commonly found in the hills above Malibu. To make the 20-mile trek to Griffith Park, the cat, labeled P-22 by researchers, had to cross two major freeways and ascend winding, mansion-lined streets. That dangerous, risky journey pretty much assures that P-22 will live out the rest of its life near Griffith Park. Scientists say it's worth it for the big cat, as he faces no real competition for food.

• **Coyotes in Chicago.** In 2007 a coyote casually strolled past the open front door of a Quizno's restaurant and attempted to jump over the counter. After scaring all the customers and workers out of the shop, the coyote jumped into the open beverage cooler while a large crowd of onlookers gathered around the restaurant. Witnesses described the wild beast as "docile" and "nonaggressive," a sign that it was probably looking for shelter, not food. After a few nights in captivity to make sure it was healthy, the coyote, now named Adrian, was set free at the Flint Creek Wildlife Rehab Center.

• **Alligators in Apopka.** Walmart's prices are apparently so good, even the gators can't stay away. In October 2013, shoppers at an Apopka, Florida, Walmart spotted an alligator casually wandering around the front entrance of the store. The six-foot-long reptile spent about an hour blocking the automatic doors until animal-control authorities arrived. Despite the alligator's calm demeanor, the Florida Fish and Wildlife Conservation Commission had to put it down. Why? Experts said the animal's tranquil attitude showed it had lost it's fear of people, and if left unchecked, it would continue to "terrorize" urban centers. And, they said, the behavior would probably spread to other gators, too.

Spoiler alert: NASA found 168 "impossible things" in the 1998 movie *Armageddon*.

ASK THE EXPERTS

Everyone's got a question or two they'd like answered—basic stuff like "Why is the sky blue?" Here are a few of those questions, with answers from some of the world's top trivia experts.

MEN IN TIGHTS

Q: *Why do superheroes wear their underwear on the outside?*

A: "According to Julius Schwartz (famed editor of DC Comics from 1944 to 1986, who edited the most famous of all external-underwear superheroes, Superman), this was modeled after the garb of aerial circus performers and wrestlers of the era. It should be noted that wrestlers, circus performers, and superheroes weren't actually wearing underpants over their leggings, but rather tight underwear-like shorts. As superheroes are generally incredibly athletic and perform amazing acrobatic stunts while crime-fighting, it was natural enough for the earliest superhero artists to adopt this style of dress for their characters." (From *The Wise Book of Whys*)

A LITTLE TO THE LEFT

Q: *Why is the computer cursor slanted and not straight up and down?*

A: "Today, there's no longer a good reason for the mouse cursor to be slanted. But in the infancy of digital displays, angling the cursor solved a real design problem. According to software developer Bart Gijssens, the mouse was first invented back in 1963 by Douglas Engelbart. The cursor was originally an arrow pointing up, but on the low-resolution displays of the day, it was often difficult to make out a tiny vertical line on a screen. So Engelbart decided to tilt the arrow to the left at an angle of about 45 degrees. The angle made the pointer easier to pick out against the pixelated background. Soon, Steve Jobs adopted the left-leaning pointer software from Engelbart, and then Bill Gates snagged it." (Carey Dunne, *FastCoDesign.com*)

SLIPPERY WHEN WET

Q: *How did the Egyptians transport massive stones across the desert?*

A: "The ancient Egyptians transported their rocky cargo across the desert sands, from quarry to monument site, on large sleds with

---

It's estimated that a common housefly can have as many as half a billion bacteria on its body.

upturned edges. Now, when you try to pull a sled carrying a 2.5-ton load, it tends to dig into the sand ahead of it, building up a berm that must be cleared regularly or become an even bigger obstacle. Wet sand doesn't do this. With just the right amount of dampness, *capillary bridges*—essentially microdroplets of water that bind grains of sand to one another through capillary action—form across the grains, doubling the material's relative stiffness. This prevents the sand from berming in front of the sled and cuts the force required to drag the sled in half. Artwork in the tomb of Djehutihotep depicts a scene of slaves hauling a colossal statue, and a guy at the front of the sled is shown pouring liquid into the sand." (Daniel Engber, *Gizmodo.com*)

THE AIR UP THERE

Q: *If heat rises, why is it colder on a mountain peak than in a valley?*

A: "Heat doesn't rise. Low density air rises if surrounded by air of higher density. Air that's heated by contact with the warm ground becomes less dense and therefore rises. As it rises, it mixes with cooler air above and cools to a point where it stops rising. Air at the top of a mountain makes little contact with the ground and is therefore cold. Air in the valley below makes a great deal of contact and is therefore warm." (From *The Last Word*, published by *New Scientist* magazine)

PULP FACT

Q: *What was in the mysterious glowing briefcase in* Pulp Fiction?

A: "After many Answer Man discussions on the briefcase, I received the following from Roger Avary, who co-wrote the film with Quentin Tarantino: 'Originally the briefcase contained diamonds. But that just seemed too boring and predictable. So it was decided that the contents were never to be seen. That way each audience member will fill in the "blank" with their own ultimate contents. All you were supposed to know is that it was "so beautiful." No prop master can come up with something better than each individual's imagination. Then somebody had the bright idea (which I think was a mistake) of putting an orange light bulb in there. Suddenly what could have been anything became anything supernatural. Didn't need to push the effect.'" (From *Questions for the Movie Answer Man*, by Roger Ebert)

The USDA once paid $46,000 for a study on how long it took Americans to cook breakfast.

TV FACTS: THE 1960s

Stuff you didn't know about some TV classics.

Bewitched. "Second Darrin" is TV-industry slang for recasting a role in the middle of a show's run...and hoping the audience doesn't notice. On *Bewitched*, Darrin Stephens was first played by Dick York, then by Dick Sargent. (*Bewitched* also had two Gladys Kravitzes and two Louise Tates.)

Star Trek. In a 1968 episode, censors made Gene Roddenberry cover an actress's exposed belly button. Five years later, when Roddenberry was making the pilot for a sci-fi show called *Genesis II*, he cast the same actress as an alien and gave her two belly buttons. He felt he was "owed" one.

The Green Hornet. The 1966–67 series is best remembered for one of martial-arts star Bruce Lee's earliest acting roles. Although Lee only played the sidekick (Kato) to the title character portrayed by Van Williams, in Asia the show was titled *The Green Hornet Starring Bruce Lee as Kato*. In Hong Kong it was *The Kato Show*.

The Flintstones. While it was clear to almost anyone familiar with both shows, *The Flintstones* creator William Hanna admitted in 1993 that he and Joseph Barbera based it on *The Honeymooners*. One person who noticed the similarity: Jackie Gleason. He considered suing Hanna-Barbera, but ultimately let it go. He didn't want to be known as "the guy who yanked Fred Flintstone off the air."

The F.B.I. The show's technical advisor, FBI associate director Mark Felt, was later revealed as Watergate informant "Deep Throat."

I Dream of Jeannie. Jeannie (Barbara Eden) was born in 64 B.C., which at the time of the show's premiere in 1965 would have made her 2,029 years old.

Rowan & Martin's Laugh-In. Canadian comedian and *Saturday Night Live* creator Lorne Michaels broke into American television in 1969 with a job writing for *Laugh-In*, at the time the #1 show on TV. He resigned in protest after less than a year. Reason: He objected to a guest appearance by President Richard Nixon.

Ripe fruit from the South American sandbox tree explodes with a sound like gunfire.

FIND...OR FAKE?

Even if you don't consider yourself a history buff, there are some bits of history that are bound to touch you—like this story of an old, wrecked violin found in an attic...or was it something much, much more?

SHOW AND TELL

In 2006 a man walked into the Henry Aldridge & Son Auction House in Devizes, Wiltshire, England, carrying an old leather case with the initials W. H. H. stamped into the leather. Inside the case were seven water-stained sheets of American ragtime music and a battered old violin that the man said had been in his family for more than 60 years. He'd recently found it again while rummaging through his mother's attic in Lancashire. On the tailpiece of the violin was an engraved silver plate that read

FOR WALLACE ON THE OCCASION OF
OUR ENGAGEMENT FROM MARIA

The violin looked to be over 100 years old. It was so badly cracked from water damage that it would have been unplayable even if it hadn't been missing a string. Value: about £12 ($20), a fraction of what it would have cost to restore it to playable condition. The instrument was unremarkable in every respect...except that it came with a remarkable story. The man, who asked to remain anonymous, said that according to family legend, this was the violin that the *Titanic's* bandleader played to comfort doomed passengers as the great ship went down. The owner of the violin wanted to know if there was any way to determine whether it was authentic.

A LIKELY STORY

The man had come to the right place. Auctioneer Henry Aldridge and his son, Andrew, had sold a lot of *Titanic* memorabilia over the years, and they were experts at sizing up the authenticity of purported *Titanic* artifacts. They knew that all eight members of the *Titanic's* band bravely went down with the ship, playing their instruments until the bitter end. Andrew Aldridge probably knew without having to look it up that the bandleader's name was Wallace Henry Hartley. That matched the W. H. H. initials on the leather case and the name Wallace on the engraved silver plate.

A little research would have confirmed that Wallace did have a fiancée, and that her name was Maria. But any scam artist could have easily found the same information and used it to create a believable *Titanic* "artifact" by making an old-looking silver plate, attaching it to a junk violin, and soaking the whole thing in a bucket of seawater.

The violin was almost certainly a fake. How could it not be? What were the odds that such a remarkable artifact—one of the most famous musical instruments in history—would have survived the sinking, and then be forgotten for almost a century? Even so, the possibility of the violin being the genuine article was so tantalizing that the auction-house staff decided to dig deeper.

THAT SINKING FEELING

Among the official records of the *Titanic* sinking are lists of bodies pulled from the water and the personal or "body effects" found on them. William Hartley was one of only three band members whose bodies were recovered; it was pulled from the water ten days after the ship sank and is listed in the records as Body #224. Items reported as having been found on Body #224 included a gold fountain pen inscribed with the initials W. H. H., a silver cigarette case, a pocket watch, a cigar holder, and pocket change...but no violin.

As part of their investigation, the auction house's researchers also studied contemporary newspaper coverage of the recovery of bodies from the *Titanic*. They found several articles that mentioned Hartley by name. The story of the band members bravely playing for the doomed passengers had already become famous, and there was great public interest when his body was recovered. More than one article states that Hartley was found with his violin. He had placed it in his leather case along with his sheet music and strapped the case to his shoulders above his life jacket, to protect it as much as possible from the seawater.

So why wasn't the violin included in the official list of body effects? "The most likely explanation was that the case containing the violin was simply not regarded as a 'body effect,'" Henry Aldridge says. Instead, it was probably considered a piece of luggage.

What do you think—is the violin the genuine article?
Part II of the story is on page 347.

Outside of the Vatican, the world's largest collection of Christian relics is in Pittsburgh.

NOTES FROM THE UNDERGROUND

Fascinating facts about nature's most down-to-earth creature—the earthworm.

• An earthworm is like a living water balloon. Between its external muscles and its digestive system, the worm has a tube of liquid that keeps its body inflated. If it gets scared by a predator, it can squirt fluid through pores in its back.

• The Australian blue squirter worm can shoot its fluid 12 inches into the air.

• Earthworms don't have lungs; they breathe through their skin. If their skin dries out, they suffocate.

• Every earthworm is hermaphroditic, meaning it has both male and female sex organs.

• Many earthworms can regrow a lost tail. Some species can also regrow a lost head.

• An earthworm can excrete as much as 10 pounds of poop per year. These "casts" are rich in nitrogen, phosphates, and potassium, all very nutritious to plants.

• Canada exports 370 million worms a year, mostly for bait and animal food.

• An acre of healthy soil may contain around 1.7 million worms. The worms under a ranch's soil may outweigh the livestock above it.

• Professional bait collectors practice "worm charming," sending vibrations into the ground that cause worms nearby to come to the surface. Certain predators, as well as falling rain, do the same thing.

• The World Worm Charming Championships take place each year in Cheshire, England. Worm charmers compete to see who can raise the most worms out of their plots (9 square meters) in 30 minutes. World record holder: 10-year-old Sophie Smith, with 567 worms (2009).

• Earthworms have no eyes, but they can sense light...and they avoid it.

• There are about 2,700 species of earthworms. Australia has about 1,000, including the world's largest—the giant Gippsland worm, which can grow to 10 feet long and weigh nearly half a pound.

At the 1976 Olympics, Nadia Comaneci became the first-ever gymnast to score a perfect 10....

LET'S PLAY KOLEJKA!

Some kids learn geopolitics from playing Risk or spelling from playing Scrabble for Juniors. But you may not believe what these games teach.

BLACKS AND WHITES (1970)

Psychology Today published this game with the intent to show white Americans what it was like to be African American in the 1960s and 1970s. The game is similar to Monopoly. Players buy real estate and build fortunes. It's different, though, in that some players are "Black" while others are "White." White players start the game with $1 million and can buy property anywhere on the board. Black players start with $10,000 and can buy in some areas only after they've amassed $100,000…but still can't buy property in the "Suburban Zone."

PUBLIC ASSISTANCE (1980)

In the late 1970s, conservatives called for welfare reform, pointing to "welfare queens," people who had grown rich by exploiting government assistance programs. Hammerhead Enterprises cashed in on the moral panic created by the notion that some elements of society were getting a free ride with this satirical, anti-welfare game. Players had a choice of two routes around the game board: "Working Person's Rut" or "Able-Bodied Welfare Recipient's Promenade." The welfare path included government checks; the working person's path included taxes. The winner: the player with the most money left at the end of the game. (It was usually the person on the welfare path.)

TRESSY CAREER GIRL GAME (1960)

This game educated young girls on the many career paths available to women. Because it was 1960, those options were "actress," "model," "secretary," "teacher," and "dancer."

DR. RUTH'S GAME OF GOOD SEX (1985)

The celebrity sex-advice writer lent her name to this game in which players—either a committed couple or up to four couples (for an especially awkward time)—roll dice and travel around the board. They earn "arousal points" by answering trivia questions about

---

…Only problem: the scoreboard couldn't display a perfect score. "1.00" was shown instead.

human sexuality (including menstruation and sexually transmitted diseases) and learning how to better please one another in the bedroom.

WHO'S HAVING THIS BABY ANYWAY? (2004)

If a round of *Dr. Ruth's Game of Good Sex* went particularly well, players might find themselves playing this game, which purports to be a replacement for pregnancy and childbirth books like *What to Expect When You're Expecting*. Players take on the role of a pregnant woman, and the game progresses through all 40 weeks of a pregnancy. First one to "dilate to 10 centimeters" wins!

THE TERRIBLE TOBACCO TALE (2013)

This game for 8- to 10-year-olds is designed to make children fear tobacco and never start smoking. Players go around the board, some taking a "smoking" path and others going the route of "chewing tobacco." Instead of points, players amass the effects of smoking, such as bad breath, poor lung capacity, discolored teeth, and cancer. Designed for schools (it includes a teacher's booklet), the game costs up to $99…about the same as 18 packs of cigarettes.

KOLEJKA (2011)

The title is a Polish word that means "line-up," as in a line that people stand in to wait for things. The game was published by Poland's Institute of National Remembrance to remind young Poles just how awful life was in Poland when it was under Communist rule, from 1945 to 1989. Players must try to find items on a shopping list and move around the board to different shops…where they wait in line endlessly or find out the store is out of the needed item. It gets worse. Draw the wrong card from the deck, and you lose your spot in line entirely. Draw the "colleague in the government" card, however, and you move up in line. In 2013 Kolejka was published in English, Spanish, and Japanese, presumably so that kids in the United States, Spain, and Japan could also learn how awful life was in Poland under Communist rule.

*   *   *

"There is a foolish corner in the brain of the wisest man."

—**Aristotle**

"POLLY WANT A LAWYER?"

You've heard of pheasant under glass—how about "parrot under oath"?
Just because bird testimony may not be admissible in court, that
doesn't mean it can't influence the outcome of a case.

Parrot: Bozo, a cockatoo owned by Argentinian couple Carlos and Rosella DeGambos

Background: Divorces aren't as easy to get in Argentina as they are in the United States, or at least they weren't in the 1980s when Rosella DeGambos tried to divorce her husband, Carlos, on grounds of adultery. What did she have as proof? "Testimony" from Bozo. When attorneys brought the bird into court and asked it, "Who loves Carlos?" the bird squawked, "Ruby loves Carlos! Ruby loves her baby!" (Ruby was Carlos DeGambos's secretary.) When the attorneys showed Bozo a picture of another woman, a young beautician said to have visited the DeGambos home when Rosella was away, the bird shrieked, "Honeybun, I love you!"

What Happened: The judge granted the divorce.

Parrot: Lorenzo, a parrot owned by a Colombian drug cartel

Background: In September 2010, police raided a suspected cartel hideout in the city of Barranquilla, Colombia. Their suspicions were confirmed when Lorenzo recognized their police uniforms and squawked, "Run! Run! You're going to get caught!" "The parrot was sending out alerts," officer Hollman Oliveira told reporters. "You could say he was some sort of watch bird."

What Happened: Police arrested four men in the raid and seized a large quantity of drugs. They also took Lorenzo and two other lookout birds into custody—not to charge them with crimes but to see if they could be coaxed into revealing anything else about the gang. "Parrots like to talk, and we are good listeners," Oliveira said. Colombian police estimate that as many as 2,000 parrots have been trained to act as lookouts for drug cartels.

Parrot: Heera, a parrot owned by Vijay and Neelam Sharma in the city of Agra, India

Background: In February 2014, Neelam Sharma was murdered by

Adolf Hitler was on the short list for the 1938 Nobel Peace Prize.

robbers who were burglarizing her home. Police had little to go on at first and were unable to identify a suspect.

What Happened: Heera the parrot was home at the time of the attack and apparently witnessed the crime. He provided the first clue about a week after the murder. When Vijay's nephew, Ashutosh Goswami, visited the house, Heera became visibly agitated. "During discussions, too, whenever Ashutosh's name was mentioned, the parrot would start screeching," Sharma told *Time* magazine. "That raised my suspicion and I informed the police." They brought Goswami in for questioning, and he eventually confessed. Police also found the murder weapon and some of Neelam's jewelry in his possession. At last report he and an accomplice were in jail and awaiting trial for murder.

Parrot: Max, an African Grey parrot owned by a Santa Rosa, California, woman named Jane Gill in the early 1990s

Background: Like Heera, the parrot in India, in November 1991, Max apparently witnessed his owner being murdered in her home. Two days passed before Gill's body was discovered; when it was, Max was found in his cage nearby, hungry and dehydrated. He was taken to a pet store to recover, and when his health returned he began screeching, "Richard, no, no, no!"

What Happened: Gill's friend and former housemate was a man named Richard, so was he charged with the murder? No. When other evidence pointed to Gill's business partner, Gary Rasp, the police arrested and charged him. At his murder trial, Rasp's attorneys tried to have the testimony of Max the parrot introduced as evidence, but the judge refused to allow it. When that trial ended in a mistrial in 1993, Rasp was tried a second time, and in March 1994 he was found guilty. Sentenced to life in prison without the possibility of parole, he maintains his innocence to this day.

*　　*　　*

OOPS!

Students at Chicago's Paul Robeson High School made a spelling goof when they chose the theme for their 2014 senior prom, and none of the staff or teachers caught it...until after the invitations were printed. The theme: "This Is 𝒜re 𝒮tory"

Surprise! On average, 54 percent of the money awarded by courts goes to cover legal fees.

"PUT NOT OFF YOUR CLOTHS"

Rules of Civility & Decent Behavior in Company and Conversation was a list of 110 rules created by 16th-century Jesuit educators to teach boys how to behave like gentlemen. Nearly 200 years later, boys in the American colonies (including young George Washington) were still expected to commit all the rules to memory. Some of them seem silly today, but others are still pretty good advice. Here are our favorites.

• "When in company, put not your hands to any part of the body not usually discovered."

• "In the presence of others, sing not to yourself with a humming voice, or drum with your fingers or feet."

• "Sleep not when others speak; sit not when others stand, speak not when you should hold your peace, walk not on when others stop."

• "Put not off your clothes in the presence of others, nor go out of your chamber half dressed."

• "Spit not into the fire, nor stoop low before it; neither put your hands into the flames to warm them, nor set your feet upon the fire, especially if there be meat before it."

• "Shift not yourself in the sight of others, nor gnaw your nails."

• "...Bedew no man's face with your spittle by approaching too near him when you speak."

• "Kill no vermin, or fleas, lice, ticks, etc. in the sight of others; if you see any filth or thick spittle put your foot dexterously upon it; if it be upon the clothes of your companions, put it off privately, and if it be upon your own clothes, return thanks to him who puts it off."

• "To one that is your equal, or not much inferior, you are to give the chief place in your lodging, and he to whom it is offered ought at the first to refuse it, but at the second to accept, though not without acknowledging his own unworthiness."

• "In visiting the sick, do not presently play the physician if you be not knowing therein."

- "Let your ceremonies in courtesy be proper to the dignity of his place with whom you converse, for it is absurd to act the same with a clown and a prince."

- "Run not in the streets, neither go too slowly, nor with mouth open; go not shaking of arms, nor upon the toes, kick not the earth with your feet, go not upon the toes, nor in a dancing fashion."

- "Play not the peacock, looking every where about you, to see if you be well decked, if your shoes fit well, if your stockings sit neatly and clothes handsomely."

- "Associate yourself with men of good quality if you esteem your own reputation; for 'tis better to be alone than in bad company."

- "In company of those of higher quality than yourself, speak not 'til you are asked a question, then stand upright, put off your hat and answer in few words."

- "Being set at meat scratch not, neither spit, cough or blow your nose except there's a necessity for it."

- "Make no show of taking great delight in your victuals. Feed not with greediness. Eat your bread with a knife. Lean not on the table, neither find fault with what you eat."

- "If you soak bread in the sauce, let it be no more bread than what you put in your mouth at a time, and blow not your broth at table but stay 'til it cools of itself."

- "Put not your meat to your mouth with your knife in your hand; neither spit forth the stones of any fruit pie upon a dish nor cast anything under the table."

- "Cleanse not your teeth with the tablecloth, napkin, fork or knife, but if others do it, let it be done with a pick tooth."

- "Rinse not your mouth in the presence of others."

- "In company of your betters be not longer in eating than they are. Lay not your arm but only your hand upon the table."

- "If others talk at table be attentive, but talk not with meat in your mouth."

- "Let your recreations be manful, not sinful."

- "Labor to keep alive in your breast that little spark of celestial fire called conscience."

GOVERN-MENTAL

Strange-but-true tales from the public sector.

DON'T PICK THIS CLASS

Controversy erupted in Oakland, California, in 2013 when mayor Jean Quan announced in her weekly newsletter that the city was sponsoring a community class entitled "How to Pick Locks." She explained that it was designed to teach people what to do if they got locked out of their residences, but a chorus of critics was quick to point out that the class was being offered at a time when home burglaries in Oakland were up 40 percent from the previous year. "What's next," asked one angry resident, "the Fundamentals of Armed Robbery?" Quan canceled the class.

LOONY ORANGE LEPRECHAUN?

British prime minister David Cameron was mocked all over the Internet in 2013 when it was revealed that he didn't know what "lol" means. According to Rebekah Brooks, the former head of News International, she and Cameron occasionally exchanged text messages, which he'd conclude with "LOL, DC." He *thought* he was saying "Lots Of Love, David Cameron" until Brooks politely informed him that the abbreviation stands for "Laugh Out Loud." It turned out that Cameron had been concluding much of his correspondence that way. (He doesn't anymore.)

SPACED OUT

In 2014, three years into a four-year term, David Waddell decided to leave his seat as city councilman in Indian Trail, North Carolina. And he submitted his resignation letter in Klingon. Weirder still, he botched the translation. Instead of using one of the many websites dedicated to the *Star Trek* characters, Waddell typed the letter into *Bing.com*, clicked "Klingon" as the language, and copied and pasted the translation. Result:

Teach (the) city (the) constitution.
I will return next time to witness victory.
Resignation occurs in 2014 the 31st of January.
Perhaps today is a good day (to) resign.

What the...? When you deliberately fail to complete a sentence, it's called *aposiopesis*.

Mayor Michael Alvarez couldn't tell whether the letter was bad Klingon or good Klingon, but he still didn't like it, saying it was "childish and unprofessional."

STRAINER IN A STRANGE LAND

Wearing a large colander on his head, Christopher Schaeffer took his oath of office in the Pomfret (New York) town council in 2014. The colander was not a joke, Schaeffer said, but a symbol of his religion—the Church of the Flying Spaghetti Monster. He is a "Pastafarian Minister." The church was founded in 2005 by a 24-year-old named Bobby Henderson, who defended Schaeffer's odd headwear, saying, "Some people will see it as obnoxious, but I am completely confident that Schaeffer will distinguish himself as a council member of the highest caliber."

THE TIMES THEY AREN'T A-CHANGIN'

Remember those 3.5-inch floppy disks that PCs used nearly 20 years ago? The U.S. government remembers them…because they're still using them today. The news came to light in a December 2013 *New York Times* article. It explained that the *Federal Register*, "the daily journal of the U.S. government," regularly gathers information from various agencies and then issues a document (online and in print) consisting of proposed rule changes, proclamations, executive orders, etc., so that it can be available for public inspection. However, a few government agencies submit their information on the antiquated floppy disks. Why haven't they upgraded to at least CD-ROMs so modern computers can actually read them? According to the *Times*, "in part because legal and security requirements have yet to be updated, but mostly because the wheels of government grind ever so slowly."

LEAVING HER MARK

Late one night in May 2011, Tennessee state representative Julia Hurley was finishing up her first term as a lawmaker. While sitting in the House chamber, she carved her initials in the desk. Only problem: It wasn't *her* desk; it belongs to the state, and when the carving was discovered, Hurley had to pay to have it repaired. Matters worsened for her when the local news aired a report about the incident. "I don't understand why it's news," she complained, "and I don't want to talk about the desk." But the press wouldn't let up, and Hurley was forced to talk about the desk. "It was like one in the morning on the last day of the session. I wasn't thinking straight."

THE HUNT FOR RED NOVEMBER

The Democratic National Committee wanted to demonstrate that the party is committed to national defense, so on the final night of their 2012 convention, they brought out a four-star general to speak, surrounded by dozens of military veterans. To really push the point home, the video screen behind them displayed an image of four warships. Only problem: The ships are in the Russian Navy. The DNC apologized and blamed the goof on "vendor error."

MINOR MAYOR

In July 2012, Bobby Tufts, age three, was elected mayor of Dorset, Minnesota. His first decree: to make ice cream the top of the food pyramid. When reporters asked what his favorite flavors were, Mayor Tufts replied, "Chocolate. And vanilla. Strawberry. Cotton candy. And rainbow sherbet." Technically, the small town (population: 28) doesn't have a local government, so Bobby's duties are ceremonial, and "elections" consist of drawing someone's name out of a hat...which makes it that much more amazing that at the end of the one-year term, Bobby, then four, was picked for a second time.

*　　　*　　　*

YOU'RE MY INSPIRATION

In 1863 Mark Twain was a 28-year-old newspaper reporter living in San Francisco when he became friends with a local firefighter. The two men shared a passion for riverboats and talked at length about them while playing cards and drinking beer. Twain was very impressed by the young man—he'd once saved 90 people from a burning steamship. At the time, Twain was preparing to work on his first novel, which was going to be about a female firefighter called *Shirley Tempest*. But he scrapped that idea and instead began a book about a boy who grew up around the riverboats of the Mississippi River. The name of Twain's friend: Tom Sawyer.

UNCLE JOHN'S STALL OF FAME

*Uncle John is amazed—and pleased—by the unusual ways
people get involved with bathrooms, toilets, and so on.
That's why he created the "Stall of Fame."*

Honoree: The Detroit Metropolitan Airport

Notable Achievement: Offering pit stops for pooches

True Story: Since 2009 the U.S. Department of
Transportation has required that airports provide designated "pet
relief areas" for people traveling with service animals. In most
airports the area is outdoors, and thus outside the secure area of the
airport. If your service dog has to answer nature's call after you've
passed through TSA security, you have to go through again, which
can take an hour or more and could cause you to miss your flight.

In April 2014, Detroit Metropolitan Airport unveiled an indoor
Service Animal Relief Area, located inside a secure area near the
departure gates. The $75,000 facility consists of two "toilets"—one
real patch of grass, one artificial—each with a small fire hydrant
in the center (to give dogs something to aim for). There are drains
beneath each patch of grass, and pushing a red button on the wall
activates pop-up lawn sprinklers that rinse your dog's pee into the
drains. (If your service dog poops, you still have to pick it up and
dispose of it yourself.)

Honoree: Karen Perrin, a senior assistant at a private family
foundation in Washington, D.C.

Notable Achievement: Not giving up when the "going" got tough

True Story: Late one evening in December 2013, Perrin was working alone in the office, finishing up some work for her boss. When
she was ready to go home, she made what should have been a quick
trip to the restroom…but she discovered the lock on the bathroom
door was broken, and she was trapped inside.

Perrin, who is claustrophobic, tried kicking the door open and
taking apart the lock. Neither worked. Then she started shoving
paper towels under the door, hoping that the security guards would

notice them on the security camera. "I probably put two hundred towels out, but nobody came to rescue me," she told ABC News. Then she tried to lift herself up through a hatch in the ceiling, but couldn't. She did, however, find a three-foot steel rod in the ceiling. She took it and started banging on the wall next to the locked bathroom door…and after pounding for more than two hours, finally smashed a hole large enough to stick her hand through and unlock the door from the outside. In all she spent more than eight hours locked in the bathroom. "I felt like I was escaping a bad dream, like when you have a nightmare and you wake up and your heart is pounding and you realize, 'Oh, I was just dreaming. Did that just happen?'"

Honoree: Donnie Lindsey, the battalion chief of the Garner, North Carolina, Fire Department and Charmin Toilet Paper
Notable Achievement: "Tight-wadding" the fire department to a one-year supply of free toilet paper
True Story: One of Lindsey's less impressive duties is making sure the department's four fire stations have enough toilet paper. In early 2014, the department's budget was stretched so thin that he thought he might have to switch from premium two-ply toilet paper to cheaper one-ply. That started the firefighters grumbling on Facebook, which caught the attention of folks at Charmin. It turns out that Charmin has a "Relief Project" through which the company donates a year's supply of toilet paper to one fire department in each of the 50 states. When they heard about Garner's situation, they made the Garner Fire Department the winner for North Carolina. A few weeks later, each of the winning fire departments received a shipment of 960 rolls of toilet paper, enough to keep 20 firefighters rolling along for a year. "We'll take what we can get. Every little bit helps," says Deputy Chief Tim Herman.

*   *   *

4 REAL CANDIES FROM AROUND THE WORLD
- Shrimps & Bananas (England)
- Uncle Urnie's Candy Ashes (United States)
- Super Osama bin Laden Kulfa Balls (Pakistan)
- Kitten Tongues (Czech Republic)

In the first five seasons of the TV show *24*, Jack Bauer killed 112 people.

THE FUTURISTS

What do today's top forecasters see looming on the horizon? That simple question introduced us to the fascinating field of "futures studies"— its checkered past, muddled present, and uncertain tomorrow(s).

NOSTRA-DUMB*SS

For most of human history, professional prognosticators could only guess what the future would bring. If you sought advice from a shaman, a soothsayer, or Nostradamus, you'd hear whatever the bones or the crystal ball "told" them. It wasn't until the last few centuries that people began to look at the future from a more scientific point of view. Why? Because for most of history the world that you died in was basically the same one you were born into. Societal changes via scientific and technological advances— fire, the wheel, agriculture, metallurgy—were few and far between and could take centuries to spread around the world.

Then, in the mid-1400s, came the printing press and with it the book industry. For the first time, the world's accumulated knowledge was available to the masses. (At least to the ones who could read.) That advance ushered in the Age of Enlightenment, followed by the Industrial Revolution. All of a sudden, the modern world was taking shape…and fast!

GULLIVER'S TRAVAILS

The first futurists weren't necessarily scientists, but a keen understanding of both history and human nature helped them project what might be on the horizon. That concept is called *foresight.* "It refers to a process of visioning alternative futures through a combination of hindsight, insight, and forecasting," explains Tuomo Kuosa in his book *The Evolution of Strategic Foresight.* "(Hind)sight is about systematically understanding the past, (in)sight is about systematically understanding the true nature of the present, and (fore)sight is about systematically understanding the future."

One of the first men to display that foresight was Irish satirist Jonathan Swift. In his 1726 novel *Gulliver's Travels,* the hero travels to a strange island full of futuristic gadgets—one of them a giant "Engine" containing "Bits" that allow even "the most ignorant

---

Ghanaians are frequently named for the day of the week on which they were born.

Person to write Books in Philosophy, Poetry, Politicks, Law, Mathematicks, and Theology." It's all "linked together by slender Wires." Swift basically described electricity, computers, and the Internet hundreds of years before they were invented.

Even more impressive, Swift wrote about "two lesser stars, or satellites, which revolve around Mars." How did he know that Mars had two moons 150 years before they were discovered? He wasn't psychic (as some assumed), just logical: the two planets closest to the Sun have no moons, ours has one, and it was known even then that the large outer planets have several moons. Mars, Swift concluded, would most likely have two. His foresight was spot-on.

TO THE MOON, JULES

Swift used fantastical settings to mock his world, but he wasn't a prognosticator by trade. French writer Jules Verne, however, *did* try to predict the future. In 1828, when Verne was born, ocean voyages took months, and there were hardly any sets of railroad tracks that stretched from one town to another. Just three decades later, steam-powered ships and locomotives were taking people across oceans and continents in only a week. Knowing that the rate of change was increasing, in 1863 Verne attempted to track it in a book called *Paris in the 20th Century.* Among Verne's predictions for the 1960s: glass skyscrapers, high-speed trains, gas-powered cars, air-conditioned houses, fax machines, and convenience stores. His publisher rejected the manuscript as being too "far-fetched."

Verne's next novel, *From the Earth to the Moon,* has since been hailed as a pioneering work of both science fiction and foresight. The plot: three wealthy men finance a trip to the moon. Their ship was launched from a cannon, so Verne got that part wrong, but he was close to the mark on other details—including the rocket's escape velocity, the Florida launch site (where NASA missions would take place a century later), the three-man crew, and the splash-down in the Pacific. Even more uncanny, Verne's moon trip cost $5,446,675—$12 billion in 1969 money. Cost of the actual moon mission: $14.4 billion.

DEEP WELLS

Like Verne, British novelist H. G. Wells witnessed significant change in his lifetime. When he was born in 1866, cities were lit by torches and oil lamps, and there were no horseless carriages or air travel. By the turn of the century, cities were being lit by gas lamps, and automobiles were steadily replacing the horse. In 1901 Wells published his groundbreaking treatise on the future, *Anticipations*. In it, he foresaw the end of the steam age and the rise of oil. He accurately predicted that the entire region from Boston to Washington, D.C., would become one long system of suburbs, cities, highways, and traffic jams. He even predicted speed limits.

Yet for all his foresight, Wells got a lot wrong: He said that airplanes were just a passing fad and that moving sidewalks would be commonplace in cities. He also predicted that the world's governments would merge into one "New Republic" ruled by scientists who would eliminate all but the white race and "establish a world state with a common language and a common rule." That future hasn't arrived.

COME TOGETHER

For the most part, however, Verne, Wells, and other early futurists worked alone. Wells realized that in order to make accurate forecasts, an incredible amount of information would be required to construct a more complete world picture. That meant bringing together scholars and scientists from disparate fields to share and compare data. So in 1932 he made an impassioned speech on the BBC, calling for "Professors of Foresight":

> It seems an odd thing to me that though we have thousands of professors and hundreds of thousands of students of history working upon the records of the past, there is not a single person anywhere who makes a whole-time special job of estimating the future consequences of new inventions and new devices. There isn't a single Professor of Foresight in the world. But why shouldn't there be? Isn't foresight as important as history?

Though Wells never saw the formation of a coalition of futurists, his use of the word *foresight* helped lay the foundation for modern futures studies. The field soon came to be viewed as not just an honorable pursuit, but a necessary one. Two world wars left much of the planet in tatters, and the Cold War threatened to destroy mankind for good. Suddenly, forecasting the future became a respected science...and a bona fide fad.

For Part II, set your Flux Capacitor for page 205.

WORST IN CLASS

Next time you're up late studying, consider what one of Uncle John's teachers once said: "College is hard—there should be some classes where you can get an easy A." Maybe that's why most schools offer "cream-puff" courses like these.

Deconstructing TV's Buffy. "*Buffy the Vampire Slayer* is an extremely 'full' text, playing on ideological fault lines. The series, self-consciously generic in conception and execution, allows this course to examine the histories, theories, and traditions of the musical, melodrama, comedy, silent film, and horror genres. Students should exit the course with a paper worthy of publication in an academic journal." (Emerson College)

Feel the Force: How to Train in the Jedi Way. "This course analyzes the real-life psychological techniques behind Jedi mind tricks and examines the wider issues behind the *Star Wars* universe, like balance, destiny, dualism, fatherhood, and fascism. Lightsabers are not provided." (Queen's University Belfast)

The Simpsons *and Philosophy*. "From philosophy to religion, from science to politics, students will explore a number of different worldviews. By taking this class, students will come to appreciate how *The Simpsons* can lead to a better understanding of, well, pretty much everything." (University of California, Berkeley)

Religions *of* Star Trek. "The course focuses on the *Star Trek* franchise and the religious issues the series frequently discusses. Students will question how religion and technology appear to be both at odds with and complement each other. The parallel and conflict between religion and science are concepts they can relate to in their technology-filled lives." (Muhlenberg College)

What If Harry Potter Is Real? "Who decides what history is? Who decides how it is used or misused? How can fantasy reshape how we look at history? The Harry Potter novels and films are fertile ground for exploring all of these deeper questions. By looking at the actual geography of the novels, real and imagined historical events portrayed in the novels, the reactions of scholars to the novels, and

Of the 31,534 different words in Shakespeare's works, 14,376 were used only once.

the world-wide frenzy inspired by them, students will examine issues of race, class, gender, the uses of space and movement, and the role of multiculturalism in history." (Appalachian State University)

Calvin & Hobbes. "Modern cartoonists consider *Calvin & Hobbes* to be incredibly influential and any fan will attest to its quality and reliability. But what makes it such a great strip? This class will explore the question, looking to the singular personality of its author, Bill Watterson, and to its wealth of themes and ideas." (Oberlin College)

South Park *and Contemporary Social Issues.* "Students will explore such controversial social issues as gay marriage, immigration, race, consumerism, business ethics, and pornography. And who better to engage students and trigger impassioned discussions than fourth-graders Kyle Broflovski and Stan Marsh, stars of the Comedy Central cartoon TV show?" (McDaniel College)

***21st Century Skills* in Starcraft.** "An eight-week, entirely online course that uses the popular real time strategy (RTS) game *Starcraft* to teach valuable 21st-century skills through a hands-on approach. With society becoming increasingly technology-based and fast-paced, it is important for professionals to be highly proficient in skills such as critical thinking, problem solving, resource management, and adaptive decision making. This course includes required weekly gameplay, viewing and analysis of recorded matches, written assignments which emphasize, analyze, and synthesize real/game-world concepts, and collaboration with other students." (University of Florida)

OTHER COURSES YOU MIGHT ENJOY

Street Fighting Mathematics (MIT)

Tattoos in American Popular Culture (Pitzer College)

Tree Climbing (Cornell University)

The Amazing World of Bubbles (Cal Tech)

How to Watch Television (Montclair State)

The Textual Appeal of Tupac Shakur (U. of Washington)

The History of Surfing (U. of North Carolina)

Politicizing Beyoncé (Rutgers University)

Getting Dressed (Princeton)

"WHERE'S MY LUGGAGE?"

You watched your bag get loaded onto the plane,
and then it was gone. What happened to it?

LOST IN SPACE

After a long flight, airline passengers shuffle to the baggage claim area and wait for their luggage to slide down the chute and onto the carousel. Most passengers see their bag, grab it, and go on their way. But not everyone. Every year, of the more than 2.5 billion bags checked onto flights worldwide, 26 million go missing—and of that 26 million, 1 million never make it back to their original owner. Bad weather and flight delays, miscoded destination tags, and the fact that some people simply forget to take one of their bags off the carousel are a few of the reasons. But the number-one reason a bag ends up lost is that it has no ID tag, and airlines don't know to whom it belongs.

Transferring luggage from check-in to departure gates to arrival gates to baggage claim is a delicate piece of timing. If the system moves too slowly, the baggage won't make connecting flights. If it's too fast, the bags may make the connection but the passengers might miss the flight. Each airport has its own way of allotting how much time a bag needs to move in transit. Denver International Airport, for example, has a sophisticated automated system that includes scanners that read luggage labels, destination-coded vehicles that travel along tracks and load and unload the bags without stopping, and sorting machines that route baggage to the appropriate gate. Even so, all that technology may not save your luggage tag from being torn off in the conveyor belt, making you the hapless owner of a bag with no name.

MISSING IN ACTION

Once a bag goes missing and the passenger files a claim, the bag is declared "mishandled" by the carrier. *Mishandled* refers to bags that have been delayed, lost, stolen, or damaged. Most delayed bags are only one flight behind their owners and can be delivered within 24 hours. The other bags are examined by airline employees for clues to their ownership and destination. If the mystery is solved, those

---

Fewer than 1% of all Google searches use the "I'm Feeling Lucky" button.

bags are returned to their owners within four or five days. Bags with no destination code or identification tag are shipped to a central warehouse, and undergo a comprehensive baggage tracing process over the next 90 days.

TOTALLY LOST

Every airline has its own investigation procedure. According to Jan Fogelberg, Frontier Airlines' vice president of customer service, "Our employees don surgical gloves and then do an autopsy of the bags." Photos, shopping receipts, and names on prescription bottles have all been used to trace a bag's owner. Airlines inventory their mishandled luggage, and many use a database to match the contents with owners' descriptions. It takes about three months to go from "missing in action" to "irretrievably lost." Once that happens, the bags are donated to charity, sold at auction, or purchased by a company like the Unclaimed Baggage Center in Alabama (see page 385), which sells the bags and their contents to the public.

NEVER AGAIN

As for the unfortunate bag owners, in the United States, airlines pay a maximum of $3,300 for a lost bag. But receipts for big-ticket items have to be produced to justify a claim that high, so travel experts recommend you never pack cameras, jewelry, electronic devices, or anything of real value in your checked baggage. Another recommendation: make sure your name is on the outside *and* inside of the bag, along with a copy of your itinerary and phone number so an agent can find it. It also doesn't hurt to have something really flashy and unique on your luggage to make sure other people don't mistake your bag for theirs.

*   *   *

R U NUTS?

In 2013 the Utah Division of Motor Vehicles released a list of 995 vanity license plate requests that were rejected because they were considered "obscene or offensive." Here are a few that we can print: PB4WEGO, LITUP, HITNRUN, WITEBOY, MOONER1, BEGAY, CARGASM, SKISLUT, NAZI, PKRWOOD, ADULTOY, COWBOYP, EZRU2, HOTWAD, UPYOURS, and FQ.

MY OLD KENTUCKY MONKEY'S EYEBROW

When you think of Kentucky, you think of bourbon, bluegrass, the Kentucky Derby, Colonel Sanders, maybe Louisville Slugger bats…but probably not towns named after animals. Yet it turns out there are quite a few.

BLACK GNAT. This tiny hamlet is located on U.S. Route 68, in both Green and Taylor Counties, pretty much right smack dab in the middle of the state. Why is it named "Black Gnat"? The traditional explanation: sometime in the late nineteenth century, the local schoolhouse got a new paint job—bright white. That was at about the same time that residents were trying to come up with a name for the little community. Someone noticed that the freshly painted schoolhouse was covered in black gnats, and commented that "There sure are a lot of black gnats here." And the town had its name.

PIG. Located about 20 miles from Bowling Green, in the central part of the state, Pig became an official town in 1880, when it got its U.S. post office. According to local tradition, the people of the area gathered in the post office to choose a name for the new town, but they couldn't agree on anything. The "discussion" got heated. Finally, a man said, "I see a small hog outside on the road," and snidely suggested they call the town "Pig." (The post office closed in 1904, but the community of Pig is still there.)

PEWEE VALLEY. This small Oldham County town in north-central Kentucky got its post office in 1856, and, like Pig, residents gathered to choose a name for the town. Just then a flock of pewees—small birds known today as eastern wood pewees—happened by and broke out in song. That inspired someone to suggest "Pewee Valley" for the name of the town. Nobody can quite figure out where the "valley" came from, however, as the town isn't in a valley—it actually sits on a ridge.

CRUMMIES. Crummies lies in Harlan County, in far southeastern Kentucky, and was named in the 1920s after Crummies Creek,

---

The Amazon River is 3,900 miles long—nearly the distance from New York to Rome.

which runs through the town. The creek's name was inspired by the sighting of a herd of cows with crooked or "crumpled" horns. To the Scottish immigrants who had settled the area, a cow with crumpled horns is called a "crummie."

POSSUM TROT. Possum Trot is located in Marshall County, in the far west of the state. According to Robert Rennick's book *Kentucky Place Names*, the name was born out of a conversation between area farmers Sol King and William "Buck" Bolen while they were hunting possums one day around the turn of the twentieth century. Having no luck, one of the men remarked, "If we don't catch one soon, these possums are going to trot across the road and be gone." Although it's not clear to anyone (including Uncle John) exactly how, that led to the town being named "Possum Trot."

BUGTUSSLE. This rural district is located in Monroe County, in south-central Kentucky, right on the Tennessee border. According to Ralph Marshall's 1969 report for the U.S. Board of Geographic Names, the name came from a farmer's joke about the profusion of "doodle-bugs," or pill bugs, pests commonly found in barns, in the town:

> According to the oldest residents in this community, the name was acquired during the time the wheat thrashers slept in beds of hay in the barns and stayed so long that it was said the bugs got so large they would tussle [with the thrashers] in the hay.

MONKEY'S EYEBROW. This sparsely populated community lies just south of the Ohio River in far southwestern Ballard County. It was settled in the late nineteenth century by brothers John and Dodge Ray, who operated a general store and blacksmith's shop there. There are at least three versions of the story of how the region acquired its odd name. One of the most popular is that a grassy, curving hill behind the Ray brothers' store looked like a monkey's eyebrow. (Why anyone would think that is not part of the legend.) Another is that a map of Ballard County sort of looks like the profile of a monkey (looking westward), and that Monkey's Eyebrow is located where its eyebrow would be. The third is that it was named after the people who lived there, who were said to resemble monkeys—right up to the eyebrows. (If you're ever looking for Monkey's Eyebrow, head northwest from Possum Trot, go through Paducah… and keep going until you hit Monkey Eyebrow Road.)

CARS THAT STALLED

*Car brands come and go—even major ones like
Pontiac, Oldsmobile, and Packard. Here are
three auto companies that ran out of gas.*

CROSLEY (1939–1952)

Starting Up: In the late 1930s, an Ohio industrialist named Powel Crosley Jr. decided that American car buyers, still suffering through the Great Depression, needed a no-frills "Car of Tomorrow" that anyone could afford. The tiny two-door convertible he came up with wasn't much larger than a golf cart, but its two-cylinder, air-cooled engine got 50 miles to the gallon. The car was sold through a network of department stores and independent appliance dealers for as little as $374. By 1942 car buyers could choose from tiny station wagons, sedans, pickup trucks, and four-seater convertibles. Crosley sold nearly 6,000 of his pint-sized cars before America's entry into World War II halted domestic auto production for the duration of the war.

Breaking Down: After World War II ended, it took a while for U.S. auto companies to resume auto production, and as long as cars were in short supply, consumers bought whatever they could get their hands on…even Crosleys. But the Great Depression was over. Consumers wanted bigger cars, and as soon as they could buy them, they did. Though Crosley had added tiny "Farm-O-Road" jeeps and Hotshot sports cars to the lineup by 1950, sales plummeted from nearly 25,000 cars in 1948 to 1,500 cars in the first half of 1952. Crosley didn't wait to see what sales would be like in the second half: that summer he shut down production and sold his factory to a tire company.

HUPMOBILE (1908–1940)

Starting Up: In 1908 a 30-year-old engineer named Robert C. Hupp quit his job at the Regal Motor Car company, lined up some financial backers, and founded the Hupp Motor Company. Operating out of a rented factory in Detroit, the company produced its first automobile in 1909—a two-speed, four-cylinder, open-air (no roof) runabout called the Hupmobile Model 20. Price: $750. If you wanted "extras" like a convertible top, a windshield, or headlights, you had to pay more.

Robert Hupp fell out with his backers and left the company in 1911. He started several more car companies after that, but they all failed. The Hupp Motor Company, however, powered on without him for nearly three decades, over the years offering a range of models from two-seater convertible roadsters to five-passenger sedans. They were stylish, well-engineered, and very popular. By 1928 the company was selling 65,000 Hupmobiles a year.

Breaking Down: In the mid-1920s, the company phased out its mid-priced four-cylinder cars in favor of pricier six- and eight-cylinder luxury sedans. Then when the Great Depression hit in 1929, the company responded by building even larger sedans, perhaps thinking that the crisis would be short-lived. It wasn't. Hupmobile would have been lucky to stay afloat selling cheap cars; with the big cars, it was doomed. It manufactured just 319 cars in 1939, fewer than in its first year of business, and went bankrupt in 1940.

SEARS ALLSTATE (1952–1953)

Starting Up: Like the Crosley, the Allstate was an industrialist's attempt to build a car that anyone could afford. This time it was Henry J. Kaiser who got into the auto business in 1945, along with his partner, Joseph W. Frazer. The cheapest car in the Kaiser-Frazer line was the Henry J, a two-door sedan introduced in 1950. Cost: $1,300. You didn't get much for your money, though. The two available engines were both underpowered, the rear windows didn't roll down, there was no glove compartment, and there were no armrests. If you wanted to put something in the trunk, you had to fold down the rear seat, because early Henry Js didn't have trunk lids, either.

Sales of the Henry J were disappointing, so Kaiser made a deal to sell them through Sears-Roebuck stores under the house-brand name Allstate, which Sears used to sell tires, spark plugs, and other auto parts. To distinguish the Allstate car from the standard Henry J, it was given a plaid interior, a special front grille, special hubcaps, and a hood ornament that looked like a jet plane. Allstates had more standard equipment—including glove compartments and trunk lids—and sold for a lower price than ordinary Henry Js,

---

Ouch! Each square centimeter of your skin contains about 200 pain receptors.

something that drove Kaiser-Frazer dealers crazy. The cars also came fitted with Sears Allstate auto parts.

Breaking Down: Sears wasn't a full-service auto dealer and had no plans to become one. If your Allstate needed repairs, even under warranty, you were on your own. And there was no guarantee that you'd get good service from your Kaiser-Frazer dealer, since you didn't buy your car from them. Few Sears stores were willing to give up floor space to showcase even a single Allstate. You were supposed to order your car sight unseen, without taking a test drive, perhaps after seeing a picture of one in a Sears catalog. Worst of all, Sears didn't take trade-ins. Not very many people wanted Henry Js in the first place; buying one from Sears—even at a lower price— was such a hassle that hardly anyone bothered. Sears sold just 1,500 in 1952 and fewer than 800 in 1953, the year it pulled the (spark) plug on the Allstate.

* * *

RESCUED FROM THE TRASH

Background: In the early 1980s, a Hollywood executive named Ed Neumeier got an idea for a film after seeing a poster for *Blade Runner*, which is about a cop who hunts criminal robots. Neumeier's idea: a film about a "robot who hunts criminals." He and scriptwriter Michael Miner wrote *RoboCop*, but a dozen big-name directors turned it down, and it looked like the movie would never get made. Then he sent the script to Dutch filmmaker Paul Verhoeven, who was looking to direct his first American movie. He hated it, too: "I skim-read it and just threw it away. I thought it was terrible."

Rescued From the Trash: Verhoeven's wife, Martine Tours, picked it up off the floor and read it more thoroughly. "I think you're wrong," she told him. "Read it again because there are many possibilities here for you to do something different and interesting." Verhoeven did read it again…and discovered layers of satire and social commentary he hadn't noticed before. So he took on the project and added even more layers of satire to the story. The "B-movie sci-fi clunker" that no one would touch ended up being one of the biggest successes of 1987 and has since become a cult classic.

TATTOOS IN THE NEWS

Some stories that will make you ask: What were they inking?

PREMATURE ILLUSTRATION

In March 2014, a Kentucky Wildcats college basketball fan named Tyler Black got a tattoo that read "2014 Nati9nal Champions." Only problem: the NCAA tournament hadn't even started yet. At the time of the inking, Kentucky was favored 30 to 1 to win the national title. And they did go pretty deep into the tournament—they made it to the title game…but then lost to the University of Connecticut. (Black claims he'll keep the not-quite-accurate tattoo.)

FACING HIS FEAR

Some psychologists say that to overcome one's fears, one must directly face them. A Florida man named Eric Ortiz was weary of his crippling fear of spiders, which he encountered daily during his job as a landscaper. So he decided to do something about it. Did he adopt a pet tarantula? Did he visit the zoo's spider-and-insect house? Nope. He decided to diminish his fear's power by getting a tattoo of a black widow spider…that now occupies the entire right side of his face.

A PET CAUSE

In 2014 "Mistah Metro" (real name: Alexander Avgerakis) posted a picture of his dog on Instagram. The dog, looking very uncomfortable, was sporting a heart tattoo. It's real. "One of the many reasons my dog is cooler than yours! She had her spleen removed today, and the vet let me tattoo her while she was under." At the time, Avgerakis worked at Red Legged Devil, a tattoo parlor featured on the reality TV show *NY Ink*. Accusations of animal cruelty over the tatoo have since led Avgerakis to resign.

NOT HAPPY TO SEE THEM

One morning in March 2014, Michael Smith of Norridgewock, Maine, awoke to find several tree-removal workers in his yard. Smith went outside—shirtless—and yelled at the men to leave his property. They did. A short time later Smith was awakened for a second time. A policeman with a megaphone was ordering Smith to come out of the house and surrender, adding that several armed state troopers were in the driveway. Smith came out with his hands up, and he and the police quickly realized that there had been a misunderstanding. The tree removers thought Smith had a handgun tucked into the waistband of his pants. He didn't—but he does have a tattoo of a handgun on his waist.

WHAT A TWIT

British rapper Dappy loves Twitter. He has more than 839,000 followers and posts messages and photos throughout the day, every day. The "hashtag"—an unspaced phrase that starts with "#"—is a tool Twitter users employ to search the site for people discussing a certain subject—click on a hashtag to find all mentions of that phrase. The most-used hashtagged subjects are listed each day as "trending topics." In 2014 Dappy got a pea-sized tattoo of the hashtag # on his right cheek so he could "stay trending forever."

MESSAGE TO MICHAEL

A Sudanese woman was discovered to have a tattoo of the name "Michael" on her right thigh. Why is that newsworthy? Because the woman is a 1,300-year-old mummy, making her tattoo one of the oldest ever discovered. The mummy, who died around the year 700, has the ancient Greek characters "MIXAHA" on her leg, which translates to the modern name of Michael. Archaeologists at the British Museum doubt the woman was declaring her devotion to a boyfriend, though. It more likely refers to the Archangel Michael, biblical leader of God's armies and patron saint of medieval Sudan.

EXHIBIT M

In 2014 Jeffrey Chapman of Kansas was put on trial for the 2011 murder of Damon Galyardt. Chapman has many tattoos, but his lawyer filed a motion with the court to allow one specific tattoo to be removed from his neck. The motion was denied, as state law requires tattoo removal to be performed only at licensed tattoo parlors, and the judge would not let Chapman be transported to one. Chapman had to stand trial with a neck tattoo that his lawyer said would be "extremely prejudicial" if seen by jurors—a large tattoo below his chin that spells out the word "MURDER."

Thomas Edison had a tattoo of five dots on his forearm.

'HOUSE RULES

Best known for his Jeeves and Wooster novels, British author
P. G. Wodehouse (1881–1975) was one of the 20th century's great wits.

"The fascination of shooting as a sport depends almost wholly on whether you are at the right or wrong end of the gun."

"It is a good rule in life never to apologize. The right sort of people don't want apologies, and the wrong sort take advantage of them."

"She looked as if she had been poured into her clothes and had forgotten to say 'when.'"

"If there is one thing I dislike, it is the man who tries to air his grievances when I wish to air mine."

"You're one of those guys who can make a party just by leaving it. It's a great gift."

"An author who expects results from a first novel is in a position similar to that of a man who drops a rose petal down the Grand Canyon and listens for the echo."

"It is no use telling me there are bad aunts and good aunts. At the core, they are all alike. Sooner or later, out pops the cloven hoof."

"Half the world doesn't know how the other three quarters live."

"He had the look of one who had drunk the cup of life and found a dead beetle at the bottom."

"However devoutly a girl may worship a man, there always comes a time when she feels an irresistible urge to haul off and let him have it in the neck."

"Insidious things, mint juleps. They creep up on you like a baby sister and slide their little hands into yours and the next thing you know the Judge is telling you to pay the clerk of the court fifty dollars."

"Unseen in the background, Fate was quietly slipping lead into the boxing-glove."

"When you have been just told that the girl you love is definitely betrothed to another, you begin to understand how Anarchists must feel when the bomb goes off too soon."

"I always advise people never to give advice."

PAYBACK!

Revenge may be a dish best served cold...but it can get quite heated.

PHONE-Y BALONEY

Background: In 2009 a Dex phone-book salesman tried to sell ad space to a Montana restaurant owner named Hunter Lacey, but Lacey decided to go with the regular listing instead. **Payback!** When the new phone book came out, Lacey was shocked to find that the listing for his Bar 3 Bar-B-Q restaurant was published in the "Animal Carcass Removal" section. He complained to Dex, and the listing was removed from the online edition...but in the next year's print edition, Lacey's listing was still in the same section, and the following year, as well. When Jay Leno made fun of the "carcass-removal restaurant" listing on *The Tonight Show* in 2011, Lacey sued Dex for defamation, claiming that the listing (and Leno's joke) reduced business at his restaurants. Result: the salesman was fired, and Dex settled for an undisclosed amount of money.

SIBLING RIVALRY

Background: In 2013 two middle-aged Norwegian brothers (names not released to the press) got into a dispute over a rundown house located on the older brother's property. The younger brother wanted to live there, but the older brother wouldn't let him. Then the younger brother heard rumors that the house was going to be razed. **Payback!** The younger brother became so angry that he drove a forklift into the house where his older brother lived with his 16-year-old son...while they were home. Father and son got out in time, but the upset uncle literally destroyed the house. He was later arrested, banned from driving, and ordered to pay the cost of repairing the home—a hefty $164,000.

PIZZA HOCK

Background: In 2013 a Pizza Hut manager from Erwin, Tennessee, named Amanda Engle let a friend drive her car while drunk. The friend was arrested for DUI, but according to Tennessee law, anyone who allows someone to drive their car drunk can also be cited for DUI. So Unicoi County sheriff's deputy Frank Rogers did just that. Engle was fined $350 and sentenced to two days in jail.

Payback! The following January, Deputy Rogers went to Engle's Pizza Hut for dinner. According to his police report: "I sat down on the bench in front of the counter....As she removed the pizza from the oven I observed her look at me. She then leaned over the pizza that she had begun to slice, and I observed her spit on the pizza." Rogers arrested Engle again. (She was fined and fired from Pizza Hut.)

UNHOOKED

Background: In 2012 Angela Potter of Waikato, New Zealand, was dumped by her boyfriend. He then packed *his* belongings into *her* suitcase and moved to Australia. Potter called him and asked for the suitcase back. His answer: No.

Payback! It just so happened that the boyfriend was an avid fisherman who kept a secret list of his most productive fishing locations. Potter found the list of fishing spots—with GPS locations—and decided to sell them on an online auction site. Her listing: "My ex-boyfriend is a very successful fisherman who asked me to protect his collection of GPS fishing-spot coordinates (with my life, no less). Not a problem." Potter thought she'd get 100 views; instead she got 90,000 and ended up making nearly $3,000. "I didn't list them to be vindictive," she insists. "I listed them as a bit of a laugh."

GRAVE MATTERS

Background: In 2014, after Kelly Stowe's elderly father passed away, she purchased a plot for him at a cemetery in Skiatook, Oklahoma, complete with a shiny black headstone. Stowe's nephew (the deceased's grandson) became upset because he wasn't consulted and he thought the headstone was ugly.

Payback! A few days later, the nephew purchased all the plots around Grandpa's grave and had a massive sandstone boulder hauled in and dropped just a few feet in front of the black headstone, blocking it from view. "I don't think there's any excuse for that right there," complained Stowe, accusing her nephew of trying to "cause trouble." She called police to the cemetery, but they said it was a civil matter. "My mom is still alive and she's having to see all this," said Stowe. "She says she doesn't even want to be buried out here anymore." At last report, the boulder and the headstone were still at the grave site, resting not so peacefully.

It is possible to become psychologically addicted to feeling angry.

TRADE DEFICITS

Being the general manager of a pro sports team requires equal parts research, foresight, and luck. Sometimes things work out…and sometimes they don't.

TRADED: Brett Favre, future NFL superstar
BY: The Atlanta Falcons
THE STORY: The Falcons selected Favre, a star quarterback at the small University of Southern Mississippi, 33rd overall in the 1991 NFL Draft. Unfortunately for Favre, he was drafted by Falcons exec Taylor Smith against the wishes of head coach Jerry Glanville, who didn't want another quarterback, and told the *Milwaukee Sentinel* that it would take a plane crash for him to put Favre into a game. The Falcons already had a starting quarterback in Favre's rookie season—Pro Bowler Chris Miller—so it made sense to trade Favre away after that season. And when the Falcons got a first-round draft pick from the Green Bay Packers for him, it looked like they'd gotten a great deal. Wrong. Favre led the Packers to their first Super Bowl in 30 years, was named MVP three times, and started a record 297 games. Miller started only 10 more for the Falcons. What did they do with the draft pick they got for Favre? They traded him to Dallas.

TRADED: Herschel Walker, Heisman Trophy winner
BY: The Dallas Cowboys
THE STORY: Four games—and four losses—into Jerry Jones's first year as the Cowboys' owner and GM in 1989, the flamboyant executive knew he had to make a critical change to the roster. He spread the word that Walker, the team's running back and brightest light, was on the trading block. Several teams made offers, but none matched that of the Minnesota Vikings' GM Mike Lynn, who thought Walker would lead the Vikings to a Super Bowl. In what remains the largest trade in NFL history, Minnesota gave up five players and eight draft picks—including three first-round selections—for Walker (and some late-round draft picks). Walker did have an incredible debut in his first game for Minnesota, running for 148 yards on 18 carries…and that was about it. After two and a half unremarkable seasons, Walker was released. Meanwhile in Dallas, Jones used that stockpile of draft picks to acquire Emmitt Smith and Darren

Woodson, cornerstones of the Cowboys' three Super Bowl-winning teams in the 1990s. Soon after Walker left the Vikings, so did GM Mike Lynn. He told the *New York Times*, "I gave up too much."

TRADED: Pedro Martinez, future baseball superstar
BY: The Los Angeles Dodgers
THE STORY: Ramon Martinez was a solid pitcher for the Dodgers in the early 1990s. His play wasn't stellar, but it was respectable enough that the Dodgers signed his brother, Pedro, even though, at 5'11" and 170 pounds, he was scrawny for a Major League pitcher. Despite Ramon's claims that Pedro was the better pitcher and had the ability to go long innings (which would make him an excellent starting pitcher) Dodgers manager Tommy Lasorda used Pedro mostly in relief situations. In 1993 second baseman Jody Reed became a free agent (he signed with the Milwaukee Brewers), and the Dodgers needed a replacement. Fearing that Pedro's body would eventually break down, the Dodgers traded him to the Montreal Expos for second baseman Delino DeShields. DeShields hit just .243 in three seasons with the Dodgers, but Pedro Martinez went on to become one of the greatest starting pitchers of all time, winning three Cy Young Awards (one with Montreal, two with the Boston Red Sox), the pitching Triple Crown, and a World Series.

TRADED: Pau Gasol
BY: The Memphis Grizzlies
THE STORY: This trade started off lopsided, but that's not how it ended. When the Los Angeles Lakers acquired Pau Gasol from the Grizzlies in the middle of the 2007–2008 season, it appeared that the Lakers got away with highway robbery. They traded a bunch of low-level draft picks and benchwarmers for him. But one piece of the trade stood out: Memphis got Gasol's younger brother, Marc. While Pau helped the Lakers make three consecutive NBA Finals, Marc was quietly improving his play. In 2011 he made the NBA All-Star team. Two seasons later he was named the NBA Defensive Player of the Year while leading the Grizzlies to its first appearance in the Western Conference Finals. It's the only time in NBA history that two brothers were traded for each other—and ended up more or less even…eventually.

BEASTLY EXPRESSIONS

You'll go wild for these phrase origins.

DARK HORSE
Meaning: An unknown contender who makes a surprisingly good showing
Origin: "Sam Flynn, a Tennessean, was a horse trader who secretly bred racehorses. It was his practice to drive his workhorses to auctions along with one of his 'secret' racehorses and enter it into a horse race. One was particularly swift—a coal-black stallion called Dusky Pete. Just before the race, a judge was told of Sam Flynn's foolish betting. The judge recognized Dusky Pete at the starting post. 'Gentleman,' he said, 'there's a dark horse in this race that will make some of you sick before supper.' Of course Dusky Pete won, and the judge's words rang prophetically true. After that it became customary at races and other contests to 'beware the dark horse.'" (From *Common Phrases and Where They Came From*, by Myron Korach)

BLACK SHEEP

Meaning: A person who doesn't fit in with his or her family
Origin: "Black sheep have had bad press since the sixteenth century when they were accused of being 'perylous' beasts, quite capable of giving a nasty nip. In Shropshire, England, there was, apparently, a superstition that if a black lamb were born into a flock, bad luck would dog the shepherd. An economic factor also contributed to the animal's unpopularity; the fleece of a black sheep could not be dyed and was therefore worthless. The term *black sheep* was applied sometime in the eighteenth century to a person who falls foul of the accepted standards of his fellows." (From *Dictionary of Proverbs and Their Origins*, by Linda and Roger Flavell)

BULLPEN

Meaning: The area in a baseball park where relief pitchers warm up
Origin: "Early in the twentieth century, the imposing Bull Durham Tobacco signs behind outfield fences in American baseball parks pictured a brightly colored bull, proclaiming that any batter whose home run hit the bull would get $50 and two bags of Bull Durham.

The average person spends 10–20 min. a week on hold (or about 43 days of their life).

Pitchers usually warmed up near these signs, which may be why warm-up areas are called bullpens today, although the word also could have been derived from the word *bull pen* that had meant a 'stockade for prisoners' since 1809." (From *God Bless America: The Origins of Over 1,500 Patriotic Phrases*, by Robert Hendrickson)

A WOLF IN SHEEP'S CLOTHING

Meaning: Someone with bad intentions who pretends to be nice

Origin: "It was Jesus who first referred to this type of person in the Sermon on the Mount, as recounted in the Gospel of St. Matthew (7:15): 'Beware of false prophets, which come to you in sheep's clothing, but inwardly they are ravening wolves.'" (From *The Real McCoy*, published by Oxford University Press)

TAKE A GANDER

Meaning: Take a look at something

Origin: "The month after a wife's postnatal confinement was once called the *gander month* or *gander moon*—in allusion to the aimless wandering of a gander while the goose sits on the eggs. During that period the husband was called a *gander mooner*—and pleaded a certain amount of indulgence in matters pertaining to sex. So originally, to 'take a gander' was to 'take a walk and give the girls the eye.' The phrase as we use it today retains some of this meaning." (From *Why Do We Say It?*, published by Castle Books)

LOUNGE LIZARD

Meaning: An idle person (usually a man) who dresses well and hangs out in nightclubs

Origin: "Mainly carnivorous, lizards are, like all reptiles, cold-blooded—meaning they keep their bodies warm chiefly by heat from their surroundings. Therefore they are often seen lounging on sunny walls, rocks, and fences, warming themselves and occasionally pouncing on prey. From these habits comes the term *lounge lizard*, a man who frequents cocktail lounges, hotel lobbies, and the like in search of ladies who are richer, and usually older, than he, on whom he sponges. The term originated about 1915 and was quite popular in the 1920s. It is heard less often today, though the practice certainly has not died out." (From *It's Raining Cats and Dogs...and Other Beastly Expressions*, by Christine Ammer)

You are slightly more likely to have twins if conception occurred in the summer.

TOM SWIFTIES

This classic style of pun from the 1920s is corny and atrocious, and makes you think before you groan…so of course Uncle John loves them.

"Shall I frost the cake?" Tom offered icily.

"Why do you accuse me of throwing softballs?" asked Tom underhandedly.

"You must draw the line somewhere," Tom ruled.

"That just doesn't add up," said Tom, nonplussed.

"I brought the dessert," said Tom piously.

"Where's the shredded cheese?" asked Tom gratingly.

"It's three dollars to cross the bridge, sir," Tom told him.

"I can't remember the name of Prince William's brother," Tom said harriedly.

"I love hockey," said Tom puckishly.

"I'm the world's most aggressive matador," Tom rambled.

"I want to speak only with women today," Tom mentioned.

"Let's attack a monarch!" said Tom strikingly.

"We might need a ten-gauge needle," Tom hypothesized.

"Crosby is my favorite crooner. Is he yours?" asked Tom probingly.

"I killed the Greek piper god," Tom deadpanned.

"That's a very large shark," said Tom superficially.

"The bank won't take my business," said Tom unaccountably.

"I hate sweet potatoes," Tom yammered.

"I wrote the book on that subject," said Tom authoritatively.

"I used to work for the railway company," said Tom extraneously.

"I'm on welfare," said Tom dolefully.

"This team needs a player who can hit sixty homers a year," said Tom ruthlessly.

"I once read a book about the Spanish Armada," said Tom fleetingly.

"That's not really Dracula," Tom discounted.

One shot of Tom Cruise walking through a door in the film *Eyes Wide Shut* required 97 takes.

"IT'S JUST BUSINESS."

The business world's most successful CEOs being brutally honest.

"Number one, cash is king. Number two, communicate. Number three, buy or bury the competition."
—**Jack Welch, GE**

"Banks do not have an obligation to promote the public good."
—**Alexander Dielius, Goldman Sachs (Europe)**

"Success breeds complacency. Complacency breeds failure. Only the paranoid survive."
—**Andrew Grove, Intel**

"If drink sales are falling off, we get the pilots to engineer a bit of turbulence. That usually spikes sales."
—**Michael O'Leary, RyanAir**

"If you put your compensation in a one-year context to define your overall level of happiness, you've got a problem that is bigger than the job. If you're really unhappy, just leave. I mean, life's too short."
—**James Gorman, Morgan Stanley, responding to employees' complaints about 30 percent pay cuts**

"I'm not a schmuck. Even if the world goes to hell in a handbasket, I won't lose a penny."
—**Donald Trump**

"Life is a game. Money is how we keep score."
—**Ted Turner, CNN**

"If any of my competitors were drowning, I'd stick a hose in their mouth and turn on the water. This is rat eat rat, dog eat dog. I'm going to kill them before they kill me. You're talking about the American way—of survival of the fittest."
—**Ray Kroc, McDonald's**

"Okay, but the notice is retroactive from two weeks ago."
—**Steve Jobs, Apple, responding to fired Pixar employees who asked for at least two weeks' notice**

"There are not enough lifeboats. Someone is going to die. So you might as well enjoy the champagne and caviar!"
—**Jamie Dimon, JP Morgan Chase**

The FBI had a file on Albert Einstein. It was 1,427 pages long.

SEVEN REASONS
NOT TO CLIMB
MT. EVEREST

*Climbing the world's most famous mountain appears on
many lists of things people want to do before they die.
But there are some very good reasons not to.*

REASON #1: IT'S HARDER THAN YOU THINK
Most people don't realize how recently it was that Edmund
Hillary and Tenzing Norgay made the first successful climb
to the top. That was 1953. Before that, starting in the 1920s, there
were many unsuccessful attempts by highly qualified western climbers, and many fatalities. Today, even with expert assistance and
canisters of oxygen, a lot of people don't make it up the mountain…
and a lot don't make it back down again.

#2: IT'S ABSURDLY EXPENSIVE
Here's what you can expect to pay before you set foot on the
mountain:
Climbing gear: $8,000–$10,000
Bottled oxygen: $3,000
Permit to climb: $11,000, regardless of group size
Transporting your gear to base camp: $2,000
Sherpa support, guide, food, etc.: $40,000–$80,000 (plus tips—the
sherpas' main source of income—for keeping you alive)
Round-trip flight to Nepal: $800–$1,200

The total cost will be between $60,000 and $120,000. What
does the high price say about your fellow climbers? Some may be
avid (and hopefully experienced) mountaineers spending their life
savings for a once-in-a-lifetime experience. Others may be rich
kids or dot-com executives trying to prove something. Regardless,
that level of investment of time and money encourages desperate
risk-taking in a place where doing so can bring on tragedy.

There's enough wood pulp in one cord of wood to make half a ton of toilet paper.

#3: IT'S RIDICULOUSLY COLD

In July, the warmest month of the year, the average temperature near the top is -2°F. It never gets anywhere close to above freezing. There's also wind chill: While winter features hurricane-speed winds (70+ mph winds for most of the season), summer winds offer little relief—they're typically 20 mph, with frequent summer snowstorms.

#4: YOU MAY LOSE BODY PARTS YOU WISH TO KEEP

The culprit: frostbite. One lucky survivor in 1996 had to have his right arm amputated below the elbow, besides losing parts of both feet, his nose, and all five fingers of his remaining hand. In Everest's subzero temperatures, frostbite is easy to get and difficult to fix.

#5: THERE'S A GOOD CHANCE YOU'LL DIE UP THERE

As you get above 26,000 feet, you enter the "Death Zone," so called because the air is thin enough that you'll slowly suffocate if you end up having to stay up there beyond your oxygen tanks' capacity. A sudden storm that makes it impossible to leave your tent for a day or two? A sprained ankle, illness, or altitude sickness? If you can't move quickly enough on your own, it can be a death sentence as extra liquid collects in your brain and a frothy sputum fills your lungs, drowning you. Rescue by helicopter or emergency personnel is virtually impossible. The death rate has been in the range of about four deaths for every hundred people who reach the top. One of the deaths was John Delaney, founder of Intrade, who, walking up a gentle slope 50 yards from the summit in 2011, suddenly crumpled and died.

#6: THE TOP IS LITTERED WITH TONS OF TRASH... AND A FEW HUNDRED HUMAN CORPSES

If you die on the mountain, there's only a small chance that your body will be recovered. Worse, your mummified body will become yet another unsightly piece of Everest's litter...or, as in the case of some longtime corpses, a landmark. Example: Green Boots, a frozen climber from India, whose fluorescent-green footwear marks the way up a popular path. Or the sitting young woman who for many years, until her body was finally blown into a crevice by a winter storm, sat leaning against her pack, her eyes open and her long hair blowing

The forehead of a bottlenose dolphin is called the "melon."

in the wind. The styles of the dead climbers' clothes date them, from baggy wool and cotton blends of the 1950s to bright synthetics of the twenty-first century. Some bodies still have cell phones in their pockets with photo-filled memory cards. There are more than 200 bodies on Everest, prevented by altitude and cold from rotting away or being eaten by predators. Many of them are visible to other climbers in the summer season. In fact, "Rainbow Valley" along a popular route just below the summit gets its nickname from the colorful nylon outerwear on the dozens of bodies scattered across the landscape.

#7: IT'S NOT AS BIG A DEAL AS IT USED TO BE

Despite its perils, more than 5,000 people have made the trip to the top. With space-age clothing, modern climbing equipment, cell phones, and satellite-assisted weather reports, the climb isn't quite the solitary human-against-nature struggle it used to be. When going up the mountain, climbers will typically have support—expedition guides and sherpas (and yaks) to carry supplies, drop off oxygen bottles along the route, set up camp, and even make dinner when they arrive. And climbers no longer have to blaze a trail with an ice ax and crampons—they can take one of two popular routes, each with permanently preset ropes and bridges. Ironically, these improvements may end up increasing the number of fatalities, tempting reckless newbies to attempt the climb and more expert climbers to attempt dangerous "firsts," such as being the oldest climber (male, 80; female, 73), youngest climber (13), first blind climber, most times to the top (21—a tie by two sherpas), first to hang-glide down the mountain, first ascent without oxygen, and so on.

*   *   *

DID THEY SEND HIM TO THE CAN?

"An 8-year-old boy in Zhuzhou, Hunan province, phoned police to ask for assistance. The boy was left at home alone by his parents and could not find toilet paper after going to the lavatory. He phoned the police hotline, saying his parents were out and he needed paper. Police then contacted the boy's parents, telling them to return home to take care of him."

—*China Daily*

Last bone in the human body to stop growing: the collarbone.

LIFE IN THE 1910s

*It's fun to look back at a long-ago era and see what the world
was like. Here's a snapshot of the 1910s, when…hold on
to your suspenders…they didn't even have YouTube!*

PRICES. Milk: 32¢ a gallon; Kellogg's Corn Flakes: 9¢ a box;
pork chops: 38¢ a pound; eggs: 34¢ a dozen; coffee: 34¢ a
pound; a first-class stamp: 2¢; a movie ticket: 7¢; the cheapest
Kodak camera: $1.25; a car: $550; a house: $6,200.

AVERAGE ANNUAL SALARY. About $750

BAD TIMES. More than 65 million men from 100 countries
fought in World War I (1914–18). Over 16 million people were
killed; 20 million more were wounded. As the war wound down, the
Spanish flu pandemic broke out and did far worse than the war had
done, killing between 50 and 100 million people in virtually every
country on Earth. In India, the hardest hit, more than 17 million
died. (America's death toll: 650,000; Canada's: 50,000.)

LIFE EXPECTANCY. 50 for men; 53 for women

SHIPPING DISASTERS. Two of the worst in history occurred
in this decade. The sinking of the *Titanic* in 1912 resulted in 1,517
deaths. The British luxury liner *Lusitania* sank in 1915 (after being
torpedoed by a German U-boat), killing 1,195 people.

BIGGEST SPORTS STARS. Baseball: Babe Ruth, Ty Cobb,
and Shoeless Joe Jackson. College football: Knute Rockne (Notre
Dame) and Jim Thorpe (Carlisle). Boxing: Jack Johnson (became
the first black heavyweight champ in 1908 and defended his title
17 times before losing it in 1915) and Jack Dempsey, "the Manassa
Mauler" (won the heavyweight boxing title in 1919). Horse racing:
Sir Barton, the first horse to win the Triple Crown (1919).

MOST POPULAR CAR. The Ford Model T, by a landslide.
Between 1910 and 1912, Ford produced a total of about 120,000
Model T's. By the end of the decade, they'd produced more than 3
million—more than every other American car company combined.
Also on the streets: Chevrolet, Dodge, Hudson, Pierce-Arrow,

Buick, and Oldsmobile, among others. (The horse and buggy remained a common sight on roads throughout the 1910s, too.)

TOP BABY NAMES. For boys: John, William, James, Robert, Joseph; for girls: Mary, Helen, Dorothy, Margaret, Ruth.

POPULAR RECORDS. "Alexander's Ragtime Band" by Arthur Collins & Byron G. Harlan; "Over There" by Nora Bayes; "It's a Long, Long Way to Tipperary" by John McCormack; "Let Me Call You Sweetheart" by the Peerless Quartet; "Rock-a-Bye Your Baby" by Al Jolson; "Tiger Rag" by the Original Dixieland Jazz Band

INVENTIONS. Stainless steel; the supermarket; the tow truck; the modern bra; the electric traffic light; the toggle light switch; formica; the condenser microphone; the modern zipper; army tanks; pop-up toasters; the electric blanket; the Brillo Pad

NEW TOYS. Erector Set (1913), Tinkertoys (1914), Raggedy Ann doll (1915), Lincoln Logs (1916, by John Lloyd Wright, son of architect Frank Lloyd Wright), the Radio Flyer red wagon (1917)

POPULAR MOVIES (all silent). *Tillie's Punctured Romance* (1914), the first feature-length comedy ever made, starring Marie Dressler and Charlie Chaplin; *His Majesty, the Scarecrow of Oz* (1914), produced by L. Frank Baum; *The Birth of a Nation* (1915), the popular pro-Ku Klux Klan epic; and *Tarzan of the Apes* (1918)

BOOKS. *Howards End*, E. M. Forster (1910); *The Secret Garden*, Frances Hodgson Burnett (1911); *Sons and Lovers*, D. H. Lawrence (1913); *Tarzan of the Apes*, Edgar Rice Burroughs (1914); *The Metamorphosis*, Franz Kafka (1915); *A Portrait of the Artist as a Young Man*, James Joyce (1916); *My Ántonia*, Willa Cather (1918)

STILL ALIVE. Some famous people born in the 1910s and still alive in 2014: author Herman Wouk, actress Olivia de Havilland, actor Kirk Douglas, poet Lawrence Ferlinghetti, banker and philanthropist David Rockefeller, and TV star Judge Joseph Wapner. Number of Americans born in the 1910s still living today: about 420,000—0.1 percent of the population.

NOT IN EXISTENCE IN THE 1910s. Television, insulin therapy for diabetes, antibiotics, 3-D movies, spiral notebooks, and the gas chamber. (Those were all invented in the 1920s.)

TAKING ON
SATURDAY NIGHT LIVE

Since 1975 NBC's Saturday Night Live has dominated weekend late-night television. Its only real competition: Fox's sketch comedy series Mad TV (1995–2009). Other shows tried to take on SNL...and all failed.

Show: *Fridays* (ABC)
Year: 1980
Story: After five years on the air, *SNL*'s original cast—the "Not Ready for Prime Time Players"—had all left the show for prime-time TV and movie roles. The ratings suffered, and ABC tried to swoop in with *Fridays*, a program it hoped would be as hip and edgy as *SNL* had been. In fact, it "borrowed" *SNL*'s basic format: a cast of unknown actors doing sketch comedy, celebrity guest hosts, hip musical acts, even a fake news segment. Only problem: where many of *SNL*'s original cast members had worked together in live comedy theater for years, the *Fridays* cast members were all hired individually in a nationwide search. But once they coalesced, the show's quality improved. *Fridays* began to beat *SNL* regularly in the ratings and provided two breakout stars: Michael Richards and Larry David, who later worked together on *Seinfeld*. With the Lorne Michaels era over (he left in 1980) and without its original cast, *SNL* was also struggling and might have been beaten permanently except for one thing: the rising popularity of *Nightline*. ABC's late-night news show was doing so well Monday through Thursday that in 1981 they decided to expand it to five nights a week. To make room for *Nightline*, they cut *Fridays* from an hour to a half hour and moved it back by 30 minutes. Starting a half hour later killed *Fridays*, and it was canceled in 1982.

Show: *The New Show* (NBC)
Year: 1984
Story: Lorne Michaels created *Saturday Night Live* and has been its guiding force for nearly 40 years...except for a five-year period in the 1980s when he quit the show (and show business). Michaels's vacation ended in 1984 when he was lured back to NBC to try

something new, but really something old: a sketch comedy show, although a taped one, that would air during the last hour of prime time on Fridays. In interviews promoting the new show, which he called *The New Show*, Michaels took shots at what his successors had done to his baby. "On *Saturday Night Live*, shocking has replaced funny," he told the *New York Times*. Michaels also aimed to reinvent the TV sketch comedy show format. Instead of hiring a large repertory cast and inviting a guest host each week the way *SNL* did, *The New Show* had just three regular players (Buck Henry, Dave Thomas, and Valri Bromfield) and multiple weekly guest stars, such as Steve Martin and John Candy. The writing staff was headed by *SNL* vets Al Franken and Jack Handey, all part of Michaels's desire to recapture the cutting satire of *SNL*'s early years. But instead of creating a show unlike anything seen on TV, Michaels created a show that remained…virtually unseen. *The New Show* was canceled after only nine episodes and was ranked as the lowest-rated TV series of the season. Michaels quickly rebounded, though. In 1985 he was rehired as the executive producer of *SNL*.

Show: *Animation Domination High Definition* (Fox)
Year: 2013
Story: When *Mad TV* went off the air after 14 modestly rated seasons in 2009, Fox gave its late-night Saturday time slot to a talk show hosted by comedian Wanda Sykes, which lasted just nine months. Then, after a couple of years of using the space to run unaired episodes of canceled and short-lived prime-time series, in fall 2013 Fox debuted *Animation Domination High Definition*, a programming block of "adult animation," similar to *Adult Swim* on the Cartoon Network. Segments included a darkly comic parody of Archie comics called *High School High*, and an adaptation of the comic book *Axe Cop*, an ultra-violent police show parody that was co-created by a six-year-old boy. In April 2014, Fox announced that ADHD was suffering from low ratings and that it would be available online only.

*　　*　　*

"As long as the world is turning and spinning, we're gonna be dizzy and we're gonna make mistakes." —**Mel Brooks**

Fingernails and toenails grow more slowly in space.

FUNNY FUNGI

Mushrooms are more than those little white things you buy at the store. There are hundreds of wild-growing varieties—some edible, some poisonous, some neither—and many have very odd names.

Octopus Stinkhorn

White Cheese Polypore

Bleeding Tooth

Violet Toothed Polypore

Ochre Spreading Tooth

Two-tone Parchment

Pig's Ear

Gypsy

Horn of Plenty

Turkey Tail

Sea Anemone

Bearded Tooth

The Devil's Cigar

Ringless Honey

Red Cushion

Ivory Funnel

Fool's Webcap

Sulfur Tuft

Mossy Maze Polypore

Jack-O-Lantern

Chicken of the Woods

Crowded Parchment

Brown-toothed Crust

The Prince

Death Cap

Judas' Ear

Butter Bolete

Gem-Studded Puffball

Blewit

Sweetbread

Shaggy Mane

Trumpet of Death

Velvet Foot

Black Saddle

Hedgehog

Belly-Button

Candy Cap

Blue Milky Cap

Deadly Parasol

Fairy Ring

Old Man of the Woods

Bird's Nest Fungi

Black Knot of Cherry

Dead Man's Fingers

Inky Cap

Jelly Ear

Lobster

Witch's Hat

Witch's Butter

Brain Mushroom

Great Felt Skirt Destroying Angel

Brown Roll-Rim

Yellow Clubbed Foot

Man on Horseback

Annual alcohol poisoning fatalities in the U.S.: 300; In Russia: 40,000.

BENSON'S BUBBLERS

*Simon Benson has been dead for more than 70 years, but if
you ever get the chance to visit the Pacific Northwest,
you can still have a drink on him.*

WATERWORKS

Very few big cities have public drinking fountains. One that does is Portland, Oregon. If you've ever walked around the downtown area, you've probably seen the many unique fountains that dot the city's sidewalks. There are two varieties: a four-bowled version and a single-bowled version. Each four-bowled fountain has a stout cast-bronze trunk, somewhat reminiscent of a fire hydrant. From the top of the trunk, four thick arms (also bronze) sprout like the arms of a candelabra. Each arm curves upward and ends in a shiny brass bowl about 11 inches in diameter. From the center of each bowl is a spout, from which water gently bubbles, allowing any passerby—and three of his friends—to get a drink. (The single-bowl version is very similar, but simply has one bowl, rather than four.) These are Portland's "Benson Bubblers," named for Simon Benson, the man who donated them to the city in 1912.

BUBBLER HISTORY

Benson was born in Norway in 1851, emigrated to Wisconsin with his family in 1867, worked a series of odd jobs across the country, finally ending up in the logging business in Portland, Oregon, in the 1880s. There, over the next three decades, he became one of the wealthiest "timber barons" in the Northwest. In 1912 Benson, by this time one of Portland's best-known civic leaders, donated $10,000 to the city (about $240,000 today) for the installation of 20 drinking fountains, or *bubblers*, around the city. (Drinking fountains are still known as "bubblers" in some parts of the U.S., especially around the Great Lakes.)

Where did he get the idea to install public drinking fountains around the city? Nobody knows for sure, but several legends persist. One says Benson was inspired after seeing a young girl at a July 4th parade, crying because she couldn't find a drink of water. Another is that Benson, a teetotaler, was tired of his loggers getting drunk

---

Gram for gram, black widow venom is 15 times more potent than rattlesnake venom.

in Portland's saloons during lunchtime, so he had the fountains installed to give them a healthier drinking option. (That's probably not true, but it is true that a drink from one of the fountains became known as a "Benson cocktail.")

MR. BUBBLER

The first of the unique four-bowled bubblers (designed by the renowned Portland architect A. E. Doyle, dozens of whose buildings are on the National Register of Historic Places) was installed at the busy downtown intersection of Southwest Fifth Avenue and Washington Street, on June 18, 1912. The remaining 19 soon followed. Quickly known as "Benson Bubblers," they were a big hit, and according to a July 1913 *Oregonian* newspaper article, the crowds that formed around the fountains—especially during hot weather—weren't typical urban crowds:

> The fountains are whirlpools of democracy. Sometimes four distinct races may be seen drinking at the same time, and the "color line," however well defined it may be at other places, recedes to the vanishing point on a hot afternoon at the corner of Sixth and Alder, Fifth and Washington, or any of the other 20 odd corners in the city where, night and day, the Benson fountains bubble their little song of welcome and generosity.

TIME IN A BUBBLE

Over the decades, the Benson Bubblers were neglected, some having one or more of their arms broken off, others simply removed to make room for new roads or other structures. Then, in the 1950s, a Portland longshoreman named Francis Murnane began a campaign to get the city to preserve the old fountains. "It is my belief," he wrote to the city council in 1952, "that the Benson fountains belong to all the city and should be restored to their beauty and usefulness." It took six years, but Murnane persisted, and the city finally responded in 1958, when efforts to repair and preserve the damaged bubblers finally began. And in the years that followed, the city even installed more fountains. (Many of these new bubblers were the same four-bowl design as the original, but others were made with a single bowl, and some people therefore do not consider them true Benson Bubblers.)

Today there are 52 Benson fountains, and an additional 74 of the single-bowl variety, bubbling away on sidewalks all over downtown Portland. The Portland Water Bureau, which maintains the fountains (they clean each one twice a week), even publishes a brochure about them for tourists, with a regularly updated map showing where each of the bubblers is located so that you can take your friends and family on a guided (and refreshing!) Benson Bubbler tour someday.

A FEW MORE DROPS

• Benson Bubblers run from 5:30 a.m. until 11:30 p.m. every day, 365 days a year, except during especially cold or dry spells—and also when it's very windy (so pedestrians don't get sprayed with water).

• Where does Benson Bubbler water come from? It comes directly from the Bull Run watershed, located 26 miles from Portland in Mt. Hood National Forest.

• A Benson Bubbler sits on the grounds of the Maryhill Museum of Art—in Maryhill, Washington. Why there? According to the Portland Water Bureau, Sam Maryhill, the museum's founder, was a friend of Simon Benson, and he simply asked Benson for one.

• Only one other Benson Bubbler can be found outside Portland. It's in Sapporo, Japan. (Sapporo is Portland's Japanese sister city, and the fountain was presented to the city as a gift in 1965.)

• All of the Benson Bubblers were cast at Portland foundries—except two, which were made in 1975 by engineering students at Benson Polytechnic High School (a Portland magnet school founded in 1915 with a $100,000 grant from Simon Benson). One of those bubblers still stands in front of the school.

• When new bubblers began to be installed in the 1960s, some were slightly outside of Portland's downtown district. This led Simon Benson's heirs to request that the city restrict the location of new Benson Bubblers to a specific downtown area, "so as to not dilute their uniqueness." The city agreed.

*   *   *

"If Jesus had known that his image would end up on Justin Bieber's calf, he would've never started Christianity."

—**Natasha Leggero**

Poet Henry David Thoreau once burned down 300 acres of forest trying to cook a fish.

ORIGINS YOU CAN EAT

How some tasty food items got their names.

BANANAS FOSTER

Richard Foster was the chairman of the New Orleans Crime Commission in the early 1950s and a friend of restaurateur Owen Brennan, who also served on the commission. Foster must have loved bananas, because in 1951 Brennan had his chef, Paul Blangé, whip up this dessert—bananas cooked *flambé* in rum, butter, and banana liqueur, served hot with a scoop of vanilla ice cream— and then named it in Foster's honor.

SACHERTORTE

In 1832 Austrian chancellor Prince Klemens von Metternich was expecting several important guests for dinner and asked his head chef to come up with a special dessert for the occasion. The chef took sick before he could think of anything, so the task fell to a 16-year-old apprentice named Franz Sacher. The dessert he came up with, a chocolate sponge cake layered with apricot jam and covered with chocolate icing, was a simple and delicious departure from the elaborate desserts of the day. It wasn't until Sacher finished his training as a cook that he began selling his creation to the public. Once he did, "the cake by this man Sacher" soon became the signature dessert of Viennese cuisine.

OYSTERS ROCKEFELLER

It's not clear that John D. Rockefeller ever ate oysters Rockefeller or even knew that they existed. What is clear is that when fancy French snails were in short supply in 1899 and a New Orleans restaurateur named Jules Alciatore replaced them with a dish of local oysters served on the half-shell topped with bread crumbs and a secret sauce, he wanted a name that let diners know that the oysters were every bit as classy as the snails. So he named them after John D. Rockefeller, the founder of Standard Oil and the richest man in the world. Antoine's, the restaurant that introduced the dish in 1899, is still in business more than a century later. It still serves the oysters, and the recipe remains a closely guarded secret to this day.

One-tenth of the world's population relies on the Ganges River for water.

CELL PHONE MYTHS

Can you really get colon cancer from butt dialing?
Of course not—that's just a myth…or is it?

Myth: Using cell phones on airplanes isn't allowed because the signal can scramble navigational and communications systems, and could cause the plane to crash.

Truth: The Federal Aviation Administration didn't ban cell phones on airplanes—the Federal Communications Commission did. When you make a cell phone call from the ground, the signal bounces around from available cell tower to available cell tower. If everyone on the same airplane made a phone call at the same time at that same high altitude and speed, the signals would have to bounce too quickly from tower to tower, jamming and clogging cell networks (and making it difficult for service providers to track—and bill for—the calls).

Myth: Cell phones cause cancer.

Truth: Dozens of studies have been done (and continue to be done), and the results remain inconclusive. The largest study, conducted in 2005 by the Institute of Cancer Research, tested 4,000 people and found no link between cancer and regular cell phone use. A 2008 Israeli study concluded that cell phone use caused a 50 percent increased risk of cancer of the salivary glands—located just below the skin where a cell phone touches the face. However, that same year, an Australian study found no link between cell phones and that kind of cancer.

Myth: You have to completely drain a battery before charging it up again, or else the battery will "remember" the point at which it started to charge as its "dead" spot.

Truth: It used to be true, but it's not anymore. In the olden days (the 1980s and 1990s), cell phones were powered primarily with nickel-metal hydride (NiMH) and nickel-cadmium (NiCD) batteries, which had to be completely drained and then completely recharged. If they weren't, the batteries experienced a "memory effect"—the point at which it started to charge up again was its "zero" point. Result: it would lead to poor battery life. Today, cell phones use lithium-ion batteries, which aren't subject to the same confusing requirements. You can safely recharge them at any time, regardless of whether they're partially charged.

Myth: Talking on your cell phone while fueling your car at a gas station can cause a fire or explosion.
Truth: Cell phones do give off a very small amount of electricity but not enough to light *anything* on fire, let alone gasoline. Both the American Petroleum Institute and the Cellular Telecommunications Industry Association have debunked this urban myth, which spread via an e-mail and warning stickers on fuel pumps in the 1990s.

Myth: Cell phones are banned from hospitals' intensive care units because they interfere with lifesaving equipment and electronic monitoring machines.
Truth: It's sort of true. It's been exaggerated…but for a noble reason. Ringing cell phones can be loud; conversations on them may also be loud, disruptive, and emotional, and that can disturb patients and their families. Experts say that only about 5 percent of the devices in use in the ICU would be affected by cell phone signals, but then only at a distance of under 40 inches, and even then, only a little.

* * *

NAME CHANGERS
• Sheila Ranea Crabtree hated her first name; she thought it was ugly. She went by her middle name as a teenager, but didn't think that one fit her personality, either. So, with the blessing of her husband and children, the Ohio woman had her name legally changed to Sexy Crabtree.
• A man in New Zealand lost a bet and had to legally change his name. Good news: His new name is one letter shy of the government's 100-letter maximum. Bad news: His name is now Full Metal Havok More Sexy N Intelligent Than Spock And All The Superheroes Combined With Frostnova.

THE MAN UPSTAIRS

*In death, as in real estate, sometimes the only thing
that matters is location, location, location.*

DECEASED: Richard Poncher, a businessman and social acquaintance of baseball legend Joe DiMaggio

DETAILS: DiMaggio married actress Marilyn Monroe in January 1954, but the marriage lasted only nine months. That fall, while DiMaggio was in New York, he ran into Poncher. "You want to buy two crypts?" the slugger asked. Now that DiMaggio was splitting from Monroe, he wanted to sell the two aboveground burial spaces he'd bought for Monroe and himself in the wall of a mausoleum at Westwood Memorial Park, a cemetery in Los Angeles.

GOING MY WAY: Poncher agreed to buy the crypts, but he did it only as a favor to his friend, nothing more. Then when Monroe died in 1962, DiMaggio had her interred in another crypt in the same wall, which turned out to be directly beneath one of the crypts he'd sold to Poncher eight years before.

Suddenly realizing he'd be spending eternity next to Hollywood's biggest sex symbol, Poncher decided to make the most of it. He took the crypt above Marilyn's for himself and gave the other one to his wife, Elsie. Before he died in 1986, he made one last request. "He said, 'If I croak, if you don't put me upside down over Marilyn, I'll haunt you the rest of my life,'" Elsie told the *Los Angeles Times* in 2009. She passed the request on to the funeral director, perhaps thinking he'd laugh it off. He didn't: "I was standing right there, and he turned him over," Elsie told the *Times*. Poncher has been lying facedown over Marilyn ever since.

UPDATE: How long he'll stay there is anyone's guess. The plaque on his crypt reads, "To the man who gave us everything and more," and he may not be done giving. In 2009 Elsie listed his crypt on eBay, hoping to sell it for enough money to pay off the $1.6-million mortgage on her Beverly Hills home. An anonymous bidder in Japan made the winning bid of $4.6 million, only to back out later. A second auction attracted no bids at all. (If the crypt ever does sell, Elsie plans to move Poncher over to her crypt, so he'll still be in the neighborhood.)

About 10% of people are left-handed. About 20% are left-footed.

FREE ADVICE

Timeless wisdom from yesterday and today.

"Do not pray for an easy life, pray for the strength to endure a difficult one."
—**Bruce Lee**

"You gotta lose 'em some of the time. When you do, lose 'em right."
—**Casey Stengel, baseball manager**

"Pray for rain all you like, but dig a well while you do it."
—**Stephen King**

"Waste no more time arguing what a good man should be. Be one."
—**Marcus Aurelius**

"Don't take life so serious, son. It ain't nohow permanent."
—**Walt Kelly**

"Make the right decision even when nobody is looking. Especially when no one is looking."
—**Oprah Winfrey**

"No one will take care of you if you don't take care of yourself."
—**Alicia Keys**

"It is not enough to swing at the ball. You've got to loosen your girdle and really let the ball have it."
—**Babe Didrikson Zaharias**

"Don't gamble; take all your savings and buy some good stock and hold it till it goes up, then sell it. If it don't go up, don't buy it."
—**Will Rogers**

"I think it's better to feel good than to look good."
—**Tom Hanks**

"I try to teach my heart not to want things it can't have."
—**Alice Walker**

"The most important thing to do if you find yourself in a hole is to stop digging."
—**Warren Buffett**

"Your time is limited, so don't waste it living someone else's life."
—**Steve Jobs**

"Keep your eyes open and your mouth shut."
—**John Steinbeck**

Typically, a spammer needs to send 12,500,000 e-mails to get one response.

MÜELLERS & MELNYKS

Most common surname in the United States: Smith (followed by Johnson and Williams). Here are the most common last names in other parts of the world.

Australia
1. Smith
2. Jones
3. Williams

El Salvador
1. Hernández
2. Martínez
3. López

Turkey
1. Öztürk
2. Yılmaz
3. Kaya

Israel
1. Cohen
2. Levy
3. Mizrahi

Azerbaijan
1. Mammadov
2. Aliyev
3. Hasanov

Italy
1. Rossi
2. Russo
3. Ferrari

Sweden
1. Andersson
2. Johansson
3. Karlsson

Malta
1. Borg
2. Camilleri
3. Vella

Latvia
1. Berzins
2. Kalnins
3. Ozolins

Estonia
1. Ivanov
2. Tamm
3. Sarr

Northern Ireland
1. Wilson
2. Campbell
3. Kelly

Czech Republic
1. Novak
2. Svoboda
3. Novotny

Vietnam
1. Nguyen
2. Tran
3. Le

Belgium
1. Peeters
2. Janssens
3. Maes

Denmark
1. Jensen
2. Nielsen
3. Hansen

Germany
1. Müller
2. Schmidt
3. Schneider

Serbia
1. Jovanovic
2. Petrovic
3. Nikolic

Ukraine
1. Melnyk
2. Shevchenko
3. Boyko

Netherlands
1. De Jong
2. Jansen
3. De Vries

Wales
1. Jones
2. Williams
3. Davies

China
1. Wang
2. Li
3. Zhang

Smallpox was named "small" to distinguish it from "great" pox, now known as syphilis.

BEAT THE PRESS

Goofs both big and small from the Fourth Estate.

• To promote its series *Chicagoland* in March 2014, CNN posted a gallery of old Chicago photographs on its website. The first one, "1837 Lake Street," depicts an Old West-style street, busy with carriages and pedestrians. CNN deleted the picture a day later after several Chicagoans complained. Reason: it wasn't "old Chicago"— it was a still shot from the 1937 movie *Old Chicago*, which was filmed on a Hollywood back lot.

• In May 2013, the Halifax, Nova Scotia, *Chronicle Herald* ran a headline that read: "Chroinicle Herald Claims Six Awards." (Apparently none of those awards were for proofreading.)

• On March 14, 1995, the *New York Times* celebrated its 50,000th edition. The paper has numbered every edition on the masthead since it was founded in 1851. But in 1999 a news assistant at the *Times* discovered an embarrassing fact: the number was off by 500. It turned out that the February 6, 1898, edition was the paper's 14,499th, and although the following day's edition should have been the 14,500th, it was incorrectly marked No. 15,000. It only took the *Times* a century to correct the goof.

• The *Toronto Star* accused local politician Margarett Best of taking a trip to Mexico while she was on paid medical leave. The proof: she had posted a vacation picture from Mexico on her Facebook page. Oops. The *Star*'s "veteran reporter" Richard Brennan based his entire story on the day the pic was posted—April 4, 2013—but failed to notice that the photo was actually taken back in 2008. The *Star* issued a lengthy apology.

• During a 2013 snowstorm, New York's CBS2 ran a crawl across the screen announcing that two counties were "without paper."

• In January 2014 on *The Five* (Fox News), Andrea Tantaros lamented, "The biggest thing that hurts this country is we don't study history. If you ask most people, they don't even know why some guy in Boston got his head blown off because he tried to secretly raise the tax on tea." The fact-checkers at Politifact.com were perplexed;

President Lyndon Johnson married his wife, Lady Bird, with a $2.50 ring from Sears.

they think the "some guy in Boston" she referred to was Charles Townshend who, as Great Britain's Chancellor of the Exchequer in the 1760s, did tax tea…but not in secret. And he died of an illness in England, not of a gunshot in Boston. And he couldn't have gotten his "head blown off" because guns back then weren't powerful enough. Politifact rated Tantaros's history lesson as "Pants on Fire."

• The Associated Press mixed up a few key details in a review of a Nine Inch Nails concert in September 2013: "NIN closed the night with a slow and smoky cover of Johnny Cash's 'Hurt,' which earned nonstop cheers from the crowd." The goof: "Hurt" was actually a Nine Inch Nails song that was famously covered by Johnny Cash.

• Scary correction in the *New York Times*: "An earlier version of a tweet in this column misstated the name of its writer. As her Twitter handle correctly noted, she is Jillian C. York, not Chillian J. Yikes! (That's a pseudonym she created for Halloween)."

• When *NBC Nightly News* reported on a July 2013 train wreck in Canada near the New Hampshire border, it displayed a wide map of the region and then zoomed in on the crash site. The following night, anchor Brian Williams showed the map again and admitted, "You'll see what a few of our sharp-eyed viewers saw, including at least one U.S. senator: New Hampshire's gone, vanished. It apparently moved to Vermont, and then New York took over a bunch of territory. Nobody knew it." Williams then apologized to New Hampshire.

• On November 19, 1863, President Abraham Lincoln gave his Gettysburg Address, in which he proclaimed the Civil War was a fight to preserve the Union. A few days later, the Harrisburg, Pennsylvania, *Patriot & Union* ran a scathing editorial: "We pass over the silly remarks of the President. For the credit of the nation we are willing that the veil of oblivion shall be dropped over them and that they shall be no more repeated or thought of." On the speech's 150th anniversary in 2013, the newspaper—now called the *Patriot-News*—ran this correction: "The *Patriot & Union* failed to recognize the speech's momentous importance, timeless eloquence, and lasting significance. Our predecessors were perhaps under the influence of partisanship, or of strong drink, as was common in the profession at the time. The *Patriot-News* regrets the error."

Croissants aren't French—they were invented in Austria.

SIGN THE PETITION

The federal government is a huge lumbering entity. That's why we're amazed whenever someone in authority comes up with a way to bring its operations into the 21st century. Behold the electronic petition.

IT'S YOUR RIGHT

In addition to guaranteeing freedom of religion, freedom of speech, and freedom of the press, the First Amendment to the U.S. Constitution affirms "the right of the people…to petition the government for a redress of grievances." For most of history, exercising this right meant placing an actual signature on an actual piece of paper. Not anymore. In September 2011, the Obama administration added a feature called "We the People" to the White House website. Purpose: to let visitors create online petitions and use them to call attention to issues they felt were important. And while the Constitution says nothing about the government actually having to respond to petitions, the administration promised that "if a petition gets enough support [initially 5,000 votes within the first 30 days], the White House staff will review it, ensure it's sent to the appropriate policy experts, and issue an official response."

SIGN HERE

Any visitor to the White House website who's at least 13 years of age can create a petition on the website. It's up to petitioners to collect the first 150 signatures themselves, by alerting friends and family and getting them to click on the e-mail link to the petition. After that, the petition becomes visible on the White House website for everyone to see and, if they wish (and they're old enough), to sign. Petitions containing offensive or threatening language are not allowed, nor are petitions that violate an individual's privacy or "that if published would violate criminal law or give rise to civil liability." Furthermore, the subject has to fit into one of the predetermined categories. But in spite of these limitations, visitors to the site have managed to create petitions on a wide variety of topics. Most deal with serious issues. As for the rest? You be the judge.

PETITION: "Immediately disclose the government's knowledge of and communications with extraterrestrial beings."

It costs about $300,000 to produce a two-minute movie trailer.

DETAILS: Within days of the launch of We the People in October 2011, two petitions dealing with space aliens crossed the 150-vote threshold and became visible on the website—one calling on the government to reveal what it knows about little green men, and another asking it to "formally acknowledge an extraterrestrial presence engaging the human race." The petitions received a combined 17,465 signatures in the first 30 days, far exceeding the 5,000 needed to qualify for an official response.

RESPONSE: The petitioners got a response, all right, but probably not the one they were hoping for. "The U.S. government has no evidence that any life exists outside our planet, or that an extraterrestrial presence has contacted or engaged any member of the human race," wrote Phil Larson, an official with the White House's Office of Science and Technology Policy. (At about the same time, the White House raised the threshold for an official government response from 5,000 signatures in 30 days to 25,000).

PETITION: "Secure resources and funding, and begin construction of a Death Star by 2016."

DETAILS: In November 2012, a petition became visible on the White House website calling for the federal government to build a *Star Wars*-like space station, both to defend against space aliens and to stimulate the economy by "spurring job creation in the fields of construction, engineering, space exploration, and more." Within 30 days, more than 34,000 people had signed the petition.

RESPONSE: The administration rejected the proposal based on cost (a estimated $850 quadrillion—about 50,000 times the current national debt), on principle ("the administration does not support blowing up planets"), and on futility ("Why would we spend countless taxpayer dollars on a Death Star with a fundamental flaw that can be exploited by a one-man starship?").

PETITION: "We, the undersigned, hereby request Barack Obama to immediately nationalize the Twinkie industry."

DETAILS: If you're a fan of Twinkies, Ding Dongs, Ho Hos, Sno Balls, and other snack cakes made by Hostess Brands, you probably remember where you were on November 21, 2012, the day that bankrupt Hostess Brands won permission from a judge to cease operation and go out of business. Twinkies disappeared from store shelves soon afterward, prompting this petition calling for the government to seize the means of Twinkie production and "prevent our nation from losing her sweet creamy center."

RESPONSE: Hostess cited falling demand for its products as the reason for going under; if anything, the petition underscored the problem. It failed to generate enough signatures—it only received around 4,000—and did not get a government response. (Not that it mattered. In June 2013 most of the Hostess brands were purchased by a new company and Twinkies returned to store shelves the following July.)

PETITION: "We, the undersigned, request that the president peacefully grant the state of [your state here] to withdraw from the United States of America and create its own NEW government."

DETAILS: President Obama received enough votes in 2012 to win reelection, but he certainly didn't win *all* the votes, and many Americans who voted for Mitt Romney or other candidates took his victory badly. How badly? In the first weeks after the election, more than 750,000 people signed petitions asking Obama to allow their states to secede from the Union. At least eight states exceeded the 25,000 signatures in 30 days needed to trigger an official response; the Texas secession petition alone received more than 100,000 signatures.

RESPONSE: Jon Carson, then director of the White House's Office of Public Engagement, had the sad duty of informing the petitioners that the Constitution does not allow states to secede from the Union. (The good news: though nearly 30,000 people signed various petitions asking President Obama to strip signers of secessionist petitions of their citizenship and deport them to other countries, he doesn't have the power to do that, either.)

PETITION: "Actually take these petitions seriously instead of just using them as an excuse to pretend you are listening."

DETAILS: The petition received more than 37,167 signatures.

RESPONSE: "We're listening," said Macon Philips, then White House Director of Digital Strategy. "Thanks for taking the time to participate....We look forward to hearing from you again."

A FREE PRIZE INSIDE!

You might be surprised by the swag that once came in cereal boxes.

PRODUCT: Quaker Oats (1891)

INSIDE SCOOP: Quaker was the first company to put a "premium" inside their product's package. For choosing Quaker Oats over a competitor's cereal, the company wanted to give the consumer something extra. But what? Quaker decided to put something into their boxes that would appeal to homemakers, since they were the ones doing the buying. The prize at the bottom of the box of Quaker Oats or Mother's Oats: a china cup, saucer, bowl, or plate. The premiums were so popular that by 1900, Quaker was ordering 48,000 bowls per week from the Homer Laughlin china company—a fifth of Laughlin's total china sales. Since the dishes and cups had to fit inside oatmeal boxes, they were smaller than store-bought china, but "oatmeal china" had the same quality as china sold in stores. The program continued for more than 70 years, right up to 1960, when Quaker finally discontinued the chinaware program.

PRODUCT: Quaker Oats (1954)

INSIDE SCOOP: In the 1940s and 1950s, the radio show *Challenge of the Yukon* followed the fictional adventures of Sergeant Preston and his dog, Yukon King. The plot: the duo tracked down evildoers and rescued damsels in distress during the 1890s gold rush. In one famous 1954 promotion, Quaker's ad agency paid $1,000 for a 19.11-acre plot upstream from Dawson City, Yukon, Canada; divided it up into 21 million plots of one square inch apiece; and then printed "Deeds of Land" for each plot.

Deeds for the stamp-sized parcels were handsomely lettered, individually numbered, and bore the seal of the "Klondike Big Inch Company." (The company wanted to mail them out in exchange for a box top, but the Ohio Securities Division ruled that exchanging deeds for box tops meant Quaker Oats needed a license to sell foreign land, so they put the deeds inside boxes of Quaker Puffed Wheat or Puffed Rice instead.) Kids loved the promotion so much that all 21 million boxes sold in just a few weeks.

Warm swarm: Honeybees keep their hives at 95°F.

And then the craziness started: deedholders began writing to Quaker and to the Canadian government, asking about their land. How could they locate it? What was it worth? One man had 10,800 deeds and wanted to merge them into one piece of land. Quaker also received hundreds of letters from people who wanted to mine their one-inch parcels for gold. (Mineral rights had not been included with the deeds—if gold was found, it didn't belong to the deedholder.) Worse still, Quaker never paid to register the titles, which made them worthless, at least at the time. Today a Klondike Big Inch Company deed in mint condition can be worth between $30 and $40 to a collector. But in 1965, the Klondike Big Inch Company was dissolved, and the land went back to Canada.

PRODUCT: Cheerios (2000)

INSIDE SCOOP: In 2000 the U.S. Mint produced one-dollar gold coins featuring the image of Sacagawea, the Native American woman who led Lewis and Clark through the West. They weren't released to the Federal Reserve Bank until January 26, 2000, but through a special promotion, collectors could find them in boxes of Cheerios starting on January 1. One in every 2,000 boxes contained one gold coin, and one in every 4,400 had a certificate good for 100 coins. The U.S. Mint struck 5,500 coins just for Cheerios. (More than a billion Sacagawea dollars went into general circulation.)

Then, in 2005, a coin collector noticed a difference between the "Cheerios dollars" and the regular coins. All the Sacagawea coins had an eagle on the back. But on the Cheerios dollars, the U.S. Mint struck the coins with more definition in the eagle's tail feathers. Then it was decided that the feathers "made the tail appear too dark," so the design was changed for mass production.

While that might not seem like a big difference, any coins with variations are big news to collectors. And since only 5,500 Sacagawea dollars had the variant, that made them rare…and valuable. One more value-added detail: since the difference wasn't discovered until five years after the coins were issued, many Cheerios dollars were taken out of their packaging and used as money. Those coins went into general circulation, and many were lost. So how much is such a rare coin worth? In 2007 a mint-condition Cheerios Sacagawea golden dollar was auctioned off for $11,500. That's a lot of money for a prize found in a box of cereal.

There was a real WWII hero named G.I. Joe. He was a carrier pigeon.

UNCLE JOHN'S PAGE OF LISTS

Some random information from the BRI's bottomless files.

6 Things Stuck in People's Noses in 2012 (according to ER reports)

1. AA battery
2. Sponge
3. Two erasers
4. Heart-shaped gem
5. Earplug
6. Plastic eyeball

3 Types of Black Holes

1. Stellar
2. Supermassive
3. Miniature

7 Movies & TV Shows Inspired by Shakespeare

1. *My Own Private Idaho* (*Henry IV*)
2. *Thor* (*Henry V*)
3. *The Lion King* (*Hamlet*)
4. *Sons of Anarchy* (*Hamlet*)
5. *She's the Man* (*Twelfth Night*)
6. *Deliver Us from Eva* (*The Taming of the Shrew*)
7. *Forbidden Planet* (*The Tempest*)

11 Most Expensive Concert Tickets (average price)

1. The Rolling Stones ($624)
2. One Direction ($460)
3. Maroon 5 ($364)
4. The Eagles ($354)
5. Justin Timberlake ($339)
6. Roger Waters ($314)
7. The Who ($314)
8. Beyoncé ($294)
9. Fleetwood Mac ($282)
10. Pink ($270)
11. Paul McCartney ($241)

6 Celebrity First Cousins

1. George Clooney & Miguel Ferrer
2. Snoop Dogg & Brandy
4. Melissa McCarthy & Jenny McCarthy
5. Rip Torn & Sissy Spacek
6. Jason Schwartzman & Nicolas Cage

5 Most Common Computer Passwords (2013)

1. 123456
2. password
3. 12345678
4. qwerty
5. abc123

10 U.S. States that have no NFL, NHL, NBA, or MLB Team

1. Alabama
2. Connecticut
3. Idaho
4. Iowa
5. Nevada
6. New Mexico
7. Vermont
8. Virginia
9. Wyoming
10. South Dakota

Top 5 Nations that Read the Most (the U.S. is #22)

1. India
2. Thailand
3. China
4. Philippines
5. Egypt

Older than you think: The world's first roller skating rink opened in New York City in 1863.

UNDERWEAR IN THE NEWS

*Here's what happens when the
unmentionables get mentioned.*

PUTIN ON PANTIES

In August 2013, a Russian artist named Konstantin Altunin fled to France and requested political asylum, claiming he faced persecution for painting an unflattering portrait of Russian president Vladimir Putin. How unflattering? Putin is wearing a woman's nightgown and combing the hair of prime minister Dmitry Medvedev, who's wearing a bra and panties. Russian authorities seized that painting and others by Altunin that poke fun at civic and religious leaders, prompting the artist to flee for his life. He hopes to remain in France indefinitely: "I want to live and work in an atmosphere of freedom," he says. (No word on whether he plans to paint *French* officials in ladies' underwear.)

STATUE OF LIMITATIONS

One Monday morning in February 2014, students at Wellesley College, an all-women's college in Massachusetts, awoke to the sight of a middle-aged man, wearing only saggy white cotton briefs, sleepwalking near the center of campus. The "man" turned out to be *Sleepwalker*, an eerily realistic statue that was part of an art exhibit at the college's Davis Museum. Many students were not amused: by the end of the week more than 500 had signed an online petition calling the statue "a source of apprehension, fear, and triggering thoughts regarding sexual assault" and demanding that it be moved indoors, where fewer people would have to look at it. No dice, said Davis Museum director Lisa Fischman; she saw the controversy as a "teachable moment" about artistic freedom and said the statue would remain until the exhibit closed in July. "I love the idea of art escaping the museum and muddling the line between what we expect to be inside (art), and what we expect to be outside (life)," she said. Tony Matelli, the Brooklyn sculptor who created *Sleepwalker*, was stunned by the response to his statue. He says he was only trying to depict a vulnerable man, the opposite of a typical "hero on a horse." "I think they're seeing something in the work that isn't there," he told WBZ radio, "but who am I to say how people should react to it?"

A FRESH START

If you're a member of the LinkedIn career networking website and started a new job in October 2013, you may have been one of the 25,000 people who received the following message from underwear maker Fruit of the Loom:

> We're all excited for you about the new gig. To show this, we're hooking you up with a complimentary pair of Fruit of the Loom. Because great-fitting underwear can help you start your workday in a great mood.

The free-underpants message may have looked like spam, but it was the real deal, part of Fruit of the Loom's Start Happy advertising campaign. Recipients were invited to choose a size and style (boxers or boxer briefs for men; bikini, high-cut, or "boy shorts" for women). Two weeks later, the free underpants, plus a $5 coupon good toward the purchase of more, arrived in the mail. "What you put on first thing in the morning really can have a positive impact on your day, and we thought about all that hope and optimism of starting a job," said Fruit of the Loom spokesperson Scott Greene.

SHORT-SIGHTED

In January 2014, utility workers called to the site of a blocked sewer in the English village of Ditton Priors found the source of the problem: dozens of pairs of men's and ladies' underwear that someone had flushed down a toilet. "You wouldn't think boxer shorts would fit down a toilet, but this is just one example of amazing things we find blocking the sewers," said Sue Fulford, a spokesperson for the water utility. (Three months later, workers responding to a report of a "fishy-smelling" blockage in the nearby town of Telford discovered a pipe clogged by half a dozen dead fish that were thought to be piranhas, but turned out to be tilapia, most likely flushed by a pet owner who got tired of caring for them.) Clogged sewer calls, said Fulford, cost the county's taxpayers an estimated £10 million (nearly $17 million) a year. Of these, 75 percent are caused by inappropriate items—like underpants—flushed down toilets.

Conquistador Francisco Pizarro overthrew the entire Inca Empire with just 150 men.

DOWN UNDER(WEAR)

The nearly 50 percent of Australian men who let their mothers, girlfriends, or wives buy their underwear for them had a new option beginning in August 2013: subscription underwear. It's the brainchild of a 24-year-old entrepreneur named William Strange. Every three months, Strange's company, Three65 Underwear, sends a shipment of underpants—briefs or boxer briefs, in white, red, or gray—to subscribers who pay from $26.95 to $36.95 per shipment, depending on whether they want a two-, three-, or four-pair subscription. Shipping is included, and Strange throws in a free pair of socks with every pair of underwear. "Subscription underwear is the revolution the underwear market needs," he says. "There are 7.5 million men age 15 to 65 in Australia and we want 75 percent of that market."

DEATH BY UNDERPANTS

In December 2013, Brad Lee Davis, 33, of McLoud, Oklahoma, was arrested and charged with murdering his stepfather, Denver Lee St. Clair. Weapon: St. Clair's own underwear. According to Davis, the two men began arguing after St. Clair made disparaging remarks about Davis's mother. St. Clair jumped Davis, who retaliated by hitting St. Clair over the head and giving him an "atomic wedgie." He pulled St. Clair's underpants out of the back of his trousers, up over his head, and around his neck, at which point the elastic waistband started choking St. Clair. Davis called 911 as soon as he realized that his stepfather had stopped breathing, but it was too late. The state medical examiner ruled the death a homicide, caused by blunt force trauma (the blow to the head) and asphyxiation. "The asphyxia is coming from the atomic wedgie," said Pottawatomie County sheriff Mike Booth. "The gentleman pulled [St. Clair's] underwear up over his head. Nobody that I've had contact with has seen anything like this before." Davis claims he administered the wedgie in self-defense.

*   *   *

"Indeed, the pun is considered by many to be more distasteful than the common expletive. You might even say the pun is mightier than the s-word."

—George Takei

THE SHINING, STARRING ROBIN WILLIAMS

Some roles are so closely associated with a specific actor that it's hard to imagine he or she wasn't the first choice. But it happens all the time. Can you imagine, for example…

TOM CRUISE AS TONY STARK (*Iron Man*, 2008). It took nearly 20 years to bring to the screen the Marvel Comics story of the billionaire who builds a super suit. After several high-profile Hollywood players—including Nicolas Cage and Quentin Tarantino—tried and failed to get *Iron Man* off the ground, it looked like a go in the early 2000s when Tom Cruise was set to produce and star. But then Cruise read *Iron Man* creator Stan Lee's script…and lost interest. The project went back into "development hell" until director Jon Favreau took over. He surprised everyone by casting down-and-out actor Robert Downey Jr., who he felt could make Stark a "likable a**h*le." (He was right.)

HELEN MIRREN AS MIRANDA PRIESTLY (The Devil Wears Prada, 2006). The role of the ruthless fashion-magazine boss earned Meryl Streep a Best Actress Oscar nomination. But the producers' first choice was Mirren, who was unavailable because she'd been cast to portray another powerful boss: Queen Elizabeth II in The Queen. And it was Mirren, not Streep, who took home the Best Actress Oscar that year. (Streep won an Oscar five years later for playing yet another boss: British prime minister Margaret Thatcher).

SYLVESTER STALLONE AS SUPERMAN (*Superman*, 1978). When production for the biggest comic-book movie in history began, Stallone lobbied hard for the lead. And having just won a Best Picture Oscar for *Rocky*, he nearly landed the part. That is, until Marlon Brando, who'd already been cast as Jor-El, Superman's Krypton father, found out. Brando had casting-veto power in his contract, and he said no to Stallone playing his son. Reason: many people in Hollywood were promoting Stallone as "the next Brando," and he reportedly found the comparison offensive.

…pronounced "sink us." (The name was changed after WWII.)

ZAC EFRON AS SUPERMAN (*Man of Steel*, 2013). Eager to break out of his boyish *High School Musical* reputation, Efron was nearly set to take the lead in Zak Snyder's *Superman* reboot. But Efron was unsure about taking the part, so he asked his idol, Leonardo DiCaprio, if it would be a good idea. DiCaprio advised against it, saying that it would be a bad idea for Efron to get "bogged down with a franchise." So Efron passed, and Snyder offered the part to Henry Cavill, who'd actually been considered for the role in *Superman Returns* five years earlier before losing out to Brandon Routh. (Cavill was also considered for the part of James Bond in *Casino Royale* in 2006, but lost it to Daniel Craig.)

HENRY CAVILL AS EDWARD CULLEN (*Twilight*, 2008). Englishman Robert Pattinson became an international star for his role as the brooding vampire in the film adaptation of Stephenie Meyer's best-selling supernatural romance novel. But Meyer initially wanted another English actor, Henry Cavill, to play the part of the 17-year-old undead teenager. Except that at 25, Cavill looked too old to be a teenager. So Pattinson (who'd played a brooding teen in 2005's *Harry Potter and the Goblet of Fire*) beat out 3,000 other actors for the role of Edward.

NO ONE…EXCEPT WILLIAM H. MACY…AS JERRY LUNDEGAARD (*Fargo*, 1996). Macy wanted the part of the bumbling salesman in the Coen brothers' dark comedy so much that—after auditioning twice and then not hearing back—he flew to New York and tracked down the Coens at their office. Macy then barged in and announced, "I'm very, very worried that you are going to screw up this movie by giving this role to somebody else. It's my role, and I'll shoot your dogs if you don't give it to me." Macy got the part.

*   *   *

CASHING IN HIS CHIPS

When Arch West, inventor of Doritos, died in 2011, his family made plans to bury his ashes alongside those of his wife. His daughter, Jana Hacker, told reporters, "We're going to let everyone toss in a Dorito. It will be just the plain flavor, though. Otherwise people will say, 'Thanks Jana, now I've got nacho all over my hand.'"

What did Gandhi and Henri Matisse have in common with Julio Iglesias? They were all lawyers.

A TREE-EATING FISH

...and other animals that seem as if they were invented by a crackpot fantasy writer but are 100 percent real.

Animal: Desert grassland whiptail lizard

Odd Fact #1: They're asexual; they reproduce via *parthenogenesis*—the females' eggs develop into embryos without the need for male sperm for fertilization. (The term *parthenogenesis* comes from the Greek words for "virgin birth.")

Odd Fact #2: Reproducing this way means that except for occasional mutations, all of the lizards in the species are genetically identical to each other—they're clones. And since they're all clones of females, there is essentially no such thing as a male desert grassland whiptail lizard.

Odd Fact #3: Even though desert grassland whiptail lizards don't need males and don't mate, they still have a mating ritual. When a female lizard is about to lay eggs, another lizard—also female, of course—mounts her, just as a male would, and the two carry out what's called *pseudocopulation*. (According to many herpetologists, the behavior is influenced by the lizards' hormone cycles.)

Animal: *Panaque* armored suckermouth catfish

Odd Fact #1: There are nearly 700 species of armored suckermouth catfish, all native to Central and South America. One of their distinguishing characteristics is that their bodies are covered in overlapping rows of bony armorlike plates.

Odd Fact #2: The species' other distinguishing characteristic is "sucker mouths"—specially adapted, roundish mouths located on the bottom of their heads. They use their mouths to attach themselves to submerged rocks and logs with a powerful suctioning grip. There they feed on organic matter on the surface of those objects.

Odd Fact #3: Seven species of suckermouths make up the genus *Panaque*. Unlike the other species of suckermouth armored catfish, panaques don't just eat what's on the surface of wood—they eat the wood, too. Once they're attached to submerged logs or tree branches, they use their spoon-shaped teeth to rasp the wood into tiny pieces, which they can digest and obtain nourishment from

---

The word "broadcast" originally referred to farmers *casting* (scattering) seeds over a *broad* area.

specially adapted stomach enzymes. Of the roughly 32,000 known fish species in the world today, the seven species of *Panaque* armored suckermouth catfish are the only ones that eat wood. (Want to see one? They're very popular aquarium fish and can be found at most pet shops.)

Animal: Gastric-brooding frog

Odd Fact #1: There are actually two species of these frogs, both found only in small areas of rainforest in Queensland, Australia. When a female gastric-brooding frog lays her eggs—about 40 of them—she waits for the male to fertilize them…and then she eats them.

Odd Fact #2: The eggs go to the mother's stomach…and stay there. Luckily, they're coated in a jelly that contains *prostaglandin E2*—a substance that stops the production of hydrochloric acid in the mother's stomach, so the eggs don't get digested during gestation. Then, when the tadpoles hatch, they excrete more prostaglandin E2, so they don't get digested, either. They just swim around in their mother's belly, which gets bigger and bigger as the tadpoles grow, even squeezing her lungs out of the way.

Odd Fact #3: After about six weeks, she finally gives birth to the babies. How? She literally just vomits them up into the water. The tadpoles then swim away and begin their froggy lives.

Note: Only a few specimens of gastric-brooding frogs have ever been seen since they were first discovered in 1914. The most recent sighting was in 1985. They are so rare that scientists now fear both species of gastric-brooding frogs—the only frogs known to carry their young inside their stomachs—may be extinct.

*   *   *

RANDOM FACTS

- Jellyfish have no brain or heart, and can evaporate if beached.
- Population of Monowi, Nebraska: 1. It's 72-year-old Elsie Eiler.
- Scotland's national animal is the unicorn.
- All the iron in your body could be used to make a 3-inch nail.

HACK ATTACKS

Computer hacking can be pretty scary—crippling corporations or even countries. These hacks, however, are more funny than scary.

TUPAC LIVES!

In May 2011, the PBS news program *Frontline* ran a story on Julian Assange, founder of WikiLeaks, the hacking organization that leaked sensitive U.S. government data. A group of hackers called "Lulz Security" didn't like the way Assange was portrayed. So they hacked into the PBS website and posted a fake story about deceased rapper Tupac Shakur, reporting that he "has been found alive and well in a small resort in New Orleans." PBS took down the story, but Lulz used Twitter to take credit for the attack and send out messages like "F*** Frontline." In 2013 the FBI arrested Hector Monsegur, or "Sabu," one of Lulz's founders. (He turned informant.)

WE'RE JAMMING

In 1990 Los Angeles radio station KIIS-FM held a huge promotion: the 102nd caller after the station played a certain three songs in a row would win a $50,000 Porsche. On June 1, 1990, the station played the songs, and the calls started coming in. The 102nd caller was a man named Michael Peters. But not really. He was really a hacker named Kevin Poulsen, who hacked into the station's phone lines the moment he heard the third song play. Jamming all but one of KIIS-FM's 25 phone lines, Poulsen easily made himself the 102nd caller and won the car. The FBI figured out what had happened and began an investigation (Poulsen also allegedly accessed classified information on U.S. Air Force computers). The story was featured on NBC's *Unsolved Mysteries*...whose toll-free tip line mysteriously crashed. Poulsen was caught, and he served five years in prison, the longest sentence ever for hacking (at the time).

THE TRUTH IS IN THERE

In 2002, just a few months after the 9/11 attacks, a bizarre message flashed on a U.S. Army computer screen: "Your security system is crap. I am Solo. I will continue to disrupt at the highest levels." The message appeared on 97 Army, Navy, Air Force, and NASA computers. Officials immediately suspected—and feared—that it was a terrorist attack. It wasn't. Security experts tracked the messages to Scotland, where they'd been sent out by one Gary McKinnon. His lawyer's defense: McKinnon has Asperger's syndrome, a condition marked by an inability to understand simple social cues but an enhanced ability to understand complex systems (such as computer networks). McKinnon had hacked into the military networks because he believed that's where the U.S. government was storing "the truth" about UFOs. The U.S. government asked the U.K. to extradite McKinnon for trial, but in 2012—after ten years of legal wrangling—the extradition was denied and McKinnon went unpunished.

FREE THE MUSIC

Illegal file sharing of music can cost recording artists millions of dollars. It's especially damaging if a hacker can get access to their songs before they're even released. Over the course of 2009 and 2010, a German teenager using the name "DJ Stolen" broke into the personal computers of top music stars, including Lady Gaga, Ke$ha, Justin Timberlake, and Mariah Carey. There he found unreleased, unfinished recordings of songs (and in the case of Ke$ha, dirty photographs) and shared them online, charging people to listen to them. In total he earned 15,000 euros (about $21,000) from the scam…before he was caught in June 2010 and sentenced to 18 months in jail and mandatory rehabilitation for Internet addiction.

E-STONIA

In 2007 the Estonian government removed a bronze statue memorializing Russia's World War II soldiers from the capital city of Talinn. Estonia was part of the Soviet Union at the time but became independent in 1991. Animosity between the two nations remains, which is why Estonia blamed Russia when, a few days after the statue came down (and riots ensued), Estonia's Internet crashed. Government websites, bank websites, ATMs, and every networked computer in the Baltic nation was suddenly off the grid. Service was restored within a week, but it took months to find the responsible party: Dmitri Galushkevich, a 20-year-old Russian (and anti-Estonian) living in Estonia. He admitted to prosecutors that he'd sent out a virus that directed tens of thousands of Estonian computers to flood dozens of websites. His fine: 17,500 kroons, or about $1,600.

Modern squirrels are nearly identical to their ancestors from 35 million years ago.

RANDOM ORIGINS

Once again, the BRI asks—and answers—the question:
Where does all this stuff come from?

OUTSOURCING

In 1989 General Electric chairman Jack Welch went to Bangalore, India, to meet with a delegation of Indian executives and prime minister Rajiv Gandhi. Purpose: to pave the way for GE's entrance into the Indian marketplace. (Specifically, Welch wanted to sell airplane parts and medical equipment.) Gandhi, in return, tried to interest Welch in buying Indian software, but Welch was more interested in something else: the country's low labor costs. After that meeting, Welch decided to shift some of GE's labor force—the phone-based customer service labor force—from the United States to India. A year later, Bangalore had its first call center, for GE products, which would lead to thousands of American jobs moving to India, labor savings for American companies, and the word "outsourcing."

RETSYN

In 1956 the British candy company Cadbury introduced Certs, a peppermint-flavored breath mint designed to compete with Life Savers. Cadbury's goal: to appeal to adults and be thought of as a mint, not a candy. So the company launched a marketing campaign designed to make Certs sound scientifically superior to Life Savers, touting it as "the only mints with Retsyn." Retsyn is a breath-freshening ingredient, and the registered trade name for a lab-created mixture of partially hydrogenated cottonseed oil, artificial mint flavoring, sugar, and copper gluconate. (The little green spots in Certs aren't little pieces of mint—they're copper gluconate flecks.)

POCKET PROTECTORS

In 1943 electrical engineer Hurley Smith had lost his job at a company that made electrical transformers. Needing to make ends meet fast, Smith racked his brain for a moneymaking idea. It was literally right in front of him—many of the pockets on the white shirts he'd worn to work were frayed around the edges and spotted with pen and pencil stains. His solution: a "pocket protector," a simple sheath

---

Peaches, avocados, cashews, and bananas are all pollinated by bats.

that held the weight of small tools and prevented stains from leaky pens. Smith experimented with a variety of plastics, eventually settling on PVC, which he formed using his wife's iron. By 1947 Smith had a patent for the pocket protector, and two years later he was producing them at a plastics factory in Lansing, Michigan. The product caught on with engineers, computer programmers, and students, but by the 1980s they'd become synonymous with nerds, thanks to the pocket-protector-wearing geeks in movies such as *Revenge of the Nerds*. Today, they've been re-embraced by self-proclaimed nerds. The MIT college bookstore, for example, sells one inscribed with the words "NERD PRIDE."

MARASCHINO CHERRIES

The marasca is a type of cherry that grows in Croatia and Italy. For more than 150 years, farmers there have preserved them in maraschino, a liqueur made from marasca cherries. These "maraschino cherries" became popular among European aristocrats and royalty in the late nineteenth century—they were expensive and hard to get because they were produced only in small quantities in just a few places. Wealthy Americans wanted the cherries, too, but after 1919 couldn't get them anymore—they were banned due to Prohibition. Around the same time, an Oregon State University agriculture professor named Ernest Wiegand came up with a way for local farmers to sweeten and preserve Queen Anne cherries in order to compete with European maraschinos. Wiegand's technique: soak the cherries in a calcium salt brine and then add large amounts of sugar. Today, maraschino cherries are prepared a little differently. The fruit is soaked in a solution of calcium chloride and sulfur dioxide, which turns the naturally pale cherries a sickly yellow. Then they're pitted, soaked in a high-fructose corn syrup solution for a month…and then dyed red. (Yum?)

* * *

MYTH-AMERICA

Myth: George Washington wore a powdered wig.
Fact: Most men—and nearly all politicians—from that time wore powdered wigs, but Washington chose not to. Instead, he powdered his own hair, which was light brown, and then tied it back so that it *looked* like he was wearing a wig.

M*A*S*H NOTES

The unlikely origin of an instantly recognizable theme song.

THE MOVIE

Early in his career, Robert Altman had a reputation for being difficult. When he was still directing TV shows like *Maverick* and *Bonanza*, he'd been fired several times over "creative differences" with his bosses. He was recognized as talented, but his rancorous nature slowed his work to a trickle.

Finally in 1969, after nearly two decades of struggling, he got a big break. He was offered the opportunity to direct a film version of *MASH*, Richard Hooker's 1968 novel about three doctors' misadventures in a mobile army surgical hospital (MASH) during the Korean War. Altman wasn't the studio's first choice. In fact, he wasn't even their tenth choice. More than a dozen other directors had rejected the project, and with good reason: at a time when the war in Vietnam was a very controversial topic, *MASH*'s mix of crude hijinks and badly injured soldiers had the smell of a box-office disaster. But Altman didn't have a lot to lose, so he took the job.

FACING THE MUSIC

Analyzing the script, Altman was aware that he was walking a tightrope between slapstick and tragedy. But if he could craft a scene that successfully combined both, he felt that he could probably figure out the rest of the movie. He settled on a scene he nicknamed "The Last Supper," in which Captain Walter "Painless Pole" Waldowski decides to kill himself after an embarrassing failure in the bedroom, and in response, his friends wine and dine with him in a pre-death "wake" in which his seat of honor is a casket.

Altman quickly saw that the absurdity of the scene wasn't quite working as written. It needed a song—solemn…but so bad that it was funny. Altman called on a friend—composer Johnny Mandel, who'd recently won an Oscar for his song "The Shadow of Your Smile" from the movie *The Sandpipers*. Mandel accepted the job, but not without some trepidation. The last film he'd done with Altman (*That Cold Day in the Park*) had been an embarrassing flop, and he knew that, in Hollywood, another flop could do serious damage to his career.

Dirty dancing: When it became popular in the 1750s, the waltz was considered scandalous.

Although a movie score is usually handled in postproduction, after filming and editing, Altman asked Mandel to be present during the planning of "The Last Supper." That's when he asked Mandel to write a song for actor Ken Prymus to sing while playing the guitar. Altman's two stipulations: the song had to be called "Suicide Is Painless," and it had to be "the stupidest song ever written."

SINS OF THE FATHER

Altman may have sensed Mandel's lack of enthusiasm in aspiring to stupidity. He told Mandel to stick with the music and forget about the lyrics—Altman would write them himself. Easier said than done. Altman discovered that stupidity wasn't as simple as it looks. "I can't write anything nearly as stupid as what we need," he reported after a few days of trying. But he had a trump card: his 14-year-old son, Michael. Whether Mike should've been flattered or insulted, his father was confident that he had within him "the stupidest song ever," and Mike didn't disappoint. He came through with lines like "The sword of time will pierce our skins / The pain grows stronger, watch it grin," and Altman declared them perfect. Award-winning songwriter Mandel wasn't so sure. In fact, he was mortified when Altman decided to use the song for the movie's title song as well. Mandel couldn't see how the "stupid song," performed in an easy-listening style, fit the scenes of helicopters, stretchers, carnage, and patients in pain. But somehow it did.

IRONIES IN THE FIRE

Amazingly, "Suicide Is Painless" became Mandel's biggest hit…and Michael Altman's only hit. When producer Ingo Preminger asked what he wanted for writing the lyrics, the 14-year-old said that all he wanted in return was a guitar. Instead, producer Preminger gave him a standard songwriter's contract. Lucky for Michael. The song was recorded by dozens of musicians, from Henry Mancini to Marilyn Manson, and it was used for the TV version of M*A*S*H.

Robert Altman went on to become a hugely successful film-maker; Johnny Mandel scored many more movies. Michael, though, retired from songwriting and focused on his career as a painter. He could afford to. In the 1980s, his dad good-naturedly complained to Johnny Carson that he'd been paid only $70,000 for directing the movie, while his son had become a millionaire from the song.

Greatest bite force of any animal: Crocodile. Its jaws can exert 3,700 psi. (Humans: 200 psi.)

HOW TO DO EVERYDAY THINGS…IN SPACE!

With the International Space Station up and running since 1998, astronauts now spend months at a time in orbit. And in between their scientific experiments, they still have to have to attend to their own personal hygiene, which, due to the lack of gravity, can be pretty tricky.

BRUSHING YOUR TEETH
There's no running water on the ISS. Reason: there's not enough gravity to push it through the pipes. But even if water was forced through pipes, once it came out of the tap, the lack of gravity would make it float everywhere and eventually get inside the machinery, shorting it out. Instead, astronauts get their drinking water from "water bags"—small plastic containers filled with water, sealed, and outfitted with a capped straw. This is what astronauts use to brush their teeth. First, they carefully squeeze a ball of water out of the straw (the water forms a ball in low gravity) and then apply it to the toothbrush to wet it. Next, they suck any excess water off the toothbrush and apply toothpaste as normal. After brushing their teeth as they would on Earth, where do the astronauts spit? They don't—they swallow it. After that, they squeeze another water ball into their mouths and rinse the toothbrush (in their mouths), swallowing all the liquid again.

WASHING YOUR HANDS
Again, there's no running water, so astronauts rely on packaged water. They're given eight-ounce liquid-filled bags called "no rinse body bath"—a premixed solution consisting of three parts water and two parts gentle soap. To wash, the astronaut carefully squirts out a large ball of soapy water and places it on the hands. He (or she) then rubs the mixture, which has a consistency of hand sanitizer or lotion, all over the hands, then wipes them dry on a towel.

GETTING SICK
Being in space takes some getting used to—the weightlessness and the lack of anything differentiating between "up" and "down" has

made numerous astronauts sick on their first day aboard the ISS. That's why they have special astronaut barf bags. It's a thick plastic bag liner inside of another thick plastic bag. The astronaut has to insert his or her entire head in the bag to make sure they catch every drop of their own vomit. The liner is absorbent, so the astronauts wipe their faces completely clean with that. Then they pack the sick bag inside the outer bag, which seals up like a Ziploc bag.

SHAVING

This is tricky business—shaving separates hundreds of tiny hairs from the skin, and those hairs could float around, infiltrate the machinery, and wreak havoc. Solution: a special NASA-developed shaving cream called AstroEdge. It's a thick blue paste that the astronaut applies to his face in a very fine layer. He then quickly shaves off his whiskers with a regular disposable razor. However, after each stroke, he must wipe the paste and hair off the razor and into a tissue. Shaving a mustache is done in a similar way—only with a small, handheld vacuum to nab the larger volume of hair.

PEEING

The ISS keeps its toilet in a private booth. It doesn't look much like a toilet, though—it's essentially a long hose, held to the wall with Velcro, with a lidded funnel on the end. The (male) astronaut places his feet and hands in holds along the wall, pops the lid off the funnel, and waits about 15 seconds for suction to kick in. The astronaut then pees directly into the tube. (Female astronauts use the same procedure—it's just slightly more difficult.) Then they wipe the funnel with a disinfectant wipe, and bag it up for trash.

But wait, where does the urine go? It's filtered…and reused. The ISS is a closed environment, and there is very little water. Astronauts get some deliveries of water (packaged in bags), but it's not enough. So in 2010, the ISS introduced a sophisticated water filtration system—more than 90 percent of all water used on the station, including urine, is reclaimed, reused, and repackaged into potable water. Using an artificial gravity system, keg-sized distillers purify the urine immediately after it leaves an astronaut. It may sound gross, but the recycled urine is actually purer than most drinking water on Earth.

Ancient Mesopotamians dusted crops using powdered sulphur as a pesticide.

WANNA BET?

We bet you five bucks you've never been this lucky.

THREE'S COMPANY

Gambler: An anonymous Welshman

Background: In December 1989, a man in Newport, South Wales, walked into the local outlet of the popular British gaming chain Ladbrokes (betting shops were legalized in the U.K. in 1961) and made a "novelty bet"—an unusual bet on something not normally wagered on, often covering a long time period.

The Bet: The man bet £30 (about $75 at the time) that when the year 2000 came around, the following things would be true:

1. Three long-running soap operas—the British-made *EastEnders* and the Australian-made *Neighbours* and *Home and Away*—would still be airing on British TV.

2. The Irish rock band U2 would still be together.

3. British singer Cliff Richards would have received a knighthood.

Ladbrokes's estimate of the odds of all three of those predictions coming true: 6,479 to 1.

Outcome: On January 1, 2000, all three items were true. So a few days after New Year's Day, eleven years after making his £30 bet, the man walked into Ladbrokes and collected his prize money: £194,400, or about $311,000. (According to Ladbrokes, the man, described only as a 40-year-old night-shift worker, wished to remain anonymous.)

CARDS SHARK

Gambler: An unnamed gambler in Las Vegas

Background: On September 12, 2011, with just 15 games left in the season, baseball's St. Louis Cardinals were five games back from taking the wild card spot in the upcoming playoffs.

The Bet: The man, who did not want his name released, bet $250 at the MGM Grand Casino that the Cardinals would not only make it to the playoffs—they'd win the National League Championship, sending them to the World Series. Odds: 500 to 1.

Outcome: The Cardinals went on a tear, winning 11 of their final

---

What are *Gabi-Gabi*, *Wagga-Wagga*, and *Yitha-Yitha?* Native Australian languages.

15 games, and made the playoffs—on the very last day of the season. They then smashed their way through the playoffs, beating the heavily favored Philadelphia Phillies to win the National League pennant. The mystery man's winnings: $125,000.

Bonus: Did we mention that the man also bet that the Cards would win the World Series? Another $250, this time at odds of 999 to 1. When the Cardinals beat the Texas Rangers in seven games, the man won $250,000. Total winnings: $375,000.

A DAY AT THE RACES

Gambler: Darren Yates, 30, of Lancashire, England

Background: Yates was described in one British newspaper as "a compulsive bettor with a failing carpentry business," who had recently promised his wife that he would stop gambling. His gambling preference: horses. His favorite jockey: celebrated Italian rider Frankie Dettori.

The Bet: On September 28, 1996, Yates broke his promise to his wife and bet £67.58 (about $100) that Dettori would win every race held that day—seven races in all—at England's famous Ascot Racecourse. Odds: 25,095 to 1.

Outcome: Yates's wife probably forgave him for breaking his promise. Why? Yates won £550,823 (more then $860,000) when Dettori won all seven races—something no British jockey had ever done before. (It's been done once since by jockey Richard Hughes, who won seven races at Windsor Racecourse in October 2012.)

Bonus: As Dettori's wins piled up through the day, more and more people heard about it…and they started betting that he'd keep winning, resulting in what U.K. betting agency William Hill called the "blackest day in British bookmaking history." Industry experts estimate the streak cost bookies more than £50 million.

SUDDEN DEATH

Gambler: Mick Gibbs, 42, Staffordshire, England

Background: An "accumulator bet" is a British term (in the U.S. it's called a "parlay" or "combo bet") for a bet in which the gambler makes a single wager on the outcomes of several different events. Every chosen outcome has to be met or the entire bet loses.

The Bet: In August 2000, Gibbs, a roofer, bet 30 pence (about 47¢)

Antarctica has 28 airports…and no paved runways. (They're all ice.)

on a "15-fold accumulator bet," predicting the winners of fifteen games—twelve soccer matches, two cricket tournaments, and one rugby match. Odds: 1,666,666 to 1.

Outcome: Gibbs picked the winner of every one of the first 14 matches. The fifteenth: Germany's Bayern Munich soccer team versus Spain's Valencia for the European Cup, which took place on May 24, 2001—a full nine months after Gibbs made the bet. (Gibbs picked Bayern Munich.) The game's regulation time of 90 minutes ended…in a 1-1 tie. They went to a sudden-death extra time period of 30 minutes…and neither team scored. They went to a five-shot penalty shoot-out round (each team gets five penalty shots)… that ended in a 3-3 tie. They went to a sudden-death penalty shot round…and both teams scored. Then they went to a second sudden-death penalty shot round…and Gibbs lost. Just kidding— Bayern Munich scored, and Valencia's do-or-die shot was blocked. For his 30-pence wager, Gibbs won £500,000 (or about $784,000).

*   *   *

PHRASE ORIGIN: *SPELLING BEE*

Meaning: A contest to determine who can spell the most words correctly

Origin: "The word *bee* had been used in conjunction with other group activities, such as a 'quilting bee,' or occasions when farmers or neighbors would help each other, such as 'husking bee,' 'apple bee,' or 'raising bee.' (More grimly, *The Oxford English Dictionary* also provides evidence of the terms 'hanging bee' and 'lynching bee.') Despite the obvious link to industriousness and teamwork, this use of the word *bee* seems to have nothing to do with buzzing insects. The word's etymology in the *Unabridged* shows that this *bee* is an alteration of a word that meant 'voluntary help given by neighbors toward the accomplishment of a particular task,' and descends from the Middle English word *bene*, which also gave us the word *boon*, understood today to mean 'blessing' but which also has the meaning of 'benefit' or 'favor.'" (Peter Sokolowski, from Merriam-Webster's blog "A Thing About Words")

DUMB CROOKS

Here's proof that crime doesn't pay.

CADDY SHOCK

There were more than a dozen police cars parked at a Houston, Texas, deli in 2013. (The officers were there for a retirement party.) But 20-year-old Johnny Deleon didn't seem to notice—he was focused on the shiny rims of a Cadillac Escalade also parked in the lot. He sneaked up to the Escalade and started removing the rims when an officer spotted him. Before Deleon knew it, nearly 30 cops were walking out of the restaurant to detain him. His response: "Oh, sh*t!"

HEY, I KNOW THAT GUY!

In 2012 a "mid-level Taliban commander" named Mohammad Ashan walked up to a U.S. Army checkpoint in Afghanistan holding a wanted poster...with his picture on it. There was a $100 reward for information leading to his capture. One of the American soldiers, Specialist Matthew Bake, told the *Washington Post* what happened next: "We asked him, 'Is this you?' He answered with an incredible amount of enthusiasm, 'Yes, yes, that's me! Can I get my award now?'" Ashan did not get the "award," but he did get arrested. A U.S. official observed, "This guy is the Taliban equivalent of the *Home Alone* burglars."

FINDERS KEEPERS

In Gaffney, South Carolina, two heater repairmen showed up at Lois Brown's house to do some work in 2010. Before they got started, Brown, 70, informed them that her late husband had hidden a large sum of money—about $100,000—in the basement, but the family couldn't find it. If the workers found the cash, Brown said, she would give them a "big reward." When the job was completed, the men—Joey Reed, 47, and Elie Spencer, 50—reported that they hadn't found the money and left. The following day they quit their jobs and went on a shopping spree, purchasing a riding lawn mower, a big-screen TV, and a car. And they paid for it all with old $100 bills. News of their spree quickly spread through the small rural town…and then to Brown. She immediately contacted Reed and Spencer and told them if they returned what they hadn't spent, she would give them a little extra money and not call the police. They told her they didn't know what she was talking about, so Brown called the police. Reed and Spencer were arrested on grand larceny charges. They face up to ten years in prison.

SNOW PROBLEM

In December 2013, just as Frederick West, 48, was stealing a briefcase from a truck parked outside of an Akron, Ohio, business, the owner walked out and confronted him. West ran away. When police arrived, they simply followed the tracks in the snow, which led them right to West. He was arrested.

THE BUTT-DIAL CONFESSION

Used-car dealer Larry Barnett, 68, owed a "large sum of money" to his former employee, James Macom, 33. Barnett figured that if Macom was dead, he wouldn't have to pay. So he hired a hit man. While discussing the plan with the hit man, Barnett pulled up Macom's contact information on his cell phone, which he then put into his back pocket, and inadvertently hit the "send" button. Macom answered and listened in as the men plotted his demise. "I don't care if you have to burn his house to the ground with him in it," said Barnett. "Just make it look like an accident." Macom hung up and called the police. Later, when investigating officers went to Macom's house, they discovered that the place had been broken into and the gas stove had been tampered with. Barnett was arrested and charged with conspiracy to commit murder.

NOT A SELF-STARTER

In 2014 a Cape Coral, Florida, police officer stopped to assist Scott Ogden, 47, who was walking a broken motorcycle (it had no battery or key) on the side of the road. Ogden explained that he was trying to get it running for a friend, but when the cop asked for the friend's name, Ogden drew a blank. So the officer called in the bike and discovered that it had been reported stolen. Ogden ran away on foot, leaving behind the bike as well as his backpack with his ID inside it…which led police right to his house. (Maybe he should have stolen a motorcycle that, you know, worked.)

Q: Can you name the three falls at Niagara Falls? A: Horseshoe, American, and Bridal Veil.

INDUSTRIAL MUSICALS

From the Dustbin of Industry comes one of the weirdest examples of entertainment we've ever come across. Or is it the weirdest example of big business we've ever come across? It's both!

L ET'S PUT ON A SHOW(™)!
In the 1950s and 1960s, the American economy was in excellent shape. Corporate profits were up, unemployment was low, and real wages were the highest they'd ever been. Result: more and more Americans could afford to buy a home, a car, and all the newfangled appliances.

Big companies spent freely, providing salesmen with huge expense accounts to wine and dine clients. That spending trickled down to marketing, too—internal marketing. Companies had to get their troops riled up to rally them to sell more products. So several times a year, big companies would gather their sales forces for conventions, meetings, lectures, product launches…and a big-budget stage musical. Really. The sales force would gather in an auditorium and watch a full-length Broadway-style musical about their employer, commissioned by the company and written by up-and-coming New York playwrights, lyricists, and composers. Often, salesmen got to take home an LP of the show as a souvenir. Those albums are now highly sought-after treasures in thrift stores and record shops.

As companies tightened their belts during the 1970s, the "industrial musical" faded away, a victim not only of cost-cutting but also of the changing times—they were just too corny. Here are some of the corniest.

Show: *Deal Me In* (1961)
Company: Presented by U.S. Steel at the National Automobile Dealers Association, encouraging carmakers to sell more cars made of steel
Details: The subtly-named car dealer, Mr. Rutt, rallies his bored salesman by describing the magical night he'd just had. While Mr. and Mrs. Rutt are sorting through boring mail like bills and magazines (in the song "Bills and Magazines"), they come across a

---

Blackboard chalk isn't chalk; it's actually plaster of paris.

U.S. Steel sales kit. They discover that U.S. Steel has an automotive design research center, and Mr. Rutt fantasizes about how great it would be to work there. Mrs. Rutt fantasizes about being named Woman of the Year at her ladies' club simply because of her husband's success. Then a U.S. Steel representative—Mr. Steelman—arrives, and the three sing about the glories of steel. (The songs were written by Bernie Wayne, who also wrote "Blue Velvet.")

Show: *The Golden Value Line of the '60s* (1960)
Company: General Electric's Major Appliance Division
Details: Twenty-two songs are almost all sung from the point of view of one of GE's appliances, or an inanimate object praising one of GE's appliances. Example: a GE Disposall boasts of how quiet it is, and a piece of china (singing in a "Chinese accent") praises a GE dishwasher. Even Satan gets a number, singing about how "when it gets hot as Hades and lovely ladies look like chicken fricassee." Everything's going great for Satan until the arrival of his sworn enemy—a GE air conditioner.

Show: *Penney Proud* (1962)
Company: J. C. Penney
Details: The department store chain was celebrating its 60th anniversary in 1962, so for its annual sales conference it hired nightclub performer Michael Brown to write a musical that told the company's history in song. Highlights: "Opening Day at the Golden Rule," depicting the day James Cash Penney began working at the Wyoming dry-goods store that he eventually bought out; and "May I Have Your Penney Charge Card?" (Sample lyrics: "May I have your Penney Charge Card? Though it's small, it's such a large card. For a hat, a zipper, or chemise, may I have your Penney Charge Card, please?")
Bonus: The souvenir record included sheet music, so Penney employees could sing the songs at home.

Show: *Go Go Bio* (1966)
Company: DuPont
Details: Millions of Americans had space fever in the mid-1960s, and DuPont cashed in on it with a space-themed sales convention.

Winner of the 1950 Tony for Best Supporting Actor: nobody. The judges felt no one merited it.

This musical was the centerpiece. NBC news anchor Chet Huntley was paid a hefty sum to record a fake newscast about the "Bio 1" rocket heading into space, which leads into songs sung by astronauts, mission control…and actual DuPont executives. Was this all to demonstrate DuPont's high-tech role in sending a man into space? No. DuPont made weed killer, and as one song notes, "There'll be crabgrass on the moon!"

Show: *Going Places with Glidden…In '72* (1971)
Company: Glidden Paint
Details: Glidden traveling salesman George Grandley is nervous about attending the annual company sales conference (like the one where this was performed), afraid that Glidden executives don't understand how hard it is out on the road. ("If you're selling paint, tell 'em paint is what it ain't. Get their eye on the doughnut, not the hole," George sings in "Advertising.") George then falls asleep and is visited by three ghosts, who assure him that Glidden will be introducing some exciting new advertising campaigns and sales tools in 1972. Bonus: the friendly ghosts were all portrayed by actual Glidden executives.

Show: *The Bathrooms Are Coming!* (1969)
Company: American Standard
Details: The show begins with a group of women asking the Greek goddess Femma, "the epitome of all women's attitudes and desires" (and not a real member of the Greek pantheon), for a "bathroom revolution." Who can deliver a revolution for the bathroom, which the show says is a woman's "private place, a very special kind of place"? American Standard, of course. One scene features a sleazy plumber lamenting how the company's new products are so good it's putting him out of business. In another, a woman sings about how dangerous her old tub was. ("It's dangerous and certainly a hazard. / It's positively lower than substandard.") The highlight: "Spectra 70," a song about the bathtub of the future—it has a shower with two heads and plenty of shelves "for books and kits, martinis, too, / a safety bar to hold, / for cigarettes, a storage shelf with lots of room to spare." Drinking martinis and smoking cigarettes in the shower? Hey, it was the 1960s.

Oil crisis? The oil that sardines are packed in costs more than the fish themselves.

IT CAME FROM THE TOILET

Are you sitting on the commode right now? Not to scare you or anything, but you might not be alone.

MEET MR. BITEY

Anthony Schofield of London was doing his business in 2013 when a vicious fox pushed its way in through the bathroom door and started attacking him. "I didn't even have a chance to wipe," said Schofield, 49, who chased the wild canine around his flat. It then attacked Jesse, the family cat. As Schofield and his partner, Tanny Chapple, wrestled the fox away from the cat, Chapple received a gash on her finger. "There was blood everywhere," said Schofield, who ultimately got the fox out of his house…with its teeth still attached to his arm. Once outside, the fox opened its jaws and ran away. Schofield, Chapple, and Jesse were all treated for cuts. (The fox wasn't rabid.) "I can't believe how strong it was," said Schofield. "It panicked. I don't blame it for that."

SHE'S GOT COMPANY

"You don't expect to sit down in the loo and be bitten by a rat," said Maxine Killingback, 55, of London. But that's what happened. The eight-inch-rodent's teeth latched onto the top of her leg in 2008 while she was alone in her flat. Despite having severe arthritis, Killingback sprang up from her seat, but then fell to the floor, injuring her back. The rat fell back into the toilet and started clawing to get out. Killingback quickly pulled the chain to flush the toilet, but the rat didn't go down. She grabbed a plunger and tried to pin the animal down, but it was wiggling its way out. Then Killingback saw *more* rat noses trying to get out of the toilet. She slammed the lid shut and weighted it down with a box of detergent and every heavy thing she could find, and then limped out of the bathroom and out of her flat. "My next-door neighbor came in to verify what had happened because I thought I was going mad."

Count 'em: A strawberry has about 200 seeds.

THE FLESH-EATING TOILET MONSTER

It's a good thing that the three-year-old Norwegian boy brought his mother to the bathroom to open the lid for him, otherwise the large black-and-yellow lizard might have escaped and attacked. Mother and son both screamed; the father ran in and slammed the lid shut. "It was not a nice experience," he said. It's unknown how the carnivorous lizard, called a *teju*, got into the toilet—it either crawled into the house through an open door or window, or winded its way through the sewer pipes all the way to the toilet. Considering these reptiles can stay underwater for 30 minutes, that's the most likely scenario. Also not known: How a lizard native to South America made it to Norway, where it's considered illegal contraband. A local reptile expert was called in to catch the animal and take it away from the frightened family.

NOT PLAYING

Thirty-nine-year-old Tim Fraser of Brisbane, Australia, was doing laundry one day when his toilet started bubbling. "What the hell is happening?" he thought as walked over to investigate. He looked into the commode and saw the pointy head of a little opossum wiggling out of the hole. The animal was all wet and slimy-looking after having traveled nearly 50 feet through the pipes to Fraser's bathroom. "It was like the toilet had given birth," he recalled. Instead of trying to flush it down or whack it with a stick, Fraser rescued the marsupial (with the help of a friend who's a plumber). "He was close to death and lucky that no one had used the toilet recently," said Fraser. Once free, the animal hissed at his rescuers and then scampered out of the house and into the woods.

POST-TRAUMATIC SNAKE DISORDER

In 2013 a man from Ghana named Kwabena Nkrumah was sitting on the toilet in a crowded public restroom when he felt a sharp, stinging pain in his private parts. He looked down into the toilet and saw the culprit: a "big black snake." Just as the reptile was about to strike again, Nkrumah ran out of the restroom, yelling, "Snake! Snake! Snake!" The other men in the restroom quickly followed him. Feeling faint and dizzy, Nkrumah collapsed and was rushed to a hospital. Luckily, the snake wasn't venomous, but the emotional trauma will likely stick with him for a long, long time.

PHONE A FRIEND

Hopefully you'll never need to call a suicide hotline, but if you do, you can thank an eccentric radio personality, who slept by the phone in case somebody called.

SUICIDE CITY

Pretend it's 1962 and you're feeling desperate enough that suicide sounds like a real option. That would be a bad choice, of course, but for people on the edge, alternatives were few. Suicide was actually illegal back then, so calling an emergency line could get you put in jail "for your own good." Talking to a minister might get you a scolding about throwing away God's gift of life. And calling a psychiatrist could get you a heavy drug regimen, electroshock treatment, and a stay in a mental institution (or on weekends, an answering service). Bernard Mayes had lived some dark days himself. When he got a job in San Francisco, America's #1 center for suicide, he wanted to see if he could help people near the end of their rope.

Here's what Mayes wasn't: a therapist or a trained counselor. But he wasn't just some guy with good intentions, either. Mayes was a radio correspondent from London, broadcasting short features for the BBC about cultural trends in the United States. While on an assignment, he'd discovered San Francisco's status as a magnet for suicide-prone people—more people jump from the Golden Gate Bridge than any other place in the world. Mayes was also an ordained Episcopal priest, and decided his calling was to minister to these desperate strangers, offering a nonreligious, nonjudgmental—and anonymous—phone service for free.

DON'T HANG UP

It's difficult to imagine that somebody had to invent the suicide-prevention line. The concept seems so logical that's its easy to assume it's been around forever. But at the time it sounded like a crazy idea. Just listening to people talk? How could that possibly help them? The idea seemed so crazy to anyone he mentioned it to that in late 1961 Mayes decided to go it alone.

Finding a place to set up his service wasn't easy. Landlords were leery of renting to him, afraid that the phone service would become a drop-in place for the mentally ill, even though Mayes assured them

Bathroom geometry: The diameter of the cardboard tube in a standard roll of toilet paper is 1.5".

the office's location would be kept secret from the public. He got rejected again and again as he told prospective landlords about wanting to help suicidal people...until one said, "You mean like this?" After rolling up his sleeves to reveal slash marks on his wrists, the man not only agreed to rent the space to Mayes—he rented it for half price.

A SLEEPLESS KNIGHT

Using a pseudonym, Mayes began spreading an intriguing message of hope on matchbook covers and on small cardboard signs in bars, phone booths, and buses: *"Thinking of ending it all? Call Bruce, PR1-0450, San Francisco Suicide Prevention."*

On the first night, he settled in on the office couch with the phone nearby in case somebody called, and it wasn't long before somebody did. Mayes got one call the first night. He did what he could: he listened and gently reflected back what he was hearing, which seemed to be what people needed most. There were 10 calls the first week; 30 in the first month. One early call was especially disconcerting: the caller said he had a gun and, to prove it, spun the cylinder, repeating, "I've got it ready! See? It's ready!" Mayes calmly responded, "Put the gun down and let's talk."

Soon there were six volunteers working the phones, all trained by Mayes and willing to work shifts at any hours. Within a year, the calls were up to 200 per month. Nowadays, San Francisco Suicide Prevention gets that many calls a day, routed to one of five volunteers on five lines, 24 hours a day.

Mayes left the program in 1971, feeling that founders don't make good administrators and risk killing what they started if they stay too long. Instead, he continued in broadcasting—he helped found San Francisco's public radio station KQED-FM in 1969, and was the founding chairman of NPR a year later. In the 1990s, he "came out" as both an atheist and a gay man.

NOT THE END

Because San Francisco Suicide Prevention is anonymous, there's no way to know how effective its intervention is. However, a half-century after its founding, the city's suicide rate dropped from 33 per 100,000 residents to 12.5. The community-based program was the first of its kind, but not the last. It has been copied by more than 500 hotlines in all 50 states and in many other countries.

Razors were rationed during WWII. Some women "shaved" their legs with sandpaper.

HAIRY SUPERSTITIONS

*We combed through our files to bring you these
headscratching superstitions. Some may be new
to you; others you may have haird about.*

SUPERSTITION: *Eating bread crusts will make your hair curly.*
TRUTH: The exact origin of this centuries-old superstition is unknown, but many sources say it originated in Europe in the 1700s. However, there's not a follicle of truth in it. The texture of your hair—curly or straight—is determined by genes, and what you eat can't change your genetic makeup. Historians believe the myth may come from the fact that people with curly hair were once associated with wealth and good health, which were associated with having enough food to eat…especially the staple part of every diet, bread (because only the wealthy could afford to have bread as a regular part of their diet). That may have led to the idea that eating bread crusts gave you curly hair. In the mid-twentieth century, straight hair became more fashionable and curly hair became less desirable, and the concept got turned around: many people avoided eating bread.

SUPERSTITION: *Pluck a gray hair and more will grow back.*
TRUTH: For starters, one hair follicle can only grow one hair, so the idea that more could grow back makes no sense. And if the idea is that plucking gray hairs just generally causes more gray hairs to grow—that's wrong, too. The reason we get gray hair is that as we age, the pigment cells in our hair follicles stop functioning, and the hairs growing from those pigment-depleted follicles become lighter, ultimately becoming gray (or white). The age at which this occurs, scientists say, is determined by genetics and can be affected by diet and health. So why would people think that plucking a gray hair could cause others to grow? It's most likely due to the fact that once you start going gray, you naturally start accumulating—and seeing —more gray hairs. If you pluck those hairs, it may *seem* that it's causing more gray hairs to grow…but it's not.

SUPERSTITION: *It's best to cut your hair while the moon is waxing.*
TRUTH: This suggests that if you cut your hair when the moon is

Crayola crayons soften at 105°F and melt at about 128°.

waxing (growing larger, from crescent moon to full moon), rather than when it's waning (getting smaller after the full moon), your hair will grow back thicker and stronger. According to scientists, that's lunar nonsense. For starters, the hair that you can see—and cut—is dead. The only part that's alive is the part under the skin, in your hair follicles, where hair cells reproduce, pushing the hair shafts out and causing your hair to grow. Before the shafts even reach the surface of your skin, the cells that make it up die. Whether it's a waxing moon or a waning moon, cutting that dead hair has no effect on what happens down inside the follicles.

SUPERSTITION: *Shaving makes hair grow back thicker and darker.*
TRUTH: This is one of those myths that teenage boys have always hoped is true—so they can grow a beard faster. At the same time, it's one that teenage girls hope is *not* true—so shaving their legs doesn't result in looking like a werewolf. Sorry, guys (and good news, gals): It's not true! Cutting your hair has no effect on how it grows back. The reason people think it grows back thicker after shaving is probably because hair is thicker at its base (and thinner near the ends of the hair), so when it grows out after being shaved, it simply *looks* like it's grown back thicker. But it will be just as thin as it was before. As for shaving making hair grow back darker: exposure to sunlight actually makes hair lighter, so new shorter hairs tend to look darker than the older, longer tapered hairs they replaced.

SUPERSTITION: *Women who experience heartburn during pregnancy will have a baby with a full head of hair.*
TRUTH: Experts say this superstition isn't true…but there may be a simple biological coincidence to explain it. Heartburn is common during pregnancy, primarily because the surge in hormones women experience during pregnancy has a side effect of causing the sphincter at the bottom of the esophagus (yes, you really do have a sphincter in your throat) to relax, which allows acid to leak from the stomach into the esophagus—which causes heartburn. And, scientists say, those hormones might also be related to fetal hair growth. So especially high levels of pregnancy hormones might cause both heartburn—and hairy babies—making it seem as if there's a direct connection between the two…but there's not.

LET'S MAKE AN ALKALINE BATTERY!

*Okay, we don't expect you to try to make a battery.
In fact, don't try to make a battery. But if you
did, here's how you'd do it. (But don't!)*

YOU'VE GOT POTENTIAL

A battery is basically a portable energy source. It's a tiny machine that converts the potential energy in a chemical into usable electrical energy. The chemical or chemicals used can vary, but the science and machinery of how batteries work is all more or less the same. When you put batteries in your gadgets, they work because of an *electrochemical reaction*.

The energy in the battery remains *potential* chemical energy until it's hooked up to something. At that point, when a "load" is applied (i.e., when you turn on the gadget), the battery becomes part of an active circuit and then begins churning out electricity.

ANODE TO JOY

To create an electrochemical reaction inside a battery, there must be two *electrodes*. One is positively charged, called an *anode*. The other is negatively charged, called a *cathode*. Inside the battery, the anode and cathode are surrounded by a solution called an *electrolyte*. That solution can be in liquid, paste, or powder form, although powders are most commonly used. Reason: those powdery grains mean there's more surface area of the electrolyte exposed, making it more reactive, contributing to more energy and longer battery life.

First, a chemical reaction causes an excess of electrons to build up in the anode. When the battery is connected to an electronic device like a flashlight and the device is turned on, the electrons flow from the anode, through the device, to the cathode. This reaction keeps happening until the electrolytic solution and/or the electrons in the anode are used up—and that's a dead battery.

Those active battery elements can be made up of almost any two metals, provided there is the possibility of a chemical reaction between them. In common household alkaline batteries (AAs, Cs,

---

Cold comfort: The average beehive needs 40–70 pounds of honey to survive the winter.

or Ds, for example), the anode is made of powdered zinc, and the cathode is made of manganese dioxide. (The electrolyte used in that case, then, is potassium hydroxide.)

CHARGED UP

Batteries are cheap and readily available in almost any store in the country, and we are *not* really suggesting you make your own—it's dangerous and more trouble than it's worth. (Nor do we know where you would purchase potassium hydroxide.) But here is a hypothetical "step-by-step" on how to construct your own battery—something battery manufacturers do with sophisticated machines and all kinds of safety equipment to prevent electric shock and chemical burns.

What you'll need:
• A hollow steel drum the size of the battery you're trying to duplicate. An AA battery, for example, would require a steel drum about two inches long.
• Powdered zinc, to serve as the positively charged electrode, or anode
• Powdered manganese dioxide, the negatively charged electrode, or cathode
• An electrolytic solution of liquid potassium hydroxide
• Coal dust
• A brass "collector pin"
• Plastic-cover seal cap
• Two external lead end caps, one positive (+) and one negative (–)
• A porous synthetic plate separator (a special paper)

MAKE IT SPARK
1. Soak the porous synthetic plate separator paper in the liquid potassium hydroxide. Set aside.

2. Take the hollow steel drum, which serves as the battery's casing, houses all the working parts, and assists the performance of the cathode.

3. Mix the powdered manganese dioxide with the coal dust.

4. Melt the manganese-coal solution and let it adhere to the inner wall of the steel drum. The cathode is now complete.

5. On top of the cathode-lined casing, fit in the electrolyte-treated paper.

6. Fill the remaining space inside of the battery (and within the porous plate separator paper) with zinc powder and more of the potassium hydroxide.

7. Insert the brass pin in the middle of the battery, from the bottom. This collector pin collects the negative charge.

8. The brass pin is in touch with the lead end cap, but just inside of that, place the plastic cover. That separates the steel drum from the caps, which have different charges. Seal the end with its lead cap: (+) on the top, (–) on the bottom.

9. Insert the battery in your electronic device.

10. Go to a hospital to get treated for chemical burns and mild electrical shock.

11. Buy some batteries for $2.99.

*　　　*　　　*

AMERICA'S FAST FOOD TEST KITCHEN

After companies create new products and before they come to you, they're usually "test marketed" in a city, state, or region. This is done to test whether consumer interest is strong enough to justify a nationwide roll-out. If not, the product can be improved…or killed. Fast food companies often test market their products in Columbus, Ohio. Wendy's corporate headquarters are located there, as are the head offices of White Castle, Bob Evans, Steak Escape, and more than a dozen other chains. Panera Bread and McDonald's aren't based in Columbus, but they almost always test new products there. Why Columbus? Because demographically speaking, it's astonishingly average, making it an ideal cross-section of America. Even the median income level there is identical to the national median. Bonus: the 57,000-student Ohio State University is located in Columbus and companies are eager to make lifelong customers out of these highly impressionable—and influential—young consumers.

The Scopes evolution trial was deliberately staged to help generate publicity for Dayton, TN.

"STICK AROUND."

One of the things we love about action movies is listening for the cheesy one-liner that the good guy delivers just as he kills the bad guy.

"Looks like you won't be attending that hat convention in July."

—Bruce Willis,
Hudson Hawk, while
decapitating the bad guy

"He's in the car."

—Kevin Costner,
The Untouchtables, after
throwing the bad guy
off a roof onto a car

"You're fired."

—Arnold Schwarzenegger,
True Lies, launching a
missile through a building
with the bad guy attached

"I think he got the point."

—Sean Connery,
Thunderball, impaling a
bad guy with a spear gun

"How do you like your ribs?"

—Carl Weathers,
Action Jackson, burning the
bad guy with a flamethrower

"Stick around."

—Arnold Schwarzenegger,
Predator, after pinning a bad
guy to a wall with a knife
through the chest

"Consider that a divorce."

—Arnold Schwarzenegger,
Total Recall, after shooting
his wife when he finds
out she's an evil spy

"He always did have an
inflated opinion of himself."

—Roger Moore,
Live and Let Die, after
making the bad guy's body
expand and then explode

"You need a bath."

—Charles Bronson,
Death Wish V,
pushing the bad guy
into a vat of molten plastic

"What a pain in the neck."

—Arnold Schwarzenegger,
The Running Man,
breaking a bad guy's neck

"Looks like they'll be import-
ing oil this year."

—Jason Gedrick,
Iron Eagle, after blowing
up an enemy's oil refinery

"It's just about time, anyway."

—Chuck Norris,
The Hitman, just
before the bad guy gets
blown up by a time bomb

Three actors from the movie *Predator* (1987) have run for governor. (Two were elected.)

POISONOUS BIRDS

We've written about oddly toxic creatures before (such as the platypus and the Komodo dragon). Here are few more—in the bird family.

THE STING

In 1989 American ornithologist Jack Dumbacher was catching birds of paradise in New Guinea when he accidentally caught several colorful little songbirds in his net. As he freed one of them, the bird pecked and scratched one of his fingers. He instinctively stuck the finger in his mouth…and his lips and tongue started to "tingle and burn." Dumbacher asked local villagers about the birds, and they told him it was a "rubbish bird" and "wasn't even good for eating." Fascinated, Dumbacher began a series of experiments with the birds, called hooded pitohuis. His study culminated with a finding in 1992 that shocked the biology world: some birds have developed a type of chemical defense, meaning their bodies produce a chemical that is a deterrent to predators. This chemical defense is well known in animals such as poison dart frogs, skunks, and many types of insects, but this was the first time it was ever found to be used by birds. And since then, a couple of other toxic birds have been discovered. Here are a few.

Toxic Bird: Hooded pitohui

Details: Pronounced PIT-a-HOO-ee, this is the bird that gave Dumbacher the stinging tongue and lips. There are actually six species of these birds, all native to New Guinea, and Dumbacher went on to discover that five of them have toxins in their bodies and their feathers. The toxin is a type of batrachotoxin, and it's extremely potent: a couple of BB-sized drops of pure batrachotoxin is enough to kill an adult human. (Smaller amounts can lead to paralysis.) Twelve years after his discovery, Dumbacher figured out how the birds produce that toxin: they don't. They acquire it by eating a type of beetle that produces the poison as part of its own defense. Scientists believe the pitohuis developed an immunity to the deadly beetle juice, and the ability to store it in their bodies and feathers. (Dumbacher later discovered another poisonous New Guinea bird, the blue-capped ifrit, that also gets its toxicity by eating poisonous beetles.)

Toxic Bird: Common quail

Details: This is a quail species found in Europe, North Africa, and western Asia. Consumption of this bird has long been known to cause fatal illness—but scientists still don't know what causes it. Making it more difficult to figure out: they're not *always* danger-ous to eat. Some populations of common quail are poisonous only during and directly after their southward migration, while other groups are poisonous only during and directly after their northward migration. Which makes it all pretty complicated...but people continue to eat them anyway! The quail-related sickness has been known for millennia—the ancient Greeks and Romans wrote about it, and it's even mentioned in the Bible. It's called *coturnism*, after the common quail's scientific name, *Coturnix coturnix*. Symptoms include difficulty breathing, impaired speech, nausea, weakness and pain in the legs, partial paralysis—and sometimes death. Some scientists believe the birds' toxicity is caused by consumption of a toxic plant, possibly the seeds of the hemlock plant, somewhere along their migration routes, but this is uncertain.

Toxic Bird: Spur-winged goose

Details: Spur-winged geese are found all over sub-Saharan Africa. They're huge, weighing in at more than 15 pounds, with a wing-span of more than six feet. And they're poisonous to eat. Like the pitohui, the spur-winged goose goes out of its way to eat a toxic beetle—the blister beetle, so named because it produces a powerful poison called cantharidin, that can cause severe chemical burns. Also like the pitohui, these geese have developed an immunity to the substance, along with the ability to retain it in their body tissue. Just how dangerous they are to eat is unknown, but there have been reports of sickness (and at least one death), so it's probably best to keep them off your menu.

*   *   *

"I saw a couple making out at Legoland. That's really creepy. It's a place for kids. So I went up to them and said, 'C'mon, you two. This is Legoland. Build a room.'"

—**Adam Heath Avitable**

Get reel: You are ten times more likely to be injured while fishing than at an amusement park.

"HOLY OLEO, BATMAN!"

The campy 1960s Batman TV series generated 120 episodes...and 359 separate utterances of Robin's "Holy [blank], Batman!" catchphrase. (That's three per episode.) Here are a few choice examples.

"Holy taxidermy, Batman!"

"Holy bank balance, Batman!"

"Holy semantics, Batman!"

"Holy wedding cake, Batman!"

"Holy stewpot, Batman!"

"Holy rats in a trap, Batman!"

"Holy squirrel cage, Batman!"

"Holy chicken coop, Batman!"

"Holy travel agent, Batman!"

"Holy contributing to the delinquency of minors, Batman!"

"Holy Long John Silver, Batman!"

"Holy Bluebeard, Batman!"

"Holy Venezuela, Batman!"

"Holy hole in a doughnut, Batman!"

"Holy oleo, Batman!"

"Holy haberdashery, Batman!"

"Holy remote-control robot, Batman!"

"Holy sardine, Batman!"

"Holy red snapper, Batman!"

"Holy costume party, Batman!"

"Holy floor covering, Batman!"

"Holy waste of energy, Batman!"

"Holy slipped disc, Batman!"

"Holy understatements, Batman!"

"Holy jelly molds, Batman!"

"Holy known unknown flying objects, Batman!"

"Holy bunions, Batman!"

"Holy astringent plumlike fruit, Batman!"

"Holy mashed potatoes, Batman!"

"Holy coffin nails, Batman!"

"Holy hors d'oeuvre, Batman!"

"Holy Benedict Arnold, Batman!"

"Holy potluck, Batman!"

...FROM CNN: THE "CAN" NEWS NETWORK

Sit right down and get all your bathroom news right here, right now!

Dateline: Wales—In 2013 an inebriated woman from Cardiff somehow got herself wedged between a toilet and a wall in a public restroom and had to be rescued by firefighters. After attempts to free her failed, the rescuers had to dismantle the toilet. According to firefighter Mick Flanagan, "It was a bit comic at the time because she was a bit tipsy and laughing."

• **Dateline: Hawaii**—To the surprise of many fans, Oprah Winfrey, one of the world's wealthiest and most powerful women, was photographed fixing one of the toilets at her Maui mansion. The pic was posted to Instagram by Winfrey's "bff" Gayle King, along with the caption: "Stars are just like us. @Oprah at her other job, plumber." Subsequent news reports (and there were many) did not reveal what was wrong with the toilet or whether the fix was successful.

• **Dateline: Belgium**—After a 2014 concert in Brussels, Steve Lukather, a founding member of the rock band Toto ("Rosanna," "Africa," and "Hold the Line") told reporters what he thought of Toto's name: "I don't like it." Some sources say the band, which formed in 1977, was named for the dog in *The Wizard of Oz*; others say it's derived from a Latin phrase that means "all-encompassing." Toto also happens to be the name of a popular toilet manufacturer, and for years, the band has been the butt of toilet-related jokes from friends and music critics...which made Lukather's next confession that much more surprising. "I am the proud owner of a Toto toilet," he said, calling it "the best toilet you can get!" But that hasn't changed his opinion of his band's name, which he calls "sh*tty."

• **Dateline: Oregon**—A new fad among coffee aficionados—drinking coffee from beans that were passed by exotic animals—has been taken to a whole new level in Portland, Oregon. In 2013 this ad appeared on Craigslist:

> I'm a home roaster and I'm noticing in the newspapers that animal poop coffee is really popular and expensive. I've been growing yellow

---

There are more people with the surname Chang in China than there are people in Germany.

bourbon arabica in my greenhouse for a couple of years and it's finally starting to produce quality cherry. I will personally ingest this cherry and mimic the "kopi luwak" process. I will be able to harvest only a couple of pounds of this special coffee so act now before it's too late. I'm 47, healthy, and will guarantee you'll like my kopi luwak style coffees. Fecal specimens available for inspection upon request.

No thanks.

• **Dateline: France**—On January 16, 2014, a truck driver parked in front of the Bourbon Palace in Paris, where France's lower parliament meets, and proceeded to unload several tons of manure on the street. A large sign on the truck read "Out with Hollande and the entire political class. Long live the Sixth Republic." (French president François Hollande was mired in a scandal at the time; the current French constitutional era, which began in 1958 under President Charles de Gaulle, is the Fifth Republic.) The manure dumper turned out to be a disgruntled horse breeder, upset over a proposed tax increase on horse breeders.

• **Dateline: Mississippi**—In February 2012, the Jones County Junior College campus was evacuated after a student found a bomb threat scribbled on a piece of toilet paper in a men's room. After a search by law-enforcement agencies turned up no bombs, investigators were able to match the handwriting to a 19-year-old student named Harold Hadley Jr. He was arrested at his home in Seminary, Mississippi. His aunt told reporters that her nephew is a good student, and this was just a big misunderstanding:

> He was in the restroom doodling on some toilet paper, and I am going to just let modesty go and tell you we are from the country, and so he calls passing gas "bombs." So, he was doodling on the toilet paper and put "I passed a bomb in the library."

• **Dateline: New Zealand**—In 2014 a reporter named Patrick Gower was covering New Zealand prime minister John Key's state of the nation speech. During a break, Gower had to pee but forgot to turn off his wireless lapel microphone…and he was live-streaming the speech on the Internet. Result: dozens of people who were logged in got to hear the unmistakable sound of Gower tinkling. He said afterward: "I've been involved in a lot of leaks in my time, but this is the first time it actually involved me taking one." He then added, "It could have been a lot worse."

OL' JAYBEARD'S BRAINTEASERS

Time to test your mental fortitude with these tricky conundrums. (Answers are on page 540.)

1. A bacterium is placed in a petri dish at noon. At 12:01 it divides into two bacteria. A minute later those two become four, and they keep doubling every subsequent minute. If the petri dish is half full at 12:24, at what time will it be full?

2. The frustrated man couldn't take it anymore. So in the middle of the night, he took his gun outside, fired one shot, and never saw another sunrise. But he showed up alive and ready to work the next day. How is this possible?

3. A king said to his three most loyal knights, "My rule will end in one month. To each of you I give one seed. Whoever grows the prettiest flowers will inherit my throne." A month later two of the knights showed up with beautiful blooming plants… but the third knight had only a pot of dirt. The king said to the third knight, "You, sir, will inherit my throne." How could that knight have won?

4. How is it possible to cut a round cake into eight equal pieces using only three cuts?

5. In what room is 99 more than 100?

6. A swindler approached a man at a bar and said, "With my extensive knowledge of music, I'll bet you $100 that I can sing an actual song lyric that includes any name you give me."

"Okay," said the man confidently, "Dame Magrathia Hamburglar-Smith the Third."

A minute later the swindler had won $100. How?

7. Why is this the most dangerous list of words in this book?

balance, begun, crossword, grimace, elbow, Shakespeare

8. Ol' Jaybeard used to work at a butcher shop. At the time, he stood 5'6" tall, had a 31-inch waist, and wore size 8 shoes. What did he weigh?

A group of gerbils is called a *horde*; a group of wombats is called a *wisdom*.

GREEN LEMON:
THE FISKER KARMA

*Think this story is going to be about fruit? The investors who financed the
Fisker Karma probably wish it had been that kind of lemon. Their
experience was bitter…but citrus had nothing to do with it.*

AHEAD OF THE CURB

In August 2007, a Danish car designer named Henrik
Fisker founded a company called Fisker Automotive and
set out to design and build one of the world's first plug-in hybrid
cars. Called the Karma, the car would be powered by two electric
motors fed by a bank of onboard batteries. If the car was driven
beyond the range of the electric batteries, a gasoline-powered
engine would spring to life, generating electricity to power the car
and recharge the batteries. The batteries could also be recharged
in as little as six hours by plugging the car into a conventional wall
outlet.

On paper, the yet-to-be-built Karma was more advanced than
any car on the market in 2007. The Chevy Volt, which would use
similar technology, was still four years off. And though the Toyota
Prius, the first mass-produced hybrid car, had been around since
1997, it used a different technology. It wasn't a *plug-in* hybrid, so
you couldn't recharge the batteries by plugging the car into a wall
outlet. And the Prius could drive for only seven miles on its electric
batteries before they were exhausted and the gasoline engine had to
take over.

OUT OF GAS

The Karma's batteries, by comparison, promised a range of up to
50 miles. If you were one of the 78 percent of American commut-
ers who drove fewer than 40 miles to work and back, that meant
you could make your daily commute without using any gasoline at
all and without generating any air pollution. Then when you got
home, you could plug your car in overnight and do it again the next
day. As long as you drove fewer than 40 miles a day, there was no
limit to how long you could go without using any gas.

Old-timey fact: According to experts, the best shaving-brush material is badger hair.

INSIDE JOB

What made Fisker Automotive different from other "green car" start-up companies that promised the moon was that Henrik Fisker had actually designed cars before. Not just any cars, either: he'd spent more than a decade at BMW, and in the late 1990s headed the team that designed the Z8, the beautiful roadster driven by Pierce Brosnan in the 1999 James Bond film *The World Is Not Enough*. In 2001 Fisker moved to Aston Martin, where he designed the stunning DB9 touring car and the V8 Vantage.

Fisker had gotten the idea for his plug-in hybrid in 2003, when he saw Leonardo DiCaprio pull up to the Academy Awards in a Toyota Prius. A lot of people like the unconventional style of a Prius, but it's easy to understand why a designer of BMWs and Aston Martins would not. "I thought, 'There's got to be a market for an environmentally friendly car that goes beyond the Prius.' That was my first inspiration," Fisker told the BBC in 2012. He resolved to give the world a high-performance hybrid car every bit as beautiful as the supercars he'd designed in the past. He called his concept "responsible luxury" and "sustainable design without compromise."

FULLY LOADED

As Fisker fleshed out the details of the Karma, he filled it with one environmentally friendly feature after another.

• If you wanted a leather interior, Fisker promised to buy the hides from a sustainable slaughterhouse (whatever that is) and to use as much of each individual hide as possible, including parts with scratches and other imperfections, to minimize the number of animals butchered for your driving pleasure. Vegans and animal lovers who wanted a cruelty-free interior could order "100 percent recycled post-industry virgin polyester ultrasuede" instead of leather.

• To save trees, the Karma's interior was trimmed with the buyer's choice of three types of wood taken from trees that were already dead: "Fallen Wood," mahogany harvested from old-growth trees knocked down in storms; "Rescued Wood," walnut salvaged from a 2007 California wildfire; and "Sunken Wood," white oak retrieved from century-old logs fished from the bottom of Lake Michigan.

• The Karma's roof incorporated a solar panel that recharged the car's batteries, in the process giving owners "up to 200 miles per year of completely emission- and cost-free driving."

More than 700 different species of dinosaurs have been identified and named.

- The exterior was painted with water-based paint that got its sparkle from flakes of recycled glass added to the paint.

Packed with all of these green features and more, plus boasting uncompromising performance and a top speed of more than 125 mph, the Karma was not going to be cheap—Fisker calculated that it would top out at more than $100,000. But he also figured that there would be plenty of Leonardo DiCaprios out there willing to pay handsomely for a guilt-free supercar.

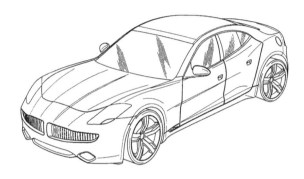

PICTURE PERFECT

The final design that Fisker came up with was every bit as breathtaking as the cars he'd designed for BMW and Aston Martin. One auto industry analyst called it "perhaps the most beautiful car ever made." Prospective investors who got a look at it, and at Fisker's impeccable résumé, eagerly ponied up the cash he needed to get his company off the ground. Between November 2007 and March 2009, he raised more than $94 million from wealthy individuals (including Leonardo DiCaprio) and Silicon Valley venture capitalists, plus component suppliers who hoped to make a bundle selling parts to Fisker Automotive once it was up and running.

The endorsement of so many sophisticated investors impressed the U.S. Department of Energy, which had a program to fund greentechnology auto companies like Fisker. In 2009 the DOE approved a $528-million line of credit for Fisker Automotive. The line of credit came with plenty of strings attached—only $169 million of the money would be used to bring the Karma to market. The rest, which would be released only if strict production figures and sales targets were met, would be used to fund the creation of a second, cheaper plug-in hybrid, to be called the Atlantic, that more people could afford. The Atlantic would also have to be manufactured in the United States, creating American jobs in the process. (The Karma, at least at first, would be built in Finland.)

SKIN DEEP

Just as the early investors had stimulated the Department of Energy to act, the DOE's endorsement prompted a surge of new investors who wanted in on the ground floor. By June of 2011 they would pump another $500 million into Fisker.

But as these investors would soon discover, Henrik Fisker was better at designing cars than he was at building and running car companies. He was a designer, after all: his area of expertise was making cars look good. Engineers would have to make the Karma run as beautifully as it looked, but rather than hire them in-house, Fisker subcontracted the engineering work to outside companies that were hired to make individual components.

No one at Fisker Automotive paid enough attention to making sure that components made by different contractors worked well together when assembled in the car. Working out the bugs caused huge delays and sent costs soaring, a problem the company made worse by stockpiling millions of dollars' worth of parts before the glitches had been fixed. Then, when it turned out that many of the problems could only be solved by re-engineering and remanufacturing the parts, the stockpiled parts became obsolete and worthless. It's estimated that the company spent as much as $100 million on parts it couldn't use, forcing it to cough up another $100 million to replace them.

RUNNING LATE

Another problem: the schedule Henrik Fisker negotiated with the Department of Energy to keep the line of credit open was wildly unrealistic. He had agreed to deliver both the Karma and the Atlantic in less than two years, something that even established auto companies wouldn't have been able to pull off. (It took GM nearly four years to bring the Chevrolet Volt to market.) Fisker either didn't realize the schedule was unrealistic, or he assumed that the Department of Energy would be flexible. It wasn't. When Fisker

---

In the Peanuts comic strip, Peppermint Patty's real name is Patricia Reichardt.

Automotive fell hopelessly behind schedule, the DOE froze the line of credit after Fisker had drawn "only" $196 million of the $528 million available.

By now Fisker Automotive had burned through much of the cash it had raised from investors and was starting to fall behind on payments to its suppliers. The pressure to have *something* to show was intense, so in July 2011 the first handful of defective Karmas began straggling off the assembly line. Leonardo DiCaprio got one of the first Karmas; no word on how well his ran. Several months later *Consumer Reports* magazine bought a Karma to road test, but before it could be put through its paces, the car died and had to be towed back to the dealership. "We buy about 80 cars a year, and this is the first time in memory that we have had a car that is undrivable before it has finished our check-in process," the magazine wrote on its blog in March 2012.

OUT OF JUICE
The problem with the *Consumer Reports* car was traced back to defective batteries manufactured by a company called A123 Systems. The same batteries in other Karmas had caused the cars to catch on fire, and A123 Systems spent so much money recalling and replacing the batteries that it went bankrupt in October 2012. Since it was the only supplier of batteries for the Karma, production of the car screeched to a halt. It never started again.

How did Fisker Automotive respond to these and other troubles? By painting a rosy picture and continuing to raise money. By the end of 2012 it had pulled in another $515 million from investors, bringing the total raised to $1.15 billion, not including the line of credit from the DOE. And it burned through the cash almost as quickly as it came in. By April 2013, it had just $20 million in the bank and Henrik Fisker was out—he resigned following "disagreements" with management.

Fisker Automotive stumbled on for another seven months, then declared bankruptcy in November 2013, after spending nearly $1.4 billion and having fewer than 2,500 finished cars to show for it—a cost of more than $500,000 per car. Today Karmas sell on eBay for as little as $50,000, though there are few takers. (If you decide to buy one, you might ask the seller to throw in a tow truck.)

A gun with a silencer attached sounds about as loud as a car door being slammed.

THE CASE OF THE CURSED CASH

Most of us have dreamed of finding a big pile of cash. But as this man's story illustrates, be careful what you wish for.

IN THE BAG

Wayne Sabaj, 49, was a chronically unemployed carpenter who was living with his father in the town of Johnsburg, Illinois. One evening in August 2011, he was barbecuing a pork shoulder in his backyard when he decided to get some broccoli from his garden to go with it. As he kneeled down over his plants, he saw a black nylon bag—the kind you stuff a sleeping bag into—lying on the ground, next to his bell peppers.

The bag was stuffed, all right, but not with a sleeping bag. It was full of cash, nearly all of it $20 bills. Some bills were older and fastened together with paper clips or wrapped in paper; others were newer, wrapped in bundles of $1,000 with the paper bands still on them, as if they'd just come from the bank. Some of the money had been carefully wrapped in plastic.

JAILBAIT

If you'd been unemployed for more than two years and you stumbled across a big bag of money in your own backyard, what would you do? Probably not what Sabaj did. He ran inside the house and told his father, "Hey, Dad, we got more problems!" He figured that the money had to have been dumped there by criminals—most likely *violent* criminals—and that they would soon be back to get it. He didn't want anything to do with what he was sure was ill-gotten gains. "With my luck, it came from a bank robbery, and I'd be charged with the bank robbery," he explained to a local TV news reporter.

After talking it over with his father, Sabaj decided to report the find to the police. When they arrived at his house, he showed them where and how he'd found the money in his garden. Amazingly, as the police investigated, they found a *second* bag stuffed with $20 bills nearby. Together, the two bags contained about $150,000, more money than Sabaj or his father had ever seen in their lives.

The town of Carter Lake, Iowa, is legally within the city limits of Omaha, Nebraska.

GOING PUBLIC

The police left their calling card next to where the money had been dumped, along with a note instructing the owner of the cash to call the number on the card. They explained to Sabaj that the law required news of the find to be made public, so that whoever owned the money would have a chance to claim it. If a year passed and no one claimed the money, Sabaj could claim it for himself.

Eleven months passed, and then, just two days before Sabaj would have gotten the money, two different parties filed claims. One was a liquor store in nearby Naperville. Lawyers for the store claimed that masked gunmen had robbed the store of nearly $150,000 in small bills in 2010.

The other claimant was Diane Howe, the daughter of Sabaj's 87-year-old neighbor, Dolores Johnson. Howe claimed that she often helped her mother count out her savings and sort it into bundles, but that one day the money disappeared, disposed of in some way by her mother. Dolores Johnson had dementia and was unable to tell Howe what she'd done with the money, other than that she'd "gotten it outside the house" and then hid it somewhere because it was "cursed." It wasn't until Howe heard about Sabaj finding a fortune in his backyard that she realized what her mother must have done with her money.

YOU CAN HAVE IT

Attorneys for the liquor store were unable to give a good description of the money, but Diane Howe was, because she'd bundled so much of it herself. She convinced the judge that the money really did belong to her mother, who had since died, and the judge awarded Howe the money.

Howe did, however, agree to pay Sabaj a finder's fee, but just ten days before he would have collected the money, he died suddenly at the age of 51 from complications related to diabetes. Sabaj's father had a heart attack after learning of his son's death…but survived.

So with two people dead (and one almost killed by a heart attack), is it possible the money really was cursed? Maybe, maybe not, but Sabaj's lawyer, Robert Burke, who would have been paid with proceeds from the finder's fee, wasn't taking any chances. "I'm thinking about waiving my fee," he told the *Chicago Sun-Times*. "I don't think I want the money."

Green sea turtles have green fat.

PLANET PIZZA

According to Mrs. Uncle John, pizza—bread, tomatoes, and cheese—is the perfect food. But in many countries, that's not how it's made.

SOUTH KOREA: Among the most popular varieties of pizza in Korea are those featuring potatoes. The dough, made with a potato-based crust, is topped with sweet-potato mousse and sour cream (instead of tomato sauce), bacon, and potato wedges.

ICELAND: Italian-style pizza is popular there, but not topped with mozzarella cheese. Icelanders prefer cream cheese and blue cheese.

BRAZIL: A thick layer of pizza sauce is unusual. Instead, a very thin layer is used and, more often, none at all. Popular toppings include sliced tomatoes, peas, and bananas.

FINLAND: There are more than 200 outlets of the Kotipizza chain in Finland. Its most popular topping is smoked reindeer, which is called the Pizza Berlusconi after Italian prime minister Silvio Berlusconi, who, in 2005, visited Finland and remarked that he had to "endure" Finnish food such as marinated reindeer.

TURKEY: The closest thing to pizza in Turkey is a flatbread dish called *lahmacun*—a round, thin piece of baked dough topped with minced lamb, parsley, and lemon juice.

SOUTH AFRICA: It looks like the usual pizza, except for the tomato sauce—it's blisteringly spicy. The most popular pizza toppings in South Africa: bananas and minced pork.

INDIA: The country's residents are predominantly Hindu, and don't eat meat. The Western-style pizza is popular, but pepperoni and sausage as toppings are not. Indian pizza eaters prefer baby corn, pickled ginger, and tofu.

NORWAY: What country's citizens eat the most pizza, per capita? Norway. Except that it's frozen pizza. More than 24 million frozen pizzas are sold to Norway's five million residents each year. The most popular brand is Grandiosa, introduced in 1980. Grandiosa is so beloved that a commercial jingle for the frozen pizza has topped the Norwegian pop chart...twice.

Nearly 20 tons of waste are generated to produce a single gold wedding ring.

WAR WIZARDRY

To help win World War II, the Allies used every skill they could come up with—including illusion, trickery…and magic.

WIZARD SCHOOL
In 1940 Britain's Ministry of Home Security created a military unit dedicated to "civil camouflage." Their job would be to provide safety through "seriously ridiculous deception." The unit of *camoufleurs*—soldiers tasked with finding ways to hide equipment and troop movements from the enemy—would be trained at the Camouflage Development and Training Centre at Farnham Castle, Surrey. The camouflage office's odd cast of characters included artists, movie set designers, cartoonists, and a third-generation stage magician named Jasper Maskelyne. (Unrelated fact: Maskelyne's grandfather invented the pay toilet.)

In 1941 the city of Alexandria, Egypt, was home to a million people. Controlling its harbor allowed Allied forces to replenish supplies and troops for the desert war raging in North Africa. That made it a prime target for German Luftwaffe bombing raids. Major Geoffrey Barkas—a former filmmaker appointed head of Middle Eastern Camouflage—called on Jasper Maskelyne and the team of camoufleurs known as the "Magic Gang." Their mission: conceal the entire port, including the battleships and merchant vessels docked in it. "We can't cover it up. We can't disguise it. And we can't hide it," Maskelyne reportedly said. "There's only one solution left to us, isn't there? Move it."

Magician's Dummy
Maskelyne and his team proceeded to construct a "dummy" port complete with mock battleships and submarines on an inland lake about three miles away from the real harbor. They installed real antiaircraft guns and searchlights, and rigged up remote-control explosives. The team consulted nighttime aerial photos of the actual city, and then planted lights in the sand and mud to make the fake site look as much like Alexandria as possible. Meanwhile, the real city of Alexandria went black.

Reports say that German bombers pounded the fake Alexandria

Henry VI was crowned king of England before the age of one.

(rather than the real one) for eight nights in a row. Sources agree that the ruse protected the real city from possible destruction. They disagree on one crucial factor: Maskelyne's role in the deception.

Official records offer little information about the magician's wartime exploits, but his ghostwritten memoir, *Magic: Top Secret*, tells tale after tale of battlefield prestidigitation led and organized by Maskelyne. A writer named Richard Stokes has devoted an entire website to debunking the memoir. According to Stokes, the book was Maskelyne's most effective piece of camouflage..."ingeniously compact, built from recycled tree carcass, and weighed only thirteen ounces. And it has fooled people for sixty years."

MAKING MINCEMEAT OF HITLER

Prior to the 1943 invasion of Sicily, a dead man became a key player in another very effective WWII deception. On April 30, a corpse washed up on the coast of southwestern Spain. The body was dressed in the uniform of Britain's Royal Marines. An ID found on the body identified the man as Major William Martin. Chained to the dead major's wrist: a black attaché case.

The Nazis couldn't wait to get their hands on that case, and before long a helpful Spanish official had given one of Hitler's agents a look at the documents inside. They identified the dead officer as an expert in amphibious landings. His mission, seemingly thwarted, was to deliver top-secret information about Allied plans to attack German-held Greece and Sardinia. The coded letter Martin carried was addressed to Admiral Andrew Cunningham, commander of the Mediterranean fleet. It asked the commander to return Major Martin to his ship and have him "bring some sardines with him"—a rather obvious allusion to Sardinia.

Hitler took the bait, transferring troops to Greece and clearing the way for Allied forces to attack the real target. On July 10, 1943, the project code-named "Mincemeat" ended with an invasion by 160,000 Allied troops...into Sicily, not Sardinia. As for the corpse? "Major Martin" wasn't a Royal Marine. He was a vagrant whose body had been spirited out of a London morgue for use in what became one of the most successful military deceptions ever staged. Note: Mincemeat's planners included Charles Fraser-Smith, the real-life model for Q in Ian Fleming's James Bond novels, and without him, the operation couldn't have succeeded. Fraser-Smith

Greece and Bulgaria fought each other in the War of the Stray Dog (1925). It lasted a week.

created the container that kept the vagrant's body "fresh" for days, until it could be dumped in the water off the coast of Spain.

TANKS FOR NOTHING

On June 6, 1944, a pair of French bicyclists watched in awe as four American soldiers picked up a 40-ton Sherman tank and turned it around. "Americans are very strong," one of the soldiers quipped. Had the U.S. Army bred a team of superhuman Captain Americas? No, they had created a top-secret unit—the 23rd Headquarters Special Troops—and manned it with a thousand artists, designers, and audio technicians. Their job was to create a deceptively realistic army division consisting of inflatable tanks, cannons, jeeps, trucks, and airplanes.

In just a few hours, the 23rd could assemble airfields filled with rubber planes, motor pools stocked with rubber jeeps, and battle formations with rows and rows of rubber tanks. To complete the illusion, 500-pound loudspeakers mounted on jeeps broadcast a barrage of combat sound effects. The 23rd's fake-outs had a serious purpose: to divert German forces from the "real" action and give Allied troops the advantage.

Many members of the 23rd were art students, recruited from schools in New York and Philadelphia, including fashion designer Bill Blass, painter Ellsworth Kelly, and photographer Art Kane. Others were showmen, such as Captain Fred Fox, a former member of Princeton University's Triangle Club musical-comedy troupe. Fox knew that rubber tanks wouldn't be enough to convince the enemy. The 23rd, he insisted, must consider itself "a traveling road show" and be ready to perform "at a moment's notice."

> The presentations must be done with the greatest accuracy and attention to detail. They will include the proper scenery, props, costumes, principals, extras, dialogue, and sound effects. We must remember that we are playing to a very critical and attentive radio, ground, and aerial audience. They must all be convinced.

And it worked. According to recent reports, the "Ghost Army," as it was known, staged more than 20 operations over the course of the war. Their deceptions are believed to have saved between 15,000 and 30,000 American lives, and they did it all without their fellow soldiers ever knowing of their existence. The Ghost Army remained top secret until 1985—forty years after World War II ended.

There are about 50 billion galaxies in the cosmos.

PARLIA-MENTAL

The U.S. Congress may have had a record-low nine percent approval rating in 2013…but at least they don't try to punch each other (yet).

T AKEDOWN IN TURKEY

In late 2013, several key members of prime minister Recep Erdogan's ruling party were arrested on charges of corruption. Erdogan's supporters in Turkey's National Assembly responded to the arrests by passing a controversial bill that gave Erdogan increased powers over the nation's judiciary branch. That set off a raucous debate on the floor of parliament in February 2014, which quickly turned into a violent scuffle. One MP who threw a punch broke a finger; another took a punch in the face and stumbled away bloodied, with a broken nose. (The bill passed anyway.)

SMACKDOWN IN SOUTH KOREA

In 1987 a student-led democracy movement resulted in South Korea's first truly free elections. One of the students' biggest allies was a lawyer named Roh Moo-hyun. Although Roh was disbarred as political retribution, he was redeemed when he was elected president as a candidate for the Millennium Democratic Party in 2002.

Roh attempted to usher in a sweeping set of reforms, but he met with stiff resistance from the Grand National Party (GNP), the nation's largest opposition group. Political tension reached a boiling point in 2004 when many of Roh's supporters left the MDP to create the Uri Party and run in upcoming parliamentary elections. Roh quickly announced his support for the group. Bad move. South Korea's constitution requires presidents to remain neutral in parliamentary elections. Pouncing on Roh's goof, the anti-Roh wing of the MDP joined forces with the GNP to impeach the president. Members of the Uri Party staged parliamentary sit-ins to stop the proceedings, but they were literally dragged kicking, shoving, and screaming from the podium to allow a 193–2 vote that sealed the impeachment.

CRACKDOWN IN CARACAS

When Venezuelan president Hugo Chavez died two months into his fourth term in 2013, the race to fill the power vacuum was on.

Representing Chavez's Socialist Party was his loyal deputy, Nicolás Maduro. His opponent: conservative Henrique Capriles, who had lost to Chavez in the presidential election just a few months earlier.

The emergency election that followed was particularly combative. Maduro insinuated that the unmarried Capriles was gay, and in response, Capriles called Maduro's wife ugly. After Capriles lost the election—and a recount—he publicly denounced Maduro and refused to accept the results. To silence Capriles, the Socialist-controlled national assembly passed a measure banning MPs (such as Capriles) from addressing the body if they hadn't publicly recognized Maduro's presidency. Capriles and his MP supporters protested by hanging banners calling for a coup. Not allowed to speak, they let their fists—as well as flying laptops, chairs, and tables—do the talking. The ensuing fracas injured seven congressmen (and Maduro retained power).

MELEE IN MEXICO CITY

Political analysts watched the 2006 Mexican presidential election to see if the Institutional Revolutionary Party (PRI)—which was defeated in 2000 after 71 straight years in office—could retake control from the National Action Party (PAN). But the PRI ended up a bystander in the real fight between the PAN and the upstart Party of the Democratic Revolution (DPR). Following an election (and charges of fraud) that gave the PAN victory by just 0.58 percent, the fight turned violent. DPR leader Andrés Obrador led marches in which he declared the election fraudulent, and proclaimed president-elect Felipe Calderón "a thief." Obrador and his allies made one final protest in the hours before Calderón's inauguration: they occupied the legislative chambers and hung banners declaring Calderón a traitor. Calderón's supporters were not happy, and fought with the protestors...with their fists...on live TV.

Hours after this parliamentary punch-out, Calderón was whisked into the Mexican congress to recite an oath of office that was drowned out by jeers from the chamber. The new president then exited to the national auditorium to give his first speech as president of Mexico to a crowd of supporters and foreign dignitaries, including California governor Arnold Schwarzenegger. As he got an up-close peek at the congressional clash, the former movie star was quoted as saying, "It's good action!"

Per capita, there are more burglaries in Canada than in America.

AMAZING SPIDERS, MAN

A lot of people think spiders are weird and creepy,
but we think they're fascinating. (And creepy.)

• **THE REDBACK SPIDER.** The female redback is 50 times larger than the male—an important advantage during mating, when the females eat the males. While females eating the males after mating isn't particularly unusual behavior among spiders and insects, what is unusual about the redback is that the female begins to eat the male *during* the act of mating, not after.

• **THE GOLIATH BIRD-EATING SPIDER.** It's the largest spider by weight, and the second-largest by leg span. From end to end, this spider is nearly a foot long. The name, however, is a misnomer—it *could* eat birds if it wanted to, but it doesn't. It lives in the Amazon River valley and eats insects, and occasionally frogs or mice, paralyzing its prey with neurotoxins that come out of its inch-long fangs.

• **THE DIVING BELL SPIDER.** Many spiders live, hunt, or mate on water some of the time, but the diving bell spider is the world's only totally underwater-dwelling spider. It lives in ponds and shallow lakes across Europe and northern Asia. It can't breathe underwater, though. It builds a bubble (like a diving bell) out of its own silk and fills it with air it gets from the surface, which it does by trapping tiny pockets of air in the hairs on its legs.

• **THE TWIG SPIDER.** Stand on your tippy-toes and reach for the ceiling with both hands. When the twig spider stretches out the same way, it looks remarkably like—you guessed it—a twig. Any insect that lands on the harmless-looking piece of plant life, or crawls out onto it, will end up staying for lunch.

• **THE PEACOCK SPIDER.** Like the bird they're named for, male peacock spiders are covered in "plumage"—blue, red, yellow, and white stripes on the back and head. During mating, brightly colored flaps around the male's abdomen expand like a peacock's tail. He then raises two of his black-and-white (and hairy) legs

---

It's on your shoulder! *Delusory parasitosis* is the delusion of being attacked by invisible bugs.

upward, and does a side-to-side courtship dance (while vibrating its abdomen), trying to attract a female's attention.

• **THE ANT MIMIC JUMPING SPIDER.** This spider conceals itself from predators and prey alike with its ability to constrict parts of its anatomy until it looks remarkably like a weaver ant. The female spider looks most like the ant; the male looks more like a large ant carrying a smaller one on its back. Real weaver ants have a painful sting, prompting predators to steer clear.

• **THE OGRE-FACED SPIDER.** To catch its insect prey, the ogre-face weaves a mini web—or rather, a net—between its front legs. Then it waits above where its prey might pass (high in a tree, for example). When it does, the ogre-face drops its net on the unsuspecting target.

• **THE BIRD-DROPPING SPIDER.** A lot of birds eat spiders, and they'd probably eat the bird-dropping spider…if they could find it. This spider cleverly camouflages itself to look like bird poop— milky white with little black spots. Bonus: the spider feeds on moths by releasing a pheromone similar to one put out by mating female moths. When male moths come near, the spider traps them with its legs, then feasts.

• **THE SMILING SPIDER.** What's weird about this Hawaiian native is the unusual pattern on its abdomen. It looks like a smiley face. The abdomen is yellow with two black dots (eyes) above a red crescent shape (mouth). It's also called a "happy-face spider."

• **THE ASSASSIN SPIDER.** It gets its name from the fact that it hunts and eats other spiders. It's also called a pelican spider because of one unusual un-spiderlike part of its anatomy—it has a neck. Fossilized remains of assassin spiders have been found dating back at least 40 million years.

• **THE RAVINE TRAPDOOR SPIDER.** Unique feature: it has an odd rear end, larger than the rest of its body and flat on the end. The outsized, blunt-ended junk in the trunk has a purpose. The spider can crawl into a burrow and use its abdomen to seal off the opening from predators, like a cork in a wine bottle.

Found in a Chinese tomb in 2010: The world's oldest bowl of soup—2,400 yrs. old & still liquid.

SEND IN THE CLONES

Drug traffickers have found a new way to smuggle contraband from Mexico to the United States: "cloned" commercial or government vehicles—ordinary trucks and buses painted to look just like the real thing…almost.

CHEATS OF LAREDO. In October 2012, a police officer in McMullen County, Texas, stopped a school bus that was marked "Property of the Laredo Independent School District." The driver stopped the bus, jumped out, and then took off on foot (although he was later caught). What made the police officer stop the bus in the first place? The students sitting in the bus didn't look quite right, and they weren't. They were mannequins… that had been stuffed with more than 2,700 pounds of marijuana.

DO'S AND DOTS. Eagle-eyed police officer Jorge Medina of George West, Texas, pulled over a government vehicle in 2007. The truck bore the insignia, stickers, and other markings of a Texas Department of Transportation vehicle, but Medina noticed that the license plate had a prefix ordinarily assigned to a school-district vehicle, not the DOT. The driver of the truck pulled over…and sped off, leading to a high-speed chase. The chase ended when the suspicious truck flipped over, spilling its cargo on the road: more than 1,000 pounds of marijuana.

GONE FISHING. Acting on a tip that clone trucks were operating in the small Arizona border city of Douglas, U.S. Border Patrol agents pulled over a U.S. Fish and Wildlife Service truck for a routine inspection. It wasn't a real FWS vehicle…but it was loaded with hidden compartments that held $1.6 million worth of marijuana.

DIRECT TARGET. Police pulled over a DirecTV service van in Mississippi in 2008. They were suspicious because the truck was decorated not only with DirecTV signage, but with signs from several of the satellite TV company's competitors as well. Another tip-off: the police called the "how's my driving" number on the truck, and it belonged to a phone-sex hotline. The truck was carrying approximately 785 pounds of cocaine.

Police once caught a drug smuggler in a truck marked "Border Patron."

HOW TO WIN AT BOARD GAMES

*Playing board games like Scrabble or Risk against a skilled
player can be aggravating. Here are a few devious tactics
and tips that may help you win (almost) every time.*

MONOPOLY
Tournament players often employ an aggressive strategy at the beginning of their matches. They purchase every property they land on. Then, after a little wheeling and dealing with other players to obtain all the properties of a single color, they start placing houses on their squares. (The cheaper ones first, because funds are typically low early in the game.) Opinions vary on which properties are landed on the most often, but many swear it's the orange ones. Buying as many of those as possible should be considered a priority, because the more property you own there, the more you get to collect in rent from the other players. Late in the game, it pays to stay in jail for as long as possible. That way you can collect rent on your properties while you remain safely behind bars, away from your opponents' rent-earning properties.

BATTLESHIP
When setting up your ships at the beginning of the game, it helps to place smaller vessels alongside or beneath larger ones. You should also put at least one ship on the edge of your board, since most players tend to aim for the middle. Another tip: never fire another peg within one space of a miss. This will help reduce your need to randomly guess where your opponent's ships are hiding by at least half. There's also the "checkerboard method," which involves imagining the board with alternating black-and-white squares and firing only on the black ones. Then, once you score a hit, you should fire pegs adjacently until you sink your opponent's boat.

THE GAME OF LIFE
At the beginning of the game, you should probably go to college. This will help you get a better job and earn a higher salary, although doing so might not help if you don't land on enough "Pay Day"

squares later on. Auto and home insurance can come in handy, but unless you're really unlucky, you'll be throwing away your hard-earned play money. Instead, invest in stocks. If you land on a "Lucky Day" square, you should always gamble instead of keeping the initial jackpot—the chances of winning are around 5 to 1.

SCRABBLE

You don't need a huge vocabulary to win at Scrabble, but it does help to know a lot of the obscure, two-letter words to use late in the game where there isn't a lot of space available for longer words. First, there's "za." Definition: "pizza." "Qi" is another simple but powerful word. (It means "life force.") And don't be afraid to swap out all your letters if you wind up with a tray full of lousy ones. Yes, you lose a turn, but it will likely aid you in the long run. Another key tactic: play defensively. Don't create words that will allow your opponents to capitalize on the triple-letter or triple-word squares. Oh, and there's one more word you should memorize: "oxyphenbutazone." It's an anti-inflammatory drug, and, theoretically, the highest-scoring word possible in Scrabble. It could earn as many as 1,778 points.

RISK

Since the late 1950s, the "Game of Global Domination" has brought out the power-hungry dictator in millions. If full-scale warfare isn't your forte, follow these tips the next time you play, and end the game quickly. At the game's outset, focus on taking over every territory in Australia and South America—two remote continents that are easy to defend—as quickly as possible. This will earn you some "continent bonuses" that will significantly boost the number of armies at your disposal. Then allow several turns to pass while your opponents attack each other. Once your forces grow big enough, launch your own invasions. It goes without saying that when you attack a territory, do so with as many armies as possible. Why? Because if you win the battle with just a few armies, you probably won't have enough left to protect the territory you invaded. Also, learn a lesson from Napoleon: don't attempt to invade both Europe and Asia at the same time.

*   *   *

"What I learned from losing: winning's better." —**Ted Turner**

Sand castle recipe: For best results, use about 8 parts sand to 1 part water.

DEACON'S DOUBLE LIFE

*Deacon William Brodie has been largely forgotten, but he was as
notorious in his day as the stock swindler Bernie Madoff is today.
He was also the inspiration for one of English literature's most
infamous villains. See if you can guess which one it is.*

FORTUNATE SON

William Brodie was born in 1741 to one of the most prominent carpenters and cabinet makers in Edinburgh, Scotland.
His father, Francis Brodie, was a leader, or "deacon," of a guild of
skilled tradesmen, a position that also gave him a seat on the city
council. Francis's standing in the community brought him access to
the highest social circles, and examples of his handiwork could be
found in many of the finest homes in the city.

When young William was old enough, he began to learn his
father's trade. Like his father, he rose in his profession until he, too,
was a deacon of his guild and a member of the city council. His status, profession, and family connections should have been enough to
ensure a comfortable life for the rest of his days...except for the fact
that there was one way that he *didn't* take after his father: William
was, at heart, a scoundrel.

SPLIT PERSONALITY

During the day, Brodie was to all appearances a morally upright
citizen and a pillar of the community. But at night he prowled the
worst neighborhoods of Edinburgh feeding a compulsive appetite
for vice. He frequented a seedy tavern in a back alley called
Fleshmarket Close, where he consorted with criminals and gambled
at dice and on cockfights. He wasn't very good with dice, even
when he played with his own crooked pair. He wasn't good at picking winning roosters, either, and lost huge sums of money at both.

Brodie had two mistresses that historians know of, and fathered
five children by them. To his credit, he supported both his families
(neither of which knew about the other), but the expense of maintaining their households plus his own, when added to his substantial
gambling losses, was more than he could afford.

Musical note: Over 20 million Americans play the piano; less than a million play the saxophone.

MAKING AN IMPRESSION

At some point in the 1760s, Brodie began stealing from the customers of his cabinetry business to support his lifestyle. His modus operandi was simple: in those days it was common practice in private homes, businesses, and even government offices to leave the key to the front door hanging on a nail next to the door. When Brodie was building cabinets in someone's home, he'd quietly case the premises while pretending to go about his work. Then, when no one was looking, he'd take the key from its nail and quickly press it into a wad of putty that he kept in a small metal case in his pocket. He'd return the key to its hook and later use the impression to make a duplicate key. Weeks or months afterward, when enough time had passed for him to avoid suspicion, he'd return with the duplicate and burglarize the home.

SEEING IS (DIS)BELIEVING

Brodie pulled off one such break-in after another for nearly 20 years. Twice he robbed homes that he believed would be empty but, in fact, were not. One belonged to a friend, who recognized Brodie even though he was wearing a mask. Perhaps because in those days burglary was punishable by death, the friend never turned him in. The second case involved an old woman who was sick in bed at a time when she should have been at church. On that occasion Brodie was, ironically, saved by his good name, as William Roughead related in his 1906 book *Trial of Deacon Brodie*:

> [The old lady] was alone in the house—her servant having gone to church—when she was startled by the apparition of a man, with a crepe [mask] over his face, in the room where she was sitting. The stranger quietly lifted the keys which were lying on the table beside her, opened her bureau, from which he took out a large sum of money, and then, having locked it and replaced the keys upon the table, retired with a respectful bow. The old lady meanwhile, had looked on in speechless amazement, but no sooner was she left alone than she exclaimed, "Surely that was Deacon Brodie!"
>
> Although the Deacon was recognized, no action was taken.... The old lady preferred to doubt the evidence of her senses—a striking proof of the advantages conferred by a respectable reputation.

*So **have you figured out which fictional villain was inspired by Deacon Brodie's double life? Part II is on page 479.***

YOU CALL THAT ART?

If dogs can play poker, then why can't fish perform surgery?

Artist: Martynka Wawrzyniak
This Is Art? Wawrzyniak, a 33-year-old "New York City-based Polish-New Zealander-American editor, photographer, model, and performance artist," recently started working in a new medium: smell. Her 2012 show "Smell Me" was the culmination of a yearlong art project in which her bodily odors were chemically extracted (with the help of some chemistry students at Hunter College in Manhattan) and "reconstituted for diffusion." Then the public got to stroll through a posh gallery and sniff Wawrzyniak's "olfactory-based self-portrait," which featured the smell of her hair, tears, and underarm sweat.
Artist's Statement: "I think I'm part canine."

Artist: Frances Wadsworth-Jones
This Is Art? Wadsworth-Jones thinks it's "lucky" when a pigeon poops on a person, so she created "Heaven Sent" pigeon-poop brooches. They're not made with real poop, but with tiny precious gems that she combines to *look* like poop. (She has a collection of hundreds of bird-poop photos she uses as models.) Her art was displayed at the Museum of London, and some of the poop-brooches sold for £2,500 ($4,250).
Artist's Statement: "The stain is very intimate."

Artist: Alexander Selvik Wengshoel
This Is Art? After living more than 20 years with a deformed hip, the Norwegian art student decided to have it replaced. For his senior project at Tromso Academy of Art, gallery patrons got to watch a video of the surgery and see the deformed hip bone in person. Another part of the project (that no one got to see): to purge himself of the pain the deformed hip had caused him, Wengshoel claims he boiled the "flesh off the bone" and then consumed the meaty broth (along with potato gratin and a glass of wine).
Artist's Statement: "It tasted of wild sheep."

Artist: Diemut Strebe

This Is Art? Strebe wanted to "regrow" Vincent van Gogh's ear (which the Dutch painter famously sliced off in a fit of rage in 1888). But she was unable to obtain a pure DNA sample, so she settled on some tissue from Lieuwe van Gogh, the great-great-grandson of Vincent's brother Theo (it has 1/16th of Vincent's DNA). Strebe grew the tissue in a lab and then used a 3-D printer to form it into the shape of Van Gogh's missing left ear. The ear is being kept alive in a vat of "nourishing fluids," and is currently on display in Germany. Strebe plans to take the ear on a world tour.

Artist's Statement: "I use science basically like a type of brush, like Vincent used paint."

Artist: Anthea Moys

This Is Art? In 2013 Moys played a soccer game against a professional team of men. She lost. Then she entered a 60-mile bike race on a stationary bike. She lost. Those were two of the performance pieces in her weeklong art project in South Africa called "Anthea Moys vs. the City of Grahamstown." Other events featured her going up against chess masters (she lost) and karate black belts (she lost). Moys, who claims she wanted to combine "conceptual engagement with ideas of play, passion, and failure," had never tried any of these activities before, which could explain why she lost every contest.

Artist's Statement: "I'm not very competitive."

Artist: Anne-Catherine Becker-Echivard

This Is Art? The 43-year-old conceptual artist builds elaborately detailed dioramas—scenes of everyday life featuring figures, each roughly a foot tall. Then she buys fresh fish and chops off the heads, which she uses to complete the scenes, which include fish-headed doctors performing surgery, fish-headed prisoners standing in a snowy prison yard, fish-headed workers in a sardine cannery, fish-headed engineers on a North Atlantic oil rig being attacked by a giant octopus, and (our favorite) a fish-headed reader sitting on a toilet with a *Batman* comic book. Once each diorama is complete, Becker-Echivard photographs it…and then eats the fish for dinner.

Artist's Statement: "My family and friends think I am crazy."

TECHNICALLY SPEAKING

Uncle John helps you navigate life's little nuances.

You might think...The Milky Way is a spiral galaxy. **But technically speaking...**It's a "barred spiral galaxy," meaning it doesn't have a round bulge in the middle with several arms spiraling outward. Rather, it's more like a thick bar of stars with the arms spiraling out from either end.

You might think...*Disinterested* and *uninterested* are synonyms.
But technically speaking...A *disinterested* person is interested in the subject but not the outcome; so a baseball coach might take interest in a game on an adjacent field but is disinterested in who wins. An *uninterested* person wouldn't give a rat's tutu about baseball and would rather be somewhere else.

You might think... Shakespeare wrote his works in Old English.
But technically speaking... Old English looks like this: *Fæder ure þu þe eart on heofonum* ("Our Father, who art in Heaven"). Middle English looks like this: *Ye been fadres of tydynges* ("You be fathers of tidings"). Shakespeare wrote in what we now call Early Modern English: "To thine own self be true." The new language began to take hold in the mid-1400s, a century before the Bard was born.

You might think... All fish have scales.
But technically speaking... Many don't—including mackerel, cod, whiting, sharks, eels, loaches, and some catfish.

You might think...*Irregardless* is not a word.
But technically speaking... According to *Merriam-Webster's Collegiate Dictionary*, "*Irregardless* originated in dialectal American speech in the early 1900s. Its fairly widespread use called it to the attention of commentators as early as 1927. The most frequently repeated remark is that 'there is no such word.' There is, however. It is still used primarily in speech, although it can be found from time to time in edited prose. Its reputation has not risen over the years, and it is still a long way from general acceptance. Use *regardless* instead."

...is his reproductive organ. (Some species rip the arm off and hand it to the female.)

MUSICAL MASH-UP

Here's a new kind of quiz. We give you the names of two popular songs. Combine the performers most closely associated with each song to form a "portmanteau." Example: "Thriller" + "Running on Empty" = Michael Jackson Browne. Got it? Good luck! Answers are on page 541.

1. "Let's Stay Together" + "American Idiot"

2. "I Believe I Can Fly" + "Since U Been Gone"

3. "Physical" + "Imagine"

4. "Go Your Own Way" + "Baby, Don't Get Hooked on Me"

5. "Faith" + "How Am I Supposed to Live Without You?"

6. "Enter Sandman" + "(They Long to Be) Close to You"

7. "My Heart Will Go On" + "A Teenager in Love"

8. "You've Got a Friend" + "We Are Never Ever Getting Back Together"

9. "The Thunder Rolls" + "Boot Scootin' Boogie"

10. "Rockin' in the Free World" + "Bust a Move"

11. "Empire State of Mind" + "Sharp Dressed Man"

12. "Holding Back the Years" + "Under the Bridge"

13. "We're Not Gonna Take It" + "We Are Family"

14. "Venus" + "Summertime Blues"

15. "Can't Get Enough of Your Love, Babe" + "Seven Nation Army"

16. "Losing My Religion" + "Lose Yourself"

17. "(Your Love Keeps Lifting Me) Higher and Higher" + "Hold On"

18. "White Christmas" + "Teach Your Children"

19. "Super Freak" + "I Feel Good"

20. "Where Were You (When the World Stopped Turning)?" + "ABC"

21. "Hey Paula" + "Opposites Attract"

22. "Stand by Me" + "The Court of the Crimson King"

Jaleel White ("Steve Urkel") was the voice of Sonic the Hedgehog in the 1990s cartoon.

STUFF IT

The word taxidermy comes from the Greek taxis, for "arrangement," and derma, for "skin." If you love animals but your landlord won't let you have a pet, maybe this is your solution.

FOR THE BIRDS

You may think of taxidermy—the art of preparing, stuffing, and mounting animal skins—as a modern phenomenon, but the practice has been around for millennia. Exactly how long people have been practicing the art of taxidermy is unknown. Experts believe it's an outgrowth of the practice of tanning animal hides for use as clothing or blankets. Oldest surviving examples: the mummified dogs and cats found preserved in ancient Egyptian tombs.

For the last hundred years, taxidermy was pretty much restricted to hunters who had the heads of dead animals stuffed and mounted for display in their living rooms or dens. Here are a few odd taxidermy fads.

• **Cabinets of Curiosities**. As early as the mid-sixteenth century, people were creating "cabinets of curiosities" in their homes. These were small rooms in which collectors displayed taxidermy, along with natural history specimens and extraordinary objects. Often called *wunderkammers*, or Wonder Rooms, they would showcase unusual finds positioned in ways that told stories of the wonders of the world. A small human skeleton draped in pearls might be positioned with a butterfly perched on an outstretched bony finger. A stuffed pelican could be grasping a conch shell in its talons. Dutch collector Frederik Ruysch (1638–1731) was so proud of his wunderkammer that he opened his Amsterdam home to the public, who called it "The 8th Wonder of the World." The popularity of cabinets of curiosities reached its height in the mid-1800s.

• **Hancock's Birds.** During London's Great Exhibition of 1851, British ornithologist John Hancock mounted an artistic display of birds that he'd shot and stuffed himself. Hancock wasn't the first to stuff dead birds—sportsmen had been doing that since at least the Middle Ages. What set Hancock apart was the artistry of his displays, which were dramatic and lifelike. One of his most famous works was *Struggle with the Quarry*, which shows a falcon preying on a heron, which in turn has an eel in its talons. Hancock won a prize for his work at the Great Exhibition, and soon nearly every middle-class Victorian's home sported at least one stuffed bird or animal, including the home of Queen Victoria, who amassed a huge collection of stuffed birds.

- **Anthropomorphic Taxidermy.** Taxidermists began dressing animals in human clothes and putting them in scenes that became known as a Victorian Whimsy. German taxidermist Hermann Ploucquet started the trend at the Great Exhibit of 1851 with his display of two mice dueling with rapiers and watched over by their seconds, two moles. Queen Victoria noted in her diary that his work was "marvelous." Another anthropomorphic taxidermist, Walter Potter, owner of the famous Mr. Potter's Museum of Curiosities in Bramber, England, began his career in the 1850s when, as a teenager, he attempted to preserve his pet canary. By the 1860s Potter had become famous for his *Rabbit School* diorama featuring 48 little bunnies reading books and writing on slates at a row of desks in a classroom. He also created *Kitten's Tea Party*, complete with Victorian dresses, teacups, and cakes. But his most famous taxidermy diorama was *The Death and Burial of Cock Robin*, with Robin in a casket surrounded by 98 species of British birds sporting black mourning sashes. The museum's collection of nearly 10,000 specimens was auctioned for £500,000 ($700,000) in 2003. British artist Sir Peter Thomas Blake, designer of the Beatles' *Sgt. Pepper* album cover, purchased many of the key pieces.

- **DIY Taxidermy.** Pinterest, a website where you can create your own cabinet of curiosities by pinning images to a virtual bulletin board, has helped to inspire real, tangible collections. This may be a reason that many old-fashioned crafts, such as urban beekeeping, bookbinding, needlepoint, homebrewing, and do-it-yourself (DIY) taxidermy, have become the rage in many cities. Carnivorous Nights, an annual DIY taxidermy contest sponsored by the Secret Science Club of Brooklyn, has become wildly popular since it began in 2009. If you like taxidermy but don't want to kill anything, you might consider joining the Minnesota Association of Rogue Taxidermy (MART). These taxidermists, many of whom are vegetarians, will only stuff roadkill, animals that have died of natural causes, or vermin, such as rats. MART is "dedicated to the showmanship of oddities," which is why if you visit their website (*roguetaxidermy.com*) you might find a two-headed chicken, a muskrat eating its own feet, or a miniature yeti.

Certain rules apply to DIY taxidermists. Most states require a permit to perform taxidermy, even if you find an animal dead on the side of the road. And it is illegal to own a single feather—let alone a full body—of any endangered species, which includes bald eagles, and practically any other bird of prey, songbird, or migratory bird. Any protected animal stuffed after 1947 must have a document certifying it died of accidental or natural causes. And if you were thinking of picking up a human skeleton, think again: there are even more regulations restricting *that* kind of acquisition.

* * *

DATELINE: FAILURE

CBS has *60 Minutes*; ABC has *20/20*. What newsmagazine does NBC have? Before it scored with *Dateline* in 1992, the network tried these 17 primetime newsmagazines…and they all failed.

- *First Tuesday* (1969–71)
- *Chronolog* (1971–72)
- *First Tuesday* (1972–73)
- *NBC News Presents: A Special Edition* (1973–74)
- *Weekend* (1978–79)
- *Prime Time Sunday* (1979)
- *Prime Time Saturday* (1979–1980)
- *NBC Magazine With David Brinkley* (1980–81)
- *NBC Magazine* (1981–82)
- *Monitor* (1983)
- *First Camera* (1983–84)
- *Summer Sunday USA* (1984)
- *American Almanac* (1985–86)
- *1986* (1986)
- *Yesterday, Today and Tomorrow* (1989)
- *Real Life With Jane Pauley* (1990–91)
- *Exposé* (1991)

TV FACTS: THE 1970s

This page isn't a rerun—these facts are about shows from the 1970s.

The *Partridge Family.* Despite being a fictional band with songs performed almost entirely by studio musicians, the Partridge Family was nominated for Best New Artist at the 1971 Grammy Awards. (They lost to the Carpenters.)

All in the Family. Today, many shows carry a "mature themes" warning, but *All in the Family* was the first, in 1971. The sitcom's first six episodes had a disclaimer to warn viewers that they were about to hear racist (although satirical) dialogue from Archie Bunker.

The Mary Tyler Moore Show. Moore's character, Mary Richards, was originally written as a divorced woman. CBS nixed that, worried that divorce was too controversial (it was 1970) and that audiences might think she was still playing her character on *The Dick Van Dyke Show*...and that she'd divorced Rob Petrie.

Kojak. Some TV cops smoked cigarettes, but Lt. Theo Kojak (Telly Savalas) sucked on lollipops. Reason: As the series began shooting in 1973, Savalas was trying to quit smoking and was using lollipops as a substitute. *Kojak* writers incorporated it into his character.

WKRP in Cincinnati. There were lots of Saturday-morning cartoon versions of popular 1970s sitcoms, such as *Mork and Mindy, Laverne and Shirley,* and *Happy Days.* Hanna-Barbera Productions also proposed a cartoon version of *WKRP* in which all the main characters...were dogs. (It never got past the planning stage.)

The Dukes of Hazzard. Half of all the hundreds of fan letters the show received each week were addressed to "General Lee." That's not an actor; it's the orange, Confederate flag-adorned 1969 Dodge Charger driven by Bo and Luke Duke.

The Odd Couple. Neil Simon wrote the play *The Odd Couple,* but not the 1968 movie version on which the TV series was based. After the first season, he asked that his name be dropped from the series' title, *Neil Simon's The Odd Couple.* He eventually came to like the series and even appeared on the show once...weirdly, as himself.

UNCLE JOHN'S MAILBAG

A reader asks; we answer.

BACKGROUND
Here at the BRI, we sometimes get questions that knock us back onto our oval seats. Example: reader Paul McMurray asks,

"Uncle John, did cavemen snore? This is a real question—in prehistoric times, with fierce beasts all about, snoring would give away a person's location."

That's a fascinating question, not only because it sounds like something *we'd* want to know, but because scientists actually have some ideas about it—somewhat contradictory, but compelling nonetheless. Which theory makes the most sense to you?

THEORY #1: Cavemen probably snored, but seldom got eaten. Although humans were prey for all of their early existence, they were also formidable predators in groups. They also weren't stupid enough to sleep (and snore) alone. Normally that could mean sleeping in caves (hence *cave*men) with restricted entrances and fires, which would keep most animals away. Even when hunting far afield in dangerous areas, they'd be likely to sleep close together around a fire, with watchmen on guard. So snoring didn't hurt them, and maybe even kept human-averse animals at bay.

THEORY #2: Cavemen probably didn't snore as much as we do, because the ones who snored got eaten.

Those who snored would have been most likely to get eaten, whether sleeping or not. That's because, as we know today, the people most likely to snore are some combination of being overweight, over 40, and sickly. When predators scout out a group of potential prey, what do they look for? The individuals who are least able to escape or fight back—for example, the older, the sicker, and the overweight. So it is possible that snorers would attract predators that had figured out that a snorer was more vulnerable than the young, healthy, skinny guy sleeping next to him. But it's just as likely that this culling of the human herd's weakest took place in daylight hours, not at night.

Opera singer Enrico Caruso drank and chain-smoked to "protect his voice." He died at age 48.

THEORY #3: Cavemen hardly snored at all.

This one's maybe the most interesting one because—besides age and weight—it depends on one more fundamental difference between cave dwellers and modern humanity. Scientists say that, in terms of genetics, *Homo sapiens* has evolved very little in the past few million years. There is evidence that if you could time-travel, you could switch a cave baby and a modern one and they'd do fine in each other's eras. Still, there's a unique thing that our modern culture has given us: Overbites. What's an overbite? It's when your front teeth don't normally meet when you close your jaw. Almost everybody now has one; back then, almost nobody did.

British anthropologist Charles Loring Brace discovered this while analyzing 19,000 skulls of modern and ancient humans. He also came up with a theory for what caused this: dining utensils—chopsticks in Asia, and the fork and knife in Europe.

For most of human history, food was served in large pieces. You ate by sinking your sharp front teeth into the food and pulling with your hands until the piece in your mouth broke off. Eating like that, your incisors in front become worn down while your back teeth keep growing, eventually stopping when top and bottom meet perfectly. Use a fork to pick up precut pieces of meat, however, and your molars get most of the action, while your little-used incisors keep growing. With those overgrown front teeth, most people now have to pull their jaws inward to close their mouths enough to chew.

You're probably asking, "What's all this got to do with snoring?"

Try this: Gently push your lower jaw as far back as it will go, and try to make a snoring sound in your throat. See how easy it is? Now jut it forward until your front teeth meet perfectly and try making the same sound. Not so easy now, is it? The fact is that your jaw position makes a big difference in whether you snore or not, and an overbite seriously constricts the flow of air in your throat. If your palate is flaccid from extra fat, age, or alcohol, it will vibrate as you breathe, making you snore. That's why anti-snoring mouthpieces are designed to position your bottom jaw more forward when you wear them.

So according to this theory, cave dwellers probably didn't snore much. (And their mates, their kids, and their pets probably slept a lot better, too.)

The first commercial dental floss, produced in 1882, was made of silk.

(B)AD CAMPAIGNS

*They say there's no such thing as bad publicity, but as
these companies learned the hard way, getting
on the news isn't always a good thing.*

SHORT SALE

Subway, one of the world's largest fast-food chains, had some explaining to do in 2013 after upset customers took to social media to post photos of their "Footlong" subs. The problem: the subs were only 11 inches long. "I will NEVER eat at Subway again!" posted one angry patron. "We've been outright lied to!" said another. "I smell a lawsuit," said another. As the complaints kept coming in, Subway finally responded…by explaining that "'Footlong' is a descriptive name, and not intended to be a measurement of length."

THE CHAIN GANG

"Got a sneaker game so hot you lock your kicks to your ankles?" That was the caption to a 2012 Adidas ad that proved so controversial, the shoes—called JS Roundhouse Mids—were recalled before they were shipped to stores and never even released. Reason: the sneakers came with rubber shackles…reminiscent of the shackles once worn by slaves. Joining the chorus of critics was Rev. Jesse Jackson, who called the shoes "offensive, appalling, and insensitive." An Adidas spokesman denied the slavery reference and said, "We're sorry if anyone was offended." Then the shackled shoes were shelved.

THAT'S DEPRESSING

Urban Outfitters came under fire in 2014 for selling a T-shirt that had the word "Depression" printed all over it. Customers, as well as mental health advocates, criticized the retail chain for making light of a disorder that affects 25 million Americans. The company tweeted, "Hey, everyone, we hear you and we are taking the shirt down from the site." But some critics suspected that Urban Outfitters knew exactly what it was doing—using a controversy to generate free publicity—and that they've done it before. "It's almost as if the hipster retailer has a formula," wrote Jessica Wakeman in

---

Hey, they can't all be *Harry Potter:* The average novel sells 2,000 copies.

The Guardian, "Once a year or more, a fresh outrage erupts on the Internet after one of their products is deemed offensive. Sometimes Urban Outfitters pulls the offending product, but other times it sells out first." Wakeman pointed to the time that the chain angered anorexics for a shirt that said "Eat Less" (worn in ads by a skinny model), the time it angered Hindus by selling socks emblazoned with a picture of the Hindu deity Ganesh (inappropriate and offensive in the Hindu religion), and the time the Navajo Nation, which has dealt with alcoholism issues, protested the use of their name on a line of flasks.

OLD KING COAL

Scholastic, one of the world's largest children's book publishers, felt the heat after distributing curriculum materials called "The United States of Energy" to teachers. Environmental and children's advocacy groups complained that the material included information about the benefits of coal, but it failed to mention coal's impact on the environment and human health. According to reports, a lobbying group for the American Coal Foundation had tried issuing the energy lesson plan itself but was only able to get it to 7,000 fourth-grade teachers. After partnering with Scholastic, that number increased to 66,0000. "It's predatory marketing," said Susan Linn, director of the Campaign for a Commercial-Free Childhood. "By selling its privileged access to children to the coal industry, Scholastic is commercializing classrooms and undermining education." In 2011, after a flurry of bad press and letter-writing campaigns from parents, teachers, and even other Scholastic authors, the publisher withdrew the lesson plan.

McBAD ADVICE

In 2013 McDonald's launched a "McResource Line" website to give helpful life advice to its 1.7 million employees. Among the advice: Don't eat at McDonald's. Really. A picture of a hamburger, fries, and a soda was labeled an "unhealthy meal choice." More advice: employees who need to ease their holiday debt should "return unopened gifts, get a second job, or sign up for food stamps." According to Reuters, the McResource line also gave suggestions on "how to tip dog walkers, housekeepers, massage therapists, personal fitness instructors, pool cleaners, au pairs, and other services McDonald's employees are definitely unlikely to make use of ever."

Myth: Peeing on a jellyfish sting can actually make it more painful. Use vinegar instead.

(This was during a time when thousands of the chain's workers had threatened to quit because of low wages.) A company spokesperson blamed the questionable advice on a "third-party vendor" hired to maintain the site, and said that McDonald's agrees with the advice. Then the fast-food giant quietly took the site down.

NOTHING TO SEE HERE

Shortly after a Thai Airways passenger jet slid off a runway in Bangkok in September 2013, a crane rushed out to the crashed plane. As emergency crews rescued the injured passengers, airport workers hurriedly raised the crane's bucket and sprayed black paint over the Thai Airways logos on the tail and fuselage. Responding to complaints that the airline cares more about its image than the safety of its passengers, a Thai Airways spokesman said that it was simply following a "crisis management" policy enforced by Star Alliance, an international conglomerate that oversees several airlines. Star Alliance denied the policy (using all capital letters in its rebuttal), and placed the blame solely on Thai Airways, which it said "acted alone." The airline later admitted as much…and then explained that blacking out its logo on crashed planes is standard procedure.

CONSOLATION PRIZE

Early one morning in February 2014, an explosion rocked Bobtown, Pennsylvania. "It sounded like a jet engine going five feet above your house," said one rattled resident. The blast came from a nearby fracking well that Chevron Corporation was preparing for natural gas production. One worker was killed; the fire lasted five days. In addition to fears of a second explosion, locals were concerned about noxious smells, polluted groundwater, a loud hissing noise, and an increase in skin rashes. That's when Chevron's public-relations team sprang into action. Each of the rural town's few hundred residents received a letter of apology from Chevron saying, "We value being a responsible member of this community and will continue to strive to achieve incident-free operations." However, it wasn't the apology that made news—it was the gift certificate that came with it…for a free large pizza and a two-liter bottle of soda. Without the offer, the story would have faded from the news. Instead, it inspired headlines like this one: "Chevron nearly destroys town, offers free pizza as compensation." (That's the kind of publicity you just can't buy.)

Legendary pool shark Minnesota Fats was actually from New York.

NAME THAT TEAM

Once an NFL team is named, who thinks about the names that weren't picked? We do.

C **INCINNATI RHINOS.** Cincinnati has a large German population, and when the city was awarded a professional football team in 1966, owners almost called it the Rhinos—a play on Germany's Rhine River. After somebody pointed out that rhinos are fat and slow, the owners went with Bengals, the name of a football team that played in Cincinnati in the 1930s.

SEATTLE D. B. COOPERS. A 1975 naming contest for the new Seattle NFL franchise brought in 20,365 entries with 1,741 suggestions. Among them: the Lumberjacks, the Soggies, the Running Salmon, the Washington Georges, the Abominable Snowmen…and the D. B. Coopers, after the mysterious hijacker who jumped out of a plane over Washington in 1971. The winning name, submitted by 150 people: the Seahawks (a rarely used nickname for the osprey).

ATLANTA DOGS. In 1965 the NFL awarded Atlanta its first pro sports franchise. But the new team had competition in the popular football programs at Georgia Tech and the University of Georgia. To lure fans from both groups, the owners considered combining Tech's Yellow Jackets with UGA's Bulldogs, and naming the team the Yellow Dogs. Bonus: "Yellow Dog" was also a term for anti-Union Southern Democrats after the Civil War. The owners ultimately decided to have a fan vote, and Falcons won out.

DALLAS STEERS. The Dallas NFL expansion team was all set to begin the 1960 season as the Steers…until owner Tex Schramm realized that his team might be mocked if their mascot was the steer—a castrated male cow raised to be turned into beef. He liked the name "Rangers" but didn't want to be confused with the then-minor league Texas Rangers baseball team. He finally decided on Cowboys.

OAKLAND SEÑORS. In 1960 the *Oakland Tribune* held a name-the-team contest, and the winner was…the Señors. It's likely that the contest was fixed, as a joke—the team's co-owner, real estate developer and local celebrity Chet Soda, called everyone he met "señor." About a week after the name was announced, owners went with the third-place voter getter: the Raiders.

No bears are native to Australia. (Koalas aren't bears, they're marsupials.)

"TAKE MY ADVICE..."

You might not want to follow it, but then again...you might.

"Always run from a knife and rush a gun."
—**Jimmy Hoffa**

"If a thing's worth having, it's worth cheating for."
—**W. C. Fields**

"When your opponent's sittin' there holding all the aces, there's only one thing to do: Kick over the table."
—**Dean Martin**

"Don't look before you leap. It'll ruin the surprise."
—**Kris Brand**

"You got drunk and peed your pants. Now your date knows you're a freedom machine, and if she can't handle that, she's BORING!"
—**Charlie Sheen**

"If everyone dropped out of school, we'd have a much more intelligent society."
—**Jaden Smith**

"Start by writing a nasty song about him, have your record come out all over the world, then make out with some hot bearded dude."
—**Ke$ha**

"Don't steal the hubcaps. Steal the car."
—**Frank Sinatra**

"You have to be a bastard to make it—and that's a fact."
—**John Lennon**

"Claim everything, concede nothing, and if defeated, allege fraud."
—**Tammany Hall political maxim**

"Don't play it too fast, and not too slow—just half-fast."
—**Louis Armstrong**

"An affair now and then is good for a marriage."
—**Bette Davis**

"Words are cheap. Be doers, not hearers."
—**Matthew Henry**

"Have you ever talked to your muscles? As you work out and bring up the two dumbbells to your body, say, 'Grow!'"
—**Sylvester Stallone**

"If you can't convince 'em, confuse 'em."
—**Harry S. Truman**

First Greek student society: Phi Beta Kappa (College of William and Mary, 1776).

IRISH FAIRY FOLK

*You've probably heard of leprechauns and banshees, but how
about the other "little people" of the Emerald Isle?*

THE POOKA

In the 1950 film *Harvey*, the main character, Elwood P. Dowd
(played by Jimmy Stewart), consults with a six-foot-tall rabbit that only he can see. He calls the rabbit a *pooka*, defined in the
film as "a fairy spirit in animal form, always very large. The pooka
appears here and there, now and then, this one and that one; a
benign but mischievous creature, very fond of rum pots, crackpots..."
That sounds benign, but in Ireland, a pooka is the most feared of all
magical creatures. Pookas appear at night and wreak havoc on farmers. In County Down, legend has it that the pooka transforms itself
into a deformed goblin who demands a share of the year's harvest,
which is why many farmers leave a "pooka's share" of crops still in
the field. But the form a pooka most often assumes is that of a huge
black horse with fierce yellow eyes. It roams the countryside, tearing
down fences, freeing livestock, and destroying crops. The only man
ever to tame the pooka was Brian Boru, the eleventh-century high
king of Ireland. According to legend, Boru made the magic horse
promise to stop tormenting the farmers and ruining their crops, and
never again to attack an Irishman going home....unless he's drunk—
and then he can give the man a good pounding.

THE CHANGELING

Fairies who give birth to sick or ugly babies may try to swap them
with healthy babies from the human world. The bad-tempered child
left in its place is called a *changeling*. Changelings bring bad luck
and misery to a human home, crying day and night. The babies most
in danger of being switched are those not baptized or those who are
oohed and ahhed over because of their beauty. A changeling looks
exactly like the human baby, but somehow seems to be different.
They have dark, penetrating eyes that show a wisdom beyond their
age. They can develop crippling diseases and live only a few years.
Most changelings are boys, which is why, even as recently as 60
years ago, some Irish families would disguise their boys in dresses till
they were seven years old, too old to be taken by fairies.

MERROWS

In *Tir fo Thuinn*, the land beneath the waves, the fairy people are called *merrows*. They mostly take the form of beautiful women who can live on land or in the sea. Unlike mermaids, who are half-human, half-fish, the merrows of Irish folklore have legs and arms. But their fingers are webbed and their feet are flat. In the northern waters off Ireland, they swim wrapped in sealskin capes and are often mistaken for seals. A merrow also wears a *cohuleen druith*, a magical red cap that helps her swim. She must abandon the cap and cape to come ashore. There are many stories of coastal fisherman taking merrows as lovers and even marrying them. The O'Sullivans and O'Flahertys of Kerry and the MacNamaras of Clare claim to be descendants of these unions.

THE GROGOCH

If you pass two large stones leaning together in the countryside, you could be passing a grogoch's house. But fear not—the half-man, half-fairy grogoch is a pleasant creature. He's small, covered in red hair or fur, and very dirty. (A mother might tell her unkempt child, "You look like an old grogroch.") Another name for this creature is *pecht*, which comes from *Pict*, the name of the Celtic people who once lived in Scotland. Like the Picts, grogochs left Scotland and settled on Ireland's northern coast and on the Isle of Man. A grogroch is friendly but shy, and he loves hard work. (He is credited with moving large marble stones and clipping the grass in a meadow.) The one thing a grogroch doesn't love: laziness. Workers who lie down in fields to rest may find themselves poked and prodded by an invisible hand until they get back on the job.

THE WATER SHEERIE

Swamp gas is often the explanation for phosphorescent balls of light that appear over bogs at twilight. In Ireland these glimmering spirits are known as *water sheerie* and are believed to be the souls of unborn children trying to return to the mortal world. A traveler making his way through the bog might see these bobbing lights and try to follow them, thinking they are people with lanterns, but the lights are illusive and never let people get near them. If you do get close, beware. Sheerie, sometimes called "corpse candles," may lead you into a bog hole…and a watery grave.

One of St. Patrick's achievements: he helped end the slave trade in Ireland.

BILLIE'S LAST RIDE

Who says you can't take it with you?

EASY RIDER

Billie Standley was a retired truck driver and former rodeo rider who lived in Mechanicsburg, Ohio, in the 1990s. Many years earlier, after he'd settled down to raise his family, he took up motorcycle riding to remind himself of his exciting younger days in the rodeo. He rode for the rest of his life.

When Standley was in his sixties, he approached the local funeral director, David Vernon, about the possibility of being buried with his beloved 1967 Harley-Davidson Electra Glide. Not just with it but actually *riding* it, and in a see-through plexiglass casket so that his biker friends could watch him make his final ride to the cemetery. Vernon explained that it wouldn't be easy and it wouldn't be cheap: Standley would have to buy three adjacent funeral plots to create a large-enough grave, and both the casket and the concrete vault it would be lowered into would have to be custom-made.

TRIP PLANNING

Standley spent the last 18 years of his life preparing for his funeral. He bought the three funeral plots, had the concrete vault poured, and designed a special brace that would allow the funeral director to secure his dead body to the Harley and give it a lifelike pose. His sons, Pete and Roy, made the steel-reinforced plexiglass casket.

"Me and my brother built the casket five years ago, and it's been sitting in his garage waiting for him to die," Pete Standley told ABC News. Standley proudly showed off the casket to anyone who came to visit. It looked like a giant aquarium.

By the time Standley passed away from lung cancer in January 2014, everything was ready. Five embalmers dressed him in his leathers, helmet, and glasses, and secured him to his Harley inside the casket. Then they towed him to the cemetery, where hundreds had gathered to cheer him on and bid farewell. "We granted him his final wish," Pete Standley says. "He rode his motorcycle to the grave…and he's still riding it today."

"The Star-Spangled Banner" didn't become the U.S. national anthem until 1931.

OOPS!

*More tales of outrageous blunders sure to make
you glad they happened to someone else.*

UN-DIG-NIFIED MISTAKE

In 1923 a British geologist named Herbert Henry Thomas made a startling announcement: He had discovered the source of the stones used to build Stonehenge. The site—called Cairn Meini—was 150 miles away in Wales. Archaeologists flocked there, and for the next 90 years they carefully excavated it, looking for clues about who cut the stones, who moved them, and how they did it. But dig after dig revealed no solid answers. Then, in 2013, a Welsh geologist named Richard Bevins made another startling announcement: Thomas goofed. Bevins's team discovered this after they X-rayed samples from Cairn Meini and found that they didn't match the rocks at Stonehenge. The actual stones came from Cairn Goedog, a similar rock outcropping located about a mile away from Cairn Meini. "I don't expect to get Christmas cards from the archaeologists who have been excavating at the wrong place all these years," said Bevins.

DEEP DISCOUNT

How does a 97-percent-off jewelry sale sound? It didn't sound good to Macy's, but they had to honor it after a typo in the department store's February 2013 mailer offered a $1,500 gold necklace for only $47. (It was supposed to be $479.) No one caught the goof until after the mailer had been delivered to thousands of homes in Dallas, Texas. Once the error was caught, most of the stores hurriedly put up signs alerting customers to the corrected price, but some stores didn't react in time. Result: the necklaces sold out in one day.

WEE GOOFED

In 2013 Target started selling a line of sandals called Orinas. The name, the company explained, was inspired by the Russian word for "peace." But no one bothered to check what *orina* means in other languages. The store's Latino customers were quick to point out that in Spanish, *orina* means "urine." Target no longer sells the sandals.

THE FLYING TOMATO

Great athletes gotta have game (required) and silly nicknames (optional).

Karl "the Mailman" Malone (NBA). Because he always "delivered."

Robert "Tractor" Traylor (NBA). The pun on "tractor-trailer" was fitting because at 290 pounds, Traylor was one of the biggest players in NBA history.

Moses "Chairman of the Boards" Malone (NBA). For his tenacious rebounding.

Shaun "the Flying Tomato" White (snowboarding). Because of his red hair and incredible hang time.

Reggie "the Minister of Defense" White (NFL). He was an imposing lineman… and an ordained minister.

Ron "the Penguin" Cey (MLB). His short legs made it look as if he was waddling around the bases, like a penguin.

Walt "Clyde" Frazier (NBA). Off the court, he wore wide-brimmed hats like the lead character in *Bonnie and Clyde.*

Charles "the Round Mound of Rebound" Barkley (NBA). Barkley was a top rebounder, and he also had trouble keeping his weight down.

David "the Admiral" Robinson (NBA). He graduated from the U.S. Naval Academy. But he never rose higher than a lieutenant.

Bill "Spaceman" Lee (MLB). An admitted fan of marijuana.

Darryl "Dr. Dunkenstein" Griffith (NBA). He wasn't really a doctor, but he was known for his frequent powerful slam dunks.

Ray "Jesus" Allen (NBA). He played a character with that name in the 1998 film *He Got Game.*

Anthony "Spud" Webb (NBA). "Spud" means small, and at 5'7", Webb was one of the shortest players in NBA history.

Shane "the Flyin' Hawaiian" Victorino (MLB). He runs fast. He's Hawaiian.

ALSO ON THIS DAY IN HISTORY

We think of historic events as being the only thing that happened that day. Yes, those days will live in our memory...but what else was going on?

November 22, 1963: President John F. Kennedy is assassinated by Lee Harvey Oswald while riding in a motorcade in Dallas.

Also: After a grueling six-day, $175,000 shoot ($1.3 million in today's dollars), one of the most expensive TV pilots to date, the first episode of *Gilligan's Island*, wraps in Hawaii.

July 20, 1969: *Apollo 11* astronauts Neil Armstrong and Buzz Aldrin become the first men to walk on the moon.

Also: After tensions over immigration from El Salvador into Honduras boil over into riots at a World Cup soccer qualifying match and lead to six days of fighting, the two nations declare a cease-fire, ending what is known as the Football War.

August 28, 1963: More than 200,000 civil-rights protesters convene on the National Mall in Washington, D.C., for the March on Washington, which culminates in Martin Luther King's iconic "I Have a Dream" speech.

Also: The Evergreen Point Floating Bridge opens to car traffic in Washington, connecting Seattle with the northern suburb of Bellevue across Lake Washington. Spanning 7,578 feet, it's still the longest floating bridge on the planet.

August 9, 1974: Facing impeachment and possible conviction for his role in covering up the Watergate break-in, U.S. president Richard M. Nixon resigns.

Also: With inflation and economic problems beginning to mount, General Motors announces that 1975 car prices will be 9.5 percent higher, an average of $480 per car. Part of that increase—$130—is to cover government pollution-control costs. The pollution control is now regulated by the new Environmental Protection Agency, an agency started by the Nixon administration.

Chew on this: The melting temperature of bubble gum is 125°F.

December 8, 1980: John Lennon is shot and killed outside his New York City apartment.

Also: The Bravo cable network debuts, providing 40,000 premium cable subscribers in New York and New Jersey with programming that includes operas, plays, and classical music performances. At first, it runs two days a week, sharing cable space with a soft-core pornography network. (Today, the network plays mostly reality shows, such as *The Real Housewives of Beverly Hills*.)

November 9, 1989: With the Soviet grasp on Eastern Europe beginning to crumble, communist East German officials announce that, for the first time since the Berlin Wall was constructed in 1961, residents of East Berlin could travel to and from West Berlin. By that evening, Germans began to tear down the wall.

Also: Solving the largest case of art theft in French history, police recover $17 million in artwork stolen from the Cannes home of Pablo Picasso's granddaughter, Marina Picasso. The stolen works include seven paintings by Picasso and a bust by Auguste Rodin. Arrested for the heist: two of Marina Picasso's security guards.

February 11, 1990: After 27 years in jail for political activities aimed at ending racial oppression in South Africa, Nelson Mandela is freed from prison. Within just four years, Mandela will win the Nobel Peace Prize and be elected president of South Africa.

Also: Boxer Mike Tyson fights Buster Douglas at Japan's Tokyo Dome. Tyson is undefeated and a 42-1 favorite to beat Douglas. But in the 10th round, Douglas sends Tyson to the mat for good. It's the first time anybody has ever knocked out or beaten Tyson. (It's also the first time anybody has knocked him *down*.)

September 11, 2001: Terrorists hijack four planes. They crash two into the World Trade Center, another into the Pentagon, and a fourth into a Pennsylvania field. Final death toll: 2,996.

Also: It's a Tuesday—the day of the week most new music albums are released in North America. A number of notable albums are released on 9-11, though few people feel like shopping. One is Nickelback's *Silver Side Up*, which will eventually sell 8 million copies, one of the top-selling albums of the decade. Another, Mariah Carey's soundtrack to *Glitter*, is not. With just 600,000 copies sold, it's the biggest flop of her career.

THE LONGEST HIGH-FIVE CHAIN IN THE WORLD!

And a few other interesting "longest" things. (Note: This is a pretty long article. So you might have to take the world's longest bathroom break to read the entire thing.)

LONGEST CAT FUR

In August 2013, *Guinness World Records* awarded its first-ever "cat with the longest fur" title. Recipient: Colonel Meow, a Himalayan Persian kitty belonging to Anne Marie Avey of Los Angeles, California. Fur length: nine inches. (The length was verified by three different veterinarians.) "We already knew that he was the best cat in the world," a proud Ms. Avey said, "but to be recognized in the *Guinness World Records* book takes it to the next level."

Bonus fact: The best part of the story is that Colonel Meow was a rescue kitty. He was in a shelter in Seattle, Washington—and scheduled to be euthanized—when he was rescued by a Seattle group dedicated to rescuing Himalayan Persian cats. They put him up for adoption online…and the rest is cat-fur history.

LONGEST CARROT

Joe Atherton of Nottinghamshire, England, grows carrots in plastic tubes more than 20 feet long, each one filled with nutrient-rich compost and positioned so they lie at an angle of about 45 degrees to ensure proper drainage. In September 2007, Atherton carefully extracted one of those tube-grown carrots, being careful not to break its long, fragile root. That particular carrot had been growing for 14 months: Atherton had extended its growing season beyond the usual two or three months by regularly nipping off any seed buds that appeared on it, thereby preventing it from going to seed. Result: the carrot was 19 feet, 1.875 inches long. It's the current record holder for "longest carrot in the world."

Bonus fact: Atherton is one of hundreds of "extreme gardeners" who participate in the National Giant Vegetables Championship, part of the Bath and West National Gardening Show, held in Somerset, England, every fall.

Paul McCartney has played an average of more than one gig a week since 1957.

LONGEST HIGH-FIVE CHAIN

In March 2014, a woman standing in a field in La Quinta, California, gave the man standing next to her a "high-five" hand slap. The man immediately turned around and gave the person standing next to him a high-five. That person gave the person next to *him* a high-five…and you get the picture. About three minutes and forty-five seconds later, the 1,113 people standing in the high-five line had established the new record for the longest high-five chain in history.

Bonus fact: The record-breakers immediately followed that feat by breaking the record for the longest "human towel chain." The first person in the chain held the end of a regular bath towel; the next person held the other end of that towel, together with the end of another towel. The next person held the end of that second towel, together with the end of yet another towel…and so on. That chain, it must be noted, was only 1,110 people long: they'd lost three people after the high-five chain, possibly to injuries caused by high-fiving (or maybe they were on a bathroom break.).

LONGEST GOLF COURSE

Australia's Nullarbor Links has 18 holes, just like a normal golf course, and par is 72, also just like most regulation courses. The longest hole—588 yards from tee to cup—is also pretty normal. So why is it the world's longest golf course? Because the first hole is in the town of Ceduna, South Australia, and the last hole is in Kalgoorlie, Western Australia, 848 miles away. The average distance between holes: 41 miles (two of the holes are 120 miles apart). Nullarbor Links, which opened in 2009, incorporates seven holes from already existing courses and has eleven of its own holes. Each is located at roadhouses and rest stops along southern Australia's Eyre Highway, part of which traverses the Nullarbor Plain, some of the flattest, dryest, and most desolate land in all of the Australian outback. Average amount of time it takes to finish a round: about four days.

Bonus: If you get a chance to play this course, be warned. Summer temperatures on the Nullarbor Plain regularly reach 100°F. (One day in January 2014, it reached 119°F.)

LONGEST ECHO

In January 2014, an acoustic scientist crawled into an underground fuel tank in Scotland. The tank, part of a secret underground fuel depot constructed in the Scottish Highlands during World War II, is huge. It's about 600 feet long, 30 feet wide, and 45 feet high, and was designed to hold 2.5 million gallons of fuel. The walls are two feet thick, and there are no doors into it: Trevor Cox, a professor of acoustic engineering at Scotland's University of Salford, had to slither through a pipe that's 18 inches in diameter to get into the tank. "The sound just goes on and on and on," Cox later told *The Independent* newspaper. "I started off just playing around, whooping and hollering." After he was done whooping and hollering, Cox set up very sensitive recording equipment inside the tank, and a fellow scientist fired a pistol—loaded with blanks—into the pipe. Result: they created an echo that lasted an astounding 75 seconds, a new record for the longest echo ever created. It actually went on longer; at very low frequencies the echo could be detected for 112 seconds. But across all frequencies, which was required for the record books, it lasted only 75 seconds.

Bonus: The previous record was, oddly enough, also set by Scots: It was the echo of the sound of the doors to the Hamilton Mausoleum, in Hamilton, Scotland, being slammed shut. It lasted a paltry 15 seconds.

LONGEST ENGLISH WORD

The longest word in the English (or any other) language:

mehionylalanylthreonylserylarginylglycylalanylserylarginylcysteinylprolylarginylaspartylisoleucylalanylasparaginylvalylmethionylglutaminylarginylleucylglutaminylaspartylglutamylglutaminylglutamylisoleucylvalylglutaminyllysylarginylthreonylphenylalanylthreonyllysyltryptophylisoleucylasparaginylserylhistidylleucylalanyllysylarginyllysylprolylprolylmethionylvalylvalylaspartylaspartylleucylphenylalanylglutamylaspartylmethionyllysyl...

Okay, we have to stop there because that word has a total of 189,819 letters—enough to fill the next 100 pages of this book. What does the word mean? It's the chemical name of what is commonly known as *titin*, or "connectin," a type of protein found in muscle and the largest protein ever discovered. That, in fact, is why the name is so long: chemical names must precisely identify every part of a chemical compound—and this one has a *lot* of them.

Bonus fact: If you happen to have 3.5 hours to kill, you can see a video of a Russian man named Dmitry Golubovskiy pronouncing the entire word on YouTube. It has currently been viewed more than two million times. (Note: some experts insist that such chemical names aren't really words, so this really shouldn't be called the "longest English word." But we say if it has letters, a meaning, and can be pronounced, it's a word.)

RANDOM LONGESTS

• **Longest dog ear:** 13.75 inches. That was the length of the right ear of Tigger the bloodhound (the left ear was a little shorter), who belonged to Bryan and Christina Flessner of St. Joseph, Illinois, and became the record holder in 2004. (Tigger died in 2009, but he still holds the record.)

• **Longest basketball shot ever made:** 109 feet, 9 inches—about 15 feet longer than a regulation NBA basketball court—made by Thunder Law of the Harlem Globetrotters in Phoenix, Arizona, in November 2013.

• **Longest reverse car jump:** 89 feet, 3.25 inches, by professional daredevil Rob Dyrdek at Six Flags Magic Mountain in Valencia, California, in February 2014.

• **Longest alphabetical e-mail address:** *www.abcdefghijklmnopqrstuvwxyzabcdefghijklmnopqrstuvwxyzabcdefghijk.com.* (Go ahead—try it!)

• **Longest time treading water:** According to the *Limca Book of Records*, a record book published in India, the record for treading water is 85 hours—or about 3.5 days. It was set, says *Limca*, by 19-year-old Ashish Singhvi in March 1997. (Note: *Guinness World Records* does not have a category for treading water. It's too dangerous!)

*　　　*　　　*

UNCLE JOHN'S HELPFUL HOUSEHOLD HINTS

• Use a staple remover to separate hard-to-separate key rings.

• Serving a lot of condiments at a barbecue? Serve them in a muffin tin—you'll have only one dish to wash.

• Use a bread-bag tab to keep the end of a roll of masking tape from sticking to itself.

• Bananas that are connected at the stems will ripen and spoil faster than bananas that are separated.

A trip around a baseball diamond is 20 yards longer than a goal-to-goal run on a football field.

VITAMIN SEA

Apparently, once you've earned enough money to buy a boat, you also develop a really corny sense of humor. These are all real boat names.

The Codfather	Breakin' Wind	My Pride and Toy
Aqua Holic	Aloan Again	Eat Drink and Remarry
Vitamin Sea	Apocalypso	Boatweiser
Colin's Tuition	Pier Pressure	Rest a Shore
Marlin Monroe	Your Place Oar Mine	Deeper in Debt
Duck Sloop	Dijabringbeeralong	It'll Do
Yacht to be Working	Sails Call	Docked Wages
Aida Fish	Ahoy Vey	Wheredahelarwe
Maid of Plywood	Unsinkable II	The Last Straw
Fah Get a Boat It	Seaductress	Seize the Bay
My Widdle Wifeboat	Knot Guilty	Fishfull Thinking
Costa Lotta	L. L. Boat	To Sea Oar Knot to Sea
Piece of Ship	Bow Down	Just for the Hull of It
She Got the House	A Crewed Interest	Weather Oar Knot
License to Chill	Bow Movement	Helmroid
Driving Miss Lazy	Half-a-Wake	Nuclear Fishin'
Seas the Day	Sea Me Smile	Never Again #2
	Lamberdinghy	

When "feminine scents" such as vanilla are sprayed in women's clothing stores, sales increase.

GERMANY'S LITTLE GREEN MANN

When East Germany passed into history in 1990, the newly reunited Germany happily set about removing every last vestige of the old Soviet-dominated police state. If you visit the capital city of Berlin today, you'll find very few signs that the old country ever existed…until you try to cross the street.

DON'T WALK

In 1961 an East German traffic psychologist named Karl Peglau was assigned to see if he could find a way to reduce the rising number of traffic fatalities in East Berlin, the capital city. Some 10,000 people had died in traffic accidents between 1955 and 1960, and as Peglau pored over the numbers he saw that many fatalities were pedestrians who were hit by cars while crossing the street. At the time, East Berlin didn't have traffic lights for pedestrians, not even at crosswalks.

Peglau thought installing some would help. He wanted them to be so simple that small children, the elderly, people who were color-blind, and people with cognitive difficulties could easily understand them. Then he hit on the idea of covering ordinary traffic lights with stencils that changed the shape of the emitted light into a symbol. The green light would look like the profile of a walking man. The red light would show a man with his arms outstretched, as if he were physically blocking people from crossing the street.

FLESHING IT OUT

Peglau handed off the idea to his assistant, Annelise Wegner, and told her to work out the details. To increase the amount of light emitted and to make the character more appealing to children, Peglau instructed Wegner to make the little men chubby and friendly in appearance. The designs that Wegner came up with—fat little men in porkpie hats—were so cheery and playful that Peglau feared they'd never be approved by the humorless communist bureaucrats that he reported to. He was wrong. The designs were approved, and the first *Ampelmännchen*, or "little streetlight men" as they came to be known, began appearing on the streets of East Berlin in the fall of 1961. Just as Peglau hoped, the Ampelmännchen were popular with children, who happily waited on the sidewalk until the little green man told them it was safe to cross. In time, the Ampelmänn became the East German equivalent of Smokey the Bear or McGruff the Crime Dog: the East German government used it in animated safety films for kids and created Ampelmänn merchandise—board games, coloring books, etc.—to teach children simple lessons about safety.

UPS AND DOWNS

The year the Ampelmänn debuted, 1961, was also the year that the communist East German government erected the Berlin Wall to keep its citizens from fleeing to the West. When the wall came down in 1989, nearly every trace of the hated old order was swept away. By the mid-1990s even the street signs, traffic lights, and pedestrian lights bearing the friendly Ampelmännchen began to be phased out in favor of their humorless West German equivalents.

Had the reunification of Germany gone more smoothly, the little green and red men might well have disappeared. But as the years passed, what had initially seemed like a joining of East and West came to feel more like a swallowing of the East by the West. The former East Germans, or *Ossis* (Easterners), as they were nicknamed, felt like second-class citizens in the new Germany. They worried about losing their identity in what felt like a foreign country, and they resented being looked down upon by the *Wessies*, or "Westerners," as backward and slow. The Ossis were glad to be rid of the old regime, but they chafed at the idea of losing even this most innocuous and cheery reminder of their old lives. They came to identify with the chubby little man in the silly hat as he was being pushed aside.

CAN'T KEEP A GOOD MANN DOWN

In 1996 Peglau banded together with fans of the Ampelmännchen to form a group called "Rescue the Ampelmännchen!" and began lobbying the Berlin government to leave the pedestrian lights alone. They had more than nostalgia on their side: the chubby Ampelmännchen gave off nearly twice as much light as their skinnier West German counterparts, making them easier to see.

Berlin officials soon realized that keeping the lights was good politics. The Ampelmännchen not only stayed up in old East Berlin, in time they became the standard for the entire city. Since then other German cities have adopted them as well.

MANN ON THE STREET

The Ampelmännchen also became pop-culture icons, thanks to a West German industrial designer named Markus Heckhausen, who first saw the lights during a trip to East Berlin in 1988, when Germany was still divided. "I loved them because they seemed like the only bright, humorous thing in a gray world. They were so happy and friendly," he says.

After the wall came down, Heckhausen converted some discarded streetlights into decorative lamps. Those sold so well that he bought the rights to the character from Karl Peglau and put it on T-shirts, hats, key chains, pens, playing cards, shot glasses, coffee mugs, you name it—hundreds of products in all. Tourists have snapped up millions of the souvenirs every year and, in the process, have turned the Ampelmänn into as iconic a symbol of Berlin as the Eiffel Tower is for Paris and the Statue of Liberty is for New York. "People just love them, as I did when I first saw them," Heckhausen says. "They are kind of naive and childlike. And fun."

*   *   *

"Poverty of course is no disgrace, but it is damned annoying."
—**William Pitt the Younger**

During WWII, the Allies used crossword puzzles to recruit codebreakers.

THE FUTURISTS, PART II

"The future" used to seem exciting. Has it gotten scarier? Here's Part II of the history of prediction. (Part I is on page 68.)

THE GOLDEN AGE OF FUTURISM

In the 1950s, World's Fairs showed millions of people what the "World of Tomorrow" would look like: Dad flies the family car to work while Mom activates the self-cleaning house and picks out a three-course meal (in the form of a pill) for dinner. In 1958 the TV show *Disneyland* predicted that by 2008 American highways would carry driverless cars, glow in the dark, and automatically melt ice and snow. Atomic reactors would burn tunnels through mountains in mere minutes. And of course, *The Jetsons* predicted that every future family would have a sassy robot maid.

In 1966 a futurist named Edward Cornish (who would later predict the 9/11 attacks) brought H. G. Wells's dream of a future-oriented think tank to life when he founded the World Future Society. Billing itself as "a neutral clearinghouse of ideas on the future," the WFS's mission was (and still is) "to enable thinkers, political personalities, scientists, and lay-people to share an informed, serious dialogue on what the future will be like." The society amassed thousands of members from all over the world. Senior members advised U.S. presidents (last one to be advised by the WFS: Ronald Reagan) and other world leaders, and the most famous futurists became household names. Here are a few:

• **R. Buckminster Fuller:** Fuller was an American philosopher, futurist, and architect (he invented the geodesic dome). After personal tragedy and alcoholism nearly led him to suicide in the 1920s, Fuller dedicated his life to helping mankind through scientific advancement. His boldest prediction: by the year 2000, the means would be available to end poverty and world hunger. That prediction was actually proven true in 1977 when a study conducted by the National Academy of Sciences concluded: "If there is the political will in this country and abroad…it should be possible to overcome the worst aspects of widespread hunger and malnutrition within one generation." So why does poverty still exist? Because another one of Fuller's predictions *didn't* come true: "By 2000

Gag me! There are, on average, 7 food-hygiene errors in every 30-minute cooking show.

politics will simply fade away. We will not see any political parties."

• **Isaac Asimov:** One of the 20th century's most respected science-fiction writers, Asimov predicted in 1942 that as robotic technology advanced, so would the need to govern robots with a set of rules. In his short story "Runaround" (which became the basis for his novel *I, Robot*), Asimov outlined "Three Laws of Robotics":

> **1.** A robot may not injure a human being or, through inaction, allow a human being to come to harm.
>
> **2.** A robot must obey the orders given to it by human beings, except where such orders would conflict with the First Law.
>
> **3.** A robot must protect its own existence as long as such protection does not conflict with the First or Second Laws.

Although robots haven't yet become as commonplace as Asimov predicted, in the early 2000s, Japan's Ministry of Economy, Trade, and Industry has urged manufacturers to include the Three Laws in the safety requirements for all of that country's robots.

• **Arthur C. Clarke:** Another science-minded writer, Clarke predicted in the 1950s that there would be a global library by 2005 (it's currently being created on the Internet) as well as a global network of satellites to transmit hundreds of TV channels and provide navigation "so no one is ever lost again." He also envisioned a "personal transceiver, so small and compact that every man carries one."

• **Alvin Toffler:** In his 1970 book, *Future Shock*, Toffler warned that by the year 2000, technological advances will come so fast that they'll actually make people's lives more complex, not easier, leading to what he called *information overload*:

> Millions of ordinary, psychologically normal people will face an abrupt collision with the future, which will lead to distorted perceptions of reality, confusion, and fatigue.

Has Toffler's prediction come true? Just consider all the passwords, remote controls, onboard navigation systems, and Internet search engines you have to deal with today. As the rate of technological advances continues to increase, predicting the future will become even more difficult. "Much like walking through a dark forest with a flashlight," says futurist Thomas Frey, "the future only comes into focus a short distance in front of us." That distance seems shorter than ever. And the field of futures studies finds itself at a crossroads.

For Part III, transport yourself to page 337.

A tossed coin is slightly more likely to land the way it was facing when flipped.

BATHROOM NEWS

*Here are a few fascinating bits of bathroom trivia
that we've flushed out from around the world.*

IS THIS SEAT OCCUPIED?

For some people, the worst fear they might face when they go to the bathroom in the morning is discovering they're out of toilet paper. Not so for a woman in Framingham, Massachusetts: one morning in February 2014, she discovered a man she did not know passed out drunk on her toilet. The horrified woman called 911 and police rushed to the apartment, where they woke up the man and promptly hauled him off to jail. A charge of burglary was reduced to trespassing when the man, 28-year-old Tyrease Slaughter, explained that he'd meant to go to the apartment of a relative who lived nearby, but in his drunken state he didn't realize he'd entered the wrong apartment. He didn't get off scot-free, though: passing out on the wrong pot got him 10 days in the can.

READY, AIM...

In August 2013, the government of Shenzhen in China's Guangdong province instituted a new 100-yuan fine ($16) for anyone who abuses the city's public restrooms by smoking, littering, spitting on the floors, or writing messages on the walls. Reasonable enough, and had the city officials left it at that, the new regulation probably wouldn't have attracted any attention. But they also decided to fine people who "aim poorly." "It's totally impossible to enforce it, unless you place someone in the restroom to monitor those who use it, which is weird and unacceptable," Zhu Rui, a visiting tourist, told the *China Daily* newspaper when informed of the new regulation.

THE TOILET THAT KNEW TOO MUCH

The Conference on Human Factors in Computing (CHI) is an annual meeting of scientists and researchers who are interested in new methods of human-computer interaction. When the meeting was held at the Toronto Convention Center in April 2014, attendees who visited the restrooms were greeted by the following sign,

---

It takes 20 people two days to install the Academy Awards' red carpet.

posted by a company called Quantified Toilets: "Behaviour at these toilets is being recorded for analysis. Access your live data at *quantifiedtoilets.com*." On its website, the company explained that it was analyzing "deposits" to determine the user's gender, blood-alcohol level, and evidence of illegal drug use. The analysis also indicated whether they were pregnant or had a sexually transmitted disease. "We use this data to streamline cleaning-crew schedules, inform municipalities of the usage of resources, and help buildings and cities plan for healthier and happier citizens," said the company.

So is toilet deposit analysis coming to a restroom near you? Not from Quantified Toilets: e-mails sent to the company in response to the signs received the following automated reply: "As you may have worked out, Quantified Toilets is a fake company, and all data reported were equally fake. It was a thought experiment at CHI, designed to engender thought and discussion regarding the issues of surveillance, data, and privacy."

COPPER CAPER

In February 2011, two thieves broke into an electrical substation in the city of Leicester in central England to steal copper wire. While one of the thieves, 50-year-old Richard Boyce, drained oil from a transformer to gain access to the wire inside, his accomplice, 36-year-old Michael Harper, decided to pee on it. You've heard the expression "never pee on an electric fence"? It also applies to 22,000-volt transformers, as Harper discovered when the one he was peeing on short-circuited and exploded, shocking him, igniting the oil, and knocking out power to more than 2,000 nearby homes and businesses. Both men suffered serious injuries in the explosion but lived to tell the tale…in court, where they were tried for burglary and for causing $42,000 worth of damage to the substation. Boyce was sentenced to four years for his role in the crime; Harper got one year. "It seems to me you have suffered a punishment already," Judge Michael Stephens said to Harper as he handed down the lighter sentence.

*   *   *

"The early bird may get the worm, but the
second mouse gets the cheese."

—Uncle John

The first casualty of war is the truth: When Spain declared war on the US on April 24, 1898…

THE MACGUFFIN

We're so fascinated by Hollywood culture that we sometimes forget that part of what we love about a good movie isn't the stars—it's having our emotions manipulated, no matter how predictable the plot devices may be.

SPELLBOUND

Suspense films often revolve around a mysterious object or important information that is stolen or missing. Someone has it, and someone else desperately wants it. It can be an important letter, a treasure map, or a secret nuclear weapon that kick-starts the whole cinematic adventure. Legendary thriller director Alfred Hitchcock referred to this device as "the MacGuffin."

According to Hitchcock, the MacGuffin is really a "nothing." The object itself is meaningless to the audience. They don't care whether the MacGuffin is a diamond necklace or a stolen painting; they are spellbound by the actions of characters running for their lives or falling in love in the midst of all the suspense.

In Hitchcock's 1935 classic, *The 39 Steps*, the MacGuffin turns out to be secret plans for an airplane engine stored in the mind of a vaudeville performer named Mr. Memory. If the plans fall into the wrong hands, the fate of the world may lie in the balance. Does the audience worry about that? No, they worry about handsome Richard Hannay (played by Robert Donat), who is wrongly accused of murder and goes on the lam with a beautiful woman while trying to clear his name and stop a spy ring. The device worked so well that Hitchcock used a MacGuffin in almost all of his films after that. He felt his most meaningless, nonexistent MacGuffin—meaning his best—was the never-explained "government secrets" in the 1959 film *North by Northwest*.

STRANGERS ON A TRAIN

In a 1966 interview, Hitchcock told film director François Truffaut that the term comes from a Scottish story about two men on a train:

> One man says, "What's that package up there in the baggage rack?" And the other answers, "Oh, that's a MacGuffin." The first one asks, "What's a MacGuffin?" "Well," the other man says, "it's an apparatus for trapping lions in the Scottish Highlands." The first man says, "But there are no lions in the Scottish Highlands." And the other

one answers, "Well, then that's no MacGuffin!" So you see that a MacGuffin is actually nothing at all.

FRENZY

MacGuffins aren't restricted to Hitchcock films; other directors have used them, too. In *Pulp Fiction*, the MacGuffin is a mysterious suitcase—you never know what's in it, but it glows ominously. In *Mission Impossible III*, it's a mysterious rabbit's foot that is some kind of biohazard. We never really find out what Unobtanium is in *Avatar*, but worlds go to battle and two people fall in love because of it. Here are some more examples of MacGuffins:

***The Maltese Falcon* (1941).** In this tale of murder, mystery, and romance, everyone is after a jewel-encrusted gold statuette of a falcon from ancient Malta. That's the MacGuffin. (And they never find it.)

***Man of Steel* (2013).** Baby Superman is sent to Earth with the "Codex" (the MacGuffin). General Zod and the bad guys will do anything to get it, including obliterate Earth.

***Labyrinth* (1986).** Baby Toby (the MacGuffin) is taken into the Labyrinth by Goblin King Jareth. Toby's half-sister Sarah has 13 hours to find him or he will be lost forever.

***Transformers* (2007).** The MacGuffin is the Allspark, which gives unlimited power to any Transformer who possesses it. Both the Decepticons and the Autobots want it.

***Citizen Kane* (1941).** The MacGuffin is "Rosebud," the final word of newspaper tycoon Charles Foster Kane, muttered on his deathbed. A reporter spends the rest of the film trying to figure out its meaning.

***Monty Python and the Holy Grail* (1975).** The cup used by Jesus Christ at the Last Supper gives the movie its title, and it gives King Arthur, Sir Lancelot, and the other knights the reason for their quest. But they never find it.

***Raiders of the Lost Ark* (1981).** The Ark of the Covenant is the chest that is said to contain the tablets of the Ten Commandments. Though we see the Ark itself, we never get to see the stone tablets—and everyone who looks inside it…well, let's just say they live to regret it.

Gasp! Humans are the only mammal that can't breathe and swallow at the same time.

NOTABLE REFS

Conventional wisdom says that if you never notice the referees, then they're doing their job correctly. Here are some unusual sports officials who, for various reasons, got noticed.

ED HOCHULI (NFL)

Details: Hochuli is a bodybuilder and has a physique that rivals those of the players' under his watch. He has become a cult figure in football because his likeness appears in the *Madden NFL* video games—unheard of for a non-player. Hochuli is also known for being extremely detailed in his penalty explanations, but that makes sense—in the off-season, he's a trial lawyer in his hometown of Phoenix, Arizona.

JOEY CRAWFORD (NBA)

Details: Crawford is one of the league's most tenured refs, having officiated more than 2,000 games since 1977. He's just as famous for his temper. Example: In a 2007 Spurs–Mavericks game, Crawford ejected Tim Duncan, one of the most stoic players in NBA history, for laughing while sitting on the bench, which Crawford thought was directed toward him. After the game, Duncan reported that Crawford challenged him to a fight. Following an investigation, Crawford was suspended for the remainder of the season and the playoffs. Crawford returned the next year and disclosed that he was seeing a sports psychologist for his anger problems.

MILLS LANE (BOXING)

Details: The highly publicized 1997 rematch of Evander Holyfield and Mike Tyson ended with a bloody chunk of Holyfield's ear lying on the mat, bitten off by Tyson. But the other shock of the night was the rise of a boxing referee to stardom. After the ear-biting incident in the third round, referee Mills Lane (a last-minute replacement when the scheduled official couldn't make it) stopped the fight, and then gave a memorable post-fight interview, wearing a blood-stained shirt. The gruff, bald-headed Lane—a Nevada district court judge outside the ring—retired a year later to take advantage of his newfound fame. He starred in two TV shows: MTV's *Celebrity*

Death Match, where he voiced a claymation version of himself, and a daytime court show, *Judge Mills Lane*. Lane's popular catchphrase "Let's get it on!" featured prominently in both programs.

TIM DONAGHY (NBA)

Details: In 2007 Donaghy was indicted on two counts of conspiracy after an FBI investigation found that he schemed with organized crime associates to fix games during the 2005–06 and 2006–07 seasons to pay off tens of thousands of dollars in gambling debts. Donaghy pled guilty and admitted calling unnecessary fouls that allowed his partners to benefit on final scores. He was sentenced to 15 months in federal prison.

JOE WEST (MLB)

Details: "Cowboy" Joe West has had a Major League Baseball umpiring career that's spanned five commissioners. He also has a side gig as a recording artist. West has released two albums: *Blue Cowboy*, a traditional country music album about which the *Cleveland Plain Dealer* said, "Roy Roger's horse, Trigger, was probably better at carrying a tune than West," and *Diamond Dreams*, a spoken word album where West waxes poetically about his life "revolving around a little white ball."

*   *   *

WELCOME TO NUDGEMS

In England, it's traditional to name estates, or even houses, with colorful, evocative names. Here are some of the kookiest ones we found.

- Autumn Twigs
- Beatle Fields
- Handcuff House
- Beggars Roosts
- Lollybogs
- Mosquito Ghur
- Sherlock's Holme
- Yoo Hoo
- Poggles Wood
- Cowpat Cottage
- Cat in the Wall
- Pratty Flowers
- Motley Rot
- Ghost Nook
- Nudgems
- Stripper Stones
- Timelock
- Crumbledown

WONDER BRAS

When Mary Phelps Jacob invented the modern bra in 1913, she started a revolution in ladies' undergarments. Since then, bras' designs, the variety of styles made, and the materials they're made of have changed a lot ...and they're still changing. Here are a few unusual examples.

THE INVISIBRA

What It Is: A bra designed to be worn with backless dresses

Details: The straps and back of the InvisiBra may seem invisible, but that's because there aren't any—this "bra" consists of cups only. How does it stay in place? The inner surface of each cup is made of silicone "with a layer of skin-friendly adhesive, making it easy to apply and stay on securely all day and night," says Lavalia, the London company that makes InvisiBra. Though the cups go on individually, they do fasten to each other with a clasp, enhancing cleavage. They look like ordinary bra cups, so that if a revealing outfit turns out to be a little too revealing, the wearer's modesty is protected. InvisiBras are available in just about every style and color that regular bras come in.

THE BREAST TISSUE SCREENING BRA

What It Is: A bra that detects breast cancer

Details: This bra, which at last report was still undergoing clinical trials and awaiting approval from the FDA, is a diagnostic medical device that would be worn for 12 hours straight as part of a routine health exam. During this period, 16 sensors would carefully monitor the wearer's breast tissue for changes in temperature associated with the growth of abnormal blood vessels that feed cancerous tumors. Pattern-recognition software would also analyze the information for signs of abnormality. First Warning, the company that is bringing the bras to market, says that they can detect tumors before they're large enough to be detected by self-exams or mammograms. And unlike mammograms, which use radiation and thus pose some risk to the patient, the bras can be worn by women below the age at which the benefits of mammograms begin to outweigh the risks associated with them. The company expects to begin selling the bras in the next few years.

THE TRUE LOVE TESTER

What It Is: A smart bra that unclasps if—and only if—it detects the presence of "true love"

Details: Embedded in the left cup of the bra is a heart-rate sensor that communicates, via Bluetooth, to an app on the wearer's smartphone. The app then compares the pattern and speed of the heart rate to those typical of a variety of stimulating activities, including watching horror movies, eating spicy foods, flirting, jogging, and receiving unexpected gifts. If the app detects the cardiographic signature of true love, "the bra hook is unlocked automatically," says Ravijour, the Japanese lingerie company that invented the bra. At last report True Love Testers were not yet available for sale—the only way to get one was by winning it in a drawing after buying $50 worth of merchandise on the company's website.

THE MICROSOFT SMART BRA

What It Is: A bra that contains "physiological sensors" to track the wearer's emotional state in order to discourage "emotional eating"

Details: The experimental undergarment grew out of a University of Southampton (England) study called "Food and Mood: Just-in-time Support for Emotional Eating." The bras contained an electrocardiogram (EKG) electrode under the arm to measure the wearer's heart activity, electrodermal activity sensors (EDAs) to detect changes in perspiration, plus a gyroscope and accelerometer to sense the wearer's movements. Four female test subjects wore the bras for four days; the information the bras collected was sent to a special app on their smartphones.

During periods of increasing stress, the smartphone app alerted the wearer by flashing a warning message, followed by suggestions for breathing exercises and other activities to bring the stress level back down without the aid of comfort foods. As the researchers hoped, the bras were remarkably effective at discouraging emotional eating. So is Microsoft planning to bring such a product to market? Nope—"While we will continue our research, Microsoft has no plans to develop a bra with sensors," says a spokesperson. (Mood-sensing underpants for men were also considered, but were found to be less effective—the waistline EKG electrodes, said researchers, were "too far from the heart to be effective" at detecting changes in mood.)

Until about 4 billion years ago, Earth had no oxygen.

NATURE'S CLEANERS

*When it comes to cleaning up humanity's messes, who
knows best? Mother Nature, of course!*

PROBLEM: 1.3 million tons of U.S. soil contaminated with TNT and other explosive residue

CREATING THE MESS: TNT is widely used in U.S. military munitions. Places the Environmental Protection Agency (EPA) commonly finds TNT contamination include hand-grenade ranges, antitank rocket ranges, artillery ranges, bombing ranges, munitions testing sites, and open burn/open detonation sites. When munitions factories are torn down or military installations are closed, TNT contamination doesn't just miraculously disappear. It remains in the soil, seeping into the groundwater. In 2008 the California Office of Environmental Health listed TNT as a carcinogen. Other possible affects of exposure to TNT include rashes, anemia, and liver-function abnormalities. TNT can also poison plants grown on contaminated land. Removing and incinerating the dirt would clean it, but that method is prohibitively expensive.

MOTHER NATURE'S SOLUTION: Sheep! There are bacteria in sheep's stomachs that can digest plants that are poisonous to any other animal. In 2004, while experimenting to find out what else a sheep's belly bacteria could break down, a veterinary scientist at Oregon State University discovered that sheep could completely digest TNT. In fact, sheep stomachs break it down so completely that there's no trace of explosives in their poop.

To decontaminate soil, scientists propose planting grass on explosive-tainted land. The grass would absorb the TNT residue through its roots, the sheep would eat the grass, and the cycle would repeat until the soil was clean. The process is still in the testing stages, but it's estimated that 20 sheep could crop an acre of grass in a month and leave the acre 100 percent TNT-free within three years.

PROBLEM: Mountains of disposable diapers in landfills

CREATING THE MESS: According to the EPA, Americans dump about 20 billion disposable diapers in landfills...every single year. That's more than 3.5 million tons of waste annually.

Casablanca **was based on an unproduced play by a high school teacher and his wife.**

Disposable diapers are made from cellulose. To make diapers, cellulose is extracted from pine trees and turned into a soft pulp. That pulp draws in liquid and retains it inside the diaper. But when a diaper is discarded and goes to a landfill, it takes *500 years* to break down.

MOTHER NATURE'S SOLUTION: Oyster mushrooms! Oyster mushrooms live by consuming cellulose, especially from dead and dying trees. A University of Mexico researcher grew oyster mushrooms on diapers in a landfill and discovered that the mushrooms broke down 90 percent of a diaper within two months and completely consumed it in four months. Growing mushrooms on diapers was just an experiment, so mushrooms aren't being planted on dirty diapers everywhere just yet. But the researcher hopes that, given her discovery of how well oyster mushrooms work, they hold promise for cleaning up landfills in the future.

PROBLEM: Metal-contaminated water

CREATING THE MESS: Areas around lead and copper mines have high concentrations of metal. So do the areas around factories that use metal to manufacture goods. If metals aren't properly stored and cleaned up, rain can cause metal residue to run off into streams, rivers, and lakes. Drinking metal-contaminated water regularly can make people feel sick and give them headaches; in high concentrations, it causes organ damage and cancer. When a body of water is identified as polluted, it has to be cleaned up, but it's pricey.

MOTHER NATURE'S SOLUTION: Banana peels! A banana peel contains carboxylic acids that bind to the atoms in metal. Scientists at São Paulo State University in Brazil used this property to remove metal residue from water. They made a filter out of minced banana peels and then ran a sample of contaminated river water through it. The metal residue stuck to the carboxylic acids in the peel on contact, and when the filter was removed from the water, the metals came with it, leaving clean water behind.

Banana-peel filters are still being studied, but results show that they work as well as more expensive filters, and can also be reused up to 11 times before they lose their water-cleaning properties. They're still experimental, but eventually banana-peel filters might be used to clean water around the world.

Two ounces of botulism toxin is enough to kill the entire population of the U.S.

ODD BOOKS

We like to include a wide variety of topics in our Bathroom Readers.
Here are some real books that have a much more limited focus.

Reusing Old Graves

Goblinproofing One's
Chicken Coop

Developments in Dairy Cow Breed-
ing: New Opportunities
to Widen the Use of Straw

Managing a Dental Practice:
The Genghis Khan Way

Hand Grenade Throwing
as a College Sport

The Humanure Handbook:
A Guide to Composting
Human Manure

The Bright Side of Prison Life

Afterthoughts of a Worm Hunter

Down Home Gynecology

Last Chance at Love:
Terminal Romances

Teach Your Wife to Be a Widow

Increasing Laundry Output

Where Underpants Come From

How to Land a Top-Paying
Pierogi Makers Job

The Radiation Recipe Book

Castration: The Advantages
and the Disadvantages

The Beginner's Guide to
Sex in the Afterlife

My Cat's in Love, or How to
Survive Your Feline's Sex Life,
Pregnancy, and Kittening

The Madam as Entrepreneur:
Career Management in
House Prostitution

Collectible Spoons of the 3rd Reich

The Sunny Side of Bereavement

So Your Wife Came Home Speak-
ing in Tongues! So Did Mine!

Old Age: Its Cause and Prevention

The Golden Fountain: Complete
Guide to Urine Therapy

How Tea Cosies
Changed the World

Ghosts: Minnesota's
Unnatural Resource

Eating People Is Wrong

1st rock album in space: Pink Floyd's *Delicate Sound of Thunder* (Mir space station, 1988).

FIRST FAMILY FAITHS

Christianity is the predominant religion in the United States. About 75 percent of Americans identify themselves as Christians (and the number used to be higher), so although the U.S. Constitution sets no religious requirements, it's not surprising that nearly all presidents have been Christians. And yet, of the nation's roughly 1,500 Christian denominations, only 11 have been represented in the nation's highest office.

EPISCOPALIANS. Twelve presidents were members of this denomination: George Washington, Thomas Jefferson, James Madison, James Monroe, William Henry Harrison, John Tyler, Zachary Taylor, Franklin Pierce, Chester A. Arthur, Franklin Delano Roosevelt, Gerald R. Ford, and George H. W. Bush. Jefferson was actually a Deist, someone who accepts God but rejects the structure of organized religion, but he was raised as an Episcopalian.

PRESBYTERIANS. There have been seven Presbyterians in the White House: Andrew Jackson, James Buchanan, Grover Cleveland, Benjamin Harrison, Woodrow Wilson, Dwight D. Eisenhower, and Ronald Reagan.

UNAFFILIATED CHRISTIANS. Five presidents never formally adopted a specific denomination: Abraham Lincoln, Andrew Johnson, Ulysses S. Grant, Rutherford B. Hayes, and Barack Obama. "I am a Christian by choice," President Obama wrote, but he has never formally joined any specific religious organization.

UNITARIANS AND BAPTISTS. These two are tied with four each, but their records span two distinct periods of time. The second president, John Adams (1797–1801), was a Unitarian, as were John Quincy Adams, Millard Fillmore, and William Howard Taft. But Unitarians have not had a White House resident since 1913. Conversely, the first Baptist president was Warren G. Harding, who took office in 1921. He was followed by Harry S. Truman, Jimmy Carter, and Bill Clinton.

METHODISTS: Next in line are the Methodists, with three chief executives: James K. Polk, William McKinley, and George W. Bush. All were members of Methodist congregations, but differed politically. Polk was a Democrat; both McKinley and Bush were Republicans. The Episcopalians almost had a thirteenth White House occupant: George W. Bush, who was raised as an Episcopalian but became a Methodist when he married Laura Welsh, a 1968 graduate of Southern Methodist University in Dallas.

DUTCH REFORMED, DISCIPLES OF CHRIST, AND QUAKERS. These three churches have each had two of its members in the Oval Office. Martin van Buren and Theodore Roosevelt were Dutch Reformed. James Garfield and Lyndon Johnson were Disciples of Christ. There have been two Quakers, both from California: Herbert Hoover and Richard Nixon. (Hoover was born in Indiana but graduated from Stanford with a degree in geology and used California as the base for his mining operations.)

CONGREGATIONALISTS AND CATHOLICS. Calvin Coolidge is the only Congregationalist president. One Sunday, as he returned from services, a reporter asked him the subject of the sermon. "Sin," was his reply. How did the minister deliver the message? "He was agin' it." There are more Catholics in America than any other individual denomination, but there has been only one Catholic chief executive: John F. Kennedy.

Some major Christian denominations not represented (so far) in American presidential history: Lutheran, Pentecostal, Mormon, Jehovah's Witness, Assemblies of God, Eastern Orthodox, Seventh-Day Adventist, and Mennonite. Also not represented are the next two largest U.S. religions after Christianity: Judaism and Islam. Also not represented in the White House: nearly 20 percent of the U.S. population that identifies as atheist, agnostic, or "nothing in particular."

*   *   *

Disneyland's Original 14 Attractions (Opening Day, July 1955): Jungle Cruise, King Arthur's Carousel, Mark Twain Riverboat, Snow White's Scary Adventures, Mad Tea Party, Peter Pan's Flight, Casey Jr. Circus Train, Autopia, Fire Engine, Main Street Cinema, Mr. Toad's Wild Ride, Disneyland Railroad, Storybook Land Canal Boats, and The Golden Horseshoe Stage

Poll results: 84% of American office workers are against unisex bathrooms.

POD SLUGS & TWIG PIGS

The next time you're handcuffed in the back of a police car and you hear the Slick Sleeves refer to a Turkey Trooper or an M.S.T, you'll know what they're talking about.

Sergeant in the Trunk: A GPS device in the patrol car that lets your supervisor track your whereabouts (so he can check up on you)

Shark in the Tank: When your supervisor is present at a crime scene you're working (so he can check up on you)

Driving Miss Daisy: Being accompanied by your supervisor when you go out on patrol (so he can check up on you)

Critter Sitter or Pod Slug: A jail or prison guard (inmates often live in units called "pods")

Working the Bubble: An officer assigned to the front desk at the precinct house (it's protected by bulletproof glass)

Smoke Eater/Hose Dragger/Basement Saver: A firefighter (the house burns down but the hole in the ground survives)

Evidence Eradication Team: Firefighters who show up at a crime scene

New Boot: A rookie

Doughnut Commando: A young officer's term for older (and flabbier) colleagues

Slick Sleeve: A long-serving officer who's never been promoted (no stripes on their sleeves)

R.O.D. (Retired On Duty): An officer who doesn't do his or her share of the work (also called a "mattress back")

M.S.T. (Morale Suppression Team): Superiors who make an officer's job more difficult than it already is

Turkey Trooper/Fish Cop/Minnow Mountie/Moose Marshal/Trout Scout: A fish and wildlife officer

Meadow Marshall/Rabbit Ranger/Twig Pig/Smokey the Pig: A park ranger

Muppet: "Most Useless Police Person Ever Trained"

Kiddie Cop: A police officer assigned to a school

The conducting gel used in electric chair executions was called Electro-Crème™.

Barneys or Town Clowns: Small-town police

Choir Practice: A social gathering of officers at the end of a work shift

Breakfast Club: Choir practice for the graveyard shift

Zebra: An unpopular sergeant or supervisor (a zebra is an "ass with stripes")

Puddle Pirates: The U.S. Coast Guard

Ticket Cricket: A highway patrol officer

Feebs or First Bunch of Idiots: FBI agents

Comma Cop: A supervisor who spends more time checking paperwork for errors than he spends in the field

Puzzle Palace: Police headquarters

Holster Hugger or Badge Bunny: A police groupie

Scarlet Fever: A badge bunny attracted to the red uniforms of the Royal Canadian Mounted Police

Rubber Gun Squad: Officers who are under investigation and assigned to special duty (that doesn't require a firearm)

Nastygram: A written reprimand

*　　　*　　　*

MUSTACHE QUOTES FROM JOHN OATES

John Oates is one-half of the popular rock duo, Hall & Oates. From 1976–1990, they scored 16 top-ten hits. Almost as famous as the music: Oates' mustache.

"A good mustache makes a man for many reasons."

"Having a mustache and never smiling became a permanent component of my persona through the quaintly self-important decade of the '70s."

"I couldn't wait to grow a mustache. I stopped shaving my upper lip the day I graduated from high school."

"My mustache has become this weird iconic representation of a certain era."

"The mustache represented the old John. I didn't want to be that guy anymore, so I shaved it off. It was ritualistic in a way."

In medieval times, the average person met about 100 people in a lifetime.

UNUSUAL CHEESES

We all know there's only one true cheese—the bright orange molten goo
they squirt onto nachos at convenience stores and movie theaters. Well,
you might be surprised to learn that there are actually hundreds of
different kinds of cheese in the world—some experts say there are
thousands—and some of them have pretty interesting stories
behind them. Here are a few of our favorites. (And in käse
you actually havarti heard of these cheeses, feel brie
to gorgonzola to another article in the book.)

FLOWER OF RAJYA

This cheese was developed in 2001 cheesemaker Jonathan White of Westchester County, New York, with the help of Tibetan nomads high in the Himalayas. White went to live with these nomadic yak herders (who live much as they have for thousands of years, grazing their yaks at altitudes as high as 13,000 feet) as part of an economic aid program, to help the wandering farmers develop a cheese they could produce for export. They have used yak milk, which has a seven percent fat content—twice that of cow's milk—to produce butter and yogurtlike products for millennia, but they had no tradition of making cheese. So White helped them develop a yak-milk cheesemaking process.

First the milk is heated in large copper vats—over a fire fueled by burning yak dung. Then enzymes are added, causing the mixture to curdle and coagulate. (This is a normal part of almost all cheesemaking.) The liquid is drained off, and cheese is molded into ten-pound wheels about 18 inches in diameter. The wheels are then dry-cured for two months to a year in one of the region's red-salt mines. Result: a semifirm, dense, fairly dry cheese with, according to White, a flavor that carries hints of wild grasses and wildflowers—and leather and wood. (He says it's really good with wines and ciders.) White named the cheese *Rajya Metok*, meaning "Flower of Rajya," Rajya being the name of a nearby village.

The yak-milk cheese wheels are wrapped in scarves, packed in bamboo crates, and shipped to Beijing for sale. (You can find this cheese—occasionally—in specialty food shops in the United States. Cost: about $20 a pound.)

CARAVANE

This cheese is made by the Tiviski dairy, which is located just outside Nouakchott, capital city of the west African nation of Mauritania. Founded in 1989 by a British woman named Nancy Abeiderrhamane, Tiviski isn't just any dairy; they make products from camel's milk, which they buy from the region's nomadic camel herders. Camel's milk, it turns out, is very nutritious—it has about three times as much vitamin C as cow's milk, and about ten times the iron content—but it's also notoriously difficult to make into cheese. It doesn't curdle easily the way cow's or goat's milk does because it lacks certain proteins found in those other milks. But in the 1990s, Abeiderrhamane, with help from scientists funded by the United Nations, came up with a process through which they were able to turn camel's milk into cheese. (The secret ingredient was apparently calcium phosphate—just in case you're wondering.) Result: an off-white, soft, gooey cheese with a white mold crust, much like camembert. *Caravane*, pronounced "caravan" (as in camel caravan), is not widely available in the U.S., but like the yak cheese described above, you can sometimes find it in specialty shops. Cost: about $30 a pound. (It's sometimes marketed under its nickname—"Camelbert.")

PULE

Pule (pronounced poo-LAY) means "foal" in Serbo-Croatian, and it's the name of a cheese made from the milk of a herd of endangered Balkan donkeys—about 130 of them, at last count—that live on a farm in a nature preserve about 50 miles west of the Serbian capital of Belgrade. The jennies (female donkeys) are hand-milked three times a day, and it doesn't add up to much; these donkeys produce only about five or six gallons of milk per year. (The average American dairy cow produces about eight gallons *per day*.) The cheese is processed in tiny vats the size of small buckets, and it's smoked after processing. The result is a moist, crumbly white cheese that is described as having a flavor like smoked cheddar, but much more robust. (According to British food writer Charles Campion, it has a "fusty-musty flavor.") Pule cheese is, of course, hard to find, but if you do, get ready for sticker shock: it costs around 1,000 euros per kilogram—or about $600 per pound. It is the most expensive, and probably the rarest, cheese in the world.

...on his lips. He removed them himself with a razor blade.

Bonus fact: The idea to make cheese from the milk of those endangered donkeys came in 2011 from farm manager Slobodan Simic, who wanted to raise public awareness about the donkeys and the wetlands they call home. It worked—especially when newspapers around the world reported in 2012 that Serbian-born tennis star Novak Djokovic had arranged to buy the entire world's supply of pule cheese for his chain of high-end restaurants. That, it turned out, was a hoax. But for a little while, it made pule one of the world's most famous cheeses.

MILBENKÄSE

Unlike flower of Rayja, caravane, or pule, which are modern cheeses, *milbenkäse* has been around a while: it's been made in Germany since the Middle Ages. The process by which it's made begins with *quark*—sour milk which has been allowed to coagulate until it has a consistency of ricotta cheese. (Quark is a popular bread spread and cooking ingredient in Germany.) The quark is flavored with salt and caraway seeds, shaped into lemon-sized balls or short cylinders, and then allowed to dry. The quark balls are then buried in a tan-colored granular substance within suitcase-sized wooden boxes and left to age for months. What's that granular substance? It's a mixture of rye flour and millions of tiny *Tyrophagus casei* bugs, also known as "cheese mites." As the mites eat the flour (the flour's in the mix so that the mites won't eat the cheese), they poop, and that poop contains enzymes that interact with the quark, causing it to ferment. It will ripen into a dense yellow cheese if the quark pieces are left in the mite box for three months, or a dark red cheese if it's left in the box for a year. The flavor is said to be very strong and very sour—with a lemony aftertaste. Today milbenkäse is made only in the village of Würchwitz, in the central German state of Saxony-Anhalt. Cost: about $60 a pound.

Bonus fact: When you buy it, it's still covered in mites and mite poop. You're supposed to eat that along with the cheese.

*   *   *

"When I get a little money, I buy books; if any is left, I buy food and clothes."

—**Desiderius Erasmus**

MAN'S ENEMY, THE TREE

Considering how many trees have been chopped down through the ages, it stands to reason that the trees are going to get a little payback once in a while.

TREE VS. THE LAW

Late one night in May 2014, Officer Jeremy Veach of the Centerville, Iowa, Police Department observed Candice Duffey driving without headlights. He pulled her over, and as he stood next to her car writing her a ticket, a 30-foot oak tree suddenly fell onto the road, striking Veach and smashing the front of Duffey's car. "I heard a couple of cracks and a very loud pop. In hindsight, I had time to think, 'Holy cow, a tree is falling,'" Veach told CNN. The blow knocked the police officer to the ground, but he suffered only scrapes and bruises, and a cut on his elbow that required three stitches. Although Duffey was unhurt, her car was totaled. The good news: she got out of the traffic citation. "You know," said Veach, "everyone asks police officers how you get out of a ticket. If a tree falls on you, you're probably going to get off."

TREE VS. THE INTERNET

In June 2013, a tree fell near the Lehigh River in eastern Pennsylvania. As it went down, it fell onto an overhead optical cable line and pulled it onto train tracks…just in time for an oncoming train to run over it and sever the cable in two places. Result: more than 8,000 customers lost their Internet, cable TV, and telephone service. It took a team of 20 repairmen three days to splice the 2,000 individual strands of optical fiber back together and restore service to the people who'd lost it.

TREE VS. LUMBERJACK

In 1984 Forthman Murff, 74, made the mistake of heading into the forest near his home in Gattman, Mississippi, to chop down some trees. An experienced lumberjack, he had taken down thousands of trees over the years, but this time his luck ran out. He'd just finished sawing through the trunk of a tree, and as it fell, it knocked a dead limb off an adjacent tree. The limb struck Murff on the shoulder, knocking him into a ditch. As the first tree fell, it pulled down a second tree that fell on Murff's leg, breaking it, crushing his foot,

---

Research shows that if you touch an item in a store, you're more likely to buy it.

and pushing him throat-first onto his still-running chainsaw. The saw cut so deep into his neck that, according to one account, "the only structures keeping his head attached to his body were the spine, carotid arteries, and the meat of the back of his neck."

The injury should have killed Murff…but it didn't. He threw the chainsaw to one side, stood up, and hobbled 150 feet on his one unbroken leg to his pickup truck, then drove himself the half-mile to his neighbor's house for help. "When I got to my neighbor's house, he was standing right there, so I jumped into his truck," Murff told an interviewer. The neighbor drove him to the nearest hospital, 17 miles away. When doctors saw the extent of his injuries, they packed him into an ambulance and sent him to a trauma center 30 miles away in Tupelo, Mississippi. He arrived there about an hour after the accident, but still made a full recovery. Murff lived another 19 years, and never chopped down another tree. Years after the accident he told a reporter that the three loves of his life were "Jesus, music," and, despite everything, "chainsaws."

TREE VS. CAR (AND NOT JUST ANY CAR)

The Toyota 2000GT, manufactured from 1967 to 1970, was Japan's first luxury sports car. Only 351 were produced, including two convertibles they made for Sean Connery to drive in the 1967 James Bond film *You Only Live Twice*. In top condition, they sell for more than $1 million and are highly sought after by car collectors… and, it appears, at least one tree. In June 2014, a 2000GT was being driven in Toyama Prefecture, west of Tokyo, when a 100-foot-tall beech tree fell to Earth just as the car was passing by. The tree struck and all but flattened the car, but somehow the driver escaped with only minor cuts and bruises. Any other car would have been loaded onto the back of a truck and hauled off to the nearest wrecking yard, but not this one. The owner plans to (somehow) restore the mangled piece of automotive history to its former glory.

TREE VS. MOURNER

In May 2014, Tony Calderon, 49, of East Los Angeles, California, was standing out in his yard waiting for a ride to his uncle's funeral when the crown of a palm tree in the next-door-neighbor's yard suddenly snapped off and fell on him, crushing him under its 2,000-pound weight. He died instantly.

CALCULATOR RIDDLES

World-famous puzzle constructor Patrick Merrell sent us these. If you still have an old-school calculator around, give 'em a try. (Answers on page 540.)

I NSTRUCTIONS: To solve each riddle, solve the math problem using a calculator…then turn the calculator upside down and read the answer.

Riddle #1
What are filled by
emptying refrigerators?
(*Calculator hint:* 2,658,869 x 2)

Riddle #2
What appears twice in a week
but only once in a year?
(*Calculator hint:* 1,755 ÷ 585)

Riddle #3
What needs to be broken
to fix what's inside?
(*Calculator hint:*
75,123,771 + 2,222,222)

Riddle #4
What can you have
in your pockets even
when they're empty?
(*Calculator hint:* 6,713 x 8)

Riddle #5
What can make you
two inches taller, but
only if you add a foot?
(*Calculator hint:*
36,672,457 x 2)

Riddle #6
What is a short order
you might give a bad cook?
(*Calculator hint:* 19.8 ÷ 22)

Riddle #7
What company is responsible
for over a billion windows
being open every day?
(*Calculator hint:*
257,797 + 121,212)

Riddle #8
What does a happy
gardener do?
(*Calculator hint:*
19,019 x 16)

Riddle #9
What can a goose walk
on that a turkey can't?
(*Calculator hint:*
10,415,001 x 9)

Riddle #10
What do you call
bears with no ears?
(*Calculator hint:* 352 ÷ 44)

Eew! Researchers found 15 different kinds of bacteria on doctors' pens.

GOING MY WAY

More examples of people who earned their fifteen minutes of fame not by how they lived their lives, but by how they left this world.

Deceased: Steve Marsh, 51, an engineer with the Ford Motor Company in England

Details: Marsh may have made his living at Ford, but his heart was with BMW—he was such a big fan of the cars that his family and friends called him "BMW Steve."

Going His Way: When Marsh, who had heart problems, died in his sleep in 2009, rather than settle for an ordinary headstone, his family ordered a gravestone monument shaped like a BMW M3 convertible. Carved from a single piece of solid black granite, the headstone sits atop the granite slab that covers Marsh's grave. It's as big as a go-kart, weighs about a ton, and cost £50,000 (over $75,000), more than most real BMWs. It looks remarkably like the genuine article, complete with headlights, taillights, a dashboard with gauges, a steering wheel, a vanity license plate that reads "STEVE 1," and BMW logos on the hood, trunk, and rims. There's a space between the front and rear seats for mourners to leave flowers.

Marsh's "car-cophagus" is a gaudy addition to London's Manor Park Cemetery, but the locals (some of them, anyway) are getting used to it. "It's definitely not my taste," Rene Dryden told the *Daily Mail* newspaper in 2010. "When I walked past it the other day, though, I have to admit that it did make me smile."

Deceased: Harry Ziarnik, of Madeira Beach, Florida

Details: Ziarnik was a fan of the 1988 film *Rocket Gibraltar*, starring Burt Lancaster. In the film, Lancaster's character asks for—and gets—a "Viking funeral." His grandkids put his body in an old rowboat, push it out to sea, and shoot it with flaming arrows to set it on fire. Ziarnik probably never thought he'd actually get it, but he told his family that he'd like a Viking funeral, too.

Going His Way: Believe it or not, when Ziarnik passed away at the age of 62 in 1996, his daughter Kathy figured out a way to honor

---

Carmageddon: In the 20th century, 5 times as many Americans died in traffic accidents as in wars.

his wishes…sort of. She had her father cremated and put the ashes in a radio-controlled model boat. Then she took the boat to the beach, set it in the surf, lit it on fire, and used the radio controller to send it out to sea. "It was a positive, beautiful remembrance," she told the *Tampa Tribune*. "We lit the boat, and dolphins came. My dad would have loved it." (But was the mini-Viking funeral even legal? Maybe…or maybe not: "I tried to get permission," Kathy told reporters, "but no one could give me an answer.")

Deceased: Wally Amendola, a coffee-loving Canadian trucker
Details: Amendola always bought his coffee (two creams, no sugar) at the drive-up window of the local Tim Hortons, the nation's largest doughnut chain. It was a nice part of his day.
Going His Way: Before he died in 1996, Amendola told his wife, Carol, that he wanted to go to his reward dressed in his favorite jeans, blue shirt, and cowboy boots. And he wanted to stop for coffee on the way. He told Carol to be sure that his funeral procession stopped by the drive-up window for one last cup of joe—to go.

"I argued with him," Carol told the *Toronto Star* in 1998. "I said, 'What are they going to do with the coffee after they buy it?'" But she eventually came around. So did Tim Hortons: they hosted the wake and even let Carol pass Wally's coffee through the drive-up window to the guy driving the hearse.

Deceased: Donald Fieldhouse, a retired English scrap dealer
Details: Fieldhouse began working in his father's junk business in Sheffield, England, at age 14 and stayed there until he retired. He joked that he and his father were like *Steptoe and Son*, the BBC sitcom characters that inspired the 1970s American sitcom *Sanford and Son*.
Going His Way: Before he died in 2013 at the age of 85, Fieldhouse told his son Darren that he wanted "a traditional scrap man's funeral." In the old days that would have meant using a scrap dealer's horse and cart in place of a hearse. But the old days are long gone, so Darren got his friend, scrap dealer James Hartley, to haul Fieldhouse to the funeral in the back of a "skip lorry"—a garbage truck. "We had to make some modifications," Hartley told Sheffield's *The Star* newspaper, "but it was easier than using a hearse because two people on the back of the skip lorry were able to slide the coffin straight into the pallbearers' hands."

The average office cubicle is half the size of the average jail cell.

THE WORLD'S LEAST EXPENSIVE...

If cheap golf and stamps are important to you, you may need to move.

BEER. In Guangzhou, China, the average price for half a liter of beer is 2.25 yuan. That works out to just 36 cents a glass.

HEALTH CARE. Turkey spends the equivalent of $906 per capita on health care annually, the lowest among industrialized nations.

BIG MAC. McDonald's signature sandwich runs 94 rupees in India. That's a mere $1.54. Only thing: it's a mostly Hindu country and cows are sacred, so it's called a Maharaja Mac and it's made from chicken.

PARKING. Quito, Ecuador, is a well-developed modern city, but it doesn't have the same high cost of living as other major world cities. Case in point: to park at the airport costs just $5...a day.

ELECTRICITY. Per kilowatt hour, China has the cheapest electricity, at 17 cents.

POSTAGE STAMPS. A standard stamp, enough to mail a letter, costs 4 taka in Bangladesh—roughly a nickel.

GASOLINE. Government subsidies keep the cost down in Venezuela: a gallon of gas costs the equivalent of 5 cents.

COLD PILLS. Local drug-makers around the world sell knockoff versions of famous medicines with the same active ingredients. In India, a box of phony Dayquil costs less than a dollar.

iPHONE. A 32-gig iPhone5 costs $299 in the United States. That may sound like a lot (and it is), but that makes the U.S. the cheapest place in the world to get one.

GREENS FEES. To play a round of golf at one of the many golf courses in Jakarta, Indonesia, will cost you about 75,000 rupiah on average—a paltry $6.

COFFEE. India wins again. A grande latte at a Starbucks in New Delhi costs the equivalent of $2.80.

83% of American office workers say their bathroom at home is cleaner than the one at work.

THE WORLD'S MOST EXPENSIVE...

The next time you complain about rising costs, think of these.

BEER. In Norway's bars, the average price for a pint of beer is 68 kroner, or about $11.50. In the city of Alta, it's higher—the equivalent of $12.50.

HEALTH CARE. The United States spends $8,509 per capita on health care each year. That's the highest among industrialized nations.

BIG MAC. McDonald's signature sandwich runs 42 krona in Norway. That's almost $7.80.

PARKING. To leave your car in central London can cost you £42 a day on average—about $70. London is also the home of the world's most expensive airport parking: at Heathrow, it costs £12 ($19) per hour.

GASOLINE. A gallon of gas in Turkey costs the equivalent of a whopping $9.98.

ELECTRICITY. Per kilowatt hour, Denmark has the most expensive electricity, at 41 cents—more than three times what it costs in the U.S.

POSTAGE STAMPS. A standard first-class stamp, enough to mail a letter, costs 9.5 kroner in Norway, roughly $1.67.

COLD PILLS. Price-gouging Westerners who work in the country's oil industry is a way of life in Gabon. Case in point: a box of over-the-counter cold medicine costs about $17.

iPHONE. A 32-gig iPhone5 costs $299 in the United States. In Brazil, a 32-gig iPhone5—which isn't guaranteed to work on many of Brazil's cellular service networks—costs 2,699 real. That's more than $1,200.

GREENS FEES. To play a round of golf at Las Vegas's Shadow Creek course, it'll cost you $500. (However, that includes a limo ride to and from the course and the use of a caddie.)

COFFEE. Norway wins again. A grande latte at a Starbucks in Oslo costs the equivalent of $9.83. (In New York, it's a mere $4.30, on average.)

Big mouth: Before he wrote *Jaws*, Peter Benchley was a speechwriter for Pres. Lyndon Johnson.

WEIRD TWIN NEWS

These stories are so odd you'll want to read them twice.

DOUBLE BIRTHDAYS. Twins might not mind having to share their birthday with their closest sibling (or maybe they do mind), but it's not an issue for Tampa, Florida, twins Marcello and Stephano Velasco. They were born on separate days, in separate years, and even in separate decades. How's that possible? Marcello was born just a few minutes before midnight on December 31, 2009. Moments later, just past midnight on January 1, 2010, his brother Stephano was born.

DOUBLE LABOR. Heather Richardson and Sarah Fidler—twin sisters from Northumberland, England—told each other the same big news on the same day in mid-2013: "I'm pregnant." On February 13, 2014, Richardson gave birth…and then so did Fidler. (Neither gave births to twins, though.) Odds of twins giving birth on the same day: 400,000 to 1.

DOUBLE, DOUBLE, EVERYWHERE. On the west side of Havana, Cuba, is a small neighborhood known as 68 A-Street. Of the 70 homes and 224 people that live in the two-block area, there are an astounding 12 sets of twins. That's about one set per 20 people—four times the average rate. There are twin babies, twin children, twin teens, even twins in their 60s. Researchers are perplexed. None of the families have used fertility treatments, nor are the families related to each other. Even weirder: a few years ago, a pair of twins moved out of 68 A-Street. A few weeks later, a family from Spain moved in…with their twins.

DOUBLE TROUBLE. A man and a woman (names withheld in media reports) met in England in the early 2000s and felt a strong connection. They bonded over the fact that both had been adopted as infants. The couple married, and later helped each other track down their birth parents…who turned out to be the same parents. The married couple were fraternal twins, who had been separated at birth and raised by different families. In 2008 a British judge annulled the marriage.

LUCKY FINDS

*Ever stumble upon something valuable or get something back
you lost decades ago? It's an incredible feeling. Here's the
latest installment of one of the BRI's regular features.*

GOOD CAR-MA

The Find: A man's wedding ring

Where It Was Found: Under a car seat

The Story: When a Sacramento, California, man named Steve
Callahan misplaced his cell phone in June 2012, his wife, Shannon,
looked inside the couple's 2004 Pontiac Grand Am to see if it was
there. It wasn't—but as Shannon reached around beneath the front
seat, she felt something metal. "It was hooked to the bottom of
where the seat goes back and forth. It was wedged in there pretty
good, so I reached in there again and moved the seat forward and
back and found a wedding ring," she told the *El Paso Times*.

The Grand Am was a used car that the Callahans bought in
California. A sticker in the trunk indicated that the car had been
purchased new in El Paso, Texas. With that information, the
Callahans were able to get the names of the previous owners, Steve
and Darlene King, from the Texas DMV. But the Kings had moved
away and left no forwarding address. The Callahans contacted
the *El Paso Times*, which ran a story on the wedding ring that was
picked up by the Associated Press. From there it was printed in the
Callahans' local paper, the *Sacramento Bee*, which tracked the Kings
to Auburn, California, just 50 miles from where the Callahans
lived. Steve King had died a year earlier, but his widow, Darlene,
was relieved to get his ring back. "I told Steve it probably went down
the drain or something. We thought it was a lost cause," she said.

BOWLED OVER

The Find: A pretty ceramic bowl

Where It Was Found: At a garage sale in New York State

The Story: A New York family, not identified in press reports, paid
$3.00 for the bowl in 2007. They displayed it on the mantelpiece
of their home, and it received so many compliments over the
years that they decided to have it appraised by Sotheby's. Only

---

Individual income tax accounts for about 50% of the federal government's budget.

then did they learn that it was more than a thousand years old, and had been made in China during the Northern Song Dynasty (A.D. 960–1127). Sotheby's predicted the $3.00 bowl would fetch between $200,000 and $300,000 at auction, but when it went under the hammer in March 2013, it sold for more than $2.2 million.

CANNED GOODS

The Find: Some old coins

Where They Were Found: In cans, buried in a backyard in California

The Story: In February 2013, a couple living somewhere in California's Gold Country and identified only as "John and Mary" were walking their dog on their property, as they had hundreds of times before. This time, however, they noticed the edge of a rusty can poking out of the ground near a spot they called Saddle Ridge. The can looked as if it had been there a long time, and when the couple dug it up, they learned just how long: inside the can were American gold coins dating from 1847 to 1894, but none newer than that. Eight cans in all were buried at the spot; together they contained nearly 1,500 gold coins with a face value of $27,000. That's just the face value—the rarest coin in the hoard was appraised at $1 million, and the combined value of the rest was more than $9 million, making the "Saddle Ridge Hoard," as it's called, the most valuable buried treasure in American history.

So how did the coins end up buried in the couple's backyard? One theory is that they were put there by the Wild West stagecoach bandit Black Bart. The fact that about a third of the coins are in mint condition also makes it possible that they were actually stolen from the mint before they entered circulation, perhaps in an inside job. But the U.S. government isn't having any of it. "There's nothing connecting these coins to any theft from our mint—nothing," says Adam Stump, a spokesperson for the U.S. Mint. That's a good thing for the couple that found the coins, because when no theft could be proven and no legitimate owner came forward to claim the coins, they got to keep them (or at least the ones they didn't have to sell to pay nearly $5 million in state and federal income taxes.) Some of the coins were put up for sale online; prices ranged from $3,250 for a single coin to $2,750,000 for the "14 Finest Coins with Original Hoard Can."

In 18th-century Paris, street vendors sold baths, carrying tubs and water into private homes.

TRY, TRY AGAIN

The Find: An unsigned landscape painting of a scene with oak trees and bushes in the foreground, with a wheat field and the ruins of a monastery on a hill in the background

Where It Was Found: In an attic in Norway

The Story: For years the owner of the painting, who was not named in press reports, suspected it was the work of the Dutch painter Vincent van Gogh, though "experts" assured him it was a fake. The man put the painting in his attic, but from time to time he'd take it down and try to have it authenticated. In 1991 the man took the painting to the Van Gogh Museum in Amsterdam. There, too, experts assured him it was not the genuine article, based partially on the fact that the painting was unsigned. But even they admitted that it *looked* like a Van Gogh. When the man brought it back to the museum in 2011, they decided to take a more serious look. Specialists spent two years investigating the possibility, comparing the chemical makeup of the paint with other Van Gogh paintings (the paints were identical) and X-raying the picture to see if the canvas matched other Van Gogh canvases of the period (it did).

Researchers also found a reference to the painting in a letter that Van Gogh wrote to his brother, Theo, in July 1888, in which he describes the painting in detail. He also remarks that the effort "was well below what I'd wished to do," which is probably why he never signed it. This and other evidence finally led the museum to conclude in September 2013 that the painting was indeed a lost Van Gogh. Titled *Sunset at Montmajour*, it is the first full-size example of the artist's work to have been discovered since 1928. If the owner ever decides to part with it, it will likely sell for a bundle: the most recent sale of a Van Gogh was *Portrait of Dr. Gachet*, which sold in 1990 for $82.5 million, the equivalent of $151 million today.

*   *   *

WITH OR WITHOUT YOU

"Thank you for submitting your demo tape. We have listened with careful consideration, but feel it is not suitable for us at present. We wish you luck with your future career."

—**1979 rejection letter from RSO Records to Paul Hewson, later known as Bono, about his band…U2**

Electric eels are not true eels. They're members of the carp family.

THE WRONG STUFF

You'd think that anyone smart enough to be an astronaut would also be smart enough not to get themselves thrown off a space mission, right? Think again.

Astronaut: Robert L. "Hoot" Gibson

NASA Résumé: Gibson commanded four space shuttle missions and served on the crew of a fifth (1984–1995).

Grounded! NASA required astronauts assigned to upcoming shuttle flights to refrain from any high-risk recreational activities. Gibson violated the rule in July 1990 when he raced his stunt plane in a Texas air show and was involved in a mid-air collision that killed another pilot. Accident investigators faulted the other pilot for the crash, but NASA still suspended Gibson from shuttle flights for a year, which cost him the command of a 1992 mission.

Astronaut: David M. Walker

NASA Résumé: Between 1984 and 1995, Walker commanded three shuttle missions and served on the crew of a fourth.

Grounded! In 1989 Walker was piloting a NASA jet when he came within 100 feet of colliding with a Pan Am airliner. For this and other aviation infractions, he was grounded for 60 days and replaced as the commander of a March 1991 shuttle mission.

Astronaut: Mark C. Lee

NASA Résumé: Lee was a crew member on four shuttle flights between 1989 and 1997.

Grounded! Why specifically did Lee lose his spot on a 2000 shuttle mission to the International Space Station? Neither he nor NASA will say, but according to news reports, he was pulled after "a breakdown of communication" with several of his superiors.

Note: The incident wasn't Lee's first run-in with NASA brass. In 1992 he and fellow crew member Nancy Jan Davis secretly got married before a space mission. NASA won't assign married astronauts to the same shuttle crews, so the couple didn't tell the space agency about their marriage until it was too late to replace them. (If history's first wedded couple in space consummated the marriage while in orbit, they aren't talking.)

JEAN SEBERG:
SMEARED BY THE FBI

*Think the government is out to get you? It turns out that
sometimes they really are. (Especially you, Kevin.)*

THE STAR

In the late 1960s, Jean Seberg was one of the most sought-after film actresses in the world. The blonde-haired, blue-eyed beauty from Marshalltown, Iowa, had made her debut as a 18-year-old in 1957, in the title role in Otto Preminger's *Saint Joan* (she had gotten the role by winning a nationwide talent search with 18,000 other contestants). In the years that followed, she'd starred in a number of critical and box-office hits in both Hollywood and Europe. They included *The Mouse That Roared*, with Peter Sellers in 1959; Jean-Luc Godard's groundbreaking "French New Wave" film *Breathless* in 1960; and the Hollywood musical *Paint Your Wagon*, with Lee Marvin and Clint Eastwood, in 1969. Seberg started off the 1970s with a bang by starring alongside Burt Lancaster and Dean Martin in the year's second-highest-grossing film—and the one that started the "disaster film" genre—*Airport*.

Then everything began to fall apart.

THE STORY

On May 19, 1970, Hollywood gossip columnist Joyce Haber ran an item in her *Los Angeles Times* column about an unnamed actress. It said she was pregnant, and rumor had it that the father wasn't the actress's husband—the father was a prominent member of the radical civil rights group, the Black Panthers. The story mentioned no names, but Haber dropped enough hints to make it clear she was talking about Seberg.

Seberg and her husband, French diplomat and novelist Romain Gary, had been married since 1962. They had a son together, but at the time the Haber column was published, they were in the process of divorcing...and Seberg was pregnant.

A white woman having a child with a black man was a powerful cultural taboo in most of the United States in the late 1960s. In

---

fact, it was still illegal for interracial couples to marry in several states. (It didn't become fully legal in the U.S. until 1967.) Because the white woman in this scenario was a Hollywood star, the story became a scandal—and more than 200 newspapers carried Haber's column. Seberg and Gary mostly ignored it…at first. Then in August 1970, just three months after Haber's piece, *Newsweek*, one of the country's most trusted news magazines, ran the story. They named Seberg as the actress, Gary as the husband who'd been cheated on, and Black Panther leader Ray Hewitt as the father of the baby. And they didn't run it as a rumor—they reported it as fact.

THE DAMAGES

The day the story appeared, Seberg went into premature labor at her Paris apartment, and later that day gave birth to a girl. The baby died two days later. Seberg and Gary blamed the baby's death on the *Newsweek* story: Gary told reporters that Seberg had read the story, had become distraught, and a few hours later had gone into labor. At the infant's funeral, Seberg insisted that the casket be open—to prove that the baby was white and that the story was a lie. The couple sued *Newsweek* for libel and defamation, and the magazine was ordered to pay $10,800.

But the damage had been done.

Seberg made just one more Hollywood film, perhaps because studio executives feared the "controversy" had damaged her box-office appeal. In 1972 she married again, to American film director Dennis Berry; made several small-budget European films, the last in 1976; separated from Berry sometime after that; and in 1978 started a relationship with an Algerian man named Ahmed Hasni. By all accounts, throughout this period, Seberg was becoming increasingly emotionally unstable.

THE TRAGEDY

On August 30, 1979, Seberg went missing in Paris. Hasni told police she had simply disappeared during the night. Ten days later, Seberg's decomposing body was found wrapped in a blanket in the backseat of her car, not far from her Paris apartment. She was 40 years old. An empty bottle of barbiturates was found beside her, along with a note, which Paris police said was addressed to her son, 17-year-old Alexandre Gary. It read, in part, "Forgive me. I can no longer live with my nerves." The death was ruled a "probable suicide" (Paris police said they could not conclusively rule out foul play). Romain Gary, who had remained close to Seberg after their divorce, said he believed that Seberg had killed herself, just as she had attempted to commit suicide every year, in late August— around the time of their daughter's death.

Six days after the discovery of Seberg's body, in response to a Freedom of Information Act request that had been filed earlier, the FBI released several classified documents about Seberg.

THE TRUTH

The documents showed that the FBI had fed Joyce Haber the false story about Seberg's pregnancy. An internal FBI memo said the story had been planted to "cause her [Seberg] embarrassment and serve to cheapen her image with the public." The smear campaign had been approved by FBI chief J. Edgar Hoover himself. Why? Because Seberg had donated money to the Black Panthers—a perfectly legal thing to do.

The smear was part of Hoover's notorious COINTELPRO operation, through which the FBI secretly—and often illegally—worked to undermine political dissent, especially targeting civil rights and antiwar groups, and celebrities like Seberg who supported them. The agency also admitted it had spied on Seberg from 1969 until 1972 and had even wiretapped her phone. (They had learned of Seberg's pregnancy long before the news became known to the public by listening in on her phone conversations.)

THE END

The FBI, to its credit, responded quickly, releasing the classified documents just days after Seberg's death, because by 1979 they were trying to distance themselves from the stains the Hoover era had left on the agency. FBI chief William Webster, who had taken over after Hoover's death in 1972, issued a public statement, saying they would no longer be taking part in such campaigns. "The days when the FBI used derogatory information to combat advocates of unpopular causes have long since passed," he said. "We are out of that business forever."

The statement did little to comfort the friends and family of Jean Seberg. Romain Gary held a press conference after the FBI's admission and bluntly stated that "Jean Seberg was destroyed by the FBI." Few could argue with him. To this day, the smearing of Jean Seberg remains one of the ugliest examples of the abuses of the FBI under J. Edgar Hoover.

AFTERWARD

• After the FBI admission about the planted story, the editor of the *Los Angeles Times*, Jim Bellows, expressed regret that he had not squashed Joyce Haber's gossip item. Haber, for her part, claimed she didn't know the story was false. She refused to name her source and took the secret to her grave in 1983.

• In 2002 Bellows finally admitted that he knew who Haber's source was: it was the paper's city editor, Bill Thomas, who later became editor-in-chief. Thomas, who had retired in 1989, admitted his role, saying he got the tip from another reporter—who'd told him the information came from the FBI. He said he passed the tip along because his source told him the FBI believed the story to be true. Thomas said he couldn't remember who the reporter was.

• In December 1980, fifteen months after Seberg's suicide, Romain Gary took his own life. His suicide note made pains to say it was not because of the death of Seberg but because he felt he could no longer write.

• The annual Jean Seberg International Film Festival has been held in Seberg's hometown of Marshalltown, Iowa, since 2011.

*   *   *

ORANGE YOU GLAD THEY'RE NOT GREEN?

California and Florida are both subject to cold spells in winter. That has an effect on the millions of oranges grown there: The cold causes the chlorophyll in the fruits' skins to break down and turn orange. Oranges grown in tropical climates, where it never gets cold enough for that breakdown to occur, are ripe when they're yellow, or even green. These oranges have been imported to the U.S., but sold poorly because green oranges appeared unripe to customers. Solution: Imported oranges are treated with ethylene gas, which causes the oranges to ripen and turn…orange.

IS *IDIOCRACY* COMING TRUE?

There's only one way to stop it—keep reading
Uncle John's Bathroom Reader!

BACKGROUND
Based on a 1951 short story by Cyril M. Kornbluth called "The Marching Morons," *Idiocracy* is a 2006 dystopian satire written and directed by Mike Judge. Initially, the movie was a box-office flop, but it has since achieved cult status and is seen by many as a cautionary tale about the dumbing down of society.

The plot: In 2005 an "average Joe" (Luke Wilson) is recruited by the U.S. Army to be frozen for one year. But he is forgotten. When he wakes up in the year 2505, America is on the brink of collapse. "With no natural predators to thin the herd," explains the narrator, "evolution began to simply reward those who reproduced the most and left the intelligent to become an endangered species." *Idiocracy*'s surviving humans have become so stupid, in fact, that Joe is now the smartest man alive. He's ordered by President Dwayne Elizondo Mountain Dew Herbert Camacho (Terry Crewes) to solve the nation's problems in one week or he will be "rehabilitated" in a gladiator-style monster-truck demolition derby.

Can Joe save himself, much less save the country? You'll have to watch the movie to find out. But to see the future that *Idiocracy* predicts, you only need to go shopping, watch TV, surf the Internet....

IN IDIOCRACY: The number-one TV show is *Ow My Balls!* It features a man getting hit in the groin...a lot.
IN REAL LIFE: In March 2012, the number-one app in Apple's iTunes Store was *Ow My Balls!*, a real game based on the fake show.

IN IDIOCRACY: Disoriented after waking up, Joe goes to the hospital. As Joe describes his symptoms, a dimwitted staffer stares at a screen full of big, colorful buttons. Each button has a simple graphic that represents a malady—a broken arm, a frowny face with a knife in its head, a baby dropping from between two legs, etc.

IN REAL LIFE: A popular new line of over-the-counter medicines comes in sparse packaging with labels in large type that read "Help! I have a headache," "Help! I can't sleep," "Help! I have an aching body," "Help! I'm nauseous," "Help! I have allergies," and "Help! I'm horny," and so on. Viewed side by side, the packages look eerily similar to *Idiocracy*'s medical screen.

IN *IDIOCRACY*: When Joe asks for some water, he gets laughed at. Water has been replaced by a sports drink called Brawndo.

IN REAL LIFE: In 2012 Gatorade released a video game called *Bolt!* To maintain his speed, sprinter Usain Bolt must keep drinking Gatorade. And he must avoid droplets of water because, according to Gatorade, "Water is the enemy of performance!" The app had two million downloads and has won numerous advertising awards.

IN *IDIOCRACY*: Joe gets laughed at for using "big words." He says, "Smart people used to be cool," and gets laughed at some more.

IN REAL LIFE: During a 2012 campaign rally, Senator Rick Santorum drew cheers when he said, "President Obama said he wants everybody in America to go to college. What a snob!"

IN *IDIOCRACY*: The world is overrun by garbage. Trash has piled up so high that it causes "the Great Garbage Avalanche of 2505."

IN REAL LIFE: In 2008 Reuters reported: "At least four people died and 20 were missing in a Guatemalan garbage dump when a mountain of trash collapsed on people foraging there."

IN *IDIOCRACY*: The taboo against profanity has all but vanished. Fast-food restaurant Carl's Jr.'s slogan is "F*ck you, I'm eating!"

IN REAL LIFE: In 2011 Frank's Red Hot Sauce ran a successful ad campaign with the slogan, "I put that sh*t on everything!"

IN *IDIOCRACY*: The number-one movie in America (and the winner of the 2505 Oscar for Best Screenplay) is called *Ass*. It is literally 90 minutes of a close-up of a butt.

IN REAL LIFE: In 2013 a Chilean band called Astro released a popular music video that consists of 2 minutes, 47 seconds of people's naked rear ends. That's it.

Consumers tend to perceive precise numbers ($329.95) as lower than round numbers ($300.00).

EUROPEAN COUNTRY NAME ORIGINS

Here's why some European countries are called what they're called.

BELGIUM. In an 1830 revolution, the southern, mostly Catholic and French-speaking provinces of the Netherlands seceded to create a new country. They named it Belgium, which derived from *Gallia Belgica*, the Roman name for the northernmost province of Gaul. Prior to the arrival of the Romans in 100 B.C., Gallia Belgica was the ancestral homeland to the *Belgae* ethnic group, from which many modern-day Belgians are descended.

THE NETHERLANDS. In the native Dutch language, the country is called *Nederland*, which translates to "low country." It is very low indeed—about 50 percent of the country's area sits no more than one meter (39.3 inches) above sea level, and more than 25 percent of the entire Dutch population lives at that elevation (or lack thereof).

FRANCE. France comes *Francia*—Latin for "the Franks' country." *Franks*, in turn, may come from the Germanic word *frankon*, which is the term for a weapon used by the people who lived there. The weapon is also known as a *francisca*, or a javelin or throwing axe.

GREECE. Greece's official name is the Hellenic Republic, or *Hellada*. That comes from Hellen, the legendary forefather of the ancient Greek tribes. The English name "Greece" comes from *Graecia*, the Latin word for the country, coined by Romans in the third century A.D.

SPAIN. Spain, or *España*, is short for *Hispania*, which is what the area was called by Romans. Some linguists believe that the word is a corruption of *I-shfania*, the Punic/Hebrew word for "island of the rabbits," or possibly a corruption of the Basque name *Ezpanna*, which means "edge." Both make sense: Spain sits on the far western side of Europe, or, as was commonly believed in antiquity, the edge of the world itself.

The beam of light from a laser pointer can travel more than a quarter mile.

NORWAY. The country's name comes from the Old Norse *nor veg*, meaning "the northward route," which it would have been for ancient nomadic tribes.

FINLAND. In Finnish, Finns call Finland *Suomi* (it literally translates to "Finnish"). That comes from a word in the early Baltic language (the root of the Finnish, Latvian, and Lithuanian languages). The word is *zeme*, which simply means "land."

POLAND. Poland consists mainly of large grassy expanses and low hills. The area came to be known in the local tribal languages as *Polanie*, which means "land of fields."

ENGLAND. In Old English, the country was called *Englaland*, which means "land of the Angles." The Angles were a Germanic tribe that ultimately settled in Britain in the Middle Ages, emigrating from the Angeln Peninsula on the Bay of Kiel, off what is now Denmark and Germany.

AUSTRIA. Today Bavaria is a state in southern Germany, but it was once an independent nation and a cultural and political powerhouse in central Europe. As such, it expanded to include other regions that are now countries or parts of other countries. One of those Bavarian-controlled areas is modern-day Austria. In A.D. 976 Austria was established as the easternmost outpost of the Bavarian realm. The German word for Austria, then and now, is *Österreich*, which translates to "eastern realm."

MALTA. "Land of milk and honey" is a poetic description of a paradise. Malta is literally that—at least the honey part. The tiny Mediterranean island nation is the only place in the world where the *Apis mellifera ruttneri* bee lives, and has long been a center of European honey production. When the ancient Greeks controlled the island, they called it *Melité*, which means "sweet as honey." Ancient Romans "Latinized" the Greek word into "Melita," and in time it became corrupted to "Malta."

*   *   *

"I think, therefore I'm single." —**Lizz Winstead**

Before *The Hunger Games*, Suzanne Collins wrote for the TV show *Wow! Wow! Wubbzy!*

PUBLIC ENEMY #1

If you've ever heard the phrase "public enemy number one,"
you may have wondered how it came to be. Here's how.

MAKING A LIST
In 1930 organized crime was terrorizing Chicago. Frank J. Loesch, chairman of the independent Chicago Crime Commission, wanted to shed light on the problem—to make both police and citizens aware of certain criminals and to help eradicate the menace. Loesch asked the CCC's director to draw up a list of the city's most notorious criminals—but not just fugitives from justice or crooks charged with one particular crime. Loesch wanted the "slippery" ones—bootleggers, "hoodlums, known murderers, murderers which you and I know but can't prove."

The list was about 100 names long. Loesch whittled it down to the 28 worst and branded them "Public Enemies," a term for criminals used by cops and politicians since ancient Rome. Loesch sent the list to every Chicago police precinct and to the media.

A few years later, the FBI adopted its own "public enemies" list. Unlike Loesch's list of undesirables to watch, the FBI's included only fugitives wanted for a particular crime, mostly bank robbers like John Dillinger, Baby Face Nelson, and Ma Barker. "Public Enemy Number One" soon became an FBI term, but here's Loesch's original list of the 28 "public enemies" from the Chicago criminal underworld, topped by Al Capone, the first Public Enemy #1:

Al "Scarface" Capone	"Polack Joe" Saltis	Frank McErlane
Ralph Capone	Myles O'Donnell	Vincent McErlane
"Bugs" Moran	Frankie Lake	William Niemoth
Frank Kline	Terry Drugan	Danny Stanton
"Machine Gun" Jack McGurn	Tony "Mops" Volpe	George "Red" Barker
Jack Guzik	James "Fur" Sammons	Jack Zuta
William "Klondike" O'Donnell	James Balcastro	William "Three Finger Jack" White
Joe Aiello	Rocco Fannelli	Leo Mongoven
Edward "Spike" O'Donnell	Lawrence "Dago" Mangano	Joseph "Peppy" Genaro
	Frank Diamond	

The Aztecs shaved with razors made of obsidian (volcanic glass).

IRONIC, ISN'T IT?

*There's nothing like a good dose of irony to put the
problems of everyday life into proper perspective.*

IRONY, M.D.

• In 2014 the U.S. Food and Drug Administration ordered a
recall of several homeopathic remedies being sold by a company
called Terra-Medica. Tests revealed that the remedies contained
trace amounts of penicillin (a natural byproduct of the fermentation
process). They were recalled because penicillin is "actual medicine,"
which is illegal for homeopathic remedies to contain.

• A recent study published by the National Cancer Institute warns
that people who wear sunscreen to protect them from skin cancer
are actually more prone to getting skin cancer. Reason: they stay
in the sun for longer periods of time, believing the sunscreen is
protecting them from skin cancer, unaware that sunscreen blocks
only some of the sun's harmful rays.

THOU SHALT NOT COMMIT IRONY

Frances Thomas, 33, of Spartanburg, Georgia, was caught shoplift-
ing items from a Walmart in 2014—including socks, cheese…and
a Bible. Had she made it home and read the book, she would have
learned that what she did was wrong.

WARNING: UNSAFE IRONY AHEAD

• In 2013 Russell Strickland of Cincinnati, Ohio, was badly
bruised when a cable pulling a car snapped loose and hit him in
the stomach. At the time, Strickland was setting up an "accident
reconstruction" event, in which participants study car collisions,
trying to identify ways to prevent accidents.

• Roger Wallace, 60, of Tucson, Arizona, was looking for a "safer
hobby" than drag racing, so he took up radio-controlled airplanes.
Not long after, he was flying a six-pound model plane when he
momentarily lost sight of it in the sun. Seconds later, the plane
slammed into his chest and killed him.

• Fifteen-year-old Andrew Owens was injured while walking to
school in Brandon, Florida, in 2013, when he stepped out into

---

The book *Bambi* was translated from German to English by Soviet spy Whittaker Chambers.

traffic and was struck by a car. The accident occurred on National Walk to School Day—in which parents are urged to "teach children to cross streets at marked crossings and always look left-right-left."

• Ron Huber, 59, was a former NASCAR driver who routinely topped speeds of 150 mph. He also flew fast planes, rode fast motorcycles, and liked to jet ski (fast). Huber was killed in 2004 after he fell on the pavement and hit his head. The accident occurred while he was riding a Segway scooter…at 5 mph.

GOVERNMENTAL IRONY

• On April 8, 2009, the New Hampshire House of Representatives debated a bill concerning transgender rights. April 8 also happens to be "Tartan Day," which celebrates Scottish heritage. That created an ironic predicament for the lawmakers who showed up to work wearing kilts…and then voted against a bill to outlaw discrimination against men who dress like women. (The bill did not become law.)

• In January 2014, Georgia governor Nathan Deal scheduled a ceremony in Atlanta to declare February 3–7 "Severe Weather Awareness" week. He had to cancel the ceremony, though, after an inch of snow and ice crippled the city for the entire week. (Critics accused the mayor of being "unprepared" for the severe weather.)

IRONY IN THE COURT

U.S. district judge Lucy Koh grew increasingly frustrated by the smartphone usage that kept interrupting her high-profile case. In addition to the onslaught of ringtones, crisscrossing Wi-Fi signals were disrupting a wireless network that was supposed to transmit real-time transcripts of the proceedings to her. At one point, she yelled at attorneys and audience members: "Phones off!" The case she was presiding over: a patent dispute between Apple and Samsung.

18-KARAT IRONY

British jeweler Theo Fennell sells a unique set of cuff links depicting the face of Indian spiritual leader Mahatma Gandhi, who once said, "It is health that is real wealth and not pieces of gold and silver." The cuff links are made of 18-karat gold. Price: $8,000.

"PEE" IS FOR PILOT

One odd fact of 21st-century aero-technology is that it's easier to make a fighter plane invisible to radar than it is to provide a toilet for the pilot, who cannot leave his or her seat during missions that can last 15 hours or more. Here are two devices created to address the problem.

ADVANCED MISSION EXTENDER DEVICE
Description: An "automated, noninvasive, in-flight, bladder relief system" for American fighter pilots
Background: In the bad old days, pilots had few choices. They could refrain from drinking liquids before a mission, but then they risked passing out from dehydration while pulling strong G-forces. Or they could "hold it" for hours on end, increasing the likelihood of a bladder infection. Then came UCDs (urine collection devices), or "piddle packs," plastic bags with a special urine-absorbing gel. But those required the pilots to take their hands off the controls long enough to unzip their fly (or flies, if they were wearing more than one kind of flight suit) and relieve themselves into the bag. Enter AMXDmax, the Advanced Mission Extender Device.
How It Works: The device, worn inside special underwear, looks like an athletic cup, except that it's connected by a hose to a battery-powered pump and a urine collection bag that fits in the pocket of the pilot's flight suit. "When the user begins to relieve his bladder, urine-detecting sensors activate the control unit pump, transferring the urine from the cup into the collection bag, keeping the user dry." The female version uses a device shaped like a sanitary pad that inflates in 30 seconds to create a watertight seal. (If the pilots have to go "number two," they're still out of luck.)

PZH-1 BRIEFS
Description: Extended mission underpants for Russian MiG fighter pilots
How They Work: "A special container has been attached to the groin of ordinary cotton undergarments. The container and a hose with an overflow valve are connected with the plane's onboard sewage disposal system, which, when the ejector, fed by hot air, is turned on, ensures that the urine is ejected overboard."

Vaseline retains its gooey consistency at temperatures as low as -40°F.

LET'S GET HYPOCRITICAL

*As these stories prove, sometimes it's wiser to trust
the message…and ignore the messenger.*

Do as I Say: McGruff the Crime Dog, created by an advertising agency in the 1980s, tells kids to "take a bite out of crime" by saying no to drugs and violence.
Not as I Do: In 2011 John Morales, an actor who played McGruff in the 1990s, was arrested in Galveston, Texas, after police raided his home and discovered "1,000 marijuana plants, 9,000 rounds of ammunition, and 27 weapons—including a grenade launcher." (The bad dog got 16 years in prison.)

Do as I Say: In 2004 Paris Hilton was a celebrity mouthpiece for the "Vote or Die" campaign, urging young people to vote.
Not as I Do: It was later revealed that Hilton herself wasn't even registered to vote. In fact, she admitted that she'd *never* voted.

Do as I Say: Fred Hiestand, general counsel of the Civil Justice Association of California, fights for tort reform by trying to make it harder for people to file "frivolous class action lawsuits that hurt small businesses."
Not as I Do: In 2009 Hiestand took his son out to eat and parked in a no-parking zone. His car was towed. Believing he should have received only a citation, Hiestand filed a class action suit against the city of Sacramento, the police chief, the cop who wrote the ticket…and the towing company that was ordered by police to tow the car. "Not all class action suits are bad," he said.

Do as I Say: State Senator Suzanne Williams (D-CO) pushed for a bill requiring children under eight be secured in safety seats.
Not as I Do: The day after Christmas in 2010, Williams was driving her family through Texas when she collided with an oncoming car. Her three-year-old grandson—who was not secured in a safety seat—was thrown from the vehicle and seriously injured. According to reports, Williams was observed retrieving the child and buckling him in his car seat as police arrived.

First arrest for a computer crime: Ian "Captain Zap" Murphy, who hacked AT&T in 1981.

Do as I Say: "There's no such thing as a free lunch!" said U.S. Representative Jack Kingston (R-GA) while opposing a federal school lunch program. He suggested that poor kids should have to clean the cafeteria before receiving taxpayer-funded lunches.

Not as I Do: A local news station investigated the congressman's own expenses and discovered that he had received nearly $4,200 worth of tax-payer funded meals since he took office.

Do as I Say: In 2012 U.S. Representative Charlie Rangel (D-NY) urged presidential candidate Mitt Romney to "come clean about the tax returns he's hiding from voters."

Not as I Do: Two years earlier, Rangel had to step down as chairman of the House Ways and Means Committee—which is responsible for drafting the nation's tax policies—after he was censured for "failing to pay income taxes and filing misleading financial statements."

Do as I Say: "Discrimination is horrible. It has no place in civilized society," said Kansas State Rep. Charles Macheers (R).

Not as I Do: Macheers made this statement while championing a bill that would make it legal for any "public and private employees the right to deny services, including unemployment benefits and foster care, to same-sex couples on the basis of religious freedom."

Do as I Say: Celebrity environmentalist Barbra Streisand urged the U.S. government to pass tougher laws in order to curb the effects of global warming. "I just hope one day soon the country will wake up and realize that we need to step up in a major way in order to avoid catastrophic demographic dislocation in the years ahead."

Not as I Do: In his book *Hollywood Hypocrites*, Jason Mattera notes that "Streisand…spends $22,000 a year watering her lawn and gardens, requests 120 bath-size towels upon arrival at production offices, and uses thirteen 53-foot semi trailers at her concerts."

Do as I Say: In 2014 England's Prince William, 31, called for a crackdown against the illegal wildlife trade in Africa. "I want my son to be able to experience the same Africa I did as a child."

Not as I Do: A week prior to making that statement, William hunted wild boars in Africa.

In one study, reminder signs in ladies' restrooms increased handwashing 36%. Men's rooms: 0%.

27 USES FOR ALOE

You've seen it as an ingredient on numerous creams, salves, and ointments, and with good reason—wellness experts call it one of the most versatile and healing plants on Earth. Is it? We don't know, but we thought it was worth including because of the variety of benefits attributed to aloe.

NATURE'S GOODNESS

Aloe vera is a *succulent*, the botanical term for certain "fleshy" plants that retain water in arid conditions. It's closest relatives are the lily and asparagus. The name comes from the Arabic word *alloeh* ("shining bitter substance") are the Latin *vera* ("true").

Humans have been cultivating and using aloe for mild, mostly topical, medicinal purposes for more than 5,000 years. The most useful part resides in the leaf of the aloe: a clear gel that's 99 percent water. All that moisture aids in soothing and rehydrating, but it's the other 1 percent that has the real power—more than 200 chemical components. Among them are vitamins (A, C, E, niacin, B_1, B_2, B_6, B_{12}), minerals (calcium, magnesium, zinc, iron, potassium, copper), and all eight essential amino acids. Result: Aloe is thought to be anti-inflammatory, anti-bacterial, and it helps the body repair itself.

Here are some of the many purported naturopathic uses for aloe vera.

IF YOU RUB IT ON YOUR SKIN, ALOE CAN...

- Shrink warts.
- Make blisters heal faster.
- Clear up rosacea.
- Remove makeup.
- Relieve the pain of sunburn.
- Soothe cooking burns.
- Make bug bites less itchy.
- Minimize tissue damage from frostbite (if applied quickly).
- Relieve rashes.

The word "paradise" comes from the Persian for "walled garden."

- Clear up acne.

- Smooth out uneven pigmentation and dark spots.

- Reduce skin discoloration from bruises.

- Clear up athlete's foot.

- Seal hair cuticles to tame frizzy hair and errant eyebrows.

- Be used as a shaving gel with less razor burn.

- Soothe post-shave redness (if you used something besides aloe to shave with).

- Be used to make a face mask. Mix with oats and a mild skin oil, leave on for 15 minutes, and wash off.

- Speed up hair growth. Massage aloe into the scalp, letting it sit for 30 minutes, and rinse.

- Reduce dandruff. Mix aloe vera juice with coconut milk and wheat germ oil, massage into scalp, and rinse.

IF YOU DRINK IT, ALOE CAN...

- Relieve redness and inflammation of eyes and ears.

- Alleviate symptoms associated with seasonal allergies. It's rich in helpful fatty acids such as campesterol, HCL cholesterol, and B-sitosterol.

- Reduce the amount of fat in the blood, and subsequently bad cholesterol levels, because of those same fatty acids.

- Reduce inflammation in joints.

- Help relieve constipation *and* diarrhea. Aloe is an *adaptogen*, meaning that it does whatever needs to be done in the digestive system. Aloe juice makes its way into the intestinal tract, where it can absorb toxins and take them with it when it leaves the body.

- Absorb and help eliminate intestinal worms.

- Promote gum and teeth health. Mix some in with toothpaste and brush as normal.

- Help relieve asthma symptoms. Boil aloe leaves in water and then breathe in the fumes.

A red blood cell will travel about 300 miles in its lifetime.

WORLD WAR WEIRD

Here are some interesting, odd—and creepy—World War I and World War II facts that you've probably never heard before.

The German navy ship *Wien* was sunk in 1918, during World War I. The Italian navy ship *Po* was sunk in 1941, during World War II. What's weird about that? It was the same ship. The sunken *Wien* was raised in 1921, repaired, and renamed by the Italians.

• Nearly 80 percent of all boys born in the Soviet Union in 1923 did not survive World War II.

• "Salon Kitty" was a high-end brothel in Berlin, frequented by German government officials and foreign diplomats in the 1930s. In 1940 it was taken over by the Nazis, fitted with secret microphones, and staffed by 20 prostitutes trained to elicit secrets from their clients. "Operation Kitty" spied on tens of thousands of men until the operation ceased in 1943.

• Penicillin, which only entered medical trial stages in the early 1940s, became so precious during World War II that it was regularly extracted from the urine of soldiers who had been treated with it—and reused.

• During World War I, the British executed 306 of their own soldiers for crimes such as desertion and cowardice. These included 25 Canadians, 22 Irishmen, and 5 New Zealanders. The French are believed to have executed more than 600. The Germans: 48. Americans: none.

• American radio stations were prohibited from doing popular "man in the street" interviews during World War II, for fear that an enemy agent might be interviewed and influence public opinion. Stations were also banned from mentioning weather conditions during broadcasts of baseball games, out of concern that enemies might be able to create national weather maps from the information.

• "Canary girls" was a term for women who worked in British artillery factories during World War I. They were so called because prolonged exposure to TNT causes skin to turn orangish-yellow.

World's biggest pile of poop: Deer Cave, Malaysia, where bats produce 5 tons of guano per night.

• During World War II, the Bicycle playing card company worked with American and British intelligence agencies to create "map decks" that were sent to Allied prisoners of war in German prison camps. Unbeknownst to the Germans, the decks contained special cards that, when soaked in water, revealed hidden maps of routes the POWs could use if they managed to escape.

• At 3:10 a.m. on June 7, 1917, British soldiers detonated 19 underground mines containing more than 900,000 pounds of explosives in a 19-second attack on German positions near the town of Messines, Belgium. The explosions were so loud they were heard in London—140 miles away, across the English Channel.

• In 1938 Yang Kyoungjong, an 18-year-old Korean, was drafted into the Japanese army to fight the Soviet Union. In 1939 he was captured by the Soviets, sent to a labor camp and, in 1942, was forced to fight in the Soviet army against the Germans. In 1943 he was captured by the Germans and forced to fight in the German army against the Allies, making him a veteran of three different armies a single war.

• Russia and Japan have still not signed a peace treaty officially ending their participation in World War II.

• Calvin Leon Graham enlisted in the U.S. Navy in 1942. Later that year he was awarded for heroism after being wounded while serving on the USS *South Dakota* in the Battle of Guadalcanal. A few months after that he was thrown in the brig for three months, and in May 1943 he was dishonorably discharged from the navy. Why? Because he lied about his age when he enlisted: he was just 12 years old. (He turned 13 in April 1943.) He was the youngest American to serve during World War II.

• In January 1943, Princess Juliana of the Netherlands—who lived in exile in Ottawa, Ontario, with her two daughters during World War II—gave birth to a third daughter at Ottawa Civic Hospital. At the request of the Dutch government, the Canadian government legally designated the hospital room "Dutch soil" to ensure the princess would be exclusively a Dutch citizen (and not also a Canadian citizen), a requirement for the new princess to remain in the Dutch royal line of succession. In thanks for its wartime kindness, the Dutch government still sends Canada 20,000 tulips every year.

FINE FEATHERED FRIENDS

You've heard the expression "an elephant never forgets"? It turns out that parrots have amazing memories as well.

PARROT: Spike, a green Amazon parrot owned by Jim and Lin Ryder in Kincardineshire, Scotland

BACKGROUND: Like many Amazon parrots, Spike was quite a talker, and learned to mimic Lin's voice and accent perfectly.

WHAT HAPPENED: When Lin died from breast cancer in 2002, her daily chats with Spike came to an end. Jim assumed that Spike would stop imitating his wife, and the bird did indeed fall silent in the days following Lin's death. But not for long. A few days later, Jim was walking through the house when he heard what he would have sworn was the voice of his wife calling to him, "Hello, Jim!" It was Spike. "Spike sounds exactly like her when he talks. If you close your eyes, she could be in the room with you," Jim told the *Daily Record* newspaper in 2003. He admits it was strange to hear his dead wife's voice at first, but once he got used to it, it actually helped him with the grieving process. "It is very comforting to hear Spike mimic her," he said. "She loved animals, and I'm sure she would be smiling now if she could see us talking together."

PARROT: Abigail, who lived through the London Blitz of World War II

BACKGROUND: In 2006 Abigail was over 70 years old and living in Great Britain's National Bird Sanctuary in Lincolnshire.

WHAT HAPPENED: The Blitz must have made quite an impression on Abigail, because she could still mimic the whistling and explosions of the bombs dropped on London 65 years earlier. Still, not all of Abigail's memories were bad: Though she outlived her owner—that's how she ended up at the sanctuary—she could still reproduce the sounds of daily life that she'd shared with him for decades: the creak of the staircase and a "Morning, Abigail!" as the man came down to begin his day, followed by the sound of running water and the man singing as he shaved. Abigail also mimicked the clinking sound of glass milk bottles being delivered to the front door. (It was probably one of the last places in the U.K. where visitors could hear the sound of long-gone milkmen making their rounds.)

PARROT: Paco, one of Abigail's neighbors at the National Bird Sanctuary

BACKGROUND: Like Abigail, Paco no longer lives with his owners (a married couple). If they were around to hear the details he was revealing about their stormy relationship, they'd probably wish he still did.

WHAT HAPPENED: Paco's cage was in the man's workshop, the place he went to calm down after arguments with his wife. It must have taken quite a while for the man to cool off because Paco picked up a lot of colorful expressions over the years and even learned to associate them with his owner's missus. When women matching her description—overweight, with red hair—visit him at the National Bird Sanctuary, he lets them have it, calling them "lard arse" (his favorite expression) and threatening, "I'll get you, you fat cow."

"People absolutely love it," the sanctuary's founder, Steve Nichols, wrote in an article in London's *Daily Mail* newspaper in 2006. "The other day I tried to whisk a group of old ladies from the local bridge team past him, but he called out, 'Oi, you fat old hags, get over here!' He swore like a trooper, putting on a real show, and they loved it…He never speaks to men that way."

PARROT: Charlie, a 50-year-old African Grey who lived at the National Bird Sanctuary with Abigail and Paco

BACKGROUND: Charlie was a frail old bird, and time soon came when Steve Nichols realized he was dying.

WHAT HAPPENED: "I was cradling him in my arms in the middle of the night, stroking his feathers and whispering to him as he went," Nichols wrote in the *Daily Mail*. Like most people, he had always assumed that parrots simply mimicked sounds in their environment without really understanding them or trying to communicate a particular meaning. That night Nichols changed his mind after Charlie "with his last ounce of strength turned his head to me and said in a crystal-clear voice: 'I love you. Thank you,' and died."

CATCH-11

Think it's easy coming up with a memorable title? Just look at what these classic books were almost called.

Working Title: *The Dead Un-Dead*
Final Title: *Dracula* (Bram Stoker)

Working Title: *Bugles Sang True*
Final Title: *Gone with the Wind* (Margaret Mitchell)

Working Title: *Twilight*
Final Title: *The Sound and the Fury* (William Faulkner)

Working Title: *Forks*
Final Title: *Twilight* (Stephenie Meyer)

Working Title: *Fiesta*
Final Title: *The Sun Also Rises* (Ernest Hemingway)

Working Title: *Catch-11*
Final Title: *Catch-22* (Joseph Heller)

Working Title: *War*
Final Title: *Paradise* (Toni Morrison)

Working Title: *Harry Potter and the Doomspell Tournament*
Final Title: *Harry Potter and the Goblet of Fire* (J. K. Rowling)

Working Title: *Beauty from Ashes*
Final Title: *Of Human Bondage* (W. Somerset Maugham)

Working Title: *All's Well That Ends Well*
Final Title: *War and Peace* (Leo Tolstoy)

Working Title: *The Last Man in Europe*
Final Title: *1984* (George Orwell)

Working Title: *The Jewboy*
Final Title: *Portnoy's Complaint* (Philip Roth)

Working Title: *The Kingdom by the Sea*
Final Title: *Lolita* (Vladimir Nabokov)

Working Title: *A Week with Willi Worm*
Final Title: *The Very Hungry Caterpillar* (Eric Carle)

Working Title: *They Don't Build Statues to Businessmen*
Final Title: *Valley of the Dolls* (Jacqueline Susann)

In 1959 the USSR launched *Luna 1* toward the Moon. It missed, and orbited the sun instead.

UNSETTLING SETTLEMENTS

Thinking of amassing some followers and starting your own town in a faraway place? You might want to first consider the ill-fated attempts by these founding fathers…whose lofty goals were squashed by the harsh realities of life.

THE SETTLEMENT: San Miguel de Guadalupe

THE STORY: In 1526 Lucas Vázquez de Ayllón set sail from Hispaniola with six ships of colonists, eager to establish a city in what is now South Carolina. Accompanying the expedition was Francisco Chicorana, a slave who was supposed to serve as guide and translator. Chicorana was a Native American who'd been captured in the Carolinas by Spanish slave hunters and sold to Ayllón. He told his master about the riches and wonders waiting back in his homeland: pearls and precious stones were abundant there, he said, the chief of his tribe was a giant, and the men of a nearby tribe had tails. He even told a story about tame deer that his tribesmen kept indoors and milked. Ayllón bought every fantastic word. He was so excited about the riches Chicorana described that he petitioned the king of Spain for permission to settle in the Carolinas and enticed 450 people to join him with the promise of fertile farmland.

THE END: Once the expedition reached the Carolina coast that July, the lead ship ran aground and destroyed most of the settlers' supplies. Chicorana, having reached the land of his birth, promptly escaped and was never seen again. Far from being fertile, the land was swamp, and it was July—too late in the season for planting. In September, Ayllón tried to move his people to Georgia, but it was a cold autumn, and their remaining supplies quickly ran out. Sickness killed many of the colonists, including Ayllón, and by November, the 150 surviving settlers boarded their ships and returned home.

THE SETTLEMENT: Fountaingrove

THE STORY: In 1875 a "religious mystic" named Thomas Lake Harris founded the Brotherhood of the New Life. He and his followers lived in a colony he named Fountaingrove, north of Santa Rosa, California. Harris had about 1,000 followers worldwide, but the population of Fountaingrove was only around 30. The Brotherhood's colonists ran a successful winery that produced 70,000 gallons of wine at its peak (1886). Harris, who called himself "Father," "Primate," and "King," convinced his followers that every person on Earth had a spiritual counterpart in the Celestial Sphere (his version of heaven). According to Harris, the ultimate goal of human life was to find that counterpart and, basically, have sex with him or her. Not surprisingly, rumors spread that Fountaingrove was simply a "free love" commune. Perhaps most scandalous of all, Harris taught that God was bisexual and Christ was the "second Eve-Adam."

THE END: Though the winery was successful, Harris's sexual theology was not—at least not outside of Fountaingrove. In 1891 a young reformer named Alzire Chevallier visited Fountaingrove. Scandalized by what she saw there, she gave lectures in San Francisco and Santa Rosa describing Harris as "a vampire," "a lecherous fiend," and the "greatest black magician" of his time. After the *San Francisco Chronicle* ran a series of unflattering articles about the Brotherhood, Harris, disgraced, left Fountaingrove and never went back. The property went to a follower named Kanawe Nagasawa, who managed the winery until his death in 1934. By that time, Nagasawa was the only brother left in the Brotherhood of the New Life, so Fountaingrove died with him.

THE SETTLEMENT: Nueva Germania

THE STORY: In 1886 fourteen German families chosen for their "racial purity" founded a town on 50,000 acres of jungle land in Paraguay. They were led by Bernhard Förster, founder of the intensely anti-Semitic German People's League, and his wife, Elisabeth, who wanted to establish "New Germany," a return to a pure, agricultural-based life. If all went as planned, Förster's intention was that the Aryans produced by New Germany would one day take over all of South America. He had chosen his settlers for their ethnicity, not their farming skills, which was a problem in a colony founded on the principles of an agrarian lifestyle. Once the settlers cleared the trees from the land, they discovered that most crops wouldn't grow.

THE END: Förster believed that vegetarianism was essential to keep their race pure, but that was difficult to achieve without crops, and the starving settlers soon abandoned their vegetarian principles. The wealthier colonists bought food from locals, creating resentment among those without funds. Tropical diseases and bad water made people sick, and tensions grew. Dejected, Förster left the colony, moved into a hotel in another town, went on a two-week drinking binge, and then killed himself with a deadly dose of strychnine. Following Förster's death, some colonists returned to Germany. Those who remained tried to retain their racial "purity" by marrying within the settlement, but gradually more and more married locals. Over time, the former racial "purists" completely interbred with their Paraguayan neighbors. Nueva Germania still exists (population: 4,300), and while around 70 families do have German ancestry, little German is spoken.

THE SETTLEMENT: Holy City

THE STORY: Holy City was nestled in California's Santa Cruz Mountains, on the only road between San Jose and Santa Cruz. It was founded by William "the Comforter" Riker in 1919 as a home for himself and the 30 followers of his quasi-religious sect.

Riker began his career as a "mentalist," with a palm- and mind-reading act. After being arrested for bigamy (he apparently didn't see *that* coming), he fled to Canada, where he developed his religious philosophy—the "Perfect Christian Divine Way," an odd-ball mix of abstention from alcohol and white supremacy. (Some of his manifestos were reportedly written in crayon.) On returning to the United States, Riker founded Holy City as a tourist attraction, hoping that visitors would come for the entertainment and stay to be converted. It had a restaurant, a service station, a zoo, and a lunar observatory but, strangely, no church. There was, however, an entertaining collection of billboards, such as one that said "See Us If You Are Contemplating Marriage, Suicide, or Crime!"

THE END: As long as Holy City was the only stop on the road, it prospered, and Riker made $100,000 a year from its attractions (close to $1.5 million today). Then in 1940, Highway 17 opened, bypassing the Old Santa Cruz Highway…and bypassing Holy City. Suddenly, tourists stopped coming. In 1959 Riker lost ownership of the land in an ill-conceived real-estate transaction, and most of the buildings were razed. Though Holy City was gone, Riker continued to live in his house among the ruins until his death in 1969. Today Riker's house and the old post office are the only buildings still standing.

First country to establish diplomatic relations with the United States: Morocco (1777).

TIME TO ADMIT YOU HAVE A PROBLEM?

If these real-life alcohol-related gadgets appeal to you, maybe it's time to get off the stuff.

Boozie Bear Flask. It looks like one of those plastic, bear-shaped containers of honey you buy at the supermarket, except that it's candy-apple red instead of honey-colored. (When you drink from it, it looks like you're sucking the brains out of a giant Gummi Bear.)

Belt-Buckle Flask. The buckle has two parts: a detachable three-ounce flask and the part that holds the flask while also keeping your pants from falling down.

Cocktail Master Electric Cocktail "Shaker." This shaker requires no shaking or pouring. Push one button to activate the motor that mixes the drinks; push the other one to squirt it into a glass. Takes all the strain out of mixing your own cocktails.

Cruzin' Cooler. A plastic ice chest that has been converted into an electric scooter with the addition of wheels, handlebars, and a seat. The motor and battery are inside the cooler, leaving enough room for 12 cans of beer plus ice. If a dozen cold ones aren't enough for you, fear not: the manufacturer also sells a "Coolagon" cooler trailer that you can tow behind your Cruzin' Cooler.

Putter Dispenser. It looks like an ordinary putter. Just place it in your golf bag with your other clubs, then whenever the urge strikes, push a button on the side of the putter to activate the battery-powered pump and dispense up to 52 ounces of wine or spirits.

Sneak Caps. Use this to smuggle booze onto cruise ships that make you buy their alcohol at huge markups. Crack open your factory-sealed bottled water, pour out the water, replace it with vodka or some other clear liquor, then reseal the bottle with a Sneak Cap. It will look like an unopened bottle of water, not booze, so you can sneak it aboard the ship.

Walter Koenig wore a toupee in his 1st season as Chekov on *Star Trek*. Later he had a comb over.

Shampbooze. Another way to sneak your hooch onto a cruise ship, Shampbooze is a 16-ounce flask disguised as a bottle of shampoo. Also available: a 16-ounce bottle of "conditioner."

Big Bobber Floating Beverage Cooler. It looks like one of those round, red-and-white bobber floats that you attach to your fishing line to tell if the fish are biting, only this one is large enough to hold a 12-pack and ice. Like a real bobber, the Big Bobber floats, so you don't have to risk life and limb getting to shore to grab another beer.

Sasquatch Flask. It looks like a conventional stainless-steel flask, except it's big enough for Bigfoot. It holds an entire gallon of spirits, just over five 750 ml bottles' worth. Also available: the Sasquatch Cocktail Shaker, large enough to let you mix ten margaritas at once.

Grill Sergeant Apron. Like a standard barbecue apron, only in camouflage colors and with enough pockets to hold barbecue tools, condiments, accessories…and six cans of beer.

Beer Belt. Like an ammo belt, but instead of having lots of small loops for bullets, its six loops are large enough to hold bottles of beer.

Wine Rack. A sports bra with a built-in plastic flask that "will turn your A cups into double Ds." Lets you sneak 20 shots of liquor or one bottle of wine into concerts and other venues where alcohol is not allowed.

Beer Belly. The same idea as the Wine Rack, but for men. It hides up to 64 shots of whiskey, or just over three bottles of wine, in a plastic flask that looks like a big fat beer belly when worn under your shirt.

BACtrack Breathalyzer. Turns your smartphone into a Breathalyzer, making it easy to post your results (and incriminating photos) to Facebook. "Want to see your BAC [blood alcohol content] from last week? Just view your history on the Tracking Graph."

Ultimate Wine Bottle Glass. It looks like a wineglass stuck on top of a wine bottle. "Finally," says the ad, "no more judgmental looks from friends when you refill." Holds an entire bottle's worth of wine.

Cane Flask. Hides ten ounces of alcohol, or a little over six shots of liquor, inside a hollowed-out walking stick. (If your gait becomes a little unsteady, you can lean on the cane.)

A hologram of a magnifying glass also functions as a magnifying glass.

NEIL'S SPIEL

Why has Neil deGrasse Tyson become one of the world's most famous scientists? For his ability to make science accessible…and fun.

"No one is dumb who is curious. The people who don't ask questions remain clueless throughout their lives."

"Know more today about the world than you knew yesterday and lessen the suffering of others. You'd be surprised how far that gets you."

"Curious that we spend more time congratulating people who have succeeded than encouraging people who have not."

"Physics is the only profession in which prophecy is not only accurate but routine."

"Based on comments from winning players, it's remarkable how much time God spends to help athletes defeat their opponents."

"The universe has many hilarious aspects. So I shouldn't get credit for a sense of humor if all I do is point this out."

"Don't know if it's good or bad that a Google search on *The Big Bang Theory* lists the sitcom before the origin of the universe."

"Knowing how to think empowers you far beyond those who know only what to think."

"The good thing about science is that it's true whether or not you believe in it."

"Some educators who are quick to say, 'These students just don't want to learn,' should instead be saying, 'I suck at my job.'"

"I know of no time in human history where ignorance was better than knowledge."

"Dinosaurs are extinct today because they lacked opposable thumbs and the brainpower to build a space program."

"Scientific inquiry shouldn't stop just because a reasonable explanation has apparently been found."

"A scientist is just a kid who never grew up."

"In five billion years, the Sun will expand and engulf our orbit as the charred ember that was once Earth vaporizes. Have a nice day."

The 1st moon landing touched down in the Sea of Tranquility. The 2nd: in the Ocean of Storms.

BEHOLD THE SLOTH

Their name is synonymous with laziness, but these small, cat-size animals of South and Central America's rain forests are really just misunderstood.

• Sloths look like rodents, but they're not—they're mammals in the order *Pilosa*, which is Latin for "hairy."

• Sloths spend only about four hours each day awake, and that's spent hanging upside down from tree limbs by their long, pointed claws. They can sleep, breed, fight predators, and even die hanging upside down.

• Sloths move very little because their typical diet of leaves and twigs provides so little energy or nutrition. It also gives them a very slow metabolism. (They poop only once a week, at most.)

• All that roughage is digested by a four-chambered stomach that can take a month to fully digest a meal.

• Only about 25 percent of a sloth's body weight is muscle (most mammals have about 50 percent), and they are unable to shiver in the cold.

• Their body temperature is the lowest and most variable among mammals, ranging from 74° to 92°F.

• The rate at which a sloth climbs a tree: six to eight feet…per minute.

• The sloths' closest relative is the anteater. Another relative: the extinct ground sloth, which fossils indicate were as large as elephants. They were hunted to extinction by primitive humans at the end of the last ice age, about 11,000 years ago.

• The sloth's lack of movement makes its fur habitable to insects, such as moths and beetles, that would fly away from more active animals. Sloth fur is also known to host incredibly slow-growing creatures…such as algae.

• The sloth lives a solitary life…until it's time to breed. In the dead of night, a female sloth will emit a bloodcurdling scream to alert the male sloths.

• Sloths are the only mammals with parted fur. It splits from the belly to the back, which allows rainwater to run off a sloth while it hangs upside down during a rainstorm—a common occurrence.

Why does spinach leave a chalky aftertaste? It contains large amounts of calcium oxalate.

FINDING PRIVATE GEORGE

*Here's the story of how two kids on the hunt for Real American Heroes
action figures ended up searching for the genuine article instead.*

MEDAL MISSION

Michael and Mauro Mazzariello are two kids who live in
Wallkill, New York. When they do well in school, their
dad, Michael Sr., rewards them by taking them to the Antique &
Collectibles Shop in nearby Newburgh, where they like to look for
G.I. Joe Real American Heroes action figures from the 1980s and
1990s. That's what they were doing on a trip to the store in April
2012, but on that visit, Michael, 11, and Mauro, 8, were more
interested in a collection of military medals on display.

Three of the medals—a Bronze Star, a Purple Heart, and a Good
Conduct Medal—had been awarded to the same man, someone
named Charles George. Bronze Stars are the fourth-highest military
service honor and are awarded for "heroic or meritorious achievement during military operations." Purple Hearts are awarded to
soldiers wounded or killed in action. Clearly, George was a war
hero…so what were his medals doing in an antique store? They
belonged with him, or if he was deceased, with his family.

The owner of the store, Terrance Berean, had no idea who
Charles George was or why the medals had left his possession.
Berean estimated they were worth about $800, but he offered to
let the boys have them for free, on one condition: they had to find
George and return the medals to him.

ON THE HUNT

Michael and Mauro accepted the challenge. They took the medals
home and started calling and e-mailing veterans' groups, elected
officials, the National Purple Heart Hall of Honor, and anyone
else they could think of that might know who Charles George was
or how to find him. They also searched online, and found one of
their biggest leads in a YouTube video of a 2007 Veterans Affairs
ceremony renaming the VA Medical Center in Asheville, North
Carolina, after George. One of the men in the video was a veteran
and American Legion officer named Warren Dupree. The boys

Of the 137 million items at the Smithsonian, about 35 million are insects.

tracked down an e-mail address for Dupree, and when they contacted him, he told them that Charles George was even more of a hero than they realized.

GIFT OF LIFE

Dupree explained that George was a Cherokee Indian who was a private first class in the U.S. Army during the Korean War. In November 1952, his infantry unit was fighting near Seoul when an enemy soldier threw a hand grenade into their trench. George, whose Cherokee name, *Tsali*, means "self-sacrifice," shouted a warning and then pushed a fellow soldier out of harm's way and threw himself on the grenade. George's body absorbed the full force of the blast, and he died a short time later. He was 20 years old.

Two years later, George was posthumously awarded America's highest military honor, the Congressional Medal of Honor, for gallantry above and beyond the call of duty. President Dwight D. Eisenhower invited George's parents to Washington, D.C., to receive the honor on their son's behalf, after which they traveled to New York for another ceremony. It's possible that the Bronze Star, Purple Heart, and Good Conduct Medal that ended up in Terrance Berean's antique shop in Newburgh, New York, were either lost or stolen during the trip. But no one knows for sure, and George's parents were no longer around to provide the answer.

COMING HOME

With Dupree's help, Michael and Mauro contacted the Eastern Band of the Cherokee tribe in North Carolina, and plans were made to return the medals to George's relatives in a special ceremony on November 12, 2012—Veterans Day. Years earlier, the family had donated George's Congressional Medal of Honor and a second Purple Heart to the Museum of the Cherokee Indian in Cherokee, North Carolina, and the family decided that's where the newly returned medals should go as well. Today, all of George's medals are on display there, thanks in large part to clever detective work by a couple of kids from Wallkill, New York.

"It was the most satisfying moment of my life, to finally give the medals back," Michael Mazzariello told reporters. "We can finally rest, knowing we did the right thing."

When tobacco ads were banned in 1971, TV lost about 20% of its advertising revenue.

WEIRD VIDEO GAMES

*Super Mario Bros. concerned a plumber who ate mushrooms and
flowers to power himself on a quest to defeat an evil dragon.
An odd premise, but nothing compared to these.*

Game: *Sneak'n Peek*
System: Atari (1982)
Details: Hide-and-seek is a simple childhood game that
requires no equipment and can be played almost anywhere. Video
games are fast-paced fantasy worlds of lasers, robots, and flashing
images. And then there's *Sneak'n Peek*—a video game version of
hide-and-seek. Only problem: the game's designers ignored the
infinite possibilities of video games. *Sneak'n Peek* offered only three
rooms and a yard to hide in, with 20 hiding spots overall. One of
those rooms has only one hiding place: under a bed.

Game: *Seaman*
System: Sega Dreamcast (2000)
Details: One of the bestselling video games of the 2000s was
Nintendogs, a Nintendo game in which players tended to the needs
of a virtual pet dog. *Seaman* is similar, except that instead of an
adorable pixelated pup, the player has to take care of a fish…with
a creepily realistic human face…and the voice of Leonard Nimoy.
The game begins with the fish-creature being birthed from a giant
squid, which it then brutally kills.

Game: *Metal Wolf Chaos*
System: Xbox (2004)
Details: This game was released only in Japan, but the gameplay
and character dialogue is in English because it takes place in a
futuristic, dystopian United States. The player controls President
Michael Wilson (supposedly related to Woodrow Wilson) as he
violently quells a military coup with the cooperation of a gigantic
robotic exoskeleton called Metal Wolf. Who's leading the coup
against the U.S.? In a not-too-subtle reference to George W. Bush's
vice president, Dick Cheney, the culprit is Vice President Richard
Hawk.

A "sonic hedgehog" is a type of brain molecule, named for the video game *Sonic the Hedgehog*.

Game: *Sensible Train-Spotting*

System: Amiga (1995)

Details: "Train spotting" has long been a popular activity among "railfans" (train buffs) in the United Kingdom. They sit out near a train station, wait for a train to pass, and then write down the make and model of the train. That's it. *Sensible Train-Spotting* recreates the riveting experience of sitting near a train station and waiting for a train to pass. In the game, the screen is blank for a few minutes… until a train slowly rolls across it. That's the entire game.

Game: *Playboy: The Mansion*

System: Xbox, Playstation 2 (2005)

Details: Many men have dreamed of being *Playboy* founder Hugh Hefner and living in the Playboy Mansion, and this game lets them live out that fantasy…but probably not the way they had in mind. This game focuses less on Hef's "social life" and more on making sharp business deals to expand his publishing empire.

Game: *Samurai Zombie Nation*

System: Nintendo Entertainment System (1990)

Details: In the distant, far-off year of 1999, an evil alien called "Darc Seed" crashes in Nevada, unleashing a virus that turns everyone in the United States into zombies…including the Statue of Liberty. It's up to the players to stop a sentient, stomping Lady Liberty, and they do so by controlling the dismembered head—in ghost form—of an ancient long-dead samurai warrior.

Game: *I Have No Mouth and I Must Scream*

System: PC (1995)

Details: An evil supercomputer called AM ignites a world war, ending with the last five survivors being tortured by AM for a century. The torture ends when the computer pits the five against each other in a series of mind games. That's the gameplay here—mostly logic puzzles. If solved incorrectly, the player is turned into a mouthless slug; if solved correctly, the player wins and escapes to the moon, where they rescue a secret colony of 750 humans who have survived the apocalypse. This game is based on Harlan Ellison's classic 1967 science-fiction story of the same name, making it one of the few video games ever based on literature.

The Inca Empire covered an area roughly twice the size of Texas.

SURVIVOR STORIES

*Why is the Reaper so grim? Because he was sure he'd
get these people…but somehow they escaped.*

IN THE BELLY OF THE BEAST

The dive team had already recovered four dead bodies from the wreck of a tugboat that sank off the coast of Nigeria in May 2014. As one of the divers was swimming through the ship, he saw a hand floating in the murky water. He reached for it…and the hand grabbed him back. "He's alive!" shouted the diver. "He's alive!" The alive man was the ship's cook, Harrison Okene, one of 13 crew members on the doomed boat. Seventy-two hours earlier, Okene, 29, awoke at 4:30 a.m. and was on his way to the bathroom when a massive ocean swell capsized the vessel. Everything went dark. Okene was caught in a torrent of water rushing down one of the tug's corridors and ended up in the bathroom of another cabin. The rising water stopped a few feet short of the ceiling (the ship was upside down, so it was actually the floor), leaving a small pocket of air for him to breathe. Wearing only boxer shorts, Okene shivered in the frigid water 100 feet below the surface. He could hear large predators in the corridors—most likely sharks—fighting over the bodies of the drowned crew. After a while, everything went silent. Minutes turned to hours, hours to days. A deeply religious man, Okene passed the time reciting psalms and thinking of his family. His only sustenance: a bottle of Coke. When the dive team finally found him three days later, he was dazed and weak but in surprisingly good health. "Good job, my friend," said one of the rescuers. "You are a survivor."

TERROR AT 12,000 FEET

Nine skydivers. Two pilots. One collision. Those ingredients should have led to catastrophe—but, incredibly, everyone survived. The two Cessnas were flying in close formation over Superior, Wisconsin, in 2013 when the trailing plane slammed into the lead plane, breaking the wings off the lead plane and sending a huge fireball into the sky. When the accident occurred, most of the skydivers were on the wing struts of the planes preparing to jump. Some were knocked unconscious, but their chutes opened and

The Eiffel Tower was almost demolished in 1909. What saved it? Its potential use as a radio tower.

they landed safely. The others were able to jump and landed safely. The two skydivers still inside the trailing plane quickly jumped out. They landed safely. The lead pilot was trapped in the wingless aircraft as it spun out of control. Fortunately, he was wearing a parachute, and the spin slowed down enough for him to jump out. He landed safely. The trailing plane sustained damage to a wing and a propeller, but the pilot was able to regain control and land the plane safely. According to survivor Mike Robinson, who was on his 937th jump, the collision wasn't even the scariest part: "The wings were falling slower than we were—one on fire, one not. We were very concerned that we'd get hit by them when we opened our parachutes." No one was injured.

GETTING ON TRACK
Andrew Faithful, 26, of Blaxland, New South Wales, Australia, was driving home from work one night in 2014 when he went into diabetic shock caused by low blood sugar. He blacked out—and his sedan sideswiped a parked car, crashed through a fence, drove off an embankment, and plunged 30 feet before landing upside down on train tracks. Amazingly, Faithful wasn't severely injured, and even though he was in a weakened state, he was able to crawl out of his wrecked car. Then he collapsed. A few seconds later, Faithful could hear people shouting at him: "Get off the tracks!" With only seconds to spare, he scuttled to safety right before a freight train roared by and slammed into his car, pushing it more than 100 feet before coming to a stop.

INTO THE WOODS
In September 2013, Gene Penaflor, 72, and a friend took their annual deer-hunting trip to northern California's Mendocino National Forest. Separated from his partner, Penaflor was stalking a deer in the remote wilderness when he slipped and fell off a cliff. He remembers hitting his head and feeling a sharp pain in his knee… and then losing consciousness. When he awoke the next day, his lips and chin were cut, and his knee hurt so badly that he could barely walk. Gathering his wits, Penaflor took inventory: He had his rifle, seven bullets, two plastic trash bags, and a lighter. His knife and water bottle were nowhere to be found. Neither was the trail back to his camp. He was lost. Going into survival mode, Penaflor cleaned his wounds and found shelter. He kept a fire going during

the days; a rotted tree and dry leaves kept him warm during below-freezing nights. Too weak to hunt deer, he limped through the forest and foraged for berries and algae. He also ate lizards, frogs, a snake, and three squirrels. Four days after Penaflor was reported missing, the search was called off due to stormy weather. His family was told to expect the worst, but they knew he wouldn't give up. Two weeks later, a hunter heard weak calls for help from the bottom of a canyon. It took several men and a makeshift stretcher to get Penaflor out of there. He was taken to a hospital and released the same day. He walked out—13 pounds lighter—on his own two feet.

DE-RAILED

In 2014 a 23-year-old pregnant woman, identified only as Liu, was driving on a highway in Chongqing, China. Her husband was in the passenger seat. All of a sudden, the mom-to-be lost control of the car and saw that it was headed straight for a guardrail. With no time to think, Liu leaned to her right just as the car was impaled by a 24-foot-long metal rod. It entered the interior right next to the steering wheel and then exited through the driver's-side window—missing Liu's head by less than an inch. When police arrived on the scene, they couldn't fathom how anyone could have survived such a horrific wreck. But Liu, her husband, and her unborn baby all made it out unscathed. "I was so paralyzed with fright," Liu later told reporters, "my husband had to pull me out of the car."

DEATH RAFT

Tseng Lien-fa can't swim, so catching baby eels at the beach was risky. But the 42-year-old Taiwanese man's girlfriend was pregnant, and they needed money. (Baby eels are a delicacy in Taiwan.) While crouched at the water's edge, a freak wave sneaked up and knocked Tseng over. Before he knew it, an even larger wave came in and swept him out to sea. He flailed about and was losing strength fast. Then something came floating by; he grabbed it and clung to it for dear life. Upon closer inspection, he realized that it was—and no one knows how it got there—a coffin lid. Without food or fresh water, Tseng clung to the coffin as he floated in the open ocean. He hoped that a ship or search plane would spot him, but none did. Nearly three days later, rough seas finally pushed him back to shore…46 miles from where his ordeal began. (He promised his girlfriend he would find a safer job.)

The inventor of ChapStick sold his idea for $5.

CHOKE AND CROAK

It figures that an industry as mistrusted as car sales would have its own slanguage. See how many of these expressions you overhear the next time you're in the market for a car.

Monroney: The window sticker on a new car (named for U.S. senator Mike Monroney, who authored the 1958 legislation that requires them)

Third Baseman: Someone who accompanies a potential car buyer because they're unable to negotiate the sale by themselves

Be-back: A potential buyer who leaves the lot without buying anything, but who promises he'll "be back"

Be-back Bus: A mythical vehicle that will someday deliver all the customers who said they'd be back

Whiskers: A car that's been sitting on the lot for a very long time

Hit Everything but the Lottery: A car with lots of dents, dings, and scrapes

Handshaker: A car with a manual transmission (a stick shift)

Bone Thrower: A sunroof

Toad: A worthless trade-in vehicle (it'll be sold for scrap)

Buried: A customer who owes more on his (or her) trade-in vehicle than it's worth

Broom 'em: Getting a non-buying customer off the lot so that he doesn't waste a salesperson's time

Choke and Croak: Disability and life insurance policies that dealerships try to include in a sale

Mooch: A customer who insists on buying the car at the dealer's invoice price.

Mop-and-Glow: Paint sealer (an add-on sold to buyers to increase the dealer's profit)

Unhorse or Dehorse: Hiding a buyer's trade-in vehicle to keep him from leaving

Friday Car: A car with a lot of mechanical problems. (It must have been manufactured on a Friday, when the auto workers were rushing to start the weekend.)

How about you? 7% of Americans suffer from *paruresis*—bashful bladder syndrome.

CAPITAL IDEA

*You probably know that the "D.C." in Washington, D.C., stands
for "District of Columbia" and that the district is not part of any
state. But do you know why America's Founding Fathers
placed such importance on creating a capital outside of
any state? We owe it all to piles of unpaid bills.*

EVOLUTION OF THE REVOLUTION

In April 1783, the U.S. Congress (then known as the
Continental Congress) gave preliminary approval to the
Treaty of Paris, which, if ratified by both England and the United
States, would end the Revolutionary War after eight long years of
fighting. Final ratification was still a year off, but it was clear that
the war was all but over and that the American colonies had won.
That was good news for the colonies...but not necessarily for the
soldiers who'd done the fighting, because it wasn't clear that they
would ever be paid for their years of service and sacrifice.

The Congress had run up huge debts to finance the war effort,
and it had no real means of paying back the money. The Articles
of Confederation, which served as the American constitution from
1781 until it was replaced by the U.S. Constitution in 1788, gave
Congress the power to declare war and the power to raise an army
to fight it. But it didn't give Congress the power to levy taxes.
Without this power, it had no way to raise the money it needed to
pay its war debts. The Congress could ask the states to contribute,
but it couldn't *compel* them to do it. The states had run up huge war
debts of their own that had to be repaid.

BEG, BORROW, STEAL

Many soldiers had been paid with IOUs or not at all. Their material
needs had often gone unmet as well. During the winter of 1777,
for example, nearly a quarter of the 10,000 soldiers camped at
Valley Forge died there—not from combat, but from malnutrition,
exposure, and disease. "We have this day no less than 2,873 men
in camp unfit for duty because they are barefooted and otherwise
naked," General George Washington complained in a letter two
days before Christmas in 1777.

One of the major causes of the fall of Rome, according to historians: runaway inflation.

FREE...FOR NOW

Soldiers with the means to do so had supported themselves during the war, and when their money ran out, they had amassed debts of their own. Now, having shed their blood to secure America's liberty, they faced the prospect of losing their own liberty in debtors' prison as soon as they were discharged from the army. "We have borne all that men can bear," one group of soldiers wrote in a petition to Congress in early 1783, "our property is expended, our private resources are at an end."

In response to this and other demands for payment from the soldiers, Congress could offer only vague promises to make good on its obligations to pay them...someday.

ON THE MOVE

On June 19, 1783, a group of about 80 unpaid soldiers stationed in Lancaster, Pennsylvania, mutinied and began marching the 60 miles to Philadelphia, then the nation's capital, to demand payment from Congress in person. As they made their way toward the city, more troops abandoned their posts and joined the march. The congressmen, meeting at the State House (known today as Independence Hall), feared that if the soldiers made it to Philadelphia they'd join forces with soldiers stationed in the city. The mutiny might then be large enough to overthrow the government, ending America's democratic experiment just as it was beginning.

Congress had no troops of its own to call on for protection. When the war ended, the Continental Army had disbanded, and command of the soldiers had reverted to the states, each of which had its own militia. Alexander Hamilton, then a congressman from New York, appealed to Pennsylvania's ruling body, the Supreme Executive Council, to dispatch the state militia to protect Congress, but the council refused to do so. Unless and until the soldiers became violent, Congress would have to fend for itself.

By then, of course, it would probably be too late.

OVER THE LINE

Having been rebuffed by the Supreme Executive Council, Hamilton dispatched the assistant secretary of war, Major William Jackson, to meet with the soldiers at the city limits and hopefully turn them back. No such luck—the soldiers marched right past Jackson and, as feared, made common cause with troops stationed in the city. The mob, now numbering some 400 angry (and, thanks to the generosity of sympathetic tavern keepers, drunken) men, raided several arsenals and seized the weapons inside. Then it marched on the State House and surrounded it while Congress was meeting inside.

STANDOFF

The mutineers delivered a petition to Congress stating their demands and threatening that if they were not met within 20 minutes, the "enraged soldiery" would take matters into their own hands. As volatile as the situation was, Congress refused to submit to the soldiers' demands, nor would it agree to negotiate with the mob or even adjourn for the day. Instead, it continued with its ordinary business for another three hours, then adjourned at the usual time and left the building to the taunts and jeers of the soldiers outside.

That evening Congress reassembled at the home of Elias Boudinot, the president of Congress. There it passed a resolution condemning the mutineers and demanding that Pennsylvania's Supreme Executive Council order the state militia to disperse the mob. If the Council refused, the Congress warned, it would leave the state and assemble in either Trenton or Princeton, New Jersey. And if Pennsylvania refused to guarantee the security of the congressmen in the future, it would never meet in the city again.

TIME TO GO

The next morning Alexander Hamilton and another congressman, Oliver Ellsworth, delivered the resolution to the president of the Supreme Executive Council, John Dickinson, in person. But Dickinson sympathized with the unpaid troops, and he feared that the Pennsylvania militia—also comprised of Revolutionary War veterans—would refuse to fire upon their brothers in arms if commanded to do so. Dickinson declined to take action.

With no help coming from the state government, Congress made good on its threat and evacuated to Princeton. It remained there for just a month before moving to Annapolis, Maryland. A year later, in 1785, it moved to New York City. It was still there in June 1788, when the U.S. Constitution replaced the Articles of Confederation. The new constitution gave Congress the power to levy taxes, which finally made it possible to pay its bills.

Anise, dill, fennel, caraway, coriander, cumin, and parsley are all members of the carrot family.

STAND DOWN

By then, of course, the mutiny was long over. Pennsylvania's Supreme Executive Council eventually did call up the state militia to disperse the mutineers, and as soon as the soldiers received word that the militia was on its way, they laid down their arms and returned to their bases. They never fired a shot or killed a single person in anger, which is one of the reasons the "Pennsylvania Mutiny of 1783" is largely forgotten today.

But the mutiny did have a big impact on American history, because the congressmen who found themselves surrounded by an armed, angry (and drunken) mob with no one coming to their aid were determined that the fledgling democracy would never face such a threat again. "The Philadelphia mutiny…gave rise to the notion that the national capital should be housed in a special federal district where it would never stand at the mercy of state governments," author Ron Chernow writes in his biography of Alexander Hamilton. When delegates met in 1787 (in Pennsylvania's State House, ironically) to draft the new constitution, they inserted in Article 1, Section 8, of the U.S. Constitution a paragraph giving Congress the power

> …to exercise exclusive Legislation in all Cases whatsoever, over such District (not exceeding ten Miles square) as may, by Cession of Particular States, and the Acceptance of Congress, become the Seat of the Government of the United States.

DETAILS, DETAILS, DETAILS

The U.S. Constitution did not, however, say where the capital city should be located or even require that one be established. All it said was that such a city *could* be created, and if it was, that Congress would exercise exclusive control over it, including providing for its security. Whether such a city would be built—and if so, where— would be the subject of battles to come.

For Part II of the story, turn to page 532.

For Part II of the story, turn to page 532.

*   *   *

"We are imperfect. We cannot expect perfect government."
—**William Howard Taft**

Funny guy: President Gerald Ford liked to fart loudly and blame it on his Secret Service detail.

MERE SKYBOSH!

We bookwrights hope these obscure, obsolete words from the 18th and 19th centuries don't leave a natkin in your mouth.

GROAK: to watch another person eat, hoping they'll offer you some of their food

SNOUTFAIR: a man with a handsome face

RESISTENTIALISM: the feeling that an inanimate object is being rude or spiteful

BEEF-WITTED: dumb, cowlike; thought to be caused by eating too much beef

WONG: a grazing meadow

JIRBLE: to pour a liquid unsteadily, with a shaky hand

SKYBOSH: to engage in practical joking, goofing off, or other nonsense

BREEDBATE: someone who engages in skybosh

CURGLAFF: the shock a person feels when he or she dives into cold water

ENGASTRIMYTH: a ventriloquist

PUSSYVAN: an angry rage

LUNTING: smoking a pipe while walking down the street

NATKIN: a foul taste or smell

FUNKIFY: to flee in terror

NIDULATION: nestmaking

SLUBBERDEGULLION: a slob

SNAWKY: nauseating

VECKE: an old woman

BOOKWRIGHT: as a shipwright makes ships and a playwright makes plays, a bookwright is an author

YEMELES: negligent

GOBEMOUCHE: from the French for "fly swallower," it refers to a person so dumb their mouth is always hanging open

DUMFUNGLED: used up

QUOP: to throb

CRINETS: hair

SCRIBBET: drawing charcoal

MISCOMFRUMPLED: wrinkled, rumpled, or creased

SLANGREL: anything that is long

Odds that a dropped piece of toast will land butter-side down: 62%.

COUNTRIES NAMED AFTER PEOPLE

Bet you didn't know that Canada was named after a guy named Bob D. Canada! (The "D" was for "Doug.") Okay, that's not true. But these stories about the origins of country names are.

BOLIVIA. The west-central South American nation of Bolivia was officially founded on August 6, 1825, after a 16-year war for independence from Spain. It was named after its most important revolutionary leader, Simón Bolívar. Bolívar, it should be noted, was not born in Bolivia—he was born in what is now Venezuela. Bonus fact: Venezuela is named after him, too. It's officially known as the Bolivarian Republic of Venezuela. (Bolívar is credited with playing an important part in the independence movements of no less that five nations: Bolivia, Venezuela, Colombia, Ecuador, and Peru, and he is still known as "El Libertador"—"the Liberator"—throughout Latin America.)

COLOMBIA. Colombia first gained independence from Spain in 1819, as part of the same independence movement that freed Bolivia. The original Colombia was enormous. In the years after it collapsed in 1830, it was divided and became the nations of Colombia, Venezuela, Ecuador, and Panama, as well as parts of Peru, Guyana, and Brazil. (The original Colombia is now referred to as "Gran Colombia," meaning "Great Colombia," to differentiate it from modern Colombia.) The name "Colombia" was chosen by another revolutionary, Francisco de Miranda, who fashioned the name after explorer Christopher Columbus—even though Columbus never set foot in Colombia. Exactly why de Miranda did this is unclear. One theory: He got the idea while touring the United States in the 1780s and early 1800s, where he met the leaders of the new nation, including presidents George Washington and Thomas Jefferson. There, historians say, de Miranda would have become familiar with the popular custom of using "Columbia" (with a "u") as a place name, in honor of Christopher Columbus. (Even the nation's capital, Washington, D.C.—District of Columbia—was named this way.) But why did he spell "Colombia" with an "o" rather than "Columbia" with a "u"? To more closely match the English pronunciation. If he'd spelled it with a "u," the Spanish pronunciation would have been "Coloombia."

DOMINICAN REPUBLIC. This country makes up the eastern portion of the Caribbean island of Hispaniola (the western part is Haiti). It is the site of the oldest permanent European settlement in the Americas, established by Bartholomew Columbus (brother of Christopher) in 1496 as "Santo Domingo," in honor of the 13th century Spanish priest also known as "Saint Dominic." The country officially became the "Dominican Republic" when it gained independence in 1844. Bonus fact: from 1822 to 1844, the Dominican Republic was ruled by Haiti and was known as "Spanish Haiti."

LIECHTENSTEIN. In 1719 Holy Roman Emperor Charles VI decreed that two tiny, unconnected, privately owned regions in the Alps, situated between Switzerland and Austria, were heretofore to be considered the official Holy Roman Empire principality of "Liechtenstein." It was basically a favor to the emperor's friend, Anton Florian von Liechtenstein, who had recently bought the two pieces of land just so the emperor could make them a principality, thereby allowing Anton to become a member of the *Reichstag*, the imperial government. (Owning a principality was a requirement for membership.) The two tiny regions grew over the decades—a little—and in 1866 became the nation of Liechtenstein. It is still ruled by the Liechtenstein family.

MAURITIUS. In 1598 a fleet of Dutch ships accidently discovered an Indian Ocean island after becoming lost on their way to India. The explorers claimed the island, naming it "Mauritius," after the leader of the Netherlands, Maurice, Prince of Orange. The French took over the island in the 1700s, changing its name to "Île de France"; the British took it in 1810, and changed the name back to Mauritius. It remained in British hands until 1968, when it became an independent nation. Bonus fact: Mauritius was the only home of the dodo bird, which became extinct 80 years after the Dutch first discovered it.

MOZAMBIQUE. In 1498 Portuguese explorer Vasco da Gama became the first European to sail to India. His route went around

Africa's Cape of Good Hope and across the Indian Ocean. On the way, he stopped at a small island off the coast of southeast Africa, and was surprised to find it populated (the island had been a major port for Arab traders for centuries). Da Gama was told the island was ruled by a sheik named Mussa Mbiki. The sheik's name was morphed by the Portuguese into "Mozambique," first as the name of the island, later as the name of the entire Portuguese colony that extended far into the mainland, and finally, in 1975, the name of the independent Republic of Mozambique.

SEYCHELLES. The French named these previously uninhabited Indian Ocean islands the Séchelles in 1756, in honor of the prominent French politician Jean Moreau de Séchelles. In the early 1800s, the British took control of the islands from the French and anglicized the name to Seychelles, as it remains today. (It's no longer British, though. It became independent in 1976.)

THE NAME GAME

• El Salvador, which means "the Savior," was named in honor of Jesus. (It was originally called the "Provincia de Nuestro Señor Jesus Cristo, el Salvador del Mundo"—the "Province of Our Lord Jesus Christ, the Savior of the World.")

• "Las Islas Felipenas" was the name given to two Southeast Asian islands in 1543, in honor of Spain's 16-year-old Prince Philip (Felipe). Today there are more than 7,000 islands in the Republic of the Philippines.

• Swaziland is an independent nation located almost entirely inside South Africa, bordering Mozambique to the east. It was named after Mswati II, warrior king of the Swazi people (who also take their name from Mswati), who ruled the region from 1840 until 1868.

• In 221 B.C., Qin Shi Huang unified several warring states and founded the Qin Dynasty—the original Chinese nation. *Qin* is pronounced "ch'in," and China is still named after him.

*   *   *

Loony Law: It's illegal in Alaska to wake up a sleeping bear in order to take its photograph.

Most accurate way to measure snowfall: by hand, with a ruler.

WATCH YOUR WALLET!

*If you've ever had your wallet stolen while traveling, you know how
disruptive it can be to a vacation or business trip. Here's how
to outsmart pickpockets before they ruin your vacation.*

THE MUSTARD SQUIRTER

Setup: An apparently absentminded person eating a hot dog or some other food bumps into you on the street and gets mustard on your jacket. Variations on the ruse include phony bird poop—which skilled pickpockets will apply themselves while pointing it out on your jacket—and other disgusting substances.

Watch Your Wallet! The person then offers to help you remove the goo from your jacket and may even ask you to take it off so that they can do a better job of cleaning it. And in the process of wiping you down, they rifle through the pockets of your garment and steal whatever they find.

THE ESCALATOR STUMBLEBUM

Setup: Just as you're about to step off an escalator and walk away, the person just ahead of you on the landing trips and falls. Or they drop some pocket change and stop to pick it up. Or they spill the contents of a shopping bag and stop to pick that up.

Watch Your Wallet! In the process of getting up or retrieving their dropped items, the person blocks you from getting off the escalator—and because it's still moving, the people behind you start to bump and press up against you. If you're being set up for a theft, the people pressing against you are the stumblebum's accomplices; they'll pick your pockets clean while you're distracted by the commotion in front of you.

THE VICTIM

Setup: A person on a crowded bus, train, or subway platform suddenly jumps up and screams, "Somebody stole my wallet!"

Watch Your Wallet! The natural reaction of all bystanders within earshot: Reach for their own wallets to see if they're still there. If the "victim" is actually part of a pickpocket ring, their accomplices are scanning the crowd to see which pockets the other passengers reach for. Now they know which ones to pick. If the passengers are distracted by all the fuss the victim is making or wrongly assume that the pickpocket has already made a getaway, they may even relax their guard, making it even easier for their pockets to be picked.

THE LOST SOUL

Setup: A person or group of people approach and tell you they're lost. They will then ask for directions and, if you agree to help, they'll unfold a large map. Or they may ask you to open your map if you have one. If the lost person appears to be alone, other people may approach the two of you and crowd around to provide extra "assistance."

Watch Your Wallet! The map serves two purposes: it distracts your attention, and it blocks you from seeing the hands of the accomplices as they steal your wallet.

THE PETITIONER

Setup: A person with a clipboard approaches you and asks you to read and sign a petition dealing with a worthy cause (such as cancer research, feeding the hungry, or housing the homeless). If you agree, the person hands you the clipboard and a pen.

Watch Your Wallet! Now that you're distracted with what you're reading and both your hands are occupied, the petitioner or an accomplice feigning interest in the petition can pick your pocket.

THE BABY TOSSER

Setup: A beggar carrying a baby will stumble right in front of you and toss her baby into your arms.

Watch Your Wallet! Believe it or not, this ruse is fairly common in parts of Italy and eastern Europe. Sometimes the beggar doesn't even bother to trip before tossing the baby. Either way, the shock of having to catch the baby and save it from harm forces you to drop any bags or other items you have in your hands. By the time you realize the "baby" is just a doll wrapped in a blanket, "Mom," her accomplices, and your belongings will be long gone.

*   *   *

"Obviously crime pays, or there'd be no crime." —**G. Gordon Liddy**

YOU'RE MY INSPIRATION

More fascinating secrets behind where the architects of pop culture get their ideas. Some of these may surprise you.

ANNIE WILKES. The psychotic nurse in Stephen King's *Misery* (played by Kathy Bates in the 1990 movie) was based on pediatric nurse Genene Jones, imprisoned for overdosing kids and then reviving them so she would be seen as a hero. (Not all of them survived.) King also based Annie on his own demons: "I was having such a tough time with dope. Annie was my drug problem, and she was my number-one fan. God, she never wanted to leave."

"I'D BUY THAT FOR A DOLLAR!" In "The Marching Morons," a 1951 sci-fi story by Cyril M. Kornbluth, a popular catchphrase of the future is "Would you buy *that* for a quarter?!" In 1987 *RoboCop* screenwriter Edward Neumeier added 75 cents and made it a popular catchphrase in futuristic Detroit.

LONG JOHN SILVER. The one-legged pirate in Robert Louis Stevenson's classic novel *Treasure Island* was based on a friend, poet William Henley, who was a loud, gregarious fellow with only one leg. "I will now make a confession," wrote Stevenson to Henley years later. "It was the sight of your maimed strength and masterfulness that begot Long John Silver."

SKULL AND ROSES. The Grateful Dead's logo was created in 1971 by Stanley "Mouse" Miller, who was designing a concert poster for the band. He found a 1913 edition of the eleventh-century Persian poem *The Rubaiyat of Omar Khayyám*, illustrated by E. J. Sullivan. One of Sullivan's drawings was the image of a skeleton wearing roses on its head. "I thought, 'That might work for the Dead.'"

MOE SZYSLAK. Matt Groening modeled *The Simpsons*' grumpy bartender after a bartender named Red Deutsch, who was known for his angry responses to prank callers. Moe's face is a combination of a gorilla and comedian Rich Hall. When Hank Azaria auditioned for the part, he mimicked Al Pacino in *Dog Day Afternoon*. Groening told him to make the voice "more gravelly," and Moe was born.

D'oh! The six main voice actors for *The Simpsons* each make $300,000 per episode.

MORE CARS THAT STALLED

Here's a look at three more automotive brands
that seemed like good ideas at the time.

MERKUR (1985–1989)
Starting Up: The Ford Motor Company has had factories all over the world for decades. In the early 1980s it decided to import some of its European-made cars to the United States, and sell them through Lincoln-Mercury dealerships under the brand name *Merkur* (pronounced mehr-KOOR), the German word for Mercury. The first car brought over was the Ford Sierra XR4i, a popular two-door compact made at a Ford plant in West Germany. Only problem: GM already sold GMC Sierras and Oldsmobile Cutlass Cieras in the United States, so Ford dropped the name Sierra but kept the XR4i. And because stricter U.S. safety regulations added nearly 300 pounds of equipment to the weight of the car, Ford gave the American XR4i a turbo-charged engine and added a "T" to the name, making it the Merkur XR4Ti.

Ford predicted sales of 20,000 cars in 1985, with total Merkur sales climbing to 100,000 cars a year by 1990 as a full range of European models were added to the brand.

Breaking Down: Though the XR4Ti's European styling (no grille in front and a "biplane" double spoiler in the rear) could be off-putting, the car had quick acceleration, tight handling, and a top speed of 130 mph—and it was a lot of fun to drive. The mistake Ford made was selling it through Lincoln-Mercury dealerships. The XR4Ti was intended to compete against BMWs and Audis, but Lincoln-Mercury dealers sold bloated "land yachts" like the Lincoln Town Car and the Mercury Marquis to older, stodgier car buyers. People who bought Town Cars weren't interested in the sporty XR4Ti, and people who bought BMWs and Audis never visited Lincoln-Mercury dealers.

The XR4Ti would have been a better fit at Ford dealers parked alongside Mustang SVOs and Thunderbird Turbo Coupes, but even there it might have been a tough sell, with a weird model name that looked like it belonged on a license plate (XR4TI) and an odd brand name that was usually mispronounced as "MER-ker." Sales peaked at 14,000 cars in 1986, well below expectations. They fell by nearly half in 1987, which meant that the 700 Lincoln-Mercury Merkur dealers were selling less than one XR4Ti a month. When sales continued to disappoint (even after the four-door Scorpio sedan was added to the 1988 lineup), Ford put Merkur out of its misery.

STERLING (1987–1991)

Starting Up: Sterling Motor Cars was a marriage of convenience between British carmaker Rover, whose quality-control problems had driven it out of the U.S. market, and Honda, which was preparing to launch its Acura luxury car division but had never made a full-size sedan before. The car that resulted, the Sterling 825, was essentially a rebadged Acura Legend with an elegant English wood-and-leather interior.

Breaking Down: The Sterling was assembled in Great Britain to give Rover a chance to learn Japanese production methods. The company didn't learn much: as soon as the Sterlings arrived on American shores in 1987, they began to fall apart. Rust was the worst problem, but the cars were also plagued with bad wiring, shoddy paintwork, faulty gauges, and other problems. Even the English interior was a mess—the wood trim came apart and leather seats turned green in the sun. (By comparison, the nearly identical Acura Legend, made in Japan, had some of the highest initial-quality ratings of any car that year.)

Sales of Sterlings, disappointing from the start, collapsed entirely once people realized how awful they were. By 1992 Rover and Sterling were gone from American shores, never to return. Rover never did fix its quality-control problems and went under in 2005.

MAYBACH (2002–2013)

Starting Up: When British defense contractor Vickers PLC put its Rolls-Royce Motors subsidiary up for sale in 1997, Daimler-Benz, maker of Mercedes-Benz automobiles, passed on the chance to buy the company because it felt the price was too high. The following year Volkswagen bought most of Rolls-Royce's assets, including its Bentley subsidiary, but did not buy the rights to the Rolls-Royce

---

Big in more ways than one: Of all dog breeds, Great Danes are the most expensive to own.

name and logo. Those were licensed to BMW, which began manufacturing Rolls-Royces in 2002. Now Daimler-Benz (which changed its name to Daimler-Chrysler after merging with Chrysler in 1998) faced the prospect of competing against not one but two ultra-luxury car brands, both reinvigorated by its two biggest competitors: Bentley, made by Volkswagen, and Rolls-Royce, made by BMW. Daimler-Chrysler responded by creating its own in-house ultra-luxury brand: Maybach (pronounced MY-bock), named after a legendary German luxury car of the 1920s and 1930s.

Breaking Down: Rather than engineer a new car from scratch, Daimler-Chrysler simply modified its aging Mercedes-Benz S-Class sedan, stretching it to make it even longer and then cramming it full of luxuries, like a liquid-crystal glass moonroof that turned opaque with the push of a button, power curtains for the side and rear windows, 16-way power rear seats that reclined until they were nearly horizontal, a refrigerator/wine chiller, a humidor, and a TV/DVD player with up to three screens and three remote controls that doubled as cell phones. Pushing a special button on the phones connected you to your Maybach's "personal liaison manager," who booked flights, hotel rooms, and theater tickets upon request. All this bling cost a bundle: prices for the Maybach started at $340,000, nearly twice the cost of the most expensive Mercedes-Benz, and climbed as high as $1.4 million.

One of the problems with Maybachs was that the name meant nothing outside of Germany. And as fancy as they were on the inside, they were nothing special on the outside. Except for their length and a special "M" hood ornament, they looked like ordinary Mercedes-Benzes. Who wants to pay $340,000 for a car that looks like its $160,000 cousin? Rolls-Royce and Bentley were distinctive cars and world-famous brands, and now they handled like German cars. The Maybach didn't—it was, as *Fortune* magazine put it, an "inferior automobile" with "all the grace of an Airstream trailer."

Daimler AG (which sold Chrysler in 2007) hoped to sell 2,000 Maybachs a year but averaged barely 250, even after it offered rebates of up to $100,000. After eleven years of trying to make the brand work, in 2012 Daimler pulled the plug and wrote off its $1 billion investment in Maybach as a total loss (though there are rumors that it might try to resurrect the brand again, so stay tuned).

LOST ALBUMS

*The music industry is notoriously difficult for artists to thrive in.
And as these examples show, not even being a platinum-selling
artist ensures that your music will be heard.*

Artist: Green Day
Album: *Cigarettes and Valentines*
Story: By 2003 Green Day was in a creative rut. They'd won a Grammy Award (for *Dookie* in 1994), sold tens of millions of albums, and were one of the biggest bands of the 1990s. But they wanted to grow—to somehow mature their sound without alienating the fan base who loved their three-chord punk rock. Not knowing quite how to do it, they went into the studio and recorded 20 tracks for an album called *Cigarettes and Valentines*. Then fate intervened. The master tapes were stolen from the studio, leaving the punk trio with nothing to release. After consulting with their longtime producer, Rob Cavallo, the band decided to go in a completely new direction and made *American Idiot*. It wasn't a punk album at all—it was a concept album and a rock opera about bored suburbanites. Result: *American Idiot* became a massive hit. It sold 12 million copies and was later turned into, of all things, a Broadway musical. Though the *Cigarettes and Valentines* tapes were never recovered, re-recordings of two of the songs, "Too Much, Too Soon" and "Olivia," later appeared as B-sides.

Artist: D'Angelo
Album: *James River*
Story: In 2000 R&B singer D'Angelo became an international sensation when he appeared nearly nude in the video for his hit "Untitled (How Does It Feel?)." But D'Angelo was more than just a pretty face and a set of rock-hard abs. His album *Voodoo* was named one of the best soul records of all time by *Rolling Stone*. So what did he do for a follow-up? Amazingly, nothing…yet. While struggling to adapt to his new fame, D'Angelo developed a drug and alcohol problem during the tour to support *Voodoo* and didn't release any music for five years. In the decade since getting clean, D'Angelo has made guest appearances on other artists' records, but has missed

every publicized release date for the highly anticipated follow-up, reportedly titled *James River*. However, according to *Voodoo* producer and Roots bandleader Ahmir "Questlove" Thompson in 2013, *James River* is "ninety-nine percent done."

Artist: Dr. Dre
Album: *Detox*
Story: *Detox*, in the works since 2001, has become legendary…as in it may be real, and it may not be. In a cameo on rapper The Game's 2005 track "Higher," Dr. Dre shouted, "Look out for *Detox!*" But the album didn't materialize, nor did it in 2008 when Dre's protégé, Snoop Dogg, told *Rolling Stone* that *Detox* was finished. A sample of *Detox* was played in a 2009 Dr Pepper commercial, but that was all that was released. The wait seemed to be over in late 2010 when Dre released two official singles, "Kush" and "I Need a Doctor," and even filmed music videos for them. Still no album. After serving as executive producer for Kendrick Lamar's acclaimed *Good Kid M.A.D.D. City* in 2012, Dre announced that he was taking a hiatus from making music to concentrate on his Beats By Dre headphone line and the USC Academy of Arts, Technology, and Business that he founded with Interscope Records' Jimmy Iovine. Like Brian Wilson, Dr. Dre has a reputation for being a perfectionist in the recording studio, so don't be surprised if his hip-hop equivalent of *SMiLE* takes another 40 years to see the light of day.

Artist: 50 Cent
Album: *Power of the Dollar*
Story: Imagine you're a record label executive who just signed an up-and-coming gangsta rapper, when word reaches you that someone put out a hit on him…and he's in the hospital with a gunshot wound. That's what happened to Columbia Records in 2000 when they discovered that 50 Cent had been shot nine times while parked in a car in Queens. But instead of taking advantage of the free publicity and mega-hype that would surround the rapper after the incident, the label dropped the former drug dealer and shelved his debut album, *Power of the Dollar*. While the album was never officially released because it still belonged to Columbia, it was heavily bootlegged. The bootleg eventually reached the ears of Dr. Dre, who quickly got 50 Cent a record deal with Interscope. His

official debut, *Get Rich or Die Trying* (2003), sold more than nine million copies.

Artist: Britney Spears
Album: *Original Doll*
Story: Spears was the world's biggest pop star in the early 2000s, but her downfall began around 2004 when she married rapper and backup dancer Kevin Federline. The damage that their marriage and subsequent divorce did to the superstar's reputation and mental state was well publicized between 2004 and 2007, but it also killed one of her albums. On New Year's Eve 2004, Spears made a surprise appearance on the Los Angeles radio station KIIS-FM to premiere the single "Mona Lisa" from her new album, *Original Doll*. The only problem was the singer didn't have permission from her label, Jive Records, to unveil the single or reveal the title. Jive responded by shelving *Original Doll*. Additional tracks from the *Original Doll* sessions have emerged on YouTube, but the album remains unreleased.

Artist: Bruce Springsteen
Album: *Nebraska*, the electric version
Story: Released in 1982, between Springsteen's massive hits *Born in the U.S.A.* and *The River*, *Nebraska* showed the New Jersey legend's more haunting side. While his lyrics about small-town life have always been dark and brooding, *Nebraska* was the first time Springsteen abandoned the sound of his E Street Band for the simple, powerful resonance of folk music. That, however, wasn't the initial plan. Springsteen's acoustic demo tapes (recorded on a four-track cassette player in his home) were just supposed to be a blueprint for a full electric version of *Nebraska*. But when Springsteen listened to the E Street Band's lush recordings of his songs about down-on-their-luck blue-collar workers, he and his producers decided that the acoustic guitar-driven demos should be the album instead. Though Springsteen has downplayed rumors of the unreleased electric version for years, in 2010 his longtime drummer, Max Weinberg, confirmed that the E Street Band's version of *Nebraska* does, in fact, exist.

* * *

"He who sings well, prays twice." **—St. Augustine of Hippo**

In 2003 the first toothbrush in space (Eugene Cernan's, 1969) sold at auction for $10,000.

THAT'S A SPICY QUIZ

They add a certain variety to life, but do you know your spices? This quiz may tell you whether thyme is on your side. (Answers on page 541.)

1. What two spices come from the same plant?
A. Pepper and peppermint
B. Mace and nutmeg
C. Basil and rosemary
D. Paprika and fennel

2. How many spices are combined to make "allspice?"
A. 1
B. 5
C. 8
D. 12

3. What spice was prescribed by herbalist John Gerard in 1597 because it "consumeth winde, provoketh urine gently, maketh abundance of milke, and stirreth up bodily lust"?
A. Ginger
B. Cinnamon
C. Spanish fly
D. Anise

4. What common spice "seeds" are actually the dried fruit of the plant?
A. Sesame seeds
B. Fennel seeds
C. Caraway seeds
D. Mustard seeds

5. What part of the plant is cinnamon?
A. Seeds
B. Root
C. Bark
D. Fruit

6. The seeds of the flavorful herb cilantro are a spice, too. What are they called?
A. Coriander
B. Black pepper
C. Green pepper
D. Cardamom

7. Grown in England since before 1550, this pungent treat was rarely eaten—it was used for driving off evil, werewolves, demons…and sometimes people.
A. Onion
B. Garlic
C. Dill
D. Cloves

8. What is the most expensive spice?
A. Goldenrod
B. Vanilla
C. Curry
D. Saffron

Al Capone estimated that in 1927 he spent $30 million in bribes.

9. Is salt a spice?

A. Yes

B. No

10. Which of these peppers is not like the others?

A. Black pepper

B. Red pepper

C. White pepper

D. Pink pepper

11. This spice was mentioned in both Testaments of the Bible, found in King Tut's tomb, and recommended by Mohammed as "a cure for every type of ailment except death." What is it? (*Hint: It also tastes good in curry.*)

A. Mustard seed

B. Hops

C. Black cumin

D. Onions

12. It's green while it's still on the plant, but it can turn hot red after it's picked. What is it?

A. Annato seed

B. Paprika

C. Sumac

D. Cayenne

13. True or false: eating poppy seed bagels can cause you to flunk a drug test.

A. True

B. False

14. What common herb—often removed from food before you eat it—is also used in killing jars by insect collectors?

A. Bay leaf

B. Wasabi

C. Wormwood

D. Marjoram

*   *   *

CORNY JOKES

Q: What do you call a fake noodle?
A: An impasta

Q: Where do boats go when they get sick?
A: The dock

Q: What did one hat say to another?
A: You stay here, I'll go on a head

Q: What do you call an alligator in a vest?
A: An Investigator

On average, American high school graduates live 9 years longer than high school dropouts.

INTERNATIONAL FUZZ

Every country on the planet has its own slang terms for the police. Some are offensive; some are harmless.

Små blå (Denmark): "Little blue ones," referring to the police's blue uniforms.

Smurfs (Poland): Another reference to the blue uniform.

Rennleitung (Germany): This term for police who catch speeders on the Autobahn translates to "racing officials."

Kyttä (Finland): "Snooper."

Asfalt kovboyu (Turkey): It means "asphalt cowboy," a term for corrupt cops, as if they lived in the lawless American Wild West.

QX (Singapore): Police cars in Singapore have license plates that begin with that prefix.

Bizzies (Liverpool, England): Stems from a distrust of police who once used to claim to be too "busy" to help out.

Batsos (Greece): It's Greek for "slaps," referring to especially brutal cops who would slap minors to keep them in line.

Bängen (Sweden): It's a Romani (Gypsy) word that means "devil."

Boton (Argentina): It means "button" or "badge" in Spanish. Argentinian police used to wear uniforms with large buttons and badges.

Droid (Hungary): Specifically, the well-armored riot police, who resemble the robots from *Star Wars.*

Yellow fever (Nigeria): Traffic police in Nigeria wear yellow.

Sinivuokko (Finland): It translates to "liverwort," a flower that's blue, like a police uniform.

Snut (Sweden): Derived from *snute,* a dog's nose, implying that police sniff around.

Mata (Malaysia): The Malay word for "eye."

Paco (Costa Rica): It comes from Francisco "Paco" Calderon, the national security minister in the 1940s.

Pandu (India): From a popular 1975 Indian movie about a policeman named Pandu Hawaldar (Title: *Pandu Hawaldar*).

GET STUFFED (ANIMALS)

They have been called "breathless zoos" and "Still Lives," but whatever you call stuffed dead animals, here are a few celebrities who collect them.

MARTHA STEWART

Many of Stewart's fans were shocked to read her 2011 blog *From My Home to Yours: Taxidermy*, in which the doyenne of gracious living disclosed that she has always had a fondness for taxidermy. "Ever since I was a schoolgirl, when I would spend long afternoons in the Newark Museum and the American Museum of Natural History, I have loved the examples of taxidermy more than anything else on display." Stewart's blog displays photos of her taxidermy collection—stuffed ducks, geese, a turkey, a baby bear, an owl, a porcupine (next to the liquor cabinet), a fox, and a lynx. The photos prompted readers to write comments like "Martha, dead animals are not decorations. What's wrong with you?" and "Appalling and disgusting!" The Academy of Achievement says that Martha Stewart "has had more influence on how Americans eat, entertain, and decorate their homes and gardens than any one person in our history," but apparently not everyone thinks taxidermy is, as Stewart puts it, "a good thing."

WES ANDERSON

Taxidermists credit Anderson, director of such films as *Moonrise Kingdom*, *The Royal Tenenbaums*, and *The Grand Budapest Hotel*, with the recent resurgence in interest in taxidermy. The term "Wes Anderson-style" is used to describe a decor that's a mash-up of time periods, with extreme colors of paint or wallpaper, weird artifacts, and, of course, some kind of taxidermied springbok or moose head over the bar or fireplace. Hipsters scour flea markets looking for the odd taxidermied squirrel or weasel to give their apartments the complete Wes Anderson touch.

AMANDA SEYFRIED

This star of HBO's *Big Love* and the films *Mama Mia* and *Les Misérables* explains her love of taxidermy in a single sentence: "Animals are easier to look after when they're dead." In a recent

photo, the blonde, blue-eyed ingénue posed reading a book surrounded by her animal friends that include Sparkle the goat,
Linda the chickadee, Beatrix the owl, Kevin the fox, and a baby
deer named Sha'Dynasty. While in Europe to promote her movie
Red Riding Hood, Seyfried purchased a three-week-old miniature
(deceased) horse that she named Antoine. "People think it's weird,"
Seyfried told the *Daily Express*. "I don't know why."

JACK WHITE

The singer, guitarist, songwriter, actor, director, frontman for the
White Stripes, and former upholsterer has his own special hobby—
collecting high-quality taxidermy. White's collection includes a
zebra head, a giraffe head, two gazelles, a kudu, an eland, a giant
white elk, and most recently, an elephant head. "I don't have much
choice in the matter," he says. "I feel like a rescuer, a Humane
Society employee. There's a majesty to these animals that I want to
preserve; I can't see them looked at in a comedic way." When rock
fans got wind of his hobby, they barraged White with new pieces
for his collection. He was not amused. White says he respects the
artistry. "Sometimes people get it wrong," he said, "and it's so insult-
ing. They'll buy me a squirrel playing pool or some s**t like that."

DAVID SEDARIS

In an interview with *This American Life*, the award-winning humor-
ist took host Ira Glass to purchase a stuffed magpie at one of his
favorite Parisian haunts, Deyrolle. Since 1831, Deyrolle, located on
the posh Rue du Bac, has been, as Sedaris calls it, "the Noah's Ark
of taxidermy." Sedaris told Glass that his fascination for taxidermy
came from seeing the trophy room at his great aunt Monie's home
when she was dying. His great uncle, a big-game hunter, had bagged
a wide variety of animals, including snow leopards and white tigers,
which are now extinct. "You would walk into this perfect room,"
Sedaris said, "and there were thousands of eyes staring at you. That's
the thing that I loved. And that's the feeling you get when you go
into Deyrolle, that all of these creatures that are stuffed and poised
to pounce, that they're all staring at you. It's the same feeling you
get from being in front of an audience." In his home in England,
Sedaris displays a stuffed dog in a Plexiglas case mounted to the
wall. The dog's name: Casey. (Get it? Case-y.) "That's the only way
I would allow a dog into my house," he says. "Dead and in a box."

UNCLE JOHN'S
PAGE OF LISTS

More random information from the BRI's bottomless files.

10 Odd Color Names
1. Razzmatazz (reddish-pink)
2. Xanadu (green-gray)
3. Smaragdine (emerald green)
4. Gamboge (dark yellow)
5. Coquelicot (orange-red)
6. Fulvous (brownish-yellow)
7. Eburnean (yellowish-white)
8. Caput Mortuum (purple-brown)
9. Wenge (dark gray-brown)
10. Arsenic (dark gray-blue)

6 Best Entry-Level Jobs (wallethub.com)
1. Web application developer
2. Information security analyst
3. Web designer
4. Attorney
5. Software engineer
6. Financial analyst

6 Things Banned by NYC Mayor Michael Bloomberg
1. Cars in Times Sq.
2. Styrofoam packaging in single-service food items
3. Putting organic food waste in landfills
4. Sodas larger than 16 ounces
5. Cell phones in schools
6. Less than a 2-to-1 female–male ratio for restrooms in new public buildings

10 Sports Russian president Vladimir Putin has been photographed playing
1. Ice hockey
2. Arm wrestling
3. Horseback riding
4. Hunting
5. Skiing
6. Judo
7. Boxing
8. Scuba diving
9. Formula One auto racing
10. Bowling

Top 4 Twitter Accounts (2014)
1. @katyperry (53 million followers)
2. @justinbieber (51 million followers)
3. @BarackObama (43 million followers)
4. @YouTube (42 million followers)

8 Largest Moons in the Solar System
1. Ganymede (Jupiter)
2. Titan (Saturn)
3. Callisto (Jupiter)
4. Io (Jupiter)
5. The Moon (Earth)
6. Europa (Jupiter)
7. Triton (Neptune)
8. Titania (Uranus)

5 Uses for Dryer Lint
1. Pillow stuffing
2. Cleaning up motor oil spills
3. Bedding for birds' nests
4. Kindling for a campfire
5. Packing material

Norman Rockwell became the art director for *Boys' Life* magazine while still in his teens.

OVERHEARD IN THE LIBRARY

When do "rude" and "stupid" become appropriate descriptors for library patrons? When things like this (actually) happen.

Mom to her kids: "BE QUIET, YOU LITTLE TURDS! THIS IS A LIBRARY!"

Library patron, explaining why he refuses to pay for a missing book: "Aliens stole it from the book drop after I returned it there."

Patron: "I'd like to see a photo of Jesus."
Librarian: "Do you mean some paintings of Jesus?"
Patron: "No. The *photo* of Jesus."

Patron request: "Can you help me find a book about the real meaning of Christmas? Nothing religious, though."

Patron, calling the library after a bad storm: "Is your power out?"
Librarian: "No."
Patron: "Well, do your phones work?"

Patron: "What is the dating capital of the galaxy?"
Librarian: "Earth."

Patron at a government library: "I need public records."
Librarian: "Which ones, specifically?"
Patron: "All of them."

Patron: "Do you have any Berenstain Bears books? Sorry, I can't remember the name of the author."

Student at college library, after the reference librarian found the book the student needed and handed it to her: "So…can you, like…rent these or something?"

Patron request: "Can you give me a map that tells where I can find caves that haven't been discovered yet?"

Teen patron: "I need info on the holocauts."
Librarian: "We have a lot of information on the Holo*caust* available. What specifically do you need?"
Teen patron: "Info. On. The. Holocauts."

Patron: "Do you have any information on fornication in the church?"

Librarian, answering the phone: "Good morning, Charleston Library, how may I help you?"
Patron: "Yes, what county is the Charleston County Public Library in?"
(long silence)
Librarian: "I believe it is in Charleston County…"
(even longer silence)
Patron: "Oh, I see. Thanks."

Patron to reference librarian: Is it "Beavis and Butthead" or "Beavis ampersand Butthead"?

Student patron: "Do you have *How to Kill a Mockingbird*?"

Patron request: "Do you have any books by the famous American author Hemingstein?"

Patron (Rolling up shirt sleeve to show the librarian her arm): "Is this herpes?"

Items found inside returned DVD cases: Live cockroaches, an unwrapped condom, Social Security checks, a love note to someone's "baby mama," a dead tropical fish, and a crack-cocaine rock (the librarian thought it was a rotten tooth).

*   *   *

MYTH-INFORMATION

Myth: The famous Italian scientist Galileo Galilei (1564–1642) once released two balls from a balcony on the Leaning Tower of Pisa. With this experiment, he became the first person to show that two falling objects dropped at the same time will hit the ground at the same time, no matter how heavy or light they are.

The Truth: According to historians, there's no evidence that Galileo ever dropped anything off a tower in Pisa. The earliest account of this tall tale was written by Galileo's student and assistant, Vincenzo Viviani. Only problem: Viviani set his story decades before Galileo completed his theory on falling bodies. And even if Galileo *had* done the experiment, he wouldn't have been the first: Another Italian scientist, Giuseppe Moletti, had already performed the same basic experiment and reached the correct conclusion in 1576—when Galileo was only 12 years old.

You can lose as much as 75% of your liver and it will grow back…in as little as 2 weeks.

THE VANPORT TRAGEDY

*Today, Portland, Oregon is known as one of the most liberal cities in America.
How did it get that way? Begrudgingly, when it had to welcome thousands
of African-Americans displaced by a horrible flood.*

FROM OREGON WITH HATE

Oregon became a state in 1859, stayed with the U.S. during
the Civil War, and anti-slavery Abraham Lincoln carried the
state in the 1860 and 1864 presidential elections. That belies deep
institutional racism in early Oregon. The state's first constitution
expressly prohibited black people from even entering the state. The
Supreme Court struck down those provisions in 1926, but blacks
were still persona non grata.

That was due in no small part to the Oregon chapter of the Ku
Klux Klan, one of the most active branches in the nation. In the
1920s, the KKK in Oregon counted 20,000 members. Among them
was governor William M. Pierce, who openly acknowledged his
involvement with the hate group, going so far as to appear on the
front page of *The Portland Oregonian* with local Klan leaders.

By contrast: In 1940, only about 2,000 black people lived in
Oregon, most of them in the state's largest city, Portland…although
they were restricted to the Albina neighborhood due to the "code of
ethics" established by the city's real estate. The only jobs available:
railroad work or as domestics.

WAR BABIES

Accurately predicting that the U.S. would at some point join World
War II, ship magnate Henry Kaiser built shipyards across the West
Coast in the late 1930s. One of the biggest sat on the Columbia
River at the northern point of Portland, Oregon. When Japanese
pilots bombed Pearl Harbor and the U.S. formally declared war in
1941, Kaiser added two more boat factories in that location to meet
the anticipated demand for warships.

Around 10,000 men and women came to Oregon to find work
at Kaiser's shipyards, a great economic boost in the post-Great

---

Boeing has a patent on a process for using the moon's gravity to control the orbit of satellites.

Depression years. The problem: a lack of housing for workers and their families, particularly the 7,000 new African Americans who arrived in the area.

A CITY IN A YEAR

Kaiser needed to act fast to ensure his employees had someplace to live. His son Edgar Kaiser, newly in charge of his father's Oregon plants, quickly purchased 650 acres of land near the factories north of Portland and signed a deal with the federal government to help fund what would become the largest public housing project in U.S. history at that point. The "Liberty ships" built in Kaiser Shipyards were known for their rapid construction—four days was their record—and the brand-new city to house the shipbuilders was built just as rapidly. Residents moved into their homes in December 1942, just 16 weeks after construction began. The ad hoc community was nicknamed Vanport—it was right between Vancouver, Washington, and Portland.

Within months, that collection of quickly built homes became a real community, a city even. Schools were constructed, as were shopping centers, nurseries, a fire station, a library, police stations, a hospital, and even a 750-seat movie theater. Like Portland—and many of the cities of the time—the residential areas of Vanport were segregated. But the schools, churches, and businesses were not. By 1945 Vanport was home to 42,000 people, making it the second-largest city in Oregon.

THE FLOOD

When the war ended in 1945, so naturally then did the need for tens of thousands of shipyard workers. The work left, and so did the people. By 1947, just two years after the end of World War II, Vanport's population shrunk to 18,000 people. It was a ghost town. Portland mayor Earl Riley proposed that his city absorb what he called a "municipal monstrosity" bulldoze it, and build a new industrial district to provide manufacturing jobs.

While civic leaders debated what to do with the town, Mother Nature intervened. The winter of 1947–48 left a massive snowpack on the nearby Cascade Mountains, which melted during the warm temperatures that accompanied a heavy May rainfall. As the Columbia River began to rise, local politicians tried to temper fears of the very real threat of a flood for citizens of Vanport and northern Portland. The Housing Authority of Portland released the following statement the morning of Memorial Day 1948:

> REMEMBER:
> DIKES ARE SAFE AT PRESENT.
> YOU WILL BE WARNED IF NECESSARY.
> YOU WILL HAVE TIME TO LEAVE.
> DON'T GET EXCITED.

But they didn't have time. That afternoon, the Columbia River breached Vanport's western dike and sent a 10 foot wall of water into the city. The hastily built wooden buildings were tossed aside like cardboard boxes by the raging water. In less than an hour, 16 people were killed in the destruction. The flood completely wiped out Vanport.

PORTLAND'S INTEGRATION

In the days following the flood, the 18,000 newly homeless former Vanport residents streamed into Portland for assistance. Because so many of the families who stayed in Vanport after the war were black it forced Portland to permanently confront integration of the city. While some residents remained hostile, many white families opened their homes to the helpless refugees.

In the ensuing decades, civil rights legislation and the liberalization of Oregon's politics would contribute to Portland's reputation as one of the most liberal-leaning cities in America. Another of Henry Kaiser's businesses was Kaiser Permanente, which today offers health-care services to more than nine million people in eight states. In 2009 the company paid to erect a memorial plaque near where Vanport stood, which now encompasses the Portland neighborhood of Kenton. That plaque, commemorating the 1948 flood, is the only trace of Vanport. What was once shipyards and housing projects is now the Portland International Raceway and a golf course.

*   *   *

"Two wrongs don't make a right, but three lefts do." —**Jason Love**

Marine iguanas get rid of excess salt by sneezing.

~~WEAPONS~~ PEOPLE MALFUNCTIONS

Gun goes bang. Bomb goes boom. People go "Ow!"

RUDE AWAKENING

On a summer night in 2013, a 34-year-old farmer from Mitchell, South Dakota, was sitting on his front porch cleaning his gun and then drifted off to sleep…with the pistol on his lap. Around 2:00 a.m., his wife checked on him and turned on the porch light. Startled awake, the farmer inadvertently squeezed the trigger and shot himself in the midsection. (Luckily, the bullet didn't hit anything too important.)

SMOOTH MOVE, CHIEF

In 2014 David Counceller, the chief of police in Connersville, Indiana, was at a gun shop looking at a .40-caliber Glock handgun. He just happened to have his own Glock with him, so he took it out to compare the two. But when Counceller went to holster his weapon, it got caught on his sweater. He tried to force it, and in doing so, pulled the trigger. The bullet went through his leg and into the floor. "I need to pay more attention," said the police chief.

LE BOMB

In 2005 a French soldier retrieved an antitank rocket from the battlefield and kept it as a souvenir. He mounted it on the wall of his office, where it remained for two years…until it suddenly became dislodged, hit the floor, and exploded. The blast didn't take any lives, but of the four men in the room, one lost both legs, another lost a foot and a testicle, and a third lost his hearing. The soldier said he didn't realize that the bomb was still armed.

KARMA

In 1999 the Israelis and Palestinians couldn't even agree what time it was. On September 2, Israel switched its clocks to standard time several weeks before the official end of daylight saving time. Reason: for more light in the mornings during a religious holiday.

Feeding by passing food mouth to mouth is called *trophallaxis*.

Some defiant Palestinians refused to acknowledge the change. When a terrorist living in a Palestinian-controlled area set two car bombs, he used daylight saving time. But the terrorists who transported the bombs were going by Israeli time. Result: both bombs blew up an hour ahead of schedule and killed all three terrorists transporting them.

DIGIT HURT?

Fred Peterson, 66, from Stockton, Minnesota, was trying to prove to his wife that it's impossible to pull a handgun's trigger if it's in its holster. So he held his holstered .38 special in one hand and pulled the trigger with the other. The bullet nearly took off his index finger. (Peterson, by the way, is an NRA-certified firearms instructor.)

FIREWORKS

On July 4, 2013, Lassiter Basket, 82, of Baltimore, Maryland, continued his 50-year holiday tradition of firing his .22-caliber handgun. For safety, he only fired the gun inside and only with blanks in the chamber. It was more of a "noisemaker" than a live weapon, he said. But this time, Basket had forgotten there was a round in the chamber. When he fired, the bullet went through a wall and hit his 17-year-old great-granddaughter. She received only minor injuries.

MORE KARMA

In 2014 an al-Qaeda instructor was conducting a training session for Sunni militants near Baghdad, Iraq. While he was showing them how to assemble a suicide bomb vest, he accidentally set it off…and took out himself and at least 21 other terrorists.

THAT'LL SHOW 'EM!

A group of neighbors living in an apartment complex in El Ejido, Spain, discovered that a man was living illegally in a vacant apartment. When they confronted him, rather than go quietly, the squatter pulled out a gun and fired several shots into the air. Not enough shots, though—there was still one round in the gun. According to press reports, "When he attempted to put the weapon back in his pocket, he mistakenly shot himself in the pubic region."

First person known to go on a diet: William the Conqueror. (He was too fat to ride his horse.)

UNCLE JOHN'S STALL OF FAME

More stories of the odd, interesting, and funny ways that people get involved with bathrooms.

Honoree: Mr. Xu, whose first name was not given in news reports

Notable Achievement: Being a roadside "arc-pee-ologist"

True Story: The 20-year-old Xu of Sichuou province, China, was driving home from work one day in April 2014 when nature called and he pulled to the side of the road to pee. As he relieved himself onto a mound of dirt, some of it washed away, revealing a small ceramic figurine of a woman. He dug the object out of the dirt with a couple of sticks and took it home. He later brought the figurine to an expert, who identified it as an object from the Song Dynasty (960–1279). Figurines of that kind were often buried beside tombs to scare away evil spirits, so if there's an undiscovered tomb nearby, Xu's pit stop may yet yield more buried cultural treasures.

Honoree: Zane Noland, a nine-year-old boy who lives in Florida

Notable Achievement: Preventing possible pot shots

True Story: In June 2013, Zane, his brother, and his father, Wesley Noland, went to see *Man of Steel* in a Tampa movie theater. Not long after the movie started, Zane had to go, so Wesley took him to the nearest restroom. Zane went into one of the stalls, where he saw a handgun sitting on top of the toilet paper dispenser. That might have been a temptation for many kids, but Zane had been taught by his dad, a Marine veteran, to tell an adult if he ever found a gun. And that's exactly what he did: "Dad, there's a gun!" he exclaimed. Wesley entered the stall and picked up the gun, a Glock 26 semi-automatic…and it was loaded. Wesley removed the ammunition clip, took Zane to a private bathroom designed for families, and called 911 to report the gun.

Wesley's fear was that the gun belonged to a criminal, perhaps even someone who wanted to shoot up the movie theater. It didn't. The gun belonged to Luke Hussey, an off-duty detective with the

Hillsborough County Sheriff's Office, who happened to be in the same theater seeing *Man of Steel* on his day off. It took him 90 minutes to realize he'd left his gun in the bathroom; by the time he went to look for it, the Tampa Police had already confiscated it. He was suspended without pay for ten days and demoted to deputy for leaving a loaded gun where children could find it.

Honoree: Arra Daquina, a maintenance worker at San Jose International Airport in Northern California
Notable Achievement: Doing the right thing after "striking gold" in the bathroom
True Story: Arra found a gold ring while cleaning one of the airport's men's rooms. She didn't know what kind of ring it was, but it was "big and heavy," she says, and encrusted with diamonds. A lot of people would have been tempted to pocket such an item, but not Daquina: she turned it right in to the airport's lost and found department. They recognized it as a Super Bowl ring, awarded to the San Francisco 49ers for winning Super Bowl XIX in 1984. And because it had "Macaulay" engraved on one side, they were able to return it to ex-49er center John Macaulay as soon as he dropped by to report it missing. Daquina's employer, HMSHost, was so impressed with her honesty that it gave her its Above and Beyond Award. "Her actions exemplify what it means to give five-star service," said a spokesperson.

Honoree: Eron Watts, a New York City resident
Notable Achievement: Helping subway riders find a place to go
True Story: Watts takes his video camera into the subway, where he roams the stations in search of restrooms that are clean enough for people to actually use. He films the clean ones—only the clean ones—and posts the videos on YouTube so that other people can find and use the restrooms. As of February 2014, he has visited 129 restrooms and given passing grades to 48. And the other 81? "The conditions inside many of them are just like what you see at the subway-station platforms: dirty, filthy, messy, smelly, stinky, rusty, and disgusting," he says.

Don't forget! According to doctors, getting 7½ hours of sleep improves memory retention.

TV FACTS: THE 1980s

Fun facts about your favorite Reagan-era sitcoms and cop shows.

Murder, She Wrote. This show—about the deadliest idyllic Maine town imaginable—is one of the most popular TV shows ever. It was the most-watched drama on television for nine straight seasons—a record. It's also among the least-awarded. Angela Lansbury was nominated for the Best Actress in a Drama Emmy 12 times. Number of times she won: 0.

Cheers. In its first season, *Cheers* finished dead last in the ratings. But NBC was the least-watched network and didn't have anything to replace it. Good move: By its fourth season, *Cheers* reached the top 10…where it remained for the rest of its 11-year run.

Miami Vice. This show made star Don Johnson so in demand for movie roles that he threatened to leave the series unless his salary per episode was raised from $30,000 to $100,000. Producer Michael Mann gave in…but not before threatening to fire Johnson, move production out of Miami, and retitle it *San Diego Vice*.

Simon & Simon. Simon and Simon's mother is named Cecilia, a reference to the song "Cecilia," written by…Paul Simon.

Kate & Allie. The CBS sitcom was about two single mothers who share an apartment and raise their children together. Network censors didn't want audiences to get the wrong idea and think that Kate and Allie were a gay couple, and so made writers include a scene in most episodes that showed Kate and Allie going into separate bedrooms at the end of the day.

Moonlighting. Most episodes had an inexplicably long sequence of Maddie (Cybill Shepherd) getting off an elevator and walking to her office. Reason: the show had so much rapid-fire dialogue that scripts were twice as long as most TV scripts and took twice as long to shoot (14 days versus 7 days). Head writer Glenn Gordon Caron needed the hour it took to shoot Maddie's elevator scene to finish the script that would be filmed that day.

If you speak Portuguese, you already know that Rio de Janeiro means "River of January."

FLUBBED HEADLINES

Whether silly, naughty, or just plain bizarre—they're all real.

Bon Jovi Surprises Fan
With Brain Cancer

*Legislation would make
child abuse training
mandatory*

Deer Season To Conclude
With Youth Hunt

Endangered Fish Holds
Up Water Plant

**University of Colorado-
Denver celebrates 40 years
of forging identity**

**Rapper Ja Rule Leaves NY
Prison In Gun Case**

Police: Middletown Man
hid crack in his buttocks

Plans made for
East Side crime wave

*1 Million Get Shot to
Save On Loans*

***Army School Suspends
Female Head***

**Vermont Town Devastated
by Irene Looking For Money**

Elderly Woman
Found Using GPS

Colon seems headed
for long relief role

NEW PRESIDENT AT
KANSAS CITY FED

**Plan To Rework Trash Hailing
Moves To City Council**

Jets Patriots jumphead goes
herey barlskdjf fkdasd fg asdf

Reporters return to
Tibet after rioting

Florida Reporter
Completes Sentence

*Community, friends, family
remember slaying victim*

Homicide Victims
Rarely Talk To Police

Survey: Seniors having
more sex than thought

**GERMANS ARE SO SMALL
THAT THERE MAY BE AS
MANY AS ONE BILLION,
SEVEN HUNDRED MILLION OF
THEM IN A DROP OF WATER**

The title of the movie *October Sky* is an anagram of the book it was based on, *Rocket Boys*.

A RIVER RUNS FROM IT

It's easy to see where a river ends (at the sea, or another river),
but it's a lot tougher to determine where it begins.

SOURCE SPOT

You've probably heard the term "source" in relation to rivers, meaning the body of water where the river begins. Well, that's a bit of a misnomer: most rivers don't get their water from just one place—they're fed from many places, including tributaries, underground springs, lakes, and snowpacks, just to name a few. Geographically speaking, "source" refers to a waterway's most distant origin point—and that's how we're going to use it here.

THE NILE. At 4,132 miles, the Nile is the world's longest river, stretching from Khartoum, in the East African nation of Sudan, all the way to the Mediterranean Sea. The Nile is fed by two main tributaries: the White Nile and the Blue Nile. Tracing the origins of those waterways is more complicated. The Blue begins at Lake Tana in Ethiopia, but experts disagree about the source of the White. Some evidence points to lakes in Rwanda; other evidence points even farther away, to lakes in Burundi. So the Nile's actual source could be in either of those countries, more than 1,000 miles from Khartoum.

THE AMAZON. This river may not be the world's longest (it's 4,000 miles long, which makes it #2), but it has the largest waterflow, discharging more than 7 million cubic feet of water per second into the Atlantic Ocean. The Amazon receives its H_2O from several waterways located across Colombia, Peru, and Ecuador. According to one study, the Amazon's most distant source is a glacial stream located on the slopes of the Nevado Mismi, a mountain in the Peruvian section of the Andes.

THE MISSISSIPPI. The Mighty Mississippi stretches a good 2,320 miles, but where it does get its water? From all over the map. It is the chief river in the largest "drainage system" in North America, which means that many other waterways flow into it. Countless tributaries located in 31 U.S. states and two Canadian provinces feed the Mississippi. However, according to officials, Ol' Man

---

First *Sports Illustrated* swimsuit model: Babette March (January 1964).

River's most distant source is Lake Itasca, a relatively small body of water in north-central Minnesota.

THE YANGTZE. Asia's longest river winds over nearly 4,000 miles and empties into the East China Sea near Shanghai. For millennia, the Yangtze has been used as a border line in military conflicts, in addition to everything from irrigation to sanitation. The river's most distant source remains up for debate. The Chinese government officially considers it the Tuotuo tributary, which flows from the Geladandong Mountains in Tibet. Others, however, contend that the Yangtze's most distant source is actually the wetlands that feed into the Dangqu tributary, approximately 200 miles away, near the border of Tibet and China's Qinghai Province.

THE GANGES. This river runs for 1,569 miles across India and Bangladesh. The Ganges is considered sacred by Hindus, who worship it as the embodiment of the goddess Ganga, and millions depend on its waters for their livelihoods, despite the fact that it is one of the world's most polluted. The river is complicated from a geographical perspective. Experts disagree over its official drainage basin and its official length and, as such, the Ganges's most distant water source has yet to be pinpointed. Some say it's the Gangotri Glacier, which is located on India's border with China in the Himalayas. Others theorize that it might actually be the snowpack on any of seven different peaks in the Himalayas.

THE THAMES. Great Britain's most famous river is only 215 miles long. Much like the Yangtze, its source is disputed. Officially, it's the appropriately named Thames Head, an underground spring near Kemble, a small town in southwest England. Some geologists, however, contend that the river's most distant source is actually Seven Springs, 11 miles north of Thames Head.

THE COLORADO. This 1,450-mile-long river passes through five states and some of America's most beautiful canyons, including the Grand Canyon. The Colorado's source is generally considered to be a tiny stream located on the La Poudre Pass, at an altitude of approximately 10,000 feet. This wetlands area, which sits atop the Continental Divide, can be found in the Rocky Mountains about 76 miles west of Fort Collins, Colorado.

OUR FLOSS? YOUR GAIN

What's in a normal serving of cotton candy? Two tablespoons of sugar and a lot of air. Nutrition: 96 calories and no fat. And that's not all.

• Who introduced cotton candy to the world? Dentists. The first, Dr. William Morrison of Nashville. In 1897 he and candy maker John C. Wharton invented a device that melted sugar and blew it through a fine screen to create "Fairy Floss." He introduced it at the 1904 St. Louis World's Fair, and sold 68,000 boxes for 25¢ each ($6.75 in today's money).

• Another dentist, Dr. Josef Lascaux of New Orleans, improved the design in 1921 and patented the name "Cotton Candy."

• What Americans call cotton candy is called "candyfloss" in the UK and India, "fairy floss" in Australia and Finland, "papa's beard" (*barbe à papa*) in France, and "old ladies' hair" in Greece.

• Modern cotton candy machines melt the sugar and spin it at thousands of revolutions per minute, using centrifugal force to shoot the molten liquid through tiny holes. When it hits the air, it immediately hardens into miles of fine threads.

• Threads of cotton candy are thinner than a human hair.

• Fabric makers use a similar melting-and-spinning process to make polyester thread for weaving into cloth.

• In theory, you could make yarn out of cotton candy and knit it into a very short-lived scarf or pair of pink mittens.

• Spun sugar has been around since the 17th century. Chefs whisk melted sugar into thin strands with a fork, using them to decorate cakes and pastries.

• Other versions of candy floss: Iran has *pashmak* (Persian for "wool-like") with sesame added to the sugar before melting; the Himalayan nation of Bhutan has *ngathrek golop lhakpa*—spun sugar with butter tea and chili pepper; China has "dragon's beard candy," with peanuts and coconut (and a texture like horsehair); and Turkey has *Pişmaniye*—spun sugar blended with buttered flour.

• National Cotton Candy Day is December 7.

...nearly 250,000 miles—and 60 miles farther from Earth than any other Apollo mission.

FLEA MARKET RENOIR

Here's the story of a painter, a shopper, a thief, a liar, and a mother.

FIRST IMPRESSION

In September 2012, an Alexandria, Virginia, auction house announced that it would be auctioning off a recently redis-covered painting by the French Impressionist painter Pierre August Renoir. The painting was owned by a woman calling herself "Renoir Girl," who preferred to remain anonymous.

Renoir Girl said she bought the painting at a West Virginia flea market in 2009. It was one of several items in a box of junk that included a plastic cow and a Paul Bunyan doll. Cost of the box: $7.00. She recognized it as Renoir's work but assumed it was a copy, so she didn't get around to having the painting appraised until 2012. Only then did she learn that it was a genuine Renoir, not a copy. Titled *Paysage Bords de Seine* (Landscape on the Banks of the Seine), the painting depicted, as its name suggested, a river scene.

This work by Renoir was unusual in that the artist had painted it on a linen napkin, not on canvas, while dining with his mistress at a café overlooking the Seine in 1879. The auction house valued the 5½ by 9-inch painting at between $22,000 and $100,000.

HOT STUFF

It's not every day that someone finds a Renoir in a $7.00 box of junk. That's what the *Washington Post* thought when they sent a reporter to cover the story. But what started out as a light human-interest piece soon turned into something darker after reporters discovered that the painting had been stolen from the Baltimore Museum of Art in 1961. The painting had been gone so long that the museum forgot that it had ever been part of their collection. Nevertheless, acting on evidence uncovered by the *Post*, the FBI seized the painting the day before it was scheduled to be auctioned and locked it away until a judge could determine its rightful owner.

THE PLOT THICKENS

Rather than give up the painting without a fight, Renoir Girl filed papers in court, arguing that because she'd had no idea the Renoir

---

Greenland's only national park is more than twice the size of California. Nobody lives there.

was stolen when she bought it, she was entitled to keep it. She had to file the court documents under her real name, and that's when the world learned that she was Martha Fuqua, 51, a former phys-ed instructor and the owner of a driver's training school in Lovettsville, Virginia.

Precisely *why* Fuqua wanted to keep her identity a secret became clearer as soon as her name became public. That's when several people came forward telling a very different story of how the painting must have fallen into her hands. They reported seeing the Renoir hanging in the home of her mother, Marcia, as far back as the 1980s. Marcia (who spelled her last name Fouquet) was a painter and had attended art school in Baltimore in 1961, around the same time the painting was stolen.

DID I SAY THAT?

According to these witnesses, when Marcia Fouquet showed the painting to visitors, both she and her daughter identified it as a genuine Renoir. "I remember looking at it and saying to them, 'Is this a real Renoir?'" one childhood friend of Fuqua's told the *Washington Post* in 2013. "One of them said yes…I immediately dismissed it as preposterous. I didn't ask where it came from because I just assumed they were lying."

Martha's brother, Matt, told the *Post* that their mother had even instructed Martha to "return the painting to its rightful owner—the museum—so that all of this goes away." (He does not believe that his mother stole the painting herself. Rather, he suspects that it was given to her by the thief, who was probably a friend.)

CASE CLOSED

At the time the story broke, Marcia Fouquet was in her 80s and dying from cancer. She passed away before the FBI could ask her where she'd gotten the Renoir or whether her daughter knew it was stolen. Since there was not enough evidence to prove that Fuqua *did* know it was stolen, she was not charged with any crime.

But she didn't get to keep the painting. In January 2014, a judge ordered it returned to the Baltimore Museum of Art. It hangs there to this day.

In one survey, 21% of Americans said they are regularly "bored out of their minds."

EUGÈNE VIDOCQ: THE WORLD'S FIRST DETECTIVE

*Sherlock Holmes, Jean Valjean, and the FBI can all trace
their roots back to one Frenchman who turned
a life of crime into a life of fighting crime.*

SPLIT PERSONALITY

In 1809 a 34-year-old petty criminal named Eugène François Vidocq (pronounced vee-DOCK) was doing yet another stint in a French prison, this time for forgery. In and out of jail since he was a teenager, there were basically two Eugène Vidocqs: One was a hard-drinking brawler and womanizer who was quick to challenge any man to a duel. The other was a charismatic family man who had a knack for gaining people's trust...so he could scam them. It was that persona that Vidocq used in prison to win the confidence of some of Paris's most notorious criminals. And then he ratted out their plans to the city's police chief, Jean Henry.

Why did the crook suddenly turn informant? For one, Vidocq was facing a long prison term and possibly the guillotine. But he was also growing tired of living life as a fugitive. He'd tried to go legit before, and this time he wanted it to stick. So after he proved his worth to Henry, in 1811 the chief arranged for Vidocq to "escape" prison, something he'd done for real many times before. After that, Vidocq became an undercover spy, working the streets of Paris. He burrowed into the city's criminal underworld, often in disguise, and brought back what he learned to Chief Henry. The information he obtained put dozens of his former accomplices in prison...and sent more than a few to the guillotine. And he was just getting started.

THE WRATH OF CON

Born in 1775 in the northern French city of Arras, Vidocq's early years were filled with one thrilling adventure after another. That is, if you believe his memoir, which historians say was quite embellished. But what is known: he spent his first stint in jail at age 13 after stealing his father's silver, and ran away at 14 after stealing 2,000 francs ($6,000 in today's money) from his parents' bakery.

People person: Over the course of his career, Charles Dickens created over 13,000 characters.

Then at 15 he joined the circus (where he ate raw meat in a freak show). By this time, the teenager was already a veteran thief and a formidable fencer—a skill he picked up from off-duty soldiers as a boy. During the French Revolution, Vidocq (now 16) joined the army. He fought bravely in two battles against the Prussian army, but his military career was short-lived. He routinely challenged his fellow soldiers to duels (he was 14–2 by his own count), and once even assaulted his commander. By the time Vidocq was 19, it was clear to him and to his superiors that a military life was not for him.

GLOVES OFF

After spending his 20s bouncing from family life (he married twice) to bachelor life (he was known as a gambler and a ladies' man) to criminal life (he once masqueraded as Austrian so he could get at a widow's money), he decided that his 1809 forgery conviction would be his last time in prison.

Once on the outside, Vidocq took to his new job as a spy with great enthusiasm, applying his skills as a keen observer and master of disguise. Those abilities, combined with his superior fighting skills, soon proved he could be even more effective than regular cops…because he wasn't a regular cop. Whereas Paris police officers were restricted to their own districts, routinely allowing fleeing suspects to get away, Vidocq simply ignored those boundaries and would doggedly hunt down his targets day and night until they were apprehended.

In 1811 Vidocq convinced Chief Henry to let him form a plain-clothes police unit that would be free to do their work unhampered. Henry agreed, and Vidocq rallied up a small band of former convicts like himself. Vidocq's secret division soon began bringing in the worst of the Paris underworld. Vidocq himself single-handedly tracked down a notorious counterfeiter and beat a confession out of him, which led to an execution.

GOOD COP…

Within a year, Vidocq and his secret agents had proven so effective that Henry made them an official unit of the Paris police called the *Brigade de la Sûreté* ("Security Brigade"). A year after that, French emperor Napoleon Bonaparte signed a decree that expanded the brigade. Now it was the official state security police force for all of

France, and Vidocq was in charge.

Over the next 15 years, Vidocq laid the groundwork for what would eventually become the modern police detective:

• He introduced law enforcement's first card-index record-keeping system—it cataloged all of France's known criminals, complete with each one's physical description, arrest history, and *modus operandi* (method of operation).

• Vidocq trained his agents to use disguises and go undercover without being discovered. No police force had ever made this a regular tactic before.

• He invented several forensics techniques, including the use of handwriting to identify a suspect, plaster of Paris to make casts of footprints, and even firearm ballistics. In an 1822 murder case, Vidocq was one of the first police investigators—if not *the* first—to have a bullet removed from a body in order to prove that it wasn't fired by the prime suspect's gun. Vidocq even tried to develop a way to record criminals' fingerprints. (It didn't work, but later became a common law-enforcement practice.)

• Another first: Vidocq recruited female agents to go undercover and gather information.

...BAD COP

As innovative as some of Vidocq's crime-fighting techniques were, many others would get him booted off any modern police force. He and his agents regularly engaged in bribery, entrapment, illegal searches, coercion, and outright violence. That didn't sit well with many of Paris's legitimate police officers, who still considered Vidocq a fugitive because he never completed his forgery sentence. In 1818 Chief Henry officially pardoned Vidocq for his crimes. But the bad blood between him and his fellow cops remained.

Meanwhile, the Sûreté kept rounding up scores of France's most notorious bandits, forgers, counterfeiters, and killers. By the 1820s, the agency, now up to 28 agents, had been credited with reducing crime in Paris by more than 40 percent. Vidocq became a household name in France—a hero to some, a villain to others.

But when Chief Henry retired in 1826, Vidocq's days on the force were numbered. The new chief was among those who objected to the Sûreté's gang of ruffians, and he went out of his way to make things difficult for Vidocq and his men. After receiving one too many complaints about the behavior of his agents—who were, Vidocq admitted, seen regularly with crooks in the city's lowliest taverns and brothels—he wrote to the new chief:

> To save you, sir, the trouble of sending me further similar complaints in the future, and me the inconvenience of receiving them, I have the honor to solicit you for accepting my resignation.

In 1827, after 15 years as head of the Sûreté, Vidocq became a civilian again.

SELF-PROMOTER

Out of the force, Vidocq tried his hand as an author and as a "legitimate businessman." He wrote *Memoirs of Vidocq: Master of Crime*, which detailed his adventures on both sides of the law. The book was a huge hit in France and was even translated into English. In 1829 a popular London theater ran a play based on the memoir, called *Vidocq! The French Police Spy*. That, too, was a hit, and Vidocq was flying high. Now in his 50s and living a comfortable life, he opened a small paper mill outside of Paris that employed ex-convicts, both male and female.

But despite his successes in civilian life, it soon became clear that fighting crime was Vidocq's destiny. In 1831, amid tumultuous political upheaval in France—and the appointment of yet another chief of police in Paris—Vidocq found himself back as the head of the Sûreté. A year later he was out again. Rather than retire, he went on to make even more history.

VIDOCQ: P.I.

In 1833 Vidocq opened *Le Bureau des Renseignements* ("The Office of Information") at No. 12 rue Cloche-Perce in the Marais district of Paris. It was the world's first private detective agency. For a fee, Vidocq or one of his agents (mostly ex-convicts) would hunt down thieves and confidence men, spy on cheating spouses, act as enforcers to collect unpaid debts, or do whatever else a paying client wanted. Not bound by police regulations, the agency, which at its peak had more than 40 agents, solved several high-profile criminal cases that made headlines all over Europe.

But those busts came at a cost. The Paris police force kept a close eye on the agency and raided Vidocq's headquarters several times. Many of his agents were arrested—sometimes with cause, sometimes without. Vidocq himself was arrested more than once, resulting in a few more stints in prison

By 1848 Vidocq had had enough and closed the agency for good. Even at 72 years old, he refused to retire. He took on a few freelance cases, continued seducing women, and was even arrested one last time for good measure. In 1854 the old man survived a bout with cholera, but his health continued to decline. On May 11, 1857, he died in his home in Paris at the age of 82.

INTO THE DUSTBIN OF HISTORY

It's surprising, given Vidocq's storied life and the impact he had on law enforcement, that he isn't better known today. But even if you're not familiar with the name Eugène Vidocq, you've undoubtedly heard of the characters and agencies he inspired:

• In the 1820s, Vidocq became friends with many of the great French writers of the era, one of whom was Victor Hugo (who some say helped Vidocq write his memoir). In his 1862 play *Les Misérables*, Hugo wove both of Vidocq's distinct personalities into the two main characters—the fugitive Jean Valjean, and the cop who won't stop chasing him, Inspector Javert. Vidocq also provided inspiration for characters in the writings of Honoré de Balzac, Émile Gaboriau, and Alexandre Dumas.

• Edgar Allan Poe based his literary detective C. Auguste Dupin on Vidocq. In the 1841 short story "Murders in the Rue Morgue," Poe's character describes Vidocq as "a good guesser, and a persevering man. But, without educated thought, he erred continually by the very intensity of his investigations." Arthur Conan Doyle's Sherlock Holmes was based, in part, on Dupin, who was modeled on Vidocq.

• In 1829 the Metropolitan Police of London, commonly known as Scotland Yard, was founded in England, using Vidocq's Sûreté as a model. The same is true of the FBI, founded in 1908.

• In 1990 an exclusive group of the world's most renowned forensic scientists, former police detectives, and FBI agents banded together to create a crime-fighting force unlike any that had ever existed. They called themselves the Vidocq Society. (That story can be found on page 445.)

At about age 7, Abe Lincoln shot a wild turkey...and felt so bad that he never hunted again.

FUNNY TWEETS

*If you spend time on Twitter, you know how difficult it is to be clever
in less than 140 characters. Yet plenty of writers manage to do it.
Here are a few examples of how to be funny and brief.*

"I always get confused by the phrase 'stop, drop, and roll.' The 'stop' part doesn't belong. That's just extra time for being on fire."
—**Jon Friedman**

"I hope you all like the haircut I gave Miley Cyrus."
—**Helen Keller**

"Some people assume that I think I'm something special. Look, I'm just a regular guy telling people what I think. Like Jesus, I guess."
—**Ricky Gervais**

"Something that's been bugging me for years: the sequel to *Scooby Doo* should have been called *Scooby Doo Deux*."
—**Michael Ian Black**

"My mechanic just told me I could pick my car up at 5 p.m. and that they 'might be having a few beers there after work.' OMG is this a date?!"
—**KatyDidSays**

"At what age does Ryan Gosling have to change his name to Ryan Goose?"
—**Megan Amran**

"I love NY and its inhabitants. I could wander the street licking people's faeces just to convey my affection. Sorry, I meant faces. Either."
—**Russell Brand**

"Obama sobs as he signs Theres No More Ice Cream Act. 'Its really all gone?!' he cries. Biden winks to crowd as he sneaks up w/giant sundae."
—**Horton Atonto**

"The girl kept her eyes on the ground as the cashier rang up her cat litter & tampons. 'I have a lot of internet friends,' she whispered."
—**Mary Charlene**

"I love that moment when you make eye contact with a dog and he slyly smiles and nods to let you know he's secretly a tiny man in a dog suit."
—**Mike Henry**

"Let me get this straight—we can put a man on the moon but we can't replace the sound of my toilet flushing with a rimshot?"
—**Conan O'Brien**

First state to have cable television: Pennsylvania, in 1948.

BLUE BIRDS

Who hasn't fantasized about owning a parrot that knows dirty words?
President Andrew Jackson had one. At his 1845 funeral, held at home, the
bird swore so much that it had to be removed from the house. Here are two
more fowl whose foul language earned them their 15 minutes of fame.

Dirty Bird: Bluey, a blue-and-gold macaw that was part of a
parrot show at a zoo on England's Isle of Wight in the 1990s
Fowl Language: In the show, Bluey's "act" was performing
simple feats of arithmetic…or at least it was until the day he made
a mistake and his trainer scolded him onstage. That's when Bluey
graduated from addition and subtraction and told his trainer (in so
many words) to "go forth and multiply," using language that many
children in the audience had never heard before.

What Happened: The zoo made repeated attempts to reform the
bird. "We even got a local elocution teacher, but Bluey told him
to go on a sexual excursion, too," a spokesperson told *USA Today*.
When those efforts failed, Bluey was given an early retirement.

Dirty Bird: Flounder, a parrot living in Charlotte, North Carolina
Fowl Language: Just as you'd expect from a bird owned by college
roommates and named after a character in the movie *Animal House*,
Flounder learned more than a few naughty words. (He could also
make a farting noise and say "excuse me" afterward.) But like a
lot of pets in college towns, there came a time when his owners
could no longer care for him, and in 2000 Flounder ended up at the
Humane Society of Charlotte.

What Happened: These kinds of birds can be hard to find homes
for, but the Humane Society found one for Flounder right away—at
the Humane Society. "The bird makes us laugh, and we don't get
many laughs, so we're keeping him," spokesperson Patti Lewis told
the Associated Press. (The group also feared that if they placed the
bird in a private home and people asked where the bird learned to
talk like that, the new owners would blame the Humane Society. "It
would not be the best PR," Lewis said.) At last report the Humane
Society was trying to teach the bird to whistle instead of swear.
What does Flounder think of that idea? "&@$*!" he says.

THE RIDDLER

*Time to test your deductive reasoning with some classic and
not-so-classic riddles. (Answers are on page 540.)*

1. I am bought by the yard
and worn by the foot.
What am I?

2. We can't breathe,
but we can run.
We can't eat,
but we can grow.
We can't see,
but we can take you away.
What are we?

3. I am made of wood,
but I have never been cut.
What am I?

4. I begin with "r"
and end with "t."
To most I belong,
yet no one wants me.
I have no mass,
yet add great weight
because I always come too late.
What am I?

5. I am not enough for one,
just right for two,
but too much for three.
What am I?

6. I pass in front of the sun
yet make no shadow.
What am I?

7. I lose two teeth
whenever I bite,
but those two teeth
keep everything tight.
What am I?

8. To every town I belong.
I am the building with the
most stories, though not
necessarily the tallest.
What am I?

9. I am the most feared beast
in the forest;
my cry can be heard
from a mile away.
Yet a man may silence me
by simply letting go.
What am I?

10. We all have tails,
and we all have heads,
but not a single arm or leg.
We are stronger than bone,
but if we weigh you down,
you will never have to beg.
What are we?

11. When you don't know
what I am, I am something.
When you figure me out,
I am nothing.
What am I?

Self-winding clocks were invented in 1783.

MYTH-CONCEPTIONS

*"Common knowledge" is frequently wrong. Here are some
examples of things that many people believe…but
according to our sources, just aren't true.*

MYTH: You lose most of your body heat through your head.
FACT: It's not just your head—heat is lost evenly through
any skin that's exposed to cold. So you can (and should)
wear a hat to keep your head warm, but it's no different than wearing
a jacket, pants, gloves, or shoes to keep the rest of you warm.

MYTH: You should change your car's oil every 3,000 miles.
FACT: It's only true for old cars. Although your mechanic may suggest you change your oil every 3,000 miles, that's the lowest end of a
range that can go up to 20,000 miles. The average is about 5,000 to
8,000 miles. So why the myth? According to Philip Reed, the Senior
Consumer Advice Editor at Edmunds.com, "This wasteful cycle
continues largely because the automotive service industry, while
fully aware of the technological advances, continues to preach the
3,000-mile gospel as a way to keep the service bays busy."

MYTH: Chimichangas are Mexican food.
FACT: They are delicious, but these deep-fried burritos were
invented in Arizona.

MYTH: *The Nightmare Before Christmas* was written and directed
by Tim Burton.
FACT: Most people assume this because the 1993 film was
marketed as *Tim Burton's The Nightmare Before Christmas*. He
did produce the film, but the screenplay was written by Caroline
Thompson and Michael McDowell, and the movie was directed by
stop-motion animator Henry Selick.

MYTH: Egypt's Great Pyramids were built by slaves.
FACT: Greek historian Herodotus (484–425 B.C.) recorded this as
fact, but he lived 2,000 years *after* the structures were built and was
actually just reporting what he'd been told. The myth persevered for

John Wayne was friends with Wyatt Earp.

another 2,000 years, right through the twentieth century—helped along by Hollywood—but recent archeological evidence reveals that the Great Pyramids were built by tens of thousands of skilled laborers who were paid handsomely. Some were even paid in beer.

MYTH: If you have a nosebleed, you should tilt your head back.
FACT: Doctors actually suggest the opposite. Tilting your head back can cause blood to flow into your esophagus and choke you or enter your stomach. Instead, tilt your head forward to drain the blood and keep your head above your heart to slow the bleeding.

MYTH: In Medieval England, streets were riddled with human waste.
FACT: According to historian Tim O'Neill: "The idea that people emptied chamber pots out windows into the street…has been taught to generations of schoolchildren.…Medieval towns and cities actually had a lot of ordinances and laws to do with waste disposal, latrines, and toilets."

MYTH: Rabbits eat carrots.
FACT: If rabbits ate carrots as voraciously as Bugs Bunny, they'd suffer horrible indigestion and possibly tooth decay because carrots have a high sugar content. The myth most likely arose because rabbits have been known to eat the leaves that grow aboveground, but *not* the carrot itself, which is technically the plant's root. Veterinarians warn that carrots should be a rare rabbit treat. Feed them store-bought pellets or hay instead.

MYTH: Half of all marriages end in divorce.
FACT: The U.S. divorce rate is actually much lower, but how much lower is uncertain because many states don't keep divorce records. The confusion began in the late 1970s, when recorded divorce rates peaked. A 1981 report then noted that there were 2.1 million marriages that year, compared to 1.2 million divorces. But it wasn't the same couples getting divorced that got married; there were more than 100 million still-married Americans that year. The erroneous statistic was also helped along by forecasters who predicted that if trends continued, the divorce rate *could* climb as high as 50 percent. But since then it's been dropping, not rising.

Agent Orange wasn't orange. It was clear—the containers had orange stripes.

HAIRY SUPERSTITIONS

On page 143 we told you the truth behind some hair-related superstitions. Hair are a few more superstitions we found during our research.

If you have worms, eating a hair from a horse's forelock will cure you.

Don't wash your hair on New Year's Day. You'll wash away all the luck from the coming year. (And don't cut your hair during the first week of the new year for the same reason.)

Dropping a comb while combing your hair means bad luck is headed your way.

A woman who pulls on the hairs of her eyebrows will have difficulty bearing children.

Don't want your baby to be born hairy? Don't beat your animals!

Love potion: pluck a hair from your head, root and all. Burn it, mix the ashes into a drink, and give it to the one you desire.

Never throw away your hair cuttings—burn them. Reason: if a bird weaves your hair into a nest, you'll go insane.

Feed your baby plenty of corn and the baby will grow up to have long brown hair.

If you want a powerful good good-luck charm, pluck a hair from an elephant's trunk.

If a young man has hairy arms, he'll be wealthy one day.

If two girls are combing the hair of a third girl at the same time, the youngest of the three will die soon.

Don't comb your hair while walking, or you'll soon find yourself in an embarrassing situation.

Cutting the hair of a very sick family member will hasten his or her death.

A woman with a "widow's peak" (a V-shaped hairline in the middle of the forehead) will outlive her husband.

Burn a strand of your hair in a fire. If it burns very brightly, you'll live a long life.

To delay going gray, eat *hijiki*—a sea vegetable found in China, Korea, and Japan. (Note: the FDA advises *against* eating hijiki. It contains toxic levels of arsenic.)

Nacho nightmares: Research shows that eating spicy foods before bed can disturb your sleep.

GANGSTERS' PARADISE

Rural Wisconsin was once the perfect place for bad guys to hide out. Today tourists can chill where crooks used to beat the heat.

NORTHSIDE STORY

During the Prohibition Era (1920–1933), when Chicago's most notorious bootleggers and racketeers needed to lie low for a while, they'd head north to Michigan, Wisconsin, and Minnesota. Al "Scarface" Capone, "Bugs" Moran, and "Polack Joe" Saltis all had hideouts in Wisconsin's North Woods. Capone's lodge sat on 400 acres on Perch Lake near Couderay, in the northwestern part of the state. Special gangster features included 18-inch walls, two stone guard towers for machine-gun-toting goons, an eight-car garage, and a light switch in Capone's bedroom that illuminated the entire grounds. He had a bunkhouse for his henchmen and a thick-walled cement jail cell for his enemies. From his fortress on the 45-acre lake, Capone greeted seaplanes smuggling in bootlegged alcohol from Canada and kept a long-distance eye on his gambling and prostitution rings back in Chicago.

Saltis, a Chicago gang leader and speakeasy operator, built his cedar lodge on Barker Lake in the town of Winter, not far from Capone's spread. Besides the main lodge, Barker Lake Lodge had a nine-hole golf course and private cabins tucked safely into the woods, where visiting gunmen, called "blazers," could lie low and get a little R&R.

FISH WITH THE FISHES

Many of America's deadliest criminals were also avid outdoorsmen. Not far from Saltis's and Capone's hideouts on the Chippewa Flowage was the Herman's Landing Resort, a popular destination for gunman who liked to fish. On October 22, 1949, according to James "Pepsi" Buono, chauffeur to mob kingpin Joseph "Joey Doves" Aiuppa, his boss caught a record-setting 69-pound 11-ounce muskelunge on the resort's river. Instead of keeping it, says Buono, he sold the muskie (for $50) to a local fisherman named Louis Spray, who registered it as his own. Is it a fish story? We'll never know for sure. What we do know, however, is that Spray's record still stands.

There are more Indian restaurants in London than there are in Mumbai (Bombay).

PUBLIC ENEMY #1

Manitowish Waters, in far northern Wisconsin, is a chain of ten
pristine lakes linked by 4,200 acres of land, and is legendary for its
gangster gatherings. The most famous one took place in April 1934
at the Little Bohemia Lodge on Little Star Lake. "Public Enemy"
John Dillinger's gang—including George "Baby Face" Nelson,
Homer Van Meter, Tommy Carroll, and John "Red" Hamilton—
was holed up at the lodge. The FBI got wind of their gathering
and planned to ambush the crooks as they left the Little Bohemia
the next morning. But Dillinger changed his mind and decided
to leave that night, which sent the FBI racing to intercept them
at the lodge. Unfortunately, the trigger-happy feds mistook three
innocent diners leaving the lodge's restaurant for gang members
and sprayed them with bullets. That alerted the Dillinger gang, who
then joined the shootout, killing two FBI agents. Dillinger and the
other gangsters escaped out the back window. Baby Face Nelson ran
18 miles to Ollie Catfish's cabin, held Catfish hostage, and hid there
for a few days before slipping away. The Dillinger gang's days were
numbered, however. On July 22, 1934, Dillinger was gunned down
by the police on the streets of Chicago. Nelson met his end in a
shootout on the Illinois Highway on November 27, 1934.

WHERE ARE THEY NOW?

• Today, tourists can stay at Nelson's hideout—it's "Cabin #5" at
Dillman's Bay Resort in Lac du Flambeau. The Little Bohemia Club
is now a supper club that plays host to "bullet-hole customers" who
come to eat and gawk at the bullet-riddled windows and walls.

• Herman's Landing is still there (now called The Landing), and it's
more popular than ever since the government stocked the Chippewa
Flowage with 4 million walleye and more than 300,000 muskie.

• Since 1954, Capone's lodge has been a tourist destination called
The Hideout, serving prime rib in the garage where the gangster's
eight limos were housed and offering tours of the lodge and cabins.
In 2009 a local bank foreclosed on the property, and the Lac Courte
Oreilles tribe bought back the land (they had owned it originally) for
$2.6 million. There is now discussion of turning it into an assisted-
living facility for the area's elderly, many of whom remember the
gangsters coming to Couderay in "fancy cars" during the Depression
and throwing dollar bills out of the windows to townspeople.

Studies show: If you work out on Monday, you're more likely to exercise throughout the week.

NUDES & PRUDES

Nudity can be shocking…and so can prudery.
Which side of the fence do you fall on?

NUDE… Sixty-three-year-old Stephen Dombeck was taking a leisurely stroll down a sidewalk in Maple Grove, Minnesota, wearing nothing but a pair of high heels. When a police car approached, Dombeck clumsily ran back to his car and drove away, but he was quickly captured and arrested for indecent exposure. He was also treated for cuts to his feet because…well, have you ever tried to run from the cops wearing high heels?

PRUDE… In 2011 the town of Coalville, Utah, purchased an outdoor sculpture called *Leaf Dancer*, depicting a nude female figure made of metal leaves connected by wire. "We thought it was immodest," said resident Bridget Wright, "so we started taking old clothes, and dressing her." Before long, other locals joined in the fun. Since then, *Leaf Dancer* has been dressed up as a chef, a nun, a pirate, and a hula girl. Town officials now sponsor a "Dress Up the *Leaf Dancer*" event every summer.

NUDE… Italian extreme-sports star Roberta Mancino has made thousands of skydives…including five with no clothes on. But she explains that the nude jumps are "never for fun" because skydiving naked is "painful and *so* cold." So why do it? For money. Mancino also happens to be a world-famous model, and she uses photos of her nude skydiving shoots to fund her other hobbies—including BASE jumping, wingsuit flying, and swimming with sharks…which she does fully clothed. (Sorry, sharks.)

PRUDE… In 2014, while at a shopping mall in Orem, Utah, with her 18-year-old son, Judy Cox was shocked to see T-shirts that featured images of "scantily dressed models in provocative poses" displayed in the window of PacSun, a trendy clothing store. She complained to the manager, who agreed that the shirts were offensive but said he didn't have the authority to remove them without permission from the corporate office. So Cox came up with her own solution: she bought all of the $28 shirts herself. Cost: $567.

To ensure its growth, World Wide Web inventor Tim Berners-Lee refused to patent the idea.

NUDE... In 2012 the National Galleries of Scotland advertised an upcoming exhibit with a poster of Picasso's *Nude Woman in a Red Armchair* in Edinburgh Airport. Typical of the Cubist painter's style, the woman's proportions are not lifelike. That didn't stop passengers from complaining, prompting airport officials to cover her naughty bits. National Gallery director John Leighton was outraged: "It is bizarre that all kinds of images of women in various states of undress are used in contemporary advertising without comment, but somehow a painted nude by one of the world's most famous artists has to be removed!" (This entry would have been in the "prude" category, but airport officials reconsidered and uncovered the poster.)

PRUDE... In 2008 Yvette Dean was walking her 7-year-old son to school in Springfield, Virginia, when she saw 29-year-old Erick Williamson standing naked in the doorway to his carport. She immediately called police, who cited Williamson for indecent exposure. He explained that he sleeps naked, and because there was no one else home that morning, he made coffee in the buff. "It was dark, and I had no idea anyone was outside looking in at me," he said. The judge found him guilty, saying Williamson "wanted to be seen." But though he wasn't jailed or fined, Williamson wanted his name cleared. So, risking a year in jail if convicted, he appealed. After a six-month court battle that cost thousands of dollars in legal fees—Williamson was finally acquitted.

NUDE... People who love being naked—and love God—have a place to worship in Southampton, Virginia. Since 2006 Pastor Allen Parker has preached au naturel at the White Tail Chapel in a nudist resort located in the rural town. Calling other churches' clothing requirements "pretentious," Parker says, "When Jesus was born he was naked, when he was crucified he was naked, and when he arose he was naked. If God made us that way, how can that be wrong?"

PRUDE... In 2013 French weather girl Doria Tillier—a former model—pledged that if France's soccer team came back from a 2–0 deficit, she would present the weather *à poil* ("in the nude"). To her horror, the team won. Staying true to her word, Tillier stripped down to her boots and read the forecast from the middle of a field hundreds of feet away from the camera. And from that distance, she was just a tiny naked dot.

I HATE BEING FAMOUS!

Oh, those poor, poor A-listers.

"There's nothing good about being famous. You can get the table you want in a restaurant. It gets you doctor's appointments. But what's that worth? Nothing."
 —Harrison Ford

"Sometimes I feel like a zoo animal. I'll be at a restaurant, and someone will put their phone in my face and take a picture without saying hi."
 —Kim Kardashian

"The worst thing for me is the fame. I've never understood why anyone wants people to know who they are. That's the thing I wish I could turn off."
 —Ricky Gervais

"Somehow you're not supporting your film if you don't go on every talk show and talk about your personal life."
 —Brad Pitt

"I don't want to be a product."
 —Johnny Depp

"I can't go out without being recognized. Simply put, it's a pain in the *ss."
 —Daniel Craig

"They wait at the end of my street in their cars. Every time I exit my home, I have company."
 —Ashton Kutcher

"When you start living in that world, you start feeling raped."
 —Charlize Theron, when asked if she Googles herself

"A certain amount of success you can mentally deal with, but there's a point where you think, 'Jesus Christ, what is this? I'm not that great!'"
 —Robert Pattinson

"It's a pretty horrific profession, really. Every photo takes away a bit of your soul. I wish I was just an insignificant speck."
 —Keira Knightley

On the other hand…
"This guy came up to me and said, 'Man, I'd hate to be you right now, no privacy at all.' And I was thinking, 'Sure thing, man, I have a @#$* Rolls Royce, a million dollars in the bank, and my own jet—and you feel sorry for me? What are you?'"
 —Noel Gallagher

Emily Dickinson wrote 1,789 poems. Only 10 were published in her lifetime, all anonymously.

BENNIES FROM HEAVEN

Does your employer provide job benefits? Not all do, of course. So if you're job hunting, here are a few companies that offer some fantastic—and unusual—perks to let their employees know they're appreciated.

• **Google** believes that happy employees work harder, so it provides many benefits, such as free breakfast, lunch, and dinner, and free oil changes and car washes at its Mountain View, California, campus. And if a Google employee dies, his or her spouse or partner receives 50 percent of the deceased person's salary...for 10 years.

• **AOL** offers eight paid weeks of maternity for new moms...and dads. Employees who've recently adopted a baby get two weeks. The company also offers pre- and postnatal baby-care courses, and on site day care.

• **Dealer.com** is an automotive consulting company. Its workers do most of their work on computers, and the company doesn't want them to get lethargic and unhealthy, so it provides free organic vegetables and salads, delivered right to their desks.

• **Chesapeake Energy** offers beauty services. Employees have free access to tanning beds, along with lesion removal, cancer screenings, and Botox injections.

• Portland-based **Umpqua Bank** requires its tellers to dress in professional business attire. That can be expensive, so the company gives new employees a "clothing advance" of up to $500. All other employees can get clothes loans of up to $1,000 per year.

• **Scottrade** is an online investing service, yet they have outlets all around the country. Reason: they'll open a new branch in an area if an employee is considering moving there. So far, they've opened 20 new locations because a Scottrade worker wanted to move there.

• **Threadless Design** produces and sells T-shirts. The company gives employees free beer. Threadless's CEO is friends with the owner of Chicago brewery Finch's Beer, and asked him to create a special beer for Threadless. Now, "Threadless IPA" is always available on tap in the employee kitchen.

The toxins in death cap mushrooms (*Amanita phalloides*) can cause your liver cells to burst.

YOU BET YOUR LIFE

Uncle John once bet a guy $100 he could walk into a 7-Eleven buck naked singing "I'm a Lumberjack" at the top of his lungs, grab an armload of beef jerky and candy bars, walk out the door—and nobody would try to stop him. (That's how Uncle John got inducted into the New Jersey "Things Not to Say to Policemen" Hall of Fame.) Here are a few more oddball gambles.

SWIMS WITH THE FISHES

Gambler: Captain Matthew Webb of Shropshire, England

Background: Webb was a British Merchant Navy captain and daredevil swimmer who, in 1875, at the age of 27, became the first person ever to swim across the English Channel. In 1883 he took his daredevil skills to the United States.

The Bet: Webb would attempt to swim through the Whirlpool Rapids, a narrow section of turbulent rapids on the Niagara River a little more than a mile below Niagara Falls and ending in a massive whirlpool. Payoff: fame—and the fortune that came with it. (Webb had tried to raise $10,000 directly for the event, but failed. Strapped for cash, and with a wife and two young children to care for, he decided to attempt the swim anyway, because if he succeeded he was already guaranteed $1,600—about $37,000 in today's money— for an exhibition the following week in Massachusetts, with hopes of many more such lucrative exhibitions to follow.) On July 24, 1883, Webb took a ferry to a point just before the start of the rapids, stripped down to his red swimming trunks, and, with 500 people watching, dove into the water.

Outcome: Webb's body was found four days later. Witnesses say he actually made it through the rapids but was sucked into the whirlpool and disappeared. His body was recovered near the town of Lewiston, New York, about five miles downstream from where he had entered the water.

A RUN FOR HIS MONEY

Gambler: Ashton Griffin of Orlando, Florida

Background: One morning in February 2011, Griffin, just 22 and a professional high-stakes poker player since he was in his teens (he made his first million gambling online when he was just 19), was talking with some friends when the conversation turned to the subject of long-distance running. That, Griffin said later, led to some "yelling" after which "numbers were thrown around." When the dust settled, Griffin had made an official wager with his room-mate, fellow poker pro Haseeb Qureshi.

The Bet: Griffin bet Qureshi $300,000 that he could run 70 miles on a treadmill over a span of 24 hours, to begin immediately. Qureshi took the bet because he knew that Griffin had had only four hours of sleep the night before and that he was hung over. And although he was physically fit, Griffin had never run farther than 13 miles in his life. Qureshi also got Griffin to give him 3 to 1 odds, meaning that if Griffin lost, he'd owe Qureshi $900,000. Griffin started running on the treadmill in their apartment complex's gym at noon that very day.

Outcome: Qureshi regretted making the bet even before the 24-hour period was over because Griffin seemed to be causing himself real harm as the hours (and miles) dragged on. Griffin's parents even drove three hours from Ft. Lauderdale to Orlando when they heard what their son was doing, and tried to talk him into stopping. Griffin refused to give up…and he finished with 45 minutes to spare. Qureshi paid up—and moved out of the apartment the next day. (But the two men say they're still friends.)

STAR WAGER

Gamblers: Steven Spielberg and George Lucas

Background: In the late 1970s, director George Lucas was in the midst of making a film when he visited his friend, director Steven Spielberg, on the set of the film *he* was working on. Lucas was so impressed with what he saw, and so nervous about his own film, that he suggested an odd wager.

The Bet: Lucas offered to trade 2.5 percent of the profits from his movie for 2.5 percent of the profits from Spielberg's. Convinced that Lucas's film would be a bigger hit, Spielberg agreed.

Outcome: The year was 1977. Spielberg was working on *Close Encounters of the Third Kind*; Lucas was working on *Star Wars*. Who got the better deal? Spielberg. *Star Wars* did a lot better at the box office than *Close Encounters* did, and, by some estimates, the friendly wager ended up costing Lucas around $40 million. And according to Spielberg, Lucas paid up. (Not that $40 million would have hurt Lucas—who's worth about $5 billion today.)

HOW DRY I AM

Gambler: Erick Lindgren of Las Vegas, Nevada

Background: Lindgren is a two-time World Series of Poker champion with lifetime gambling earnings upwards of $9 million. He's a pretty good golfer, too. In June 2007, he was at a bar with friends when he made an offhand comment about spending an entire day golfing. One thing led to another, and…

The Bet: Lindgren bet several of the friends a total of $340,000 that he could play four rounds of golf in one day, between sunrise and sunset. The rounds had to be played at Las Vegas's Bear's Best Golf Course. Lindgren had to walk (no cart), he had to carry his own bag, he had to shoot from the farthest tee placements—and he had to shoot under 100 in each of the four rounds.

Outcome: Lindgren won…barely. He started golfing at 5:30 a.m. and finished 14½ hours later, just before official sunset, racking up scores of 83, 85, 94, and 94. The hardest part: the temperature had reached 106°F that day, and by the final round, Lindgren was in seriously bad shape, suffering from fatigue and dehydration. "At one point I saw him lying on the ground," Lindgren's agent, Brian Balsbaugh, said later. "He told me that he couldn't hear." Lindgren said the bet "may have taken a year or two off my life," but added, "I won the bet, and that's all that matters."

HOUSE IT GOING?

Gambler: Henry Dhabasani of Iganga, Uganda

Background: Dhabasani is a fan of the English soccer club Arsenal, one of the most popular and widely followed sports clubs on Earth. In November 2013, Arsenal was slated to play archrival Manchester United—and Dhabasani decided to prove just how dedicated a fan he was.

The Bet: Dhabasani—who has three wives and five children—bet a friend, Rashid Yiga, that Arsenal would win. The stakes: his family's home. And to make it official, the two men put the bet in writing in front of local town leaders and other witnesses.

Outcome: Arsenal lost 1–0. According to the *Uganda Reporter* newspaper, Dhabasani fainted when the final whistle blew. The

---

"StripeSpotter" software can track individual zebras, reading their stripe pattern like a bar code.

paper went on to say that the next day "several Manchester United fans stormed Dhabasani's home and threw him and his family out." (What had Mr. Yiga wagered in return? His car, a brand-new Toyota Premio luxury sedan, and one of his wives.)

OH, CRAP

Gamblers: Four dudes

Background: *The Buried Life* was an MTV reality show that aired in 2010. It followed the lives of four guys—Duncan Penn, Jonnie Penn, Ben Nemtin, and Dave Lingwood—as they attempted to complete their "bucket list." Number 75 on the list: make $1 million. Toward the end of season two, the guys received a $100,000 sponsorship from Pizza Hut and were able to increase that to $125,000 on the stock market. For the season two finale, they headed to the Golden Gate Casino in Las Vegas.

The Bet: The guys bought $125,000 in chips—and bet them all on "red" on a single spin of the roulette wheel (meaning that if the roulette ball landed on any red number, they'd double their money).

Outcome #1: They won. They now had $250,000—a quarter of a million dollars—and they immediately bet all of it on another spin. This time they chose black.

Outcome #2: They made the single largest bet in Las Vegas roulette table history....and lost. (They lost again when their TV show wasn't picked up the next season.) But the friends haven't given up their quest: they wrote a book about their adventure, and they're still traveling the world, attempting to cross off all the items on the list, keeping fans updated on their website. At last report, #75 still hasn't been crossed off.

CATCH YOU LATER

Gambler: Yasuhiro Kubo of Tokyo, Japan

Background: On September 2, 2000, Kubo, an accomplished skydiver, was in an airplane flying at an altitude of 3,000 meters (9,840 feet) when he jumped out of the plane...without a parachute.

The Bet: Kubo was taking part in a "sport" known to its few practitioners as "banzai skydiving." He had thrown his parachute out of the plane before he jumped himself—literally betting his life that he would be able to direct himself to it, grab it, put it on, and open it before he fell to his death.

Outcome: Kubo was able to snag the parachute in midair and put it on—after an incredible 50 seconds in parachuteless freefall. He then floated safely to the ground. (*Guinness World Records*, which normally doesn't recognize such dangerous stunts, recognized this one, acknowledging that Kubo's 50-second banzai skydive holds the record for the longest amount of time between jumping from a plane and hooking up with a parachute that had already been thrown out of the same plane.)

WHAT A BOOB!

Gambler: Brian Zembic of Las Vegas, Nevada

Background: Canadian-born Zembic is a professional high-stakes gambler. In 1996 he was hanging out with some of his gambling buddies, with whom he often made outlandish bets, when the subject of breast implants came up.

The Bet: One of the friends bet Zembic $100,000 he wouldn't get breast implants—and keep them for a year. After thinking about it for a few months—and after suffering some heavy gambling losses that left him in need of cash—Zembic took the bet. In October 1996, he underwent silicone breast implant surgery in New York City, ending up with size 38C (and hairy) breasts.

Outcome: Zembic not only won the bet by keeping the implants in for a year (the $100,000 was promptly deposited in his Swiss bank account), he still has the breasts today, more than 18 years later. He says he got used to them and has even grown attached to them. He's even made a career out of what he calls his "man boobs," having appeared in numerous TV shows and documentaries. There is even talk of a Hollywood movie based on Zembic's life. Since getting the implants, Zembic has married, and he now has a daughter. (It took his daughter some time to get used to her dad's breasts, but now, he says, she's fine with them.)

*　　*　　*

"Success makes life easier. It doesn't make living easier."

—**Bruce Springsteen**

Philadelphia-brand cream cheese was originally made in New York City.

EAST MEETS WEST

Visit European cities…re-created as housing developments in China.

PLACE: Venice Water Town
DETAILS: In the late 2000s, economic and population increases led to a housing boom in China. Most of the quickly constructed bedroom communities are typical—large blocks of apartment buildings. And then there's Venice Water Town in Hangzhou. Like its famous Italian namesake, it's lined with canals that feature gondolas, although residents travel by train or car. It also contains replicas of Venetian landmarks, such as Doge Palace, St. Mark's Square, and the Campanile. Despite its novelty, Venice Water Town is well-populated, mostly because it's home to many of the workers employed by a nearby amusement park.

PLACE: Spring Legend
DETAILS: Oddly, this suburban Beijing community (built in 2009) bears little resemblance to the German alpine villages that inspired it. Instead of rustic wooden ski chalets, most of Spring Legend's buildings are painted in pastel colors. Reason: residents said they found traditional Bavarian houses too dark and depressing. Another odd feature: For some reason, there's a statue of former British prime minister Winston Churchill standing outside a restaurant in the town's center. Spring Legend has a 60–70 percent occupancy rate, but most of its homeowners only live there on the weekends.

PLACE: Tianducheng
DETAILS: The architecture here lovingly re-creates the best parts of Paris…or it would, if anybody actually lived here. Though it was completed in 2007, Tianducheng's poor location (it's a 40-minute drive from the closest city, Hangzhou) and high prices (the average villa runs $800,000) have kept people away in droves. Designers expected a subway stop to be built nearby, but that never happened. Result: most of this ghost town's fountains are turned off and its 354-foot replica of the Eiffel Tower seldom gets visitors. But although the streets are lined with fake storefronts and empty shops, the town's management still regularly sends out a street cleaner. The vehicle loudly blasts "It's a Small World" while making its rounds.

DINO-GIRL

Looking for shells and other interesting things in the sand is one of the best parts of going to the beach. But how many people ever find anything important? Say hello to nine-year-old Daisy Morris.

THE NATURAL

Daisy Morris's parents knew they had a special kid on their hands when she was only a toddler. Where other kids were interested in toys, Daisy had an insatiable curiosity about the natural world around her, particularly animal bones. When her mother, Sian, made fish for dinner, Daisy wanted to be the one who cut the heads off the fish so that she could see what was inside. If she found the bones interesting, her parents let her keep them.

It must have been tempting for Daisy's parents to steer their child toward more "normal" interests for someone her age, but rather than stifle her curiosity, they decided to support it. "This is what Daisy enjoys, so her dad and I have never said 'ugh!' We've tried to encourage her," her mother told the London *Daily Mail* in 2013.

The neighbors contributed, too. They gave Daisy any dead animals they found, including any mice or birds killed by their cats. Friends and family living far away sent her dead critters by mail, and Daisy also had the pick of any roadkill she saw when the family was out driving. Any animals not already reduced to bare bones were placed under a crate in the garden, then left there for as long as it took for worms, flies, maggots, and other scavengers to pick the skeletons clean. After the bones were cleaned, Daisy got to bring them into the house and add them to her collection, which included a bull's skull, a shark's jaw, a tortoise shell, miscellaneous animal teeth, seashells, skulls, and a mummified frog. Daisy also collected stuffed animals—stuffed by taxidermists, that is.

DARK BONES

Daisy's family lived on the Isle of Wight, off the southern coast of England. The island has been called the "dinosaur capital of Great Britain" because so many fossils have been found there. It was probably inevitable that she would collect those, too, and that's what she was looking for one winter day in 2009 when she and her family

---

King Henry VIII once tried a man for heresy...even though he'd been dead for 300 years.

went walking along the beach near their home. Daisy, then five, spotted some dark bones poking out of the clay at the base of a cliff that runs along the beach. She knew that dark bones are often fossils, so she carefully dug them out of the clay and took them home.

Daisy was so excited about her find that, rather than simply add the fossils to her collection, she and her mother brought them to paleontologist Martin Simpson at Southampton University. Simpson had a 50,000-fossil collection of his own, but didn't have much to offer about Daisy's fossils because he'd never seen any quite like them before. That made him wonder if *anyone* had ever seen fossils like Daisy's before. "You don't get many dinosaur fossils like that. I knew it was important," he said.

PTER-RIFIC FIND
Simpson got Daisy's permission to send the fossils to two paleontologists named Darren Naish and Gareth Dyke, who spent the next five years studying them. In 2014 they published their findings: the bones were from an entirely new species of *pterosaur*, or flying reptile, the earliest *vertebrate* (an animal with a backbone) capable of powered flight. Daisy's pterosaur was about the size of a crow; it lived during the Cretaceous period, more than 115 million years ago. The fact that her fossils were in better condition than most other petrosaur fossils that have been found added considerably to the importance of the find. "This fossil was so well preserved," said Darren Naish, "that we could compare it to all sorts of other pterosaurs. Nobody had really done this before, so it allowed us to look anew at the evolution of pterosaurs."

A MORRISAURUS
Had Daisy not recognized and collected the fossils when she did, the waves crashing against the cliff would likely have washed them away within a few days, and the new species of petrosaur would have been lost, perhaps forever. To honor Daisy's contribution to paleontology, Naish and Dyke named the species *Vectidraco daisymorrisae* ("Isle of Wight Dragon Daisy Morris"). "When I told my friends about it, they said it was cool," she says. She has since donated the fossils to London's Natural History Museum.

So does Daisy want to be a paleontologist when she grows up? "I just want to keep collecting things," she says.

THE FUTURISTS, PART III

The prognosticators we introduced you to in Part II (page 205) had it easy compared to today's futurists. Here's a glimpse into the mind-bogglingly complicated field of modern futures studies.

WHAT IF...?

The scene: World War I—a small village in northern France. Private Henry Tandey of the British Army spots a German soldier; Tandey aims his rifle and prepares to shoot...but then he notices that the soldier is wounded and doesn't even have the strength to raise his weapon. Tandey hesitates—and then makes a fateful decision: he spares the enemy soldier's life.

That soldier, it turned out, was a 29-year-old lance corporal named Adolf Hitler.

What if Tandey *had* killed the man who would one day attempt to conquer Europe? Would World War II have happened? Would humans have ever created the atomic bomb or traveled into space? (Would there be an *Uncle John's Bathroom Reader*? Gasp!)

Those are the kinds of questions that today's futurists ponder all the time. (Okay, maybe not the one about Uncle John's.) Some have argued that because Hitler was only one man, his premature death couldn't have altered the timeline too significantly. Another view: it was only Adolf Hitler's unique blend of hatred and charisma that could have brought the Nazis to power. If so, his removal from history would have *drastically* altered humanity's future. Tandey's decision to spare Hitler's life was the metaphorical butterfly in what's known as the "butterfly effect."

E UNUM, PLURIBUS

The concept was originated in the 1960s by a meteorologist named Edward Lorenz, who put it like this: "The fluttering of a butterfly's wing in Rio de Janeiro, amplified by atmospheric currents, could cause a tornado in Texas two weeks later." Lorenz had that revelation while he was trying to write a computer program that could predict the weather. At one point, he decided to rerun an earlier weather scenario, but he took a shortcut and substituted a slightly rounded-down number in the program. Result: the weather scenario

---

Michael Jackson wanted to do a Harry Potter musical. (J. K. Rowling told him to beat it.)

that followed differed drastically from the original one. Surprised, Lorenz checked his data and saw that the number he'd rounded down—from 0.506127 to 0.506—was to blame. That miniscule change was enough to create a completely different weather pattern.

CHAOS ENSUES

Lorenz's revelation set the foundation for the field of *chaos theory*, which he defined as "when the present determines the future, but the approximate present does not approximately determine the future." In other words, because weather is *chaotic* as opposed to *linear*, it's impossible to accurately predict exact atmospheric conditions more than a week or so out—even with today's advanced computer models. If one flap of a butterfly's wing really can affect distant weather patterns, what effects do thousands of airplanes taking off and landing every day have on the weather?

Worse, we can know that the flap of a butterfly wing will affect the future, but we don't know how—or, as Lorenz put it: "An acceptable prediction of an instantaneous state in the distant future may well be impossible." It would be akin to witnessing Private Tandey spare Corporal Hitler's life and telling him, "Way to go, dude—you've just ensured that we're going to have a *second* world war." No one could have known that.

SO WHERE IS MY FLYING CAR?

That could be why for every prediction that futurists like Arthur C. Clarke and Buckminster Fuller got right, they got a lot more wrong. Some examples:

• Clarke posited in his 1968 novel *2001: A Space Odyssey* that, by the turn of the twenty-first century, civilian space travel would be an everyday thing. That didn't happen.

• Those "World of Tomorrow" rides from the 1950s bear little resemblance to today's world. We still have to clean our houses and cook our meals and drive our own cars (for now). In the 1980s, the *Back to the Future* film trilogy (which used futurists as consultants) predicted that by 2015 lawyers would be outlawed and teenagers would be riding around on hoverboards. Wrong and wrong—not to mention the fact that the movie failed to foresee the proliferation of mobile phones and handheld devices. (*Star Trek* did predict those

---

Household hint: Talcum powder repels ants.

two things, but they weren't supposed to arrive for another couple of centuries.)

• More recently, in 1999 a futurist named Watts Wacker (that's really his name) confidently announced that within two years, the United States Post Office would offer free e-mail accounts.

In fact, very few futurists foresaw that personal computers—not transportation and space travel—would come to define the new millennium. How could they have all been so wrong? "The future is uncertain," admits Paul Saffo of California's Institute for the Future. "And thanks to technology, that uncertainty is increasing." Every new advance leads to more advances, so even if you can accurately predict the world that today's technology will bring, it's next to impossible to predict what *that* world's new tech will bring.

TAKING A RISK

Ray Kurzweil calls this concept a "technological singularity," a point beyond which it is impossible to predict what will happen. That will come, he says, by the year 2030. As one of today's most renowned futurists (and director of engineering at Google), Kurzweil's words carry weight. In the 1980s, he was one of the few to accurately predict the fall of the Soviet Union and the rise of the Internet. But he also predicted that by 2000, speech-recognition software (which his company invented) was going to replace keyboards. That hasn't happened yet—and therein lies the modern futurists' dilemma: no matter how many predictions they get right, every wrong one puts another chink in the armor of the entire discipline.

According to futurist Paul Saffo, "Single-scenario forecasts are useless. We don't live in a deterministic world; the best any of us can do is postulate reasonable alternatives and warn our clients what they should keep their eyes on." Result: today's futurists aren't the celebrated thinkers they once were—they're "risk-assessment specialists" hired by companies to draw road maps of the next 10 or 20 years and help them avoid pitfalls. For example, if General Motors had been warned in the mid-1990s that rising U.S. health-care costs for retirees were going to be a factor in the company's bankruptcy, perhaps it could have structured benefits differently and avoided the need for a government bailout a decade later.

What's next? We predict you'll find out on page 460.

What does the Relative Dentin Abrasivity Scale measure? The abrasiveness of toothpaste.

LIFE IN THE YEAR 1973

A look at life in the not-so-distant (but it sure seems like it!) past.

World population: 3.9 billion (2014: about 7.2 billion)

Average life expectancy in the U.S.: 71.4 (2014: 78.7)

Average annual income: $12,900 (minimum wage: $1.60 per hour)

Average cost of a...

- new home: $32,500
- new car: $3,200
- gallon of milk: $1.31
- gallon of (reg.) gas: $0.40
- first-class stamp: $0.08

Television

- Shows that ended their runs in 1973: *Bonanza*, *Laugh-In*, *Mission Impossible*, *The Mod Squad*
- Shows that premiered in 1973: *Kojak*, *Barnaby Jones*, *Schoolhouse Rock*, *Police Story*, *The Young and the Restless*
- Highest-rated shows of the year: *All in the Family*, *The Waltons*, *Sanford and Son*, *M*A*S*H*, *Hawaii Five-O*

Movies

- Top-grossing films: 1. *The Sting*; 2. *The Exorcist*; 3. *American Graffiti*; 4. *Papillon*; 5. *The Way We Were*

- Other notable films: *Soylent Green*, *Enter the Dragon*, *Mean Streets*, *Serpico*, *Day of the Jackal*, *Sleeper*, *Paper Moon*

Sports

- The Miami Dolphins win Super Bowl VII.
- The Oakland Athletics win the World Series.
- The New York Knicks win the NBA Finals.
- The Indiana Pacers win the ABA Finals.
- The Montreal Canadiens win the Stanley Cup.
- George Foreman is the heavyweight boxing champion.
- Jack Nicklaus is the PGA money leader.
- Secretariat wins horse racing's Triple Crown.

Music

- Top five hits: 1. *Tie a Yellow Ribbon* (Tony Orlando and Dawn), 2. *Bad, Bad Leroy Brown* (Jim Croce), 3. *Killing Me Softly* (Roberta Flack), 4. *Let's Get It On* (Marvin Gaye), 5. *My Love* (Paul McCartney and Wings)
- Notable album releases: *Dark Side of the Moon* (Pink Floyd), *Houses of the Holy*, (Led Zeppelin),

An average baby has its diaper changed up to 10,000 times before being potty trained.

Quadrophenia (the Who), *Innervisions* (Stevie Wonder), *There Goes Rhymin' Simon* (Paul Simon), *Good-bye Yellow Brick Road* (Elton John)

News

• After 12 years, the U.S. ends all military operations in Vietnam.

• The Supreme Court makes its landmark *Roe v. Wade* ruling, making abortion, with some exceptions, legal.

• The 1973 oil crisis begins. Oil-producing Arab nations cease exports, causing oil prices to soar, setting off a worldwide energy and economic crisis.

• Chilean president Salvador Allende is overthrown in a coup later revealed to have been aided by the CIA.

• The Watergate scandal, the roots of which were first uncovered in 1972, blows wide open. President Richard Nixon gives his famous "I am not a crook" speech in November. (Less than a year later, he resigns in disgrace.)

• Construction is completed on the world's tallest building: the World Trade Center.

Science News

• *Skylab*, the first American space station, is launched.

• The American Psychiatric Association officially declares that homosexuality is not a "mental disorder."

• The first handheld mobile phone call is made by Motorola engineer Martin Cooper on April 3.

• The Oldsmobile Toronado becomes the first car offered to the public with airbags.

Deaths: Bruce Lee, Bobby Darin, Veronica Lake, Gram Parsons, Jim Croce, Edward G. Robinson, Betty Grable, Lon Chaney Jr., Noel Coward, J. R. R. Tolkien, Lyndon Johnson, Pablo Picasso

Births: Seth MacFarlane, Adrien Brody, Tori Spelling, Juliette Lewis, Heidi Klum, Neil Patrick Harris, Pharrell Williams, Kate Beckinsdale, Dave Chappelle, Tyra Banks, Ichiro Suzuki, Monica Lewinsky

New Books: *The Princess Bride* by William Goldman, *Burr* by Gore Vidal, *Gravity's Rainbow* by Thomas Pynchon

Potpourri

• Percentage of U.S. homes with air conditioning: 52 percent (today: 87 percent)

• Automobile deaths in U.S.: 54,052 (in 2012: 34,080)

• The first worldwide concert telecast, featuring Elvis Presley, is seen in 40 countries by almost a billion people.

AIRPLANES THAT JUST…DISAPPEARED

*The disappearance of Malaysian Airlines flight MH370 was
one of the most tragic events of 2014—but it was far
from history's only story of a vanished aircraft.*

INTO THIN AIR

Since the dawn of flight, there have been a surprising number of airplanes that have simply vanished, never to be seen again. How many? According to the best records available, since the 1940s—and not counting military aircraft lost during combat operations—more than 70. Many of them were small private planes with just a few people on board, some were military transports, and several were commercial airliners, sometimes carrying 50 or more passengers, whose fates remain a mystery to this day. Here are the stories of some well-known tragedies, along with some that you have probably never heard about.

1944: USAAF 44-70285. On December 15, 1944, Glenn Miller, one of the most popular big band leaders in the United States ("In the Mood," "Tuxedo Junction," "Moonlight Serenade"), and at the time *Major* Glenn Miller, leader of the Army Air Force Band, climbed aboard a single-engine U.S. Air Force Norseman light aircraft at a Royal Air Force station in the southeast of England. Miller was headed to Paris to set up a Christmas concert for American troops stationed there. The plane took off in heavy fog around 2:00 p.m.—and was never seen again. It is believed to have been lost in the English Channel. (One theory says the plane may have been hit by bombs jettisoned by British planes over the English Channel.) Number of people lost: three, including Miller, Flight Officer John Morgan (the pilot), and Lt. Colonel Norman Baessell.

1950: Northwest Orient Airlines Flight 2501. On the evening of June 23, 1950, this Douglas DC-4, four-engine *propliner* (a propeller-driven airliner) left LaGuardia Airport in New York City, bound for Seattle, with a stopover in Minneapolis. At 12:13 a.m., the plane was over Lake Michigan when the pilot radioed a nearby air-traffic control tower, requesting permission to change altitude from 3,500 feet to 2,500 feet in order to avoid a storm. Because of other airplane traffic in the area, the request was denied. That was the last anyone ever heard of Flight 2501. In the search that ensued, an oil slick, some seat cushions, airline blankets—and some unidentifiable human body parts—were discovered in the lake. But the plane, despite numerous searches over the following days and more still over the years, including some by professional shipwreck hunters, has never been discovered. Number of people lost: 58. At the time it was the deadliest commercial airline accident in American history.

1951: Canadian Pacific Airlines DC-4. The flight took off from Vancouver, British Columbia, on the evening of July 20, 1951, bound for Anchorage, Alaska, with a final destination of Tokyo, Japan. It had been chartered by the United Nations as part of the Korean Airlift, an operation assisting UN efforts in the Korean War. The plane radioed in at several checkpoints along the route, the last coming at 12:31 a.m., at Cape Spencer, about 80 miles south of Juneau. Final words from the flight: "All's well." The next scheduled checkpoint, at Yakutat, Alaska, never got a report. No trace of the airplane has ever been found. It is unknown whether it went down in the sea or ventured off course and crashed into nearby mountains. Number of people lost: 38. The victims included 29 Americans and 9 Canadians, many of them military personnel. (Extra fact: Six days after the crash, searchers had to split up to look for a single-engine bush plane carrying three people that disappeared in the same area. That plane has never been found, either. On August 8, a human leg was found on a beach near Yakutat. Investigators believe it wasn't related to either missing airplane.)

1962: Flying Tiger Line Flight 739. This Lockheed Super Constellation propliner had been chartered by the United States military through the Flying Tigers military transport service for use in early operations in the Vietnam War. On March 16, 1962, the plane took off from the western Pacific island of Guam, in clear and calm weather, heading for the Philippines. About 80 minutes after takeoff, the pilot radioed the plane's position as about 280 miles off Guam—and was never heard from again. The most massive air and sea search ever conducted at the time, by the U.S. Navy, Air Force,

Typically, the larger an animal, the less sleep it needs.

Coast Guard, and Marines, failed to find the plane or any debris. The only evidence: about an hour after the plane's last contact, a tanker reported seeing a bright flash of light in the sky in what would have been the approximate location of the plane if it had continued flying west. Based on that sighting, investigators believe the plane exploded in midair, but no explanation for how or why this could have happened was ever given. Number of people lost: 107, including 93 U.S. Army Rangers, 3 South Vietnamese soldiers, and 11 American civilian crewmembers.

1965: Fuerza Aérea Argentina C-54. This plane, a four-engine Douglas C-54 Skymaster cargo plane, had been leased by the Argentine air force, and was headed from the city of Cordoba, Argentina, to San Francisco, California. It made a stopover in Panama, and took off on November 1, 1965. About 40 minutes after takeoff, while flying over the Caribbean Sea just off Costa Rica, the pilot made a mayday call, reporting one of the plane's engines had failed and another was on fire. A nearby plane maintained contact with the C-54 for a short time, and then it disappeared. Conflicting reports about the plane surfaced over the following weeks, including accounts that life jackets were found in the sea (they turned out not to be from the plane), and that indigenous people in the mountainous jungles of eastern Costa Rica reported seeing the remains of the crashed plane on land. Numerous searches over the decades, of both the coastline and those jungles, have found nothing. Number of people lost: 68. Most of them were recently graduated cadets from the Argentine air force, between 20 and 22 years old.

1979: Varig Boeing 707-323C. On January 30, 1979, just 30 minutes after taking off from Narita International Airport in Tokyo, this cargo aircraft, owned by Varig Brazilian Airlines en route to Rio de Janeiro, Brazil, lost radar and radio contact over the Pacific Ocean, just east of Japan. Its fate remains unknown. The plane was carrying 153 paintings by Japanese-Brazilian artist Manabu Mabe, valued at more than $1.2 million. Number of people lost: six, all of them Brazilian crewmembers. (Extra fact: the pilot, Captain Araújo da Silva, also piloted Varig Brazilian flight RG 820, a Boeing 707 that crashed near Paris in 1973, killing 123 of the 134 people on board.)

1986: LIAT Flight 319. This relatively small twin-engine passenger plane, operated by Leeward Islands Air Transport (LIAT) out of the Caribbean island of Antigua, took off on August 3, 1986, from the island of Saint Lucia. The flight was scheduled to take 30 minutes; it was headed to the island of Saint Vincent, just 44 miles to the north. And it almost made it. The pilot tried to land twice but was forced to abort both times due to stormy weather. But despite how close the plane had come to landing, after the second aborted attempt it simply disappeared. No wreckage was ever found. (The sea reaches depths of more than 6,000 feet in regions right around Saint Vincent.) Number of people lost: 13.

THE UNFRIENDLY SKIES

• On December 21, 1923, the *Dixmude*, a zeppelin operated by the French navy, was crossing the Mediterranean Sea from Tunisia to the island of Sicily when it disappeared in a storm. It is believed to have exploded, probably sparked by lightning. Number of people lost: 49. (One body was recovered: the body of Jean du Plessis de Grenédan, the ship's commander. It was pulled up in a fisherman's net five days after the disappearance.)

• Aircraft with the most disappearances: the Douglas DC-3 twin-engine airliner—with 19 vanished. (This includes variants of this aircraft type, such as the C-47 military version.)

• Number of planes lost in or near the Bermuda Triangle: six.

• The disappearance of Malaysian flight MH370 in 2014 was the worst disappearance in aviation history. A total of 239 people were lost when the plane disappeared on March 8, 2014.

*　　*　　*

THAT'LL GET THEIR ATTENTION

A Canadian outdoorsman broke his foot and became stranded on a remote island in Norway in 2012. After three days and no rescue in sight, the man decided to light a fire and then use smoke signals to call for help. But the fire got out of control and engulfed his tent, and the man had to hop away on one leg. Before long, nearly half of the island was up in flames. *That* they saw. Fire crews helicoptered in, put out the blaze, and rescued the man, who was not charged.

It figures: The word for the study of pronunciation, *orthoepy*, can be pronounced two ways.

BASKET CASES

Some of your favorite NBA teams almost ended up with these names.

ORLANDO JUICE. Orlando, Florida, scored an NBA expansion team in 1987. Naming it was put to a vote in the *Orlando Sentinel*. Of the 4,300 entries, four finalists were selected by the team's owners: Heat, Tropics, Juice, and Magic. They decided on Juice, alluding to the area's orange groves...until a team executive's seven-year-old daughter remarked after a trip to Orlando that "This place is like magic." Magic it was.

CHICAGO MATADORS. Original owner Dick Klein wanted the city's NBA team to have a name that alluded (indirectly) to its meatpacking district, and his original idea was the Matadors. He nixed it when research showed that the only pro sports team with a three-syllable (or longer) name that had any lasting success was the NHL's Montreal Canadiens. So he picked a one-syllable name: Bulls.

NEW ORLEANS ROUGAROU. The Charlotte Hornets kept their name when they moved to New Orleans in 2003. But in 2012 the team announced it would change its name and filed trademarks for five possibilities: Mosquitos, Bull Sharks, Swamp Dogs, Pelicans, and Rougarou. What's a Rougarou? It's a mythical werewolf said to reside in the swamps of New Orleans. In the end, the team went with the Pelicans, after Louisiana's state bird.

OKLAHOMA CITY WIND. The Seattle SuperSonics moved to Oklahoma City in June 2008. (It cost them $45 million to get out of their lease on Seattle's KeyArena.) With just four months to come up with a new name in time for the 2008–09 season, owners considered Marshalls and Bison, reflecting the city's Wild West heritage, but ultimately wanted a weather word. Result: they rejected Wind and selected Thunder.

MIAMI VICE. The NBA expanded into Miami in 1987. A number of names were suggested in a fan vote, with the finalists being the Sharks, Barracudas, Beaches, Flamingos, and Heat, which was the final selection. However, owners almost went with another finalist, a reference to something else Miami is known for: Vice, as in *Miami Vice*, the 1980s NBC crime drama.

FIND…OR FAKE? PART II

*So is the violin found in a Lancashire, England, attic a hunk
of junk or the "Holy Grail" of Titanic artifacts? Here's
Part II of our story; Part I is on page 54.*

Part I is on page 54.

PAPER TRAIL

As the researchers for the Henry Aldridge and Son Auction House pored over accounts of the sinking of the *Titanic*, they also looked into the background of Wallace Hartley's fiancée, Maria Robinson, who, if the silver plate on the violin was to be believed, had given the violin to Hartley as an engagement gift.

It turned out that after losing her sweetheart on the *Titanic*, Robinson never married and died in 1939 at the age of 59. But the researchers were able to locate members of her extended family and even located her diary. And in an entry dated July 19, 1912, three months after the *Titanic* went down, Robinson made note of the text of a telegram that she had sent to an official in Nova Scotia, requesting that he "convey my heartfelt thanks to all who have made possible the return of my late fiancé's violin"—further proof that Hartley's violin had survived the sinking and was returned to his fiancée.

CHARITY CASE

The current owner of the violin said he inherited it from his mother, but she was not related to Maria Robinson. So how did she come to possess the instrument? After more than 60 years, the details were sketchy, but from what the man could tell the auction house, they managed to trace the violin's *provenance*, or trail of ownership, all the way back to Robinson.

When Robinson died in 1939, the violin passed to her sister. The sister donated it to her local Salvation Army band, and it ended up with the band's music teacher. In the early 1940s, she gave it to a student named Evelyn, along with a letter saying that she hoped Evelyn's brother would be able to repair it so that she could practice with it. Evelyn eventually put the violin away in her attic, and there it stayed for more than six decades until her son, the current owner, came looking for it in 2006.

Bill Clinton's homeowner's policy covered the legal fees of his sexual harassment lawsuit.

UNDER THE MICROSCOPE

In all, the auction house spent more than seven years and many thousands of dollars researching the authenticity of the violin, including two years of forensic analysis of the instrument itself.

The engraved silver plate with the inscription "FOR WALLACE ON THE OCCASION OF OUR ENGAGEMENT FROM MARIA" was consistent with the period. So were the screws fastening it to the violin. Scanning the instrument with an electron microscope found no evidence that the plate had been recently added or was a replacement for an earlier plate. Analysis by a hospital CT scanner found glue in the cracks of the violin and evidence of a second layer of varnish, different from the original layer, confirming that Evelyn's brother did try to repair it.

But perhaps the most convincing physical evidence of all was the corrosion damage on the violin and in the lining of the leather case. Chemical analysis found it to be not only compatible with immersion in seawater but also consistent with similar corrosion found on proven *Titanic* artifacts.

CHANCE OF A LIFETIME

In March 2013, the auction house announced its verdict: the violin was authentic. The "Holy Grail," possibly the most famous artifact of the most famous maritime disaster in history, had been found. Not only that, but it was for sale. After making a tour of *Titanic* museums in Great Britain and the United States, where hundreds of thousands of people turned out to see it, Wallace Hartley's violin went up for auction in October 2013.

The Aldridges expected the violin to sell for something in the neighborhood of £400,000, or about $680,000. They were wrong. The bidding started at just £50 (Alan Aldridge wanted his friends to be able to bid on it)…and then quickly soared out of sight. After just ten minutes, the violin was sold to an unidentified British collector for £900,000—more than $1.7 million—making it the most expensive *Titanic* artifact ever sold, not to mention the one with the greatest hold on the public's imagination.

"In my twenty years as an auctioneer, I don't think any article has made people show as much emotion as this one," Andrew Aldridge told reporters in 2013. "People pick it up and start crying."

You've got company: antelope and porcupines are also susceptible to the Ebola virus.

HITCHCOCK'S BLONDES

Two things you can usually find in an Alfred Hitchcock film: a cameo appearance by Hitchcock…and a pretty blonde actress in a starring role. Hitchcock directed 22 movies with 16 different blonde-haired leading ladies. Can you match the blondes to their films? (Answers on page 541.)

1. *Spellbound* (1945)	**a)** Kim Novak
2. *North by Northwest* (1959)	**b)** Ingrid Bergman
3. *Psycho* (1960)	**c)** Tippi Hedren
4. *Vertigo* (1958)	**d)** Eva Marie Saint
5. *The Wrong Man* (1956)	**e)** Joan Fontaine
6. *The Birds* (1963)	**f)** Marlene Dietrich
7. *Family Plot* (1976)	**g)** Janet Leigh
8. *Rebecca* (1940)	**h)** Barbara Harris
9. *Notorious* (1946)	**i)** Doris Day
10. *I Confess* (1953)	**j)** Ingrid Bergman (again)
11. *Torn Curtain* (1966)	**k)** Anne Baxter
12. *To Catch a Thief* (1955)	**l)** Vera Miles
13. *Topaz* (1969)	**m)** Carole Lombard
14. *Marnie* (1964)	**n)** Tippi Hedren (again)
15. *Stage Fright* (1950)	**o)** Joan Fontaine (again)
16. *Rear Window* (1954)	**p)** Julie Andrews
17. *The Man Who Knew Too Much* (1956)	**q)** Dany Robin
18. *Suspicion* (1957)	**r)** Grace Kelly
19. *Mr. and Mrs. Smith* (1941)	**s)** Grace Kelly (again)
20. *Dial M for Murder* (1954)	**t)** Grace Kelly (and again)

Hand grenades were invented by the Chinese around 1000 A.D.

EGGS BENEDICT XVI

Some people have a food named after them because they are famous,
and some people become famous only because they've had a food
named after them. Here are a few of each. Bon appétit!

L OGANBERRIES
James Harvey Logan was a superior court judge in Santa
Cruz, California, from 1880 to 1897. He was also an avid
gardener. He spent years crossbreeding different varieties of blackberries, trying to improve their fruit. He did have some successes
with blackberries, but he's best known for creating a *new* variety of
berry…by accident. In 1883 he planted some blackberries too close
to his Red Antwerp raspberries. With a little help from Mother
Nature, the blackberries crossbred with the raspberries to create the
tangy reddish-purple fruit that bears his name.

CREPES SUZETTE

A dessert served *flambé*, these crepes are made with a sauce containing butter, sugar, the juice and zest of an orange, and orange
liqueur, which is ignited when preparing the dish. There are two
explanations for how they got their name: The first is that they
were created for future King Edward VII and named in his honor
when he was dining in Monte Carlo. But rather than accept the
compliment, Edward asked that they be named, instead, for one of
his dinner companions, a French woman named Suzette.

The second story is that they were named in honor of a French
actress named Suzette Reichenberg, who played a maid in a popular
1897 comedy. In one scene Reichenberg served crepes to the other
actors onstage. A local restaurant owner was responsible for preparing the crepes backstage and handing them to the actress during the
performance. To make the scene a little more interesting, the story
goes, he started setting the crepes on fire.

WOOLTON PIE

Unless you lived in England in the 1940s, you've probably never
heard of Woolton pie, and there's a very good reason. Lord
Frederick Woolton was Great Britain's Minister of Food during

World War II and was responsible for overseeing the country's strict wartime rationing of meat, butter, sugar, and other scarce food items. His job also involved encouraging people to do more with the foods that weren't subject to rationing. For one project, he enlisted the aid of the chef of London's Savoy Hotel, François Latry, in coming up with a meatless "meat" pie made with ingredients people could grow in their victory gardens. The dish Latry came up with, boiled vegetables baked beneath a mashed-potato crust, was neither tasty nor popular—the name "Woolton pie" was not a compliment—and as soon as rationing ended, people went back to regular meat pies with actual meat in them.

KUNG PAO CHICKEN

There are a number of explanations for how this famous dish came to be associated with Ding Baozhen, a popular governor, or *kung pao*, of China's Sichuan Province in the 1870s. According to one story, Ding had bad teeth, so his cook created this meal of diced, stir-fried chicken in a spicy sauce because it was easy to chew. According to another, Ding first ate it in a restaurant while sneaking around Sichuan in disguise to see how his subjects lived. Whatever the case, Ding served it to guests so often that it became known as "the governor's chicken."

EGGS BENEDICT XVI

When Cardinal Joseph Ratzinger became Pope Benedict XVI in 2005, it was probably inevitable that someone would cash in by creating a fresh take on this breakfast standard of a poached egg and ham, served on a toasted English muffin and covered in Hollandaise sauce. Enter Chicago's Polo Cafe, which added Eggs Benedicto XVI to its Saturday Bloody Mary Brunch lineup. The dish consists of "a trinity of poached eggs atop 'whol-y' wheat toast and grilled German bratwurst sausage with creamy St. Basil pesto Hollandaise sauce." Bonus: a framed portrait of Pope Benedict accompanies the dish to your table, as you dine by the light of the altar candle that is also provided. Eggs Benedicto XVI has proved so popular that the restaurant kept it on the menu even after Benedict retired in 2013.

*   *   *

There is no bad food in a famine. —**Filipino proverb**

From the 1970s–1990s, the U.S. had a psychic spy program, code-named Operation Stargate.

THEY'RE NOT COMING TO DISNEYLAND

What rides at Disneyland and Disney World have the shortest lines? These do...because although they were planned, they were never actually built.

ATLANTIS EXPEDITION

"Submarine Voyage" was one of three Tomorrowland attractions that opened in 1959. (The other two: the Matterhorn and the Monorail.) Guests boarded a submarine in a pool, and it gave the impression of a deep-sea voyage. When the ride closed in 1998, plans were made to refurbish it into "Atlantis Expedition," a new deep-sea voyage based on *Atlantis: The Lost Empire*, a Disney animated movie set to open in 2001. Coming in the wake of a string of smash hits—*The Lion King, Pocahontas, Tarzan*, and others—*Atlantis* was expected to be a massive hit. It wasn't. Disneyland executives then canceled the ride, and "Submarine Voyage" remained closed. Fortunately, in 2003 Disney's Pixar Animation released *Finding Nemo*. That one was a huge hit, and in 2007 "Submarine Voyage" became "Finding Nemo Submarine Voyage."

NOSTROMO

In the early 1980s, Disney acquired the rights to make a scary ride based on the 1979 horror-science-fiction movie *Alien*. Mirroring the plot of the movie, riders would sit inside armored vehicles on a rescue mission to find the missing (and presumed-dead) members of the *Nostromo* spaceship crew, as they were being chased by a gigantic, horrific alien. George Lucas was brought in to help develop the attraction, but Disney bosses forced developers to scrap the ride. Reason: they were afraid that because the R-rated *Alien* was so scary, the ride would be too scary for family-friendly Disneyland.

MARY POPPINS'S JOLLY HOLIDAY

Of the major animated movies released by Disney during its 1930 to 1960s heyday, only one has never been turned into a ride at Disneyland or Disney World: *Mary Poppins*. Even getting the movie

---

The leathery "armor" plates on armadillos' heads are like fingerprints: no two are the same.

made was difficult—Walt Disney only persuaded *Mary Poppins* author P. L. Travers to sign off on the rights after 20 years of asking. Travers hated the film and refused to sell Disney the right to make any sequels. That's also what prevented "Mary Poppins's Jolly Holiday" from being constructed in the late 1960s. Proposed for Fantasyland, guests would have ridden on a turn-of-the-century carousel, in upside-down umbrellas. It never got past the planning stage.

MOUNT FUJI ROLLER COASTER

Epcot, part of Disney World in Florida, is home to several pavilions representing the cultures of various nations around the world. The Japan pavilion features a traditional pagoda, Japanese gardens, and Japanese restaurants. For its opening in 1982, designers planned an indoor roller coaster housed inside a gigantic replica of Japan's Mount Fuji. And like the Matterhorn at Disneyland, with its mechanical Abominable Snowman lunging at riders, the Mount Fuji Roller Coaster was set to feature a Godzilla-like lizard scaring patrons. So what stopped the ride from getting built? Its name. Kodak, one of Epcot's largest sponsors, objected to Disney building a ride with a name so similar to that of Kodak's biggest competitor, Fujifilm.

LILLIPUTIAN LAND

Part of the pitch used to interest potential investors in the original Disneyland was an attraction called "Lilliputian Land." Named after the race of tiny people in *Gulliver's Travels*, this area of the park was intended to be a tiny village, populated with nine-inch-tall singing and dancing robots. The area was going to feature a miniature train that guests could ride to see the sights of the little town and an Erie Canal barge to take passengers on a scenic tour of "the famous canals of the world" (in miniature). Ultimately, though, Lilliputian Land was called off. Reason: Disney technicians couldn't figure out the animatronics to make the miniature robots work.

*   *   *

"I don't like that man. I must get to know him better."
—**Abraham Lincoln**

Chuck Yeager broke the sound barrier in 1947, two days after he broke 2 ribs falling off a horse.

ZERO TOLERANCE FOR ZERO TOLERANCE

We had to fire the guy who wrote this article because he came to work in a suit and tie on Casual Friday. Hey, how can we keep someone on who won't follow the rules?

BEHAVIOR MODIFICATION
The term *zero tolerance* was coined in the 1970s by police in reference to law enforcement in high-crime areas, but it gained popularity in 1994 after the U.S. Congress required states to expel for one year any student who brought a gun to school (or lose federal funding). School districts across the U.S. and Canada later implemented "one strike, you're out" policies to curb drug use and violence. The main principle of a zero-tolerance policy: school administrators *must* mete out punishment—ranging from suspension to pressing criminal charges—to any student who breaks one of the rules, regardless of any extenuating circumstances.

In 2013 the Vera Institute Center for Youth Justice released the results of a study that showed no correlation between zero tolerance and improved behavior. In fact, the institute reported that zero tolerance policies might be doing more harm than good by punishing otherwise good students for a single infraction. In the wake of those and similar findings, many school districts have announced plans to reevaluate their disciplinary tactics. Could this mean the end of zero-tolerance policies? To help you decide, here are some head-scratching examples of zero tolerance in action.

CRIME: In 2002 seven fourth-grade boys at Colorado's Dry Creek Elementary School were playing "Army" in gym class, but because toy guns were not permitted at the school, they pointed their fingers at each other and said, "Bang!"
PUNISHMENT: All seven students were suspended for violating the school's weapons policy, which included "facsimile" guns.

CRIME: In 2013 Josh Welch, 7, a second-grade student from Baltimore, Maryland, bit his Pop-Tart into the shape of a mountain.

A teacher walking past his lunch table thought it was a gun and "freaked out." Josh insisted that it was a mountain (he'd drawn one earlier in art class and was trying to re-create it in his Pop-Tart), but the teacher didn't believe him.

PUNISHMENT: Josh was suspended for two days. His dad is suing the school district to keep the blemish off his son's record. "I mean, it's a pastry," he said.

CRIME: While he was a senior at Fayette County High School in Georgia in 2002, Jamie Gilman had a part-time landscaping business. One day he drove his truck to school. In the back were his tools, one of which was a machete used for clearing brush. A security guard saw the machete and alerted school officials, who called the police. Gilman insisted that it was a tool, not a weapon.

PUNISHMENT: He was suspended for 10 days and arrested for "possession of a deadly weapon on school grounds." (The charges were later dropped, but the suspension stood.)

CRIME: In 1998 eight band students from Colorado high schools admitted to "having a taste of alcohol" in their motel room during a field trip to Indianapolis. They knew drinking wasn't allowed but expected they would get three- to five-day suspensions.

PUNISHMENT: Not only were they all expelled, they were expelled *retroactively* to the beginning of the semester so none of the credits they'd earned counted. After several appeals, the expulsions stood. "Zero tolerance is exactly that: zero tolerance," said a school official.

CRIME: In Leesburg, Virginia, 18-year-old senior Chet Maine went on a spring camping trip. When he returned to Lee County High School, he hadn't completely cleaned out the bed of his pickup truck…where school officials found two steak knives.

PUNISHMENT: Although it was just three weeks from graduation (and Maine was a good student with no record of violence), he was suspended for the rest of the year. The knives cost him his diploma and a college scholarship he'd been working for. His mother cried at the hearing: "This is one of the worst things that's ever happened to me, to see such a good kid done so wrong."

"We're just following state law," school district superintendent Bill Lewis said.

Food for thought: It takes 1,000 tons of water to produce 1 ton of grain.

CRIME: In 2013 Kiera Wilmot, 16, a Florida high school student, was working on her science-fair project before class one morning when she combined a few pieces of aluminum foil and some toilet cleaner in a bottle of water. The reaction set off a loud "pop" not dissimilar to a firecracker. There was no damage and no one was injured, but several students and teachers heard the "explosion."

PUNISHMENT: Kiera was arrested and charged with domestic terrorism for "detonating a bomb on school property." She was also suspended for 10 days and then reassigned to a charter school. But Kiera, a bookish cello player who said she wants to build robots when she grows up, insisted that she was just doing an experiment. An online "Justice for Kiera" petition sprang up, calling on authorities to drop all charges, and it generated nearly 200,000 signatures.

HAPPY ENDING: The criminal charges were later dropped, and that's not all that happened. News of the suspension reached Homer Hickam, who trains astronauts for NASA. Turns out that when Hickam was a high school student in the 1980s, he and his friends launched some homemade rockets, one of which started a small forest fire. Hickam's high school principal and physics teacher both intervened with the police on his behalf, and he was cleared of the charges, free to pursue a life in science. So when Hickam heard about Kiera, he presented her (and her twin sister Kayla) with a scholarship to attend Space Camp. "I'm really excited about going," Kiera told reporters. "Especially the zero-gravity tank, I've always wanted to do that."

*　　　*　　　*

LONDON CALLING

Frustrated British officials made the following embarrassing statistics public in the hope that Londoners "would stop calling the fire brigade just because you don't want to pay for a locksmith." From 2009 to 2013, the London Fire Brigade received:

- 3,012 calls from people who were trapped in bathrooms
- 103 people who were locked in parking garages
- 69 people who were locked in offices and shops
- 12 people who were trapped in cemeteries
- 4 people who were trapped in allotments (gardens)

Makes sense: Beaver poop looks like sawdust.

BEFORE THE WHITE HOUSE

George Washington was inaugurated as president in 1789 and John Adams was inaugurated in 1797…but the White House didn't open its doors until 1800. So where did America's first two presidents live?

First Presidential Address: 3 Cherry Street, New York City

Moving In: New York served as the nation's capital from 1789 to 1790. One week before George Washington was inaugurated on April 30, 1789, he moved into an elegant three-story brick mansion on Cherry Street, on the east side of Manhattan, that Congress rented for him at a cost of $845 per year. Washington lived there with his wife, Martha; her two grandchildren, Nelly and George Washington ("Washy") Parke Custis; and more than 20 paid servants, indentured servants, presidential staffers, and slaves.

Moving On: As large as it was, the mansion soon proved too small for Washington's needs—some secretaries had to sleep three to a room, and the dining room could accommodate no more than 14 people at state dinners. When Washington learned that the French ambassador, the Count de Moustier, was returning to France and was giving up the house he rented at 39–41 Broadway, he snapped up the lease and moved there in February 1790.

Aftermath: By the 1850s, the area around 3 Cherry Street had degenerated into a district of seedy taverns, brothels, and flophouses; in 1856 the house was torn down as part of a street-widening project. Then in the 1870s, the entire neighborhood was leveled to make room for the Manhattan approach to the Brooklyn Bridge. Today, the only reminder of the nation's first presidential residence is a commemorative brass plaque on the anchorage of the bridge. Even that's off limits to the public: After 9/11 the anchorage was fenced off for security reasons.

Second Presidential Address: 39–41 Broadway, New York City

Moving In: This four-story mansion, located on Manhattan's prime thoroughfare, close to Trinity Church and just north of Bowling Green, was, as one historian put it, "the finest house in the city and in the most fashionable quarter." A visitor who saw it and several neighboring buildings in 1787 when they were being built said they were "by far the grandest buildings I ever saw." Washington supervised much of the interior decoration himself, filling the rooms with hundreds of pieces of furniture, fixtures, and other items that he bought from the departing Count de Moustier, and doing the rooms up in his favorite color: green. "Green was the omnipresent color of the house, which had green silk furniture and a green carpet spotted with white flowers," biographer Ron Chernow writes. "Washington's love of greenery was further reflected in his purchase of ninety-three glass flowerpots scattered throughout the residence." The house was also one of the best lit in the city: Washington had a new kind of whale-oil lamp installed that produced twelve times the light that candles did.

Moving On: Washington lived there for just six months, from February to August 1790. That July he signed the Residence Act into law, which required that the capital move to Philadelphia for ten years while the permanent Federal City, soon to be known as Washington, D.C., was being built.

Aftermath: By the 1820s, the house at 39–41 Broadway was doing business as the swanky Mansion House Hotel. It later served as a boarding house and was eventually demolished. In 1928 a 36-story office building was built on the site. That building still stands; today it houses a pharmacy, medical offices, and other businesses.

Third Presidential Address: Government House, New York City

(Not) Moving In: In 1789, perhaps thinking it would remain the nation's capital permanently, the New York state legislature passed a resolution to build a presidential mansion at the foot of Broadway, at Bowling Green. The mansion was built, but Washington never lived there. By the time the building was completed in the spring of 1791, the federal government had already relocated to Philadelphia.

Aftermath: At this time New York City was also the state capital, so when the federal government decamped to Philadelphia in 1790, Government House served as the official governor's residence. Just two governors lived there before the state capital moved to Albany in 1797. The building served briefly as a boarding house and then as the Customs House for the Port of New York from 1799 until it burned down in 1814. The city sold the site at public auction the following year, and in 1892 the federal government bought it back. A new Customs House was built on the site in 1901; today the building is the home of the city's National Museum of the American Indian.

Fourth Presidential Address: 190 High Street, Philadelphia

Moving In: Washington moved to this location in November 1790, after the capital was relocated to Philadelphia. The 3½-story brick house was one of the largest in the city. Years earlier, when the British occupied Philadelphia during the Revolutionary War, General William Howe used it as his headquarters while Washington and his soldiers suffered through the winter at Valley Forge. After the British left the city, Benedict Arnold, whom Washington had appointed military governor of the city, used it as his headquarters. Arnold is believed to have begun his treasonous communications with the British while living in the house.

As big as the house was, Washington—who lived there with as many as 30 people at a time, including family members, servants, slaves, and aides—still found it to be too small for his purposes. Since there were no larger houses to move to, Washington stayed put and had some of the public rooms enlarged by extending them out into the gardens. (He also had the tub removed from a second-floor bathroom so that he could use the room as his private office.)

Moving On: Washington served out the remainder of his two presidential terms in the house. When he left office in March 1797, his successor, John Adams, moved in. Adams was none too impressed by the condition of the place when he took office. "The furniture belonging to the public is in the most deplorable condition," he complained to First Lady Abigail Adams. "This house has been the scene of the most scandalous drinking and disorder among the servants that I ever heard of." Adams and his wife lived there until the capital relocated to Washington, D.C., in 1800 and they became the first residents of the White House.

Aftermath: After the Adamses moved out, the house in Philadelphia was operated as a hotel, but that failed after just three years. The house was then converted into retail stores on the ground level and a boarding house on the upper floors. Most of the building was torn down in 1832, and what little remained was demolished in the 1950s. By then the precise location of the

---

Start singing! Habitual singing causes the body to release *leptin,* an appetite-suppressing protein.

house had long been forgotten, and a public restroom was built on the site in 1954. Nearly 50 years passed before anyone realized that Washington and Adams had lived where people now squatted. A plaque was then installed on an exterior wall of the toilet; then in 2003 the restroom was torn down and replaced with an open-air pavilion that shows the footprint of the house and also profiles the lives of nine slaves who lived with Washington during his presidency.

Fifth Presidential Address: 9th and Market Streets, Philadelphia

(Not) Moving In: Philadelphia's city fathers knew that when the capital moved there from New York in 1790, the move was only temporary. But that didn't stop them from trying to keep the federal government in the city permanently. As part of that effort, the city spent more than $110,000 constructing the "President's House," an enormous mansion on Ninth Street for future presidents to live in.

The building, three times the size of the house at 190 High Street and two-thirds the size of the White House being built in Washington, D.C., was nearly completed during George Washington's presidency. But he refused to move there—and so did John Adams, even after the city doubled Adams's rent on the High Street house. (Washington didn't want to interfere with the move to Washington, D.C., and Adams feared he wouldn't be able to afford such a big house on his $25,000-a-year salary. In those days presidents had to pay all their living expenses out of their own pockets.)

Aftermath: The city held on to the "President's House" until the federal government packed up and moved to Washington, D.C., in the summer of 1800; then it threw in the towel and sold the building at public auction to the University of Pennsylvania in July 1800. The university demolished the building in 1829 and built two new ones in its place.

*　　　*　　　*

"I don't stop eating when I'm full. The meal isn't over when I'm full. It's over when I hate myself."

—**Louis C.K.**

Every year, about 6,000 American babies are born in vehicles heading to the hospital.

DUMB CROOKS: U.K. EDITION

'Allo, guvnuh! Time to take a merry ride across the pond and read about some of the thickest hooligans in the British Isles. Bob's your uncle!

CLEARLY, BAG MAN

"Ridiculous" is how police described the robbery attempt by Jamie Neil, 41, and Gareth Tilley, 20. The two inebriated men burst into a gas station in Cornwall in 2013 and demanded all the money. Tilley wore a scarf over his head to hide his identity. Neil's disguise: a clear plastic bag. A few moments into the holdup, Tilley's "gun" suddenly lit up (it was his phone). The quick-thinking clerk hit the alarm and refused to hand over any cash, only to be head-butted by Tilley. The robbers then ran off with some liquor…but they didn't get away. Thanks to Neil's creative disguise, his face was easily recognizable on the CCTV footage. Both men were arrested and sentenced to two years in prison.

ELEMENTARY, MY DEAR IDIOT

• In 2013 Billy Joe Donnelly, 22, ransacked a home in the village of Preston in northern England, stealing valuables and a car. He also burgled the victim's greenhouse—where he took a big bite out of a cucumber. The next day, police collected DNA samples from the half-eaten fruit, which they used to trace (and arrest) Donnelly.

• Darrell Shaw stole several thousand dollars' worth of computer equipment from a school in Kent. But during the heist, he raided the fridge and took a swig from a bottle of champagne. Detectives dusted the bottle, and the fingerprints led them right to Shaw.

DEAR DIARY: I'M A DOOFUS

In 2011 Portsmouth police were investigating an armed robbery. DNA evidence left at the scene (a dropped balaclava) led them to Rashad Delawala, 21, who was arrested for robbing a bookkeeper of £500 ($820). Police suspected that his friend Jonathan Ochola, also 21, was the getaway driver, but had no evidence. Ochola claimed he was at home with his brother watching a soccer match that day.

I ❤ cordiforms! Something described as "cordiform" is heart-shaped.

That alibi might have kept Ochola out of jail…until investigators found his diary and opened it to the date of the heist. At the top of the page, he'd written:

Go Portsmouth
robbery happens

"You don't normally get such a good piece of evidence like that," said Detective Mel Sinclair. "But he was foolish enough to put it in his diary, and he admitted in his interview that it was stupid."

HEY! IT'S ME!

• A pair of technically challenged burglars broke into a British auto-repair shop in 2007 and promptly deactivated the TV camera, the alarm system, and the phone system. But amidst all their button pressing and switch flipping, one of them unwittingly activated a voice-recording system. Then for the next few minutes, as they were stealing thousands of dollars in cash and merchandise, they not only said each other's names (Sean and Johno), they talked about past crimes and discussed the best ways to break and enter. Police had little trouble tracking them down and arresting them.

• Peter Addison and a friend vandalized a children's campsite building in Cheshire. How did the cops find them? Because Addison wrote on the wall, "Peter Addison was here." Inspector Gareth Woods of the Cheshire Police commented, "There are some pretty stupid criminals around, but to leave your own name at the scene of the crime takes the biscuit."

• Troy Hamilton's crime was so dumb that he was actually sentenced to take a "thinking skills" course. In 2012 the 27-year-old Welshman went to a gas station in Holywell, walked up to the CCTV camera, and removed it from the wall without being seen by witnesses. Hamilton apparently didn't realize that all the camera does is *record* video—it doesn't store it. Result: Investigators got an up-close look at the thief's screen-filling face before the screen went black. They recognized Hamilton and arrested him at his home. (He said he stole the camera for "security reasons.") At his trial, the public defender was at a loss for words: "It's just one of those things. I think the less I say about it the better."

*   *   *

"The crisis of today is the joke of tomorrow." —**H. G. Wells**

The Scottish dress kilt was created by Tom Rawlinson, an Englishman, in 1727.

TV FACTS: THE 1990s

Must-read facts from the "Must See TV" era.

Seinfeld. Jerry Seinfeld decided to end the show after its ninth season, in 1997–98. It was the #1 show on TV for the year. NBC wanted a tenth season, and Seinfeld turned them down…along with an estimated $110 million.

Friends. David Schwimmer co-starred as paleontologist Dr. Ross Geller. Unbeknownst to the series' creators, there's a real paleontologist (in Ohio) named Dr. David R. Schwimmer.

Quantum Leap. Of the 96 times Sam (Scott Bakula) "leaped" through time and into the bodies of other people, every year he visited was between 1953 and 1987, including leaps into the bodies of Lee Harvey Oswald, Elvis, and Dr. Ruth.

3rd Rock from the Sun. Over its six seasons, NBC changed its time slot 15 times—a TV record.

Home Improvement. When reruns were sold into syndication in 1995 (for a then-record $600 million), the producers included one brand-new episode to air as part of the rerun package—a TV first.

NYPD Blue. Acclaimed for its gritty realism, the show was also the first to routinely feature obscured nudity. Of the 24 regular cast members over the series' 12 seasons, only one, actor Bill Brochtrup, never appeared nude, seminude, or in revealing clothing.

Full House. ABC unexpectedly canceled the top-30 hit in 1995 after eight seasons. Why? It was going to sell the show to the WB Network. The cast balked—John Stamos felt it was an unceremonious dumping. He threatened to walk, and the deal was scrapped.

Northern Exposure. Marilyn Whirlwind, the near-silent receptionist for Dr. Joel Fleischman, was portrayed by Elaine Miles. It was her first-ever role, and she wasn't even looking to become an actress. She accompanied her mother to the audition…and producers asked her if she was interested. (She was.)

Attila the Hun's burial party was killed to hide his grave. (It has never been found.)

TALES FROM
THE CRYPTIDS

*Cryptids are creatures that are imaginary (or maybe just unverified). The
Loch Ness Monster? Bigfoot? Before you dismiss them, remember that the
platypus, kangaroo, giant squid, and okapi were also once thought to
be myths. (European zoologists dismissed the okapi as "the African
unicorn" before British explorer Harry Johnston sent a skull and
skin back home in 1901.) Here are some creatures even
weirder…yet some people swear they're real.*

Name: Bunyip
Home: Australia
Story: Aboriginal Australians have long told tales of the
bunyip (translation: "evil spirit"), a creature that swims like a frog,
walks on its back legs, shrieks like a banshee, and eats people. In
the 1800s the natives' stories were so vivid that European settlers assumed the bunyip was just another frighteningly strange
Australian animal that they just hadn't seen yet. Even if they *had*,
it's not clear they'd recognize it. It has been variously described as

• looking like an enormous starfish;

• having a dog's face, a duck's bill, an anteater's shaggy fur, a horse's
tail, a walrus's tusk, and a body "4 paces wide" and "11 paces long;"

• having an alligator's legs and body, an emu's head and feathers,
a stingray's long bill with serrated edges, and giant lobster claws
to squeeze human-size prey to death (and laying large, leathery,
turtlelike eggs).

Name: Dobhar-Chu (pronounced "do-war coo")
Home: Lakes and riverbanks of Ireland
Story: Although it's also known as "the Irish Crocodile," this
7-foot-long albino otter with orange feet is clearly not a reptile. It
was described in 1896 as "half wolf dog and half fish" (*dohar-chu*
is Celtic for "water hound"), able to move at great speed on both
land and in water. A headstone in County Leitrim is purported
to be the resting place of a woman who was killed and mutilated

by a dobhar-chu in the 1600s. The story goes that her husband, summoned by her screams, stabbed the monster in the heart. It died, but not before screaming for its mate, which rushed the man and also died by his blade. Despite the dobhar-chus' ferocity, they haven't wiped out Ireland's selkies (seals that can take the form of humans) or kelpies (peaceful water horses), which continue to be sighted as well.

Name: Mamlambo
Home: Mzintlava River near Mt. Ayliff, South Africa
Story: According to modern mythology, this 65-foot-long creature (reported to look like a sea serpent with a horse's head) killed nine people in 1997, hiding under a bridge and grabbing solo travelers, then dragging them into the water and eating their faces in order to more easily suck out their brains. The mighty beast doesn't hide well at night, based on its tendency to glow a bright green in the dark.

Name: Manananggal
Home: The Philippines
Story: There are several classes of the *Aswang*—Filipino vampires that appear as normal humans by day and fly by night. One type, known as the manananggal, is supposedly female. At night they can sever themselves in half, their bottom halves left standing in place while the top grows large, batlike wings and flies off in search for prey. Upon finding a sleeping pregnant woman, the manananggal's sharp, elongated tongue pierces the woman's navel and sucks out the heart of its fetus. As with their eastern European vampire cousins, you can repel the manananggal with garlic. You can also kill them by finding their lower torsos and rubbing garlic, ash, or salt into their exposed interior.

Name: Ya-Te-Veo
Home: Africa and South America
Story: Imagine you're a weary explorer, bushwhacking your way through the jungle. You see a large tree and decide to rest under it for a while. Big mistake. As you make yourself comfortable, you wonder why there's a human skull at its base, and realize too late that the tree's tendrils have quietly surrounded you, pulling you helplessly toward the tree's trunk. A week later, the tendrils will

open to reveal that there's nothing left of you but a skull for the next victim to wonder about. Unlike most cryptid creatures, the man-eating tree seems to have no basis in native folklore. It's one of many variations of the "man-eating tree of Madagascar" myth that was invented by a writer for the *New York World* newspaper in 1874.

Name: Mongolian Death Worm
Home: The Gobi Desert
Story: Mongolian death worms are around three feet long and bright red. And despite having no arms, they pack a one-two punch. First, they spew an acid that corrodes metal in minutes and kills on contact. Second, they shoot lethal jolts of electricity over long distances. They hibernate most of the year and emerge from the desert sand in June and July, after heavy rains. They mostly eat plants, but kill camels in order to reproduce, by laying eggs in the camels' intestines.

Name: The Friendly Monster of Ayia Napa
Home: Cyprus, along the coast of Ayia Napa
Story: Fishermen from the resort town of Ayia Napa call it *to filiko teras* ("the friendly monster"). Not known to harm people, sink ships, or even scare children, the six-headed monster's worst misdeed is occasionally tearing fishing nets. There have been attempts to capture the monster alive to put it in an aquarium, but that would be a tragic end to stories of the mysterious monster, which is a magnet for tourists who pay for monster-seeking boat rides and buy its image on pottery, paintings, and other souvenirs.

*　　*　　*

KNOW YOUR CARTOON BIRD SPECIES
Heckle and Jeckle: Yellow-billed magpies
Tweety Bird: Yellow canary
Woody Woodpecker: Part acorn woodpecker,
part pileated woodpecker
Daffy Duck: Mallard
Donald Duck: American Pekin duck (so's the Aflac duck)

RUSH, RUSH & DELAY

Some lawyers start a firm together…either not realizing or not caring how funny their names sound when they're combined. (Lucky us!)

Gunn & Hicks
(Mississippi)

Dumas & McPhail
(Alabama)

Bull & Lifshitz
(New York)

Payne & Fears
(California)

Jeep & Blazer
(Illinois)

Butts & Butts
(Virginia)

Weiner & Cox
(Michigan)

Eggers, Eggers, Eggers & Eggers
(North Carolina)

Low, Ball & Lynch
(California)

Smart & Biggar
(Toronto)

Bickers & Bickers
(Pennsylvania)

Pope & Gentile
(California)

Recht & Greef
(Montana)

Boring & Coy
(Indiana)

Angst & Angst
(Pennsylvania)

Lies & Bullis
(North Dakota)

Slappey & Sadd
(Georgia)

Slaughter & Slaughter
(California)

Sexter & Warmflash
(New York)

Titsworth & Grabbe
(Georgia)

Ball & Weed
(Texas)

Walkup & Downing
(California)

Rush, Rush & Delay
(Arkansas)

You & Me
(South Korea)

Lawless & Lawless
(California)

Collectively, Americans spend about $300 billion per year on lawsuits.

STRANGE LAWSUITS

These days, it seems that people will sue each other over practically anything. Here are some real-life examples of unusual legal battles.

THE PLAINTIFF: Madalin Ciculescu, a Romanian lawyer
THE DEFENDANTS: Constantin Argatu, an Orthodox bishop; and four priests
THE LAWSUIT: In 2013 Ciculescu claimed that he was being terrorized by "flatulent demons" at his law office. At his request, the bishop and the four priests performed a series of exorcisms, after which they declared the demons were gone. But according to the 34-year-old lawyer, that only made the flatulent demons angrier. They followed him home and opened and closed doors, turned the TV on and off, and manifested themselves as scary crows. And they stank up the whole house (especially the fridge). "They roam unhindered," he claimed. Ciculescu called the bishop and the priests back out to finish the job, but they refused. Reason: the remaining "demons" were figments of his imagination. So the lawyer took the clergy to court, claiming "religious malpractice." "If they represent the way of God," he said, "then God's ways are crooked."
THE VERDICT: Case dismissed. Ciculescu was ordered to pay legal costs. At last report, he was taking his case to the European Court of Human Rights.

THE PLAINTIFF: Evelyn Paswall, 82, of Queens, New York
THE DEFENDANT: Apple, Inc.
THE LAWSUIT: In 2011 Paswall went to an Apple Store in Long Island to return her iPhone. Unfortunately, she didn't see the glass door and walked right into it at full speed. The impact broke her nose. Paswall claimed it was Apple's fault that she walked into the door because of the company's quest to appear "cool and modern." She said, "They have to appreciate the danger that this high-tech modern architecture poses to some people." There were small white stickers on the glass, but Paswall claimed they weren't big enough to be noticed. "I may be elderly, but I'm very active," she told the *New York Post*. "And I'm still driving, too." Paswall sued for $1 million.

THE VERDICT: Apple settled out of court for an undisclosed amount of money…and added larger stickers to their glass doors.

THE PLAINTIFF: Louis Helmburg III, a baseball player at Marshall University in Huntington, West Virginia

THE DEFENDANTS: Fellow student Travis Hughes, the Alpha Tau Omega fraternity, and Marshall University

THE LAWSUIT: Late one night in May 2011, Helmburg was standing on the deck at a frat party when Hughes decided to shoot a bottle rocket…out of his butt. Instead of launching, the firework exploded, and the BANG so startled Helmburg that he fell backward off the deck—it had no railing—and landed on the ground three feet below. (No word on whether Hughes was injured.) Helmburg claimed his injuries from the fall caused him to miss baseball games. According to his lawsuit, Hughes is liable because he got so drunk that he thought shooting a bottle rocket out of his butt was a good idea. Helmburg claimed the fraternity was negligent for failing to put a railing on the deck and that the university was negligent because it allowed the fraternity to be negligent.

THE VERDICT: The case against Marshall University was dismissed because Helmburg failed to notify the school 30 days before filing the suit. His suit against the frat and Hughes continued. According to reports, Helmburg received a settlement from the property management company that owns the frat house.

THE PLAINTIFF: Jose Martinez of San Pedro, California

THE DEFENDANT: Disneyland in Anaheim, California

THE LAWSUIT: In 2009 Martinez and his wife were on the "It's a Small World" ride when it broke down. The other riders were evacuated, but Martinez, who is confined to a wheelchair, had to sit in the car for 40 minutes while the song "It's a Small World" played over and over and over….

Martinez's ordeal was made worse because he suffers from *dysreflexia*, a condition common among people who have spinal-cord injuries and are put into stressful situations. If not treated soon enough, dysreflexia can cause a stroke or even death. Still worse—Martinez had to pee the whole time. After he was finally free and recovered from the incident, Martinez sued the amusement park for "violating federal and state laws and being unable to evacuate disabled guests in the event of an emergency." He said, "This is Disneyland, for crying out loud!"

THE VERDICT: In 2013 Martinez was awarded $8,000. Disney officials were ordered to make sure the ride is in compliance with the Americans with Disabilities Act.

THE PLAINTIFF: Jason Selch, an assets manager
THE DEFENDANTS: Bank of America
THE LAWSUIT: Selch was angry. In 2005 B of A acquired the New York-based asset management firm where Selch worked and lowered everyone's salary. When he heard about the pay cut, Selch marched into his bosses' office and asked them if he had a non-compete agreement (if not, he was free to work for another bank). They said he didn't, so Selch turned around, pulled down his business slacks, and mooned the executives. Then he marched out, expecting that to be his last day working for B of A. But to Selch's surprise, he *didn't* lose his job. In fact, his supervisor defended his actions. Result: Selch received an official warning to behave himself or he *would* be fired. So he went back to work...until Selch's supervisor's boss found out that Selch had displayed his assets and, saying the act was too "egregious" to ignore, fired him.

Selch sued for wrongful termination. His argument: because he was given an official warning with a directive to behave—which he claims he did—that firing him was a "breach of contract."

THE VERDICT: Selch lost. Adding insult to injury, the judge called his behavior "insubordinate, disruptive, unruly, and abusive."

* * *

BETWEEN A ROCK AND A CARD PLACE

Sometimes even the most experienced poker players have trouble hiding their excitement when they're dealt a good hand. That's why Dr. Jack Berdy, a plastic surgeon in New York, came up with "Pokertox." He injects Botox into various points on players' faces, inhibiting their ability to raise their eyebrows, squint, furrow their brows, or display any other "tells." "What someone sees across the table is no movement," boasts Dr. Berdy. The treatment costs about $800; the effects can last up to four months.

IT'S A WEIRD, WEIRD DEATH

There's an old joke that goes: "I'd like to die like my grandpa, peacefully in his sleep—not screaming in terror like his passengers." Here are some deathly stories that may sound like jokes, but they really happened.

Mouse Trapped: At a London factory in 1875, a mouse caused a panic when it ran across a table. A female worker screamed; a man rushed in and tried to catch the mouse but couldn't hold on to it. The rodent then ran up his arm and darted into the only hole it could find: the man's open mouth. According to the *Manchester Evening News*: "The mouse began to tear and bite inside his throat and chest, and the result was that the unfortunate fellow died after a little time in horrible agony."

Unscripted: In 2014 Mahmoud al-Sawalqa, a popular actor in Jordan, was filming his character's death scene in the TV soap opera *Blood Brothers*. At one point—while cameras were rolling—he said to the actor who was playing his son, "Son, I think I'm really going to die." The other actor replied, "You're joking." He wasn't.

Light Eater: In Wolfhalden, Switzerland, a woman (unnamed in press reports) decided to embark on a "spiritual journey" by living only on sunlight. She got the idea after seeing a documentary about an Indian guru who claimed he hadn't had any food or water for 70 years. She tried it…and starved to death in a matter of days.

Undertaken: In 1982 French undertaker Marc Bourjade was crushed to death when a poorly stacked pile of coffins fell over. According to reports, he was buried in one of the coffins.

Trumped: Eighty-year-old Wendy Davis was one of England's highest-ranked bridge players. During a tournament in 2014, she got a high-scoring hand so rare that she'd never seen it in her 50 years of playing. Moments after playing the once-in-a-lifetime hand, Davis slumped over in her chair and died. A friend called it "the perfect bridge player's death."

Doggy Downer: In 1988 a poodle named Cachi killed three people after falling out of a 13th-story window in Buenos Aires, Argentina. The first one was Marta Espina, 75, who died when Cachi landed on her. The second was Edith Sola, 46, who was crossing the street when the dog fell—she stopped and was hit by a passing car. The third was an unidentified man who saw the other two people die and then suffered a fatal heart attack. (Sadly, Cachi didn't make it, either.)

Collared: Rob Emslie, 47, of Cape Town, South Africa, was so sad after his pet mongrel, Sheevah, died in 2012 that he wore the dead dog's collar and leash around his neck. One night, after ten glasses of wine at a local bar, Emslie got into his 4X4, shut the door, started the truck, and put it in reverse. Unbeknown to Emslie, however, the end of Sheeva's 10-foot-long leash had become entangled in the wheel well, so when Emslie drove away, it snapped his neck.

Run Down: In 2010 Robert Gary Jones, 38, was jogging on a beach in South Carolina. At the same time, Edward Smith was attempting to land his small plane after it lost its propeller. Oil had smudged the windshield, which is why Smith didn't see Jones running on the beach. Jones was listening to music on his iPod, which is why he didn't hear the plane about to land on him.

Wire You Not Saying Anything? Late one night in 2004, two friends—Frankie Brohm, 22, and John Hutcherson, 21—left a Georgia bar *very* drunk. As Hutcherson was driving them to his parents' house, Brohm stuck his head out the window to vomit. Bad idea. Just then, Hutcherson veered off the road and sideswiped a guy wire for a telephone pole…decapitating Brohm. Thinking his friend had merely passed out, Hutcherson drove 10 more miles, parked in the driveway, and stumbled to bed. He didn't find out what had happened until he was awakened by police the next morning. Hutcherson was arrested and later sentenced to five years in prison.

Unhappy Ending: In 1893 Wesley Parsons, a farmer from Laurel, Indiana, started laughing at a friend's joke. He kept laughing…and laughing…and laughing. After an hour or so, the uncontrollable laughs had become uncontrollable hiccups. Parsons kept on hiccupping until he collapsed and died. (We'd tell you the joke, but we don't want to be responsible for what might happen.)

King Tut's wife was also his half-sister (and his cousin).

TOILET TECH: URINAL EDITION

Your number-one source for the latest developments in urinal technology.

PRODUCT: L'Uritonnoir

HOW IT WORKS: It's a large funnel made out of sheet metal that pokes into a bale of straw, turning it into a waterless, environmentally friendly *pissoir*, or open-air urinal. Invented by the French design studio Faltazi, L'Uritonnoir was created to provide a cheap solution to the problem of public urination at music festivals and other large outdoor gatherings. (The name is a play on the French words for urinal, *urinnoir*, and funnel, *entonnoir*.)

BONUS: When nitrogen in the urine comes into contact with carbon in the straw, it speeds the straw's conversion into compost that can be used in the garden. "Are you used to going for a number one in the back of your garden? Do not waste this valuable golden fluid by sprinkling it on inappropriate surfaces!" says Faltazi.

PRODUCT: The Guitar Pee Musical Urinal

HOW IT WORKS: It's a standard urinal that has been retrofitted to look like an electric guitar and even play like one…sort of. Inside the bowl of the urinal are seven vertical tabs that act as the guitar "strings," each of which plays a different note when you pee on it. A guitar amplifier mounted on the wall above the urinal plays the music as you make it, and when you're finished, a number appears on a small display below the amplifier. Enter that number in the Guitar Pee website, and you can download your composition as an "M-PEE-3 file."

PRODUCT: "Be Clear on Cancer" urinal signs

HOW IT WORKS: Launched by Public Health England in October 2013, the Be Clear on Cancer campaign hopes to raise awareness of blood in urine as a symptom of kidney and bladder cancers. Heat-reactive signs were placed in urinals in the restrooms of sports stadiums around Great Britain. When the signs are not "in use," they look like sheets of black plastic. When someone pees on them, the heat of the urine causes the black to fade away, revealing a red sign with white lettering that reads "If you see blood in your pee even if it's 'just the once' tell your doctor." Public Health England hopes the signs will save lives by encouraging people to seek treatment as soon as there's a sign of trouble. Each year in the U.K., some 16,600 people are diagnosed with kidney and bladder cancers, but if they're caught early enough, the survival rate is as high as 95 percent.

PRODUCT: The Pollee, an "open-air, no-touch pissoir for ladies"
HOW IT WORKS: One of the problems with open-air urinals like L'Uritonnoir is that while they provide a solution for men, the ladies are out of luck. Enter the Pollee, a product of Denmark's "Peebetter Project" (motto: "Human solutions for peeing in public spaces"). Each Pollee consists of four wedge-shaped troughs arranged 90 degrees from one another around a central hub. Four women can use the Pollee at once, one at each trough. "It is used in a semi-squat stance that requires no touching—although handles on the sidewalls are there to support balance," says the Peebetter website.

Three prototypes made their debut at the 2011 Roskilde Music Festival: "Pollee Shy," with high walls that provided complete privacy; "Pollee Topless," with lower walls that allowed users to peek over the top and "keep an eye on the goings-on outside"; and "Pollee Naked," with even lower walls "for women who don't mind letting it all hang out." Peebetter also makes the Simple P—a pissoir for men that looks like a piece of copy paper rolled into a cone. When it's not designing urinals, the Peebetter Project develops "strategic approaches to pee culture" (whatever that means).

*   *   *

4 PRODUCTS WHOSE NAMES ARE SENTENCES
- I Can't Believe It's Not Butter
- Gee Your Hair Smells Terrific
- I Wish My Hair Could Borrow Volume From My Butt
- Kiss My Face

CHEESE JOKES

Uncle John loves cheesy jokes. Literally.

Q: What was left after an explosion at a French cheese factory?
A: Nothing but de brie.

Q: What kind of cheese is a lion's favorite?
A: Roar-quefort.

Q: What did the cheese say after it heard a funny joke?
A: "That's a gouda one."

Q: What cheese is the most religious?
A: Swiss (because it's hole-y).

Q: What cheese is made backward?
A: Edam.

Q: What dance do cheesemakers do at Halloween?
A: The Muenster Mash.

Some kid threw a block of mild cheese through our living room window the other day. I went outside and shouted after him, "Well, that's not very mature!"

Q: How do you make sheep cheese?
A: Ewes milk.

Q: What cheese should you use to protect a castle?
A: Moatzerella.

Q: What kind of cheese can fly and hunt?
A: Curds of prey.

Q: Who was the first cheese-man on Earth?
A: Edam.

Q: What's a cannibal's favorite cheese?
A: Limburger.

Q: What cheeses should you eat on a windy day?
A: Bries.

Q: What kind of cheese can perform miracles?
A: Cheeses of Nazareth.

Q: What hotel did the cheese say in?
A: The Stilton.

Q: Why did the cheese get lost?
A: It didn't know the whey.

I hate cheese jokes.
I camembert them.

ACTOR LINGO

Ever watch an actor go up and then corpse? That's stage talk. Here's more.

Paper the house: When producers give out free tickets to fill all the seats so it looks like the show is a hit.

Peas and carrots: The words actors in crowd scenes murmur to each other to sound as if they're reacting to a speech.

Corpse: To get the giggles on stage (especially bad when an actor is playing a dead person).

Gypsies: Members of the chorus who have worked for years going from show to show on Broadway.

Downstage and upstage: In earlier days, stages were often "raked," meaning tilted toward the audience so they could see the actors at the front and back of the stage. The back of the stage was "upstage" and the front was "downstage."

Lazzi: Unscripted comic improvisation within a play.

Eleven o'clock number: In a musical, the big blockbuster song just before the end of the play (examples: "Memory" from *Cats* and "What I Did for Love" from *A Chorus Line*).

Actor-proof: When a play is so good it doesn't matter who plays the parts.

George Spelvin: A fake name that actors use in the program when they don't want to use their real names or don't want the audience to know they're playing multiple characters.

Dead house: An audience that doesn't respond to anything.

Apron: The stage area in front of the curtain, closest to the audience.

Go up: Forget your lines.

Al Italian: Run the play really fast.

Toi toi toi: Wishing good luck in the opera or theater. It's the equivalent of spitting over your shoulder to ward off evil spirits.

Ad lib: To make up lines when you can't remember the real ones. (From *ad libitum*—Latin for "at one's pleasure.")

Summer stock: Some theaters do a full season of plays in the summer, sometimes with only a week of rehearsal for each show. (Hey, it's a job.)

Funkotriplogynium iagobadius is a species of mite named in honor of soul singer…

COVERS UNCOVERED

With today's CDs and MP3s, album-cover art isn't as important as it once was. But from the 1960s to the 1990s, some album covers became cultural icons unto themselves, and many have great stories about how they came to be.

Artist: Supertramp
Album: *Breakfast in America* (1979)
Story: In 1978 the British rock band Supertramp moved to Los Angeles to record their sixth album. Having come from an economically depressed England, band members were overwhelmed by both the opportunity and abundance the U.S. presented. That sentiment led them to give their album the hopeful title *Breakfast in America*—which cover designers Mike Doud and Mick Haggerty took literally. They created an airbrushed illustration of the New York City skyline made entirely out of cups, mugs, saucers, and kitchen utensils. They planned to hire a model to pose in front of it as the Statue of Liberty until they got the idea to go "full diner" and use a matronly, middle-aged woman dressed as a diner waitress instead. Actress Kate Murtagh (a character actress best known for bit parts on *My Three Sons* and *Daniel Boone*) was hired to play "Libby" and was photographed holding a menu and a glass of orange juice instead of a stone tablet and torch. The cover became so iconic that Murtagh, as Libby the waitress, went on tour with the band, and introduced them each night.

Artist: Fleetwood Mac
Album: *Rumours* (1977)
Story: *Rumours* sold more than 38 million copies despite (or perhaps helped by) its cryptic cover. The design was simple: a yellow background featuring drummer Mick Fleetwood holding a crystal ball while two wooden balls dangle from his belt, and singer Stevie Nicks twirling. What does it mean? The crystal ball was featured on the cover of the band's 1975 self-titled album; the wooden balls are toilet-pull chain handles that Fleetwood stole from a bar in the 1960s and always wore onstage as a good-luck charm. Nicks, dressed in black, was in character as Rhiannon, the mythical Welsh witch (and the subject of the Fleetwood Mac hit "Rhiannon"). As for why

---

...James Brown. (*Iago* means "James" and *badius* translates as "Brown.")

this picture was taken…the band played around with a bunch of props, and hundreds of pictures were taken. The band liked this one best.

Artist: Nirvana
Album: *Nevermind* (1991)
Story: While recording *Nevermind*, Nirvana singer Kurt Cobain saw a TV documentary about water births, which proponents claim is a gentler way for babies to enter the world. Cobain thought the innocence of babies combined with the pain of childbirth expressed Nirvana's music perfectly, and asked Geffen Records art director Robert Fisher to use a water-birth picture for their album cover. Fisher found pictures of water births, but Geffen execs nixed the plan because they felt the photos were too graphic, and suggested a picture of a *swimming* baby instead. Cobain agreed. He and Fisher found a photo they liked, but Geffen execs nixed that because it cost too much (an annual royalty of $7,500). So the band hired photographer Kirk Weddle to take pictures of five different nude babies (all children of friends), in a kiddie pool. The shot the band liked most was of a three-month-old named Spencer Elden. The dollar-on-a-fishhook, a wry comment on the band's apprehension about "selling out," was edited in later.

Artist: Bruce Springsteen
Album: *Born in the USA* (1984)
Story: When Springsteen began discussing ideas for the cover of *Born in the USA* with famed *Rolling Stone* photographer Annie Leibovitz, they agreed on one thing: include an American flag to illustrate the album's title track, a scathing indictment of the poor treatment Vietnam vets received when they returned home. To complement the flag, Springsteen wore red, white, and blue—blue jeans, a white T-shirt, and a red baseball cap sticking out of his back pocket. Shot from behind (so the baseball cap is visible), the cover photo is essentially a close-up of Springsteen's rear end. Some critics thought the juxtaposition of flag and fanny was disrespectful—some even thought it implied that Springsteen was urinating on the flag. "That was unintentional," the singer later said. "We took a lot of different types of pictures, and in the end, the picture of my *ss looked better than the picture of my face."

The "Italian" calzone was invented in a Chinese restaurant in Canada.

WHY ARE THEY CALLED "SCHNAUZERS"?

We talked about doggie origin stories in our canine-based release, Uncle John's Bathroom Reader Dog Lover's Companion—*but we didn't tell you the origins of the names of these dogs. Why? Weimaraner out of room!*

BASSET HOUND. These stout, low-slung dogs are of French origin. They were used for hunting—especially badgers and rabbits—in France since medieval times. The name, which goes back to the early 1600s, was a direct reference to the dog's low-slung appearance: *bas* means "low" in French, and the *et* suffix is simply a diminutive, so basset basically means "little low dog."

ROTTWEILER. Ancient Romans traveled throughout Europe with large, powerful cattle-herding dogs. Centuries later, during the Middle Ages, butchers in the city of Rottweil (in what is now southern Germany) used descendants of those dogs as guard dogs, and they became known as *Rottweiler Metzgerhunds*—or "Rottweil butcher dogs." That was later shortened to just "rottweiler."

HUSKY. "Husky" is a general name for several types of Arctic-based sled dogs, although there are a few recognized breeds that use the name, including the Siberian Husky and Greenland Husky. The term "husky" originated in the mid-1800s as a derivation of "hoskey dog," or "esky dog"—both as variations of "Eskimo dog." (Eskimo people are more properly known today as Inuit.)

DALMATIAN. The famously spotted dalmatian was named in the early 1800s, after the region where it was believed to have been first spotted, er, bred—Dalmatia, on the Adriatic Sea coast of Croatia.

CAIRN TERRIER. These small terriers originate in the Scottish Highlands, where they were bred to hunt small pests, such as rats and mice. A common feature in the Highlands: *cairns*—large man-made stone piles, which were used as landmarks and memorials. These tough little terriers were known for their ability to rouse prey from those cairns, hence their name. "Terrier" comes from the Old French *chien terrier*, literally "earth dog." Never heard of the cairn terrier? You've almost certainly *seen* one: A cairn terrier named Terry played a little doggie named Toto in 1939's *The Wizard of Oz*. (Uncle John's dog, Felix, is a cairn terrier.)

WEIMARANER. The swift, long-legged Weimaraner was bred for hunting—by royalty and royalty only—in the early 1800s. They were named for one of their early enthusiasts, the Grand Duke Karl August of Weimar. (Today, Weimar is a state in central Germany.)

CHOW CHOW. The Chinese call this large, fuzzy, black-tongued dog *songshi quan*, or "puffy-lion dog." The name "chow chow" is a nonsense word, a pidgin English term that was once applied to all knick-knacks and goods from China, probably because the Chinese names were too difficult for English-speaking people to pronounce. So when the dogs were first introduced to Great Britain in the 1880s—they were called "chow chow," too…and the name stuck.

SCHNAUZER. The German schnauzer is known for its distinctively long, squarish snout—and that's where they got their name: the German word for "snout" is *Schnauze*.

BEAGLE. The name "beagle" first entered the English language in the late 1400s. According to etymologists (and the American Kennel Club) it came from the Old French word *beeguele*, or *begueule*—meaning "wide open throat," or "gaping throat," probably because of the beagle's tendency to howl at its prey while on a hunt.

WHIPPET. Whippets are descended from the English greyhound, and, in fact, look like small greyhounds. Their name goes back to the early 1600s and is believed to come from the verb *whip*, referring to the whippet's great speed. They're also known as "snap dogs," after the quick manner in which their jaws "snap up" prey.

SHIH TZU. *Shih tzu* is derived from the Chinese name for these dogs, which translates to "little lion." These tiny long-haired dogs weren't actually thought to resemble lions, but they did resemble lions as they were depicted in ancient Chinese painting and sculpture. (And who doesn't like saying "shih tzu"?)

HAIR OF THE DOG

We hope you never need one…but just in case you do, here are some strange hangover cures from around the world.

TURKEY: Tripe soup (that's part of a cow's stomach boiled up with garlic, onions, and cream).

VIETNAM: Powdered rhinoceros horn mixed with hot water and drunk as a tea.

ANCIENT ROME: A deep-fried canary.

THE OLD WEST: Gold miners and cowboys in the nineteenth century reportedly consumed "pellet tea"—rabbit poop steeped in hot water.

JAPAN: A pickled plum called *umeboshi* is far too mouth-puckeringly sour to eat on its own, so it's generally steeped in a cup of green tea and consumed that way.

HUNGARY: Sparrow droppings in a glass of brandy.

POLAND: A glass of the liquid from a jar of sauerkraut.

NAMIBIA: A "hair of the dog" cocktail, consisting of Irish cream liqueur, two kinds of rum, and cream.

MONGOLIA: Pickled sheep eyeballs in a glass of tomato juice.

IRELAND: Burying oneself up to the neck in river sand.

ANCIENT GREECE: Cooked sheep lungs…and a couple of owl eggs.

THE PHILIPPINES: *Balut*, a poached fertilized duck egg.

PERU: A cold soup of fish scraps, fish stock, lemon juice, garlic, and ginger.

GERMANY: *Katerfruhstuck*, or "hangover breakfast"—raw pickled herring wrapped around pickles and onions.

RUSSIA: A special treat called *Nikolashka*—a slice of lemon topped with sugar and ground coffee, swallowed whole.

LAS VEGAS: A mobile clinic called Hangover Heaven offers IV "therapy" (saline solution plus vitamins, antioxidants, and medication). It cruises the Strip, picking up patients, and also makes house calls.

In 1971 the FBI listed Groucho Marx as a "potential threat to the life of Richard Nixon."

AFTER SPACE

*More than 500 people have traveled into space—and more than
260 of them were NASA astronauts. Going to outer space
is a hard act to follow, but some busied themselves
in interesting ways after they left NASA.*

Astronaut: Neil Armstrong
In Space: He served as commander on the *Apollo 11* voyage in which he became the first man to walk on the moon.
After Space: Two years later, in 1971, Armstrong left NASA to teach aerospace engineering at the University of Cincinnati. He purposely chose a university with a small aerospace department so he wouldn't appear to be leapfrogging over other applicants.

Astronaut: Alan Bean
In Space: He piloted the lunar module for the *Apollo 12* mission in November 1969 and spent a day exploring the moon's surface. In 1973 he served as commander of the *Skylab 3* space station mission.
After Space: He left NASA in 1981 to become a painter. Most of his paintings are moonscapes with astronauts (some actually contain trace amounts of moon dust mixed into the paint) and can sell for anywhere from $35,000 to more than $400,000.

Astronaut: Buzz Aldrin
In Space: He was *Apollo 11*'s lunar module pilot and the second man to walk on the moon.
After Space: Like Armstrong, Aldrin left NASA in 1971. He wrote books, gave lectures, and founded a private aerospace company. He's also been all over TV. He appeared as himself on *Punky Brewster* in 1986 to reassure kids that it was still okay to want to be an astronaut after the *Challenger* tragedy. In 2010 he competed on *Dancing with the Stars* (age 80) and had a cameo role on *30 Rock* in which he shook his fist at the moon and yelled, "I walked on your face!"

Astronaut: Jim Lovell
In Space: He commanded 1970's ill-fated *Apollo 13* mission in which an oxygen tank exploded and the crew struggled to return to Earth.

See for yourself: Mimas, one of Saturn's moons, looks a lot like the Death Star in *Star Wars*.

After Space: In 1994 Lovell wrote *Lost Moon*, an account of the *Apollo 13* voyage, the basis for the 1995 movie *Apollo 13*, starring Tom Hanks as Lovell. Five years later, he opened a restaurant in suburban Chicago called Lovell's of Lake Forest. On display were real NASA artifacts as well as props from the movie *Apollo 13*. Until it closed in 2013, his son James Lovell III was the chef.

Astronaut: Harrison Schmitt

In Space: The only moonwalker with no military experience (he was a geologist), Schmitt piloted the lunar module for *Apollo 17* in late 1972.

After Space: He resigned from NASA in 1975 to run for the U.S. Senate in his home state of New Mexico. He was elected in 1976, but lost a reelection bid in 1982. One notable aspect of his brief tenure: He manned the "candy desk," a Senate tradition in which a Republican senator sitting closest to a chamber door keeps a stash of hard candy to pass out to senators during overly long Senate sessions. (Otherwise, food isn't allowed on the Senate floor.)

Astronaut: John Glenn

In Space: In February 1962, Glenn, one of NASA's original "Mercury Seven" astronauts, became the first American to orbit Earth (and the fifth human in space overall), traveling around the planet three times in a five-hour flight on his ship, the *Friendship 7*.

After Space: Later that year, Glenn met Robert F. Kennedy, who advised him to take a shot at a U.S. Senate seat from Ohio in 1964. That's precisely what Glenn did—he left NASA to run for office. He withdrew before the primary, after hitting his head on a bathtub and suffering a concussion. He tried again in 1970, but narrowly lost in the primary, and finally won the seat in 1974 (and again in 1980, 1986, 1992, and 1998). In 1999 Glenn returned to NASA and became the first sitting senator—and at age 77, the oldest person— to go to space, part of the crew on *Discovery*.

Astronaut: Michael Collins

In Space: As command module pilot on *Apollo 11*, Collins remained in orbit while Armstrong and Aldrin walked on the moon's surface.

After Space: Collins left NASA in 1970 for a position with the

U.S. State Department, and a year later became the director of the Smithsonian's National Air & Space Museum—home to the *Apollo 11* command module that he once piloted.

Astronaut: Dick Gordon
In Space: As the *Apollo 12* command module pilot, Gordon orbited the moon, photographing potential landing sites for future missions while Alan Bean and Pete Conrad walked on the lunar surface.
After Space: He retired from NASA in 1972 and was immediately appointed the executive vice president of the New Orleans Saints.

Astronaut: Wally Schirra
In Space: In 1962 this Mercury Seven astronaut orbited Earth, in 1965 he completed the first-ever "space rendezvous" of two vehicles, and in 1967 he commanded the low-orbit *Apollo 7* mission.
After Space: He left NASA in 1967…for television. He was hired as a special space consultant by *CBS News*. During live coverage of NASA's moon mission, Schirra coanchored the broadcasts with Walter Cronkite. But Schirra might have been most famous for having a head cold during the *Apollo 7* flight, which he treated with the pseudoephedrine-based prescription cold medicine in his medical kit. When that medicine—Actifed—became available for over-the-counter purchase in 1983, Actifed's producers signed up Schirra to be its commercial spokesman.

Astronaut: Edgar Mitchell
In Space: He was the pilot of the *Apollo 14* in 1971 and the sixth person to walk on the moon.
After Space: Mitchell is outspoken about his belief in the supernatural and paranormal. He claims that on returning from the *Apollo 14* moon mission, he experienced *savikalpa samadhi*, a mystical Hindu experience in which a person loses his own consciousness and becomes inhabited by the spirit of the god Brahman. Such experiences weren't new for Mitchell—a year before *Apollo 14*, he published the results of ESP experiments he conducted in the *Journal of Parapsychology*. NASA co-worker Buzz Aldrin later reported that Mitchell once tried to relay information from space to Earth…with his mind. Mitchell left NASA in 1972 and founded the Institute of Noetic Sciences to study the nature of consciousness.

Good start: The first thing hummingbird parents teach their babies is to poop outside the nest.

"WHERE'S MY LUGGAGE?" (PT. II)

On page 73 we told you how luggage ends up getting lost and what airlines do to try to reunite lost bags with their owners. But what happens to baggage that never gets home?

BAG MAN

In 1970 Doyle Owens was working as a part-time insurance salesman in Scottsboro, Alabama, when he got a call from a friend who worked for the Trailways Bus Company in Washington, D.C. The friend asked if Owens was interested in buying Trailways' unclaimed luggage. He was, so with a $300 loan and a borrowed pickup truck, Owens drove to Washington, brought the bags back to Scottsboro, and the Unclaimed Baggage Center was born. Owens started small, selling the luggage items on card tables in a rented house. Within four years, he was buying unclaimed luggage from airlines, trains, car rental companies, cargo ships, and cruise lines. Today, the inside of the UBC looks like a department store, and it takes up an entire city block.

Once lost luggage finds its way to the Unclaimed Baggage Center, the bags are unpacked, and items are sorted and prepared for sale. More than 20,000 pieces of clothing are laundered and dry-cleaned each day. (The UBC operates the largest commercial dry cleaner in the state of Alabama.) Phones, iPads, and laptops are wiped clean; jewelry and art are appraised. Ski equipment, rifles, diamond rings, wedding dresses, and everything else that might be found in a suitcase or crate is priced and put out for sale. Shoppers hoping to find their lost belongings at the UBC will be disappointed. Only once in 40 years of operation has anyone found an item from their own luggage—a pair of ski boots.

BAG IT!

Thanks to features in newspapers and magazines stories on *Oprah, Good Morning America*, and other TV shows, the UBC has become a tourist destination for more than a million shoppers a year. Seven thousand new items are put out every day. Mostly just what you'd

---

Iceland's very first armed robbery didn't take place until 1984.

expect to find in unclaimed baggage—clothing, electronics, books, and suitcases. But some unusual items have also shown up, including a full suit of armor, a shrunken head, a 40.95-carat emerald, and a live rattlesnake. Most of these items the UBC keeps. It did, however, return an F-16 guidance system to the U.S. Navy (worth $200,000) and a space shuttle camera to NASA. One item it did not return was a famous piece of movie memorabilia.

OUT OF THE BOX

In 2005 a worker began unpacking a large crate that had arrived at the UBC warehouse. After prying off the lid, the man dug through the Styrofoam peanuts and shredded newspapers to discover something so startling it sent him diving for cover. Peering out through the mound of packing material was a four-foot-tall monster with pointy ears, bushy eyebrows, and bulging eyes. A metal mask covered in decaying foam latex shaped the face he recognized as Hoggle, the dwarf-goblin puppet from the 1986 movie *Labyrinth*.

Jim Henson's Creature Shop built the puppet in 1985 from illustrator Brian Froud's conceptual designs. At the time, Henson said, "Hoggle is the most complicated puppet creature we have ever built." It took 18 motors operated by four people with remote controls to create its facial expressions. A fifth operator performed the body and head movements from inside the puppet. *Labyrinth* (directed by Henson, written by Terry Jones, produced by George Lucas, and starring David Bowie and 16-year-old Jennifer Connelly) cost $25 million to produce but was a box office failure.

IT'S A WRAP

After filming, Hoggle was packed in a crate and shipped off on tour, only to be lost in transit for 19 years. During that time, his latex face and hands had disintegrated and his clothing decayed. Once the crate was purchased by UBC, they owned its contents, and John Marshall, CEO of UBC, began looking for someone to restore it. Marshall called the well-known doll doctor Gary Sowatzka in Lake Tomahawk, Wisconsin, and he accepted the job. The restoration was completed in 2006, and Hoggle now stands at the entrance to the UBC Museum of Found Treasures, greeting the hundreds of thousands of shoppers who visit the baggage center every year.

HELP! I'M STUPID AND I CAN'T GET OUT!

Sometimes it doesn't take a cop to catch a criminal—it just takes simple physics.

IT'S A LOCK

Early one morning in 2013, police were called to the scene of a burglary at a motel in St. Ignace, Michigan. When they arrived, they found the suspect, a 42-year-old woman whose name was not released, stuck inside her car. She had apparently crammed a load of loot—food, dishes, silverware, furniture—into her getaway car... and then couldn't get away. According to police: "During the theft, the suspect unknowingly lost the keys to the vehicle and after loading and getting into it, realized she was locked inside because the inside-door latches were broken." She sat there until the cops freed her and took her to another place she couldn't escape from—jail.

WAKE-UP CALL

In November 2013, a homeowner in Hull, England, woke up at 5:30 a.m. one morning and went to use the bathroom. When he opened the door, he saw a man's head and shoulders wedged in the small bathroom window. "I'm stuck!" yelled the man. "Call the police!" The homeowner closed the door and did as he was told. Officers showed up, freed the burglar, and arrested him.

PINKY AND NO BRAIN

Three migrant fruit workers in Quebec were siphoning gas from a pickup truck but couldn't get the hose out when they were done. So one of the men stuck his pinky into the hole and tried to pry it out. He couldn't. And then the tank's air flap prevented him from pulling his pinky out...without pulling it off. The other two men fled the scene and called the fire department. Paramedics arrived, but they couldn't free the pinky, either. Neither could the cops. Then came the firefighters; they couldn't free it, either. Needing more working room, they moved the truck—with the man still attached to it—into the street. They removed the tank and took it and the

Fukashi Kazami's claim to fame: First person to ride a motorcycle to the North Pole (1987).

thief to a hospital where doctors performed a "tank-ectomy." The man received stitches, probation, and a $500 bill from the truck's owner.

UPSIDE-DOWNTON ABBEY

In 2008 British police were called to an upscale home in Kent where local "troublemaker" John Pearce was hanging upside down by his shoelace from a window. Pearce had apparently caught his foot while attempting to break into the house. Local residents responded to Pearce's calls for help by taunting him and taking photos. Pearce was freed, arrested, and then linked to 50 other burglaries in the area. He was sentenced to three years in prison.

DUMB SANTA

In 2004 two burglars from Houston, Texas, reportedly fueled by alcohol, tried to break into a restaurant in the middle of the night. They climbed to the roof, and one of the men tried to slide down the chimney. He almost made it to the bottom when he found himself wedged in. Unable to reach him, his friend climbed back down and broke a window to get in, but that set off an alarm. The friend ran away. When officers arrived a few minutes later, they slowly entered the building...and discovered two feet dangling in the fireplace. "He was pleading, begging, 'Oh please, please get me out of here! I don't mind going to jail, just get me out!'" said the restaurant's owner, Joe Mannke, who showed up just after the cops. Firefighters had to lower a rope down the chimney to fish out the sooty thief. "All you could see was his eyes and teeth," said Mannke. "It was the most hilarious thing I've ever seen in my life."

THE HUMAN DOOR STOPPER

In 2012 Manuel Fernandes, 54, tried to burgle a Rent-A-Center in Brockton, Massachusetts. He used a metal bedpost to pry open a garage door a few inches, and then tried to squeeze in through the small opening. But the bedpost didn't hold, and the large metal garage door slammed down on Fernandes's head, pinning his right cheek to the floor. He stayed that way for nine hours. When the shop's manager, John Rodriguez, arrived the next morning, Fernandes was still stuck. Amused, Rodriguez told the burglar to "hang tight" while he called the police. Only after they showed up did

---

Of types of smiles, the insincere smile uses the least energy and the fewest muscles.

Rodriguez raise the door. Fernandes had a huge bruise on his head but was otherwise okay. He was arrested for breaking and (almost) entering.

VENTING HIS FRUSTRATION

In September 2013, a 19-year-old Milwaukee, Wisconsin, man stripped down to nothing before he crawled into a vent above a veterinary clinic in order to steal drugs. But he got stuck inside the vent and had to wait there for nearly 12 hours until workers arrived Monday morning and heard him yelling for help. Why was he naked? He said he didn't want to get his clothes caught on a screw because "he could get stuck." (No word on what actually *did* get the naked man stuck.)

THE EASIEST BUST EVER

In 2013, while goofing around with his friends, Michael Logan Brown, 19, got stuck in a pair of handcuffs. No one had a key. After several unsuccessful escape attempts, Brown didn't want to spend the money for a locksmith, so he went to the College Station, Texas, police station, hoping to get the cuffs taken off for free. While there, an officer decided to run Brown's name through the computer…and discovered that Brown had an outstanding warrant for criminal mischief for an incident in which he dove headfirst into a stranger's windshield and then fled the scene. The cops removed the cuffs and arrested Brown. When they booked him, they found a bag of marijuana in his pocket. "He came in with handcuffs, a warrant, *and* marijuana," said the arresting officer. "In my twenty-seven years of doing this job, that has never happened before."

*   *   *

WHAT'S THE DIFFERENCE?

Q: What's the difference between a stamp and a girl?
A: One is a mail fee, and the other is a female.

Q: What's the difference between a fisherman and a bad student?
A: One baits his hooks, and the other hates his books.

Countries with higher chocolate consumption have higher suicide rates but fewer murders.

BOWLED OVER

In 2013 a newspaper reporter uncovered the NFL's "Host City Specifications and Requirements," a confidential 153-page list of the league's demands for any city bidding to host the Super Bowl. Here are a few items on the list.

• Sixteen months before the game, the NFL will send 180 people to the host city for a "familiarization trip" to inspect the region. The host city must cover all the expenses.

• Hotels where players stay must carry the NFL Network on their cable TV systems for a year prior to the Super Bowl.

• The host city must give the NFL the use of at least 20 billboards at no charge.

• The city must cover the expense of providing the NFL with a task force devoted strictly to busting game-ticket counterfeiters.

• The NFL must be allowed to install ATMs in the stadium that accept "preferred" credit and debit cards. The league may also cover up or remove ATMs belonging to other banks if they wish to do so.

• If cell phone signal strength at the team hotels is too weak, the host committee must install boosters or erect portable cell towers.

• In the event of a snow or ice storm on game day, the city must give priority to the NFL "over all other ice and snow removal projects" (except in the case of threats to public safety).

• On game day, the NFL gets access to 35,000 parking spots near the stadium at no cost.

• The league requires exclusive access to three area golf courses (at no cost) so it can host a tournament on Super Bowl weekend.

• The NFL also requests the use of two "top quality" bowling alleys (at no cost) for a bowling tournament the Wednesday before the Super Bowl.

• After the game, the host city must remove the playing field at its own expense, and, if the league requests it, give those pieces of green back to the NFL so it can sell them as "licensed products."

When Orson Welles won the 1941 Screenplay Oscar for *Citizen Kane*, the audience booed.

HAVE A DRINK ON ME!

Remembering your hometown in your will with the gift of a water fountain is a centuries-old tradition. Some of the stories behind these spectacular fountains are pretty cool. (And refreshing!)

T**HE ROSENBERG FOUNTAIN**
Where: Grant Park, Chicago, Illinois
Background: Joseph Rosenberg was born to German immigrants in Chicago's South Side in 1848. When he was still a boy, he vowed that if he ever became rich, he'd have a public drinking fountain installed in his neighborhood. Why? Because shopkeepers would never let him have a drink of water when he became thirsty while delivering newspapers. When he died in 1891, it was clear that Rosenberg had never forgotten that vow. He'd moved to San Francisco as a young man, where he had indeed become rich—and in his will left $10,000 (roughly $200,000 today) to the City of Chicago for the sole purpose of having a fountain built near his childhood home "to provide the thirsty with a drink."

The Fountain: The Rosenberg Fountain is a 25-foot-tall gazebo-like structure emulating a Greek temple: its base is a granite bowl, roughly 10 feet in diameter. Six Doric columns rise from the bowl's rim to a domed, elaborately carved granite roof, and the dome is topped by an 11-foot-high bronze statue of the (partially nude) Greek goddess Hebe, cupbearer to the gods. (The statue was cast by German sculptor Franz Machtl in Munich, Germany—as stipulated in Rosenberg's will.) The water flowed from a system of spouts rising from the bowl and protruding slightly from between the columns, making them easily accessible to anyone wanting a drink—especially kids. The Rosenberg Fountain still stands today (it's in Grant Park, near Rosenberg's childhood home on South Michigan Avenue), but the water now flows only from one central spout and is no longer used for drinking....but thirsty kids can still splash cool water in their faces if they want to (which would probably be just fine with Joseph Rosenberg).

THE HAMILTON FOUNTAIN
Where: Riverside Park, Manhattan, New York

1st-ever use of the word "bump": *Romeo and Juliet*, Act I, Scene III. (Shakespeare invented it.)

Background: Born in Manhattan in 1851, Robert Ray Hamilton was a member of a wealthy, elite New York family (he was the great-grandson of American Founding Father Alexander Hamilton). He drowned in a hunting accident on his Idaho ranch in 1890 at the age of 49. In his will he directed that $9,000 of his fortune go to the construction of a fountain.

The Fountain: The Hamilton Fountain is made of white Tennessee marble, its main body consisting of a huge Baroque-style carved plaque, reaching more than 11 feet into the air, topped by a giant eagle with outspread wings. Water flows from a carved gargoyle's head (below the eagle) into a shell-shaped bowl that juts from the plaque's center. From there, the water spills into a large, shallow basin about one foot deep and 17 feet wide. Hamilton decreed that the fountain be "so arranged that it can be used by the thirsty as well as serving an ornamental purpose." And by "the thirsty"—he meant horses: horses and horse-drawn carriages were still the most common mode of transport in New York City at the time, and decorative horse troughs were once a common sight in the city. Hamilton's fountain, which can still be seen today at 76th Street in Riverside Park on Manhattan's Upper West Side, is called one of the finest examples of these and is one of the last remaining in the city.

Bonus: The fountain's construction was controversial. Shortly before his death, it was discovered that the highly respected Hamilton, who had just been reelected to a fifth term in the New York State Assembly, had been secretly married, according to the *New York Times*, to a "notorious woman" named Eva Mann. She had tricked Hamilton into thinking she'd had his baby and had been blackmailing him for years. Having a fountain erected to the memory of someone involved in such a scandal was scandalous in itself, so construction was delayed for several years. The fountain wasn't unveiled until 1906, sixteen years after its benefactor's death.

THE GALVESTON ROSENBERG FOUNTAINS

Where: Galveston, Texas

Background: Henry Rosenberg (no relation to Joseph) left his family in Switzerland in 1843, at the age of 19, to work as a clerk in a dry-goods store in the Texas port city of Galveston. (The store was owned by the son of his employer in Switzerland.) He taught himself English, worked hard, saved his money, and bought the business. When he died in 1893, he was worth about $730,000 (about $20 million today). And Rosenberg left almost all of it to the City of Galveston: for schools, orphanages, a home for elderly women, a massive public library (still operating), and $30,000 "for the erection of not less than ten drinking fountains for man and beast in various portions of the city of Galveston."

The Fountains: Seventeen fountains, all designed by the world-renowned Scottish sculptor J. Massey Rhind, were installed around Galveston in 1898. They were carved from light gray granite and, similar to Chicago's Rosenberg Fountain, were all designed in the classical Greek style that was popular at the time. Most important, they all lived up to Rosenberg's requirement that they be for "man and beast." Along with flowing spouts and bowls placed so that people could reach them, they also featured low troughs and basins that continuously filled with fresh water, so that horses, cows, sheep—even dogs and cats—could easily drink from them. They've been renovated over the years (and some have been relocated), but several of the original Galveston Rosenberg Fountains are still in working condition today.

THE JAMES SCOTT MEMORIAL FOUNTAIN

Where: Belle Isle Park, Detroit, Michigan

Background: When James Scott died in 1910 at the age of 80, he left the bulk of his estate—$200,000 (almost $5 million today)—to his home city of Detroit. And Detroit almost didn't take it. Why? Because Scott was, by most accounts, an egomaniac who wanted part of the money to go to the construction of an enormous public fountain bearing his name—along with a life-size statue of himself. Scott had inherited his real-estate fortune from his father and was, according to his critics, a mean-spirited, lazy, hard-drinking womanizer who spent much of his time in gambling houses. (Detroit historian William Hawkins Ferry called Scott a "vindictive, scurrilous misanthrope" who "seemed to delight in feuds, lawsuits, and practical jokes.") City officials felt it would be a disgrace to erect an enormous monument to such a man, so the fight over the bequest went on for years. The city finally decided to take the money and in 1925, fifteen years after Scott's death, the fountain was finally finished.

Turkey gave women the right to vote in 1934, well before France (1944) or Switzerland (1971).

The Fountain: The James Scott Memorial Fountain sits in Belle Isle Park, situated on Belle Isle, a tiny island in the Detroit River (which runs between Detroit and Windsor, Ontario). And it is enormous. Designed by architect Cass Gilbert, who later designed the U.S. Supreme Court Building in Washington, D.C., the base bowl measures 510 feet across (that's almost two football fields), with two highly ornamented bowls made from Vermont white marble rising in layers inside the larger bowl. From a distance, the layered bowls make it look like a gigantic marble wedding cake. From the top bowl, more than 40 feet high, water shoots as high as 75 feet into the air. Water also sprays from the mouths of 109 lions, turtles, dolphins, humans, large horns, and other figures elaborately carved into and around the fountain. And, as stipulated in Scott's will (and perhaps the last of his practical jokes), overlooking the fountain is a large bronze statue of James Scott, seated on a throne.

*   *   *

THE EMOTICON THAT STARTED IT ALL :-)

In 1982 a computer scientist at Carnegie Mellon University named Scott Fahlman realized that communicating online—which was just starting to catch on at universities—had an inherent problem: It was difficult to tell if someone was joking unless they wrote "I am joking." So he had an idea and posted it to an online bulletin board:

> I propose the following character sequence for joke markers: :-) Read it sideways. Actually, it is probably more economical to mark things that are NOT jokes, given current trends. For this, use :-(.

"It was a little bit of silliness," he recalled 30 years later. "I expected my note might amuse a few friends, and that would be the end of it." But it wasn't—the smiley-face emoticon caught on in a big way.

Ironic twist: Fahlman doesn't like the *emoji* craze that his idea spawned—animated gifs of smileys that appear when you type an emoticon. "I think they're ugly," he says. "They ruin the challenge of trying to come up with a clever way to express emotions using standard keyboard characters. But perhaps that's just because I invented the other kind."

CURSE OF THE VICE PRESIDENCY

U.S. vice presidents have long complained about how useless the position is. "Once there were two brothers," said Thomas Marshall, the nation's 28th vice president. "One ran away to sea. The other was elected vice president. And nothing was ever heard of either of them again." Here some of the bad-luck cases, bad actors, and bad apples among America's vice presidents.

VP: William Rufus DeVane King, 13th vice president
Served: March 4, 1853–April 18, 1853, under Franklin Pierce
Bad Luck: Died before he assumed his duties
Story: For 24 years, King served as a popular senator from Alabama before being nominated for the vice presidency. After he and running mate Franklin Pierce won the 1852 election, King became seriously ill with tuberculosis. Seeking a cure in the comfort of a warmer climate, he traveled to Cuba for the winter months. As his inauguration approached, he felt no better and described himself as looking like "a skeleton." The U.S. Senate passed a special resolution that allowed King to be sworn in on foreign soil. Not long after he took his oath at a friend's plantation in Matanzas, Cuba, he decided returned to his Alabama plantation on April 16. He died two days later.

VP: Schuyler Colfax, 17th vice president
Served: 1869–1873, under Ulysses S. Grant
Bad Decision: Caught taking bribes
Story: The owners of the proposed transcontinental Union Pacific Railroad intended to make money the old-fashioned way—by feeding from the public trough. This required some assistance from Congress. No problem: Union Pacific created a finance company called the Crédit Mobilier, largely in order to distribute its stock—and unusually generous "dividends"—to key members of the government, including Vice President Colfax. That made sense because the vice president presided over the Senate and cast a vote in the event of a tie. But then he got caught. He categorically

Female drivers get whiplash injuries 3 times as often as males. (They sit closer to the steering wheel.)

denied everything, even after a congressional committee gathered documents and testimony that amounted to a damning critical mass of evidence against him. A resolution to investigate Colfax (for the purpose of impeaching him) failed to pass in February 1873, but only because his term in office was set to end a few weeks later.

VP: Spiro Agnew, 39th vice president
Served: 1969–1973, under Richard Nixon
Bad Decision: Caught taking kickbacks
Story: In an eerie echo of Schuyler Colfax's career, Spiro Agnew was elected 100 years after Colfax, and left office 100 years after Colfax. But that isn't all that the two shared: Like Colfax, Agnew had a fondness for bribes. In Agnew's case, it began in 1962, when he became the Baltimore county executive, collecting a five-percent kickback from building contractors for each contract they were awarded. This arrangement continued when Agnew became governor of Maryland, netting him at least $147,000 (the equivalent of more than $1 million today). And it didn't stop when Agnew became vice president—Vice President Agnew offered a $100,000 federal contract to a Maryland contractor for the traditional five percent in cash. This time, though, Agnew was caught. He negotiated a plea of no contest to one count of income tax evasion before resigning, becoming the only vice president (so far) to be convicted of a crime while in office.

VP: Dan Quayle, 44th vice president
Served: 1989–1993, under George H. W. Bush
Bad Luck: Exposed as a doofus
Story: Once thought of as an adequate senator from Indiana, Dan Quayle's election to the vice presidency revealed his lack of political and speaking skills. He made enough verbal gaffes in four years to fill a book. (Several books, actually.) His most famous political moments were ones in which he looked ridiculous, for example, "correcting" a kid's correct spelling of "potato" by insisting he add an "e" at the end, or criticizing Murphy Brown, a fictional character on a TV sitcom, for having a baby out of wedlock. And there were repeated public gaffes, such as:

• "What a waste it is to lose one's mind. Or not to have a mind is being very wasteful. How true that is."

- "The Holocaust was a obscene period in our nation's history. I mean in the century's history. But we all lived in this century. I didn't live in this century."
- "I stand by all my misstatements."

It was enough to convince both supporters and detractors to pray that George Bush survive his term as president. (He did.)

VP: John C. Breckinridge, 14th vice president
Served: 1857–1861, under James Buchanan
Bad Decision/Bad Luck: Joined the wrong side in the Civil War had to flee to Canada
Story: At 36, John Breckinridge of Kentucky was the youngest vice president ever elected, but he was also the only one to turn his back on his country and fight *against* the United States. President Buchanan distrusted his vice president and avoided Breckinridge, refusing to consult with him on matters of government. At the end of his term, Breckinridge was elected to the senate, and when the Civil War broke out, he joined the Confederate army (as a brigadier general). He was called a traitor and was expelled from the Senate. Later promoted to major general, he was charged with being drunk while losing battles at Chattanooga and Stones River, Tennessee, and removed from command. When the Confederacy fell, he and some others escaped capture by Union troops by heading south in a borrowed lifeboat, hijacking a boat in Florida—which they lost to pirates—then floating aimlessly for three weeks in a mastless dinghy until they washed ashore on a Cuban beach. Breckinridge sailed from Cuba to Europe, and then to Canada, where he waited until President Andrew Johnson issued an amnesty for Confederate soldiers in 1868. He returned home to Kentucky in 1869, but declined to re-enter politics for the rest of his life. Meanwhile, in 1861, the town of Breckinridge, Colorado, once proud to have been named in honor of a U.S. vice president, officially changed the spelling of the town's name to "Breckenridge" to sever any association with a traitor.

*   *   *

Don't send a dog to the butcher shop. —**Yiddish proverb**

Eew! Banana slugs were used as food by some Pacific Northwest natives.

WINTER BLUNDERLAND

*There's something about winter that makes some people not think all
that clearly. (Of course, the same thing could be said about the
other three seasons, but these stories all took place in winter.)*

ICE BREAKER

In January 2014, a 34-year-old pool cleaner named Alfredo
Bahena-Benitez was draining a pool outside of a Norwalk,
Connecticut, home. He drained the water into the backyard, and
it flowed out into the road. Only problem: the temperature was
hovering right around freezing, so when the water reached the
road—which is on a hill—it turned into a sheet of ice. Result:
several cars slid down the icy hill and crashed, including one that
slid into a salt truck that was stuck at the bottom. By that time, the
pool cleaner was long gone, oblivious to the mayhem he'd set in
motion.

GET THE BALL ROLLING

The two math majors (who should have paid more attention in
physics class) decided to make a big snowball at Oregon's Reed
College in 2014. The ball got bigger…and bigger…and bigger…and
before they knew it, they were at the top of a hill with a giant snowball. By this time a crowd had gathered, and they were chanting,
"Roll it! Roll it!" So the math majors pushed the snowball down the
hill, but they miscalculated the slope. So instead of rolling safely
into a clearing, the ball veered toward a dormitory. Several terrifying seconds later, the four-foot-tall, 800-pound snowball crashed
into a wall, causing $3,000 in damage. The two students said they
"feel awful." Because it was an accident and no one was hurt, they
escaped punishment.

BURNING NOT SO BRIGHTLY

Two men were driving home late one night in Alberta, Canada,
when they got stuck in a ditch on a rural road. To keep warm in
the below-freezing temperatures, they pulled the seats out of their
Honda and lit them on fire. Then they tossed all of their belongings
in, but the fire didn't last long. So they lit the entire *car* on fire.

The value of a house drops an average of $3,500 if any room is painted bright pink.

As daybreak approached, the men saw they were within walking distance of a nearby house, so they went there to get warm. That's where police later found them after a passerby reported the still-smoldering car. Not seeing a house in the dark is kind of understandable, but here's the weird part: both men had cell phones, and there was service. Why they burned everything they had instead of calling for help remains unclear.

CRANIAL VORTEX

During the polar vortex that brought prolonged subzero temperatures to much of the United States in early 2014, hundreds of people across the country tried to re-create a trick they saw on the Internet: throw boiling water into the frozen air and watch it turn into a "snow cloud." But several of them made a crucial mistake: They threw boiling water *into* the wind. Many got burned, some severely. Twitter lit up with embarrassing admissions, such as this one: "I tried to do the whole throw boiling water outside and it flew back and burned my arm so happy snow day to all."

LOST AND FOUND

One drunken winter night in 2013, a Dent, Minnesota, man called police to report that his wallet had been stolen. Good news: the police found his wallet. Bad news: they found it later that night while they were arresting him for DUI. (He flipped his snowmobile.) His wallet had been in his back pocket the whole time.

AIRHOG DAY

At New York City's 2009 Groundhog Day celebration, a groundhog named Staten Island Chuck bit Mayor Michael Bloomberg's finger, drawing blood. Five years later, a new mayor, Bill de Blasio, took over the groundhog duties. Determined not to suffer Bloomberg's fate, he said at the ceremony, "Chuck and my predecessor didn't always get along, but I'm hoping we can start anew. I'm reaching out a hand to Chuck, and I hope he will shake it rather than doing other things." But the ten-pound rodent was quite squirmy that morning, and Mayor de Blasio, who was wearing large safety gloves, was unable to hold on…and dropped him. The crowd gasped as the groundhog landed with a thud on the concrete. Shaken but okay, Chuck predicted six more weeks of winter (probably out of spite).

On average, one square inch of your skin has 60 hairs, 90 oil glands, and 19 ft. of blood vessels.

SAAB STORY

Auto companies are a lot like automobiles. Some seem to run forever; others never ran very well in the first place. Here's a look at a stylish carmaker that was beloved by its fans…but still ended up in a ditch.

FLIGHT PLAN

In the years leading up to World War II, the Swedish government founded a company called Svenska Aeroplan AB (Swedish Aeroplane Company, Ltd.), or SAAB, to build fighter planes to defend the country's neutrality if war did come. After the war, the company went looking for new products to manufacture to keep its factories humming. It considered building prefabricated housing, washing machines, and boats, but ultimately decided on cars.

Saab assigned 16 designers, aeronautical engineers, and craftspeople to the car project. None had ever designed an automobile before (and only two had driver's licenses), so to get an idea of how cars were built, they bought several from a junkyard, including a Volkswagen Beetle, an Opel Kadett, and an Audi DKW, and took them apart. They used what they learned to build the Ursaab, or "first Saab," the prototype that would serve as the basis for the company's production models.

KEEPING IT SIMPLE

The Ursaab differed in many ways from most cars of the day:

• Like the DKW, the car had a simple "two-stroke" engine, the kind more commonly associated with chainsaws and leaf blowers, instead of a "four-stroke" engine found in most cars.

• The engine was installed *transversely*, or sideways, underneath the front hood of the car, instead of being lined up front-to-back.

• To avoid the complexity and expense of connecting a drive shaft to the rear wheels, the Ursaab had front-wheel drive.

• As might be expected with a car designed by an airplane company, the Ursaab was one of the first cars tested in a wind tunnel. The futuristic teardrop shape that resulted was the most aerodynamic design of its day. In fact, when viewed from the side, the Ursaab looked like the cross section of an airplane wing.

In 2000 there was a rain of fish in Great Yarmouth, England.

LIFTOFF

The Ursaab may have been designed a little too much like an airplane wing, because when the finished prototype was taken out for road testing, the rear end had a tendency to lift off the ground at high speeds. The engineers fixed that problem by making the Saab 92—the company's first production vehicle—look more like a conventional European compact car and less like an airplane. Even so, when it went on sale in late 1949, it was still the most aerodynamic car on the market.

The Saab 92 was zippy and fun to drive. Even though it only had a tiny 25-horsepower engine—smaller than some riding lawnmowers—the car's light weight and streamlined shape gave it a top speed of 65 miles per hour and quicker acceleration than many larger cars with more powerful engines. The engine didn't use much gas and it was cheap and easy to repair, and the car's front-wheel drive gave it excellent traction in snowy Swedish winters. The 92 quickly developed a following, not just among ordinary car buyers, but also among racecar drivers, who entered them in road rallies and began racking up one victory after another.

IF IT AIN'T BROKE...

The Saab 92 was followed by the Saab 93 in 1956, the Saab 96 in 1960, the Saab 99 in 1968, and the Saab 900 (*the* classic Saab) in 1979. Beginning in 1956, engines were mounted *longitudinally*, or front-to-back instead of sideways. (In some models they were installed backward and tilted 45 degrees from vertical.) Four-stroke engines replaced two-stroke engines in 1967.

A number of changes over the years were safety improvements. The 1958 Saab GT 750 was the world's first car with seat belts included as standard equipment. In 1968 the Saab ignition switch was moved from the steering column to between the driver and passenger seats, to protect the driver's knee from smashing into it in a car accident. Saabs made after 1971 were the first cars to have steel beams in their doors to protect against side-impact collisions.

In spite of these and other changes, Saabs remained remarkably consistent over the years. The front-engine, front-wheel-drive configuration worked well, so the company stuck with it. And though the odd shape of the Saab evolved over time from its aerodynamic origins to the angular shape of the 900 (which looked to Uncle

John like a duck bill), it never stopped being odd. Whether you liked the way a Saab looked or not, when you saw one there was no doubt that it was a Saab.

AN ACQUIRED TASTE

The unique nature of Saabs, combined with the company's emphasis on solid engineering, strong performance, and uncompromising safety, helped the cars attain cult status with nonconformists looking for an alternative to the cars everyone else drove. Saab enthusiasts, or "Snaabs," as they came to be known, were well-educated: a higher percentage of Saab owners had PhDs than did owners of any other make of car. They had a strong psychological attachment to their Saabs, and just as strong a dislike of other makes of cars—especially BMWs, for some reason—not to mention contempt for the people who drove them.

And yet as popular as Saabs were with people who liked Saabs, they remained a niche product that appealed to comparatively small numbers of car buyers. Saab had trouble growing its business beyond its three main markets of Sweden, Great Britain, and the United States. Though it offered multiple variants of the same basic models over the years, including two- and four-door versions, hatchbacks, station wagons, convertibles and, beginning in 1978, models with turbocharged engines, the company struggled to grow beyond one or (from 1968–1980) two compact car platforms. It wasn't until 1984 that the company introduced a full-sized sedan, the Saab 9000, to its lineup, and only then after sharing the development costs with Fiat. The Italian automaker sold its 9000s as Fiat Cromas, Alfa Romeo 164s, and Lancia Themas.

START SAABING

Saab lost money most years, and some years it lost a lot of it. In 1989 Saab's aerospace parent company threw in the towel and spun the carmaker off into an independent company, Saab Automobile AB. The new company wasn't independent for long. Half of it was snapped up by General Motors; then in 2000, GM bought the other half, turning Saab into one of its wholly owned subsidiaries, not much different from Oldsmobile or Buick.

The acquisition offered the promise of Saab finally getting the resources it needed to expand its lineup and bring its aging models up to date. But for that to work, GM would have to let Saab be Saab. It didn't—instead, it replaced Saab's iconic styling with "half-hearted, dumbed-down…homogenized blobs," as *Car and Driver* magazine put it, alienating Snaabs without attracting new buyers. In 1994 GM ditched Saab's best-selling car ever, the beloved Saab 900, in favor of a dull replacement called the Saab 900 NG ("New Generation") that was built on the same platform as GM's Opel Vectra. Snaabs refused to buy them—the whole point of buying a Saab, after all, was that it wasn't like any other car.

By 2005 U.S. sales had fallen so precipitously that GM began "rebadging" Subarus, Chevys, and even Cadillacs as Saabs to give struggling Saab dealerships more cars to sell, so that they wouldn't abandon the brand altogether. No one was fooled: the fake Saabs sold worse than the real Saabs. And because GM itself was in a tailspin, it couldn't spare any more money to help turn Saab around. By the time GM filed for bankruptcy in 2009, annual sales of Saabs had plummeted from 133,000 cars in 2000 to fewer than 40,000.

GONE…FOR GOOD?
In 2009 Saab went into "administration," the Swedish equivalent of bankruptcy, while GM shopped it around to BMW, Fiat, Renault, and other major automakers. None of the big companies were interested, so in February 2010, GM sold Saab to tiny Spyker Cars, a Dutch maker of high-performance sports cars whose sales averaged fewer than 30 cars a year.

Spyker didn't have the resources to keep Saab afloat either; it filed for bankruptcy in December 2011. The following June a Hong Kong-backed company called National Electric Vehicle Sweden (Nevs) bought Saab's assets in bankruptcy court. In late 2013, it began building ten gasoline-powered Saabs a week at the old Saab factory in Trollhättan, Sweden, with plans to introduce electric vehicles in the future. Because Saab dealerships have gone out of business, the cars are sold on the company's website.

As of 2014, Nevs was focusing on sales to Sweden and China. It hopes to expand into other markets "over time," but don't hold your breath: "It's hard to imagine how anyone could make a go of Saab as a stand-alone business," auto industry analyst Garel Rhys told *The Guardian* in 2010. "There have only been a few years that the company hasn't made a loss since it first started making cars."

GRINDERS & FLOPPERS

More colorful expressions from the wonderful world of auto sales.

Paper Boy: A customer who brings the dealership's latest print ad to the lot and wants to buy a car at the advertised price

Roasting the App: Changing the information on the buyer's loan application to make it more likely that a third-party lender will approve a car loan

Whopper with Cheese: A car deal with a huge profit margin

Ham Sandwich: A car deal that brings in only a modest profit for the dealership

Shout Out: Announcing a pending sale over the car lot's public-address system (to keep the buyer from backing out at the last minute)

Service Lane Walk: Trying to sell new cars to people bringing their cars to the service department for repair

Eyeballer: A flashy car, often a bright-colored sports car

Grinder or Chiseler: A customer who, no matter how good a deal they're offered, insists on trying to get a better one

First Pencil: The first (and therefore highest) price that a dealership quotes to a buyer

Flopper: A customer who agrees to the first pencil price (like a fish that jumps into a boat and flops around before you've even put your fishing pole in the water)

Back Door the Trade: Not revealing that you have a trade-in vehicle until after you've negotiated a low price on the car you want to buy

Roach: A customer with credit so bad that there's no chance they'll qualify for a car loan

Gold Balls: A customer with excellent credit who pays the hefty down payment in cash

Candy Store: A dealership with a large selection of cars

Mickey Mouse: When the dealer has to finance even the down payment to sell a car

Lay Down: A buyer who agrees to every extra proposed by the dealer, adding thousands to the car price in the process. (They've been "run over.")

Surprised? Most fatal car accidents take place in good weather.

NOVA: MAKING SCIENCE COOL SINCE 1974

When PBS executives started planning a new science show in the early 1970s, people in the TV business were baffled. A show about…science? Were they crazy? Audiences wanted Happy Days *and* M*A*S*H*, *not educational shows! Luckily for us, they were wrong.*

IN THE BEGINNING…

In 1971 an American television producer named Michael Ambrosino was in London and happened to see some episodes of a science-based British TV show. Ambrosino worked at Boston's legendary public television station WGBH, and he'd been there since 1956—just a year after it went on the air.

WGBH was a pioneer in the American public television business and by 1971 had produced several groundbreaking shows, including *The French Chef* (1963), the cooking show hosted by Julia Child; *Evening at Pops* (1970); and *Masterpiece Theatre* (1971). In 1970 the station had become part of the brand-new, government-backed Public Broadcasting Service (PBS), with new funding that allowed WGBH to begin thinking bigger. That's why Ambrosino was in London: The 40-year-old was taking part in a yearlong fellowship program with the BBC—the British equivalent of PBS—to learn production techniques. There he observed the making of several episodes of *Horizon*, an educational science-based series that, to the surprise of BBC officials, was actually pretty popular with viewers.

SUPRA-NOVA

Horizon was a groundbreaking series of its own, having proven that television shows based on scholarly subjects could make for riveting TV. First airing in 1964, and roughly twice a month since then, *Horizon* covered a wide array of subjects. The 1969–70 season alone featured episodes on the science of insanity, the psychological and physical effects of alcohol consumption, the history and science of bread, an examination of wolves (and werewolves), and the role of expert scientific witnesses in the courtroom. The format employed a narrator who spoke over footage taken mostly in the field, and

---

In one day on some parts of Mercury, the sun appears to rise, reverse direction, set, & rise again.

regularly included appearances by some of the era's leading thinkers, who spoke directly into the camera in a loose, informal setting. It was nothing like a dull classroom session—and audiences liked it.

BRINGING IT ALL BACK HOME

Ambrosino felt there was a disappointing lack of educational science programming in the U.S., and seeing the success of *Horizon* spurred him to do something about it. "Science is a part of our heritage, our present culture, and a major force in determining our future," Ambrosino said in 1998. "Its absence from television, our most public medium of communication, spoke to the ignorance of its gatekeepers, who thought mostly in terms of news and the arts. Science, medicine, technology, engineering, architecture all impact our culture by determining how we live our lives. They also make for great story-telling."

In May 1971, shortly before returning home to Boston, Ambrosino wrote a five-page letter to Michael Rice, vice president of WGBH, outlining in detail a science show for PBS. His idea: to air a series of shows on a wide variety of science-based subjects, just like *Horizon*. And, also like *Horizon*, WGBH wouldn't make all of the shows themselves—they'd produce some of their own episodes, make others in collaboration with teams from around the world, especially at the BBC, and air already-finished pieces made entirely by other people. This approach solved several problems, not the least of which being that WGBH didn't have the resources to make all the shows on their own, but also that it would broaden the show's range of subjects, making them more international and encompassing, and hopefully, more interesting to the viewers. And it was also a good foundation on which to grow into the future.

NOVA TO THE GRINDSTONE

That was the vision Ambrosino laid out in his letter to Michael Rice in 1971…and Rice loved it. The letter has essentially remained the blueprint for *NOVA* ever since. But there was still a lot of work to do.

Ambrosino had done almost every job in television production during his years at WGBH—he'd been a writer, director, camera operator, set builder, and even hosted a documentary series (*Michael Ambrosino's Show*)—but he'd never taken on a project quite like this before. So…he got to work. He read science books, watched science programs, met with scientists (including Jonas Salk, who discovered the polio vaccine), and attended science conferences. Not only did he try to fill his head full of science, he tried to learn what scientists thought about science, and, more important, what scientists thought the public would most benefit from in learning about science. This was important—because if Ambrosino could get scientists and national scientific organizations behind the show, it would be a lot easier to get the funding to support it.

EUREKA! (NO, NOT EUREKA)

As the pieces started falling into place, Ambrosino realized the new show needed a name—and a good one. He made a list of possible titles, circulated it to his staff and bosses, and they came up with more. (Two of the names: *The Asymptotic Struggle* and *Eureka!*)
"I remember Ambrosino's entire office door covered with colored three by five cards with lots of potential names for the series," Ben Shedd, one of the show's original filmmakers, said years later. But Ambrosino wasn't happy with any of them. He stopped soliciting ideas and came up with his own title—*NOVA*. "A nova," he explained, "is a sudden, brilliant star in the firmament; so dazzlingly bright that it's noticed and admired by all. It delights the eye and turns the mind to a joyful appreciation and questioning about the wonders of the universe."

LIFTOFF

Ambrosino had hoped the show would air in 1972—but it took until mid-1973 to get enough funding to get the project off the ground. Just as Ambrosino had hoped, a major science foundation—the American Association for the Advancement of Science—got the ball rolling when they donated the first $40,000 to the project. Another early major donor: the Polaroid Corporation—which was founded and headquartered in Boston and had been a longtime supporter of WGBH.

Once funding was secure, hiring began. A lot of *NOVA*'s producers and assistant producers were hired away from the BBC (which didn't make the folks at the BBC very happy), and for the rest of 1973, three separate production teams went to work, first on the road, then in the tiny WGBH studios, making the first episodes.

Hamsters and stray dogs are *crepuscular*—primarily active in the twilight hours of dawn and dusk.

Ambrosino, as executive producer, was involved in every aspect of the series except actually being in the field and running the cameras. He spent the next several months choosing episode subjects or reviewing and okaying those he didn't pick himself, assisting in the editing process, all the while taking care of scheduling, budgeting, hiring, and all the other jobs that had to be done.

NEAR THE *HORIZON*

On March 4, 1974, *NOVA* made its debut with the tagline "Science adventures for curious grownups." The first episode: "The Making of a Natural History Film"—a behind-the-scenes look at the techniques used by four nature documentary makers, which showed how filmmakers captured footage of wasps laying eggs in trees, the mating habits of the oft-studied stickleback fish, and the hatching of a chicken from an egg—all very high-tech back then. To get an idea of just how much the BBC's *Horizon* influenced *NOVA*, "The Making of a Natural History Film" was a *Horizon* episode that had aired on the BBC in 1972.

THE SHOW MUST GO ON

The first *original* episode of *NOVA* aired just a week later. "Where Did the Colorado Go?" was an examination of the history of the management—and mismanagement—of the Colorado River in the American Southwest. The rest of that first season's 13 episodes featured topics that included the world's whaling industry (the antiwhaling movement was growing rapidly around this time), the ancient Anasazi people of the American Southwest, and the testing of new medications on humans—including children. The response was immediate: People loved it. Member PBS stations in dozens of the country's largest markets aired the show in prime time (mostly on Monday evenings), and the show received high marks from viewers and critics alike. *NOVA*, said *Time* magazine, was "filling the gap between deadly-dull 'educational' lecturing and pop-science trivia." *Variety* added, "With its scope, *NOVA* should be good for seasons to come."

NOVA THROUGH THE YEARS

Ambrosino was *NOVA*'s executive producer for its first three years on the air. He left the show in 1976, after the exhausting schedule

---

Comic strip quiz: What does Charlie Brown's dad do for a living? A: He's a barber.

finally got to him. (He was taking both Valium and sleeping pills by this time, he later admitted, to cope with the stress of the job.) During those three years he had supervised the airing of 50 episodes of NOVA, 19 of them made by WGBH, the rest either collaborations or outside projects, including documentaries made in Switzerland, Sweden, Yugoslavia, and other countries. By the end of that third year, Ambrosino had helped establish NOVA as one of PBS's most important and most-watched programs, garnering between four and seven million viewers for each episode. The show is now seen as one of the main reasons that the fledgling PBS network survived.

RANDOM FACTS AND HIGHLIGHTS

• NOVA has been on the air for more than 40 seasons and has aired more than 700 episodes.

• The show airs in more than 100 countries.

• NOVA won a prestigious Peabody Award in 1975, its second year on the air, being cited as "an imaginative series of science adventures" with "a versatility rarely found in television today." It has won five more Peabodys—and more than 25 Emmys—in the years since.

• Some of the highest-rated NOVA episodes over the years: "Here's Looking at You, Kid" (1982), the story of an 11-year-old boy's fight to recover from an accident that covered more than 70 percent of his body with burns; "Suicide Mission to Chernobyl" (1989), following a group of scientists attempting to secure the extremely dangerous former Soviet nuclear plant, which had exploded in 1986; "The Spy Factory" (2009), a study of U.S. intelligence agencies' failure to cooperate in the lead-up to the terrorist attacks of September 11, 2001; and "The Fabric of the Cosmos" (2011), a four-part special looking at the complex, baffling, and fascinating laws that govern our universe. After watching, said the New York Times, "you may rise from the couch with your faith in common sense stirred if not shaken."

• Michael Ambrosino continued working for public television in various capacities until he retired in the late 2000s. At last report he was living in a cabin in Maine. (No word on whether he has a TV there, but if he does…we're guessing he watches NOVA.)

On a single day in 1997, 127 million people in India were vaccinated against polio.

LOOKIN' FOR LOVECRAFT

Behold the odd tale of horror writer Howard Phillips Lovecraft, whose ghastly creations have terrorized readers for a century—and are now popping up in Facebook feeds. Who was he? Read on…if you dare.

I T'S A FAD!
Nearly 80 years after his death, H. P. Lovecraft is considered one of the most influential horror writers of all time. Stephen King called him "the twentieth century's greatest practitioner of the classic horror tale." From 1917 until his death in 1937, Lovecraft wrote hundreds of poems, short stories, and essays. Among his best known works: *At the Mountains of Madness* and *The Dunwich Horror*.

Even if you've never read Lovecraft, you may have seen one of his stories adapted into a cheesy horror movie (*Reanimator*, *Splatterhouse*, most Roger Corman films). References to his works have shown up in *Batman*, *Alien*, *It*, *Hellboy*, *The Evil Dead*, *The Blair Witch Project*, *Buffy the Vampire Slayer*, *Monsters Inc.*, and *Ghostbusters* (to name a few), and in the lyrics of songs by Black Sabbath, Iron Maiden, Metallica, the Fall, Arctic Monkeys, and Blue Öyster Cult. Perhaps you've seen Lovecraft's most famous creation: Cthulhu—the tentacled monster that has become a meme on the Internet, and adorns T-shirts, phone cases, and lunch boxes. There are even Cthulhu plushies.

And yet Lovecraft died in poverty, almost unknown, never having published a single book in his lifetime. So how did the horror writer's literary tentacles appear from beyond the grave to get such a grip on pop culture?

OF MONSTERS AND MEN

It certainly wasn't his writing skills. Unlike his more literary counterparts such as Edgar Allan Poe, Lovecraft is not celebrated for his cohesive plots or his three-dimensional characters. Many have criticized him for his long maze-like sentences filled with obscure words like "eldritch," "rugose," and "gibbous." He wrote in old-fashioned prose (even for his time) because of his lifelong devotion to antiquity. Lovecraft pictured himself as a bewigged eighteenth-century English gentleman, and he wrote like one.

Lovecraft was all about the monsters. He created an entire pantheon of extraterrestrial deities called the Great Old Ones, who are worshipped by secret cults. They have strange names like Nyarlathotep, Yog-Sothoth, and the Fungi from Yuggoth. "I could not write about 'ordinary people' because I am not in the least interested in them," he said. "Man's relations to man do not captivate my fancy. It is man's relation to the cosmos—to the unknown—which alone arouses in me the spark of creative imagination." He saw himself as "a floating, disembodied eye which sees all manner of marvelous phenomena without being greatly affected by them."

His most famous Great Old One is Cthulhu, described as "a monster of vaguely anthropoid outline, but with an octopus-like head whose face was a mass of feelers, a scaly, rubbery-looking body, prodigious claws on hind and fore feet, and long, narrow wings behind." The name Cthulhu, Lovecraft explained, was "a fumbling human attempt to catch the phonetics of an absolutely non-human word." There is some debate about how Cthulhu should be pronounced (Uncle John says "kuh-THOOL-hoo"), but since it's an alien word, unpronounceable by humans, it doesn't really matter.

THE FORBIDDEN TOME

Lovecraft's other lasting legacy: the "dreaded occult masterpiece" called the *Necronomicon*. Featured in many of his works, this ancient book is usually locked away and fiercely protected by nervous librarians. They are right to be cautious—the book is full of blasphemous incantations that if uttered aloud could open doors to other dimensions and let in all manner of creepy-crawlies.

The most often asked question about the *Necronomicon*: "Is it real?" Lovecraft insisted it was, of course, but the book did not exist before it was introduced in the 1922 short story "The Hound." That, of course, hasn't stopped numerous "genuine" *Necronomicons* from surfacing, most notably one attributed to someone calling himself "Simon," published in 1977. The paperback version has never been out of print. (The *Necronomicon* even has its own page on *HowStuffWorks.com*.)

THE MAN BEHIND THE MYTHOS

Apart from two years in Brooklyn, New York (which he found very unpleasant), Lovecraft spent his entire life in Providence,

Only ex-Beatle not in the Rock & Roll Hall of Fame as a solo artist: Ringo Starr.

Rhode Island, where he was born in 1890. Most people think of Lovecraft as a "sickly recluse," which isn't quite accurate. He did have a broad circle of friends, mostly other writers. But he never actually met most of his friends in person—he corresponded with them in letters...*a lot* of letters. Estimates put it between 70,000 and 100,000. And they were much more than "Hey, how's it going? Your pal, Howie." His letters were often 40 or more double-sided pages, ranging in topics from philosophy, science, religion, writing, and the macabre, to amusing anecdotes about buying a suit or eating an ice-cream cone. In the midst of his bleakest financial woes, Lovecraft was known to go without food so he could afford postage.

He was briefly married to a woman named Sonia Greene, but his odd habits and lack of income strained their marriage, and they soon parted. Lovecraft made almost no money from his fiction and supplemented his meager earnings by editing and ghostwriting. He died a sad, painful death, succumbing to intestinal cancer in 1937 at the age of 46.

CTHULHU CALLING

Lovecraft had no heirs. His closest living relative, an elderly aunt, inherited the rights to his work, and she died soon afterward. It was his literary friends—including his protégé, Robert Bloch, who would go on to write *Psycho*—who kept Lovecraft's words alive by publishing his stories in anthologies. They were repaying his generosity. Though he never made a dime from it, Lovecraft had encouraged other writers to use his characters (like Cthulhu) and settings (like Arkham, a fictional city in Massachusetts featured in many Lovecraft stories) in their works. This separates Lovecraft from other fantasy franchises like *Star Wars* and *The Lord of the Rings*, which are closed off by their copyright owners. Because of that, Lovecraft's fiction is still being expanded upon by countless writers. So if you feel like dabbling in the *Necronomicon* yourself, have at it. Just be prepared for whatever indescribable horrors you may conjure up.

*   *   *

"The world is indeed comic, but the joke is on mankind."

—**H. P. Lovecraft**

EURO-CAFÉS

When in Europe, why settle for a French café or Italian bistro? These wacky restaurants offer much more interesting experiences to travelers.

Restaurant: Lady Dinah's Cat Emporium
Location: London
Details: What is a "cat café"? Exactly what you'd think—a restaurant were a bunch of cats wander around, rubbing up against patrons' legs and shedding their hair in your food. And yet, this mixture of food and pets is surprisingly popular. The first cat café opened in Taiwan in 1998. The concept spread to Japan (where there are more than a hundred) and now London, thanks to a $183,000 online crowdsourcing campaign. Diners can enjoy brunch, afternoon tea, and dinner at Lady Dinah's, but they have to follow certain rules. Flash photography isn't allowed, nor is feeding the cats, holding the cats, or bringing in outside cats. When Lady Dinah's opened in March 2014, it received so many reservation requests that the booking system crashed. There's currently a six-month waiting list.

Restaurant: Disaster Café
Location: Lloret de Mar, Spain
Details: A sign on the building says "a dangerous place to eat," but other than that, it looks like an ordinary restaurant. It's not. Upstairs there's a space-themed eatery. But take the elevator down to the basement ("the depths of the earth") to find the main attraction: a cavelike café where every meal comes with a simulated 7.8 earthquake. The waitstaff wear hard hats and construction gear, and deliver food on dishes that are weighted to prevent them from sliding off tables when "the big one" hits. Then, without warning, it hits. The lights go out, the ground rumbles, and the room shakes like a roller coaster. Thirty-two seconds later, it's over.

Restaurant: Le Refuge des Fondues
Location: Paris
Details: What's weird about this café isn't the food (classic Swiss fondue), it's the way the wine is served—in babies' bottles with rubber nipples.

Odds that two British men with the same last name are related: about 1 in 4.

Restaurant: Fortezza Medicea Jail Restaurant

Location: Volterra, Italy

Details: There are several jail-themed restaurants in the world, but this is the only one housed in a real, fully operational correctional facility. Members of the staff, from waiters to cooks, are inmates doing time for crimes ranging from racketeering to murder. Under the attentive watch of prison guards, they prepare fancy meals for diners who undergo background checks before they're seated. (Helpful tip: Don't complain about the food.)

Restaurant: The Hellfire Club

Location: Manchester, England

Details: This gothic restaurant, decorated with crucifixes, skeletons, and coffins, is located next to an old cemetery, and according to the owners, it's haunted. Customers drink from goblets splattered with fake blood and order menu items with names like "Cannibal Holocaust" and "Kiss of the Vampire" (both are steaks).

Restaurant: Le Restophone

Location: Montpellier, France

Details: If you're one of the few people on the planet who wishes *more* people would talk on their phones in restaurants, this place is for you. Why? Because each table comes with its own telephone. This allows its patrons to call people at other tables or put in requests with a DJ who plays records near the dance floor. The concept is geared toward singles or anyone "looking to make new friends."

Restaurant: Klo

Location: Berlin

Details: Klo takes features from zoos, theme parks, and weird Asian cafés, and mashes them together into one of Europe's oddest restaurants. Several menu items are served in enamel toilets; beer comes in urine specimen jars. Customers have the option of sitting on toilet seats or coffins, or bar stools that spin around at the push of a button. If that isn't enough, papier-mâché rocks fall out of a trapdoor in the ceiling every so often, and animatronic skeletons jump around when diners first cross the threshold. Be sure to check out the mannequin in the ladies' room. (It sounds an alarm at the bar if anyone peeks under his kilt.)

Fatal dog attacks outnumber fatal shark attacks 5 to 1.

DREAM TEAMS

*Fantasy football lets people who could never afford to buy a pro football
team imagine what it's like to own one. So it's a bit ironic that it was
invented by someone who did own part of a pro football team.*

NIGHTMARE

Bill "Wink" Winkenbach was a limited partner in the Oakland Raiders in 1962, at a time when owning a piece of an American Football League franchise wasn't exactly good for a person's financial or psychological health. The league—and the Raiders—were only three years old, and it wasn't clear that either would survive. The upstart AFL had been created by people who wanted NFL franchises but couldn't get them because the NFL refused to expand beyond 12 teams and into new cities like Boston, Miami, and Oakland.

No rival football league had ever been able to compete against the NFL, and the AFL, like other leagues that had come before it, was struggling. So were the Raiders: they had a losing 6–8 first season in 1960, and lost so much money that five of the eight general partners who founded the team abandoned ship. The 1961 season was even worse, with 2 wins and 12 losses. And by the fall of 1962, when Winkenbach accompanied the team on a 16-day East Coast trip to play the Boston Patriots, the Buffalo Bills, and the New York Titans (later renamed the Jets), the Raiders were well on their way to a 1–13 season, the worst in the AFL.

ESCAPE

Under the circumstances, it's understandable that Winkenbach would want a distraction of some kind to take his mind off the Raiders' problems as he whiled away long hours in hotel rooms between games. A few years earlier he'd invented a betting game that he played with friends while watching golf tournaments on TV. Each person assembled an imaginary "team" of players in the tournament, then watched to see how they performed. The winning team was the one with the fewest number of strokes at the end of the tournament.

Since then, Winkenbach had come up with a similar game for

baseball. But he couldn't play either of these games now, because there wasn't much golf on TV and no baseball either, since the World Series had ended a few weeks earlier. Why not create a similar game for football? At this point in the Raiders' short, sad history, the temptation to escape into an imaginary team must have been irresistible.

TOUCHDOWN

Winkenbach shared his idea with Bill Tunnel, the Raiders' P.R. man, and Scotty Stirling, an *Oakland Tribune* sportswriter who was covering the team. They liked the idea (or maybe, like Winkenbach, they were just bored). They spent the rest of the evening helping him formulate rules for the game, deciding how much points to award for touchdown passes (25¢), how much for rushing touchdowns (50¢), and other aspects of the game. The team that won the entire season would win $60, to be spent buying dinner for the other teams.

By the time the Raiders returned home to Oakland, Winkenbach had enough details worked out to show to other people connected with the team. When they expressed interest, he formed the Greater Oakland Professional Pigskin Prognosticators League, or GOPPPL (pronounced "gopple") for short. The league had eight teams, just like the AFL, and each team had an "owner" and a "coach," which meant that 16 people could play.

DRAFTED

In August 1963, the participants met at Winkenbach's house to draft their players. Working from a list of all active pro football players, each team drafted a team of 20 players. As many as eight could be from the NFL, but no more than that. (The Raiders were in the AFL, after all.) The remaining 12 had to be from the AFL.

George Blanda, a quarterback/kicker for the AFL's Houston Oilers, was the first player ever drafted onto a fantasy football team. He was picked by Scotty Stirling and his team partner, Andy Mousalimas, the manager of an Oakland bar that was a popular Raiders' hangout. Blanda proved to be a disappointing pick, though, and by the end of the season his team was in last place. As such, they were awarded the league's "dunce trophy," shaped like a football wearing a dunce cap, and they had to display it at their home until the next season. If the dunce trophy wasn't displayed, and other GOPPPL members found out, the loser could be fined.

X MARKS THE SPOT

GOPPPL was a small, tight-knit group limited to people closely associated with the Oakland Raiders. That was the way Winkenbach wanted it, and that was the way it stayed. Had Andy Mousalimas not been one of the original participants, the hobby might never have grown beyond Oakland to become "fantasy football" as we know it today. But when Mousalimas bought his own neighborhood bar—called the King's X—in 1968, he created his own league and invited his customers to play. He also changed Winkenbach's rules a bit, awarding points for yardage, so that players who ran, but did not score, had a value similar to players who scored, but did not run. Tweaking the rules got him booted out of GOPPPL, but it didn't matter because the rapidly growing King's X league took up all his time anyway.

By the mid-1970s, the King's X league had grown from ten original teams to sixty, organized into six divisions of ten teams each. One division, the Queens, was all-female. As the game grew in popularity, people from San Francisco began driving to Oakland to play, including many people who worked at the Pacific Stock Exchange in the financial district. As these people moved on to new jobs on Wall Street and in other cities, they took their love for fantasy football with them. Soon Mousalimas was fielding calls from bar owners all over the country who wanted to start their own fantasy leagues. Luckily for fans of the game, he happily obliged.

FREE AGENTS

Today, if you want to play fantasy football, all the information you need is just a few keystrokes away. If you play on a website, your team's points are tallied automatically. But in the 1970s, there was no Internet and no cable sports channels, either. The networks broadcast football games, but when they reported the scores of the games, they reported only the score itself, not which players scored which points. Fantasy football fans had to dig up this information on their own, and if the sports page of the local newspaper didn't provide the details, they were out of luck. This slowed the growth of the hobby, and it wasn't until the first fantasy football websites began popping up on the Internet in the late 1990s that it mushroomed into the worldwide phenomenon that it is today. Nowadays more than 30 million Americans play fantasy football each year, generating more than $11 billion of economic activity in the process. Millions more play all over the world. And that's just the football sites—today just about every professional and amateur sport has a fantasy equivalent, from NASCAR to bass fishing.

FANTASY PROFITS, TOO

So how much of the money generated by this multibillion-dollar "industry" goes to the Winkenbach estate (he died in 1993 at the age of 81) or to Andy Mousalimas (at 88, he was still playing fantasy football in 2013)? Not a cent. At least not directly—fantasy football brought a lot of business into the King's X over the years, and when Mousalimas retired and sold the bar in 1991, he got a good price for it. (Today it's a tiki bar called the Kona Club. The King's X league still exists, but it now meets in another sports bar.)

Because neither Mousalimas nor Winkenbach ever copyrighted fantasy football, it is in the public domain; anyone can play for free. Neither man really needed the money—Winkenbach owned a piece of the *Raiders*, after all—but that doesn't mean that over the years they didn't wish they had some of it. As Winkenbach said to *Oakland Tribune* sportswriter Scotty Stirling in the early 1990s not long before he passed away, "I told you we should have copyrighted the damn thing!"

*　　*　　*

AN OLD JOKE

A bus driver was taking a group of senior citizens on a tour when one of the seniors handed him some almonds. "Thanks!" said the driver and ate them. A little later, the senior gave the driver some more almonds, and the driver graciously accepted them. A little later, the driver was given more almonds. "Wait a second," he said. "Why aren't you eating these yourselves?" The senior replied, "Our teeth are too brittle to bite into the almonds." The bus driver asked, "So why'd you buy them?" The senior answered, "Because we just love the chocolate around them!"

Swan song? When a western scrub jay dies, its fellow birds gather around and sing.

LOCAL HEROES

Right place + right time + cool head = lives saved.

BOWLING FOR BABIES

A toddler wanted to see where the bowling balls go, so when his mother wasn't looking, he ran down the lane of a bowling alley in Eau Claire, Wisconsin. He reached the pin area and crawled in, tripping a sensor that activates the automatic pin-setting arm. It swooped down and scooped the pins *and* the boy into a pit, where the ball-return machine was about to try to return him. As the frantic mother was screaming, alley worker Andy Gardner sprang into action: He ran toward the child as fast as he could, dove into the pin area, and hit a switch that stopped the machine. Then he shimmied inside and retrieved the crying boy. Gardner got there just in time to save the kid from being seriously injured.

IN HARM'S WAY

"Don't do it!" shouted Donnie Navidad. "Please don't jump!" The 61-year-old former Marine was one of several people trying to calm a young woman who was standing on a ledge in the upper deck of the Oakland-Alameda County Coliseum shortly after an Oakland Raiders home game in November 2013. But the distraught woman jumped anyway. The concrete was 50 feet below her. Navidad positioned himself directly underneath her, reached his arms out, and tried to catch her...but she was traveling too fast. He couldn't hold on, and both of them tumbled down onto the concrete. Navidad suffered a severely bruised arm but saved the woman's life. She was taken to the hospital with serious but survivable injuries. "I couldn't live with myself if I didn't do anything," said Navidad.

LI'L HELPER

In 2010 firefighter Captain Robert Villalovoz was at the fire station in Manteca, California, when a toddler walked into the garage. "My daddy is frozen!" said three-year-old Alesaundra Tafoya. She grabbed Villalovoz's hand and walked him two blocks to her house, where her father, Frank, was passed out in the living room. He was rushed to the hospital, where doctors determined that he had accidentally taken two medications that shouldn't be combined. They said that if Alesaundra hadn't gone for help, Frank would probably have died. The hero toddler's parents later explained that they'd instructed her that if she was ever in trouble, to go to the fire station to get help…and that's exactly what she did. "I've been here over twenty years," said Villalovoz. "It's the first time I've had a three-year-old walk up to the station."

DON'T FENCE HIM IN

In 2013 a fencing coach named Franco Scaramuzza was returning from practice when he pulled into the parking lot of a shopping center in Bellevue, Tennessee, and saw two men—Michael Butt and Zachary Johnson—robbing two women. Butt was using pepper spray to incapacitate the women while Johnson snatched their purses. "The first thing that went through my head is somebody should do something," said Scaramuzza, "and I got really upset with myself because I realized *I* had the opportunity to do something. And I didn't want to be a hypocrite who just tweeted about it." So he grabbed his épée (fencing sword) and ran at the robbers while yelling at the top of his lungs. Butt and Johnson dropped their loot and ran away, but were later captured and arrested. "You have to overcome your own fears," said Scaramuzza.

TANK YOU VERY MUCH!

On a Saturday afternoon in January 2014, a swap meet outside Maricopa, Arizona, was interrupted by a screaming mom. "My baby fell down in the hole!" As several people ran over, Emily Howard frantically told them that her one-year-old girl, Kylie, had fallen through a cracked plastic lid…into a septic tank. Without hesitating, Henry Ricketts, 27, jumped into the vat of raw sewage and started looking for the girl. "I inhaled some of the nasty water," he said, so he had to come back up. Another man, Audencio Rios, 29, was lowered by his feet, headfirst into the tank. After more than three minutes searching through four feet of sewage, he pulled Kylie out. She wasn't breathing. Then Chelsea Cunningham, a 28-year-old Canadian rancher who was on vacation, ran up and administered CPR and mouth-to-mouth resuscitation to the toddler. After a few more tense moments, Kylie started breathing again. "It's just amazing that complete strangers would go that far to help me and Kylie," said the grateful mom.

One acre of hemp could produce four times as much toilet paper as an acre of trees.

ALL ABOUT BACTERIA

Q: What do you call the bacteria that work in your favorite restaurant? A: The staph. (And now, a fascinating look at everybody's favorite microorganisms—bacteria.)

SMALL MIRACLES

The first things that come to mind for most people when they hear the word "bacteria" are germs and disease (and possibly gas station restrooms). And while there is a certain amount of truth to such negative preconceptions, there's much more to bacteria. For starters, your gut couldn't digest food and provide you with the energy you need to survive if it weren't for bacteria. They're also important in breaking down waste in septic tanks and sewage-treatment plants, they aid in the breakdown of harmful pollutants like oil from oil spills, and they're essential in the production of cheese. It goes further than that: bacteria played a crucial role in making Earth hospitable for higher life-forms…like us.

WE ARE LIVING IN A BACTERIAL WORLD

To get an idea of just how extraordinary bacteria are, ponder this. Scientists believe there are as many as 10 million different plant and animal species on Earth. The number of different bacteria species on Earth? A 2006 study found about 20,000 different species of bacteria—in a single liter of seawater. A similar study found too many different bacteria species to even estimate how many there were *in a single gram of soil*. (The number was at least in the tens of thousands, but probably much higher.) Scientists simply have no idea how many different species of bacteria exist on Earth; estimates range as high as a billion.

As for total numbers, a 1998 study at the University of Georgia determined that there are about 5,000,000,000,000,000,000,000, 000,000,000—that's 5 million trillion trillion—individual bacteria on the planet. (To put it in perspective, that's several million trillion bacteria…for every one of the 7 billion humans on Earth.)

SINGULARLY SENSATIONAL

What makes a bacterium a bacterium? (*Bacterium* is the singular

---

Myth-understood: The ancient Romans used chariots for travel and racing, not for battle.

form; *bacteria* is plural.) No single trait, really. All species of bacteria have a combination of characteristics in common. Some of the most significant:

• Bacteria are *unicellular* (single-celled) microorganisms. This means that bacteria do not bond together to form larger, more complex organisms, as happens in *multicellular* organisms—plants and animals. Each single bacterium cell is its own independent creature.

• They are microscopic. Bacteria average from 0.5 to 5 micrometers (*millionths* of a meter) in diameter. For comparison, the smallest amoebas are about 90 micrometers in diameter, and plant and animal cells range between about 10 and 100 micrometers.

• Bacteria cells are *prokaryotic*. There are two main types of cells in living creatures: *Prokaryotes* and *eukaryotes*. Think of them as old, and new and improved, respectively. Prokaryotic cells are more ancient and primitive, having no membrane-bound nucleus. Eukaryotic cells evolved from prokaryotic cells and are more complex. Prokaryotes are almost all single-celled; eukaryotes can be either single-celled or multicellular, and include all higher life-forms (even you).

WHO GOT HERE FIRST?

Before about 3.6 billion years ago, there was no life on Earth at all. Then…life! Nobody knows exactly how life started, of course, but we do know that bacteria were among the very first life-forms to appear on the planet. In fact, the oldest physical evidence of life ever found was discovered in 2012: the fossilized remains of bacteria that lived in western Australia—3.49 billion years ago.

For the next couple of billion years or so, bacteria ruled planet Earth…and made it hospitable. Photosynthesis-capable bacteria, such as blue-green algae, produced the massive amounts of oxygen that led to the formation of Earth's atmosphere, thereby making it possible for oxygen-loving higher life-forms—which eventually included humans—to appear.

What does all this mean? That bacteria not only played a huge part in making life for higher organisms possible—bacteria *are* where higher life came from. All higher life-forms, including all plants and animals, extinct and extant, are the evolutionary descendants of those ancient bacteria. (A 2012 University of Buffalo study of similarities and differences in the DNA sequences of thousands of different life-forms found that a specific kind of bacteria called *actinobacteria*, still commonly found in soil and seawater, is the most likely candidate for the common ancestor of all life on Earth.)

HI, I'M ROD

Bacteria come in three basic shapes: *coccus*, *bacillus*, and *spiral*.

• Coccus-shaped bacteria (or *cocci*) are spherical. The most familiar type of coccus-shaped bacteria is probably *streptococcus*, species of which cause several common ailments, including strep throat, scarlet fever, meningitis, and necrotizing fasciitis (better known as "flesh-eating disease"). Another familiar type: *staphylococcus*, or "staph," which can also cause several ailments.

• Bacillus-shaped bacteria (*bacilli*) are rod-shaped. Examples include *Clostridium perfringens*, which causes gangrene, and *Bacillus anthracis*, which causes anthrax.

• Spiral-shaped bacteria (*spirilli*) range from comma-shaped to very spirally, kind of like the tendrils of climbing plants. Familiar examples: *Borrelia burgdorferi*, which causes Lyme disease, and *Treponema pallidum*, which causes syphilis.

• Not all bacteria follow the rules—there are a few oddball species, including star-shaped bacteria and almost perfectly rectangular-shaped bacteria.

The shape of the bacteria, along with how they tend to arrange themselves in groups, is important information for scientists. It provides a fairly simple way to identify the cause of a bacterial infection just by looking at samples through a microscope. If a patient has a streptococcus infection, for example, a doctor can tell from the ball-shaped bacteria attached to each other end-to-end in chains—because that's how streptococci arrange themselves. If you've got another kind of infection and the doctor sees twisty, spiral-shaped bacteria, it's probably syphilis.

SUN, IRON...AND GONAD EATERS

Bacteria need energy to survive, as all living things do, and they acquire that energy in lots of different ways. Some bacteria actually survive by consuming inorganic substances, such as minerals and metals. Example: *Iron bacteria*, so named because it actually survives by breaking down iron. (If you've ever seen a reddish-brown, slimy, smelly sediment in a local waterway, such as around a stormwater drain, there's a good chance it's the result of iron bacteria.) Other types get their energy the same way plants do—via photosynthesis, converting energy from sunlight into food. An example of this is *cyanobacteria*, more commonly known as blue-green algae, which lives in a wide variety of environments, including freshwater and seawater.

Still other kinds of bacteria exist by eating only organic matter, meaning plant and animal matter. These include the kinds that inhabit your digestive system, surviving—and helping you survive—by breaking down the foods you eat. They also include the kinds that cause dead animal and plant matter to decay. And from the too-weird-to-be-true department, there's this: Certain strains of *Wolbachia* bacteria survive by infecting and consuming the contents of mosquito gonads. In the process, they can kill the infected mosquitos, change the mosquito's gender, or infect the mosquito's offspring, thereby furthering the spread of the bacteria.

HERE, THERE, AND EVERYWHERE

Bacteria live in your nose, your mouth, your skin, your gut, your hair, your underwear, all your friends' underwear, in your kitchen, in your bathroom, in your car, in your workplace, in trees, rivers, glaciers, deserts, and in all the world's oceans. Even in the air. (Yes, there are bacteria that live in the air.) There are, of course, places where bacteria *don't* live. Scientists are pretty sure, for example, there are no bacteria on the sun or in the molten core of the Earth…but after reading this next paragraph, you might even wonder about that.

There's an area of Pacific Ocean seafloor, around the equator, that has been experiencing an extremely low amount of sediment buildup for millions of years. According to scientists, it takes about 5,000 years to accumulate just one millimeter of fresh sediment there. That means that if you dig just a few feet down into this area of seafloor, you come into contact with sediment millions of years old. In 2009 Danish microbiologist Hans Roy led a team of researchers to the area and drilled nearly 100 feet down. Roy found bacteria living in the ancient mucky clay. The bacteria living in that clay, Roy said, have been there since it was deposited—roughly 86 million years ago—and have been living there ever since, feeding, ever so slowly, off the trace amounts of nutrients in the clay. Roy believes that each individual bacterium living in that ancient muck might be thousands or tens of thousands—or millions—of years old.

RANDOM FACTERIA

• The word *bacteria* was coined by German naturalist Christian Gottfried Ehrenberg in 1838, from the Greek *bakterion*, meaning "small staff or rod"—after rod-shaped bacteria.

• If you like cheese, thank bacteria. The conversion of milk sugars into acid in the production of cheese (called *curdling*) is carried out by bacteria. The "eyes" in Swiss cheese are the result of carbon dioxide gas production by bacteria during the cheese's aging process.

• Gross fact: About 30 percent of human poop is bacteria.

• Two species of *cyanobacteria* (blue-green algae) live in the fur of sloths, giving the sloths' fur a green tinge.

• In 2014 researchers found that specific species of bacteria like it when people eat chocolate—and do us a big favor for providing it to them. These bacteria consume the chocolate we eat, breaking it down in our guts and converting it into anti-inflammatory agents, which reduce swelling in our arteries and heart, thereby reducing the risk of cardiovascular disease.

• NASA has "clean rooms"—super-sanitized rooms cleaned and heated to kill bacteria and other microbes. Reason: to prevent contamination of space with Earth-based microbes. But in 2007 scientists discovered a previously unknown species of bacteria in one of those rooms—the one that had been used in developing the *Phoenix* Mars Lander, the craft that was sent to Mars. Did the *Phoenix* take bacteria to Mars? Nobody knows for sure.

*　　　*　　　*

SAVE THE LAST DANCE

Cai Jinlai, the oldest man in the village of Taichung, Taiwan, claimed that he kept young by visiting strip clubs. When Cai was in his 90s, his son promised that if the old man lived to be 100, he'd hire a stripper to perform at the funeral. Cai died in 2008 after walking three miles into town to vote in an election. He was 103. True to his word, Cai's son paid a stripper $170 to dance around his father's casket.

HIDING IN PLAIN $IGHT

There may be valuable—even priceless—objects lying around your yard, your house, or your community, just waiting to be discovered. If the idea seems ridiculous, consider what happened to these folks.

In Plain Sight: A "stinky yellow rock"
Location: On a beach near the town of Morecambe, Lancashire, on the northwest coast of England
The Story: No one knows how many people walked past the weather-beaten lump without giving it a second thought after it washed up on the beach in January 2013. Some people may have mistaken it for a rock that had been there for ages. But as Ken Wilman walked along the beach, his dog, Madge, took a special interest in it, sparking his own curiosity. "It smelled horrible. I left it, came home and looked it up on the Internet," he told England's *The Sun* newspaper.

The odd substance turned out to be *ambergris*, a waxy material found in the digestive tracts of sperm whales. From time to time the whales eject the stuff, either by vomiting it up or pooping it out. It can float around on the surface of the ocean for years before it finally washes ashore, usually in small, hardened chunks weighing a couple of pounds apiece. Ambergris, sometimes called "floating gold," is prized by high-end perfume makers for its ability to make scents last longer. It can sell for more than $8,000 a pound, depending on quality. Wilman's seven-pound chunk is estimated to be worth around £60,000, or more than $100,000. "It was like finding a bag of cash," said Wilman, who was unemployed when his dog made the discovery.

In Plain Sight: Another rock, this one about the size and shape of a tablespoon of sugar and weighing just over half an ounce
Location: On the ground in Henningsen Lotus Park, in the gold rush town of Lotus, California
The Story: Stay-at-home mom Brenda Salveson walks Sheldon, her collie, in the park every day. That paid off in April 2012 when a meteor the size of a minivan exploded over California as it entered Earth's atmosphere, rattling windows over a wide area and setting

off car alarms 100 miles away in Carson City, Nevada. Fragments of the meteor fell to Earth over an area three miles wide and ten miles long, including in Henningsen Lotus Park. An article Salveson had read in the local newspaper said to keep an eye out for dark, delicate rocks that looked "out of place."

And when Salveson took Sheldon out for his next walk, she *did* come across a dark rock that looked like nothing she'd ever seen in the park before. "It was sitting at my toes like an Easter egg," she told CBS News. Salveson picked up the rock and brought it to a group of people—geologists, she learned—who were sweeping the area with metal detectors, looking for meteorite fragments. "I opened my hand, and they all let out a collective gasp." Her rock was a rare carbonaceous chondrite meteorite and may be as much as six billion years old. (The sun, by comparison, is only about 4.6 billion years old.) Estimated value of Salveson's rock: $20,000. She sold it for an undisclosed price to a private collector who plans to exhibit it at the Field Museum of Chicago.

In Plain Sight: A "creepy" bronze statue of a naked woman with her head bowed, sitting cross-legged on a rock
Location: Next to a gerbil cage in the childhood home of a Maryland woman named Elizabeth Tillson
The Story: When Tillson, 55, and her two siblings were growing up, they didn't pay much attention to the creepy statue, other than to be "freaked out" by her, as Tillson puts it. No one in the family cared much for it, which is how it ended up next to the gerbil cage. It wasn't until 2013, when Tillson's father became ill and had to move into a nursing home, that she had it appraised for possible sale, since nobody wanted it.

The first appraiser told them it was a casting of *Despair*, a sculpture by Auguste Rodin, the French artist most famous for another sculpture called *The Thinker*. But because the appraiser couldn't tell if the statue was authentic or just a cheap copy, they estimated its value at $1,500 to $2,500. Not bad for a creepy piece of junk, but Tillson wanted a second opinion. Matthew Quinn, an appraiser who has appeared on the PBS show *Antiques Roadshow*, took the extra step of carefully separating the woman from the rock she was sitting on, so that he could get a look at the underside of the figure. There he found the raised signature "A Rodin," which proved

---

A greyhound (dog) can go from 0 to 40 mph in 1.5 seconds; a Ferrari F50 takes 2.5 seconds.

not only that the object was authentic but that it had been cast during the sculptor's lifetime, making it even more valuable. Quinn appraised the statue at $200,000; when it went under the hammer in May 2014, it sold for $306,000.

Update: Tillson, who split the proceeds with her siblings, has had a change of heart about the statue: "I have come to quite love the piece."

In Plain Sight: An old portrait of a woman with two children
Location: Hanging on the wall of a farmhouse in Scotland
The Story: Owner Fiona McLaren didn't care much for the painting that has been in her family since the 1960s, when her father, a physician, received it as a gift from a patient. Several times over the years she considered tossing it out, and when she repainted the room it was in, she didn't bother to cover it up. As a result, specks of housepaint can still be seen on the portrait today.

But no matter how much McLaren disliked the painting, she couldn't bring herself to throw it away without having it appraised first. Good move: In 2001 she took it to Sotheby's auction house, and when she showed it to the appraiser, he gasped and then fell silent (something that doesn't happen very often at Sotheby's). After he regained his composure, the appraiser explained that the painting was in the style of the Renaissance master Leonardo da Vinci, and likely was painted by one of his pupils. It's even possible that it was painted by da Vinci himself.

Though McLaren and her father believed the painting was of the Virgin Mary, the baby Jesus, and John the Baptist, art experts believe it is actually a portrait of Mary Magdalene, her son, and another child. At last report, the painting was safely locked in a vault at the University of Cambridge, where Renaissance art historians continue to study it. If they're ever able to prove definitively that it is the work of Leonardo, the "apparently worthless" house paint-speckled portrait may be worth more than $150 million.

*   *   *

"If people make fun of you, you must be doing something right."
—**Amy Lee**

Times change! In 1900 Americans spent twice as much on funerals as on medicine.

THIS BUD…AND THAT BUD…AND *THIS* BUD'S FOR YOU

Three distinctly different brews from three different eras all claim to be the one true Budweiser. Which Bud's the true brew?

FIRST BUD: Ceské Budejovice, a city in what is now the Czech Republic, is more commonly known by its German name: Budweis. Breweries have operated there since the thirteenth century, and in 1795 a group of German residents opened a new one, called Budweiser Bier Bürgerbräu. Their signature beer was a light-colored, mild German-style lager they called Budweiser.

SECOND BUD: In the late 1860s, American brewer Adolphe Busch was looking for ways to improve the quality and shelf life of the beers being made at the St. Louis brewery he co-owned with his father-in-law, Eberhard Anheuser (mostly dark ales, which were the most popular style at the time). Busch toured Europe, studying brewing methods and sampling many different types of beer. His favorite was the one he drank in Budweis: Budweiser. So in 1876, Busch's brewery developed a beer similar to Budweiser to sell in the United States, and he called it…Budweiser. On the strength of that beer, by the turn of the twentieth century Anheuser-Busch became America's biggest beermaker.

THIRD BUD: In 1895 King William II of Württemberg (today a part of Germany) made Bürgerbräu's Budweiser his official court beer. With William's endorsement, Bürgerbräu's sales skyrocketed. Result: A group of enterprising brewers decided to cash in on Budweiser's popularity. They opened the Budvar Budweiser Brewery, and rolled out the *third* lager with the name of Budweiser.

BUDS TOGETHER
Around 1900 the two Budweis-based Budweiser breweries learned

that Busch's version of Budweiser was selling extremely well in the United States. Both Bürgerbräu and Budvar began exporting their Budweisers to America. That put three different beers called Budweiser—all of which were technically very similar—into the U.S. marketplace. Surprisingly, though, this didn't lead to consumer confusion. Reason: there was a lot more of Busch's Budweiser in stores—by a ratio of 10 to 1. The three brands coexisted…but not for long.

BUTTING HEADS

It all came to a head in 1901 at a brewing-industry trade fair attended by representatives from all three breweries. The parties met…and argued about which was the real Budweiser and who should get the rights to the very lucrative and very recognizable brand name.

• The Bürgerbräu brewers argued that *they* should have the rights to "Budweiser" because they made their lagers in Budweis, and they'd been doing it since 1795.

• Anheuser-Busch representatives conceded that fact but contended that they owned the *North American* trademark on the Budweiser name and had the paperwork to prove it.

That led to a ten-year courtroom battle.

BUDS AGAIN?

In 1911 the legal dust finally settled. The agreement: each brewer could continue to use the name Budweiser, but could sell their product only in certain territories. Anheuser-Busch was granted the right to sell its Budweiser in North America only. The two European brewers agreed to share the name and the European market. The two breweries kept a tenuous peace for another few years…until the conclusion of World War I, when both operations were seized by the Czech government.

The Bürgerbräu brewers were expelled to Germany. And because Germany's armies had ravaged much of Europe, the name "Budweiser" became loathed there, leading the Czech government to ban the name altogether. The new operators of the Bürgerbräu brewery began selling their beer under names like "Crystal" and "Samson." The owners of the Budvar brewery had no choice but to drop the Budweiser name. They renamed their beer Budejovický Budvar.

BREW HA-HA

The three breweries kept out of each other's hair, all the way to the 1990s. By then, Anheuser-Busch had become one of the world's largest brewers and was selling its Budweiser lager all across Europe, but under the name "Bud" in order to avoid another round of legal bickering. After the fall of communism in Czechoslovakia and the creation of the Czech Republic in 1993, the Budvar and Bürgerbräu breweries decided to start selling beer under the name of "Budweiser" again.

That led to another round of complex legal entanglements and a bitter dispute between the three breweries that continues to this day. Who will win? It's anybody's guess. You can find any of these three lagers all across Europe and North America, but depending on where you are, they might be called something else.

* * *

YELLOW JOURNALISM

On The Simpsons, *it seems there's a funny magazine on every weird topic imaginable. Oh, how we wish some of these were real!*

Oatmeal Enthusiast	*TV God*
Loud Workplace	*Coping with Scurvy*
Gravy Aficionado	*Danger Liker*
Bad Boy's Life	*Fabergé Egg Owner*
Dream Denied Magazine	*Gum Disease Bi-Yearly*
Eleventeen	*High Strung Child*
Clown Car and Driver	*Obnoxious Co-Worker*
Barely Senile	*Schmoozeweek*
Better Homes Than Yours	*Overpass Monthly*
Smothering Mother	*Peace Pipe Aficionado*
Obsessive Bride	*Science-y Stuff Magazine*
Hooters Digest	*Seltzer World*
Bazookas Illustrated	*The Ugly Reader*
Tub Lover	*USA Yesterday*

HORVATS & HANSENS

More of the most common last names around the world. (Note: Surnames are uncommon in many African and Arab countries.)

Korea
1. Kim
2. Lee
3. Park

Russia
1. Smirnov
2. Ivanov
3. Kuznetsov

England
1. Smith
2. Jones
3. Taylor

Spain
1. García
2. Fernandez
3. Gonzalez

Finland
1. Korhonen
2. Virtanen
3. Mäkinen

Costa Rica
1. Díaz
2. Morán
3. Rodríguez

Slovakia
1. Horvath
2. Kovac
3. Varga

Ireland
1. Murphy
2. Kelly
3. Sullivan

Norway
1. Hansen
2. Johansen
3. Olsen

Philippines
1. Santos
2. Reyes
3. Cruz

France
1. Martin
2. Bernard
3. Dubois

South Africa
1. Naidoo
2. Govender
3. Botha

Japan
1. Sato
2. Suzuki
3. Takahashi

Romania
1. Popescu
2. Ionescu
3. Popa

Scotland
1. Smith
2. Brown
3. Wilson

Portugal
1. Silva
2. Santos
3. Ferreira

Hungary
1. Nagy
2. Kovacs
3. Toth

Taiwan
1. Chen
2. Lin
3. Huang

Croatia
1. Horvat
2. Kovacevich
3. Babic

Austria
1. Gruber
2. Huber
3. Bauer

Poland
1. Nowak
2. Kowalski
3. Wisniewski

Number of US families with the surname Obama: 20. (Clinton: 11,000; Bush: 60,000.)

WILL SING FOR CASH

One of the perks of being a popular recording artist: If you suddenly find yourself in deep financial doo-doo, you can make a new album to pay off your debts…and hope people will buy the album.

WILL SMITH

In the 1980s, DJ Jazzy Jeff and the Fresh Prince (Jeffrey Townes and Will Smith) became rap and pop superstars while they were still teenagers with family-friendly hits (and comic videos) like "Parents Just Don't Understand" and "A Nightmare on My Street." They became millionaires, but being so rich at such a young age with so little financial maturity, Smith spent his money freely. Result: in 1989 he received a letter from the IRS demanding he pay more than $1 million in back taxes. He rushed to record a new album, *And in This Corner*, to pay off the bill, but the rap climate had changed—hard-edged gangster rap had taken hold, and DJ Jazzy Jeff and the Fresh Prince were passé. The album didn't sell very well, and by 1990, Smith was preparing to default on the debt and declare bankruptcy. That's when a producer named Benny Medina approached Smith with an idea: star in a sitcom he'd conceived loosely based on his life as a poor inner-city kid who moves in with a rich foster family. Apart from his music videos, Smith had never acted, but he agreed to star because he had no other options. Good move. *The Fresh Prince of Bel-Air* became a smash hit for NBC, and enabled Smith to pay off his tax bill. He's now one of the biggest stars in Hollywood, commanding more than $20 million a movie.

LAURYN HILL

Hill was one of the most popular and promising music stars of the late 1990s. With her group, the Fugees, Hill rapped at breakneck speed but also possessed a remarkable singing voice, as evidenced in her hit cover of Roberta Flack's "Killing Me Softly." Her solo debut, *The Miseducation of Lauryn Hill*, sold 18 million copies and won the 1998 Grammy for Album of the Year. Hill recorded one more album—an *MTV Unplugged* live album in 2002—and then retired from music to raise her six children. It didn't last. A decade later, she was essentially forced to come out of retirement. In 2012 she pled guilty to charges that she failed to pay more than $1 million

---

How did UPS shave 28.5 million miles off delivery routes? By minimizing left-hand turns.

in taxes. Owing the government big bucks, she signed a $1 million deal with Sony to record five new tracks. She released two, as digital singles: "Consumerism" and "Neurotic Society (Compulsory Mix)." Unfortunately, the songs didn't earn enough to pay the taxes she owed, and Hill ended up spending three months in prison.

WILLIE NELSON

A few months after Nelson released the album *Born for Trouble* in 1990, trouble came: the IRS placed liens on his Texas ranch and virtually everything else he owned to account for a staggering $16 million delinquent tax bill. Nelson had no idea he hadn't paid his taxes, nor had he consciously avoided paying them. The accounting firm he'd hired, Price Waterhouse, had invested his fortune in weak ventures and illegal tax shelters...and hadn't paid Nelson's taxes in more than a decade. In 1990 and 1991, the IRS auctioned off Nelson's assets, but his fans stepped in—they bought virtually all of it and then returned it to the singer. (His ranch was bought by a group of farmers—a show of solidarity owing to Nelson's longtime support of the Farm Aid relief fund.) Nelson's lawyer talked the IRS down to a $6 million bill, but the assets didn't cover it all, so in 1992 Nelson recorded *The IRS Tapes: Who'll Buy My Memories?* Nelson recorded it on the cheap, with no band—it's just him and his guitar, playing his greatest hits. The album earned $3.6 million. Five years later, Nelson had finished paying off his debt.

MARVIN GAYE

Gaye's problem wasn't taxes—it was alimony. In 1975 his wife, Anna Gordy Gaye, served him with divorce papers, asking for child support and alimony. Gaye refused, claiming he didn't have enough money to pay his own expenses, let alone hers. In 1977 a settlement was reached: the advance and all royalties from Gaye's next studio album would go to Anna. Intending to record a quickie mediocre album without much effort—since all the proceeds were going to his ex-wife—Gaye found the recording sessions to be deeply therapeutic. The resulting album (comically titled *Here, My Dear*) became a meditative two-record concept album about his bittersweet relationship with Anna. Although it was a commercial failure, *Here, My Dear* was one of the most critically acclaimed albums in Gaye's career.

MOTHER OF THE FATHER OF HIS COUNTRY

Even extraordinary people suffer from ordinary problems. And having a difficult relationship with a parent is a pretty common one. (No, not us, Mom.) Say hello to George Washington's mother, Mary Ball Washington.

THE ORPHAN

Mary Ball was born on a Virginia farm in 1708. Her father, Joseph Ball, died when she was three years old, and her mother, also named Mary, died when she was twelve. Afterward, the girl was raised by George Eskridge, a family friend. At 23, she married Augustine Washington, a 37-year-old widower with three children. The couple had six children together (one died in infancy) before Augustine died in 1743, leaving Mary to raise their five surviving children alone.

George Washington, named in honor of George Eskridge, was Mary and Augustine's oldest son. He was only eleven when his father died. As the oldest male in the house, it fell upon him to help raise his younger siblings and also to help run the farm, and because Mary did not remarry, George had to shoulder these responsibilities for the rest of his childhood.

TOO CLOSE FOR COMFORT

Perhaps because she had suffered so much loss over the years—or because as a single mom raising five kids on a farm, she just needed a lot of help—Mary became extremely possessive of George. She took no interest in his personal ambitions other than to feel threatened by them, and she was jealous of any time that he spent away from the farm. She habitually accused him of neglecting or even abandoning her, even though he was by all accounts a devoted and dutiful son.

When George was 14, his older half-brother Lawrence and some well-connected family friends hatched a scheme to get him out of the house and away from his mother by securing a position for him as a midshipman on a Royal Navy frigate. After a lot of persuading, Mary agreed to the plan, but she changed her mind at the last

---

An estimated 7,000 Americans die every year as a direct result of a doctor's bad handwriting.

minute, and George, bags packed and ready to go, had to unpack and remain on the farm with her.

LAND LOTS OF LAND

Mary didn't know it (and even if she had, she probably wouldn't have cared), but she'd done George a big favor by keeping him out of the navy. Denied his chance for adventure on the high seas, George opted to became a surveyor, which could be a lucrative profession in the 1740s. The population of the American colonies was growing, and as people carved new settlements out of the wilderness, they needed skilled surveyors to parcel up the land. Cash was often in short supply in the back country, so surveyors were commonly paid in land. With the knowledge they gained on the job, the surveyors were able to select some of the best parcels for themselves. Young George made the most of the opportunity: By the time he was 20 he owned more than 2,300 acres in northern Virginia, which served as the basis for his personal fortune.

MOTHER MAY I?

Washington's knowledge of the back country made him valuable to the British, who by the 1750s were locked in a struggle with France for control of the Ohio Country (modern-day Ohio and Indiana, plus parts of Pennsylvania and West Virginia). In March of 1755 he was offered a position as an aide to General Edward Braddock, who'd been sent from England to drive out the French. Washington accepted and asked his younger brother Jack, who lived with their mother on her farm, to move to his farm, Mount Vernon, to look after the place.

That, of course, would have made life more difficult for Mary. When she learned what her sons were planning, she was furious. "Perhaps feeling bereft of family help at [her] farm, Mary Ball Washington arrived at Mount Vernon hell-bent upon preventing George from joining Braddock," biographer Ron Chernow writes in *Washington: A Life*. "Mary, appearing like the wrath of God, insisted upon settling her son's future plans on the spot."

This time George stood firm. He resolved to join the general's staff as planned, but his mother's haranguing caused him to miss an interview with the general's staff in Alexandria, Virginia. "The arrival of a good deal of company, among whom was my mother,

---

Loony fact: Coral only spawns in the week after a full moon.

alarmed at the report of my intentions to attend your fortunes, prevents me the pleasure of waiting upon you today as I had intended," he admitted in a letter to Braddock.

TRIAL BY FIRE

If Washington hoped to see action, he would not have long to wait. On July 9, 1755, General Braddock and 1,400 troops (including Washington) had just crossed the Monongahela River in Pennsylvania when they were attacked by a force of some 900 Indians and French soldiers from Fort Duquesne, where the city of Pittsburgh is today. More than 400 British soldiers died in the battle, and hundreds more were wounded, including Braddock, who died a few days later. Washington was luckier: Two horses were shot out from under him and at least four bullets ripped through his uniform (and his hat), but they missed his body, and he survived the fight with barely a scratch.

By any measure, the Battle of the Monongahela was a rout. As Washington had been warning Braddock for months, the British tactic of fighting out in the open and shoulder-to-shoulder was no match for the French and Indians, who fired from behind rocks and trees and scattered when fired upon, only to reappear in unexpected places to renew the attack. Only 23 of *their* men died in the battle and only another 16 were wounded.

But Washington had shown great courage and leadership on the battlefield, riding back and forth to rally the troops and organize an orderly retreat to safer ground. He returned home "the Hero of the Monongahela," and one month later was named supreme commander of all the military forces in Virginia. He was 23.

THE HOME FRONT

None of this mattered a whit to Mary Washington, who was still angry with her son for abandoning her to fight in a war that, as far as she was concerned, was none of his business. And her "suffering" wasn't over: Washington spent the next three years as head of the Virginia forces and was often away from home, defending frontier settlements from Indian attacks. He finally retired from his post in December 1758, much to his mother's relief. There had been "no end to my trouble while George was in the army," Mary Washington wrote to a relative, "but he has now given it up."

THE OTHER WOMAN

A few weeks later, Washington gave his mother a new reason to be mad at him when he married a wealthy widow named Martha Custis in 1759. There's no record of Mary having attended the wedding, even though she lived nearby, and it's possible she didn't even meet her daughter-in-law for another year. And though Mary lived for another 30 years, historians believe she never visited her son and his wife at Mount Vernon.

Washington made regular trips to visit his mother on her farm (always keeping the visits short), and he frequently gave her gifts of money. By the early 1770s, Mary, now in her sixties, was too old to manage the farm, so Washington bought her the house next door to his sister Betty's home in Fredericksburg, Virginia, where she lived for the remaining 17 years of her life. In spite of this and other acts of kindness over the years, the relationship between mother and son never healed.

A TWO-FRONT WAR

Duty called again in June 1775, when Washington was appointed commander in chief of the newly formed Continental Army at the start of the American Revolution. Before he went off to war, he arranged for a cousin to look after his mother and to take care of any financial needs she might have. That would have satisfied most mothers, but not Mary. Just as in the French and Indian wars, she was furious that her son would place his country's needs ahead of her own, and she complained "upon all occasions and in all companies," as Washington put it, that he had abandoned her and left her destitute. More than one person who met Mary Washington during the war and listened to her bellyaching assumed she'd sided with the British against her own son. If that wasn't enough, in 1781 Mary petitioned the Virginia state assembly to provide her with an emergency pension to help her pay some taxes that were due. Washington managed to get the matter quashed before it caused him public embarrassment, but the incident only further strained his difficult relationship with his mother.

Washington led the American forces to victory, of course, but even that didn't impress his mother, something she made clear following the British surrender at Yorktown, when someone made the mistake of referring to her son as "His Excellency" in her presence. "His Excellency? What nonsense!" she sputtered.

BITTER END

Just as Washington continued to provide for his mother after the war, Mary continued to complain. "I never lived soe pore in my life....I should be almost starved," she wrote in one letter to her son while he was presiding over the Constitutional Convention. In time, her whining became so incessant that George suggested she sell her house and live with one of her children—one of her *other* children—but Mary stayed put. She lived long enough to see her son inaugurated as the first president of the United States in April 1789, but his biographers have found no record of her ever congratulating her son on his achievement.

Four months later, on August 25, 1789, Mary Washington died from breast cancer at the age of 81. She left her oldest son some of her most treasured possessions, including a mirror, her bed, and a favorite quilt. But rather than accept the items, Washington gave them to his sister.

POST-MORTEM

Washington did attend his mother's funeral, but neither he nor anyone else delivered a eulogy, and more than 40 years passed before anyone put a marker on her grave. By then Washington himself was long dead, and the location of his mother's grave had been forgotten, something that stunned presidential biographer Jared Sparks when he went looking for it in 1827: "The grave of Washington's mother," he wrote, "is marked by no visible object, not even a mound of earth, nor is the precise spot of its locality known....For a long time a single cedar tree was the only guide to the place; near this tree tradition has fixed the grave of Washington's mother, but there is no stone to point out the place.".

*   *   *

QUITE CONTRARY

Q: What do Meryl Streep, Mae West, Lily Tomlin, Farrah Fawcett, Debbie Reynolds, Kathleen Turner, Sissy Spacek, Dusty Springfield, Debra Winger, Sean Young, and Elle Fanning all have in common?

A: Their real first name is Mary.

George Washington's false teeth were stolen from the Smithsonian in 1981.

STRANGE CELEBRITY LAWSUITS

Stars are just like us—only they have better lawyers.

THE PLAINTIFF: Nicolas Cage

THE DEFENDANTS: Former co-star Kathleen Turner, Associated Newspapers, and Headline Publishing Group

THE LAWSUIT: An excerpt from Turner's 2008 memoir *Send Yourself Roses—Thoughts on My Life, Love, and Leading Roles* was reprinted in London's *Daily Mail* newspaper. It described Cage's "difficult" behavior on the set of the 1986 movie *Peggy Sue Got Married*: "He was arrested twice for drunk driving and, I think, for stealing a dog. He'd come across a Chihuahua he liked and stuck it in his jacket."

It's no big Hollywood secret that Cage is somewhat eccentric, but he insists that he's never had a DUI or stolen a dog. He sued Turner, her publisher, and the British tabloid for libel. "As an actor who stars in family-friendly films," said his lawyer, "Mr. Cage was understandably upset at having been wrongly depicted as condoning that sort of reckless, dangerous, and criminal behavior."

THE VERDICT: Cage won. The passage was removed from future printings of the memoir; the publishing company paid for his legal costs and agreed to donate money to a charity of his choosing. Both Turner and the *Daily Mail* publicly apologized.

THE PLAINTIFF: Jennifer O'Neill, Lady Gaga's former best friend forever (BFF) and personal assistant (PA)

THE DEFENDANT: Lady Gaga

THE LAWSUIT: It was a dream job turned nightmare for O'Neill. In 2009 Gaga hired her BFF to be her PA. For $75,000 a year, O'Neill helped the pop superstar do everything from choose her outfits (not an easy task considering Gaga once wore a dress made of raw meat) to making sure Gaga had full makeup on *every time* she appeared in public. It also meant sleeping in Gaga's bed so O'Neill could be on hand to change a DVD, turn off a light—basically whatever Gaga needed. "I was by her side virtually twenty-four hours a

---

The *charango*, the national instrument of Bolivia, is traditionally made from armadillo shells.

day, seven days a week," complained O'Neill. For 13 months, she said, she couldn't even get a haircut or call her family from the road without Gaga throwing a fit. In 2011 O'Neill quit, citing the diva's "diva-like behavior" as the reason. Furthermore, O'Neill claimed her salary had only paid her for 40 hours per week, so she added up all the hours she *didn't* get paid for—7,168—and sued Gaga for overtime pay of $393,000. Gaga was livid. She lashed out at O'Neill in a video deposition (we left out all the swear words):

> I am going to tell you exactly what happened...which is my ex-best friend is a hood rat who is suing me for money that she didn't earn. SHE thinks she's just like the Queen of the Universe. And, you know what? She didn't want to be a slave to one—because in my work and what I do, I'm the Queen of the Universe every day!

THE VERDICT: A month before the December 2013 trial date, the case was settled out of court. According to insiders, the Queen of the Universe didn't like the fact that news reports about the lawsuit were painting an unflattering picture of her.

THE PLAINTIFFS: 34 European Michael Jackson fans
THE DEFENDANT: Dr. Conrad Murray, Jackson's doctor
THE LAWSUIT: Claiming they were unable to cope with the 2009 death of the King of Pop, in 2013 the fans filed a class-action suit for "emotional damage" in French court against Murray, who had already served two years in prison for his role in Jackson's death. The case actually went to trial. There was even witness testimony describing how sad the fans were.
THE VERDICT: The judge found that 5 of the 34 litigants had indeed suffered emotionally from the pop star's absence and awarded each of them one euro (about $1.34).

THE PLAINTIFF: Janet Clover of Tampa, Florida, a nurse who moonlighted as an exotic dancer
THE DEFENDANTS: Viacom, Stan Lee, and Pamela Anderson
THE LAWSUIT: In 2002 legendary Marvel Comics publisher Stan Lee (*The Hulk*, *Spider-Man*) allegedly went to a strip club in Tampa ("allegedly" because Lee has never spoken publicly about this case). According to Clover, 37, over the course of two private "dance sessions," she told Lee that she was leading a double life as a "sensual dancer" named Stripperella who gives back to the

community by nursing and helping homeless people.

A few months later, Clover saw a commercial on TNN (a cable channel now called Spike TV) for an animated series called *Stripperella*, "created by Stan Lee." Clover read the synopsis of the show about a "stripper by night, superhero by later at night" (voiced by Pamela Anderson) and realized it was based on her persona. She said she tried contacting Lee several times but was ignored. Clover tried to sue to keep the show from airing, but she didn't have enough money to hire a lawyer in time.

VERDICT: The case never made it to court, but *Stripperella* lasted only one season. The publicity generated by Clover's lawsuit has been cited as one of the reasons for the cartoon's cancellation. The final irony, though, may be that Clover actually liked the show. "It was kind of cute," she said.

THE PLAINTIFF: Meat Loaf, the singer (Marvin Aday)

THE DEFENDANT: Meat Loaf, the impersonator (Dean Torkington)

THE LAWSUIT: Torkington, an English singer, began impersonating the American rocker in 1996. His website is *Meatloaf. org*. The real Meat Loaf, best known for his 1977 hit "Paradise by the Dashboard Light," owns the domain *Meatloaf.net* but wanted *Meatloaf.org* as well. Torkington offered to sell it to him for $12,500. Meat Loaf refused. (Neither singer was able to afford *Meatloaf.com*, which at the time was owned by an "Internet squatter.") Angry, the real Meat Loaf showed up backstage at one of the fake Meat Loaf's shows and sternly ordered him to hand over the *.org* domain name—and to remove all of the Meat Loaf-related artwork from his van. Torkington refused; he told Meat Loaf that he was actually helping the rocker's flagging career by "keeping the legend alive." Meat Loaf didn't buy it. Unable to settle their beef, he threatened to sue the impersonator for $100,000.

THE VERDICT: Torkington lost. The judge ordered him to pay the singer $25,000. "He won't get a penny from me," said the defiant impersonator. "I used to love Meat Loaf, but now I hate him. He's trying to ruin me." Torkington has since moved on to impersonating Elton John, which he says is "much less of a hassle." If you go to *Meatloaf.org*, it redirects you to *Meatloaf.net*. And if you go to *Meatloaf.com*, it takes you to a website about meat loaf, the food.

Bhutan has issued some stamps made from silk and others made from steel.

WEIRD ANIMAL NEWS

Strange tales of creatures great and small.

DOMESTIC DISTURBANCE
A concerned neighbor in the town of China, Maine, called police in 2014 after hearing screams coming from the property next door. Four officers rushed to the house. When they got there, a woman came to the door. The screams, she explained, were coming from her "overjoyed" hog that had just been given access to a pen—where five sows were in heat.

TOO MUCH INFORMATION
Guillermo Reyes, 49, and his pet parrot go everywhere together. While driving in Mexico City after having a few drinks one night, Reyes was stopped at a police checkpoint. He knew that if he played it cool, he'd be okay. But when the officer arrived at his car, the parrot started squawking, "He's drunk! He's drunk!" so the cops gave Reyes a Breathalyzer test, which he failed.

OUT ON A LIMB
After seeing a small cat get stuck in a tall tree across the street from a Queens, New York, elementary school in 2013, the students urged their teacher to call the police. A squad car showed up, and with all eyes upon him, veteran officer Dane Natto started climbing the tree. When he got near the cat, it climbed up farther. Natto continued in pursuit. Even when the cat crawled out to the edge of a limb, Natto scampered out after it…and then suddenly realized he was 30 feet above the street. Neither man nor beast could move. Natto reluctantly asked his partner to call for help. His partner obliged, but only after laughing at him (in front of the kids). When firefighters arrived, they rescued the cat, then the cop. The kids all cheered when he finally got down.

OUCH!
In 2013 Sandra Nabucco, 52, was walking in Gavea, Brazil, when she felt a "thud" on her head. She instinctively reached up with both hands. Bad idea. "The pain was enormous," she said. For some

---

Our blood is red because it contains iron. Lobster blood is blue because it contains copper.

reason, a porcupine had climbed to the top of a lamppost and then fell—or jumped—onto Nabucco's head. It took a surgeon more than an hour to remove the 200 quills from her scalp and hands.

SURF AND TURF

In 2013 Derrick Chaulk was driving in Newfoundland when he saw an eight-foot-long shark on the beach, choking on a large brown thing, part of which was sticking out of its mouth. Then Jeremy Ball walked up. The two strangers worked together to save the animal. First, they pulled out the brown thing—it turned out to be a moose hide—and then Chaulk tied a rope to the shark's tail. He pushed (with his boot) while Ball tugged, and they finally got it into deeper water. It still wasn't moving. "Then all of a sudden," said Chaulk, "the water started coming out of his gills and he started breathing." The shark rested for a few minutes, then swam away.

DIG IN

Hendrik Helmer of Darwin, Australia, awoke to excruciating pain in his ear. Afraid a poisonous spider had taken up residence, he tried to suck whatever it was out with a vacuum cleaner. It dug in deeper. Helmer rushed to the emergency room, where a doctor told him it was most likely a "little cockroach." She tried to flush it out with olive oil. But it dug in deeper….and suffocated. That, said Helmer, was the worst part: "It was in the throes of death, twitching." The doctor finally pried the thing out with a pair of forceps. "You know how I said it was maybe a little cockroach?" she asked. "That may have been an underestimate." It was a cockroach, all right—that was nearly an inch long. (But at least it wasn't a poisonous spider.)

WE'RE GONNA NEED TWO MORE DOVES

In January 2014, Pope Francis gave his weekly speech from his apartment window at the Vatican to tens of thousands of onlookers. At the end, the pope, who was flanked by a little boy and a little girl, called for peace. Then each of the children released a white dove into the air as the faithful cheered. Within seconds, one of the doves was attacked by a large gull, and the other was chased by a crow. According to *The Guardian*, "The pope embraced the noticeably upset boy and patted his head, while the young girl just laughed." It's uncertain whether either dove was able to escape.

There are species of wasps with the scientific names *Heerz lukenatcha* and *Heerz tooya*.

THE VIDOCQ SOCIETY: COLD CASES SOLVED

On page 312 we told you about Eugène Vidocq, the pioneering police detective of 1800s France. Part of his legacy is the Vidocq Society—a group of modern-day investigators who follow in his footsteps.

THE GAME IS AFOOT

In September 1990, three friends in Pennsylvania—William Fleisher, a former police officer; Richard Walter, a forensic psychologist; and Frank Bender, a forensic artist—founded a crime-solving club. The idea: Invite investigators like themselves to join the group and use their skills to solve cold cases—specifically, long-unsolved cases of murder and disappearance. They founded the new organization in honor of and in the spirit of pioneering detective Eugène François Vidocq, calling it the Vidocq Society.

Today the group has more than 150 members from dozens of crime investigation fields, who meet regularly (usually over long lunches) to discuss potential cases. Cases are taken on a first-come, first-served basis and are taken *pro bono*, meaning members work for free. Criteria: Cases must be at least two years old, the victims cannot have been involved in criminal activity, and requests must be presented by legitimate law-enforcement agencies at one of the club's Philadelphia luncheons. The Vidocq Society has grown over the years to become a highly respected organization, and its members have helped solve (or resolve) many cases.

Here are a few of those stories.

HUEY COX. In March 1991, Huey Cox, a 30-year-old manager of a Little Rock, Arkansas, restaurant, was beaten to death with a golf club in his apartment. Nine months later, Derrick Carlock, a dishwasher from the restaurant, was arrested for the murder. But Cox's family didn't believe Carlock had done it. (Cox was white and Carlock was black, and Cox's family believed race was a factor in Carlock's being charged.) Cox's sister, Theresa Baus, contacted the Vidocq Society and actually asked them to help get Carlock off. After reviewing the case, they agreed to take it on. Richard Walter and another society member, a fingerprint expert, both studied the evidence, and both testified at the trial in Carlock's defense. They developed evidence that pointed to another suspect, which was so convincing that the jury acquitted Carlock after less than an hour of deliberations. (While not the outright solution of a case, this was the Vidocq Society's first success. And, as you may have noticed, the case doesn't meet any of the three criteria listed in the introduction. That's because those criteria were implemented after this case was resolved. The Huey Cox murder remains unsolved.)

DEBORAH LYNN WILSON. In 1992 the Philadelphia Police Department contacted the society, asking for assistance in the unsolved murder of 20-year-old Deborah Lynn Wilson. She had been found strangled to death in a stairwell at Philadelphia's Drexel University eight years earlier. Society members focused on one mysterious aspect of the case—that Wilson had been found barefoot, and her shoes and socks had never been accounted for—and recommended that police check their files for known foot fetishists. It took a long time, but a year later investigators discovered that a previous suspect, a Drexel University security guard named David Dickson Jr., had been charged with stealing a woman's sneakers while in the army in the 1970s. That tip allowed police to obtain a search warrant for Dickson's apartment, where they found several pairs of women's shoes and socks—all white sneakers and white socks, just as Deborah Wilson had been wearing, which was apparently part of Dickson's fetish. Dickson was convicted of Wilson's murder in 1995.

ROGER SCOTT DUNN. In May 1991, Roger Dunn, 24, went missing in Lubbock, Texas. Dunn's girlfriend and roommate, Leisha Hamilton, told police that Dunn had simply disappeared. An investigation found blood in the living room of the couple's apartment—on the floor, on all four walls, and even on the ceiling—and police were able to determine that it was Dunn's. In addition, police discovered Hamilton had been cheating on Dunn with a man named Tim Smith. But because there was no body, they couldn't be sure that Dunn was, in fact, dead, so no charges were filed. Years went by. Then, one day in 1996, Roger's father, James Dunn, who had never given up on the case, saw something on TV about the Vidocq Society, and convinced the Lubbock Police Department to formally request the group's help with the case. A Vidocq Society blood expert studied the evidence from the apartment living room and concluded that not only had Dunn been viciously attacked there, but that based on the amount of blood found, he could not have survived that attack. Then Richard Walter, the Vidocq Society founder and forensic psychologist, profiled Leisha Hamilton and basically concluded that she was a manipulative psychopath. He told the Lubbock police that there was more than enough circumstantial evidence to charge Hamilton and Smith with the murder. With the Vidocq Society to back them up, Lubbock police arrested the pair, and, in 1997, despite the fact that no body had ever been found, both were convicted of murder. Hamilton was sentenced to 20 years in prison; Smith received a lighter sentence. **Update:** In May 2012, more than 20 years after his disappearance, Roger Dunn's remains were found in a shallow grave just down the road from the apartment in which he had been killed. His parents buried his remains under the monument they had erected in his honor in their family plot years earlier.

TERRI BROOKS. On the morning of February 4, 1984, the body of Terri Brooks was found inside a Roy Rogers restaurant in Falls Township, Pennsylvania. The 25-year-old, who had closed up the restaurant by herself late the night before, was severely beaten, stabbed, strangled, and suffocated with a plastic bag that had been put over her head. Police concluded that it was a robbery gone wrong: The restaurant's safe was open and its contents—more than $2,500—were missing, but the case went unsolved for 14 years. Then, in 1998, a new Falls Township police chief brought the case to the Vidocq Society. They quickly concluded that the original investigating officers had gotten the motive wrong. The attack, they said, was much too vicious and personal for the motive to be robbery. Whoever did it knew Brooks—and knew her well. Police reopened the case, and this time focused on the young woman's fiancé, Alfred Keefe. At the time of the murder, friends of the couple had told investigators that Brooks and Keefe were having trouble, but nothing more came of it. Now they obtained a warrant to test Keefe's DNA. Genetic testing wasn't available at the time of Brooks's murder, but plenty of blood evidence had been taken from the crime scene, including some from under Brooks's fingernails. They compared it to a sample of Keefe's DNA (taken from cigarette butts found in his trash). Result: It was a perfect match. Keefe was arrested—and he confessed to the crime. In 1998 he was sentenced to life in prison without parole.

IT'S A MYSTERY

• The Vidocq Society has 82 full members—the maximum number allowed. The society's founding charter limits the number of full members to the number of years lived by Eugène François Vidocq. They have many associate members from all over the world as well.

• In 1997 the Vidocq Society signed a deal with actor and producer Danny DeVito's Jersey Films company for options on film rights about the society. So far, the deal has gone cold—the film has not yet been made.

• In 1989, a year before becoming one of the society's founding members, forensic artist Frank Bender appeared on *America's Most Wanted*, in the case of wanted killer John Emil List. Eighteen years earlier, List had murdered his entire family—his wife, his mother, and his three children—in their Westfield, New Jersey, home. He left a note confessing to the crime, then disappeared. At the request of *America's Most Wanted*, Bender, using old photographs, sculpted a bust of what List might look like if he were still alive. A woman in Richmond, Virginia, saw the show, thought the bust looked a lot like one of her neighbors—and two weeks later, List was in jail. He had been living in Richmond under a fake name since the early 1980s, and had even remarried. List died in prison in 2008.

• The Vidocq Society has taken on more than 300 cold cases, and claims to have helped resolve roughly 80 percent of them.

*   *   *

LIKE, ENOUGH ALREADY

*From a Marist College poll, here are
the most annoying words of 2013:*

1. Whatever
2. Like
3. You know
4. Just sayin'
5. Obviously

FIRST LOOK:
THE SONOGRAM

*If you have kids, there's a good chance that the very first time
you laid eyes on them was via a "sonogram" image taken before
they were even born. The grainy images are so common that
they've become a rite of passage for parents all over the
world. Here's the story of how they came to be.*

SHIP SHAPE

In the summer of 1955, Dr. Ian Donald, a professor of midwifery at the University of Glasgow in Scotland, was invited to take a tour of Babcock & Wilcox, a firm that manufactured steam boilers for the city's shipbuilding industry. That's not the kind of tour that would typically interest a physician who specializes in childbirth, but Donald wanted to see the company's "industrial flaw detectors"—devices used to check for cracks in the welds that held the steel boilers together.

Industrial flaw detectors were a peacetime extension of sonar technology, which had been used during World War II to detect enemy submarines. Warships equipped with sonar sent bursts of sound energy in the form of "pings" through the water. If a submarine was lurking below the waves, the pings would strike the hard surface of the sub and bounce back to the warship as echoes. Analysis of the echoes would (hopefully) reveal the location of the submarine, so that it could be attacked and sunk.

The industrial flaw detectors used by B&W worked in much the same way, by bouncing ultrasound waves off the welds in steel. The resulting echoes were analyzed to see if they revealed any unseen defects in the welds.

LUMPING IT

Dr. Donald wondered if the technology could also be used to see things hidden inside the human body. The demonstration on the tour showed promise, so Donald wangled a second invitation to the boilermaker. This time he brought a selection of cysts, tumors, and other medical samples to analyze; B&W gave him a piece of steak that he could use as a control sample of healthy tissue that contained no tumors or cysts. The results were "beyond my wildest expectations," Donald remembered 20 years later. "I could see boundless possibilities in the years ahead."

MAD MAN

Donald could see the possibilities, but his colleagues could not. They'd long ago given him the nickname "Mad Donald" for his fascination with gadgets and his attempts to incorporate them into medicine. Though he'd had some successes, including a device that assisted struggling newborns in taking their first breath, the idea of taking tumors and cysts to a shipyard boilermaker, of all places, did not help his professional reputation one bit.

Donald wasn't the only person interested in ultrasound: Researchers in Europe, Japan, and the United States were also experimenting with it, and their research was starting to appear in medical journals. But if Donald's colleagues knew this, it made no difference. When he borrowed an old flaw detector from a London neurologist who'd tried (and failed) to scan human brains from outside the skull, all it did was give the other doctors a chance to drop by his office and laugh at his experiments in person.

To be fair, those experiments were quite a sight in those early days. The only way he could get his flaw detector to work was to smear the bottom of a plastic bucket with petroleum jelly and balance it precariously on a patient's abdomen, then fill the bucket with water and immerse the ultrasound probe in the bucket. As often as not, the only result was water spilled all over the patient, the doctor, and the floor, forcing Donald to start all over again—assuming the patient was willing to risk a second drenching.

HELPING HAND

Those early results were so disappointing that Donald might have ended his research right then and there if some electricians with Kelvin & Hughes, the company that made the flaw detectors, hadn't happened to be installing lights in a nearby operating room. When the electricians saw him bucket-scanning patients with the antiquated detector, they passed word of the ridiculous sight to Tom Brown, a brilliant 23-year-old Kelvin & Hughes engineer assigned to the flaw detector department. Intrigued, Brown looked up Mad

Donald in the phone book, gave him a call, and asked if he could drop by his office for a look. The doctor agreed, and Brown soon observed that not only was Donald's flaw detector old and obsolete, it had been modified in a way that made it all but useless. He made a few calls to his bosses at Kelvin & Hughes, and a brand-new, state-of-the-art flaw detector was soon on its way to Donald's office.

PRESSING THE FLESH

With the new machine, balancing buckets of water on the bellies of patients was no longer required: All Donald had to do was smear the patient's abdomen with olive oil and run the ultrasound probe over the area. Sound waves penetrated the body, and the echoes that resulted appeared as electrical impulses on the screen of a device called an oscilloscope.

Donald had long suspected that cysts, which were filled with fluid, would have a different ultrasound "signature" than tumors, which were dense masses of tissue. His earliest experiments at the boilermaker had suggested as much, and now the new equipment confirmed it. Once again, however, his colleagues dismissed his findings. Then a professor of surgery asked him to examine one of his hopeless cases, a woman dying from inoperable stomach cancer.

Donald smeared the woman's severely distended abdomen with olive oil and ran his probe over the area. A couple of swipes was all it took: Instead of getting a reading consistent with a cancerous tumor, the industrial flaw detector revealed a pocket of fluid with clearly defined edges to it, characteristic of a cyst. The "dying" woman wasn't dying at all. She didn't have cancer, either, and after Donald operated and removed what he correctly diagnosed as a benign ovarian cyst, she made a full recovery.

SOUND'S GOOD

Mad Donald suddenly didn't seem so mad after all. His strange shipyard contraption was no longer an embarrassment to be kept hidden, either. Soon every doctor had a tricky patient they wanted scanned. "As soon as we got rid of the back-room attitude and brought our apparatus fully into the Department with an inexhaustible supply of living patients with fascinating clinical problems, we were able to get ahead really fast," Donald recounted years later. "From this point, there could be no turning back."

How'd the woodland jumping mouse get its name? It lives in woodlands and can jump 6 feet high.

COMING INTO FOCUS

As much as the new machine was an improvement over the one it replaced, it still left a lot to be desired. When Donald scanned patients, all he saw on the oscilloscope was squiggly lines. Telling one type of squiggly line from another was how he distinguished tumors from cysts, and that was good enough for him. But Tom Brown, the young engineer from Kelvin & Hughes, thought he could build something better. By late 1957, he had finished work on an improved machine that kept track of where the probe was on the patient's body and plotted the echoes on the screen of the oscilloscope accordingly. In the process, he invented the first ultrasound scanner able to produce images—sonograms, as they came to be known—instead of squiggly lines. (Money was so tight that he actually built the machine using a borrowed hospital bed table and parts scrounged from an Erector set.)

PRE-VIEW

By the summer of 1958, Donald, Brown, and a third researcher named John MacVicar had scanned more than 100 human subjects. They published their findings in the British medical journal *The Lancet*, along with images of what sonograms would become best known for—human fetuses in the womb. Believe it or not, the researchers discovered ultrasound's ability to produce these images by accident, while scanning a woman thought to be suffering from a tumor in her uterus, a condition that can cause distension of the abdomen. It wasn't until a baby's head appeared on the screen that they realized the distension was caused by a much more common condition: pregnancy.

But was it safe to bombard a fetus with ultrasound waves? Donald, Brown, and MacVicar didn't see why not, but they needed to be sure, so they cranked up the machine to more than 30 times the amount of energy needed to produce images and bombarded four anesthetized kittens for an hour. When the kittens survived unharmed, the relieved researchers concluded that it was safe to use ultrasound on pregnant mothers. In the process, an entire new field of prenatal medical imaging was born—one that, unlike X-rays, produced images of soft tissue, not just bones, and posed no risk whatsoever to mother and child.

Study: 4% of the complaints the British Rail receives are about how they handle complaints.

HARD TO SEE

If you've ever struggled to pick out a fetus from the grainy, grayscale chaos of a modern sonogram, you can imagine how difficult it must have been to spot them in images produced by those first, primitive machines. Even more difficult, it turns out, was the task of convincing obstetricians, gynecologists, and other specialists that such images were useful. These professionals had always gotten by on observation, touch, and no small amount of guesswork when practicing their profession. They'd never needed ultrasound images in the past—so why did they need them now? It also took time for hospitals that had never purchased ultrasound equipment before to understand its importance, and even longer to find the money in their budgets. Thanks to this professional and bureaucratic inertia, nearly a decade passed before ultrasound imaging began to take off.

BLIND

By then Kelvin & Hughes had already exited the business. Thanks to the genius of one 23-year-old employee, the industrial flaw-detector company had a billion-dollar industry land in their lap but early sales had been too slow to convince the company's managers that the business would ever turn a profit. So in 1967 they closed the factory in Glasgow and sold their medical imaging business to another firm.

What happened to Tom Brown, the brilliant young man who started it all? He bounced between jobs in academia and medical imaging for more than 20 years. In 1973 he signed on with another medical-imaging company and led the team that invented the world's first ultrasound scanner capable of producing 3-D images, but again sales were slow to materialize and the company went under, taking Brown's career with it. "I had to take the professional consequences of being associated with failure," he told an interviewer in 1995. "No one wanted to employ me after the collapse of the 3-D project. I was unemployed and unemployable." He spent the rest of his career in the oil industry, operating a crane. He retired in 2002 and today ekes by on a modest pension.

Decades passed before Tom Brown, Ian Donald, or John MacVicar received any recognition for their contributions to medicine. In spite of their pioneering efforts, the United Kingdom never did become a leader in the ultrasound medical imaging field.

If you ran—literally—at a snail's pace, it would take you 18 months to finish a marathon.

Instead, the technology passed to Japan, Germany, the United States, and other countries, where long-sighted companies were willing to invest millions on research and development and wait years for it to pay off. Today you can still have an ultrasound done in Glasgow, the city where it all began, but if you do, it will be done using a machine imported from someplace else.

SIGHT FOR SORE EYES

Tom Brown never made any money off the invention of medical ultrasound scanners: Though he's named as the inventor on the original patent, the commercial rights were assigned to his employer, Kelvin & Hughes. (They never made any money from it, either.) Today he gets more credit for his contribution to medicine than he used to, but his greatest personal satisfaction came in 2007 when his pregnant daughter, Rhona, received a sonogram and was diagnosed with *vasa praevia*, a condition in which the blood vessels can rupture during natural childbirth. If they do, there's a very high risk of the baby bleeding to death during delivery.

Before the invention of ultrasound imaging, the condition was very difficult to detect; the first sign of it often came only when the baby died as it was being born. But now it can be detected on an ultrasound scan, and because of it, Rhona had a Caesarean section and her son, named Tom in honor of his grandfather, is alive and well today. "The baby was safely delivered and is now an extremely bright, lovely little boy who wouldn't be here but for his grandpa's work in the past," Brown told the BBC in 2013.

*   *   *

MORE NICKNAMES FOR COPS IN OTHER COUNTRIES

Kapplständer (Austria): "Hat rack"

Små Blå (Denmark): "Little Blue Ones" Also Æggeskal ("eggshell"), for motorcycle police, a reference to the white helmets they wear

Kalevet (Israel): "Rabies"

Fjällko (Sweden): A black and white patrol car, named after cows of the same color

Kraweznik (Poland): "Curbnik," a cop who walks a beat

Yellow Fever (Nigeria): A traffic cop—they wear yellow uniforms

THE "TOILET-TO-TAP" MOVEMENT

*Booming populations in places where the supply of fresh water is inadequate
or declining has forced many cities around the world to consider solutions
to the problem that, while technologically sound, would have been
unthinkable in years past. How unthinkable? You're sitting on it.*

SUN CITY, U.S.A.

If you've ever visited San Diego on the coast of southern California, you can understand why so many people like to live there. The second-largest city on the West Coast and one of the fastest growing, San Diego enjoys mild weather year-round. It has an average daytime temperature of just 57°F in January, the coldest month, and 77°F in August. It has only 41 rainy days in a typical year.

All those sunny days at the beach come at a price, though: San Diego averages less than 11 inches of rainfall per year, enough to meet only 15 percent of the city's water needs. And that's in an average year—in drought years there may be even less rain. The rest of the water the city needs must be piped in from elsewhere, including the Colorado River to the east and the Sacramento River Delta several hundred miles to the north.

Transporting millions of gallons of water over that great a distance isn't cheap, and there's no guarantee the water will even be available in the future. Seven U.S. states (plus Mexico) lay claim to the water of the Colorado, and as the population of the Southwest grows, less of it will be available for San Diego. The supply from the Sacramento Delta is no more reliable. In recent years environmental groups have successfully sued to block water sales to San Diego on the grounds that it's too damaging to the delta environment.

POT-ABLE WATER

In the late 1990s, San Diego's inability to meet its water needs with its own guaranteed supply of water forced civic leaders to consider a pretty drastic option: treating the city's wastewater—including its toilet water—for reuse as drinking water.

The word *mallemaroking* means "seamen carousing aboard icebound Greenland whaling ships."

ONE, TWO, THREE

The technology to convert wastewater into *potable* (safe to drink) water has been around for decades; it is straightforward and scientifically sound. First, the water is subjected to microfiltration, in which it passes through filter material with holes so tiny that anything larger than 1/300 the width of a human hair is filtered out, including bacteria and protozoa. Next, the water is forced, under great pressure, through a plastic membrane in a process known as *reverse osmosis*. That removes just about everything else except for the water molecules themselves, including viruses and any pharmaceuticals that may have been flushed down the toilet. Finally, the water is treated with hydrogen peroxide and high-intensity ultraviolet light to kill any trace amounts of pathogens that might have survived the first two processes.

The treated water is then carefully tested to ensure that its purity approaches that of distilled water. And because the EPA (which regulates drinking water) sets higher standards than the FDA (which regulates *bottled* water), it's actually less risky to drink than the water you buy at the supermarket. Even so, California law does not allow recycled water to be added directly to drinking water. Instead, it must be returned to the environment, by pumping it into underground aquifers or into reservoirs. There, it must mix with ordinary water for least six months before it's treated (again) and used as drinking water.

TOUGH TO SWALLOW

Understanding the science behind "potable reuse," as it's called, is one thing; actually drinking the stuff is another, as San Diego officials discovered when they proposed a potable reuse plant for the city in the late 1990s. Opponents attacked the idea as a "toilet-to-tap" scheme (a term that, while technically accurate, is loathed by potable reuse advocates). They made such a fuss that the San Diego City Council abandoned the proposal rather than risk being tossed out of office in the next election.

San Diego's experience isn't unique. When the drought-parched community of Toowoomba, Australia, 80 miles west of Brisbane, proposed a similar plant in 2006, it was defeated by a grassroots organization that sprang up to kill the idea. The group's name: Citizens Against Drinking Sewage.

TAPPED OUT

In the tiny island nation of Singapore in Southeast Asia, advocates of potable reuse have had better luck. One of the world's most densely populated countries, Singapore imports much of its drinking water from Malaysia, its neighbor to the north. Malaysia has contracted to supply Singapore with water until 2061, but there's no guarantee that the country, with its own growing population, will be able to supply Singapore after that. Or willing. Relations between the two countries haven't always been good—Singapore was part of Malaysia for two years after winning independence from Great Britain in 1963, but simmering political and economic disputes prompted the Malaysian government to expel Singapore from the country in 1965.

Singapore has set a goal of being self-sufficient in water by the time their contract with Malaysia expires in 2061, and a big part of this effort has been the construction of four giant water-recycling plants around the island. Together, the four plants produce more than 113 million gallons of potable water per day, about a third of the country's freshwater needs. Most of that is used for irrigation and industrial uses; what's left after those needs are met is added to the drinking-water supply. Result: only about five percent of Singapore's drinking water comes from the potable reuse plants.

SOMETHING NEW

Singaporeans have adopted potable reuse with little fuss, demonstrating that if the crisis is real and the public is given enough information and time to get used to the idea, they can eventually come around. The country's example provides lessons on how other communities struggling with critical water shortages can sell the idea to an understandably skeptical public:

• **Watch Your Language.** Terms like "recycled wastewater," "toilet-to-tap," or—worst of all—"purified sewage" only harm the cause. "Recycled water," "reclaimed water," or "purified water" sound better. Singapore calls theirs "NEWater." That may sound a bit Orwellian to Western ears, but it's worked well in Singapore.

• **Don't Skimp on Public Relations.** In 2003 Singapore opened an elaborate visitors' center next to one of the NEWater plants. The country is home to almost five million people, and over the next decade nearly a million of them passed through the doors of the

---

World's largest pearl: Found inside a giant clam, it weighs 14 lbs. and is worth $60 million.

visitors' center to learn about NEWater and tour the plant.

• **Try Some!** At the end of the NEWater tour, each visitor is given a glass of NEWater to taste. Millions of bottles of the stuff have also been given away free at public events as a way of increasing public awareness of the program. The labels on the bottles are changed from time to time and from one public event to the next; many of the bottles have become collectors' items.

IF AT FIRST YOU DON'T SUCCEED…

In 2009 the City of San Diego decided to try again to build public support for a potable reuse plant, not because residents wanted it, but because businesses did. The city is home to a number of water-intensive industries, including biotech and manufacturing firms. When California entered the third year of a severe drought in 2009, many of these businesses threatened to leave the area if the reliability of future water deliveries was not assured. That's what prompted the city government to take another stab at building a potable reuse plant.

Public opinion polls had repeatedly shown strong opposition to potable reuse. But when civic leaders (and environmental groups, which oppose the discharge of wastewater into the ocean) began a public information campaign to promote the idea, the polls began to change. By 2011 public opposition was down to 25 percent. That year the city began building a $12 million Water Purification Demonstration Project to "determine the feasibility of turning recycled water into purified water that could be sent to a reservoir and later be distributed as drinking water," as the city put it.

LOOK UP

In truth, the Demonstration Project wasn't so much a study in "feasibility" as it was another step in the campaign to prepare the public for the prospect of someday having to drink recycled water. If the city had really been interested in finding out if recycling waste-water was "feasible," they would have had to look no farther than Orange County, California, 90 miles to the north. There, in 2009, the county's water district opened the spigots on the largest potable reuse water-recycling plant in the world. Called the Groundwater Replenishment System, the $481 million plant produces 75 million gallons of recycled water every day, enough for 600,000 residents, and the county plans to expand the plant's capacity to 100 million gallons a day.

Orange County's system exceeds state and federal standards for drinking water, and because state law requires that it be returned to the environment before it's used as drinking water—hence the name "Groundwater Replenishment System"—the public can legitimately think of it as groundwater, even though it may eventually be tap water. "If you take the water back to the environment, the public's memory of where it has been has been taken away," says Professor David Sedlak of the University of California Berkeley's Water Center.

NOT QUITE THERE YET

As of 2014, San Diego has not yet moved beyond the demonstration phase, though there's little doubt that it will do so eventually, if for no other reason than it hasn't got much choice.

If you live in a place where sunshine is plentiful and water is scarce, a potable reuse plant may be in your future, too. "It's really a natural and cost-effective solution when you don't have another resource available," Sedlak told the *Christian Science Monitor* in 2011. "We have to recognize that as the population of the country continues to move out into the West and as climate change continually reduces the water supply, these issues are going to become more and more important."

*   *   *

GREETINGS FROM DALLAS

If your community gets its drinking water from a river, there's a good chance you're drinking "recycled" wastewater. The city of Houston, Texas, for example, gets about a third of its drinking water from the Trinity River. That's the same river that the city of Dallas, some 200 miles upstream, releases its treated wastewater into every day. In drought years it's estimated that as much as half of the water in the Trinity flowing downstream from Dallas—and thus about a sixth of Houston's drinking water—is wastewater released from plants in the Dallas/Fort Worth area.

Déjà vu decreases with age—so the more places you go, the less you ask, "Have I been here before?"

THE FUTURISTS, PART IV

Despite the fact that the golden age of futurism is in the past (see Part III on page 337), futurists still make grand predictions. Here's what we (might) have to look forward to.

CYBORGS: In 2013 futurist Ray Kurzweil projected the next big leap forward in technology: "brain-uploading." If he's right, you'll be able to transfer all of your thoughts and memories into a computer, and perhaps even get a new robotic body. "When you talk to a human in 2035," says Kurzweil, "you'll be talking to a combination of biological and nonbiological intelligence." Author Zoltan Istvan calls this "transhumanism"—using science and technology to enhance and lengthen lives. He predicts that by 2100, humanity will consist of cyborgs living in harmony with intelligent machines that have solved all of the world's environmental, poverty, and overpopulation problems.

• **ANDROIDS:** Today's robots make cars and vacuum floors, but will they ever talk to us like people? Yes, says futurist Dick Pelletier. He predicts that by 2025, your household android will be more important than your car. "Priced from $30,000 to $100,000, these electronic household workers will wear skin made of soft, sensitive nanomaterials—tough, but with the gentle touch of a masseuse. They will understand and speak perfect language and perform butler, chef, and cleaning services; even carry disabled patients up stairways. People will wonder how they ever got along without them."

• **THE GLOBAL BRAIN:** Futurist Kevin Kelly, cofounder of *Wired* magazine, forecasts that all of the world's computers will become one sentient being. "The next stage in technological evolution is a single thinking/web/computer that is planetary in dimension," he says. "This computer will be the largest, most complex, and most dependable machine ever built. It will also be the platform that most business will run on." Kelly says this process has already begun; today's Internet is the Global Brain's "first OS" (operating system).

• **INCREASED LIFE SPANS:** According to computer scientist Aubrey de Grey, the first human being who will live for 1,000 years has already been born. De Grey isn't just predicting this; he's

working to make it come true by attempting to identify and eliminate aging factors. De Grey's critics argue that it's not that simple...
and that he's not a doctor. His response: "The only difference
between my work and the work of the whole medical profession is
that I think we're in striking distance of keeping people so healthy
that at ninety they'll carry on waking up in the same physical state
as they were at the age of thirty. What I'm after is not living to
one thousand. I'm after letting people avoid death for as long as
they want to." Thanks to recent advances in genetics and stem cell
research, eliminating diseases and regrowing limbs and organs is no
longer the stuff of science fiction.

• **"THE INTERNET OF THINGS":** Patrick Tucker, an editor at
The Futurist magazine, forecasts that soon "big data" will not only
know where everyone on Earth is—it will anticipate their needs.
"Computerized sensing is being incorporated into our physical environment, creating an 'Internet of things,'" he says. "Data from RFID
tags, surveillance cameras, unmanned aerial vehicles, and geo-tagged
social-media posts will telegraph where we've been and where we're
going. These data streams will be integrated into services, platforms,
and programs that will provide a window into the lives and futures
of billions of people." If you saw the 2002 movie *Minority Report*—
which used futurists as consultants—you saw this in action when
Detective Anderton (Tom Cruise) walks into a Gap clothing store,
a scanner reads his eye, and a hologram pops up to suggest items he
might want to purchase.

• **SPACE ELEVATORS:** Instead of choosing a floor when
entering an elevator, you choose an orbiting ship or a space station.
Arthur C. Clarke proposed the idea in 1979, and the technology
to make it happen is real—at least in theory. The elevator would
travel on a tether consisting of nanomaterials (such as bonded
carbon atoms) that would be up to 100 times stronger than steel.
Centrifugal force would keep the tether in geosynchronous orbit
above Earth. A four-year study by the International Academy of
Astronautics concluded that space elevators are "feasible." We
might see them in this century.

• **UNIVERSAL TRANSLATOR:** In a world with more than
6,000 languages, having everyone able to understand each other
would have a huge impact. The computing power required to

translate not just words, but syntax, tone, and grammar isn't quite here yet (as anyone who's tried using an Internet translator knows). But as technology continues to advance, an accurate real-time translator may not be far off. The universal translator might be part of a wearable computer (something else to look forward to) that you won't even see, but you'll hear English whenever anyone is talking to you. Later versions will be implanted in people's brains.

• **ANIMAL TRANSLATOR:** Imagine ordering your dog not to go in the neighbor's yard and have him not only understand you but be able to answer you back: "No, *you* stay!" In 2004 researchers Susan Clayton and Bruce Lloyd wrote that someday soon we may all be real-life Dr. Dolittles: "It is not difficult to see tomorrow's sophisticated computers rapidly processing complex data from animals and transmitting it in a useful form to humans via an earpiece, handheld device, or spectacle-lens display. Similarly, computers are likely to be able to translate messages from humans into stimuli that suit the cognitive style of the intended animal recipient."

• **RODENTS OF UNUSUAL SIZE:** Of course, none of these glorious futures will come to pass if some of the more dire forecasts come true and humanity gets wiped out (due to war, climate change, or an asteroid impact). If our species does become extinct, which animals will take over? Rats, according to British futurist Jan Zalasiewicz. He says that despite our efforts to control rat populations, their numbers are always rising. Their intelligence is unequaled among mammals their size, and they can adapt to almost every environment on the planet. And once all the larger animals are gone (usually the first to go in mass extinctions), the rats will increase in size, to perhaps "twenty pounds or larger," Zalasiewicz says. But like any modern futurist worth his salt, he doesn't call his theory a prediction: "It's a guess, a thought experiment."

INTO THE UNKNOWN

For the most part, all of these "guesses" are just short-term forecasts. Looking into the future is fun, but it's impossible to do it with confidence. Who knows what today's young minds will do with the technological advances of tomorrow? Their world will undoubtedly look very different from ours. As World Future Society founder Edward Cornish candidly said in 2007: "I long ago gave up being sure of anything."

Study: Overpaying for something activates the part of the brain associated with guilt and pain.

TV FACTS: THE 2000s

Stuff you didn't know about the stuff on your TiVo.

The Office. In 2009 producers planned to spin off Andy Bernard (Ed Helms) to his own show. Following the same "mockumentary" format, the show was set to be about Bernard's home life with his wife. Why didn't it happen? Because *Modern Family* happened, and it used virtually the same premise.

Game of Thrones. George R. R. Martin's books contain a few words of the fictional "Dothraki" language, but when HBO adapted the books into a TV series, linguist David J. Peterson was hired to expand it into a speakable language. Peterson developed more than 3,000 words and phrases, used extensively on the show (all subtitled).

Two and a Half Men. Highest-paid actor on a sitcom: Ashton Kutcher, at $750,000 per episode of *Two and a Half Men*. Second-highest: Jon Cryer, at $650,000 per episode of the same show.

Breaking Bad. Jesse Pinkman (Aaron Paul) was supposed to die at the end of the first season. The 2007–08 writers' strike shortened the season prematurely, which gave creator Vince Gilligan time to realize there was a lot more he could do with the character. Pinkman remained on the show until the end; Paul won two Emmys.

How I Met Your Mother. Alyson Hannigan starred on the series. Former *Full House* star Bob Saget was also on the show, as an unseen, uncredited narrator. In the late 1980s, Hannigan was the regular babysitter for Saget's children.

Arrested Development. Creator Mitchell Hurwitz got the name for Maeby Funke (Alia Shawkat)—a reference to a running joke that she was "maybe" adopted—by combining the names of his daughters: the "ma" from Maisie; the "be" from Phoebe.

The West Wing. In the Roosevelt Room of the real White House, Teddy Roosevelt's portrait is traditionally hung during Republican administrations; FDR's portrait is hung during Democratic administrations. In *The West Wing*'s Roosevelt Room, portraits of both presidents are visible. (Producers didn't want the show to seem partisan.)

Burrowing owls line their burrows with cow dung to attract insects...which they eat.

THE GREAT SALAD OIL SWINDLE

*Start with a New Jersey businessman who has questionable ethics,
add soybean oil, and let it stew in a broth of fraud and greed.
Pretty soon you've got yourself a nice little scandal.*

YELLOW GOLD

In the late 1940s, a combination of several factors led to an enormous increase in the production of soybean oil in the United States. The factors: soybeans are relatively cheap and easy to grow; they produce beans quickly; advances in technology allowed for better extraction of oil from the beans (as well as the production of safer and better-tasting oil); and in the post-World War II economic boom, the demand for products that could be made from soybean oil grew enormously. Those products included nonedible items, such as paint and plastics, and a wide variety of foods and cooking products, including margarine, salad dressings, and cooking oils. Before World War II, the most popular cooking oils in the U.S. were butter, lard, and Crisco, which was made from cottonseed oil. By the 1950s, the United States was the world's leading soybean oil producer, and by the early 1960s, there was a soybean oil surplus.

Enter Tino De Angelis.

THE MAN WITH THE PLAN

Anthony "Tino" De Angelis was born in the Bronx in 1915, the son of Italian immigrants. He worked for a few years as an apprentice butcher. Then, while still in his 20s, he bought his own hog-meat company, and in 1946, bought controlling interest in Adolf Gobel Inc., a large meatpacking business in North Bergen, New Jersey. De Angelis quickly learned what so many others have learned over the years—that the U.S. government could be an extremely lucrative cash cow. That same year, President Harry S. Truman had signed the National School Lunch Act, establishing a federally funded school-lunch program. De Angelis landed a contract to supply the program, and over the next several years made a fortune selling

---

Hey, big fella: Chimps and gorillas have been known to proposition their human trainers.

millions of pounds of meat to the government. Somewhere along the line—maybe from the start—De Angelis turned the operation into a scam. In 1952 that scam was discovered, and the government charged De Angelis with systematically overcharging the government and, worse (considering the meat went to schoolkids), selling uninspected meat. De Angelis paid $100,000 in damages (almost $900,000 in today's dollars), and Adolf Gobel Inc. went bankrupt.

Three years later, De Angelis reemerged, this time in the soybean oil business.

FOOD FOR PIECE (OF THE ACTION)

In 1955 De Angelis, described by *Wall Street Journal* writer Norman C. Miller as "a fat little man…with a bland moon face and a somewhat squeaky voice," founded the Allied Crude Vegetable Oil Refining Company. This was a massive vegetable oil refinery and storage facility in Bayonne, New Jersey, across the Hudson River from Brooklyn and right in the heart of the bustling Port of New York and New Jersey. Allied Oil was another De Angelis operation aimed at taking advantage of a government initiative, this one the "Food for Peace" program signed into law by President Dwight D. Eisenhower in 1954. Through this program, the U.S. sold surplus agricultural products to foreign governments at low cost, with the combined goals of helping struggling nations, building up good relations with those countries, and providing another market for U.S. farmers.

Allied quickly became a major player in the program, buying raw vegetable oil from U.S. farmers—primarily soybean, but also some cottonseed oil—refining it in the Bayonne facility, then selling and shipping it to foreign countries. By the late 1950s, the company was selling more than $200 million worth of vegetable oil a year (almost $2 billion today), and De Angelis was an international business tycoon, making deals with businessmen and politicians all over the world. But things were not exactly what they seemed.

SOY YOU LATER

In 1957 De Angelis set up a deal with a company known as the American Express Field Warehousing Corporation (AEFW), a subsidiary of financial giant American Express. "Field warehousing" is a financial arrangement wherein a company gives a financial institution control of their warehouse and inventory. The financial institution monitors how much inventory is being held and issues "warehouse receipts" based on the value of that inventory. Those receipts can then be used as collateral at a bank or brokerage house against a loan.

TANKS A LOT

In this case, AEFW oversaw Allied Oil's storage yard—138 massive tanks—and started writing large warehouse receipts, which De Angelis quickly and happily used as security for borrowing cash. For all intents and purposes, American Express was underwriting enormous loans for Allied. Over the following couple of years, because a respected company like American Express was giving De Angelis the thumbs up, other companies, including Bank of America and Proctor and Gamble, started loaning money to Allied Oil, too.

Almost from the start, De Angelis was scamming and AEFW was blind to it. In the normal setup for field warehousing, AEFW hires "trusted" employees of the client company (Allied Oil) as "custodians," to keep tabs on the inventory, and AEFW inspectors show up regularly to make sure the inventory checks are accurate. Only problem: AEFW let Tino De Angelis pick the custodians. He picked his friends and relatives—and they just made up the numbers.

MONEY FOR NOTHING

And when AEFW inspectors *did* show up, De Angelis and his gang had a simple way of tricking them: to check how much oil was in any given tank, an inspector would climb up to the top of the tank, open a hatch, and measure down from the top of the tank to the surface of the oil. A little math then allowed the inspector to determine how much oil was in the tank. The scam: oil floats on water, and many of Allied's tanks were almost entirely filled with water, with just a little oil on top. So the inspectors, looking down from the top of a tank, thought they were looking at a tank full of oil. What's more, the tanks were all interconnected by a maze of piping, so De Angelis's custodians could pump oil from one tank to another—to the ones being tested—at will, making it look like they had more oil than they actually did. As far as the American Express inspectors could tell, Allied Oil had huge stores of oil…and the loan money kept rolling in.

THE BIG PLAN

By 1962 De Angelis, now many millions of dollars in debt and without enough soybean oil to back it up, came up with a new plan: 1) borrow more money and use it to buy up massive amounts of soybean oil, thereby cornering the market and causing the price of soybean oil to soar; 2) buy a huge amount of "futures" in soybean oil, meaning that when the price of soybean oil rose, he could still buy it at current prices, and then resell it at a profit; 3) pay back the loans and have plenty of money left over for himself.

This was not a great plan.

De Angelis followed up on the second part of the plan—buying a huge amount of soybean oil futures—which in and of itself actually did cause the price of soybean oil to rise (because it looked like investors were confident the price would keep going up). But he didn't have enough money, so he couldn't buy enough oil to corner the market. In fact, he didn't buy much oil at all. By early 1963, a growing number of customers were complaining that oil that had been paid for was not being delivered. At the same time, banks were complaining about missed loan payments. By mid-1963, the complaints grew loud and numerous enough that AEFW—*finally*—made their inspectors do a thorough check of De Angelis's tanks. By November 1963, the jig was up.

BOOM, AND OILY BUST

The truth about Allied Crude Vegetable Oil Refining Company hit the market like a financial atomic bomb: Tino De Angelis's company had borrowed more than $150 million from 51 different financial institutions, many of them among of the oldest and most prominent Wall Street firms in existence...and he actually had only $6 million worth of oil. The price of soybean oil plummeted immediately—meaning that the little oil that De Angelis did have was now worth even less.

On November 19, Allied Oil declared bankruptcy. It was such an enormous scandal—at the time, the largest case of financial fraud in history—that New York Stock Exchange officials had to scramble to avoid a stock market crash. Three days later, on Friday, November 22, 1963, President John F. Kennedy was assassinated, adding to the financial panic. With a crash now seemingly imminent, stock exchange officials organized a bailout of two of the largest and hardest-hit Wall Street brokerage firms, and were able to avert a crash.

WHERE'S THE MONEY?

Of the 51 institutions that ended up victims of De Angelis's slippery swindle, two were knocked out of business for good; the rest lost money, in amounts ranging from substantial to gargantuan. American Express, probably deservedly so, was the hardest hit. Their stock price tumbled more than 50 percent, and they ended up losing somewhere around $58 million.

Tino De Angelis was convicted of charges related to fraud and conspiracy in 1965 and was sentenced to 20 years in prison. During the trial, it was revealed that he had hidden more than $500,000 in a Swiss bank account, but millions more of the loan money was never accounted for. De Angelis was released from prison in 1972 after serving seven years. Not long after that he did another stint in prison, this time for a scam involving a Missouri meat company. De Angelis was last heard from in 1992, when he was arrested in yet another food-related scam. (The 78-year-old had been caught trying to buy $1.1 million worth of meat from a Rochester, New York, company with a forged check.) De Angelis was sentenced to 21 months in prison. His fate after that…is simply unknown.

IT'S OIL OVER NOW

In 1964, when American Express was still reeling from the massive hit to its finances and its reputation caused by the salad oil scam, an investor swooped in and bought $20 million worth of AmEx stock, garnering a five percent stake in the company. At the time, American Express was a leader in the new credit card industry, which the investor believed would one day become a part of daily life around the world. He was right. That investor: Warren Buffett. As of today, he has made in the neighborhood of $3.7 billion from the deal.

*   *   *

"What comfort can the vortices of Descartes give to a man who has whirlwinds in his bowels?"

—Ben Franklin

PICK A NAME

Professional guitarists probably spend more time with their guitars than they do with their spouses, so it's not surprising that they name them.

Guitarist: B. B. King
Guitar: Lucille
Story: During the winter of 1949, the young blues guitarist was playing at a nightclub in Twist, Arkansas. On cold nights, the club was heated with gas—a barrel half-filled with kerosene in the center of the dance floor was lit to keep the place warm. That night, while King was playing, two guys got into a fight and knocked over the barrel, spilling flaming kerosene onto the wood floor. "It looked like a river of fire," King said, "so I ran outside. But when I got on the outside, I realized I left my guitar inside." He raced back into the burning building to save his budget model Gibson L-30 acoustic guitar…and nearly lost his life. The next day, King found out the men were fighting over a woman named Lucille, who worked at the dance hall. So King decided to name his L-30 (and every Gibson that he played after that) Lucille, as a reminder to himself never to do anything so risky again. The "King of the Blues" later wrote a song about his famous succession of Gibson guitars. MCA Records released the album *Lucille* (his 15th studio album) in 1968. During recordings of his nearly 130 albums, King often played a Fender Telecaster, but he is best known for playing Gibson ES-355 guitars. In 1980 the Gibson Guitar Corporation launched the "B. B. King Lucille" model guitar, and for King's 80th birthday in 2005, Gibson made 80 special edition "B. B. King 80th Birthday" Lucilles.

Guitarist: Willie Nelson
Guitar: Trigger
Story: In 1969 Nelson and his band were playing at the John T. Floore Country Store, a dance hall in Helotes, Texas, when one of the patrons (he was drunk) accidentally stepped on the singer's Baldwin acoustic guitar and destroyed it. Nelson sent it to Shot Jackson, a Nashville guitar maker, hoping it could be fixed. It couldn't. Jackson pronounced it dead on arrival. But he told Nelson that he had a really nice nylon-stringed Martin N-20 and he could

transfer the Baldwin pick-up onto it. Cost: $750. That was a lot in those days, but Nelson decided to go for it sight unseen. He says he named it Trigger because "Roy Rogers had a horse named Trigger. I figured this was my horse."

Though Martin is best known for their steel-string guitars, this instrument has become as famous as any they've ever built. Nelson has played it on more than 100 albums, including the chart-toppers *Red-Headed Stranger*, *Stardust*, and *Always On My Mind*. Now, after 10,000 shows and 45 years of being ridden hard and put away beer- and sweat-soaked, Trigger shows its age. The face of the guitar is covered in scars—more than 100 autographs carved with knives, pens, and sharpies by the likes of Gene Autry, Johnny Cash, Leon Russell, and Kris Kristofferson. The frets are so worn, other musicians wonder how it has any tone at all. And next to the bridge is an enormous hole—the result of Nelson's ring finger and pinkie drilling through the soft Sitka spruce over time. Nelson won't have it repaired, though, comparing it to fixing the crack in the Liberty Bell.

Nelson, who's had his share of troubles over the years with several divorces, a house fire, IRS tax liens, and the loss of his son, says, "Trigger's like me—old and beat-up." But at more than 80 years old, Nelson is still touring and recording, and Trigger still goes to a *luthier* (someone who repairs guitars) for regular maintenance. This duo has been producing gold for nearly half a century, and Nelson says, "When Trigger goes, that's when I'll quit."

Guitarist: Eric Clapton

Guitar: Blackie

The Story: Clapton had already reached the fan status of "guitar god" after his stints with the British rock bands the Yardbirds and Cream when he built his dream guitar. In 1970, while on tour with Derek and the Dominos, he popped into the Sho-Bud guitar shop in Nashville and discovered a gold mine—six 1950s-era Fender Stratocasters stacked up in the back. As old Strats were not in vogue at the time, Clapton snapped them up for $100 apiece. When he returned to England, he gave one to Steve Winwood, one to Pete Townshend, another to George Harrison, and kept the other three. Clapton then took the best components from the remaining guitars (circa 1956 and 1957) and put them into the one shiny black guitar that would become "Blackie." In 1973 Clapton debuted it at the Rainbow Theatre in London at the concert organized by Pete Townshend to support Clapton's recovery from drug addiction. Clapton admits to getting seriously attached to all of his guitars, but says there is something magical about this one. "A guitar like Blackie comes along maybe once in a lifetime."

Clapton played Blackie for 15 years on the road and in recording studios. It was the sonic powerhouse behind such hits as "I Shot the Sheriff," "Cocaine," and more. Finally, in the mid-1980s, the guitar was retired. Clapton put Blackie up for auction in 2004 to support the Crossroads Centre, the rehab facility he founded. The iconic rock guitar was purchased by Guitar Center for a record-setting $959,500. It now goes on tour at Guitar Center stores around the U.S. as the headliner—no player necessary.

Guitarist: Bonnie Raitt

Guitar: Brownie

Story: Raitt spent nearly 20 years as a cult favorite, singing and playing bottleneck blues in clubs and recording albums that garnered critical, if not commercial, success. It wasn't until 1989, with the release of the Grammy-winning *Nick of Time*, followed by 1991's *Luck of the Draw*, that Raitt achieved star status. Today this modern "Baroness of the Blues" has 10 Grammys to her credit and her own signature line of Fender Stratocasters—a first for a female guitarist. She has a number of Fenders and Gibsons in her collection, but the guitar most likely to be strapped to Raitt's shoulder whenever she takes the stage is a paintless, beat-up brown Fender Strat hybrid tuned to open G, with a body that dates from pre-1965 and the neck from a couple of years later. She has played "Brownie" at every gig since the day in 1969 when she purchased it at 3:00 in the morning for $120.

Guitarist: Keith Richards

Guitar: Micawber

Story: The legendary lead guitarist of the Rolling Stones suffers from a bad case of GAS (Guitar Acquisition Syndrome). Richards owns more than 3,000 guitars, but of his entire collection, his favorite and probably most famous is a blonde '53 Fender Telecaster he calls Micawber. (The name comes from a character in Charles

---

There's only one movie theater in Saudi Arabia—an IMAX theater that shows science films.

Dickens's classic novel *David Copperfield*.) When Richards bought the guitar in 1971, the Stones were already huge rock stars and working on their classic album *Exile on Main Street*. Customized to Richards's specifications with a bridge that features individually adjustable saddles and a humbucker replacing the original Fender single-coil neck pickup, Micawber is always kept in open G tuning (GDGBD), with the low-E string removed. "My favorite phrase about this style of playing," Richards says of his unique tuning and stringing arrangement, "is that all you need to play it is five strings, three notes, two fingers, and one a**h*le." He uses Micawber to punch out the Rolling Stones' iconic sound on classics like "Brown Sugar" and "Honky Tonk Women." To this day it remains his "go-to" guitar at every Stones concert.

Guitarist: Stevie Ray Vaughan
Guitar: Lenny
Story: It was the fall of 1980, and fame had not yet come to blues guitarist Stevie Ray Vaughan when he and his Double Trouble band members took a stroll through an Austin, Texas, pawnshop. Like most guitarists, Vaughan was always on the lookout for that hidden gem, and he found it—a 1965 Fender Stratocaster with a rosewood fingerboard and an elaborate inlaid design along the lower bridge, believed to be from a 1910 mandolin. At the time the $350 price tag seemed like a fortune to the struggling musician, but his 26th birthday was coming up, and his wife Lenora "Lenny" Bailey came up with the perfect surprise: She asked his friends to kick in $50 each, and together they bought him the vintage Strat. He promptly named it Lenny, and that night wrote a song for her, which he titled (you guessed it) "Lenny." Soon after, Billy Gibbons of ZZ Top gave him a new neck with a maple fingerboard, which Vaughn had installed on Lenny, along with his name and the year he received the guitar etched into the neck plate. Vaughn rocketed to stardom after playing the solo on David Bowie's 1983 chart-topping hit "Let's Dance." He recorded his first album, *Texas Flood*, that same year; the song "Lenny" was the tenth and final cut. Over the years, Vaughan's usual guitar was a battered '63 Strat that he nicknamed "Number One" (as in First Wife). But any time he played the song he wrote for Lenora in concert, he always used his pawnshop '65 Fender Stratocaster, Lenny.

90% of the world's piano production is in Asia.

FOIA: KEEPING GOVERNMENT HONEST

*The Freedom of Information Act was passed in 1966—and it was the very first
law in American history that gave regular citizens the legal footing to
compel the government to release internal documents. Before that—
not for you! Getting it passed was a long, tough battle.
(And it's still going on.) Here's the whole story.*

MR. MOSS GOES TO WASHINGTON

In 1952 a 37-year-old businessman named John E. Moss was elected to a seat in the U.S. House of Representatives, representing California's 3rd congressional district, which included his home city, Sacramento. Moss had lived a tough life: His mother died when he was twelve, and his father, an alcoholic and an unemployed coal miner, left shortly thereafter; Moss and his brother, both still young teens, were left to fend for themselves. Then the Great Depression came. Somehow, Moss not only survived those difficult years, by 1938, through nothing but hard work, he was the owner of a successful Sacramento appliance store. In 1948, after a stint in the Navy during World War II, he was elected to the California state assembly.

Over the course of two terms, Moss earned a reputation as someone who didn't play the game the way it was "supposed" to be played. He didn't go to lobbyists' parties, he didn't schmooze with party bosses—he just went to work. The focus of that work, not surprisingly, given his background, was fighting for the little guy. In 1952, after winning election to the U.S. Congress, it was time to take that fight for the little guy to Washington.

D.C.-CRETS

When Moss arrived in Washington in 1953, he quickly became acquainted with an issue that had been heating up over the previous few years: excessive government secrecy. During his first year on the job, 2,800 federal employees were fired for "security" reasons—meaning they were suspected of being Communists, or of having Communist leanings. (This was the height of the McCarthy

Era.) Moss, a relatively liberal Democrat, had unfairly faced such accusations many times himself, and asked to see the fired employees' records. He was refused. Those documents, he was told, were government secrets, and off limits, even to a member of Congress.

In 1955, after being elected to a second term, Moss decided to make government secrecy the main focus of his work. That same year, as a member of the powerful Government Operations Committee, he talked the committee chief into forming a Special Subcommittee on Government Information. Amazingly—for a still very junior member of Congress—he got himself appointed committee chairman. And so began what would become an 11-year mission: to open up the government to the people.

INFORMERICA

The struggle between government and citizens over access to information is as old as democracy itself. Which makes a lot of sense: The whole idea behind democracy is that ordinary citizens participate in the functioning of their government—and they can't do that if they don't know what the heck is going on. America's founding fathers gave the average citizen a considerable boost in the battle over government secrecy. During the intense negotiations around ratification of the new country's constitution Patrick Henry, of "Give me liberty or give me death!" fame, and one of the most outspoken proponents of open and transparent government, wrote in 1788:

> The liberties of a people never were, nor ever will be, secure, when the transactions of their rulers may be concealed from them.

From these sentiments came such Constitutionally-enshrined rights as the freedom of the press and freedom of speech—which gave regular citizens legally protected rights to inquiry and criticism of government. But the founders also gave Congress the right to withhold information about its proceedings from the public. The criteria for determining what could be kept secret: Anything that "in their judgment require secrecy." (It really does say that in Article I, Section 5, Clause 3, of the U.S. Constitution.)

FAST FORWARD

Remarkably, that was basically how things stayed for more than 170 years. The main reason for this, historians say, is that the

U.S. government's structure remained fairly simple and relatively small, for so long. In 1900, for example, there were still just eight U.S. federal government agencies (Treasury, Post Office, State, Agriculture, Labor, Justice, Interior, and War). By 1940 the number of agencies had grown to 51. Because laws regarding public access to government hadn't progressed as the government grew larger, by the late 1940s, there were big problems. The U.S. government, now a gargantuan and labyrinthine maze of an organization, had become a virtual black hole of government secrecy. And now people were starting to get upset about it.

MOSS GETS CROSS

In 1951, four years before John Moss formed his committee, the American Society of Newspaper Editors commissioned Harold L. Cross, legal counsel for the *New York Herald Tribune*, to investigate the issue of excessive government secrecy. In 1953 Cross's report was published as a book titled *The People's Right to Know*.

He wrote that virtually every part of American government operated under what amounted to an "official cult of secrecy"; that this secrecy had become a breeding ground for corruption; that it was leading to a rise in public mistrust in government; and that all of these things combined were doing serious damage to American democracy itself. Over the course of more than 400 pages, Cross made the case that Congress *must* craft new legislation that gave American citizens greater access to the inner workings of their government. In the early 1950s, *The People's Right to Know* became a manual for the blossoming "freedom of information" movement, and in 1955 that movement finally got the champion it needed from inside the government: John Moss.

HEARING PROBLEMS

The Special Subcommittee on Government Information—soon dubbed "The Moss Committee"—began its investigations with a series of hearings in November 1955. Moss issued subpoenas; berated bureaucrats; interviewed journalists, professors, and constitutional law experts (including Harold Cross); he wrote volumes of reports; and basically made a big congressional pain of himself for the next 11 years. He simply refused to give up, even when fellow members of Congress tried several times to close down his committee by cutting its funding.

Here are just two of the many examples of excessive secrecy highlighted by the Moss Committee:

• During World War II, the U.S. Army did top secret work developing a particular new weapon, and information on the project remained classified until the committee exposed it in the late 1950s. The weapon: a new and improved bow and arrow.

• In 1959 the Postmaster General ruled that information about the salaries of postal employees (including him) was secret because the public was not "directly concerned" with such information. He also ruled that the public had no right to know the *names* of postal employees. (Those rules remained in effect until 1966.)

IT'S THE LAW!

By the mid-1960s, the burgeoning Civil Rights and Vietnam War protest movements had increased the public's suspicion of government dramatically. As a result, the Moss Committee hearings became big news, and members of Congress—fearing for their jobs—finally got behind Moss. On October 13, 1965, the Freedom of Information Act, legislation based on the work of the Moss Committee, with language and recommendations taken directly from Harold Cross's *The People's Right to Know*, passed the Senate. On June 20, 1966, it passed the House—by a vote of 306 to 0. It was then sent on to President Lyndon Johnson.

Johnson hated the bill (he had made no secret of *that*). The other presidents in office during Moss's 11-year campaign, Eisenhower and Kennedy, had felt pretty much the same as Johnson. But now the tide had turned and on July 4, 1966, Johnson, reluctantly, signed the bill into law. American citizens finally had a legal "right to know."

FOY-YUH OWN GOOD!

So what exactly does the Freedom of Information Act, more commonly known by the acronym FOIA (and commonly pronounced *foy*-yuh) do? It creates a process through which anyone—journalists, activist organizations, universities, plain old citizens, and even noncitizens—can request documents from U.S. government agencies, and it requires those agencies to either produce those documents or provide a legal reason for not doing so.

- FOIA does not pertain to Congress or the courts. It deals with the executive branch of the federal government only. (This is primarily because, in terms of numbers of employees and agencies, the executive branch is *much* larger than the other two branches.)

- FOIA applies to federal "agencies," but the term is applied broadly. FOIA can be used to access records from the White House; federal departments, such as the Departments of Defense and Education; independent agencies, such as the Veterans Administration and the CIA; and most other offices that fall under the control of the executive branch.

FOR YOUR INFORMATION...

- Since its passage in 1966, FOIA has been used millions of times to secure the release of classified government documents. It has been called one of the most important laws regarding the rights of citizens ever enacted in the U.S.—right up there with the Bill of Rights—and it has been used as a model for similar laws in countries all over the world.

- More than 650,000 FOIA requests were made in 2012 alone. Of those requests, 30,000 were denied outright, roughly half were granted in full, and the remainder were partially granted, meaning the documents turned over were partially redacted.

- John Moss was reelected 12 times, and served in Congress until 1979. After FOIA passed in 1966, he went on to champion consumer rights, and in 1972 he authored the landmark Consumer Product Safety Act. Moss died in 1997 at the age of 82.

- In 1766, ten years before the American Revolution, Sweden passed the "Freedom of the Press Act." Among other things—it gave Swedish citizens access to uncensored government documents. And while Sweden was not a proper democracy at the time—and the law was suspended just six years later—it is recognized today as the first "freedom of information" law in history.

*   *   *

"I was born at home on newspapers. I still have a story on my butt, although now the print is much larger." —**Phyllis Diller**

Time it takes a drug-sniffing dog to completely check a car: 6 minutes.

BROWN TOWN

There are many slang terms for that bit of solid waste we all leave behind in the bathroom. They are truly disgusting…yet oddly compelling. (Enjoy?)

Fudge babies	Butt nuts
Poonami	Intestinal sewage
Butt beans	Frightened turtles
Lovely lumps	Hungry, Hungry Hippos
Hell frosting	Toilet bowl stew
Blind eels	Stink pickles
Gorilla fingers	Sea pickles
Body boulders	Turd troopers
Product of Uranus	Dog logs
Smelly pebbles	Prairie dogs
Mississippi mud	Space slugs
Keester cakes	Corn-eyed butt snakes
Boneless brown trout	Cleveland Browns
Corn massacre	Baby Ruths
Chocolate bananas	Brownie bits
Diaper gravy	Butt dumplings
Bootie buddies	Cattle cookies
Tushy tots	Mudfat balls
Brown dragons	Colon cannonballs
Meat Loaf's daughters	Sewer serpents

49% of Americans polled chose toilet paper over food as a desert island necessity.

DEACON'S DOWNFALL

People aren't always what they seem—sometimes the most respectable people turn out to be the biggest crooks. Here's Part II of the story of 18th-century Scottish scoundrel, Deacon William Brodie. (Part I is on page 173.)

THINKING BIG

A few cases of (un)mistaken identity aside, Deacon Brodie had a pretty good thing going. He might have kept it going even longer than he did, were it not for one thing: he wanted to pull even bigger jobs, and for that he needed help. Since he was already a fixture at some of the seediest establishments in Edinburgh, he had no trouble finding three accomplices: George Smith, a crooked traveling salesman with experience as a locksmith; Andrew Ainslie, a compulsive gambler; and John Brown, a convicted swindler on the run from the law.

The gang pulled its first job in October 1786, when it broke into a goldsmith's shop and made off with the gold. Burglaries of hardware stores, tobacconists, jewelry shops, grocers, silk merchants, and other businesses soon followed. At each location the gang stole money and any goods they could lay their hands on that were valuable and easy to fence. Tea was a rare, pricey commodity in those days, and in one burglary of a grocer they made off with more than 350 pounds of the stuff. When they broke into the library at the University of Edinburgh in October 1787, they took the school's ceremonial silver mace.

TAX COLLECTOR

In early 1788, Brodie planned his biggest burglary yet: robbing Scotland's General Excise Office of its tax receipts. He'd done work there and was familiar with the layout. And like other visitors to the office, he'd noticed that even in a building supposedly as secure as this one, the key to the front door was still hung on a nail next to the door. Brodie had no trouble distracting the cashier at the front desk while George Smith took the key from its nail and made a quick impression in some putty he had in his pocket.

But the burglary didn't go as well as the gang's earlier heists had. All they managed to find was £16 worth of banknotes (around

$1,600 today), missing the £600 (almost $60,000) hidden under the cashier's desk. Then, when a tax official unexpectedly entered the building while they were burglarizing it, the thieves panicked and fled rather than pounce on any intruders as had been planned. (The official didn't even realize there were burglars in the building; he only learned about the heist when someone told him about it later.)

TURNCOAT

By now there was a £250 reward (nearly $25,000) for the identification and capture of the burglars, plus the promise of a king's pardon for any of the criminals who informed against their accomplices. John Brown, already a wanted man, decided to take the deal. He figured (correctly) that the prosecutor would agree to pardon all of his crimes, even the ones he committed before joining up with Deacon Brodie, in exchange for his testimony.

As soon as Brown collected his £4 cut of the General Excise Office burglary, he marched straight to the sheriff's office and ratted out Ainslie and Smith…but not Brodie, whom he hoped to blackmail. Brodie naturally assumed he *had* been implicated, and when Ainslie and Smith were arrested he fled to Holland, where he hoped to catch a boat to America. He never made it. After both Ainslie and Smith implicated him, he was tracked to Amsterdam, arrested, and hauled back to Scotland for trial.

THE END(?)

The evidence against the gang was overwhelming. A search of Brodie's home turned up more duplicate keys, a metal case filled with the putty they used to make impressions, plus several lock picks and other burglary tools. As if that wasn't bad enough, Ainslie joined Brown and turned King's evidence against Brodie and Smith. Both men were found guilty and were sentenced to death by hanging. On October 1, 1788, in front of a crowd of some 40,000 people, the largest ever for a hanging in Edinburgh, Brodie and Smith were executed…or were they?

There was little doubt that *Smith* met his maker, but rumors abounded that Brodie had bribed the executioner for a "short drop," or shortened length of rope, to prevent his neck from breaking when the trapdoor on the gallows was sprung. Different versions of the story had him wearing a metal band around his neck, a harness

In 1907 Kellogg's offered a free box of Corn Flakes to any woman who winked at her grocer.

under his clothes, or a silver tube in his throat to prevent choking. A doctor had supposedly hidden nearby to revive him as soon as his family claimed the body. "If this succeeded," William Roughead relates in *Trial of Deacon Brodie*, "the Deacon was to lie quiet in his coffin, exhibiting no signs of life, till such time as it could be safely removed to his own house....Whether or not this remarkable program was ever carried out was never recorded."

BY ANY OTHER NAME

Regardless of whether Brodie survived, his legend certainly did, thanks in no small part to his day job as a cabinet maker. After his double life was exposed, the cabinets, chests and other furniture he'd made became instant conversation pieces. For years afterward, people in many of the finest homes in Edinburgh delighted in showing off Deacon Brodie's handiwork as they told his story to friends.

One such man was a lighthouse engineer named Thomas Stevenson. He had one of Brodie's cabinets in the nursery of his home, and his young son, Robert, never tired of the nanny telling the story of the man who was one person by day and another by night. Robert—whose full name was Robert Louis Stevenson— would grow up to become an excellent storyteller in his own right. He wrote his first play about Brodie in 1864 when he was only 14, and returned to the story repeatedly over the years. In 1882, when he was in his 30s, he and a friend brought a version titled *Deacon Brodie, or the Double Life* to the stage.

But Stevenson's most famous story inspired by Deacon Brodie came about in 1885, when publisher Charles Longman asked him to write a ghost story for Christmas. Legend has it that much of the plot, about a doctor who invents a potion that turns him into a homicidal madman, came to Stevenson in a dream, that he wrote the story in only three days, and that when his wife didn't like it, he threw it on the fire and rewrote the story in another three days. First published in January 1886, the novella *Strange Case of Dr. Jekyll and Mr. Hyde* has been in print ever since.

* * *

"The key to immortality is first living a life worth remembering."
—Bruce Lee

Musician Moby is the great-great-great grandnephew of Herman Melville, author of *Moby Dick*.

THE DISAPPEARANCE OF BOEING N844AA

On page 342 we told you the stories of several airplanes that disappeared. Here's one that deserves its own article.

RUNAWAY ON THE RUNWAY

On the evening of May 25, 2003, air-traffic controllers in the tower at Quatro de Fevereiro Airport, in the city of Luanda, Angola, watched in confusion as a Boeing 727-223 airliner that had been sitting idle on the airport grounds for over a year left its hangar, took an erratic back-and-forth path toward a runway, and motored up, as if it were readying for takeoff. The plane wasn't scheduled to depart, and whoever was in it hadn't contacted the tower. Flight-control officers tried desperately to contact the plane—and received no reply. They then watched in shock as the plane—which hadn't turned its flight lights on—took off, heading southwest, over the Atlantic Ocean.

The plane has not been seen since.

PLANE FACTS

That Boeing 727-223, with the registration number N844AA, was manufactured in 1975 and was originally owned by American Airlines. American used the plane for passenger service for just over 26 years, until August 2001. The plane was stored for a short time at an airport in Mojave, California, then was transported to Miami International Airport in Florida. There it was purchased by a Jacksonville, Florida-based company called Aerospace Sales and Leasing, which was owned by a man named Maury Joseph—who had a bit of a shady past. (More on that later.)

In early 2002, Joseph sold the plane to a South African business-man named Keith Irwin—but only after agreeing to remove most of the passenger seats and replace them with ten 500-gallon fuel tanks. Reason: Irwin planned to use the plane as part of a new—and risky—business he was forming, flying shipments of fuel to diamond mines in the war-torn nation of Angola. The plane was flown by its U.S. crew across the Atlantic Ocean, finally landing in Angola.

If you're average, you'll spend about a year of your life searching for items you've lost.

That's when things started to go wrong.

OH LORD, STUCK IN LUANDA

As soon as it landed in Luanda, the Angolan government grounded the plane. Irwin, they said, hadn't filed the proper paperwork (including the paperwork required for converting the 727 from a passenger plane to a cargo plane). Compounding his problems, Irwin's business partners, who were supposed to supply additional funds for the operation, including payments to Maury Joseph for the plane itself, which had not yet been fully paid for, backed out of the deal. Irwin spent a month finding other backers and getting his paperwork in order, then, in April 2002, the company finally started doing what it had been formed to do—flying fuel to diamond mines. (This, one of the pilots told *Air & Space Magazine* reporter Tim Wright in 2010, required flying down to the landing fields near the diamond mines in tight spirals to avoid small-arms fire from rebels trying to take over the mines.) Less than two months later, the operation had gone belly-up—and Irwin simply left the plane at the Luanda airport.

Almost a year passed.

REPO MAN

In early 2003, Maury Joseph, who was still owed several hundred thousand dollars for the plane and was still listed as the plane's owner, hired a man to fly to Angola and repossess the aircraft. The man Joseph sent: Ben Charles Padilla, a 51-year-old aircraft mechanic, flight engineer, and small-plane pilot from Florida. Padilla arrived in Luanda in March 2003 and immediately began preparing the 727 for flight. (It had gone from very good condition when it was in Miami to fairly wretched condition after making several diesel-fuel runs in Angola.) Padilla spent about two months working on the plane, near the end of that time hiring an assistant, a young man from the neighboring Republic of the Congo named John Mikel Mutantu.

Maury Joseph showed up in mid-May, telling Padilla he had found a buyer for the plane in South Africa. Padilla hired a pilot and copilot to fly the plane, planning to serve as engineer himself (a 727 normally requires a three-person crew), and told Joseph they would deliver the plane to Johannesburg, South Africa, on May 26.

What's *dartitis*? The psychological condition that prevents a dart player from releasing his dart.

WEAPON OF MASS DESTRUCTION

At about 6:00 p.m. the day before the scheduled flight, Padilla and his assistant, Mutantu, climbed into the 727's cockpit in a remote hangar at Quatro de Fevereiro Airport. Shortly after that, the plane, with Padilla and Mutantu aboard, started on its erratic path to the runway and took off, never to be seen again.

News of a missing airliner reached U.S. authorities the next day and set off a scramble by the FBI, CIA, and NSA, along with intelligence agencies from Angola and several other countries. Why? Because the 727 was carrying ten 500-gallon fuel tanks inside it, possibly full. Less than two years after the 9/11 attacks, it was no stretch to think the plane might be used in a terrorist attack. And with a range of more than 2,100 miles—along with the fact that a 727, a relatively small airliner, can land on small, remote airstrips—there was no telling where the plane was headed. There were numerous locations all over Africa that had been the targets of terrorism in recent years, and with just two hops it could reach locations all over the Middle East or Europe.

WHODUNIT?

When the hours after the plane's disappearance turned to days, then weeks, the threat of a terrorist attack lowered dramatically. Investigators then turned to other possible scenarios. Suspicion naturally fell on Padilla. Had he stolen the aircraft for some reason? It seemed unlikely. Padilla had no criminal record, and he was being well paid by Maury Joseph. On top of that, according to everyone who knew him, Padilla didn't know how to fly a 727. And his assistant, Mutantu, had no flying skills at all. (Again, it normally takes a crew of three to fly a 727.) Besides, why would Padilla steal the plane and simply disappear?

Padilla was staunchly defended by his family, particularly his younger brother, Joseph Padilla, who has appeared on news shows about the missing plane numerous times over the years. Joseph Padilla claims his brother was very close to his family and had always made a point of staying in contact with them. He believes there were people, probably terrorists, lying in wait on the airplane, and that those people took control of the plane. The erratic, back-and-forth path to the runway described by air-traffic controllers, says Joseph Padilla, speaks to this. "That tells me," he told Florida's

St. Petersburg Times in 2004, "my brother was trying to fight off whoever was trying to take control of the plane."

OTHER THEORIES

Investigators also looked into possible insurance fraud—especially when they discovered that Maury Joseph, still the aircraft's official owner, had been charged with fraud by the Securities and Exchange Commission just a few years earlier. (He was charged with defrauding investors in another failed airline company, and was fined $50,000.) Joseph, for his part, cooperated fully with investigators, as did Keith Irwin, but that investigation turned up nothing. (Whether the plane was insured and, if so, whether Joseph collected on the policy is unknown.)

Investigations into other theories—including one that the plane was stolen by drug smugglers, and another that it was flown to one of the region's many unattended landing strips, broken down, and sold for parts—also came up empty. Another mystery: in the hours before the plane's disappearance, someone paid the airport's fuel depot $93,000 in cash to fuel up the plane. Who? Nobody knows. News reports from the time say it was "an unidentified man." (And it does not appear to have been Maury Joseph.)

FINAL DESTINATION

Over the years there have been several purported sightings of Boeing N844AA in various locations around Africa—and one in Beirut, Lebanon—but investigations into each of those reports found them to be mistaken. The family of Ben Padilla continues to pressure the FBI and other agencies. Joseph Padilla was interviewed on CNN during the investigation of the missing Malaysian airliner in 2014. He says he believes his brother is dead; he just wants to know what happened to him.

Investigators have also looked into the possibility that the plane, regardless of why it was taken in the first place, simply crashed into the sea. And while they found no wreckage, and no oil or fuel slicks, a common characteristic of airplane crashes at sea, investigators believe a crash at sea is the most likely explanation of the plane's disappearance. Ultimately, we may never know the truth.

WHEN ZIGGY MET GARY

*Parrots have an instinctive ability to mimic the sounds they hear around them;
that's what makes it possible for them to imitate human speech. But how
many of them ever really have anything to say? This one sure did.*

PARROT: Ziggy, an eight-year-old African gray parrot
owned by Chris Taylor, a 30-year-old software engineer from
Yorkshire, England

BACKGROUND: Taylor raised Ziggy from a chick and named
him after Ziggy Stardust, the 1970s persona of pop star David
Bowie. Over the years Ziggy learned to imitate Taylor and his
friends (including his girlfriend, Suzy Collins) as well as the sounds
of the phone, the doorbell, the microwave, the TV, the radio, and
the songs that Taylor played on his stereo. One of the bird's favorite
expressions was "Put on your red shoes and dance the blues," from
David Bowie's hit single "Let's Dance."

NOW YOU'RE TALKING: In 2004 Taylor moved in with
Collins, but she and Ziggy never really got along. Then, sometime
in 2006, he noticed that Ziggy had started squawking "Hiya Gary!"
in Collins's voice whenever her cell phone rang. Taylor didn't know
anyone named Gary; Collins said she didn't, either. "I just dismissed
it as something he'd picked up from the telly. I thought it was hilarious," Taylor later told London's *Daily Mail* newspaper. When Ziggy
started making "long slurping kissing noises" whenever the name
Gary was said on TV or the radio, Taylor laughed that off, too. It
wasn't until Ziggy began saying "I love you, Gary!" in Collins's voice
that Collins finally admitted she'd been bringing a coworker named
Gary home for intimate lunch-hour trysts. Ziggy had witnessed it all.

UPDATE: Collins moved out of the flat…and eventually so did
Ziggy: "I couldn't get Ziggy to stop saying that bloody name," Taylor
told the *Daily Mail*. "It felt like I'd been stabbed through the heart
every time my phone rang or he heard the name on the telly." He
finally had to find his feathered friend a new home. "I know I'll get
over Suzy, but I don't think I'll ever get over Ziggy," he says. So
how's Suzy Collins holding up? Better than Taylor or Ziggy, it seems:
"I'm surprised to hear Chris got rid of the bird. He spent more time
talking to it than he did to me."

How do parrot fish fend off parasites? They sleep in a cocoon of mucus. (Just like Uncle John.)

SPECIAL BRAS

If you find it embarrassing to read about bras, here's some uplifting information and supporting facts about new developments in bras that might change your mind. (Whew! We're glad to get that off our chests.)

T HE DIGNI BRA
What It Is: A bra that women can wear during surgery
Details: When women are wheeled into surgery, they are usually wearing nothing more than their hospital gowns. Some British hospitals offer women disposable paper underpants to wear beneath the gowns…but no bras. This makes surgery, already a very stressful event, even more so for many women, because they feel so exposed. In 2013 two Welsh nurses named Natalie Reid and Fiona Cartwright started making bras out of the same blue paper material used to make the underpants. "We'd been working with female patients for a long time and we just thought, 'Why aren't there any bras to match the pants?' Reid told the *South Wales Echo* newspaper in June 2013. The bras are being tested at a private hospital in Wales and have been well received by patients and doctors alike; Reid and Cartwright hope that the National Health Service will soon offer them in hospitals all over the U.K. "It's not about vanity, it's about dignity," Reid says.

THE HOSPITAL BRA

What It Is: A bra for women recovering from breast surgery
Details: Elle Terry-Dawson owns a lingerie store in the town of Tring, north of London, England, but when she had breast surgery even she couldn't find a post-surgery bra that was acceptable. So she made one herself. The Hospital Bra is a compression garment (like sports bras or bike shorts), which aids in the recovery process after surgery. It contains no wires and has a triple closure (for additional support) that fastens in the front instead of the back, so it's easier to put on and take off. The shoulder straps are adjustable to accommodate swelling after surgery and are padded for extra comfort. Bonus: the fabric is made from natural bamboo fiber that is soft, stretchable, breathable, and has antibacterial properties that help prevent infection. "Designers of post-surgery bras should listen to people

who have had breast surgery," Terry-Dawson says.

THE BRA-HIJACK INITIATIVE

What It Is: A campaign by CoppaFeel!, a British breast cancer charity, to turn ordinary bras into reminders for breast self-exams

Details: CoppaFeel! works with bra manufacturers to sew labels into the garment that say "Checking your boobs could save your life." The labels also have the CoppaFeel! website address so that wearers can get more information. "There's no better time to check your boobs than when you've just taken off your bra," says CoppaFeel! founder Kris Hallenga, who is battling breast cancer herself.

THE TWEETING BRA

What It Is: A bra that tweets breast self-exam reminders

Details: The Tweeting Bra is a high-tech version of CoppaFeel! labels…except that there's only one bra. It's worn by a Greek celebrity named Maria Bakodimou, who has been described as the "Oprah of Greece." Every time Bakodimou removes her bra, a sensor in the clasp communicates with her smartphone via Bluetooth and tweets a message to the bra's followers on Twitter, reminding them (sometimes in English, sometimes in Greek) to examine their breasts. "Boobs, I did it again! And by 'it' I mean self-examination. How about you?" says a tweet sent on November 25, 2013. As of mid-2014, the bra has 6,215 Twitter followers.

THE FUNKYBOD MUSCLE TOP

What It Is: A support undergarment for men with "man boobs"

Details: The padded Muscle Top shirt was originally intended for skinny guys who were insecure about their lack of muscle mass. Slip on the Muscle Top and put an ordinary shirt on over it. The foam padding in the pecs, shoulders, and arms makes you look like a guy who can bench-press 200 pounds. But as Funkybod notes on their website, they soon discovered a second market for the undershirts:

> We found that some of the smaller men had man-boob issues which were covered well by the Muscle Top. This led us to experiment with larger men and look into the man-boob issue further. Indeed, the shirt's ability to lift and separate is undeniable….Finally, a push-up bra for men!

From 1931 to '97, *The Joy of Cooking* included recipes for armadillo and stuffed boar's head.

DUSTBIN OF HISTORY: THE CHECKER CAB

Even though they haven't been manufactured for more than 30 years, Checker Cabs remain one of the most iconic cars ever made. Here's a look under the hood of this unique piece of American automotive history.

TAILOR-MADE

Morris Markin was a Russian-Jewish tailor who emigrated to the United States in 1913 when he was in his late teens. He settled in Chicago, found work in the city's garment district, and within a couple of years had his own business making ready-to-wear suits. When America entered World War I in 1917, he switched to making uniforms for the army.

At war's end Markin began looking outside the garment industry for new business opportunities. In 1920 he loaned $15,000 to a fellow immigrant named Abe Lomberg, who had a business manufacturing auto bodies for Commonwealth Motors, an assembler of purpose-built taxicabs. Markin may have wished he'd stuck to the garment industry, because Lomberg's business and Commonwealth failed within a year of each other. Rather than cut his losses, Markin assumed control of both companies, merged them into a single firm, and renamed it after the company's biggest client, Checker Taxi of Chicago.

APPLES AND ORANGES

The automobiles that the Checker Cab Manufacturing Company made in the 1920s and 1930s had little in common with modern taxis. In those days cabs were hired almost exclusively by the wealthy. Everyone else took the bus, the streetcar, or the subway (or walked). Taxi passengers expected to ride in comfort, and Markin's vehicles delivered. Early Checker Cabs were big, beautiful cars with well-appointed interiors. Some models came with down-filled seats that smartly uniformed cabbies fluffed up with a special paddle between fares. The cabs also developed a reputation for being rugged, reliable, and easy (and cheap) to repair, which made them popular with taxi companies and independent drivers alike.

Poll results: The top 3 favorite smells in Britain are bread, fresh-cut grass, and coffee.

By the end of the 1920s, nearly half the cabs in New York City were Checkers, and the company had made inroads in Pittsburgh, Chicago, Minneapolis, and other American cities.

The Great Depression of the 1930s, while bad for business, helped Markin to consolidate his hold on the taxi industry. General Motors, Markin's biggest competitor, got out of the taxicab-manufacturing business altogether. And because Checker sold its cabs on credit, when taxi owners defaulted on their payments, Markin had little choice but to repossess the cabs and hire his own drivers to run them. By 1940 he was one of the nation's largest operators of taxicabs, as well as a manufacturer. And since Markin was the one buying the cabs, that, in turn, guaranteed plenty of business for Checker Manufacturing.

NEW AND IMPROVED

When the U.S. entered World War II in 1941, domestic automobile production was suspended as auto manufacturers retooled to supply matériel for the war effort. Checker was no exception: it made truck components and other equipment for the military. Then as soon as the war was over, it went back to making cabs. The first postwar Checkers were based on prewar designs; it wasn't until 1956 that Checker (which by then had renamed itself Checker Motors) introduced an all-new car, called the A8, later renamed the Checker Marathon. It served as the basis for every taxicab the company made for the rest of its 25-year run.

The Marathon was a far cry from the fancy cabs of the 1920s and 1930s. The interiors were as austere as school buses: its ceilings were made using a hard fiberboard material instead of fabric. Rubber floor mats took the place of carpeting, so drivers could clean the interior with a hose. And seamless, unpleated bench seats (seams and pleats trap dirt) replaced the down-filled cushions of yesteryear.

What people remember most about the Marathon is the spacious interiors that seemed larger than many cramped Manhattan apartments. How much legroom do you have in the backseat of your car? The Checker Marathon had 46.3 inches—nearly *four feet*. That was enough room for two folding jump seats, allowing the cab to accommodate six passengers comfortably—three on the bench seat, two on the jump seats, and one in the passenger seat next to the driver. The trunk was large enough to hold all of their luggage. When the

Chronicles of Narnia author C. S. Lewis flunked his driver's test 17 times.

jump seats were stowed away, there was enough room to roll a baby stroller right in, and the ceiling was high enough for passengers to ride without having to remove their hats.

RIDING HIGH

Checker's sales peaked at 8,100 cars in 1962. (Cost of a Marathon that year: $2,542. Power steering, power brakes, and air-conditioning were extra.) The following year, more than 35,000 of all taxis operating in the United States were Checkers.

The company sold a number of specialty vehicles based on its famous cabs as well, including ambulances, hearses, limousines, and 12-passenger "Aerobuses" that shuttled people around airports and vacation resorts. More than 22 feet long, the eight-door Aerobus still holds the record for the longest mass-production passenger car.

Checker also sold thousands of its taxis for use as personal vehicles, though these never proved as popular as the company hoped. One drawback of owning one was that when you stopped at a light there was a good chance that a stranger, thinking you were a taxi, would pull open the door and climb in the back.

STILL THE SAME

Checker's reluctance to change anything about the car was one of its selling points; Morris Markin promised that as long as there was demand for the cars, he would continue making them the same way. About the only changes he made were when parts supplied by other companies became unavailable, or when government regulations required the changes. Marathons made after 1964, for example, have lap seat belts in the front seat (they weren't required in the back); cabs made after 1969 have headrests on the front seats; and cabs made after 1978 have no jump seats—they failed crash tests and were ordered removed.

In the 1950s, it was difficult to tell a Checker from the Fords, Chryslers, and GM cars of the day. Checkers look quite a bit like '57 Chevy Bel Airs, for example. But as those cars evolved over the years and the Checker Cab did not, it gradually became one of the most recognizable vehicles in the world and a rolling, anachronistic icon of New York City. That gave the car much of its charm, but it also left it vulnerable when the soaring gasoline prices of the 1970s sent shock waves through the auto industry. As long as gasoline was

---

At age 12, Fidel Castro wrote FDR and asked for a $10 bill. (He got a reply, but no money.)

cheap, Checker Cabs were inexpensive to operate. When the price soared from 36¢ a gallon to $1.27 a gallon in less than a decade, they weren't anymore.

As the Big Three automakers began to downsize their cars, Checker was hurt in a number of ways. For one thing, the company got most of its mechanical components (engines, transmissions, brakes, etc.) from the Big Three. But as these companies re-engineered their own cars to make them smaller and more fuel-efficient, there was no guarantee that parts for the Checker Cab would be available in the future.

Ironically, the failure of the Big Three to shrink their vehicles faster also hurt Checker. That's because when GM, Ford, and Chrysler lost market share to the smaller, more fuel-efficient cars manufactured by Volkswagen, Datsun, and Toyota, they tried to goose their flagging sales by offering special fleet prices to customers who bought cars in volume. Customers like taxi companies, for example.

CHECK...

As Checker's sales dwindled from one year to the next, there was less money available to design a car more suited for the times. By the 1970s, Morris Markin was gone; he'd died in 1970 and his son David took over the company. In 1976 David sold half of Checker to Ed Cole, the recently retired president of GM, for $6 million and Cole became Checker's CEO.

Cole had some successes at GM, but he was also closely associated with the Chevy Corvair and the Chevy Vega, two of the most problematic cars that GM ever built. His plans for Checker didn't seem much better: He wanted to buy unfinished Volkswagen Golfs (then called Rabbits) from VW's factory in the U.S., then raise the roofs several inches and stretch the cars until they were long enough to hold six passengers. He was also considering a similar model based on a stretched Chevy Citation. Both of these plans came to naught when he died in a plane crash in May 1977.

...AND CHECKMATE

Checker struggled on for a few more years, but falling sales and soaring interest rates in the late 1970s made it impossible for the company to finance any further attempts at redesigning the Checker Cab. In 1981 sales hit a new low of 500 cars, and the company

---

Death row lethal injections are usually performed by prison staff, not medical professionals.

declared its first loss in nearly 50 years. A few months later Checker Motors announced it was ending production of its cars. The last Marathon rolled off the assembly line in July 1982.

END OF THE ROAD

Checker Motors continued on for nearly 30 more years as a manufacturer of parts for GM and other companies. But when rising gas prices and an economic recession made GM's sales tank in 2008, Checker's fortunes soured with it. David Markin's ability to keep the company afloat using his own funds had already been damaged when he divorced his wife in 2005 and she was awarded half of his $106 million fortune. Then, when Markin lost much of the rest of his fortune by investing it with Bernie Madoff, Checker's hopes for survival vanished entirely.

Just one month after Madoff was arrested in December 2008 and charged with running the largest Ponzi scheme in history, Checker Motors filed for bankruptcy and went out of business. Today all that's left of the company are the remaining Checker Marathons themselves…and surprisingly few of them are still around. Of the tens of thousands produced over the years, only about 700 survive. Why so few? They were *taxis*: most were driven into the ground and then towed to the wrecking yard and scrapped. The older Checkers are rarest of all; only about 15 made before 1960 are known to exist.

OUT OF SERVICE

Another thing that's hard to find nowadays is a cabbie who has ever driven a Checker. That's not just because of the passage of time, but also because there's nothing quite like driving a Checker. When the cabs became scarce in the late 1980s and could no longer be had, either new or used, many Checker cabbies got out of the business rather than drive any cab that wasn't a Checker.

That's what Earl Johnson, New York's last Checker Cab driver, did when his cab flunked its safety inspection in 1999 and had to be taken off the road after 21 years and 994,000 miles on New York City streets. Rather than stoop to driving a Ford Crown Victoria or any other car, he retired four years early. "I would never settle for driving any one of those," he told the *New York Times* on his last day on the job. "This is the only real taxi." (Sotheby's later sold his cab at auction for $134,500—$125,500 more than Johnson paid for it new in 1978.)

First service uniform to be patented: The Playboy Bunny outfit.

THINKING OUTSIDE THE BOX

Just because traditional funeral viewings involve mourners filing past an open casket doesn't mean that's the only way to do it. This odd funeral fad may be coming to an undertaker near you.

TAKING A STAND

Angel Pantoja Medina was only six years old when his father was murdered in San Juan, Puerto Rico, in 1990. The shock of the loss was made even worse a few days later at the wake, when Angel saw his father laid out in his casket. He never forgot the sight; years later Angel told his family that when his time came, he wanted his wake to be different. "If something happens to me, I want to be seen standing," he said.

In 2008 Angel, 24, followed in his father's tragic footsteps when he was murdered in a gangland-style shooting. Though the Medina family wanted a traditional burial in a pearl-white casket, they asked San Juan's Marin Funeral Home if there was any way to honor Angel's wishes and show him standing at the wake.

It was an odd request to be sure, but the funeral director thought it could be done. When they delivered Medina's embalmed body to his parents' house, where the wake was to be held, they knocked two holes in the wall in a corner of the living room and strapped Medina's corpse to the wall, posing it as if it were standing under its own power. Medina was dressed in his favorite clothes: jeans, a brown T-shirt over a white long-sleeved shirt, a New York Yankees cap, a silver cross around his neck, and his designer Dolce & Gabbana sunglasses.

DÉJÀ VIEW

Hundreds of people attended the three-day viewing, including plenty who didn't know Medina and were just there to gawk at *el muerto parao*—"the dead man standing." One of the visitors may well have been a young man from the neighborhood named David Morales Colon, because when he was gunned down two years later at the age of 22, his family went to the Marin Funeral Home

---

Prehistoric punk: In 2003 a 2,300-year-old mummy with a mohawk was discovered in Ireland.

and asked for a similar kind of wake—except with a motorcycle theme—for Colon, who'd loved riding his Honda CBR 600 racing bike. The funeral home dressed Colon in his jeans, black riding jacket, dark sunglasses, and black baseball cap; then posed his corpse atop the motorcycle, hunched over as if he were racing at high speed.

VERTICAL HOLD

For fans of "exotic wakes," as they've come to be known, it didn't help that the first two people who got them were murder victims from the same rough neighborhood in San Juan. Puerto Rico's more conventional funeral directors, who no doubt feared losing business to unorthodox competitors like the Marin Funeral Home, were also justifiably concerned that the wakes glorified the violence that has claimed the lives of too many young men in Puerto Rico.

Was it even legal to display a dead body outside of a casket? Or sanitary? There was nothing in Puerto Rican law that prohibited exotic wakes, nor was there anything in the health code that required the use of coffins or that the deceased be displayed horizontally. Though Puerto Rican lawmakers have looked into banning them, as of January 2014 exotic wakes were still legal. That's when a third young man murdered on the streets of San Juan, 23-year-old Christopher Rivera Amaro, got his.

Amaro was an amateur boxer, so his family asked the Marin Funeral Home for a boxing-themed wake. They dressed him in his boxing gloves, shorts, and shoes, plus a gold satin hoodie and sunglasses, and displayed him standing upright in the corner of a social hall that was decorated to look like a boxing ring. Slightly hunched over, with his fists raised in a defensive posture, Amaro really did look like he was entering the ring for a fight.

THE LATEST THING

It's likely that exotic wakes will become more mainstream over time. Throngs of people file past viewings whenever they're held, and many visitors have expressed a desire for a similar wake. Some have already made their arrangements: the Marin Funeral home has performed a wake for a man who wanted to be seated in a chair smoking a cigar, and in 2010 it staged a viewing for a paramedic killed in a car accident who wanted to be displayed behind the

In boxing, a blow to the head can have the force of more than half a ton.

wheel of his ambulance. The day may not be far off when the exotic wakes of ordinary people who die accidentally or from natural causes outnumber those of urban toughs who live fast and die violently while still young.

ON A ROLL

It's also possible that the trend may catch on in the United States. In 2009, several months before David Colon got his motorcycle wake in San Juan, a Puerto Rican immigrant named Julio Lopez died in Philadelphia, reportedly after choking on a home-cooked meal. Like Colon, Lopez was a motorcycle buff, and after he died his family arranged for a local funeral director named Charlene Wilson-Doffoney to pose his corpse atop his motorcycle as if he were riding it.

Wilson-Doffoney didn't do quite as good a job as the Marin Funeral Home: in some pictures Lopez looks like he landed on the motorcycle after falling out of a tree. But like the Marin Funeral Home, Wilson-Doffoney says that her first out-of-the-box wake has attracted a lot of interest from people who want the same thing for themselves. "I got a lady who just asked me if I can put her in a truck," she told an interviewer in 2010. "I will take her and have her sitting in her truck. I'll do anything they want me to do."

*   *   *

LOONY LAWS IN THE NEWS

• Sixty-five-year-old Elizabeth Millard of Surrey, England, was charged with breaking a 167-year-old law against "furious horse riding" in February 2014 after she rode past a woman and her 10-year-old daughter at a fast pace while "shouting at her horse." After the mom complained to police, Millard, who'd never spent a day in court in her life, was "mortified." She admitted to shouting and said she didn't mean to scare the little girl, but she was nonetheless fined £100 ($170).

• In 2014 city leaders in Grand Rapids, Michigan, repealed a 38-year-old ordinance that made it illegal to "willfully annoy another person." Reason: It's "unconstitutional in terms of being vague." So now it's the legal right of every Grand Rapids citizen to tap on a stranger's shoulder and then pretend it wasn't them.

Why do humans have shorter guts than their ancestors? They eat more meat and fewer plants.

GONE WITH THE SEQUELS

What happens when the fans of a hugely popular novel and every book publisher in the world demand a sequel that the author doesn't want to write? The author's family waits 50 years, then hires someone to follow up Margaret Mitchell's Gone With the Wind.

NEVER GO HUNGRY AGAIN

Gone With the Wind, published in 1936, is one of the most successful and enduring books of all time. It won author Margaret Mitchell a Pulitzer Prize, has sold more than 30 million copies (and it's still in print), and was adapted into a film in 1939 that became the most commercially successful movie ever. While the novel ends ambiguously (Rhett Butler up and leaves poor Scarlett O'Hara, and she doesn't quite know what to do next), Mitchell felt her 1,037-page novel told a complete story, and despite major interest from her publisher and the public, she had no interest in writing a follow-up. Mitchell died in 1949 at age 49, having never published another novel.

MADE IN CAROLINA

In 1987, shortly after the novel's 50th anniversary, Mitchell's estate announced that it was commissioning a sequel to *Gone With the Wind*. Why? The book's copyright was about to expire. Once the novel fell into the public domain, anyone could write a sequel, and the Mitchell estate would lose control of the characters. Not only that, they feared a slew of bad, unauthorized sequels flooding the market that could devalue the original work.

The family and its attorneys interviewed 12 writers before selecting Alexandra Ripley, a Southern author best known for romantic historical novels set in the South (like *Gone With the Wind*), such as *Charleston*, *On Leaving Charleston*, and *New Orleans Legacy*. Mitchell's family gave Ripley free reign to write whatever kind of follow-up she wanted…provided she follow an extensive set of guidelines (primarily "no raw sex") and have the first two chapters completed by April 1988. "My hand just won't write

---

Sloth bears (native to India) carry their young on their backs. They're the only bears that do.

'fiddle-dee-dee,'" Ripley said about the style guidelines. "But I figure I'll have to give them at least three and throw in 'God's nightgown!' 'Great balls of fire!' and 'As God is my witness!'"

That April, the estate sent the first 39 pages of the still-untitled novel to every major New York publisher and gave them all 10 days to make an offer. The highest bidder: Warner Books, which agreed to pay $4.94 million, edging out a $4.8 million offer from Dell Books. Ripley was given 18 months to finish the book. (It took Mitchell 10 years to write *Gone With the Wind*.)

Expectations were high, and Ripley had no delusions about the task at hand. "This one will never be mine," she told the Associated Press. "I am trying to prepare myself for a universal hatred of what I'm going to do. Margaret Mitchell may write better than I do. But she's dead."

In September 1991—almost two years after Ripley's original deadline—the 823-page *Scarlett* hit bookstores. The plot: Scarlett goes to Charleston to look for Rhett and confront his family, and then settles down in her family's ancestral homeland in Ireland.

SCARLETT FEVER

Scarlett was a pop-culture phenomenon. It was the best-selling book of 1991, selling more than six million copies—more than triple the number of the runner-up, Tom Clancy's *The Sum of All Fears*. It spent 28 weeks on the *Publishers Weekly* best-seller list. CBS quickly announced plans to adapt it into a TV miniseries.

The only problem: Just as Ripley had predicted, book critics and literary purists hated it. Critic Janet Maslin of the *New York Times* called it "stunningly uneventful." Jack Miles of the *Los Angeles Times* lamented that *Scarlett* was an indicator of the triumph of lazy commerce over literary art. "Frankly, my dear," quipped John Goodspeed of the *Baltimore Sun*, "it stinks."

RIPLEY'S GAME

The public didn't care what the critics thought. They welcomed the idea of continuing the story of Mitchell's beloved characters. The *Scarlett* miniseries, starring Joanne Whalley as Scarlett O'Hara and Timothy Dalton as Rhett Butler, aired over four nights in November 1994 to big ratings and later won two Emmy Awards. To this day, the book is still a steady seller, with a few thousand copies

Because of its funny shape, the first electric guitar was called the Frying Pan.

still bought each year (though not as many as *Gone With the Wind*). Ripley was able to weather the storm and returned to writing her own novels. "There are two reasons why I'm doing this book," Ripley told *Contemporary Authors* in 1987. "I can't resist it, and as soon as this is done I will be able to write anything I want to," meaning she would never have to worry about paying the bills again. She was right; she never had to sell out again. She wrote two novels after *Scarlett*—both published by Warner Books—*From Fields of Gold* (1994) and *A Love Divine* (1997). Both became best-sellers.

THE ENGLISH, PATIENT

The Mitchell estate (essentially three lawyers who acted on behalf of Mitchell's two surviving nephews) liked the success that *Scarlett* brought, but they reportedly didn't care for the novel itself. So in 1995 they commissioned English novelist Emma Tennant to write another sequel to *Gone With the Wind*. Tennant was best known for writing what was actually a well-received sequel to an immensely popular book by a well-loved author—*Pemberley* (1993), a follow-up to Jane Austen's *Pride and Prejudice*. They gave Tennant the same guidelines they'd given to Ripley, requiring her to imitate Mitchell's voice and stick to the original novel's characters. She also wasn't allowed to write in any "acts of incest, miscegenation, or sex between two people of the same sex." St. Martin's Press bought the rights to publish Tennant's book, paying the Mitchell estate $4.5 million.

TARA, GONE

The estate had the full right of refusal of any finished manuscript... and that's exactly what they did. Tennant submitted a 575-page novel called *Tara*, and while she had followed the Mitchell estate's guidelines, they didn't like the book. The estate had wanted a reboot, to wash away the bad feelings left by *Scarlett*, but Tennant's book picked up right where *Scarlett* left off. The estate told Tennant they would not be publishing *Tara* (official reason: because it read "too British") and then filed an injunction to prevent it from ever seeing the light of day. And it never has.

But Mitchell's people were still on the hook with St. Martin's Press for the $4.5 million advance. In 1996 they approached another high-profile author: Southern novelist Pat Conroy, who

---

Safety tip: Nearly ⅓ of burglars gain entry through an unlocked door or window.

had penned *The Prince of Tides* and who had just finished writing an introduction for a 60th-anniversary reprint of *Gone With the Wind*.

Conroy was interested, of course, but he wasn't willing to sacrifice his artistic freedom the way Ripley and Tennant had. Nor did he want to spend months slaving over a manuscript only to have it rejected for not being "true" enough to the source material. Conroy made the estate nervous when he mocked the "guidelines" to a reporter. He joked that he'd open the book with a scene of Rhett Butler and Ashley Wilkes in bed together with Rhett saying, "Ashley, have I ever told you that my grandmother was black?"

Publicly, a lawyer for the estate praised Conroy as "an artist" and promised not to restrain him in any way. Privately, however, Conroy claims that the attorneys refused to let him follow through with some of his plot points...which included killing off Scarlett O'Hara. Ultimately, contract negotiations fell apart and Conroy moved on.

AN ELF ON THE SHELF

By 2000 St. Martin's was getting fairly anxious over the fact that it had spent more than $4 million and five years on a book that never materialized. The executives working on the project, publisher Sally Richardson and editor Hope Dellon, began researching potential sequel authors on their own, without the knowledge of the Mitchell estate. One day, while browsing in a New York bookstore, Dellon found a solid candidate: She picked up *Jacob's Ladder*, a historical novel set during the Civil War (sound familiar?) by a writer named Donald McCaig.

Dellon tracked down McCaig and asked if he'd be interested in writing a sequel to *Gone With the Wind*. She expected him to immediately jump at the offer, but he didn't—because he had never read *Gone With the Wind*. (But then he did, and he signed on.)

WAR CHANGES EVERYTHING

McCaig's concept for his sequel: to not make it a sequel at all. Instead, he decided to set the novel in the Civil War and depict the events of *Gone With the Wind* from Rhett Butler's point of view. Why? He felt that the book would lack emotional resonance without that backdrop. A simple sequel, said McCaig, would be dull and lack tension (which might have been the problem with

---

Mata Hari's body was donated to science, but her head was somehow lost.

Scarlett). "You take the Civil War out of it and have the epic love story, and everything else is kind of 'Oh dear,'" McCaig told the *New York Times*.

PEOPLE WHO READ *PEOPLE*

McCaig spent six years working on the novel, doing research in libraries and document archives throughout the South. He even took a boat out into Charleston Harbor to help him understand how Rhett Butler could have navigated through fierce naval blockades. McCaig turned in chapters to St. Martin's as he finished them, which were then individually reviewed by the Mitchell estate's lawyers—a mutually agreed-upon arrangement to prevent them from rejecting (or hating) the full manuscript after the fact, as had happened with *Scarlett* and *Tara*.

In 2007 *Rhett Butler's People* was finally published, although to less fanfare than had greeted *Scarlett*, but to slightly better reviews. It nearly sold out its first print run of a million copies, again less than *Scarlett* numbers, but enough that the Mitchell estate and St. Martin's Press asked McCaig to write another entry in the *Gone With the Wind* saga. It's a prequel that will follow the life of *Gone With the Wind*'s Mammy, or "Ruth," as she'll be called in McCaig's *Ruth's Journey*.

WENT WITH THE WIND

But try as the Mitchell estate did to keep tight control over who wrote about the further adventures of the fictional characters that Margaret Mitchell first concocted more than 80 years earlier, they couldn't fully suppress unauthorized sequels. In 2001 a North Carolina teacher named Kate Pinotti self-published her first novel, *The Winds of Tara*, her own idea of what happened to the characters of *Gone With the Wind* after that book wrapped up. The book directly follows *Gone With the Wind* (ignoring the other sequels and offshoots), with Scarlett leaving Atlanta and returning home to Tara, her family's Georgia plantation.

DOWN UNDER

Self-published books are rarely cash cows or attention-getters, but the ever-vigilant Mitchell estate got wind of *Winds* and sent a cease-and-desist letter, demanding that Pinotti stop printing and distributing the book (even though it had a print run of just a few hundred copies). A legal battle ensued, with Pinotti claiming that her book was a parody, which is considered "fair use" under U.S. copyright laws. Mitchell's estate argued infringement and won an injunction banning the publication of *The Winds of Tara* in the United States.

But that's just the United States. Australian publisher Fontaine Press followed the case, did some research, and discovered that the Australian copyright to *Gone With the Wind* had expired in 1999. That meant that Fontaine could legally publish a sequel in that country...which they did, releasing *The Winds of Tara* in 2008. Reviews were mixed, but if you ever manage to find a copy of the original banned self-published 2001 edition, hold on to it—it routinely sells for more than $300 online.

*　　*　　*

STRANGE CELEBRITY LAWSUIT

Plaintiff: Dave Hester, former castmember of A&E's *Storage Wars*

Defendant: Trey Songz, hip hop artist

The Lawsuit: Before he was fired from *Storage Wars* (see page 528), Hester became famous for his catchphrase "Yuuup!" Songz also says "Yuuup!"—in his songs. Believing that Hester stole it from him, Songz sent Hester a cease-and-desist letter in 2011, ordering him to stop using the phrase. An indignant Hester countersued, claiming that *he* came up with the catchphrase first and had even attempted to trademark it three times since 2009 (to no avail). Furthermore, according to Hester's countersuit, the two entertainers pronounce the word differently. Songz's take "resembles an animal-like squeal which begins with a distinct 'yee' sound before finishing with a squeal-like 'uuup' sound," while Hester's is a "monosyllabic sounding guttural auction bidding phrase."

The Verdict: Did either man get sole custody of the catchphrase? Nooope. The suit was settled out of court in 2012, and both Songz and Hester continue to use it. (Hester even sold a little button on his website that said "Yuuup!" when you pressed it. Did it sell well? Nooope!)

GOOD TEAM, BAD OWNER

Any fool with a billion dollars can buy a sports team and run it into the ground. But it takes a special type of owner to trash his own reputation in the process.

Owner: Daniel Snyder

Team: Washington Redskins

Story: You'd think Snyder, who made his fortune in telemarketing, would understand the importance of communication. But when *Washington City Paper* columnist Dave McKenna published a laundry list of the billionaire's "heinous deeds" in 2010, Snyder's response was to sue the paper for libel. Never mind that every item listed, from charging fans $25 to attend Fan Appreciation Day, to suing a 75-year-old grandmother for being unable to pay for her season tickets during the height of the recession, to charging fans $10 to watch the team practice (plus $10 for parking), to making local sportscasters pay to become "media partners" before they were allowed in the stadium, was true. Snyder's crafty goal—to push the paper into bankruptcy from legal fees—was foiled when angry Washingtonians pitched in with cash donations to the *City Paper's* legal fund, prompting Snyder to drop the lawsuit. During Snyder's tenure, the Redskins haven't made it past the first round of the NFL playoffs, but they've remained in the news because of Snyder's adamant defense of his team's controversial nickname, defined as a racial slur by both the Oxford and Merriam-Webster dictionaries.

Owner: The Maloof brothers

Team: Sacramento Kings

Story: Joe, Gavin, and George Maloof Jr. are Las Vegas hoteliers and heirs to a beer distribution company. In 1999 they followed in the footsteps of their father, onetime Houston Rockets owner George Maloof Sr., and bought the Sacramento Kings. The Maloof brothers initially spent a lot of money to attract top-shelf talent to the Kings, and in doing so took them from being a perpetual last-place finisher that frequently entertained offers to move to other cities to a title contender playing in an arena where games were sold out months in advance. That lasted until 2002, when the team's—and the Maloofs'—fortunes started to decline. By 2004 the Maloofs were having serious financial problems and sold off a lot of their holdings…while also appearing in Lil Wayne videos and Carl's Jr. commercials touting their wealth. Shortly after that commercial debuted, the Maloofs asked Sacramento taxpayers to pay for a new arena…threatening to move the team to Anaheim or Las Vegas if they didn't get it. Voters rejected the measure (and the NBA Board of Governors refused to allow the team to move). In 2013 the Maloofs sold the team to an ownership group committed to keeping the team in Sacramento, giving Kings fans something to cheer about for the first time in a decade.

Owner: Jeffrey Loria
Team: Florida Marlins
Story: Loria bought the Florida Marlins in 2002, and a year later managed to win the World Series with a motley crew of mostly little-known rookies and unknown players. But the following offseason, Loria unloaded almost all of his players, many of whom had become stars and could suddenly command higher salaries. The team's play suffered; so did attendance and so did Loria's standing with fans. To combat the loss in revenue, in 2004 Loria announced a rebranding drive. The team, he announced, would build a rectractable-dome stadium, change its name to the Miami Marlins, introduce new uniforms, and sign some new players. It didn't work. The new roster and the new stadium, Marlins Park, opened on April 4, 2012, but the Marlins finished the 2012 season in last place. Loria promptly began to trade or sell all of the team's best players, reducing the payroll from $95 million to $19 million and leaving fans with a shell of a team to root for. To top it all off, financial records indicated that Miami citizens, who voted to fund 80 percent of the new stadium's cost, would be paying for the stadium—at least $2.4 billion—until 2048. Appearing as a contestant on *Survivor* in 2013, Loria's son-in-law and Marlins president David Samson bragged about how he got the city to pay for his stadium. (He was voted off the island in the first round.)

THE CAVES OF XANADU

Here's the story of how two ordinary guys discovered an extraordinary cave and, vowing to protect it, kept it a secret for 14 years.

THE SCENE

One Saturday in 1974, two young men affiliated with Southern Arizona Grotto, a *spelunking*, or "caving," group based in Tuscon, Arizona, were out exploring, looking for new caves near the Whetsone Mountains. Randy Tufts and Gary Tenen traveled about an hour outside of Tucson, where they were roommates at the University of Arizona. As they often did, Tufts and Tenen carried only the minimum amount of caving equipment they needed: two miners' hard hats with gas carbine lanterns affixed to the top, some rope, hammers and chisels, and snacks.

Tufts had been introduced to spelunking by an uncle, and on this day he wanted to explore an area he'd first seen seven years earlier, when he was still in high school. He recalled a large sinkhole with a narrow crack descending into bedrock. On a recent walk, he'd rediscovered the sinkhole and also noticed that the U-shaped hill next to the sinkhole had what appeared to be a collapsed cave entrance. He wondered whether there was something interesting under the hill.

THE DISCOVERY

Tufts and Tenen found the spot and lowered themselves into the 15-foot-deep sinkhole, a dry and dusty space with a skull and crossbones carved in one wall. They found footprints, a couple of broken *stalactites* (mineral formations, or "dripstones," that hang like icicles from the ceiling of a cave), and a 10-inch-wide crack. But most important, they noticed a breeze moving through the crack—a moist, warm breeze that carried the smell of bats, a sure sign of an interesting cave.

At 5'7", Tenen was the smaller of the two, so he pushed his body through the crack first. Tufts was nearly six feet tall and 170 pounds, and had to exhale deeply and practically turn a somersault to push his body through. But another five feet down, they entered a living room-sized chamber with a *stalagmite* (a cone-shaped dripstone that

---

George O. Squier, who supervised testing of the Wright brothers' plane, also invented Muzak.

rises from the floor of a cave) in the center. They knew there had to be more, so they continued until they found a 10-inch-high passageway, the source of the air current. They followed it, crawling on their bellies through 20 feet of gravel until it ended in a rock barrier with a single hole the size of a grapefruit—which cavers refer to as a "blowhole."

SODA STRAWS

For hours, the two men chiseled at the blowhole until both were able to squeeze through. They found a corridor with damp stalactites hanging from the ceiling, as well as delicate "soda straws," tubular mineral formations that grow about a tenth of an inch every century and can eventually form into stalagmites. It was dank and humid, and there were no signs that any humans had ever been in this part of the cave.

But that was just the beginning. As they moved through the cave, they found a series of "rooms" filled with wondrous formations. Orange stalactites hung overhead, soda straws dripped, calcite scrolls unrolled before them, and piles of bat guano towered (and stunk). Some of the rooms were so vast that Tenen and Tufts's lamps, which threw light for only about 50 feet, couldn't illuminate them. They wanted to explore and see how far the cave went, but they were experienced spelunkers and knew better than to go too far without additional light sources and without anyone else knowing where they were. Stunned by their discovery, they returned the way they'd come and decided to come back the following week.

IT'S ALIVE!

The two men had just discovered a cave on par with the finest caves in the world. And unlike some other popular caves, this one was still alive. By comparison, the world-famous Carlsbad Caverns is mostly dry. Another famous cave, Colossal Cave, is dry and dusty. But the wet, dripping quality of this newly discovered cave meant that the 40,000- to nearly 200,000-year-old flowstone, stalactites, and stalagmites were still growing.

Later visits unearthed more astonishing discoveries. One soda straw was an unheard-of 20 feet long. Another formation towered nearly 60 feet as a stalagmite grew up from the floor and eventually met a stalactite, all intricately rippled and lined in cascading drips and bulges. The two men named this massive formation Kubla Khan, after the poem by Samuel Taylor Coleridge, and dubbed the cave Xanadu, after the capital of Khan's empire, another reference to the poem (purportedly written following an opium-fueled dream).

TOP SECRET

Tufts and Tenen were worried about what would happen if this cave was widely discovered…and they had good reason. As cavers, they were careful never to touch formations, but looting, carelessness, and even garbage dumping at caves were rampant. And Xanadu wasn't even remote—it was located just a half mile from a major highway. With fears for the protection of the cave on their minds, the two men decided to keep it a secret, even from their spelunking group. When they drove to visit the site, they covered up their spelunking equipment and carefully sealed up the entrance when they left. But they also knew that simply keeping the cave a secret might not be enough to protect it. If they had found it, why couldn't others?

THE OWNERS

As the two young cavers looked for ways to protect the cave, they found that Xanadu wasn't on public land; it was owned by a man named James A. Kartchner. Tenen and Tufts did extensive research on Kartchner, and every indication suggested he was a civically minded man, a leader in the local Mormon community. His wife, Lois, was a retired teacher, and six of the couple's 12 grown children were doctors. In February 1978, Tenen and Tufts called Kartchner and told him, "We found something on your land we think you should know about."

When they met Kartchner and his wife, they brought along slides with photos of the formations in Xanadu as well as images of Peppersauce Cave, a once-stunning Arizona cave that was now stripped of its formations and littered with trash and graffiti. Tufts and Tenen presented their plan to the Kartchners: they thought the best way to preserve the cave was not to seal it off but rather to commercialize it, to turn it into a tour cave and use profits to fund cave research and preservation.

By that April, Tufts and Tenen had brought Kartchner, as well as five of his sons, belowground. (One of the sons nearly got stuck in the blowhole.) Once they began to explore the wonders of the cave, they understood the majesty of what was below. To the Kartchners, the cave was a representation of the divine. The Kartchner family agreed to a partnership with Tufts and Tenen.

SIGN HERE

Tufts, Tenen, and the Kartchners all believed secrecy would be key to protecting the cave while they tried to figure out how to develop it. They took the secret so seriously that when Gary Tenen met his future wife in 1977, he made her sign a contract on their second date, promising to keep all information about Xanadu secret. The Kartchners also kept the cave secret from younger members of the family. (The 12 Kartchner children had 70 children and 19 grandchildren.) It was a rite of passage in the family to be taken into the cave. The first secret trip to the cave tended to take place as the children were beginning high school. The family's photos of the cave were kept hidden, separate from other family photos. Mrs. Kartchner had a large framed color photo of Kubla Khan, but she kept it in her bedroom, away from public view.

Years passed as Tufts and Tenen researched ways to commercialize the cave. Tenen took jobs at commercial caves under an assumed name in order to learn more about how they might operate the cave. They hired a cartographer to chart Xanadu; they wrote letters to cave owners looking for information about how to run the financial side of the operation. But no matter how they looked at it, it was clear that there would be considerable expense involved in making the caves open to the public while also protecting them.

By 1980 the Kartchners' enthusiasm for the venture began to wane. The economy was sputtering and gas prices were soaring. But perhaps most important, Mr. Kartchner met Howard Ruff, a financial adviser and the best-selling author of the book *How to Prosper During the Coming Bad Years*. Kartchner asked about the advisability of spending the $300,000 they estimated would be needed to develop the cave for profit.

Ruff told him to forget it.

GOING PUBLIC

Once the Kartchners decided against investing their own money in the project, it seemed that the best route would be turning the cave

---

The word "bless" originally meant "sprinkle with blood."

into a state park. There were serious concerns about how the process would work. In order for the state or federal government to acquire it, there would have to be a public process, which would mean unveiling the secret cave. But it seemed they had no other choice.

In January 1985, Tufts and Tenen met with Arizona State Parks official Charles Eatherly without telling him what they were going to see, and even got the man's permission to blindfold him so he wouldn't be able to find his way back later. That was the beginning of a long and complicated political process, spanning the terms of multiple Arizona governors. In order to keep the cave secret, its purchase was slipped into a legislative bill without most of the legislators who were voting on the bill being aware of what they were voting on. On April 4, 1988, the Arizona state senate impeached Arizona governor Evan Mecham. The turmoil of the impeachment seemed a perfect time to sneak a bill through the legislature, granting appropriations for purchasing "the property known as the J.A.K. property"—that is, the property of James A. Kartchner.

The bill passed on April 27, 1988, and the secret finally got out: stories about the secret cave broke at several local TV stations and newspapers. One headline that day proclaimed: "Fairy Tale Cave to Become Arizona's 25th State Park." Only after the bill had passed was Tenen finally able to tell his children about the cave he'd been working to defend for more than a decade.

TODAY

Studying, mapping, and opening the cave to the public was a major undertaking for the state of Arizona. It took 11 years and cost $28 million. On Friday, November 5, 1999—25 years after Tufts and Tenen first entered Xanadu—two rooms of Kartchner Caverns State Park opened for public view for the first time.

Today, visitors to Kartchner Caverns can go on tours of many of the rooms of the cave, including the Throne Room (which contains one of the world's longest soda straws), the Strawberry Room, and the Big Room, which is closed each year from mid-April through mid-October to accommodate nursery roosting for cave bats.

*   *   *

"Life's a marathon, not a sprint." —**Dr. Phil**

All dogs are descended from gray wolves that were first domesticated in China.

CELEBRATION, FLORIDA

*Disney World may be a nice place to visit
...but would you want to live there?*

WHEN YOU WISH UPON A STAR
By the early 1960s, Walt Disney was no longer content to be an animator, movie director and producer, theme-park designer, and TV show host. What he really wanted to do was build a city in central Florida. But not just a city—a "planned community" that would serve as a utopian example for future urban planners. He called it "Experimental Prototype Community of Tomorrow," or EPCOT for short.

Top-level executives at the Walt Disney Company (not to mention Disney's financial advisors) thought he was out of his mind. But they had to give him the benefit of the doubt—just a few years earlier, the same people thought that building a "kiddie park" in a California orange grove would bankrupt Disney and his company. They were wrong, of course. Disneyland, which opened in 1955, became one of the most popular tourist attractions in the world.

Even so, Disney's plans for EPCOT were fairly bold. He'd never built a community before. But he had overseen the complex design and development of Disneyland, and he wanted to draw on that experience to build EPCOT. For example, he wanted to install small elevated trains like Disneyland's People Mover, as well as a citywide monorail. What automobile traffic that was left, Disney planned to limit to underground tunnels, like the ones used by park staff. EPCOT would also be laid out, like Disneyland, in a circle, with businesses in the center and residential areas (with enough housing for 20,000 people) along the perimeter.

GET A JOB
But Disney also wanted to make sure the community ran smoothly and according to his vision. That meant that EPCOT residents would not be allowed to own property—homes would be rental-only, and tenants would have no voting rights or any say in community lawmaking. And while that sounds very similar to a modern-day elderly residence home, Disney actually didn't want

---

First commercial antibiotic: Prontosil, invented by Bayer in the 1930s.

any retirees living in EPCOT. Everyone (except for children) would have to be employed, and employed at EPCOT. Disney actively wanted the town to be a showcase for advanced technology and to serve as a tribute to American ingenuity and the benefits of American capitalism.

"CENTER" OF THE WORLD

The Disney Company aggressively developed the idea of EPCOT until 1966, when it came to an abrupt halt. What happened? Walt Disney died…and so did his dream of EPCOT. With Walt out of the way, Disney executives no longer had to pretend they wanted any part of the massive undertaking of creating and running a city.

Besides, they had much bigger fish to fry—they had to get the company's second theme park, Magic Kingdom in Orlando, Florida, up and running by its announced 1971 opening date. When that park proved to be even more successful than Disneyland, the company announced plans to expand the Florida complex into Walt Disney World, which included plans for a second park—EPCOT Center. It opened in October 1982.

It was not the EPCOT that Walt Disney had imagined—it wasn't a town; it was an amusement park. But it was based on EPCOT's original conceptual art, and it does positively ponder the future. Visitors to Future World can see cutting-edge technology and innovation. The rest of the park, called World Showcase, is like a permanent world's fair—a series of small areas, each representing a different country.

A DREAM IS A WISH YOUR HEART MAKES

But the original EPCOT dream failed to die, probably because of the lasting—and lucrative—success of Walt Disney World. The company had long since established "Disney" as a clean, whole-some, family-friendly, all-American brand. The company also deified Disney, and looked to his old playbook for new ideas. Result: in the early 1990s, the Disney Company created the Celebration Company, charged with building a "perfect community" on a 4,900-acre plot just eight miles south of Walt Disney World.

Michael Eisner, the company's CEO at the time, challenged Celebration's designers to, as he put it, "make history." Their ideas had little in common with what Uncle Walt had planned for

EPCOT. Instead of building a futuristic utopia with people-movers, monorails, underground tunnels, and shiny angular buildings, they created a community based on "new urbanism," a design philosophy that stresses the need for walkable neighborhoods, open spaces, and traditional architecture.

Several noted architects designed many of the town's buildings, among them Michael Graves (Celebration's post office), Phillip Johnson (the Welcome Center), Robert A. M. Stern (the Celebration Health building), and Robert Vernturi and Denise Scott-Brown (the SunTrust Bank). Ironically, lots of its other buildings resemble the nostalgic all-American small-town buildings created for Main Street in Disneyland. However, Celebration doesn't have a "Main Street," because of a local law that says no two streets in the same county can have the same name.

CELEBRATE! OR ELSE

But Celebration did retain one element of Uncle Walt's vision: strict control over the community's politics, services, and appearance. Small alleyways were built behind houses for trash collection and the parking of residents' cars (most houses don't have garages that face the street). Tight neighborhood regulations dictated the color of residents' curtains (white only) and the height of the grass on their front lawns, along with a slew of other nitpicky rules. The company also hand-picked the businesses that were allowed to set up shop in its commercial districts.

Nevertheless, thousands of people wanted to live in Celebration. In 1996 the first 700 people started moving into one of the town's "villages," which was what it called its residential areas. (Average cost of a house in Celebration: $377,000.) Early promos called Celebration "a place that takes you back to that time of innocence."

Other people thought the Disney-town was creepy. "It is kind of Stepford Wife-like," a relative of a resident told the *New York Times*. Perhaps contributing to the uneasiness, Celebration's downtown contains several weird "seasonal" features. Every October, for example, leaf-shaped confetti flies out of lampposts along one street, much like the timed fireworks and parades that occur at Disney theme parks. The event, which attracts hundreds of Floridians who rarely get to experience fall foliage, occurs nightly on Fridays and Saturdays. In December, fake snow made out of soap fills the air while Christmas music trickles in from hidden speakers. (Other annual highlights include a pie festival that's televised on Food Network and a "Posh Pooch" event in which local residents dress up their dogs in fancy clothing.)

PARADISE LOST

As Celebration grew, so did discord among its residents. The one thing that Disney and his successors wanted to hold on to in Celebration—control—is what ultimately sank the community. Homeowners became frustrated by the company's control over the town, its government, and its businesses. Hundreds of homes remained unsold; many others were sold by fed-up residents for far less than they'd paid. And reality continues to shake up "the perfect community" every now and then:

• In 2010 vandals covered Celebration's memorial for veterans in black graffiti.

• Around that same time, the local elementary school was put on lockdown after a woman reported that her estranged husband was driving around town wielding a gun.

• That same year, a SWAT team and a tank were called in to deal with the owner of a failing security business who barricaded himself in his house. A 14-hour standoff ended in tragedy when the man committed suicide.

America's "Great Recession" of the late 2000s didn't help the town much, either. It caused property values to plummet 60 percent within four years. Nearly 500 houses had to be repossessed by banks and lenders. Local residents also began contending with problems that impact most American communities: burglaries, vagrancy, and divorce. Several homeowners say that the town's blandness ruined their marriages. (The term used to describe the phenomenon: "Celebration Separation.")

THE GOOD AND THE BAD

Those who stayed relish Celebration's relatively good safety record and quality of life. Many of them refer to it as "the Bubble" and, as a homeowner once joked to a reporter, Celebration will feel like a real town when a bike finally gets stolen. While we don't know if that has happened yet, Celebration's first reported homicide occurred in 2010. A retired schoolteacher named Matteo Giovanditto was

---

Abbott and Costello were insured for $250,000 against having a career-ending argument.

found dead in his condo. The murderer was a transient who claimed Giovanditto tried to drug and assault him. It was later revealed that the victim had a history of sexually abusing children.

END OF THE LINE
In 2004 the Disney Company sold off much of its property in Celebration's town center and started scaling back its role in the community. According to some insiders, that was the plan from the start; Disney intended to stick around only long enough to make a huge profit off the real estate. Depending on whom you ask, Celebration may have just been a shrewd business venture all along. But while Celebration may no longer be an official "Disney town"… it's still just a ten-minute drive from Walt Disney World.

*   *   *

26 GENERIC AND STORE BRAND VERSIONS OF DR PEPPER

Dr. Zip (Sobey's)

Dr. A+ (Albertsons)

Dr. Perky (Food Lion)

Dr. Zing (Giant)

Dr. Wow (Food Club)

Dr. Extreme
(Harris Teeter)

Dr. Wild (Kroger)

Dr. Thunder (Walmart)

Dr. Weis (Weis markets)

Dr. Good Guy (Kalil)

Dr. Sparkle
(Price Chopper)

Dr. Riffic (Eckerd)

Dr. Radical
(P&C Foods)

Dr. K (K-Mart)

Dr. W (Wegmans)

Dr. U
(United Supermarkets)

Dr. Skipper (Safeway)

Dr. Thirst (Marquee)

Dr. Springfield (Bi-Rite)

Country Doctor
(Fareway)

Dr. Celeste (The Pantry)

Mr. Pig (Piggly Wiggly)

Mr. Sipp
(Smart & Final)

Mr. Aahh (Giant Eagle)

The Dr. (Buehler's)

Doctor (Econo Foods)

THERE BE DRAGONS!

You've heard of Puff the Magic Dragon; Smaug, the dragon in The Hobbit; *and Norbert, the dragon in the Harry Potter books. Here's a look at some dragons you may not have heard of.*

B ACKGROUND
Stories of enormous, terrifying reptilian beasts have been part of folklore around the world for longer than the written record can tell us. And while the beasts in these stories vary greatly, they have several traits in common: they are virtually always depicted as having snakelike or lizardlike bodies, they're almost always covered or partially covered in scales, and they often (but not always) have wings. Here are some of the most historically significant dragonlike beasts ever recorded.

APEP

One of history's earliest recorded mythical creatures with dragon-like characteristics, this ancient Egyptian god, also called the "Evil Lizard," was the god of darkness and evil. Depictions of Apep vary. In the *Egyptian Book of the Dead*, which dates to 2100 B.C., he is described as a giant serpent, more than 50 cubits (about 75 feet) long, with a head made of flint. In some paintings he looks like a long skinny snake; in others he is part snake, part crocodile. Yet other images show him with a large, stout body; a long tail; and the arms, hands, and face of a human. He was also said to have magical powers, including the ability to hypnotize other gods with his gaze—very similar to a characteristic later attributed to other dragons.

HUMBABA

Another of the earliest dragonlike monsters, this beast is in one of the oldest known pieces of literature, the *Epic of Gilgamesh*, found etched into clay tablets in the ancient Assyrian city of Nineveh. The tablets, which date to the eighteenth century B.C., tell the stories of Gilgamesh, the legendary warrior king of Uruk, a city in Sumer. In one tale, Gilgamesh sets out to kill the guardian of the Cedar Forest, a terrifying beast known as Humbaba. Humbaba is

---

Scientists say that by now, UV radiation has turned all the American flags on the moon white.

described as having the head and paws of a lion, the horns of a bull, the claws of a vulture, a body covered in scales, and a long tail which ended in the head of a snake. He has magical powers, including the ability to change the shape of his face and that most dragonlike characteristic: the ability to breathe fire.

KAMPE, THE SHE-DRAGON

Ancient Greek mythology tells of literally hundreds of dragonlike creatures, going back to at least the eighth century B.C. In fact, the Greeks gave us the root of the word "dragon"—*drakon*, their name for these monsters. An interesting twist on this: the *drakainae*, or "she-dragons," of which Kampe was one of the most bizarre. She had the head and upper torso of a beautiful woman and the lower body of a serpent. Her hair was made of venomous, spitting snakes; long, curved claws grew out from her hands; her feet were made of more spitting snakes; the heads of dozens of snarling beasts—including lions, wild boars, and dogs—sprouted from around her waist; and she had the huge upward-curving tail of a scorpion. With dark wings that grew from her shoulders, Kampe was prone to flying around, shooting sparks from her eyes, and causing storms (and being generally unfriendly).

BIBLICAL DRAGONS

Dragons make several appearances in the Bible. The book of Revelation, the final book of the New Testament, even refers to Satan as "the dragon, that ancient serpent." In another instance the Apostle John describes seeing "an enormous red dragon with seven heads and ten horns." He says this dragon's body "resembled a leopard, but had feet like those of a bear and a mouth like that of a lion." (In the Old Testament, some angels are even depicted as dragonlike beings. The *seraphim*, meaning literally "burning ones," are regularly depicted as accompanying God in the visions of various biblical characters and are described as huge, six-winged flying serpents.)

THE INDIAN DRAGON

In the second century A.D., a Roman scholar named Aelian wrote *On the Nature of Animals*, a collection of stories relating to animals. Among the stories was one called the "Indian Dragon," about a beast said to live in the exotic faraway land of India. Aelian's description of the dragon's hunting technique (from a 1958 translation by Alwyn Faber Scholfield):

> In India, I am told, the Elephant and the Drakon are the bitterest enemies. Now Elephants draw down the branches of trees and feed upon them. And the Drakones, knowing this, crawl up the trees and envelop the lower half of their bodies in the foliage, but the upper portion extending to the head they allow to hang loose like a rope. And the Elephant approaches to pluck the twigs, whereat the Drakon springs at its eyes and gouges them out. Next the Drakon winds round the Elephant's neck, and as it clings to the tree with the lower part of its body, it tightens its hold with the upper part and strangles the Elephant with an unusual and singular noose.

Another work of the era tells of Indian dragon hunters who are able to lull a dragon to sleep by placing special stones outside the beast's lair. The hunters then kill the sleeping dragon with their axes, decapitate it…and remove magical gems from inside its head.

THE SERPENT OF CARTHAGE

In the year 256 B.C., Roman general Marcus Atilius Regulus was leading an army against the city-state of Carthage in North Africa when they set up camp on the banks of the Bagradas River. Some of the men went to get water from the river and, according to a legend repeated—and believed—for centuries, several of the soldiers were promptly devoured, armor and all, by an enormous water serpent. (Many of mythology's most famous dragons are associated with rivers, lakes, and oceans.) The creature was said to be more than 100 feet long, covered in scales that repelled spears, with huge red glowing eyes and poisonous breath that made the soldiers go mad. Another interesting feature: while it had no legs, it had a network of ribs that it used to walk on land. According to the legend, the serpent was finally conquered and its skin taken to Rome, where it was displayed in the Roman senate for more than 100 years…until it disappeared sometime in the second century B.C.

ST. GEORGE'S DRAGON

A familiar motif in dragon tales: a brave knight saves a damsel (often a princess) from a dragon. This one revolves around St. George, a Roman soldier who was executed around A.D. 303 for his Christian beliefs, leading to his canonization nearly 200 years later. Over the following centuries, St. George was somehow transformed into a dragon slayer. In the most popular version of the story, which became a best-seller of sorts all over Europe starting in the thirteenth century, brave St. George is wandering through Libya when he comes across a king who is about to offer his daughter, the princess, to the local dragon. Normally the dragon, which is more than 50 feet long and lives in a nearby lake, is happy with the two sheep the people offer it daily—but they ran out of sheep. St. George attacks and wounds the dragon, puts it on a leash, and has the princess lead the dragon into town. There he promises to kill the dragon—if the king and all his people agree to become Christians. They agree, and St. George chops off the dragon's head.

* * *

OTTO DEIFIED OTTO

A palindrome is a word or a phrase that reads the same backward as it does forward. Here are some we collected.

Nate bit a Tibetan.

Bursitis rub

Mirror rim

I saw a crow, orca was I.

A butt tuba

Wasilla's all I saw.

Salt an atlas.

Drat, Saddam! Mad dastard!

Niagara, O roar again!

Elk rap song? No sparkle.

"Rum? Rum…" I murmur.

Not so, Boston.

Dumb mud

Liam's mail

Nemo's omen

Stunt nuts

Pose as Aesop.

Eva, use Suave.

Harass Sarah.

My gym's my gym.

Yawn a more Roman way.

Otto deified Otto.

Marge, let's telegram.

God smote Tom's dog.

Solo gigolos

Rotator

Won't lovers revolt now?

Mega gem

Yo, Jay-Z, all lazy, a joy!

A Toyota's a Toyota.

Eli, bleed eel bile.

Amy, must I jujitsu my ma?

Pass mom's sap.

Galoots, too, lag.

Is it I? It is I!

UNCLE JOHN'S STALL OF SHAME

Not everyone can make it into the Stall of Fame.
That's why Uncle John created the "Stall of Shame."

Dubious Achiever: Joaquin Phoenix, 37, actor
Claim to Shame: Destroying a piece of porcelain history
True Story: In 2012's *The Master*, Phoenix starred as a troubled man who joins a religious cult. During a scene in which his character has a temper tantrum in a jail cell, Phoenix improvised and stomped on the cell's toilet, smashing it to smithereens. It just so happened that the scene was filmed in a historic building, and the "irreplaceable" toilet was also historic. "I didn't intend to break the thing," Phoenix said. "I didn't know that was possible."
Outcome: According to director Paul Thomas Anderson, the building's owners "were really pissed off."

Dubious Achiever: Emma McDonald, a baker from New Zealand
Claim to Shame: Baking the world's crappiest cake
True Story: In 2013 McDonald, owner of Oh Cakes in Southland, New Zealand, became upset with a customer who'd ordered a cake for her sister's engagement party. The customer had won a $50 voucher for a cake, but owed McDonald $20 for a separate business deal, making the voucher worth only $30. McDonald didn't think that was enough for a cake to feed 100 guests, so she scheduled a meeting with the customer, which then had to be rescheduled… and then rescheduled *again*, all of which made McDonald angry. But what really sent her over the top was that the customer wasn't specific about how the cake should look. All she said was "chocolate."
Outcome: No one at the engagement party had a chance to see the cake until it was removed from its box in front of the guests. To their horror, McDonald's chocolate cake was shaped like a pile of you-know-what (with little pieces of yellow corn strewn throughout). On top of the cake was a small flag with the words "Eat Sh*t." Just to make sure the Harrises got the message, McDonald posted this message on her Facebook page:

Your left with a $30 voucher and you want a cake still?? ok cool – give me some ideas?? oh wait you have none apart from wanting chocolate. I have a brilliant idea for your cake!!! – so here it is, your turd cake! Hope you learn your lesson.

McDonald later told the *New Zealand Herald*, "I have no regrets at all about what I did. I feel she got what she deserved."

Dubious Achiever: Rosemary Vogel, 65, of Sun Lakes, Arizona
Claim to Shame: Trying to commit a murder most foul
True Story: In 2014 nurses at Chandler Regional Medical Center were alerted to an alarm coming from the room where Vogel was visiting her 66-year-old husband, who had just undergone heart surgery. When the nurses entered the room, they found Vogel, who is a former nurse at the hospital, manipulating the IV line. (That's what set off the alarm.) They quickly wrestled the IV away from her and then discovered a brown substance inside the tube that was inserted into the husband's arm. The tube was removed and Vogel was detained. Lab tests of the brown substance revealed it to be… fecal matter.

Outcome: Vogel was arrested for attempted murder (no motive was given). Her husband recovered.

Dubious Achiever: Kings of Leon, a rock band from Tennessee
Claim to Shame: Hogging half the heads at a British music festival
True Story: In 2010 the Kings of Leon and several other bands were at the V Festival in England. Andy Cato of the English electronic group Groove Armada later wrote this blog post about the Kings' backstage behavior:

> Over in the artist area there was already a queue for the washrooms. Then I noticed the empty shower block just on the other side of some temporary fencing. A couple of us found a gap. Out of nowhere came a very large man. "Reserved for the Kings of Leon," he said, "and so is this half of the artist toilets." It's hard to believe that someone actually phoned their agent and said, "Listen, I know that Paul Weller, Kasabian, Florence, Stereophonics, Groove Armada, and co. are all sharing the artist village and facilities, but we require that you put a fence down the middle of the toilets and showers and put a large man there to keep them just for us." But somebody did…. This was all happening backstage in the area shared by all the bands. Was Paul Weller going to hound them for autographs?

Outcome: Kings of Leon had no comment.

Dubious Achiever: Christian Lusardi, 42, a poker player from Fayetteville, North Carolina

Claim to Shame: Trying to cash in his chips in the wrong place

True Story: In January 2014, Lusardi was competing in the Winter Poker Open's "Big Stack, No Limit Hold 'Em" event at the Borgata Casino in Atlantic City, New Jersey. One of thousands of entrants, Lusardi had already won $6,814 with a few days left in the tournament. But when officials discovered that 160 counterfeit chips (total value: $800,000) had been entered into play, they traced the chips to Lusardi. Knowing they were on to him, Lusardi rushed to his room at nearby Harrah's Casino and flushed all of his remaining fake chips—worth $2.7 million—down the toilet. Needless to say, the hotel's plumbing couldn't handle hundreds of poker chips, so Lusardi quickly checked out of Harrah's and hid at a nearby motel, which is where police nabbed him before he was able to get out of town.

Outcome: Lusardi was arrested and charged with "rigging a publicly exhibited contest, criminal attempt, and theft by deception." Because fake chips had been introduced into the tournament, the event had to be canceled, even though 27 players were still competing. Lusardi faces several years in prison.

*   *   *

LOVED SHACK

What's the highest-rated restaurant in the United States? Not some high-end joint in New York City. In 2014 statisticians at *Yelp.com*, the online customer review site, crunched the numbers and compiled a list of the 100 best places to eat in the U.S. The winner: Da Poke Shack, a small, nondescript (but apparently very good) café in the middle of a condominium complex in Kona, Hawaii. It earned a five-star review, the highest possible, from 612 separate reviewers. It sells a regional favorite called poke bowls—salads made with Japanese greens and topped with fresh, raw ahi tuna. Price: about $8 a person.

THE HARSH REALITY OF "REALITY" TV

If you're like us, you probably tell people that you never watch reality TV shows…well, except for that one (or two or three) that you never miss. After you read this, you won't watch them the same way again.

AS SEEN ON TELEVISION

The proliferation of reality TV started in the United States with MTV's *The Real World* in 1992, and spread globally with *Survivor* and *Big Brother* a few years later. The success of these programs proved that nonscripted shows full of nonactors could deliver huge ratings at a fraction of the cost it took to produce scripted shows. Production companies and TV networks took notice, and by the early 2000s, the prime-time schedule was being taken over by so-called reality.

Today, reality programming consists of two broad categories: the "fly on the wall" show in which cameras document the lives of ordinary people, and reality game shows in which groups of people compete for cash and prizes. In both cases, viewers expect drama, conflict, humor, and a satisfying conclusion, just like scripted television. How do producers accomplish that with an "unscripted" show? By leaving very little to chance. The extent to which many of these shows are rigged might surprise you.

SHOW: *House Hunters*, HGTV

"REALITY": Cameras follow home buyers as they choose between three properties shown to them by a real-estate agent.

REALITY: In 2012, after the Jensen family appeared on the show, wife Bobi told the real-estate website Hooked On Houses that just about everything they did on the show was faked:

> The producers said they found our (true) story—that we were getting a bigger house and turning our other one into a rental—boring and overdone. They didn't even accept us for the show until we closed on the house we were buying. Then when they decided to film our episode, we had to scramble to find houses to tour and pretend we were considering. The ones we looked at weren't even for sale…they

---

A group of eggs is called a "clutch."

were just our two friends' houses who were nice enough to madly clean for days in preparation for the cameras! Only a few months earlier, *Slate* magazine had quoted HGTV general manager Kathleen Finch as insisting that "we are a network of journalistic storytelling, not dramatic storytelling. We're very conscious of not allowing any kind of fake drama."

SHOW: *Duck Dynasty*, A&E

"REALITY": Cameras follow the Robertson family of Louisiana, headed by patriarch Phil, who owns a successful business selling duck calls. The show portrays the Robertson men as bearded hillbillies in full camo gear.

REALITY: Hillbillies? More like yuppies. In 2013 several photos emerged of Phil's adult sons and their families that were taken before the show started. Not only were the men not bearded, they were dressed in khakis and pressed shirts. And in one photo, the clean-cut sons are armed with…golf clubs. In a *Washington Monthly* exposé about *Duck Dynasty*, Daniel Luzer wrote, "A&E appears to have taken a large clan of affluent, college-educated, mildly conservative, country-club Republicans, common across the nicer suburbs of the old South, and repackaged them as the Beverly Hillbillies."

SHOW: *Call of the Wildman*, Animal Planet

"REALITY": Cameras follow Ernie "Turtleman" Brown as he helps fellow Kentuckians whose properties have been invaded by nuisance wildlife. He catches the critters with his bare hands and then lets them go in the woods.

REALITY: *Call of the Wildman* now airs with a disclaimer: "The preceding program contains some dramatizations." They're not kidding. A 2014 article in *Mother Jones* magazine accused the show of not only faking some of the rescues but also treating animals inhumanely. The article focused on a July 2012 episode in which Brown captures a raccoon (possibly rabid) living in a family's house. "Fluffy doesn't have rabies," he yells after catching the animal, "she's got *babies!*" Then Brown uses the mom to help him find her offspring in the crawl space. The *Mother Jones* investigation discovered that "Fluffy" (Turtleman names all the critters he catches) couldn't have had babies…because Fluffy is male. The baby raccoons, it turned out, were delivered to the house by a trapper. As always, Brown promised to release them into the wild. But when the raccoons were delivered to a wildlife sanctuary a week after filming, they were reportedly "emaciated" and clinging to life. One didn't survive. Other allegations: the show "used an animal that had been drugged with sedatives in violation of federal rules"; and in one scene where Brown identifies an animal by its droppings, the "droppings" were made from "Nutella, Snickers bars, and rice."

A spokesperson for Sharp Entertainment, which produces *Call of the Wildman*, insisted that "the humane treatment of our animals is a top priority." But the spokesperson also explained that Sharp is in the business of "guided reality." And even though Brown really does catch the critters with his bare hands, an anonymous source from the show said that "99 percent of Turtleman's lines are scripted."

SHOW: *Real Housewives*, Bravo

"REALITY": Cameras follow the exploits of cliques of well-to-do women from various American cities. Episodes feature fights, betrayal, drinking, and sexual situations.

REALITY: The gossip website RadarOnline posted photos of the cast and crew of *Real Housewives of New York City* filming a "spontaneous" street scene: "Carole Radziwill and Heather Thompson were taking instructions from producers, shooting multiple takes, and waiting for breaks in dialogue to ensure cameras were set up." The gossip site also reported that *Real Housewives of Atlanta* cast member Walter Jackson confessed that—at the behest of producers—he pretended to be Kenya Moore's boyfriend "to give Kenya a story line." Contrary to what viewers saw, the two were not a couple.

SHOW: *American Idol*, Fox

"REALITY": At the beginning of each season, thousands of aspiring singers line up in various cities for a chance to audition in front of the celebrity judges. If the judges deem a singer good enough, he or she gets a "golden ticket" to compete on the show in Hollywood. Singers not good enough are often ridiculed (on national TV) before being sent home.

REALITY: By the time most singers get in front of the celebrity judges, their fate has already been determined. In 2011 a former contestant who identified herself by the fake name "Maria Saint" revealed that several of the top singers didn't even have to audition.

They'd been "recruited" for the show by talent scouts. And those huge lines full of hopefuls we see on TV were actually filmed weeks or months before the celebrity judges showed up. The hopefuls sing for the show's producers, after which, according to Saint, each singer is given a piece of paper with the producer's name along with a code: "Y" means the singer is good enough to move on; "K" means the singer isn't great but has potential; and "N" means the singer's not good enough for the show…but still might still get in front of the judges. "Take my advice," wrote Saint, "if you're an 'N' and you want to see the process and you're okay with the fact that you may be humiliated and that's all right with you, then by all means, take the chance-of-a-lifetime experience." Saint kept her identity secret, fearing she could be sued for up to $5 million for breaching a confidentiality agreement that all hopefuls must sign.

SHOW: *Kourtney and Kim Take New York*, E!

"REALITY": Cameras follow the exploits of the Kardashian sisters as they navigate the perils of life, love, and family. In one episode in 2011, Kim flew to Dubai to have a heart-to-heart talk with her mom, Kris Jenner, to tell her that she was going to divorce her husband, Kris Humphries.

REALITY: After the show aired, a photograph of Kim and her mother leaving a soundstage in Los Angeles wearing the exact same outfits, hairstyles, and makeup they had in "Dubai" showed up on the Internet. And the photo was taken on December 6, 2011—a full week *after* news broke that Kim was divorcing Humphries. Not only was the location faked, so was the entire conversation between mother and daughter.

SHOW: *Toddlers & Tiaras*, TLC

"REALITY": Cameras follow the highly competitive world of child beauty pageants.

REALITY: When RadarOnline broke the story about the scripted scenes in *Real Housewives of New York City*, one of the online commenters was former *Toddlers & Tiaras* pageant mom Darci McHenry, who wrote: "We had to 're-shoot' things that started out spontaneously. We were re-fed lines to re-create a 'missed' moment. Plus, you're mic'd the whole time. You can be addressing one person, and editors can come in and splice it to make it look like you're addressing someone else because it makes for better television." She added that one scene of a little girl "spontaneously" singing a song was shot six times.

In 2012 Maxine Tinnel, who was hired to stage pageants for the show, told the *New York Post* that everything on *Toddlers & Tiaras* is preplanned to ensure that the competitive kids and squabbling parents are always at each other's throats. Capturing this is difficult, says Tinnel, because the pageants aren't nearly as combative as the show makes them out to be: "When we have downtime, the kids are sitting on the floor coloring or playing together." The real trick to creating a tense atmosphere, she says, is in the casting: "They find the crazy families first, then find a pageant near them."

SHOW: *Hell's Kitchen*, Fox

"REALITY": Twenty contestants compete for a chance to become head chef at one of Gordon Ramsay's restaurants. Each episode features a dinner service where the British celebrity chef yells bleeped-out profanities at the contestants, smashes poorly cooked meat with his bare hand, and often shuts down the service early. One chef is eliminated each week, at the sole discretion of Ramsay.

REALITY: Regular viewers often ask, "How did some of these clueless chefs even get on the show?" In a 2013 interview with *Emmy* magazine, Ramsay answered that question during a rant about "the muppets I have to work with." He said, "There's fifty percent cast for character, and there's fifty percent cast for talent." That explains why obviously inferior chefs remain on the show after better chefs have been eliminated—it makes for better drama. But regardless of how they're selected, if being lambasted by Ramsay looks tough on the screen, it's even tougher in real life. For five weeks, the chefs are completely isolated from the outside world—no TV, no Internet, no calls home. There are cameras everywhere, even in the bathrooms. Most of their work days last from dawn until 2:00 a.m., and the contestants must do all of their cooking and cleaning themselves. It's so stressful, in fact, that after a contestant is eliminated, he or she is immediately sent to a psychiatrist to be evaluated. Why? According to a show insider who spoke to the *New York Post*, the producers "want to make sure you don't want to kill yourself—or someone else."

So is it worth it? Out of the dozen or so winners in the show's history, only half received the promised job of head chef—some were given lesser positions, and a few didn't get any job at all. (They got a cash prize instead.)

SHOW: *Mystery Diners*, Food Network
"REALITY": Cameras follow restaurant "fixer" Charles Stiles as he assists restaurant owners who are losing money and can't figure out why. Stiles's company comes in at night and secretly installs hidden cameras. Then company operatives pose as employees and customers while Stiles and the restaurant owner sit in a control room and watch what transpires. In every episode, restaurant employees are caught engaging in some kind of shady activity, which leads to a heated confrontation, dramatic firings, and a grateful owner.
REALITY: If it seems as if some of the "problem employees" that Stiles's company exposes are paid actors (because who would act like that and then allow themselves to be on TV?), it's because they are. In 2013 a former employee of Big Earl's Greasy Eats in Cave Creek, Arizona, told the *Sonoran News* that when the *Mystery Diners* production crew filmed an episode there, they brought in paid actors. The confrontations were staged, and some required several retakes.

SHOW: *Breaking Amish*, TLC
"REALITY": Cameras follow five young adults—four Amish and one Mennonite—who decide to leave their rural, technology-free, religious upbringings in Lancaster County, Pennsylvania, and go to New York City. They live the "English" life for a while before deciding whether or not to go back to their traditional homes.
REALITY: Almost immediately after TLC aired the first episode in 2012, accusations arose that *Breaking Amish* is fake. According to London's *Daily Mail*: "While each cast member claims to have grown up in the strict communities, evidence has surfaced suggesting they have decidedly dark pasts—involving divorce, children, and time away from the faith." In fact, two cast members supposedly met each other for the first time on the show, but a Facebook photo taken a year earlier shows the two of them together. TLC execs say they never implied that cast members lived a completely Amish lifestyle before the show, but Hot Snakes Media, which produces the show for TLC, says on its website that *Breaking Amish* "follows

the lives of courageous young Amish men and women as they experience life, for the first time, outside of the Amish community."

As the allegations of fakery kept coming in, TLC revised the storylines throughout the first season to reflect the fact the young men and women weren't as "pure" as the show had made them out to be. The show was renewed for a second season.

SHOW: *Bug Juice*, Disney Channel
"REALITY": Cameras follow boys and girls at a summer camp.
REALITY: In an article posted on the Writers' Guild of America's website, veteran script writer David Rupel explains how reality TV really works: "The first thing is that the term 'unscripted' is a fallacy. No, we don't write pages of dialogue, but we do create formats, cast people based on character traits, and edit scenes to tell a powerful, intriguing tale." He cited an example from *Bug Juice*:

> We faced a major problem with our boy-girl love story. After weaving this story line through nine episodes, we were caught flat-footed when our boy, Connor, had the nerve to dump his girl, Stephanie, off camera! We had enough interview bites to explain what happened, but we needed a good visual to make it work. If you catch a rerun of the show, you will see a happy Stephanie obliviously bounce up to Connor, who solemnly takes her hand and leads her off, as his interview bite explains he needs to end things. With the help of a tender music cue, it turned out to be a touching and bittersweet end to our summer romance. The reality: Steph walked up to Connor, gushed about his Adidas T-shirt, and they headed off to have lunch. We used the interview bites and music cue to shape the otherwise innocuous scene to approximate the reality that we failed to shoot.

SHOW: *Storage Wars*, A&E
"REALITY": Cameras follow professional buyers as they bid on the contents of abandoned or unpaid storage units.
REALITY: Former cast member Dave Hester sued *Storage Wars* for wrongful termination in 2012. He says the show fired him because he publicly claimed it was rigged: "The producers staged entire units, planted items in lockers after having them appraised weeks in advance, and funneled cash to weaker teams to buy lockers they could not have otherwise afforded." A&E's defense: "The composition of the show is covered by the First Amendment." A judge agreed and ordered Hester to pay the network's legal costs. But

---

The 452 active volcanoes circling the Pacific Ocean are known as the Pacific Ring of Fire.

Hester is sticking to his story. He knows the show is rigged because he helped rig it. According to RadarOnline, "Hester planted items that he owned in lockers he bought and was even paid by the production company for 'renting' those items."

SHOW: *Snooki & JWoww*, MTV
"REALITY": Cameras follow Nicole "Snooki" Polizzi and Jennifer "JWoww" Farley in this *Jersey Shore* spin-off as they—like *Kourtney and Kim* (and many other reality shows)—navigate life and love.
REALITY: In her book *Baby Bumps: From Party Girl to Proud Mama, and All the Messy Milestones Along the Way*, Polizzi confessed that the story lines on *Snooki & JWoww* are all planned out in advance. In 2012, when she informed the show's producer that she was pregnant, the first thing he said was, "Get me a rewrite, ASAP!" Then the producers threw out their plans for filming in bars and quickly "concocted" scenes "in a pet store, in a baby-clothing store, at a psychic's, and at the doctor's office." Critics and viewers complained that the ensuing season felt "painfully scripted."

SHOW: *The Voice*, NBC
"REALITY": Popular music artists mentor up-and-coming singers who are chosen via "blind" auditions. The mentors can only listen to the contestants' voices before deciding whether to take them on as students. Winners are ultimately determined by a fan-voting system.
REALITY: NBC Universal is very adamant that its hit show is not rigged in any way. "We have never manipulated the outcome on this show—NBC and *The Voice* producers take the fairness and integrity of this competition far too seriously." But you wouldn't know that from the 32-page contract every contestant must sign. The *New York Daily News* broke the story in March 2014 after an anonymous Twitter user leaked the "dehumanizing" contract online. Some highlights:

• A contestant may be removed from the show at any time "for any reason whatsoever," even if they are "winning" with the public.

• A contestant must agree that the show "may portray me in a false light" that "may be disparaging, defamatory, embarrassing (and) may expose me to public ridicule, humiliation, or condemnation."

• The producers can "change the rules at any time," "ignore the show's voting system," and force contestants to "undergo medical or psychological testing and, under certain circumstances, release the results on TV."

• Failing to follow the rules or divulging inside information could result in the contestant being sued for $100,000 to $1 million.

A legal expert told the *Daily News* that this type of contract is now the norm in reality programming because several shows have been sued by bitter contestants and cast members. Result: the production companies can treat the reality stars pretty much however they want. Happy viewing.

*   *   *

THE GOLDEN FLEECE AWARDS

Sen. William Proxmire of Wisconsin created this "award" in the 1970s to call attention to wasteful government spending." A few honorees:

The National Endowment for the Humanities, "for making a $2,500 grant to Arlington County, Virginia, to study why people are rude, ill-mannered, cheat and lie on the local tennis courts."

The Federal Highway Administration, for spending $222,000 to study 'Motorist Attitudes Toward Large Trucks.' "

The National Institute on Alcohol Abuse and Alcoholism, "for spending millions of dollars to find out if drunk fish are more aggressive than sober fish, and if rats can be turned into alcoholics."

The Agency for International Development, for using part of a $97,000 grant to study "behavior and social relationships in a Peruvian brothel."

The National Institute of Neurological and Communicative Disorders, for spending "$160,000 to study in part whether someone can 'hex' an opponent during a strength test by drawing an 'X' in the air in front of his opponent's chest."

The National Highway Traffic Safety Administration, "for spending $120,126 to build a low-slung, backward-steering motorcycle that no one could ride."

The National Oceanic and Atmospheric Administration, "for spending at least $6,000 to determine if pot smoking has a bad effect on scuba divers."

FICTIONAL BOOZE QUIZ

Crack open an imaginary cold one and try to match these fictitious drinks to the movie, book, or TV show that served them. (Answers on page 541.)

1. Pan-Galactic Gargle Blaster
2. Shotz Beer
3. Romulan Ale
4. Moloko Plus
5. Pawtucket Patriot Ale
6. Panther Pilsner
7. Black Death Malt Liquor
8. Wharmpess Beer
9. Schraderbrau
10. Ent Draught
11. Old Dusseldorf
12. Lobrau
13. Butterbeer
14. Alamo Beer
15. Elsinore Beer
16. Spice Beer
17. Dharma Initiative Beer
18. Victory Gin
19. Buzz Beer
20. "Beer"

a) *Laverne and Shirley*

b) *The Three Stooges*

c) *How I Met Your Mother*

d) *The Hitchhiker's Guide to the Galaxy*

e) *The Lord of the Rings*

f) *Futurama*

g) *Family Guy*

h) *Magnum, P.I.*

i) *A Clockwork Orange*

j) *King of the Hill*

k) *Breaking Bad*

l) *Harry Potter*

m) *WKRP in Cincinnati*

n) *Strange Brew*

o) *Lost*

p) *South Park*

q) *1984*

r) *Star Trek*

s) *Dune*

t) *The Drew Carey Show*

The United Kingdom's poet laureate is entitled to 630 bottles of Spanish sherry per year.

CAPITAL IDEA, PART II

On page 273 we told you how a pile of unpaid bills led to the creation of a capital city for America that was outside of any state. So how was the site for Washington, D.C., chosen? Among other things, we have slavery, mosquitos, and that same pile of unpaid bills to thank for it.

S ITE FIGHT

The U.S. Constitution did not require that a new federal city be built from scratch. All it said was that Congress, if it wanted to, could create a federal district "not exceeding ten miles square" (a site ten miles wide and ten miles long, for a total of 100 square miles) where it would have exclusive jurisdiction. The simplest and cheapest solution would have been to designate a portion of an existing city, such as Philadelphia, Boston, or New York, as the federal district, and for the city and state in question to cede jurisdiction to Congress.

More than one city recognized the financial and other benefits that would accrue from providing the site for the new national capital. Philadelphia, then the country's largest city, was an obvious choice. The Continental Congress had met there during the war, and both the Declaration of Independence and the U.S. Constitution had been signed in the State House (Independence Hall). And though Congress had vowed never to return to the city after the Pennsylvania Mutiny of 1783, the Pennsylvania delegation was eager to forgive and forget. New York City had served as the nation's capital since 1785, and prominent New Yorkers like Alexander Hamilton, now the secretary of the treasury, wanted it to be named the permanent national capital.

DOWN UNDER

So why did neither city get the nod? Because Southern states didn't like the idea of *any* established urban center, let alone one in the North, serving as the national capital. The rural, agrarian South was suspicious of big cities and the merchants, bankers, manufacturers, stockbrokers, and other sharpies who lived there.

Southern states were also determined to preserve the institution of slavery, which was on its way out in the North. Congressional delegations from the South feared that if the capital was located in a Northern city, slavery would be under constant attack. Southern congressmen also worried that if they brought their slaves to live with them in New York or Philadelphia while Congress was in session, the presence of large numbers of abolitionists and freed slaves in these cities would make it easy for the slaves to escape. (George Washington had the same fear; it was realized in 1796 when a female slave named Oney Judge escaped from the presidential household and never returned.)

IN THE HOLE

As the United States debated where to put the capital city, it also wrestled with a much more daunting challenge: the country's staggering Revolutionary War debts. Thanks to the ratification of the Constitution in 1788, Congress now had the power to tax, which gave it the ability to generate revenue to pay down the debt. It was certainly going to need it. The nation was nearly bankrupt. In 1790 the federal government's war debt stood at $54 million (the equivalent of around $1.2 billion today) at a time when the population of the United States was fewer than four million people. Individual states had also piled up millions of dollars in debt, more than $25 million of it still outstanding.

How to repay all that money—and indeed *whether* to repay it at all—was the subject of much debate. Many Americans felt a stronger allegiance to their home states than they did to the new union; they would have cared little if the national government defaulted on its debts. Some states had already reneged on their obligations. New York stopped making interest payments on its bonds in order to drive down their market value, then bought them back for a song to avoid paying back the money in full.

FORTUNE OF SOLDIERS

Complicating the issue were the thousands of IOUs that had been issued to Revolutionary War soldiers in lieu of their pay. Many soldiers, either out of desperation or simply in despair that they would ever be paid, had sold their IOUs to speculators for pennies on the dollar. If the IOUs were paid off now, the speculators, not the soldiers, would benefit. So why not default on the IOUs and find some other way to pay the soldiers directly?

CREDIT HISTORY

Alexander Hamilton, the New York congressman whom George Washington appointed secretary of the treasury in 1789, felt otherwise. He believed that if the young country was going to develop, it would need access to capital and plenty of it. If it wanted to borrow the money at favorable interest rates, it needed to demonstrate to lenders that it would always honor its debts.

The treasury secretary drew inspiration from the British, who had built the Royal Navy with borrowed money and then used the navy to extend the British Empire to every corner of the globe. England's reputation for honoring its debts was unquestioned; the government's bonds were considered as good as cash. People could even use them as collateral for loans, which injected even more money into the British economy.

ALL FOR ONE, ONE FOR ALL

Hamilton believed it was important for the federal government to assume responsibility not only for its own debts but also those of the states, and to consolidate them all into a single, giant pool of war debts that would be repaid in full. Since everyone had benefited from the Revolution, he reasoned, everyone should pitch in to pay for it, not just the states that had done most of the fighting (and thus most of the borrowing).

In January 1790, Hamilton published his ideas in *The First Report on the Public Credit*, which he presented to Congress. His plan aroused strong opposition from the start; some states, like Virginia and North Carolina, had already paid most of their war debts, and they balked at having to pay a second time to settle the debts of other states, like Massachusetts and South Carolina. And nobody relished the idea of enriching speculators at the expense of destitute Revolutionary War veterans.

Hamilton believed that making good on the IOUs, even those that had been sold to speculators, was a necessary evil. The only reason the IOUs had sold for a fraction of their value in the first place, he argued, was because people had assumed the government would never pay up. Demonstrating the government's intent to honor its obligations would prevent those debts from ever selling for a fraction of their face value again, depriving future speculators the ability to profit from wild swings in their value. (Hamilton also had a grudging admiration for the speculators because they'd shown faith in the new government and risked their own money to buy the IOUs that so many people assumed were worthless. He believed they deserved to be rewarded for taking the risk.)

THANKS...BUT NO THANKS

As Hamilton's debt-payment plan made its way through Congress in the early months of 1790, it lost some key preliminary votes, thanks to strong opposition from such luminaries as Secretary of State Thomas Jefferson and James Madison, then an influential member of Congress. Both men were from Virginia, an agrarian Southern state that was then the most populous in the Union.

Unlike Hamilton, Jefferson and Madison were not inspired by the British model of a worldwide empire ruled by a single government in London. They envisioned the United States as something more akin to what the European Union and the United Nations are today: a coalition of independent, sovereign states linked (when necessary) by a comparatively weak central government. Jefferson and Madison feared that Hamilton's financial plan would strengthen the federal government at the expense of the states. They also sympathized with the Revolutionary War veterans and wanted to see that they, not the speculators, were paid in full.

DOUBLE TROUBLE

Either of the two great issues of the day—where to put the capital city and how to deal with the Revolutionary War debts—was divisive enough in its own right to dissolve the fragile new nation just as it was coming into being. So why didn't it happen? Because as badly as Alexander Hamilton wanted to see New York or some other Northern city as the national capital, he wanted his debt-payment plan even more. And as much as Jefferson and Madison loathed Hamilton's debt plan, they understood that America defaulting on its debts was even worse. They were willing to support Hamilton's plan, but they had a price: They wanted the new capital city to be located somewhere in the rural South.

MEAL DEAL

That was the deal that was worked out at a famous dinner that Jefferson hosted for Hamilton and Madison at his home in New

York in June 1790. There, Hamilton agreed that the capital city would be located somewhere along a 65-mile stretch of the Potomac River, on the border between Maryland and Virginia, with the exact site to be chosen later. In return, Jefferson and Madison agreed that Madison would round up the votes needed to get Hamilton's debt-payment plan through Congress. To win the support of the Pennsylvania delegation, it was agreed that Philadelphia would serve as the temporary capital for ten years while the permanent capital was being built.

The bill placing the capital city on the Potomac was called the Residence Act; it passed both houses of Congress in early July 1790 and was signed by President George Washington on July 16. Hamilton's debt plan was signed into law a few weeks later.

The Residence Act also specified that Washington would decide precisely where along the Potomac the federal city would be located. He selected a spot just 15 miles north of his estate at Mount Vernon. In 1791 the new city was named Washington in his honor, and the federal district in its entirety was named Columbia.

STAY (JUST A LITTLE BIT LONGER)

One of the reasons the Pennsylvania delegation was willing to vote for the plan in exchange for Philadelphia being named the "temporary" capital was that many Pennsylvanians assumed it wouldn't be temporary. With so much money needed to pay the Revolutionary War debts, how much would be left over to build the new capital? Washington, D.C., was supposed to be completed by 1800…but what if construction fell behind? Pennsylvania officials were so certain that the new capital would never be finished that they began constructing their own buildings to house the federal government, including a house for the president (see page 357), to entice the government into staying in Philadelphia for good.

And even though the state had been phasing out slavery for a decade via the Gradual Abolition Act of 1780, that law specifically exempted slaves owned by members of Congress from the law. That meant that congressmen from slave states could bring their slaves into Pennsylvania without fear of them winning their freedom under the law. (The slaves could still *escape* to freedom—and many did—but at least they had no means of obtaining their freedom through the legal system.)

PHILADELPHIA FREEDOM

The building of Washington, D.C., actually *did* fall behind, and there must have been plenty of times when it seemed like the project would end in failure. Who knows? Philadelphia might well have been named the permanent capital, were it not for one more problem: mosquitos. In August 1793, Philadelphia was hit by a yellow fever epidemic—its first in over 30 years and far worse than any that had come before. A tenth of the population died in just three months, and another two-thirds fled the city, leaving it a virtual ghost town. George Washington decamped to Germantown, ten miles outside the city, and ran the executive branch from there for about a month until moving to Mount Vernon in September. He survived the epidemic, but four of his servants did not.

No one understood at the time that mosquitos were the carriers of yellow fever, but when the disease returned to Philadelphia in 1797, 1798, and 1799, people assumed that *something* had to be wrong with the city, perhaps the climate, or the air, or the water. Whatever it was, what little chance Philadelphia had for remaining the capital city was gone for good. When 1800 rolled around and Washington, D.C., still wasn't completed, the federal government went ahead and moved there anyway.

It wasn't perfect, but it was better than staying in Philadelphia.

*   *   *

AN UNUSUAL "SPORT"

The World Memory Championship. This intense set of contests, which dates back to 1991, pits "mental athletes" against each other to determine who can remember the most information in a given period of time. Each tournament features ten memory games, including "Names and Faces," "Spoken Numbers," and "Random Lists." The 2014 "Speed Cards" winner was Johnny Briones. After studying a deck of cards for 60 seconds, he was given another deck, which he successfully put in the same order as the first one. (Sound easy? Try it sometime.) His time of 60 seconds set a U.S. record, but Briones, who's only 19, has his sights set on the *world* record for memorizing the order of an entire deck of cards: 21.9 seconds.

IT'S A WEIRD, WEIRD WORLD

Here's proof that truth is stranger than fiction.

THE DIRTIEST MAN IN THE WORLD

Amou Haji took a bath in 1954…and he hasn't bathed since. Not surprisingly, he lives alone. Haji, 80, has few possessions and lives a nomadic life in southern Iran. He says that he stopped washing because he believes "cleanliness brings me sickness." In addition to being really dirty, Haji eats a regular diet of rotten meat (his favorite: porcupine) and smokes a pipe packed with animal dung.

NO TASTE AT ALL

A beauty queen named Wi May Nava—who came in second place in the 2013 Miss Venezuela pageant—revealed the secret to maintaining her slim figure: She had a cosmetic surgeon sew a piece of plastic mesh to the top of her tongue. It makes eating solid food so painful that her diet consists of liquids only, helping keep off those pesky pounds.

BONK = MC²

Jason Padgett *hated* math. A college dropout who sold futons for a living, his two hobbies were "sports and partying." But everything changed one night in 2002 when Padgett was leaving a bar in Tacoma, Washington. Two men mugged and beat him, leaving him with a severe concussion. When he awoke in the hospital, his world was different: he could see geometric lines connecting and surrounding everything, and crystalline patterns in running water. As time passed, Padgett's mathematical abilities increased, though his social life withered away. He stayed home drawing complex fractals, calculating "the end of pi," and boasting of his genius online. Doctors at the University of Miami diagnosed him with *acquired savant syndrome*. (Although rare, there have been other cases of brain-trauma patients becoming geniuses.) Now in his 40s, Padgett sells his fractal art online and is working toward a geometry degree. He still has

---

On Halloween 1988, presidential candidate George H. W. Bush wore a George Bush mask.

trouble going out in public, but says it's all worth it: "I see shapes and angles everywhere in real life. It's just really beautiful."

ONE TWISTED TWISTER

In 2008 a tornado swept through Hugo, Minnesota, leaving some things oddly untouched…and other things touched very oddly.

• A local named Terry Clarkin found four steak knives stuck into his front lawn. Each blade was submerged three inches into the ground, and they were deposited in the form of a perfect square.

• At one house all the leaves were ripped off a tree and replaced with pink insulation wads. Neighbors said it looked like a cartoon.

• Jeff Janus ran inside as he saw "people's houses flying by," but wasn't able to make it to the basement before the twister hit his house. He was in his hallway cradling a pet in each arm when two doors flew off their hinges and gently landed on top of him. The doors shielded Janus and his pets from (other) flying debris.

• And our favorite: the tornado reportedly picked up a roll of toilet paper in Jason Akins's bathroom. "It draped it across the counter top, then rewound it in the sink," he said. "The toilet paper didn't even rip. I was like, 'You've *got* to be kidding me!'"

LOW ON CASH

Customers at a Sainsbury's supermarket in Basford, England, have to get on their knees if they want money—not to beg, but to use the ATM. Reason: the control panel is located about a foot above the sidewalk. After photos of the weird installation showed up online in 2014, the store's manager explained that the ATM *had* to be that low because it's "located on a hill," but couldn't explain why that would make any difference. He said that they've thought about raising it but haven't yet because "no one has complained."

REVERSE PSYCHOLOGY

Since 1989 Mani Manithan of Tamil Nadu, India, has been trying to promote world peace…by only walking backward. Bad news: so far, it isn't working. More bad news: he's no longer able to walk forward. "My mind has forgotten how to do it," he says, adding, "I have become very comfortable walking like this." He promises to continue walking backward until there is world peace or until he dies, whichever comes first.

ANSWERS

OL' JAYBEARD'S BRAINTEASERS
(Answers from page 154)

1. 12:25

2. The man shot a rooster that was cock-a-doodle-dooing all night long. With the rooster gone, he would finally be able to sleep through sunrises.

3. The king soaked the seeds in salt water so they wouldn't grow. The third knight was the only one who didn't try the old "go to the nursery and buy a flowering plant" trick.

4. First: Cut the cake in half. Second: Cut the halves into quarters (with a single cut). Third: Cut it horizontally, from edge to edge, so that you have four quarters above the cut and four quarters below the cut. That's eight equal pieces.

5. In the kitchen. If you press "100" on a microwave, it will run for one minute. If you press "99" then it will run for one minute and 39 seconds.

6. The swindler sang the "Happy Birthday" song, which includes the line, "Happy birthday, Dame Magrathia Hamburglar-Smith the Third."

7. Each word contains the name of a weapon: ba**lance**, be**gun**, cros**sword**, gri**mace**, el**bow**, Shake**spear**e

8. Meat.

CALCULATOR RIDDLES
(Answers from page 227)

1. BELLIES; **2.** E; **3.** EGGSHELL; **4.** HOLES; **5.** HIGH HEEL; **6.** GO; **7.** GOOGLE; **8.** HOE HOE; **9.** GOOSE LEG; **10.** B

THE RIDDLER
(Answers from page 319)

1. Carpet; **2.** Your legs; **3.** A tree; **4.** Regret; **5.** A secret; **6.** The wind; **7.** A stapler; **8.** The library; **9.** A chain saw; **10.** Coins; **11.** A riddle

---

Red Bull energy drink is illegal in Norway, Denmark, Uruguay, and France. (Too "unhealthy.")

MUSICAL MASH-UP
(Answers from page 178)

1. Al Green Day
2. R. Kelly Clarkson
3. Olivia Newton-John Lennon
4. Fleetwood Mac Davis
5. George Michael Bolton
6. Metallicarpenters (Metallica + Carpenters)
7. Celine Dion and the Belmonts
8. James Taylor Swift
9. Garth Brooks & Dunn
10. Neil Young MC
11. Jay-ZZ Top
12. Simply Red Hot Chili Peppers
13. Twisted Sister Sledge
14. Shocking Blue Cheer
15. Barry White Stripes
16. R.E.M.inem (R.E.M. + Eminem)
17. Jackie Wilson Phillips
18. Bing Crosby, Stills, and Nash
19. Rick James Brown
20. Alan Jackson 5
21. Paul and Paula Abdul
22. Ben E. King Crimson

HITCHCOCK'S BLONDES
(Answers from page 349)
1. b), 2. d), 3. g), 4. a), 5. l), 6. c), 7. h), 8. e), 9. j), 10. k), 11. p), 12. r), 13. q), 14. n), 15. f), 16. s), 17. i), 18. o), 19. m), 20. t)

FICTIONAL BOOZE QUIZ
(Answers from page 531)
1. d), 2. a), 3. r), 4. i), 5. g), 6. b), 7. m), 8. c), 9. k), 10. e), 11. h), 12. f), 13. l), 14. j), 15. n), 16. s), 17. o), 18. q), 19. t), 20. p)

THAT'S A SPICY QUIZ
(Answers from page 290)
1. B. Nutmeg is the seed; mace is the skin that covers the seed.
2. A. Allspice is just one herb. The name was coined in 1621 by cooks who thought it had the combined flavors of nutmeg, cinnamon, and cloves.
3. D. Like many herbal remedies, anise was thought to be a cure for many conditions. However, its use during the Civil War as an

antiseptic for open wounds was later found to be toxic.

4. C. Caraway "seeds" are actually tiny dried fruits from a plant in the carrot family.

5. C. It's a spice with a bark and a bite. A seventeenth-century Dutch sea captain noted that he could smell cinnamon 25 miles downwind from the island of Sri Lanka.

6. A. *Cilantro* is the Spanish name for what is called the coriander plant in England and France. Most Americans learned of the herb through Mexican food, hence the Spanish name, but it's also common in Indian, Thai, Vietnamese, Chinese, and some Middle Eastern cuisines.

7. B. Oh yeah, and vampires, of course. A Muslim myth had it that when Satan left the Garden of Eden after tempting Adam and Eve, garlic grew in his left footprints and onions in his right.

8. D. Saffron is made from the three stigmas inside a fall-flowering crocus flower. A pound of saffron sells for $500–$5,000 and requires 20 hours of plucking the three stigmas from 50,000–75,000 flowers.

9. B. The definition of spice is that it is made of plant matter. Salt, the only rock we eat, is a seasoning, but it isn't a spice.

10. B. Black, white, and pink pepper all come from the *Piper nigrum* plant. Red pepper, from the *Capsicum annuum* plant, isn't even in the same family.

11. C. Black cumin, darker and sweeter than ordinary cumin, may have been included in Egyptian burials to bribe gatekeepers in the afterlife—perfect for both currying favor and flavoring curry.

12. D. Cayenne, named after the city of the same name in French Guiana, doesn't always turn red, but no matter how mature, it never turns red until separated from its plant.

13. A. True. The amount of poppy seeds on a bagel or two can make you look like a heroin/morphine user to a drug test.

14. A. Bay leaves release a slightly toxic chemical that kills insects without alarming them. (Collectors don't want to damage their wings before pinning them to a display.)

* * *

"Half of everything you learn in college is a complete waste of time. But you will never know which half." —**Thomas Frey**

What do Chicago, Miami, and Houston have in common? More annual rainfall than Seattle.

More UNCLE JOHN'S than you can shake a stick at!

Per capita, more board games are sold in Germany than in any other country.

THE LAST PAGE

FELLOW BATHROOM READERS:
The fight for good bathroom reading should never be taken loosely—we must do our duty and sit firmly for what we believe in, even while the rest of the world is taking potshots at us.

We'll be brief. Now that we've proven we're not simply a flush-in-the-pan, we invite you to take the plunge: Sit Down and Be Counted! Log on to *www.bathroomreader.com* and earn a permanent spot on the BRI honor roll!

If you like reading our books…

VISIT THE BRI'S WEBSITE!

www.bathroomreader.com

- Receive our irregular newsletters via e-mail
- Order additional Bathroom Readers
- Find us on Facebook
- Tweet us on Twitter
- Blog us on our blog

Go with the Flow…

Well, we're out of space, and when you've gotta go, you've gotta go. Tanks for all your support. Hope to hear from you soon.

Meanwhile, remember…

Keep on flushin'!